SASHA AND EMMA

SASHA
AND
EMMA

The Anarchist Odyssey of Alexander Berkman and Emma Goldman

Paul Avrich and Karen Avrich

The Belknap Press of Harvard University Press
Cambridge, Massachusetts · London, England
2012

Printed in the United States of America

Library of Congress Cataloging-in-Publication Data

Avrich, Paul.
Sasha and Emma : the anarchist odyssey of Alexander Berkman and Emma Goldman / Paul Avrich and Karen Avrich.
p. cm.
Includes bibliographical references and index.
ISBN 978-0-674-06598-7 (hbk. : alk. paper)
1. Berkman, Alexander, 1870–1936. 2. Goldman, Emma, 1869–1940. 3. Anarchists—United States—Biography. 4. Anarchism—United States—History. I. Avrich, Karen. II. Title.
HX843.5.A97 2012
335'.83092273—dc23
[B] 2012008659

For those who told their stories to my father

For Mark Halperin, who listened to mine

Contents

II

PALACES OF THE RICH

III

OPEN EYES

Preface

When my father, Paul Avrich, died in 2006 after a long illness, he left behind an unfinished manuscript about the passionate half-century friendship between legendary activist Emma Goldman and Alexander Berkman, a Russian-born anarchist who achieved notoriety when he attempted to assassinate the industrialist Henry Clay Frick in 1892. My father published a number of books on Russian history and anarchism, yet he was endlessly fascinated by the magnetic Goldman, a leading figure in early twentieth-century America, and the brilliant Berkman, who served fourteen years for the attack on Frick, and was rigidly, fervently devoted to the anarchist creed. It was the story of Berkman and Goldman's intense connection and intertwined lives that my father planned to write, and he spent decades gathering material for the book.

In my father's last days, he asked me to take over the project and see it through to publication. Over six years I shaped *Shasha and Emma*, using an early draft, his notes, the hundreds of interviews he conducted during his forty-year career, and the information he collected in the United States, Russia, and Europe. To this bounty I added my own research, examining hundreds of newspaper and journal articles from the period; the works of Berkman and Goldman, including their editorials, tracts, and memoirs; scores of letters exchanged with their comrades; and numerous other primary sources. I also retraced my father's steps, visiting sites instrumental to the narrative. The scope and depth of my father's scholarly effort was nothing short of extraordinary; I alone accept full responsibility for errors or omissions in the book.

Many of the quotations in *Sasha and Emma* come from contemporaneous letters, journals, and newspapers, and from Paul Avrich's conversations with people mentioned in these pages, whose memories remained sharp, their stories comprehensive and clear. Other quotes can be found in the documents of Berkman and Goldman, who on occasion infused their recollections with zest, ideological portent, and a touch of bravado. In Goldman's autobiography, *Living My Life,* published in 1931, she recounts her tale with characteristic verve and dramatic flair, describing events long since passed. Some of her comments are necessarily colored by time and temperament.

In writing *Sasha and Emma,* I endeavored to preserve not just the story Paul Avrich was eager to share, but also the sensibility and integrity of his scholarship. It was a curious, and curiously fulfilling, way for me to experience my father's life work after his death. I have come to understand why the lush, remarkable histories of these two dauntless radicals entranced him for so long.

KAREN AVRICH

SASHA AND EMMA

PROLOGUE

On July 23, 1892, a young anarchist named Alexander Berkman armed himself with a revolver and a handmade dagger, burst into the Pittsburgh offices of industrialist Henry Clay Frick, and shot and stabbed Frick as onlookers rushed to intervene. Berkman was wrestled to the ground, hauled off to the police station, then hastily tried and convicted. He spent the next fourteen years behind bars. Frick survived, but Berkman described his shocking crime as "the first terrorist act in America."[1]

Berkman may no longer be remembered as a leading player in modern American life, but he remains anchored in its history by Emma Goldman, perhaps the nation's most famous female radical. Berkman was Goldman's closest companion and confidant, and their bond lasted nearly half a century, ending only with his death in 1936. Both were born and raised in tsarist Russia, emigrated to the United States as teenagers, and met as young adults in 1889 in a coffee shop on the Lower East Side of Manhattan. They became fast friends, briefly lovers, and then loyal comrades, their lives and destinies forever intertwined.

Though at times separated by prison terms and circumstance, they always reunited, working together, living together, lecturing together, fighting for an improbable ideal of an anarchist utopia in which society could exist without government, the poor might be elevated from their wretched conditions, labor would have a voice, and full equality would be shared by all. It was a cause Berkman cherished as "the finest thing that humanity has ever thought of."[2]

By striking down Frick, a wealthy business leader whom he regarded as the emblematic enemy of the working people, Berkman believed he was serving the human cause. Without apology, he embraced violence as a tool for social transformation, convinced such methods were justified in the battle for a better country, a better world. Berkman imagined that his attack on Frick would "shed light on the questions involved" and "draw the attention of the world."[3] With surprise, he soon discovered that what he considered a heroic act was viewed with confusion, horror, and disdain by a reproving society; he achieved nothing but a lengthy prison sentence.

While Berkman spent his twenties and early thirties locked away, Goldman saw her unlikely star rise as an activist and revolutionary, developing a national reputation as an orator and becoming personally acquainted with many of the great thinkers of the age. After his release in 1906, Berkman rejoined Goldman's efforts and served as her most constant source of support. But their extreme views and aggressive actions frightened the public and provoked government leaders. They were deemed menacing symbols of revolution and chaos, and eventually were deported to Russia in 1919 for violating the Espionage Act. Despite the unremitting censure at home and abroad, they remained participants in the intellectual and political upheavals across the United States, Europe, and Russia, offering potent descriptions of what they witnessed firsthand.

Berkman, known as Sasha, was an "eternal rebel" whose disturbing acts of violence were tempered by his tireless efforts to improve the lot of the oppressed.[4] Serving his sentence for his assault on Frick, he wrote the celebrated chronicle *Prison Memoirs of an Anarchist,* which detailed his bleak experience and exposed corruption in the American penal system. Between his release in 1906 and his deportation in 1919, he edited the two most prominent anarchist periodicals of the era, organized mass protests on behalf of radical and labor causes, and gave speeches around the country about his tribulations and beliefs. A spare but strong man with a soulful countenance, he was plagued by bouts of melancholy, the consequence of years spent in a cell. Admired by his friends for his brains and his nerve, he also could be self-centered and dogmatic, and his twin desires for justice and revenge met with disastrous results. Yet he possessed a gentle demeanor, a disarming humor. Within him mingled the visionary and the subversive, the humane and the harsh, the passionate and the pitiless.

As a child growing up in tsarist Russia, Sasha was captivated by the notion of revolution as a means of expression and defiance. When he immigrated to New York as a youth and found himself disillusioned by the policies and politics of the United States, he adopted the anarchist philosophy as a distillation of his early radical dreams. After his deportation from America, he languished abroad as a political exile for the rest of his days, without roots in any soil, clinging to his faith in the ultimate triumph of his anarchist ideals. As one friend observed, Berkman "spent his whole life in active rebellion to help the submerged and oppressed masses, without even counting the cost to himself and the comparative hopelessness of succeeding."[5]

THE BLAZING SUN TO SASHA'S MOROSE MOON, Emma Goldman was zealous, swaggering, and indefatigable. She championed a variety of causes, from women's equality, sexual liberation, and birth control to freedom of speech, labor activism, libertarian education, and artistic choice. Keenly intelligent, powerfully persuasive, she promoted her ideas with restless coast-to-coast tours, defying critics, police officers, journalists, and bureaucrats with equal ferocity.

Goldman became the object of suspicion and persecution, living her life in the steady glare of notoriety. When she defended Leon Czolgosz, the assassin of President William McKinley, she further incensed the authorities and shocked the public. Branded as a sponsor of violence, free love, and revolution, she was assailed in the press as "Red Emma," "Queen of the Anarchists," "the most dangerous woman in America." Yet Goldman was passionate about her adopted country. She loved it for its promise, longed for it when she was in exile, and viewed herself as an American champion, striving for an enlightened nation. While Berkman remained indifferent to any particular land, committed only to his ideology, Goldman considered the United States her true home.

Ignoring the storms forever swirling around her, Goldman continued to flout social and political conventions. Her reputation grew as the twentieth century took shape, and she became an international figure known to governments and agitators worldwide. With her audacity, her curiosity, her physical daring, and her resolute endorsement of controversial causes, she emerged as one of the most influential women of her time. The novelist Theodore Dreiser, while dining with her in Paris, assured Goldman that her life was "the richest of any woman's of our century."[6]

Emma's personal experiences were wide-ranging. She labored in factories, ran a restaurant, served as a trained nurse and midwife, lectured across the United States and around the globe, studied modern drama, founded the acclaimed journal *Mother Earth,* and authored a sweeping autobiography, *Living My Life.* A sharp critic of American capitalism and Soviet communism, she spent the last years of her life decrying the rise of Nazism and fighting the threat of fascism during the Spanish Civil War.

Charismatic, domineering, and sexually free, Goldman was a whirl of willful determination. Unapologetically menacing in her rhetoric, remembered as abrasive and imperious by her friends, she nevertheless was a driving force within the radical community, and no one questioned her commitment to her causes. "The spirit that animates Emma Goldman," said her comrade Voltairine de Cleyre, "is the only one which will emancipate the slave from his slavery, the tyrant from his tyranny—the spirit which is willing to dare and suffer."[7]

Both Alexander Berkman and Emma Goldman embodied that brave spirit. But scarred by childhoods in autocratic Russia, where dissent was possible only through rebellion, they nourished their lethal impulses as well. As angry young immigrants in America they were confounded by the rosy promises—and crushed by the perceived lapses of democracy—in the New World. Convinced that explosive expressions of propaganda by the deed were the only way to challenge government defects, they became warriors in what Berkman considered the first American age of terror, seeking an untenable path of aggression and inciting fear in the citizens they wished to inspire. Yet despite their brutal choices, Sasha and Emma ultimately exhorted a future of kinship and goodwill. And in the end, it was not their hostile pursuits but their energetic and eloquent commentary, their steadfast idealism, their quest for a just, harmonious society that made a lasting impact on contemporary America.

PART I

IMPELLING FORCES

1

MOTHER RUSSIA

Alexander Berkman entered the world a child of privilege, but while still a boy he was infused with the radicalism that would guide his whole life. He was born on November 21, 1870, in the Lithuanian capital, Vilnius, a bustling city located in the western provinces of the Russian Empire. The youngest of four children, he originally was called Ovsei, although he later adopted the more traditional Russian name Alexander. To his family and friends, he was known by the diminutive, Sasha.[1]

His father, Osip, or Joseph, Berkman, was a prosperous leather merchant, whose business selling "uppers," the top pieces of shoes and boots, brought him sufficient success to qualify him as a member of the first guild of merchants. Sasha's mother, Yetta Natanson, the elegant daughter of an affluent mercantile family, was a devoted presence with "beautiful black eyes" and a "sweet, tender voice." His siblings, Sonya (the eldest child and only girl), Boris, and Max, were gifted and bright.[2]

With ample wealth and a solid domestic foundation, Sasha enjoyed as many opportunities as Jews or other minorities could attain in tsarist Russia, even as they were compelled to live within the Pale of Settlement, an area established in the late eighteenth century to segregate Russian Jews. When Sasha was two or three years old, his family relocated to Sventsiany, a small town about fifty miles away on the St. Petersburg–Warsaw railroad, home to his maternal grandparents, the Natansons. The Berkmans settled in comfortably for the next few years, enjoying the opportunities brought about by changes instituted by the reigning tsar, Alexander II, one of the last of the Romanov dynasty.

Alexander II acceded to the Russian throne in 1855 during the Crimean War, which pitted Russia against Britain, France, and the Ottoman Empire. The conflict was messy and unwieldy on all sides, with poorly executed battle plans and sloppy strategy. For Tsar Alexander, it exposed just how ineffectual and regressive his country had become. At the war's sorry conclusion, Alexander was faced with an empire in social disarray, and, fearing revolt, he took drastic steps to modernize Russia, most notably by emancipating the serfs and promising a regime of "equal education, equal justice, tolerance, and humaneness" to all.[3] He abolished or relaxed a number of laws established by his father, Tsar Nicholas I, some of which affected Jews, such as a conscription act, employment restrictions, and educational limitations.[4] By the time of Sasha's birth, many among the mercantile elite, including the Natansons and Berkmans, were optimistic that the rule of the "tsar-liberator" would bring further reforms and that Jews would eventually be accepted as equal citizens, admitted to all circles of Russian society.[5]

In 1877 Osip Berkman, as a merchant of the first guild, was granted the right to live outside the Pale, and he moved to Russia's sprawling capital, St. Petersburg, a city previously barred to him. There his business flourished. The family acquired a lavish house in the city and a country place in a fashionable suburb, with a staff of servants to attend them. The children were provided with tutors and sent to a classical *gymnasium,* a school reserved for the private elements of St. Petersburg society.

Yet the seven-year-old Sasha, an intense and emotional child, soon grew agitated by the events churning around him. During the 1870s St. Petersburg was alive with revolutionary activity, and Sasha's brother Max, who displayed a boyish enthusiasm for civic mischief, related stirring stories of insurgents and rebels, dramatic acts of daring, and tragic tales of sacrifice. It was a period, as Emma Goldman later noted, "when everything in Russia was being torn from its old moorings, and the seeds for a new conception of human society—political, religious, moral, economic and social—were being planted," an experience that Berkman, "sensitive and idealistic, could not escape." It was also a period of escalating violence, directed against the autocracy. Clouds of a widespread revolutionary movement had gathered, convincing many in the ruling class that insurrection was inevitable, Tsar Alexander's reforms notwithstanding.[6]

In an effort to forestall full-blown revolution, the government rounded up a number of people suspected of sedition and staged a mass trial of 193 populists, most of whom were radical young students and elites intent on galvanizing the Russian peasantry into enlightenment and revolt. They were charged with a range of subversive activities, and although many were acquitted, the event sparked further protest. On January 24, 1878, the day after the trial concluded, a well-educated twenty-nine-year-old named Vera Zasulich shot and wounded the police chief of St. Petersburg, General F. F. Trepov, who had ordered the flogging of a political prisoner. Zasulich was tried and found not guilty by a jury, but her act triggered a flurry of assassinations. In May 1878 a captain in charge of the Kiev gendarmes was struck down by revolutionists. In August the head of the security police, General N. V. Mezentsev, was stabbed to death in broad daylight in the capital. The following February the governor-general of Kharkov, Prince Dmitri Kropotkin, a cousin of the prominent Russian anarchist Peter Kropotkin, was shot and killed as he left the theater.

In April 1879 the tsar himself became a target. While out for his morning walk in the grounds of the Winter Palace, Alexander was shot at five times by a young populist, and escaped with a hole in his overcoat. In November the People's Will, a Russian terrorist group, tried three times to blow up his train as he returned from a holiday in the Crimea. These attempts, all unsuccessful, were followed in February 1880 by the dramatic dynamiting of the Winter Palace, from which the emperor again escaped unharmed. Proud of his achievements as a reformer, aware of the improvements he had labored to bring about, Alexander II was incensed and baffled by his attackers. "What," he asked, "have these wretches got against me? Why do they hunt me down like a wild beast?"[7]

The assaults continued, reaching a climax in 1881. On March 13 the terrorists struck a mortal blow. Tsar Alexander was on his way to the Winter Palace when a bomb was hurled at his carriage. The carriage was wrecked and a score of people were injured, including a royal guard and a delivery boy who died soon after. The tsar himself initially was unhurt. But when he emerged from the carriage, a second bomb was thrown, inflicting grievous wounds upon him. Rushed to the palace, he died an hour later.

Alexander II's violent death stunned government leaders, as well as the country at large. The police went in search of revolutionary conspirators, and Sasha later recalled a "terrorized city." His parents were on edge and apprehensive, dreading the reaction bound to follow. Young Sasha, however, was intrigued by the martyrdom of the populist militants, five of whom were sent to the scaffold.[8]

As Osip and Yetta feared, the assassination of Alexander II ushered in a period of repression. The policy of the new emperor, the late tsar's thirty-six-year-old son Alexander III, was to crush all political opposition while also reversing the liberal reforms of his slain father. Soon followed mass arrests and deportations, strict censorship of the press, and tightened control of the schools and universities, where student organizations were banned and disciplinary codes enforced.

Jews became primary targets for renewed persecution, caused in part by resentment over their growing role in the economic and cultural life of the nation. Educational and professional quotas were reintroduced, and restrictions were placed on where Jews could own or purchase land, including within the Pale, resulting in mass evictions. A rash of pogroms broke out in the southwestern provinces and spread to hundreds of cities and towns, destroying property and claiming lives. The new tsar himself set the tone. When presented with a report about the progressively dire condition of the Russian Jewry, he wrote on the document, "We must not forget that it was the Jews who crucified our Lord and spilled His precious blood."[9]

The turmoil and suppression spurred rebels around the country to redouble their efforts, causing mayhem in all areas of society. Before long the unrest intruded directly on the Berkman family's life. In November 1882, a week before his twelfth birthday, Sasha came home from school, excited to tell his mother that he had just passed his exams. He found the house tense, doors closed. He overheard his mother arguing with her brother, Nathan Natanson, a wealthy businessman from Kovno, and caught the word *Nihilist,* a reference to the Russian rebels who protested the tsarist government with violence. Sasha soon learned that Maxim Natanson, the youngest Natanson brother, was in trouble. A revolutionary exiled in Siberia, Maxim had been sentenced to death.[10]

A pall descended on the Berkman home. Sasha himself was miserable—the charismatic Maxim was his favorite uncle. Yet a "deep interest" had been aroused in his consciousness, a curiosity about the perilous drama surrounding the fate of Maxim, whose name was now spoken only in whispers. His parents and elders may have been aghast, but for Sasha, the term

Nihilist was illicit and thrilling, and "conjured up visions of dreaded gendarmes, iron chains, and the frozen steppes of Siberia." He later said, "Vaguely I felt that these forbidden people, the Nihilists, somehow suffered for the sake of others—I did not know why or how—but my young heart glowed with admiration."[11]

For Sasha, Uncle Maxim became a primary source of inspiration, "my ideal," he afterward put it, "of a noble and great man." Mark Andreevich Natanson, as he was formally known, was in fact one of the most celebrated figures in the Russian revolutionary movement, and his activities spanned a half-century, from the height of the populist movement in the 1870s to the Russian Revolution of 1917.[12]

Natanson was a brilliant youth who graduated from the gymnasium with honors in 1868 and was admitted to medical school in St. Petersburg. Inspired by the French socialist philosopher Charles Fourier and the Welsh reformer Robert Owen, he organized the radical Chaikovsky circle, of which Peter Kropotkin, Sasha's future mentor, was a member. He also founded Land and Liberty, the largest revolutionary society of the era, and traveled across the country and abroad to rally his allies. He quickly drew the ire of the law, and was imprisoned in Archangel Province and in Finland before escaping and returning to St. Petersburg in 1875, where he lived as an outlaw and engaged in activities such as masterminding Kropotkin's own dramatic jailbreak. Natanson was arrested again in 1877, spent two years in St. Petersburg's notorious Peter and Paul prison, and then was banished to Siberia for a decade.

It was during this period of incarceration in the frigid wasteland that Maxim's family feared for his life. In the end, Maxim was not condemned to death but was transferred from Irkutsk to Yakutsk, a more remote and grueling place of exile. Sasha later came to suspect that the Natansons' distinguished connections had saved his uncle from the gallows. When Sasha told Emma Goldman about his childhood, she recalled that he dwelled "particularly on his beloved Uncle Maxim and on the shock he had experienced on learning that he had been condemned to die." The threat to his uncle marked Berkman's first real motivation to learn about revolutionists and their goals.[13]

More hardship followed. Shortly after Sasha turned twelve, Osip Berkman fell ill and died. Sasha's life underwent a drastic change. In addition to the trauma of losing his father, he was forced to grapple with the realities of financial instability. The business had to be sold, and the Berkmans lost their right to live in St. Petersburg. In need of aid, Yetta took her children to Kovno, a river port city and industrial center, to seek help from her brother Nathan. An affluent entrepreneur of conservative views, Nathan owned a bank and dabbled in real estate. He was generous with his assistance. Settling his sister in one of his buildings, in a second-floor flat above police headquarters, he arranged for private tutors and enrollment at a top-quality school for her children.

Small, dark, and earnest, Sasha was a spirited boy with a distinctly antagonistic bent. He never ran from a fight, tangling with "our warring school gangs" on the banks of the river Nieman. In his early teens, he discovered the mysteries of sex. "My heart beats tumultuously," he later reminisced, "as I meet little Nadya on the way to school. Pretending I do not see her, I turn around to admire the golden locks, when I surprise her stealthily watching me." With his playmates, he trailed Nadya and other schoolgirls on their way to swim in the river, and cut peepholes in a door to watch them undress. He recalled seeing another girl, "pert Masha," smile at him from her window across the street, and kissing the household chambermaid Rosa, who threatened to tell his mother.[14]

Sasha had other interests as well. He was a voracious reader who steeped himself both in the Greek and Roman classics and in the great Russian writers of his time, favoring Turgenev, Dostoevsky, and Tolstoy. He absorbed Turgenev's *Fathers and Sons,* caught up by the Nihilist philosophies described in its pages. During Sasha's early years at the gymnasium he was one of the most promising students, destined for a coveted gold or silver medal awarded to the finest scholars. As he grew older, however, he fell increasingly under the spell of radical ideas, which distracted him from his studies.

Sasha's favorite literary character was Rakhmetov, the protagonist of *What Is to Be Done?,* a novel written by the Russian philosopher and journalist Nikolai Chernyshevsky while he was in prison for criticizing the government; the book's publication resulted in his banishment to Siberia. The protagonist, Rakhmetov, was created as a prototype of the new revolutionary—hard, austere, single-minded—and he gripped Sasha's imagination. Rakhmetov welcomed physical privation, eating raw meat and sleeping on a bed of nails. He had no personal life, no wife, no friends, and no family ties that might soften or divert him. He adopted a deliberately brusque manner of conversation to discourage personal connections and social interaction, and bestowed his money upon the revolutionary cause rather than on comforts for himself. The figure of Rakhmetov remained a profound influence on Berkman, who would later borrow his name as an alias when he went to shoot Henry Clay Frick in 1892.[15]

Mesmerized by the exciting new ideas he found in the pages of Turgenev and Chernyshevsky, enthralled by the worldly older boys at school, awed by the exploits of the most daring revolutionaries of the era, Sasha began to question the social and political values on which he had been reared. His transformation from a cosseted boy into an avidly committed rebel was astonishingly rapid. The autocracy and the social systems of Russia, Sasha decided, were politically corrupt and socially exploitative. Craving a cause to serve, he adopted populism as his new creed, inspired by the bleak fate of the rebels who did not abandon their ideals despite the hard life, or early death, that awaited them.

Sasha followed the activities of the populists with adulation. He developed a special admiration for the women in their ranks, among them Sofya Perovskaya, who was executed by the state for her role in the assassination of Alexander II, and Maxim Natanson's comrade Vera Figner, who spent twenty years in harsh confinement. "Perfect comrades they were," he wrote, "often stronger than the men. Brave, noble women that fill the prisons and *étapes,* tramp the toilsome road."[16]

As personal models, though, it was the men he viewed as paragons. In addition to his Uncle Maxim were the young terrorists who relentlessly plotted the death of the tsar, constructed bombs, planted dynamite, and martyred themselves for the cause.[17] Berkman considered these men "a hallowed treasure," and he nurtured in his deepest fantasies a desire to follow their path.[18] He dreamed of a life of intrigue and danger, of suffering and sacrifice, of extreme dedication to what he was convinced was a righteous purpose.

Sasha joined a secret group at school to read and discuss revolutionary literature, an activity prohibited during the reign of Alexander III. He circulated banned material and, according to a fellow student, drafted revolutionary tracts and printed them with supplies stolen from the school. He still was recognized as a bright student, but one saddled with a disrespectful and defiant nature. "He was an unruly pupil," the schoolmate later recalled, "difficult to manage, and was frequently involved in trouble with the teachers."[19] Publicly breaching convention, Sasha presented an essay in class titled "There Is No God," for which he was punished with a year's demotion on the grounds of "precocious godlessness, dangerous tendencies and insubordination." Forced to take classes with younger children, he felt himself "disgraced, humiliated."[20]

Yetta saw that Sasha was becoming a radical like her brother Maxim, who was languishing in Siberia, and she worried about her son's future. Their relationship became strained. They quarreled over his beliefs and behavior, over Yetta's strict management of the servants, over Sasha's ideas about class structure and government. Yetta grew so incensed during one argument that she struck him on the head with a ladle, and he stormed from the house in a rage. The rift only grew wider, and never healed. In 1887 Yetta became very ill. She withdrew to the Natanson home in Sventsiany for the summer, where she was treated by the family physician and attended by two nurses. Sasha was awash in guilt, convinced that his surly and wayward behavior had exacerbated her condition. But before he could apologize, she died.

At sixteen, Sasha was left an orphan. He became the ward of Uncle Nathan, a man for whom he felt contempt. Conventional and comfortable with his lot, Nathan was anxious to preserve order and avoid hassles, and adhered without argument to the repressive policies of Alexander III, hoping for improvement in the future. Despite all the financial and practical assistance his uncle had provided him and his siblings, Sasha considered Nathan materialistic and cowardly, unworthy of respect. Nathan, in turn, thought Sasha was an ungovernable hothead, a source of continual headache and embarrassment. He could not understand what attracted his nephew to radical ideas, and worried that Sasha would antagonize the authorities, disgrace the family name, and get them all into serious trouble.

Indeed, Sasha soon faced a crisis. In the fall of 1887 he was caught bribing a janitor and stealing copies of the annual school exam. He was expelled and branded as a "nihilist conspirator."[21] At seventeen, he was without parents, without a school degree, without any idea what to do next.

As an adult, Sasha often wondered why he had chosen a path of rebellion. He said to Emma Goldman, "My brothers Max and Boris and my sister all grew up with me in the same early environment. They were all conservative. But my Uncle Max was a rebel. No doubt he got it from some distant ancestor, as I also got it from the same source, no doubt. That merely shows heredity influences, but the why and how of it we don't know of course."[22] Goldman concurred in this view. Even without his uncle's inspiration, Emma wrote, "The intense youth would have, no doubt, consecrated himself to the cause of humanity. The creative revolutionary, like the true artist, is conditioned more by the impelling forces within him than by outer influences. Alexander Berkman's whole life is proof of it."[23]

Emma Goldman was subject to many of the same impelling forces and influences. She was born in Kovno on June 27, 1869, to Taube Bienowitch and Abraham Goldman, well-educated Jews from middle-class families. Bienowitch had lost her first husband, a physician, to tuberculosis, and, left alone with two young daughters, Helena and Lena, she remarried with some reluctance. She and Abraham had four children together: Emma, born first, followed by boys Louis, Herman, and Morris. Emma moved several times as a child, first to Popelan, in the Baltic province of Kurland; then in 1876 to Konigsberg, Prussia, where she lived with her grandmother and attended a German school; and in 1881 to St. Petersburg.

The Goldman family unit was not a happy one. Taube continued to grieve over the death of her first husband, and Emma found her mother aloof and withdrawn as a result. But it was Abraham Goldman who caused Emma profound anguish. "Since my earliest recollection," she later wrote, "home had been stifling, my father's presence terrifying."[24] Viciously abusive to his family, Abraham was also frustrated by persistent money problems; he mishandled Taube's dowry and failed to maintain a successful business or steady income. He had no interest in his daughter's education or aspirations, demanding that she abandon school and help support the family. Emma was forced to neglect her studies and take a series of jobs, including working in a glove factory and as a seamstress.

Emma was sharply alert and fiercely outspoken from an early age, and the range of injustices she witnessed—social, governmental, and personal—inflamed her moral sense. As a child and young woman, she was repeatedly mistreated by teachers and employers, by her parents, and by men young and old. Her first experiences with sex were confusing and coarse. One violent encounter with a handsome hotel clerk—he courted her for a time, lured her to an empty room in the hotel, plied her with wine, then assaulted her—left her forever scarred. "Strange," she later wrote, "I felt no shame—only a great shock at the discovery that the contact between man and woman could be so brutal and painful. . . . After that I always felt between two fires in the presence of men. Their lure remained strong, but it was always mingled with violent revulsion."[25]

The increasing political repression in Russia affected Emma most acutely; like Sasha, she sympathized with the revolutionaries of the People's Will and read the works of Turgenev and Chernyshevsky's *What Is to Be Done?* She, too, had a maternal uncle who was involved with the Nihilists, a source of distress for Taube. Sasha noticed these similarities, along with their shared Kovno backgrounds, when they met years later. "We have much in common, haven't we," he remarked. Emma was as captivated as Sasha by the dynamism of the Nihilist rebels. As she wrote in her memoirs, the radicals of whom she learned as a girl ultimately became her "heroes and martyrs, henceforth my guiding stars."[26]

Emma continued to clash with her father. When she was fifteen, he tried to marry her off, asserting that women were useful only to cook and to bear children. Emma was defiant. "I would not listen to his schemes," she recalled. "I wanted to study, to know life, to travel." The following year, 1885, she saw an opportunity to escape. Lena had recently married and moved to Rochester, New York, and Helena was preparing to emigrate there as well. Emma begged her father to let her join her older sisters in America; after much debate, he finally agreed. As Emma later wrote, "the exciting anticipation of what the new land would offer stimulated my imagination and sent my blood tingling."[27]

In December Emma and Helena traveled to the German port of Hamburg, where they set sail for New York. Arriving on a freezing January day, they thrilled at the prospect of a fresh start, praying they would "find a place in the generous heart of America."[28] They struggled through the chaos at Castle Garden, an old fort at the Battery that served as New York's Emigrant Landing Depot from 1855 until 1891, through which some eight million immigrants entered the United States. There they greeted their adopted country.

Emma and Helena moved into Lena's tidy little flat, and Emma got a job in a clothing factory, sewing overcoats for $2.50 a week, a wage barely enough to live on, with nothing left over for the treats she so enjoyed—books, theater tickets, personal luxuries. It did not take her long to become disenchanted with her new surroundings. The dreary grind, the drabness of factory life, quickly disabused her of the belief that America differed fundamentally from Russia. Soon she grew convinced that she merely had moved from one oppressive land to another. Rochester, she later wrote with sour contempt, represented "my inauguration into the beauties of American factory life; the place where I first learned the brazenness of American liberty." She left her job and found better pay at a small factory near Lena's home.[29]

The rest of her family—her parents, and brothers Herman and Morris (Louis had died as a small child)—arrived from St. Petersburg in the fall of 1886, and Emma and Helena moved with them into a cramped four-room house that afforded little peace or privacy. Toward the end of the year, Emma took up with a fellow worker at the factory named Jacob Kershner, a Russian Jew who had come to the United States about five years earlier. He was attractive and attentive and pursued her with earnest devotion, proposing after four months. Although she considered herself too young for marriage, Emma was bored and lonely. Jacob "filled a void" in her life, and they wed in February 1887.[30]

The marriage proved unhappy. The couple argued frequently, and Kershner struggled with impotence. Goldman soon lost interest in her new husband, and Kershner, discouraged and insecure, turned to cardplaying, which consumed his salary. Convention deterred Emma, a married woman, from holding a job, and the rapid depletion of the household funds to his gambling added to their woes. When matters did not improve within a year, Emma took a dramatic step, and divorced him.

Single again, Emma went to New Haven, Connecticut, where she found work in a corset factory and befriended a group of young Russian immigrants, most of them socialists and anarchists. In the evenings they gathered to discuss political and cultural issues, sometimes inviting speakers from New York City. Emma enjoyed these lively discussions and the independent life in Connecticut, but she fell ill, and was forced to return to Rochester. Once more she began seeing Kershner, and he begged her to reconcile, threatening suicide if she refused. The union again failed, and she left her husband, this time for good. Reviled by the conservative Jewish community, Goldman departed Rochester in August 1889 to seek her future in New York City.[31]

As for Sasha, the start of 1888 found him still in Kovno, still at loose ends. He had no school diploma, little chance for a university education, and, with his eighteenth birthday looming, scant hope of avoiding enlistment in the military. Uncle Nathan, in an effort to rescue his floundering nephew, put him to work as a clerk in his bank, but Sasha could not get along with the other employees and had to be dismissed.[32] His reputation as a troublemaker made it difficult for him to find another job, and he chafed under the patronage of Natanson, the "dictator of Kovno," he called him.[33] As the weeks went by, Sasha found his situation increasingly intolerable. Russia seemed a grimmer place than ever. He resolved to emigrate to America.

From what he had gleaned at school and from friends, the United States seemed a golden republic, a beacon of equality and brotherhood. It was a country that knew no tsar, no Pale, no discrimination laws. It was a haven for the persecuted and oppressed. In the Kovno library he scanned "every line of American news" and was filled with hope. "There," he wrote, "beyond the ocean, was the land of noble achievements, a glorious free country, where men walked erect in the full stature of mankind—the very realization of my youthful dreams."[34]

The more Sasha learned of America, the more impatient he became to depart. An occasion arose in the winter of 1888, when his brother Max was preparing to enter medical school at the University of Leipzig.[35] The two traveled together as far as eastern Prussia, where Sasha went on alone to Hamburg and secured steerage passage to New York.[36] He sailed in early February 1888 and landed in New York on February 18. His name on the manifest is given as Moses Berkmann, most likely derived from the name Ovsei. His age is listed as "17," his occupation, "Dealer," and his place of origin, "Kovno."[37] Like Emma before him, Sasha entered the United States at Castle Garden. Four years later, on January 1, 1892, it was replaced by the freshly constructed immigrant station on Ellis Island; Castle Garden was then converted into the city aquarium.

Berkman arrived in America alone and friendless, without even a name or address to turn to. "I did not know a single soul in the whole country," he later wrote, "but I looked upon the New World as the promised land of Liberty and Justice, and I was happy to have at last escaped from the tyranny of the Romanoffs."[38] Yet despite his raw childhood memories, Sasha's nostalgia for Russia never quite left him; during his years in America he thought often, and wistfully, of his homeland.

2

PIONEERS OF LIBERTY

Once on American soil, Sasha stood "a lone stranger, bewildered by the flurry of Castle Garden, yet strong with hope and courage to carve my fate in freedom. . . . How inspiring is liberty! The very air breathes enthusiasm and strength, and with confident ardor I embrace the new life." But that life proved hard for the young émigré. He settled on the Lower East Side, the Jewish immigrant quarter of New York. The neighborhood, while vibrant, was hectic, congested, impoverished. He found lodging in a succession of cheap rented rooms and dark, airless apartments, overrun with bedbugs and cockroaches. Seventeen years old, he spoke no English, knew no trade, and had only sixty rubles in his pocket to keep body and soul together until he could find employment. He took whatever work he could get.[1]

His first job was clearing streets of snow from the great blizzard of 1888, which overwhelmed New York City in mid-March. Soon afterward he was hired by a jersey factory on Greene Street, but thanks to his customary belligerent behavior, he left after a quarrel with other workers. He got a job packing boxes in a shirt factory on East Eleventh Street at six dollars a week. He then learned the cigarmakers' trade and worked for three months as a buncher, preparing and shaping the inside part of cigars. After this he served as an operator in a ladies' cloak factory, toiling fourteen hours a day on a sewing machine for miserable pay. "A slave driver," Berkman called the foreman.[2]

Thus did Sasha, a well-born student with a classical education, become a pauperized worker. Raised in upper-middle-class affluence, he was now often forced to go without necessities, including shelter or food. At such moments, according to Emma Goldman, he lived on only a few pennies a day, reduced to sleeping on park benches and in alleys and doorways of buildings. "Ah, the wretchedness of those first years in America!" he later moaned, "the sordid misery of my 'greenhorn' days." Adding to his gloom, he faced the scorn of his relatives in Russia, who chastised him for having disgraced his late parents' good name by becoming "a low, dirty workingman."[3]

Not that Berkman was personally ashamed of being a worker. On the contrary, he was proud of his proletarian status, happy, in theory, to "join the ranks of the world's producers" and experience "the full manhood conferred by the dignity of labor."[4] Nevertheless, Berkman could not escape a feeling of disenchantment. He had carried to America a dream of freedom and equality, eager to turn his back on the cruel despotism of Russia. Instead he found a world of crowded slums, hard conditions, stark contrasts of poverty and wealth—a new world that differed all too little from the old. The values of industrial capitalism were to him vicious and repugnant. Immigrants were treated carelessly, callously. He saw American society as heartless and unjust, its culture materialistic, the desire for power and riches dominant.

The country, with President Grover Cleveland serving his first term in the White House, was still suffering the aftershocks of the Civil War and Reconstruction. Race relations were tumultuous, the economy was unstable, and immigrants faced constant harassment. From Sasha's perspective, the ideal of American democracy, the land of opportunity, now seemed little more than a myth. "Life in the tenements is sordid," he wrote, "the fate of the worker dreary. There is no 'dignity of labor.' Sweatshop bread is bitter. Oppression guards the golden promise, and servile brutality is the only earnest of success."[5]

But the notorious Haymarket incident had the most profound influence on Sasha's view of American society. Three months before he left Hamburg, a hanging had occurred in Chicago that, more than anything else, entrenched his disillusionment with his newly adopted country. The Haymarket affair, a landmark in the history of anarchism, had been set in motion on May 4, 1886, when anarchists held a meeting near Chicago's

Haymarket Square to protest against police brutality. As the meeting was drawing to a close, a contingent of policemen marched in and ordered the participants to disperse. At that moment a bomb was thrown into the ranks of the police, killing one and injuring others. The officers responded by opening fire on the crowd, killing and wounding a number of civilians as well as many of their own men—sixty-seven policemen were hurt, eight of whom afterward died.[6]

The bomb thrower was never apprehended. But eight Chicago anarchists were brought to trial and speedily convicted of murder. On November 11, 1887, after unsuccessful appeals to higher courts, four of the defendants, Albert Parsons, August Spies, George Engel, and Adolph Fischer, were hanged. A fifth, Louis Lingg, committed suicide in his cell the day before the executions with a small explosive device he put into his mouth, and the remaining three were sentenced to long terms in prison.[7]

The eight Chicago anarchists became martyrs to the cause. Their pictures were displayed at anarchist meetings, and November 11 was observed in their honor. The last words of Parsons and Spies, respectively—"Let the voice of the people be heard!" and "The time will come when our silence will be more powerful than the voices you strangle today"—were often quoted in anarchist speeches and writings. Just over six years later, in 1893, the three survivors, Samuel Fielden, Oscar Neebe, and Michael Schwab, were pardoned by Governor John Peter Altgeld, who assailed the judge for conducting the trial with "malicious ferocity" and found that the evidence did not show that any of the eight anarchists had been involved in the bombing.[8]

The case of the Chicago anarchists, prominently reported in the press, kindled public interest in anarchist individuals and ideas. The unfairness of the trial, the harshness of the sentences, the dignified bearing of the defendants, and the horror of their hangings fired the imagination of young idealists and won converts to the cause. By giving the anarchists their first martyrs, the Haymarket executions stimulated the growth of the movement, especially among recently arrived immigrants who were finding their new country indifferent and the authorities undependable. After 1887 the number of anarchist groups rose swiftly. While still in Russia, Berkman had learned cursorily of the executions from an account in the Kovno library: "Anarchists hanged in Chicago," he read. To a student nearby he whispered, "What is an anarchist?" "Sh-sh," came the response, "Same as Nihilists." Not until he arrived in America, however, would Sasha feel the full impact of the event.[9]

Emma Goldman had also been affected by the Haymarket affair. The Chicago anarchists had been arrested four months after her arrival in Rochester, and, agonizing over their fate, she learned as much as she could about the case. "I devoured every line on anarchism," she said, "every word about the [defendants], their lives, their work. I read about their heroic stand while on trial and their marvelous defense. I saw a new world opening before me."[10]

Then came November 11, 1887, the date of their execution. Goldman's spirits were shattered. Yet she felt that something "wonderful had been born in my soul. A great ideal, a burning faith, a determination to dedicate myself to the memory of my martyred comrades, to make their cause my own, to make known to the world their beautiful lives and heroic deaths." The execution of the Chicago anarchists, she said, "was the decisive influence of my life."[11]

When Berkman was getting settled in New York, Haymarket remained a hot topic of discussion. The Chicago anarchists reminded Sasha of the populists he had revered in Russia, and he, too, avidly consumed as much information as he could in the aftermath of their deaths. What he read left him deeply disturbed. "The trial of these men," he later wrote, "was the most hellish conspiracy of capital against labor in the history of America. Perjured evidence, bribed jurymen, and police revenge combined to bring about their doom." America, Berkman concluded bitterly, was no less despotic than Russia.[12]

In many ways, it was Haymarket that brought Berkman to anarchism. The example of the Chicago anarchists, he wrote, was "a potent and vital inspiration," and he wholeheartedly adopted their philosophy. "I studied the life around me," he told a friend many years later, "and the political and social conditions of the New World. My vision of America as the land of freedom and promise soon became dead ashes. I realized that political freedom without economic equality was an empty sound. I saw the coarseness, brutality, and inequalities of American life as due to the system of capitalism. I became an Anarchist and decided to devote my life and energy to the cause of the Chicago Martyrs."[13]

THUS INSPIRED, BERKMAN BRUSHED ASIDE the practical annoyances he faced as a new immigrant and immediately set about immersing himself in radical activities. The Lower East Side at that time was the center of a thriving immigrant culture, reflecting every shade of political opinion. In its restaurants and cafés, its meeting halls and clubs, its basements and tenement rooms, gathered an assortment of youthful rebels, artistic as well as social, who argued into the night through a haze of tobacco smoke over endless cups of coffee and tea.

Before fastening on the anarchists, Berkman mingled with radicals of various stripes, mostly immigrants from Russia and Germany. They were political exiles; former members of the People's Will who had fascinated him as a boy; and adherents of left-wing circles such as the Russian Progressive Union. He talked with the German socialist Alexander Jonas, who advocated a gradual and mainstream approach to governmental reform and criticized the impetuous anarchists, saying they had been driven "more or less crazy," as he put it, "by the cruelties and revolting injustices of our present law and order."[14]

But Sasha regarded gradual reform as the equivalent of surrender. Small or measured improvements to the workingman's plight, such as shorter hours and higher wages, were just feeble distractions, useless balms, bribes to prevent rebellion. He wanted change now. The idea of a grand upheaval, of complete and immediate transformation, was far more satisfying for someone like Sasha—young, emotional, and militant. "Our whole civilization, false to the core as it is, must be destroyed, to be born anew," he declared. "Anarchism alone can save the world."[15]

During the summer of 1888 Sasha joined the Pioneers of Liberty, the first Jewish anarchist group in America. The group had been formed as a direct consequence of the Haymarket case, on October 9, 1886, the day the sentence was pronounced on Parsons, Spies, and their associates. The founders, about a dozen Jewish laborers with chewy names such as Faltzblatt, Bernstein, Strashunsky, and Yudelevich, were soon joined by a number of young writers and speakers, including Saul Yanovsky, Roman Lewis, Hillel Solotaroff, Moshe Katz, J. A. Maryson, and David Edelstadt. They opened headquarters at 56 Orchard Street, a four-story tenement in the heart of the ghetto, and quickly became a force on the Lower East Side.

The Pioneers of Liberty sponsored lectures at Cooper Union, the celebrated institution on Astor Place; arranged rallies in Union Square; and held Friday night meetings at its Orchard Street club. It affiliated itself with the International Working People's Association, the group to which the Haymarket anarchists had belonged, and honored the Chicago defendants as martyrs. The Pioneers commemorated major events in the anarchist movement, such as the Paris Commune, so named after a band of French activists seized control of Paris for seventy-two days in 1871. Since the bulk of Pioneers members were workers, many in the garment trades, the group took part in strikes against sweatshop labor and helped organize some of the first Jewish unions in New York City, including the cloakmakers and kneepants workers.

Members of the group spoke on street corners and in rented halls, denouncing capitalism as evil and condemning the rich as materialistic hypocrites, beseeching workers to awaken from their enslavement, and calling for a new society without formal government. They opposed voting on election day, criticized religion as mere superstition and a dangerous ally of the state, and encouraged young radicals to emulate the Russian revolutionaries who sacrificed all for the sake of the poor and did not shy from violence to achieve their goals. As a softer counterpart to this abrasive rhetoric, the Pioneers arranged entertainment for the group's friends and followers, such as dances, picnics, and concerts, providing an alternate society of recreation and companionship to fuse with its revolutionary underpinnings.

THE PIONEERS OF LIBERTY WAS JUST the thing for which Sasha had been searching, and he became a leading member of the group. Extreme and confrontational in concept, it suited both his fierce instincts and his uncompromising vision of a world of equality and freedom. The cause gave him purpose and direction, a defined code. It helped him channel his energy, his resentment, and his passion. "We were just a handful then," he later recalled, "young men and women fired by the enthusiasm of a sublime ideal."[16]

Still a teenager, he was one of the youngest in the group, and at only five-feet-five-and-a-half-inches tall, he hardly cut a commanding figure. He had dark hair, brown eyes, protruding ears, and a bulbous mouth, which won him the nickname "Tolstogub" (the Russian term for "thick lips"). But he was wiry and tough, and his high forehead and rimless glasses gave him a serious, cerebral look, accentuated by the intense, almost severe expression that his face habitually wore. Like many of his friends he was an incessant smoker, though not a heavy drinker. He never drank whiskey, and "beer very seldom."[17]

In spite of his youth, Berkman's comrades regarded him with respect. They admired his earnestness and independent spirit, his sharp and lucid intelligence, and his eagerness to toil for the cause. He was meticulous by nature and as Goldman later observed, "always a scholar . . . well-acquainted with all sorts of scientific works." His fluency in Russian and German, as well as a general facility with languages, added to the esteem of his peers. Coming principally from Yiddish-speaking shtetls, the majority of Jewish immigrants knew little if any Russian, let alone other European languages. Berkman, by contrast, had grown up in a Russian-speaking family and had attended elite Russian schools where he had acquired his knowledge of German and a familiarity with Greek and Latin. To some extent he had also been exposed to Yiddish and Hebrew, but Russian was his primary tongue. "I really learned Yiddish in America," he afterward wrote, "through association with my many Yiddish friends and comrades." In New York, he also began to pick up some English.[18]

Berkman's aptitude for languages enabled him to widen his familiarity with anarchists of different backgrounds. In New York at that time existed English, Yiddish, French, Italian, German, and Czech anarchist groups and organizations. Sasha became acquainted with them all. One of his favorite haunts was Frank Hall at 123 West Houston Street, a ballroom where a French league met on Saturday evenings. Another was Justus Schwab's basement tavern at 50 East First Street, advertised as a "gathering place for all bold, joyful, freedom-loving spirits," a rendezvous for revolutionaries from across the world. Schwab's clientele was predominantly German-speaking; in the 1880s New York contained the third-largest German population of any city in the world, following only Berlin and Vienna. The quarter of the Lower East Side concentrated between Houston and Fourteenth Street was known as "Little Germany" or "Kleindeutschland," and a number of Austrian and Swiss immigrants lived in the neighborhood as well. The German-speaking anarchists in New York formed the largest ethnic component of anarchists in the city, many of whom were disciples of Johann Most.[19]

Johann Most was the leading German anarchist in America. Born in Augsburg in 1846 to unwed parents, he endured the early death of his mother from cholera, mistreatment from a cruel stepmother, and social humiliations caused by his deformed jaw, the result of an operation when he was thirteen. Awkward and sensitive, the young Most aspired to be an actor, but his physical disfigurement ended this dream. Instead he was apprenticed to a bookbinder, a harsh man who reinforced Most's introversion. Most left the apprenticeship and traveled through Europe, eventually encountering a group of socialist workingmen in Switzerland, who accepted him as a friend and roused him with their ideology. Most found his calling as an agitator, and put his dramatic skills to use as an orator. He began to write and publish his thoughts in activist journals and soon gained acclaim throughout Europe as a popular speaker and a savvy editor. Authorities retaliated with multiple arrests and orders of expulsion.

When Most relocated to New York in December 1882, already a hero and martyr in radical circles thanks to seven years of hard prison time and his fearless devotion to the cause, he advocated violent reaction and disdained limited reform. Eventually he would reject such extremism and adopt a more conciliatory, less destructive approach. But when Sasha first met him, Most firmly believed that compromise was futile, that it would dull the motivation of the laboring class, and that revolution was the only means of curing social disharmony. He went so far as to urge the workers to arm themselves with weapons in order to exterminate the "reptile brood," the "race of parasites," as he deemed capitalists and rulers. A year before the Haymarket incident Most published his handbook, *Science of Revolutionary War,* alternately called *Revolutionary War Science,* in which he provided detailed instructions on the manufacture of explosives and the ways they could be employed in the war of the poor against the rich.

Perhaps because of his fanaticism, Most was one of the most effective radical orators and communicators of his time. Slender and spruce, with blue eyes, prematurely gray hair, and a thick beard worn to conceal his distorted jawline, Most possessed a dazzling eloquence and a cutting wit. His blazing, incisive rhetoric was inspirational to his devoted followers, and his newspaper, *Freiheit,* or "Freedom," which he edited for twenty-seven years, earned a prime place in the ranks of German activist literature. Long after his death in 1906, German-speaking workers in Europe and America continued to sing Most's rousing "Hymn of the Proletarians" ("Die Arbeitsmaenner") to express their radical sympathies. With his revolutionary ardor and mesmeric delivery, Most enthralled even those who could not understand German, even those who scorned his message—including the police officers sent to monitor his speeches.

Although he was a gentile, he held a particular appeal for Jewish militants on the Lower East Side, who regarded him as their "high priest." His sharp phrases, said one member of the Pioneers of Liberty, had "the impact of the bombs and dynamite" he advocated. "It is an understatement to say that Most had the ability to inspire an audience," another comrade recalled. "He electrified, all but bewitched, every listener, opponent as well as friend."[20]

Berkman, too, fell under Most's powerful spell and became a fervent admirer. He had first heard of Most while reading in the Kovno library, and later recalled, "It stirred my soul" to note that *Most* means "bridge" in Russian: "Johann Most, the Bridge of Liberty!" Sasha eagerly went to hear Most speak in person soon after he came to New York, and when the two were eventually introduced, Berkman was impressed by Most's "forceful, outstanding personality" and felt "much attached to him." Most, in turn, took a liking to the "smart fellow." With the passage of time these opinions would change, drastically altering their relationship. For the moment, however, Berkman cherished Most as his principal mentor, the "hero of my first years in America."[21]

SHAKING OFF THE LONELINESS of his early months in New York, Berkman now had friends, a place to belong, and a mentor. Adding to his well-being was the arrival of a cousin, who became his inseparable companion. Modest Aronstam, nicknamed Modska, was the son of one of Berkman's uncles, a prosperous druggist in Kovno. Berkman later gave his cousin the pseudonym "Fedya" in his autobiography, *Prison Memoirs of an Anarchist,* to protect Modest's identity when the book was published in 1912; Berkman also used "Fedya" when referring to him in letters that might be screened by the authorities. Three months younger than Berkman, Modska had attended the same gymnasium, and the two were very close friends.[22]

Modska, as a young boy, possessed an unquenchable passion for art. Every night, after his parents went to bed, he would go downstairs and begin to draw or paint. More than anything else in the world, he wanted to study art, for which he believed he had a natural talent. His father disapproved of this ambition, so Modska, determined to pursue his dream, dropped out of school and emigrated to America at the age of seventeen. He reached New York on August 4, 1888, and ran into Sasha "almost as soon as he arrived." In appearance as well as outlook the two were strikingly similar. Both were small, strongly built, and excitably militant in their political views. Their friends took to calling them "the Twins." "If I happened to appear anywhere alone," Berkman said, "they would inquire, anxiously, 'What is the matter? Is your chum sick?' It was so unusual; we were each other's shadow."[23]

Modska fell in with Berkman's crowd straightaway, becoming an active member of the Pioneers of Liberty. With a third comrade in the group, a Russian immigrant named Michelman, they moved to a room on East Broadway. Together they struggled to make a living. When their money ran out at one point, they were forced to leave their home, and huddled on a bench in Union Square. "The night wind sweeps across the cheerless park," Sasha later recalled, "chilling us to the bone." Sasha felt tired and hungry, exhausted from the day's search for work. He soon dozed off, only to be awakened by the blows of a policeman's club on the soles of his shoes. Unceremoniously he and his two companions were ordered out of the park. Between them, they had twelve cents, which they pooled. Michelman, who was feeling ill, was given ten cents for a bed; the remaining two cents were spent on cigarettes. Sasha and Modska ended up sleeping on the steps of City Hall. In due course, jobs materialized, and the men were able to return to their East Broadway quarters. Michelman later moved to Boston, according to one source.[24]

When not at work, Modska painted and sketched, as much as his funds would permit for the cost of supplies. Whatever time remained he devoted to the anarchist cause, "and together," he and Sasha were "absorbed in the music of the new humanity." The Pioneers valued their membership; as a comrade remarked, the cousins were "looked upon as shining lights of the organization."[25]

3

THE TRIO

One evening in 1889, as Berkman recalled, he was having dinner at Sach's café on Suffolk Street, a meeting place for Lower East Side radicals. The door opened and in came Hillel Solotaroff, a fellow member of the Pioneers of Liberty. Accompanying him was a young woman, whom Sasha did not know. "Well-knit," wrote Berkman, "with the ruddy vigor of youth, she diffuses an atmosphere of strength and vitality."[1] His curiosity was piqued.

Emma Goldman had met Solotaroff when she lived in New Haven and he lectured there; the two hit it off and stayed in touch. She contacted him immediately when she moved to New York. At Sach's he introduced her to Anna and Helene Minkin, sisters who lived with their father in a two-room flat and were looking for another woman to join them. Then Solotaroff brought Emma over to meet Berkman. Sasha and Emma felt a powerful connection right away, and soon they were talking like old friends. "I like her simple, frank confidence; the 'comrade' on her lips thrills me. She is one of us," declared Sasha. Yet Berkman and Goldman's accounts of their first meeting differ on many points. Sasha believed they met on a chilly day in November; Emma was certain that their first encounter occurred on August 15, 1889, in stifling heat. Emma thought August 15, 1889, was a Sunday; it happened in fact to be a Thursday. The presence of Solotaroff at the first meeting has also been questioned.[2]

Sasha invited his new friend, whom he dubbed "Comrade Rochester," to hear Johann Most speak the next evening. Emma was already an ardent fan of Most's work—she had started reading his journal, *Freiheit,* shortly after the arrests of the Haymarket anarchists—and she was eager to see the man close up. The pair walked to the event together, and as they crossed Delancey Street, Emma stumbled; Sasha caught her arm and steadied her before she fell. "I have saved your life," he said with a smile. "I hope I may be able to save yours some day," she replied.[3]

Most's lecture was delivered in a small hall in the back of a saloon, "crowded with Germans, drinking, smoking, and talking." Emma found Most physically unappealing at first, with his bushy gray hair and a face "twisted out of form by an apparent dislocation of the left jaw."[4] But his eyes were a "soothing" blue, and his words were "a scorching denunciation of American conditions, a biting satire on the injustice and brutality of the dominant powers" that ruled the country. Emma marveled at his wit, the "music of his voice," the way he spoke "eloquently and picturesquely." He seemed "transformed into some primitive power, radiating hatred and love, strength and inspiration." Most, she wrote, "stirred me to my depths."[5]

One day soon after the lecture, Sasha came over to the Minkin flat to see Emma. Hot-tempered as always, he had just quit his job at the cigar factory after a quarrel with the foreman, and was free to show Emma around town. They rode the elevated train to the Brooklyn Bridge, went to the Battery, and afterward had a bite to eat at Sach's café. The high point was a visit to the office of *Freiheit,* located at 167 William Street. Most was busy and had little time to chat, yet he was intrigued by the bright, attractive Emma. He gave her some books to read, and suggested that she return to the office the next week to help prepare the paper for mailing.

In the following days, Sasha and Emma spent many pleasant hours together. Berkman took her to his favorite haunts, including Prospect Park in Brooklyn, which he preferred to Manhattan's elegant Central Park because he found it "less cultivated, more natural."[6] All the while, they talked without stop, exchanging stories about their childhood years, describing the experiences that had moved them, discussing books and ideologies, revealing their hopes and plans. They shared their opinions about the Haymarket affair, which had changed both of them irreparably.

By the time Goldman arrived in New York, she was already on the path to becoming an anarchist, and her meeting with Berkman accelerated the process. After her introduction to Most, the "Great Man," as she called him, Berkman escorted her to a Friday night lecture given by Solotaroff in

Yiddish at the Pioneers of Liberty club on Orchard Street. There she met his cousin Modska Aronstam, as well as other members of the group, "young men," she thought, "of ability and promise."[7]

In addition to the members of the Pioneers of Liberty, Goldman befriended a number of local radicals, including Annie Netter and her father, Jacob, whose grocery store at 16 Suffolk Street was a major center of anarchist activity in the neighborhood; the poet David Edelstadt, "whose songs of revolt were beloved of every Yiddish-speaking radical"; and Moshe Katz, who was a Berkman acquaintance from the Kovno gymnasium.[8] Goldman, now twenty years old, relished this circle of encouraging comrades, the rich intellectual life of the city, and the exhilarating message of the anarchist movement. In the future she would celebrate August 15, 1889, as the anniversary of her "spiritual birth." As she later wrote, all that had happened before in her life she left behind, "cast off like a worn-out garment. A new world was before me, strange and terrifying."[9]

Throughout her first summer in New York, Emma remained in the Minkins' apartment while working in a corset factory, as she had done in New Haven. In the fall of 1889 she left the factory and the Minkins and rented a small room on Suffolk Street for three dollars a month, not far from the Netters' grocery and Sach's café. There, using her own sewing machine, she stitched and repaired shirtwaists and frocks, painstaking work to be sure, but less onerous, she felt, than the monotony of factory labor.

Once established on her own, she began to assist with preparations for the November 11 Haymarket commemoration, to be held in Cooper Union. Berkman spearheaded the planning, and Johann Most was the event's main speaker. Most unleashed before the crowd "a wild, passionate cry against the terrible thing that had happened in Chicago—a fierce call to battle against the enemy, a call to individual acts, to vengeance." Both Emma and Sasha were profoundly moved. After the meeting they walked together to her Suffolk Street room. "An overpowering yearning possessed me," Emma wrote, "an unutterable desire to give myself to Sasha." That night they became lovers.[10]

From their first encounter at Sach's Emma and Sasha had been drawn "like a magnet" to each other. Emma had never met a person more dedicated, more principled than Sasha, with his all-embracing commitment to anarchism. "His earnestness," she said, "his self-confidence, his youth—everything about him drew me with irresistible force." Sasha, for his part, saw Emma in a similar light, as a "real Russian woman revolutionist."[11]

Small wonder that their friendship should have ripened into love, a love that was destined to endure nearly half a century. For all their subsequent disagreements and long separations, for all the other men and women in their lives, they maintained a devotion and mutual respect, remaining each other's most steadfast companion. When they found each other, they were young, on their own, far from their native land, severed from parents and siblings—fundamental similarities that were heightened by shared idealism, mutual understanding, intellectual curiosity, and raw passion. This instinctive kinship seized them both, and bound them uniquely for the rest of their days. Goldman foresaw their spiritual union on that November 11 night. "Deep love for him welled up in my heart," she said, "a feeling of certainty that our lives were linked for all time."[12]

Before the year was out, Berkman and Goldman moved in together, renting a four-room flat on 42nd Street, and inviting Modska Aronstam and Helene Minkin to join them. Their idea was to establish a little commune based on principles of cooperative living, women's equality, and social rebellion, inspired by Chernyshevsky's novel *What Is to Be Done?* Everything was shared among them, as befitted revolutionary comrades, and all contributed to fill the household coffers. Sasha got a job in a ladies' cloak factory, and Helene in a corset factory. Emma did the housekeeping and continued to stitch shirtwaists on her sewing machine at home. Modska focused on his art, occasionally able to "sell a picture to some dealer for fifteen or twenty-five dollars."[13] His income was supplemented by money sent from his parents in Kovno, but his financial input was by far the smallest of the group, and, furthermore, his costly oils and canvas supplies were usually funded by his comrades.

Modska began working with crayons as well, creating large-size portraits from photographs for private clients, but his proceeds remained paltry, and the expense of his artistic endeavors put a strain on the communal treasury. He felt a little guilty that his comrades were supporting him, but he remained true to his nature: high-spirited, impetuous, and indulgent. Sometimes when he sold one of his paintings, he would celebrate by bringing home flowers. Sasha was outraged that his cousin would waste money on insignificant luxuries instead of donating it to the anarchist movement, particularly when the impoverished working class continued to suffer. But his anger had little effect. Modska merely shrugged off Sasha's remonstrations, laughing that his cousin had no sense of beauty.

The friction continued. One day Modska arrived home in a fashionable new blue-and-white striped silk jersey. Sasha was furious when he saw it, calling Modska an incorrigible wastrel who would never amount to anything in the movement. "If I let him," Sasha fumed, "he'd spend all of his money on useless things—'beautiful' he calls them." The two almost came to blows, and Sasha had to leave the flat to cool off. On another occasion Sasha actually struck Modska for spending twenty cents on a meal, when a few cents, he felt, should have sufficed. "It was not mere extravagance," Berkman insisted. "It was positively a crime, incredible in a revolutionist. I could not forgive him for months."[14]

Sasha tried to justify his heated reaction. "Every penny spent for ourselves was so much taken from the Cause," he explained. "True, the revolutionist must live. But luxury is a crime, worse, a weakness. One could exist on five cents a day. Twenty cents for a single meal! Incredible. It was robbery." While Sasha was willing to concede that Modska was a legitimate anarchist, he believed that by clinging to the habits of a bourgeois upbringing his cousin was not adequately dedicated to the cause. Additionally, Sasha contemptuously disapproved of Modska's acceptance of money from his parents, calling him a "momma's boy."[15]

Berkman was, as Goldman put it, a "fanatic to the highest degree." He could not abide any weakness or self-indulgence when the revolution was at stake; for him, anarchism was serious business. Consequently Berkman's severe standards for an anarchist's life were more restrictive than his comrades were able or willing to attain. And his stringent, judgmental extremism often made him difficult to get along with.[16]

It was not that Berkman had no appreciation for beauty, as Modska claimed. But Sasha was able to curb his appetites and desires ruthlessly on behalf of the movement. For the anarchist cause, he declared, he would gladly give up anything, including his life. "Why, the very life of a true revolutionist has no other purpose, no significance whatever, save to sacrifice it on the altar of the beloved People," he said. He vowed to divorce himself from "all doubt, all regret," and become a "revolutionist first, human afterwards. My own individuality is entirely in the background. I am simply a revolutionist, a terrorist by conviction, an instrument for furthering the cause of humanity."[17] Sasha aspired to be like Rakhmetov, the imaginary hero from Chernyshevsky's book: "No luxury, no caprices, nothing but the necessary." Sasha used Rakhmetov as a model of self-discipline, self-sacrifice, and resolve, even if it alienated his closest comrades. "Such a revolutionist I feel myself to be," Sasha said. "Indeed, far more so than even the extreme radicals of my own circle."[18]

Another idol for Sasha was a man who, in many ways, resembled the fictional Rakhmetov character. This was the real-life Sergei Nechaev, one of the most outlandish and troubled figures in the annals of the Russian revolutionary underground, whose brutal murder of a fellow student provided the inspiration for Dostoevsky's *The Possessed.* To his admirers, Nechaev was a paragon of the new revolutionary: cold-blooded, unyielding, and lethal. Nechaev's credo, the *Catechism of a Revolutionary,* saw the ideal rebel as one divested of morals and integrity. Basic human instincts, such as a sense of ethics, sympathy, a taste for pleasure, were to be "absorbed by one exclusive interest, one thought, one passion—the revolution." The rebel's "one aim—inexorable destruction."[19]

Berkman echoed Nechaev's views in his comments and writings, and his own sentiments could be equally pitiless and drastic. The cause, said Berkman, "often calls upon the revolutionist to commit an unpleasant act; but it is the test of a true revolutionist—nay, more, his pride—to sacrifice all merely human feelings at the call of the People's Cause. If the latter demanded his life, so much the better." What Sasha did not yet know was that his beloved Uncle Maxim, Mark Natanson, had been a sworn enemy of Nechaev from their student days in St. Petersburg. Natanson decried Nechaev's bitter embrace of total immorality, and instead sought a revolutionary ethic based on liberty, humanity, and compassion, rather than on cruel and dogmatic methods. Peter Kropotkin, too, strongly criticized Nechaev and all that he stood for.[20]

But Berkman clung to this unbending philosophy, and some of his acquaintances came to think of him as inflexible and unfeeling. When the poet David Edelstadt fell ill with tuberculosis, the Pioneers met to discuss allocating treasury funds to send him to a sanatorium in Denver, an idea supported by Hillel Solotaroff, now a trained physician. Although Berkman and Edelstadt were close friends—they had once shared a room—Sasha argued that funds belonging to the movement must not be devoted to private purposes, no matter how crucial.

"Do you mean to help Edelstadt, the poet and man, or Edelstadt the revolutionist?" he asked. "Do you consider him a true, active revolutionist? His poetry is beautiful, indeed, and may indirectly even prove of some propagandistic value. Aid our friend with your private funds, if you will; but no money from the movement can be given, except for direct revolutionary activity." The group rejected Berkman's position, withdrew treasury funds for the medical treatment, raised more money with a theater benefit, and sent Edelstadt to Denver. But it was too late; his illness had already progressed beyond aid. He died on October 17, 1892, at the age of twenty-six.[21]

Emma was saddened by Edelstadt's death, and later remembered him as "a great poet and one of the finest types of anarchists that ever lived." She found Berkman's opposition to paying for the treatment callous. She respected Sasha's "singleness of purpose," his "selfless devotion" to the cause, but in this case felt that he had gone too far. Emma did not believe herself capable of such willpower. She was dedicated to anarchism, but embraced other aspects of life as well, such as comfort, romance, art, theater, and music, believing amusements were essential to a full and fulfilling life.[22]

In particular, she loved to dance, and boasted that she was "one of the most untiring and gayest" on the dance floor. Berkman, unsurprisingly, did not approve. Once, at a party, he sent someone to whisper to her that it did not "behoove an agitator to dance," at least "not with such reckless abandon." Her frivolity, he warned, would only harm their serious goals. Goldman refused to forsake her high spirits and sense of fun, or to restrain her appreciation of pretty treats and feminine finery. "Emma always liked the good things in life," her comrade Kate Wolfson said later. "But that didn't detract from her sincerity as an anarchist. She was a very physical woman; she enjoyed food, dancing, sex, and all the things that people *should* enjoy."[23]

Emma was growing weary of Sasha's strictness, his judgments, his endless sermons against squandering money on material pleasures. All she wanted was a little happiness—surely that was not asking too much. "I was tired," she declared, "of having the Cause constantly thrown in my face.

I did not believe that a Cause which stood for a beautiful ideal, for anarchism, for release and freedom from conventions and prejudice, should demand the denial of life and joy. I insisted that our Cause could not expect me to become a nun and that the movement should not be turned into a cloister. If it meant that, I did not want it." Sasha stuck to his guns. He told Emma that she was "too romantic and sentimental for a revolutionist," that "the task before us was hard and we must become hard."[24]

As the days and weeks went by, their relationship became progressively tense. The couple quarreled and clashed. Sasha, perpetually exasperated with Emma, grew attracted to Helene's older sister, Anna Minkin, who often visited the apartment. Emma noted their interest in each other. Unlike the rather dour Helene, a slight woman with black hair, plaintive dark eyes, and a downcast manner, the eighteen-year-old Anna was lively and alluring, with a beautiful singing voice. While Sasha apparently did not consummate his dalliance with Anna, he moved out of the flat for several weeks to sort out his emotions.

Emma, meanwhile, formed an attachment to Modska. An artist with a sensitive and considerate nature, Modska possessed many attributes that Sasha lacked. He was lighthearted, relaxed, and thoughtful. He never pressured Emma to live up to the principles of the cause, nor did he share Sasha's "aggressive manner." Emma also liked his wavy brown hair, fair complexion, neat mustache, and eyes that held a "dreamy expression."[25] Her feelings were reciprocated. As Aronstam's daughter recalled years later, "Father said that, except for my mother, he never met a more attractive woman than Emma. I knew her and she was quite good looking with her blond hair and blue eyes."[26]

One morning, at Modska's request, Emma posed for him in the nude. Soon afterward the two became lovers. But Emma had no intention of abandoning Sasha, with whom she remained on intimate terms despite their disputes and differences. She determined she could care equally for both men, cherishing "my passion for the one, my budding love for the other." Emma decided to tell Sasha how she felt. As it happened, he was already aware of her affair with Modska and accepted it without protest. "I believe in your freedom to love," he told her. He admitted that he had possessive tendencies, which he attributed to his "bourgeois background," but wanted to overcome them. In the weeks that followed, he, Emma, and Modska lived as a companionable ménage à trois, and, unexpectedly, their conflicts dissipated. As for Helene Minkin, the fourth member of the group, she played no role, as far as is known, in its convoluted sexual relationships.[27]

THE ROMANTIC TRIANGLE NOT ONLY BROUGHT increased personal coziness to Sasha, Emma, and Modska; it also bound them more closely together as revolutionary comrades. Sasha, the natural zealot, assumed the leading role and inspired them with his enthusiasm and dedication. He maintained a mood of intensity, had a flair for dramatic rhetoric, and kept the focus on their anarchist goals. The three talked late into the night about their plans for action, eyes "riveted upon the Dawn, in thrilling expectancy of the sunrise." They agreed to someday commit a "supreme deed" that might require them to sacrifice nothing less than their lives.[28]

The threesome chose Louis Lingg as their anarchist archetype. Lingg, magnetic, audacious, and strikingly handsome, was the youngest of the Haymarket defendants, and an unapologetic believer in violence. He had manufactured bombs, looked for any opportunity to use them, and ultimately killed himself on the eve of his execution with a small explosive hidden in his mouth. "If you cannonade us, we shall dynamite you," he warned the police after his arrest. During his trial, he told the court, "I despise you. I despise your order, your laws, your force-propped authority. Hang me for it!"[29]

Lingg's defiance in the courtroom, followed by his violent suicide in his cell, gave him a larger-than-life quality of daring. Fanatical young anarchists in New York copied his hairstyle and jaunty manner of walking, and considered it the highest compliment to be called by his name.[30] To the trio, Lingg "stood out as the sublime hero among the eight [Haymarket defendants]. . . . His unbending spirit, his utter contempt for his accusers and judges, his will-power, which made him rob his enemies of their prey and die by his own hand—everything about that boy of twenty-two lent romance and beauty to his personality. He became the beacon of our lives."[31] Goldman later wrote a commentary dedicated to Lingg, the "young giant who preferred to take your life rather than allow the hangman to desecrate you with his filthy touch."[32]

Sasha was pleased that Emma and Modska, following his lead, had become the "true revolutionists" on whom he could rely implicitly.[33] Modska, spurred by his cousin, grew more aggressive, taking advantage of his sinewy physical strength. Nicknamed "Hercules" by his friends despite his modest height, Modska became something of a heavy, called upon to apply strong-arm methods for the cause. When a comrade who worked in a bank planned to embezzle funds for the movement but was reported by a fellow employee, it was left to Modska to beat up the unfortunate informer. Emma, too, was becoming more militant. One day, incensed by the unflattering press caricatures of Johann Most, she asked Sasha if he did not believe one of the "rotten newspaper offices should be blown up—editors, reporters, and all." Sasha, however, did not think the newspapers needed to be taught this kind of lesson, for the press was merely "the hireling of capitalism." The object, he said, was to "strike at the root."[34]

Johann Most had at this point joined the list of Goldman's romantic suitors and often visited her at the 42nd Street flat. Some six months had passed since Emma had first heard him speak and then made his acquaintance at the *Freiheit* offices. She had returned the following week, as he requested, to help with the journal's distribution, and he took her to dinner to get to know her better. She was honored by his attention. "To me he was a man apart," Emma wrote of him, "the most remarkable in all the world." Not long afterward, Most took her to a performance of *Carmen* at the Metropolitan Opera House, and they began socializing frequently. "He opened up a new world to me," Emma recalled, "introducing me to music, books, the theatre. But his own rich personality meant far more to me—the alternating heights and depths of his spirit, his hatred of the capitalist system, his vision of a new society of beauty and joy for all. Most became my idol. I worshipped him."[35]

A physical relationship developed between the forty-three-year-old Most and the twenty-year-old Goldman. Most took the lead, certainly in the intellectual sense, but the pair initially was mismatched. He "cared a great deal about me," wrote Goldman, "and I about him, but he was already too set in his views and habits, and I was a mere slip of a girl without experience, without the necessary ways to influence anyone of his caliber."[36]

Goldman became a protégé of "the man of magic tongue and powerful pen."[37] Under his tutelage she became a force within the movement, particularly as a speaker, displaying a strong natural talent for oratory. Petite and intense, with a clear, melodic voice, she infused her talks with her own vital personality and brisk conviction. She was, said one observer, "wholly free of affectation and mannerism."[38] The dynamism of her speaking made her an authority in anarchist meetings.

It was at Most's urging, in early 1890, that Emma embarked on a two-week speaking tour, her first experience facing a large audience. In Rochester, Buffalo, and Cleveland she lectured to groups of German workers, addressing their quest for the eight-hour workday. To her delight, Emma found that she was able to hold the attention of a crowd, and the tour was a resounding success.

A few months later, in October 1890, she lectured to German workers in Baltimore. She told them of arriving in New York City, of seeing the great buildings everywhere, and of wondering how "such magnificent things can exist so close to such wretched misery."[39] The same conditions, she said, prevailed in all the capitalist countries, and the anarchists were ready to help teach the workers how to throw off the yoke of oppression. She gave more talks in New York and was called on regularly to rally workers during conflicts between labor and management.[40] The tenets of anarchism infused her speeches, but her fundamental message of equity and enfranchisement attracted many members of the working class, immigrants, and the poor, who sought consolation and inspiration.

During this period the 42nd Street commune disbanded when Helene returned to live with her sister Anna. Sasha, Emma, and Modska moved together to an apartment downtown, where they continued to engage as a ménage à trois. Johann Most found this arrangement difficult to tolerate, his own views on sexuality being far more conventional. "Like all of us," noted one anarchist paper that advocated free love, "[Most] has his faults and is often prejudiced against new theories of social life, as against the question of sex freedom, of which he cannot speak without getting into a frenzy."[41]

While Most's attitude about sexual behavior was perfectly reasonable, no doubt an element of jealousy was also involved, since he had designs on Emma. In any case, as Most's son remarked years later, "He strongly disapproved of the three of them—Berkman, Goldman, and their artist friend—living together as a threesome. 'Degenerates,' he called them. Emma had guts and brains but was lacking in character, he thought. He never forgave her."[42]

Sasha had his own problems with Most's value system, especially where money was concerned. When Emma departed for her first speaking tour, Most, to Sasha's disgust, escorted her to Grand Central Station in a taxi;

when she returned to New York, Most took her out to dinner and presented her with a bouquet of violets. Sasha was indignant. "Most," he said, "has no right to squander money, to go to expensive restaurants, drink expensive wines. He is spending money contributed to the movement. He should be held to account."[43]

For the time being, however, Berkman and Most remained on cordial terms, and Sasha still regarded his mentor with respect, occasionally soliciting his advice. In 1890, when Sasha read a report by journalist George Kennan in the *Century Magazine* about a massacre of prisoners in Siberia, at a camp where his Uncle Maxim had once been exiled, he considered returning to Russia to seek vengeance.[44] Most encouraged both Sasha and Modska to move to Russia (perhaps in part to get his romantic rivals out of the country), and suggested that Sasha apprentice himself to a printer so he could launch an underground press in Russia and be better equipped to disseminate his message.[45]

It soon was arranged for Berkman to go to New Haven, Connecticut, and he left in the fall of 1890 to begin his printer's training there. He found temporary lodgings boarding with a local family and worked as an apprentice for Paul Gephardt, the editor of a German weekly paper, the *Connecticut Volks-Blatt.*[46] His friends decided to join him in New Haven, and soon Emma and Modska, along with both Helene and Anna Minkin, moved into a small house at 25 Silver Street, reassembling their 42nd Street commune and adding a fifth member. Sasha tried to rekindle his brief romance with Anna, to no avail.[47]

While Sasha labored to master the printer's craft, Modska worked at a variety of jobs, among them drawing, painting, and shirtmaking. For a time he served as a night clerk in a drugstore; his father, Lazar Aronstam, a pharmacist in Russia, had taught him about the trade.[48] Emma and the Minkin sisters opened a dressmaking shop, like one featured in Chernyshevsky's novel. They rented a storefront on Congress Avenue and hung a shingle reading "Goldman & Minkin, Dressmakers," but business was slow and they were forced to close.[49] Emma and Helene got jobs at the corset factory where Emma had worked after her separation from Jacob Kershner nearly three years earlier. Anna remained at home, doing finishing work on dresses.

For a few months, various professional disappointments aside, life in New Haven was good. The five friends organized a club to discuss societal issues with other neighborhood radicals and kept up with their New York counterparts, including Most, who often came to Connecticut to visit them. They enjoyed local dances and theater. In March 1891 the group saw the legendary actress Sarah Bernhardt in Victorien Sardou's *Fédora,* a melodrama about Nihilists in Russia.[50] (Berkman recalled seeing Sardou's *Tosca* instead.)[51] But after six months, the New Haven commune began to dissolve. The dressmaking shop had failed. Modska could find no steady work and went back to the Lower East Side. When Anna, who had been ailing for some weeks, started to exhibit signs of consumption, Berkman brought her to a sanatorium in New York and, having acquired sufficient printing expertise to allow for new job opportunities, decided to return to the city as well.

As for Helene Minkin, she and Most, to everyone's surprise, had fallen in love during his frequent visits, and she went to New York to be with him. Despite the nearly thirty-year age gap—Helene was still a teenager—they became companions, and by 1893 were living together as husband and wife. They had two sons, Johann Junior and Lucifer, and Helene helped Most manage *Freiheit.*[52] (Johann Jr.'s own son, Johnny Most, later found national fame as a sportscaster.) Helene was intelligent and strong-willed, but the union with Most was strained. "Mother was too young for him," Johann Jr. explained, although he considered his father "a very brave man. I loved and admired him. He was a thousand years before his time, morally, mentally, and intellectually."[53]

With Helene's departure, only Emma remained to wind up the commune's affairs. By April 1891 she was back in New York, resuming the ménage à trois with Sasha and Modska. The trip to Russia never materialized. Sasha later recalled the missed opportunity wistfully. "Perhaps," he said, "I might have done something important there."[54]

4

AUTONOMISTS

After reuniting in New York, Sasha, Emma, and Modska rented a flat at 201 Forsythe Street on the Lower East Side. They fell back into their old routine, attending meetings, lectures, and an 1891 May Day rally in Union Square. Emma took up sewing and dressmaking as before, while Modska returned to his painting and portraits. Johann Most gave Sasha a chance to try out his new skills as a printer, and hired him as a compositor, or typesetter, at *Freiheit.*

The trio, however, was becoming increasingly disenchanted with Most. Sasha bristled at Most's temperamental nature, flinched at his extravagant habits, and begrudged the older man's romance with Emma. The two began to quarrel over anarchist doctrine and message. Sasha found Most dictatorial and haughty, resistant to any criticism or challenge, and seethed to Emma that Most was "a tyrant who wanted to rule with an iron hand under the guise of anarchism."[1]

Sasha's sympathies were briefly aroused when Most was taken to prison in June 1891. Three and a half years earlier, Most had been charged with using "incendiary language" during a speech on November 12, 1887, the day after the Haymarket hangings, in which he publicly denounced the executions as judicial murder. All appeals had now been exhausted, and Most was summoned to begin his sentence at the prison on Blackwell's Island (since renamed Roosevelt Island), a narrow strip of land in the East River. Berkman was among the supporters who saw Most off on the ferry trip to Blackwell's, and afterward hosted a fundraising event on his behalf. But barely two weeks later, on July 4, their truce was shattered. Berkman was fired from his position on Most's *Freiheit* because, as one newspaper account later put it, his "rabid anarchist utterances" proved too radical for the editors.[2] Goldman claimed that Berkman quit of his own accord, but in this she was almost certainly mistaken.

As their loyalty for Most was slipping away, Sasha, Emma, and Modska developed an interest in the Autonomist faction of anarchist thought. The Autonomy Group had been founded in London in 1885 by Josef Peukert, an Austrian housepainter, and Otto Rinke, a German locksmith. Rinke, born in 1853, was a highly regarded anarchist figure with a long, lively career as a rebel, and his close friendship with the esteemed Peter Kropotkin boosted his status within the movement. Peukert was a rather dour man with delicate features and a black mustache and beard; Goldman later described him as dry and "pedantic, utterly devoid of humor."[3] But Peukert was an anarchist of strength and sway—and he was Johann Most's bitterest rival.

The Autonomist anarchists, as their name suggested, emphasized individual independence, freedom from bureaucracy, and resistance to all forms of authority. Convinced that any established organization contained the seeds of tyranny, they feared the emergence of a single leader within the anarchist movement. To them, therefore, the prominent and domineering Most presented a threat.

To counteract Most's influence in radical circles, they started the London-based journal *Die Autonomie* in 1886 as a direct competitor to Most's *Freiheit.* The volatile Most had little patience for his critics, and instantly considered *Die Autonomie* and its advocates his particular foes. He also had a nasty personal history with Peukert, holding him responsible for the capture and arrest of his friend and *Freiheit* colleague Johann Neve, a popular and enterprising German anarchist who had been detained in Belgium in 1887 for smuggling radical literature. Most was certain that Peukert had informed the authorities of Neve's activities and was to blame for his arrest and incarceration.[4]

Thus accused, Peukert fled London and the movement. After spending two and a half years on the Continent, he showed up in America and resumed his radical activities; eventually an anarchist commission in London determined there was no evidence he was a spy. Otto Rinke immigrated to America as well, living first in Elizabeth, New Jersey, then moving to St. Louis, where he worked as the foreman in a factory that made electric motors. With Rinke and Peukert both settled in the States, America became the new center of the Autonomist faction and the main battleground of the feud with Johann Most.

The first American Autonomist group had been formed in Chicago in the fall of 1885, and included Haymarket anarchists George Engel and Adolph Fischer, both of whom were hanged after the trial. The group produced a journal called *Anarchist* that offered the blunt motto "We Hate Authority." The paper, which expressed scorn for Johann Most, listed no editors or managers on the masthead, both to protect its members and to drive the message that leaders of any kind were irrelevant. A casualty of the Haymarket bombing, only four issues were published.[5] As a result of the government scrutiny and repressions following the Haymarket incident, a second American Autonomist paper, *Der Anarchist,* did not get off the ground until August 1889. The biweekly was launched in St. Louis, and its philosophy was unreservedly extreme and militant: "Dynamite in the hands of the people will play a great role in the social struggle!" it declared. Letters from readers were signed "Rebel," "Red Devil," and, most baleful, "Satan."[6]

The editor of *Der Anarchist* was Claus Timmermann, a twenty-three-year-old German born in 1866 in Schleswig-Holstein who had come to America at the age of eighteen. Far gentler in appearance and manner than his journal's rhetoric would suggest, the bespectacled Timmermann was of medium height with light brown hair, and had a strong command of English. A typesetter by trade and a poet by avocation, he joined the anarchist movement soon after arriving in America, having been inspired by Johann Most. Before long, however, he quit the Most camp and threw in his lot with the Autonomists. He had been based in Chicago during the Haymarket affair, and afterward left for St. Louis. He regarded his new journal as the "faithful pioneer of the Social Revolution of anarchism, a defender of the principles of our Chicago martyrs."[7]

In addition to the Autonomist groups established in Chicago and St. Louis, fresh ones sprang up in New Jersey—in Elizabeth, Newark, and Hoboken—as well as in Brooklyn and Manhattan. They all maintained a loose association, and together made up only a small minority of the anarchist movement, no more than a few hundred members in all. As Berkman put it, "a mere handful, quite insignificant, kept alive mainly by the Most and Peukert feud."[8]

INDEED, THE FISSURE BETWEEN MOST and the Autonomist founders only widened. What the Autonomists lacked in numbers, they made up in zeal—and in a chilling advocacy of violence. They called for imminent social revolution and justified individual acts of terrorism to achieve the goal, including the use of dynamite and assassination. They believed the rich and powerful had to be eliminated in order to make way for a harmonious, equal society, and that every employer, policeman, and bureaucrat had forfeited his very right to exist.

In contrast, Johann Most had lately altered his stance on violence. Once so militant, Most had begun to soften his views, substantially toning down his appeals for violence and indiscriminate acts of terrorism. Although he still advocated social change, he now doubted the rationale for brutality and random attacks as valid weapons in the struggle against capitalism. This was particularly true, he felt, in a country like the United States, where attitudes were more open-minded and the anarchist movement was generally weak and unpopular.

Ultramilitant anarchists were outraged by Most's tempered position, and they accused him of backsliding and cowardice. It was while the Autonomist-Most feud was heating to a boil that Sasha, Emma, and Modska transferred their allegiance. Not long after Sasha's dismissal from *Freiheit* in July 1891, the trio began frequenting a New York–based Autonomist group affiliated with the Radical Workers' League, which met every Saturday evening in a tavern at 209 East Fifth Street, located between Second Avenue and the Bowery. The tavern's name, Zum Groben Michel—Tough Mike's—corresponded with the rough exterior and gruff manner of its owner, Michael Kretschmann, described in the *New York World* as "a giant in stature with a pigeon chest."[9]

The three were impressed with the League, and they found the absence of a chairman or supervisor refreshing, a pleasant contrast to Most's brusque leadership. They soon befriended a number of young Autonomists. Among them were Josef Oerter, known as Sepp, who became a lover of Goldman's, and his brother, Fritz. They also met Claus Timmermann, who had moved from St. Louis to New York during the summer of 1891, leaving *Der Anarchist* to be edited by Peukert.[10] Emma thought Claus a "likeable fellow and entirely trustworthy" with "considerable poetic talent," though a heavy drinker.[11] Timmermann soon became one of their closest friends and a member of their tight-knit unit. "They were really a foursome," Modska's daughter said, "though he wasn't amorously involved with Emma as were Father and Berkman."[12]

Emma, Sasha, and Modska also became acquainted with Peukert, and while they recognized that he lacked Most's ability as writer and orator, they respected his strict philosophy and unswerving approach to the cause. He enjoyed their company, and was especially fond of the solemn Sasha. The friends focused on *Der Anarchist* as the mouthpiece of their agenda; Emma submitted articles, and when money was available, they contributed it to Peukert's paper. By the end of the year they had fully abandoned the Mostians for the Autonomists.

Not surprisingly, Most felt betrayed. He considered anyone who sided with Peukert an enemy, and he sorely resented the trio's defection. Most directed a special fury toward Berkman, calling him a "hypocrite" and "as phony as a three-dollar bill."[13] How dared this youth, barely twenty years old, sit in judgment of a veteran revolutionary? Most had taken him under his wing and even brought him into *Freiheit,* only to see him shift loyalties to his archrival. All of this was compounded by petty jealousy, generational conflict, and competition for Emma's affections. The rift, explained Goldman, was caused by "differences of conception, experience and temperament. We [were] at the height of religious zeal, of passionate faith. We had not yet been tried in the crucible and did not know agony of spirit."[14]

Berkman became an outspoken Autonomist advocate (and blatant detractor of Most), notably at an anarchist convention held in Clarendon Hall on East 13th Street at the end of 1891, when he conspicuously proclaimed his support for Peukert. Most, midway through his term in Blackwell's prison, heard what had transpired and was livid. Also during the convention, Berkman learned that Peter Kropotkin, whom he considered his "ideal of revolutionist and Anarchist," had cancelled a planned American lecture tour on the grounds that such an expensive undertaking was too extravagant for the struggling movement.[15]

Sasha was disappointed, but applauded his hero's thrift, and was inspired anew to study Kropotkin's writings, some of which had been appearing in *Die Autonomie* and *Der Anarchist,* and to compose related commentary. He finished two pieces by early 1892, one a Yiddish adaptation of Kropotkin's

"Order and Anarchy," the other an essay on the meaning of freedom. These were Berkman's first significant anarchist editorials, and they appeared in the *Fraye Arbeter Shtime* (Free Voice of Labor), the organ of the Pioneers of Liberty, and the most influential Yiddish-language journal in the movement's history.

TEMPERAMENTALLY, BERKMAN WAS WELL SUITED for the literary life, but he had to make a living. After his firing from *Freiheit* in July 1891, he had taken a number of jobs, including one at the Singer Sewing Machine factory in Elizabeth, New Jersey, but his unchecked attitude problem kept him on the move. By the fall, he and Emma were sewing boys' jumpers in their apartment, often laboring eighteen hours a day. Modska was still committed to his artwork, but, unable to contribute to the communal treasury and at last beset by guilt, he moved to Springfield, Massachusetts, where he got a job in a photographer's shop. Working with crayon, as he had done in New York, he made portraits of individuals and families based on snapshots provided as examples. After a while, he wrote to Emma letting her know a job was available at the same establishment, processing the orders. She leaped at the opportunity, glad to get away from the tedium of the sewing machine. Springfield would be a welcome relief.[16]

Emma arrived in January 1892. The work, she discovered, was not difficult, and Modska's portraits were so well received that the pair decided to go into business for themselves. They wrote to Sasha to join them. In February the trio relocated to Worcester, Massachusetts, "the heart of the Commonwealth," as it was called, where they rented a room in the City National Bank building on Main Street. They named their shop the French Art Studio, and Modska hung a large crayon portrait of Emma on the wall. The room was rented in Goldman's name; Modska told their neighbors that Emma was his sister and Sasha her husband. Modska created all the artwork, while Sasha made the frames for the portraits and Emma took the orders. A local journalist described Modska as "a skillful artist" and reported that his "sister appeared remarkably intelligent and possessed business ability enough for three."[17]

Despite this promising beginning, the French Art Studio began to falter. Modska hired an agent, Simon Lufkin, who canvassed for out-of-town orders. Lufkin thought Modska was "a great artist," yet only a trickle of orders came in. The trio's savings were running out, so to bolster their income, Modska drew sketches for the *Worcester Commercial* and for F. S. Blanchard & Co., a printing house. Sasha and Emma rented a horse and wagon to solicit nearby farms for orders, but they found the farmers "inhospitable and close-fisted" and often had to travel for hours before getting any work.[18]

To conserve their income the three slept and ate in their little studio, all in a single room. Other tenants thought them educated and hard-working, Goldman making the strongest impression. "I talked with the three people in the room," said a dentist with an office in the building, "and always found them quiet appearing. The woman was quite a talker and was intelligent." Berkman was remembered as an inveterate smoker, "the worst cigarette fiend ever in the block."[19]

Though reliable tenants, the friends cooked "herring and other viands" over a kerosene stove, filling the floor with an unpleasant odor. This sparked complaints, and they were ordered not to cook or sleep in the room. Barely able to pay the rent for their studio, they now were compelled to search for lodgings. In April they found a place at 45 Winter Street in the Jewish section of town. The landlord, Benjamin Sapiro, rented rooms in the rear of his grocery. The cost of the room was by no means exorbitant but it added to their financial burden, and when the portrait business did not improve, the three were at the point of giving up.[20]

They had two choices, as they saw it: reestablish themselves in New York City or return to Russia, where a cholera epidemic had broken out, accompanied by serious famine. Peasants were dying by the thousands and there was a revival of radical activity as students moved from the universities to the countryside to assist the sick and needy and agitate for improved conditions. Sasha, Emma, and Modska felt the familiar yearning to engage in radical work in their homeland. But their savings were insufficient even to cover their short-term expenses, let alone travel overseas, so Mr. Sapiro suggested they stay in Worcester and lent them money to open a lunchroom. At 86 Winter Street, three blocks from Sapiro's grocery, they leased a vacant store. In a matter of weeks they turned it into an attractive luncheonette.

Emma, an excellent cook, put her culinary talents to use. The sandwiches, coffee, and desserts she prepared attracted a swelling stream of customers. This time their business was a success, and before long they paid back

Sapiro's loan and purchased a soda fountain and a new set of colorful dishes. Emma and Sasha waited on the customers, fried pancakes, and served "Arctic-cold ice cream."[21] Modska at first remained at the studio, working on his crayon portraits. But as the lunchroom's profits increased, he spent more of his time there, assisting Emma and Sasha with the customers. By June he was in the lunchroom nearly every day, neglecting his portraits almost entirely.

Having money in their pockets enabled the trio to make trips to New York, to catch up with their Autonomist comrades, and to participate in anarchist events around the city. On May 1, 1892, Goldman addressed a rally in Union Square, speaking from a wagon that was festooned with a red flag. Berkman now had time and money enough to submit articles to *Der Anarchist* and to donate five dollars to help with production costs. The three devoted most of their energy to the thriving lunchroom, and by midsummer they had saved quite a bit of cash for the journey to Russia.

One day at this time, a customer came in for ice cream while Emma was alone in the store. As she set the dish down at the man's table, she glimpsed the headline in his newspaper. A lockout had occurred at the Carnegie steel mill in Homestead, Pennsylvania. The workers had responded by declaring a strike and sealing off the mill to prevent outside labor from entering. Emma, with a rush of thrilled tension, closed up the store and ran at "full speed" the three blocks home. Sasha and Modska were in the room resting up for the evening shift, and she told them what had happened.

The trio had been following news of the escalating trouble in Homestead and were fascinated by the dramatic events. "To us," Emma later declared, "it sounded the awakening of the American worker, the long-awaited day of his resurrection. The native toiler had risen, he was beginning to feel his mighty strength, he was determined to break the chains that held him in bondage."[22] All thoughts of returning to Russia were instantly swept away. "Homestead," said Berkman, "had sounded the prelude of awakening, and my heart had echoed the inspiring strains."[23]

5

HOMESTEAD

THE HOMESTEAD AFFAIR WAS A PIVOTAL EVENT in the struggle between business and labor in the steel industry. The Amalgamated Association of Iron and Steel Workers, an affiliate of the American Federation of Labor, was the most powerful union in America. Founded in 1876, it had 24,000 members and was the largest craft union at the time. But it had never been able to organize all the plants of the Carnegie Steel Company, the biggest firm in the industry. Of the three major steel mills in the Carnegie system, the union was a force in only one, the Homestead plant, some eight miles east of Pittsburgh.

Andrew Carnegie, the famed steel magnate, had acquired the Homestead works in 1889 and signed a three-year contract with the union. The Amalgamated, as a craft union, excluded unskilled workers from membership; at Homestead, in 1892, it represented 800 men from a workforce of close to 4,000. Their contract was due to expire on June 30, 1892, and in February they began negotiations for a new agreement. Since steel prices were booming, the Amalgamated asked for a raise. Henry Clay Frick, the manager at Homestead and chairman of the board at Carnegie Steel, countered with a request for a decrease. The union rejected his offer. From this point on the negotiations did not go well. The imposing Frick, it became clear, intended to suppress the Amalgamated. He would do it, he declared, "if it takes all summer and all winter. . . . Yes, even my life itself."[1]

Carnegie, who prided himself on being a progressive employer, had expressed public sympathy for the workers on many previous occasions. "My experience," Carnegie had written in *Forum* magazine, "has been that trades-unions upon the whole are beneficial both to labor and capital."[2]

Despite this pro-union comment, Carnegie demonstrated full support for Frick's tough position. "There has been forced upon this Firm," Carnegie wrote to Frick, "the question whether its Works are to be run 'Union' or 'Non-Union.' As the vast majority of our employees are Non-Union, the Firm has decided that the minority must give place to the majority. The workers, therefore, will be necessarily Non-Union after the expiration of the present agreement." Carnegie then departed for his annual vacation in Scotland.[3]

Frick, with Carnegie's approval, planned to "teach our employees a lesson."[4] Around the plant at Homestead he erected a high board fence and covered it with barbed wire. Every twenty-five feet, loopholes were cut at a shoulder height compatible for rifles, though Frick later testified before a congressional committee that the holes were meant solely for observation. Inside the grounds, moreover, stood platforms mounted with searchlights. The workers saw all this as a declaration of war and christened the plant "Fort Frick." After three months of negotiations the situation had reached a deadlock. Yet Frick sensed that he had gained the upper hand, and on May 29 he handed the Amalgamated an ultimatum: either settle on his terms by June 24 or the company would cease to recognize the union. As the date for the expiration of the ultimatum approached, tensions in Homestead mounted. On June 23 Frick held a final meeting with a committee from the union in the Carnegie company offices in Pittsburgh. No agreement could be reached. It was time, Frick decided, to act. He terminated negotiations and announced that the company would bargain only with individual workers.

On June 28 Frick shut down part of the plant, putting 800 people out of work. That night, angry employees hanged Frick in effigy from a pole on company property. Frick reacted by dismissing additional men, several hundred at a time. By July 2 he had discharged the entire workforce and ordered everyone to go home. A massive lockout, without precedent in American industry, was thereafter in effect. Frick then moved to bring in alternate workers, known as scabs in unionists' parlance, in order to resume production. Employment agencies and labor agents sought steel workers in large cities, placing advertisements for recruits in Boston, St. Louis, and Philadelphia.

The workers at Homestead did not take these developments lying down. On June 29, after the lockout had begun, 3,000 unskilled laborers voted to stand with the 800 union members in solidarity against the company. To supervise the strike, an advisory committee was formed, which threw a line of pickets around "Fort Frick." Routes to the mill were closely watched to prevent the entry of replacement workers and a signaling system was arranged so that reinforcements could be summoned within minutes.

Frick himself had not been idle. As early as June 20, before his ultimatum to the union had expired, he had begun to deal with the Pinkerton Agency in New York. For the previous forty years, Pinkerton guards had been used by industrialists whenever there were strikes to be broken or unions disrupted. "They were the scum of the earth," a former U.S. Secret Service agent said. "There was not one out of ten that would not commit murder."[5]

On June 25 Frick asked the Pinkerton guards to take control of the Homestead plant and help the replacement workers enter the facilities. "We think absolute secrecy essential in the movement of these men," he wrote to Robert Pinkerton, head of the agency and a son of its founder.[6] From New York, Philadelphia, and Chicago, Pinkerton assembled a force of several hundred men, armed with Winchester rifles and other weapons. On July 5 the men were moved by train with darkened coaches to a point six miles below Pittsburgh. There, late at night, they were loaded onto two barges and towed up the Monongahela River toward Homestead.

Efforts to maintain "absolute secrecy" were in vain. By the end of June the advisory committee had been informed that Pinkertons would be dispatched. Thus forewarned, the strikers prepared to meet the invaders with force. As the barges passed Pittsburgh at three in the morning on July 6, a lookout wired the committee: "Watch the river. Steamers with barges left here."[7] An hour later a patrol sighted the barges a mile below Homestead. Whistles sounded the alarm, and strikers rushed to the landing, armed with rifles, shotguns, pistols, stones, and clubs. When the barges arrived at dawn, the workers were ready for them, determined to prevent the Pinkertons from docking. Someone fired a shot, and the battle was on, one of the bloodiest in American labor history. It raged from early morning until late in the afternoon, twelve or thirteen hours in all.

The climax came when the strikers deployed a twenty-pound brass cannon—generally used by the town in holiday celebrations—in an unsuccessful effort to sink the barges. They tried a smaller cannon belonging to the Homestead Grand Army Post, also without results. They loaded oil and waste onto a railroad car, set it on fire, and sent it down the tracks into the water, but it did not reach the barges. Sticks of dynamite were tossed into the barges, blowing holes in the sides, but otherwise doing little damage. Attempts to ignite the barges with a burning raft and with flaming oil poured on the water both came to naught.

Human casualties, mostly from gunfire, proved considerable on both sides. Although the final count was never ascertained, at least ten men were killed and many more later died of their injuries. According to the coroner's statement, three Pinkertons and seven strikers perished.[8] The *Pittsburgh Commercial Gazette* reported that ten Pinkertons and six workers died or were fatally wounded in the battle, and that additionally, "scores are injured and many victims will die."[9]

At five in the afternoon the Pinkertons decided that they had had enough. Raising the white flag, they surrendered their weapons and were promptly removed from the barges, which the workers then set aflame. "The barges drifted slowly down stream," reported the *New York Times,* "furnished a brilliant sight for some time, and sank when the fire reached the water's edge."[10]

As the Pinkertons were marched from the landing to the town skating rink, they ran the gauntlet of an angry crowd of strikers' wives, who inflicted indignities of such a nature that a congressional committee felt it could not publicly describe them. The *New York Times* recounted the suffering of the "battered, bruised, and maltreated" Pinkerton captives, subjected to an "uncontrollable mob of women, who not only used their fists, but clubs, stones, bricks, broomsticks, mophandles, and any missile upon which they could lay their hands."[11] In the evening the Pinkertons were unceremoniously escorted from the rink and sent away to Pittsburgh by train. Despite the violence, the people killed and wounded, the encounter was perceived as a great victory for the strikers, who remained in control of the plant. Frick, in his attempt to resume production in a nonunion shop, had, for the moment, conspicuously failed.

News of the Homestead battle captured the attention of the nation, and the defeat of the Pinkertons electrified organized labor. Unions throughout the country gave vent to their outrage in protest meetings, passing resolutions denouncing the use of Pinkerton guards. In Chicago 90,000 workers celebrated "Homestead Day" and raised $40,000 for the strikers. Further contributions poured in from other cities and towns. Public opinion in general was on the side of the strikers, chiefly because of the company's hiring of Pinkertons. "Father was killed by the Pinkerton men," ran a popular song of the era.[12] Citizens everywhere were outraged by the spectacle of a private army being employed to end a labor dispute.

The press, too, largely favored the workers. The Pinkertons were nothing but "a band of hired Hessians," said the populist paper *Topeka Advocate,* using a popular analogy for the private guards as mercenaries, and placed the blame for the bloodshed on Frick. The *New York World* decried "the attempt of an arbitrary and tyrannical man to impose his will upon men as free as himself."[13] Even some conservative papers chastised Frick for his inflexible attitude toward the workers.

Nor did Andrew Carnegie escape criticism from the press, which pointed out the contradiction between his public support for labor's rights and his determination to crush the Amalgamated. Carnegie, in the words of the *St. Louis Post-Dispatch,* had "run off to Scotland out of harm's way, to await the issue of the battle he was too pusillanimous to share. A single word from him might have saved the bloodshed—but the word was never spoken."[14] Carnegie remained unmoved. "The handling of the case on the part of the company has my full approval and sanction," he said, and counseled Frick not to soften his stance. On July 7, the day after the clash, he sent Frick the following telegram: "All anxiety gone since you stand firm. Never employ one of these rioters. Let grass grow over the works. Must not fail now."[15]

Frick had no intention of failing. Although the Pinkertons had been defeated, there remained a more powerful force: the Pennsylvania National Guard. After the chaotic July 6 battle, the sheriff of Allegheny County asked Governor Robert E. Pattison to call out the military guard to restore order. When John McLuckie, the burgess of Homestead and a member of the union advisory committee, heard the news, he sent a telegram to the governor, assuring him that the townsfolk were orderly and there was no need to bring in troops.

Under prodding from the sheriff, however, the governor ordered the entire militia—8,500 men—to Homestead. On July 12, under the command of Major General George R. Snowden, the troops marched off the train and were met by a welcoming committee, complete with a band. "On the part of the Amalgamated Association," said Hugh O'Donnell, the chairman of the advisory committee, "I wish to say that after suffering an attack of illegal authority, we are glad to have the legal authority of the State here." General Snowden replied, "I do not recognize your association, sir. I recognize no one but the citizens of this city. We have come here to restore law and order, and they are already restored."[16]

Thus began what would be the longest occupation of an American community in the country's history. The militia force, which included a cavalry detachment and field guns, took possession of the town, pitching camp on a hill overlooking the mill. The strike, as Snowden saw it, amounted to "revolution, treason, and anarchy," and Homestead was placed under martial law. From then on the locked-out workers fought a losing battle. Entire families were evicted from their company-owned homes. Under the protection of the troops, the company began to bring in replacement workers, until 2,000 laborers were operating the plant. The militia had been used "not for the purpose of restoring peace and arresting the treasonable organization of Pinkerton thugs," stated the *Topeka Advocate*, "but for the purpose of intimidating the union workingmen, protecting capital and crowding down wages through the introduction of non-union men."[17]

In the face of this new challenge, the strikers struggled to maintain their ground. According to the *New York Times*, "The average striker will tell you that this is not a strike for his bread and butter alone, but for his home. He claims the town of Homestead as his own. He denies that Mr. Carnegie built it. 'We, the workingmen of Homestead built it,' he says with pride. 'We are interested in it more than Mr. Carnegie for we made the place and we don't want to be driven out of it for a new set of workmen who have done nothing to make it what it is.' "[18] During this time, worker solidarity held fast within the community. Nearly the entire town came out in support of the Amalgamated and its crusade against the company. Shopkeepers, clergy, and municipal leaders assisted the workers in various ways, the merchants extending credit and selling goods at cost. Elsewhere, the country's labor organizations were raising $10,000 a week to feed the strikers.

Frick, unruffled and determined, used every means at his disposal in an effort to demoralize the union. He never once changed his position on the strike, repeatedly vowing to "fight this thing to the bitter end." The company brought warrants against Hugh O'Donnell, John McLuckie, and five other members of the advisory committee, charging them with the murder of a Pinkerton. Counter charges from the workers went nowhere. When a grand jury met on September 22, it handed up 167 indictments against union leaders on charges of murder, conspiracy, and riot, although only two men were tried, both were acquitted, and the cases of the rest were dropped. For two more months the strikers held out. But the influx of scabs and the arrest of their leaders ultimately proved too much. With the dwindling of funds, following the loss of wages, morale began to decline. In desperation, some returned to their jobs as nonunion workers.

On November 20, with winter approaching, the Amalgamated Association of Iron and Steelworkers called off the strike. Frick cabled Carnegie the following day: "Strike officially canceled yesterday. Our victory is now complete and most gratifying. Do not think we will ever have any serious labor trouble again. We had to teach our employees a lesson and we taught them one that they will never forget." Carnegie replied in a jubilant mood. "Life worth living again. Congratulations all around."[19] Carnegie had vowed that he would let grass grow over the works before he would hire back any of the strike leaders. He kept his word. O'Donnell, McLuckie, and the others were blacklisted from the industry. From 1892 onward, not a single union man was ever again employed in a Carnegie mill.

The Homestead strike ended in utter defeat for the workers, inflicting wounds that never healed. After five months out on strike, they were forced to accept the company's harshest terms, including a twelve-hour day and a wage cut of almost one-half. Pinkerton spies were installed in the mill, grievance committees were done away with, and workers' meetings were banned. Total victory, as Frick had foreseen, lay with the company. He had proved that a modern corporation, combined with the authority of the state, could destroy the strongest union in America. Not until 1936 would another union emerge in the steel industry. The defeat of the Amalgamated Association also weakened the American Federation of Labor and set back the progress of organized labor all over the country.

It was at the end of June, in the midst of the drama, when Emma saw the newspaper headline and informed Sasha and Modska that there had been a lockout in Homestead. They agreed to shut down the luncheonette immediately and return to New York. Their landlord exclaimed at the decision; the luncheonette was enjoying great success, and the three were well on "the way to fortune."[20] But they saw an irresistible opportunity to disseminate their anarchist philosophy to a primed audience. Modska remained in Worcester to liquidate affairs at the French Art Studio, but Sasha and Emma left the very next day on the early morning train.

Arriving in New York, they went directly to the home of Frank Mollock, an Austrian comrade in the Autonomy group. A baker by trade, with a wife and two children, he occupied a three-room apartment in a tenement at 340 East Fifth Street, a block east of the Zum Groben Michel tavern. They also conferred with Claus Timmermann and Fritz and Sepp Oerter. Sasha and Emma announced their plan to head to Homestead and distribute a written appeal to the workers, "to help them see that it was not only for the moment that they must strike, but for all time, for a free life, for anarchism." Berkman hoped that "Homestead might prove the first blush of the glorious Dawn."[21]

The group drafted the appeal, titled "Labor Awaken!" but before they could deliver it, news of the July 6 riverbank war between the strikers and the Pinkertons changed their plans. "The great battle has been fought," Sasha crowed. "Never before, in all its history, has American labor won such a signal victory. . . . What a humiliating defeat for the powers that be!"[22] The time for leaflets had passed. Instead, they decided, they were ready to perform the "supreme deed" they had talked about for two years. With the nation's attention focused on Homestead, it was the "psychological moment" for an *attentat,* or assassination, a shocking act of propaganda by the deed designed to galvanize the workers to revolt.[23]

The target would be Henry Clay Frick himself. Frick had broken off negotiations with the union, locked out the Homestead workers, and imported an army of Pinkertons to fight his battle. Therefore, believed the trio, he bore the responsibility for the bloodshed. "A blow aimed at Frick," said Goldman, "would re-echo in the poorest hovel, would call the attention of the whole world to the real cause behind the Homestead struggle. It would strike terror in the enemy's ranks and make them realize that the proletariat of America had its avengers." To the three anarchists, Frick was no longer to be seen as a flesh-and-blood person, but as an object, a symbol of the capitalist class, or, said Goldman, "not as a man, but as the enemy of labor."[24]

Berkman rationalized that the assassination of Frick was not "to be considered as the taking of a life. A revolutionist," he said, "would rather perish a thousand times than be guilty of what is ordinarily called murder. In truth, murder and *Attentat* are to me opposite terms. To remove a tyrant is an act of liberation, the giving of life and opportunity to an oppressed people." Such language evoked the tenets of the People's Will, the heroes of Sasha's youth in Russia. As the populists had assassinated the tsar, so would he assassinate the tyrant at Homestead, and he was ready to suffer the ultimate penalty. Sasha was yearning for a martyr's death, like those of the executed legends of the People's Will. "Could anything be more noble than to die for a grand, a sublime Cause?" he wondered.[25]

Of course, in Berkman's Russia, revolutionists had little means of expression—for them, a dramatic act of violence followed by a lone chance to state their beliefs publicly (before exile or execution) was the single route to representation. America, for all its flaws and limitations, was a far more open place, with many opportunities for protest and communication. But Sasha had been imprinted by the impressions and obsessions of his childhood. To him, a true attentat was the only worthy form of sacrifice for his ideals.

Emulating his idols, Berkman chose bombs as the means to destroy Frick. He had never before made bombs, but gamely went ahead with the plan. Procuring dynamite from a comrade, he used as his guide Johann Most's *Science of Revolutionary War,* descriptively subtitled *A Little Handbook of Instruction in the Use and Preparation of Nitroglycerine, Dynamite, Gun-Cotton, Fulminating Mercury, Bombs, Fuses, Poisons, etc., etc.* Berkman worked on the bombs in the apartment at night, when everybody was asleep. His awareness that a bomb might explode prematurely left him undeterred. "All means," he wrote, "are justified in the war of humanity against its enemies. Indeed, the more repugnant the means, the stronger the test of one's nobility and devotion. All great revolutionists have proved that."[26]

Goldman was more concerned about the obvious dangers of the project, especially for the innocent people in the building. What if there was an accident and the tenement blew up? "I lived in dread every moment for Sasha, for our friends in the flat, the children, and the rest of the tenants." But she brushed her fears aside, believing that their mission was worth it. "What if a few have to perish?" she wondered. "The many would be made free and could live in beauty and comfort."[27]

That young idealists imagined they were helping humanity by building bombs in a crowded tenement must give pause to any reasonable person. But reason was given little weight, and after laboring every night for a week,

Berkman managed to build two bombs, one to test and the other to use against Frick. The first he took to Staten Island for testing. It did not go off. Berkman attributed the malfunction to poor directions in Most's handbook or to the dampness of the dynamite. In either case, Berkman felt the second bomb would most likely also fail; he decided to use a handgun instead. A week's preparation had been lost and forty dollars wasted.

Time and funds were now running short. The anarchists wanted to strike as soon as possible, before the nation's attention drifted to another matter. But their savings, once so bountiful with the success of the little luncheonette, had now dwindled to fifteen dollars, barely enough to bring Sasha to Pittsburgh, where Frick lived and worked, and leave him a dollar for the first day's food and lodgings. Berkman therefore would carry out the attentat alone, and Goldman, the "born speaker, the propagandist," would stay behind, to explain his act to the world. Emma also was charged with raising money for a revolver and a proper suit of men's clothes, the latter to help Sasha gain admittance to Frick's office.[28]

Sasha packed the leftover dynamite and other bombmaking paraphernalia into a mechanic's tool satchel and made a brief trip to Worcester to drop it off with Modska and inform him of the plan. If Sasha failed, his cousin might complete the mission. "In all the movement," Sasha later wrote, "I know of no one capable of propaganda by deed, or of an avenging act, except the twin."[29]

Sasha returned to New York to make his final preparations. "If you had met Berkman," Goldman remarked to a comrade years later, "you wouldn't have thought him capable of shooting a fellow human being, but he was captivated by the ideal of anarchism and he believed that Frick's behavior was antisocial and antihuman, so that he had to be eliminated."[30] On the evening of July 13, 1892, a farewell supper was held in the apartment. Then Emma and a group of comrades went to the train station to see Sasha embark on what was to be the most fateful journey of his life.

6

ATTENTAT

Berkman traveled on the Baltimore & Ohio Railroad, taking the night train to Washington, D.C., the first leg of his journey to Pennsylvania. As he dozed on the train, in a stillness broken only by the clicking of the rails, memories of his childhood flickered through his mind, mingling with images of the present. After a fitful sleep he awoke in Washington as the train was pulling in. It had to make a six-hour stop before proceeding to Pittsburgh. The sun had just risen, he later recalled, "pouring a flood of gold upon the Capitol. The cupola rears its proud head majestically above the pile of stone and marble."[1] It was not until the evening that he arrived at his destination.

With him he had the addresses of two German anarchists, Henry Bauer and Carl Nold, whom he was counting on to find him a place to stay. Sasha had never met either man, and both were disciples of Johann Most, now his sworn enemy, yet he nonetheless planned to ask them for assistance. For one thing, there was no Autonomist group in Pittsburgh that he could approach. For another, he knew that Bauer and Nold had been active in the struggle against Frick. Bauer had called Frick "the meanest man the nineteenth century has produced," and Bauer and Nold, along with a comrade named Max Metzkow, had distributed 5,000 copies of a leaflet to the workers at Homestead on July 7, the day after the battle with the Pinkertons. "Brothers," the leaflet began, "there is no course left but to meet force with force. The factories, mills, machinery, property, in short, the wealth that Carnegie calls his, was created by us, the workers, and of right should belong to us. Therefore we should stay in the mills that

OF RIGHT BELONG TO US, and thus strike and defend ourselves against any intruders." It ended with an appeal for "revolutionary methods" and the call of "Brothers! Become Anarchists!"[2]

The leaflet was not well received at Homestead. The workers rejected it, the three men were treated with scorn, and the police were summoned. Metzkow managed to slip away, but Bauer and Nold were arrested and detained, then driven out of town and admonished not to return. Had they been forced to stay overnight, Metzkow speculated, they very likely would have been lynched.[3]

Arriving in Pittsburgh, Sasha went to see Nold, who lived in a three-story house on Cherry Street in Allegheny City. The first floor was occupied by a fellow anarchist, Paul Eckert, and his wife; the second by Nold; and the third by the printing press of the local Most group, where Nold and his friends had printed the Homestead leaflet. Originally from southern Germany, Nold had come to the United States in 1883 when he was fourteen years old. By the age of eighteen he was well read in anarchist literature and active in an anarchist group, in which he recited poetry and took part in a singing society.

Nold was a small, slight man with prominent eyebrows. He affected, said the *New York Times*, "the truly Anarchistic style of hair, pompadour, dark mustache, a restless manner, and well-worn clothing."[4] Good-natured and outgoing, he was beloved by his comrades, who enjoyed his sense of humor and love of life. From an uncle in America, he learned the trade of locksmith and later became a skilled machinist. Since 1890 he had been employed by the Taylor & Dean wire works and was said to have "given entire satisfaction as a good and steady workman."[5]

The affable Nold invited Sasha to stay with him. Bauer, however, initially was highly apprehensive—a stranger's sudden arrival at the height of the Homestead trouble made him uneasy—and he spent the night hidden in Berkman's room, a loaded gun in hand. "At the first sign of a suspicious move on my part, he was determined to kill me," wrote Berkman afterward.[6] Nold and Bauer contacted Most about the new houseguest, who cautioned them that Berkman and Emma Goldman had allied themselves with Peukert and must be considered "dangerous and suspicious individuals."[7] But Nold liked Sasha and ignored the warning. The two soon became good friends.

Bauer also warmed to Berkman. A hefty, jovial German with a ruddy complexion, Bauer was described by one newspaper as a "large, fine looking man . . . well proportioned, full in the face, has a heavy black mustache and eyebrows and hair."[8] The son of peasants, he was thirty-one years old and a carpenter by trade. He had immigrated in 1880 and settled in Pittsburgh, where he became the foreman in a carpentry shop but was fired for participating in a strike. By then he was an anarchist and a follower of Most, though by no means an avid disciple. After losing his job, he abandoned his carpentry work and became a bookseller and distributor of anarchist literature. In addition to Most's *Freiheit,* he circulated Peukert's *Der Anarchist.*

Like Nold, Bauer resided in Allegheny City, at 73 Spring Garden Avenue in a two-story frame house. He and an anarchist cobbler named Maxwell Albrecht shared the first floor. It was divided into three compartments, in which the men lived and conducted their business. On one side was Albrecht's shoe shop, on the other Bauer's bookstore, with hundreds of German and English books displayed on the shelves. At the rear, behind a curtain stretched across the threshold for privacy, were their tiny sleeping quarters. The upstairs floor was used by a German couple who apparently had nothing to do with the anarchists.

Berkman stayed at Carl Nold's from July 14 to 21. During this time he met a number of local anarchists in addition to Bauer and Nold. Among them was Albrecht, whom Berkman described as a "philosophic old shoemaker," whose shop was "a center" of the radical intelligentsia.[9] Another, Max Metzkow, the man who had helped distribute the leaflets in Homestead, became a friend of Sasha's for life.

Metzkow was a Most supporter, yet he treated Sasha as a comrade, indifferent to the Peukert-Most feud. A printer by trade, he was older than the others, born in Germany in 1854. He was first imprisoned in his home country at twenty-two for distributing antimilitary leaflets. Later he became a follower of Most and circulated *Freiheit* in Berlin, but he was arrested for treason under Otto von Bismarck's antisocialist laws and spent another two years in prison. On his release, Metzkow found sanctuary in London. There he took an active part in the anarchist movement, as well as in the Socialist League, founded by the celebrated artist and writer William Morris. He met leading anarchists, including Peter Kropotkin and the

French activist Louise Michel, and published an English translation of Most's 1887 pamphlet *The God Pestilence.* In 1888 Metzkow immigrated to New York, where he worked as a compositor. The following year he moved to Pittsburgh. He was known in his circle as a modest, unshowy man; tireless, plainspoken in manner, yet passionately devoted to the cause.

SUCH WERE THE COMRADES Berkman got to know in Pittsburgh and who were ready to come to his aid. They provided him with shelter, companionship, and money, and accompanied him when he made a sojourn to Homestead. There the signs of the July 6 battle were still in evidence. Sasha saw the high fence with its barbed wire, the cannon, empty shells and oil barrels, piles of breastworks, the charcoal remains of the Pinkerton barges at the blood-spattered dock, a testimony, he said, to the "really strong, to the victim who dared."[10] He returned to Pittsburgh with renewed vigor, determined to carry out his attentat.

During the next few days he mapped out his plan of attack. His original intention was to kill Frick at his home, a twenty-three-room mansion in the Homewood section on the outskirts of the city. To inspect the layout he went and had a look around, only to find that the premises were heavily guarded. From then on he focused on Frick's business offices, located in the Chronicle Telegraph Building on Fifth Avenue between Smithfield and Wood Streets in central Pittsburgh. The Carnegie Steel Company occupied the entire building except the top floor, which was used by the *Chronicle Telegraph* newspaper. Frick had offices on the second and fifth floors. Berkman scouted the site several times, sometimes joined by Bauer and Nold.

While Sasha was making his plans, Emma was busy raising money in New York. At first she had no success, but then she recalled the character of Sonya Marmeladova in Dostoevsky's *Crime and Punishment,* who became a prostitute to support her family. After a night of agonizing, Emma felt she could do no less to help Sasha. She scrutinized herself, wondering if she could be "attractive enough to men who seek out girls on the street," and decided her complexion was good, her blond hair and blue eyes were appealing, and her body could be ably enhanced by a corset. With a bit of money borrowed from a neighbor, she bought high-heeled shoes (she had never worn a pair before), silk stockings, and fabric for sewing decorative underclothes.[11]

That Saturday evening, July 16, she joined the women plying their trade on 14th Street. But her courage failed her when she observed the men, "saw their vulgar glances and their manner of approaching the women." Whenever a prospect advanced she hastily walked away. She was just about to give up when a tall, white-haired man, distinguished and well-dressed, came over to her. He invited her to a nearby saloon and bought her a beer. He said he could tell she was a novice streetwalker, and she admitted it was her first time, although she concealed her true identity. "It would be too dreadful," she thought, "if he should learn that Emma Goldman, the anarchist, had been found soliciting on Fourteenth Street. What a juicy story it would make for the press!"[12]

Much to Emma's surprise, the man made no physical overtures but handed her ten dollars and advised her to give up streetwalking because she did not "have the knack" for it and would "hate it afterwards." He was amiable and courteous, unlike any man she had met before; her previous experience suggested that men fell into only two categories: "vulgarians and idealists." She and the stranger parted in a friendly manner. She repaid her neighbor and then wired her sister, Helena, in Rochester, claiming that she was ill and needed fifteen dollars. Receiving the money, she sent a total of twenty dollars to Sasha in Allegheny City.[13]

With the funds from Emma, Sasha made several purchases. At Kaufmann Brothers he bought a conservative light gray suit with narrow stripes, a white shirt, and a white necktie. He ordered calling cards bearing the alias of "Simon Bachman," the purported head of a New York employment agency. This, thought Berkman, would attract the attention of Frick, who was still in need of strikebreakers. Last, he bought a cheap, 38-caliber, short-barreled "bulldog" revolver.

On Tuesday, July 19, Berkman was ready to carry out his plan. He dressed himself in his new set of clothes and put on an old black derby purchased on the Lower East Side that bore the label "Margulies, 70 Stanton Street, New York." In one of his hip pockets he stashed the revolver, in the other a dagger with a twelve-inch blade. The dagger consisted of a file set in a wooden handle, ground to a point, and sharpened at the edges. Sasha had made it himself in New York.

Arriving in the morning at the Chronicle Telegraph Building, Berkman went up to Frick's fifth-floor office. Not finding Frick there, he came down to the second floor. He told the attendant that he was from a New York employment agency and wanted to meet with Frick. The attendant took down his name but said that Frick was too busy to see him. Berkman departed. On Thursday, July 21, he returned, only to be told again that Frick could not see him. That night was the last he stayed with Nold in Allegheny City. On Friday he took a room at the Merchants' Hotel on Water Street, opposite the Baltimore & Ohio station. Signing the register, he used the name "Rakhmetov," his fictional idol from Chernyshevsky's *What Is to Be Done?*

On Saturday, July 23, the day of reckoning arrived. Berkman was awake by dawn, had breakfast in his room, and walked to the Carnegie offices. Arriving about eleven, he went up to the second floor and found the place abuzz with activity. A bundle of nerves, he retreated downstairs and loitered about the building. Meanwhile Frick left for lunch at the Duquesne Club, where he dined with his friend and physician Dr. Lawrence Litchfield. Frick returned after 1:30, went briefly to a fifth-floor room, descended to the second floor, then seated himself in his office with John Leishman, vice-chairman of Carnegie Steel.

Berkman, standing outside the building, watched as Frick came back from lunch. He hurried upstairs to the second floor and nearly collided with his target, emerging from the elevator. Berkman was unable to gather his wits and pull out his gun; Frick, unaware of the danger, continued on into his office. Berkman entered the reception room and handed his card to the attendant, who withdrew into Frick's office and told his boss that the New York employment agent who had called before was back again and wished a moment's audience. Berkman, increasingly agitated, stepped out of the reception room. Then he steeled himself, retraced his steps, pushed past the attendant, and burst into Frick's office.[14]

There sat Frick, engaged in conversation with Leishman. Berkman reached into his pocket and drew out the revolver as Frick began to rise from his chair. At that moment it occurred to Sasha that Frick might be wearing an armored vest, so he aimed the weapon at Frick's head. Frick averted his face as Berkman pulled the trigger. The bullet grazed the lobe of Frick's left ear, entered his neck at a downward angle, and lodged under his right shoulder blade.[15] Frick dropped to his knees and slumped against the chair. As Berkman moved closer, Leishman, a small man, jumped him from behind. Unwilling to fire upon Leishman—"I would not hurt him," Sasha thought, "I have no business with him"—he shook himself loose and aimed again at Frick.[16]

The second bullet caught Frick on the right side of the neck and embedded itself below the left shoulder. Berkman was pointing the weapon for a third shot when Leishman caught his wrist and pulled his hand upward, so that the bullet went into the ceiling. Leishman and Berkman grappled furiously. Frick, dazed and bleeding from his wounds, nevertheless struggled to his feet, seized Berkman around the waist, and brought all three tumbling to the floor. Berkman managed to work his left hand free and drew his dagger from his pocket. With this he stabbed Frick in quick succession in the side above the hipbone, again in the lower back, and a third time in the thigh above the knee.

The blade wounds were deep and serious, and Frick cried out in pain. Hearing the commotion, a carpenter who had been working in the building rushed in and hit Berkman on the back of the head with a hammer. The blow only stunned Sasha, and he continued to stab at Frick. The shots, "sharp and distinct," had sounded all over the building, across the avenue, and out in the street, where the struggle was witnessed by pedestrians staring up from the sidewalk.[17] In a minute Frick's office was filled with people: clerks, workers in overalls, policemen, Frick's attendant, and an assortment of shouting individuals.

Berkman, slight but fiercely strong, continued to resist, and it took several more men to overpower him. His arms were pulled and twisted until he was pinioned to the floor, and his captors set about "punishing him severely." A deputy sheriff who happened to be in the building at the time of the attack drew his revolver and aimed it at Sasha. "Don't shoot," called Frick with singular poise. "Leave him to the law. But raise his head and let me see his face." An officer jerked Berkman's head back by the hair. "Mr. Frick," he asked, "do you identify the man as your assailant?" Frick nodded without a word.[18]

Sasha stared at Frick, taking in his victim. "His face is ashen gray," he saw, "the black beard is streaked with red, and blood is oozing from his neck." Fleetingly, Frick was no longer merely a symbol, a means to an end, but a man, wounded and weak. "For an instant a strange feeling, as of shame, comes over me," Berkman later wrote, "but the next moment I am filled with anger at the sentiment, so unworthy of a revolutionist."[19]

Berkman was placed under arrest. Police headquarters was notified, and detectives hurried to the scene, along with additional policemen. Disheveled and disoriented, his necktie ripped off and his suit stained with Frick's blood, Berkman was taken downstairs and out of the building, where an angry crowd had gathered. The news of the "attempted assassination spread like wildfire . . . from Market to Wood street," and cries of "Shoot him!" and "Hang him!" filled the air. "Let him have what he gave Frick," yelled an outraged citizen.[20] A few in the throng offered words of approval ("Served Frick right!"), but "the sentiment of the crowd" was palpably hostile. "There was strong feeling manifested against" Berkman, wrote the *New York Times,* "but he did not shrink or betray fear." One bystander asked Sasha, "Are you hurt? You're bleeding." Sasha passed his hand over his face. "I've lost my glasses," he replied. An officer snapped, "You'll be dammed lucky if you don't lose your head!"[21]

The officers brought Berkman to a patrol box on Wood Street and Fifth Avenue. Soon a paddy wagon arrived, and he was taken to the central station. A mass of excited people pursued the wagon, and from all sides were more shouts of "Lynch the villain!"[22]

Doctors meanwhile had begun to attend to the wounded Frick, who was sprawled on a lounge in his office. The first to arrive after the shooting was a man named Buchanan, from Washington, Pennsylvania, who had heard the shots fired as he passed by in the street and had come inside to offer his medical assistance. Frick's personal physician, Dr. Litchfield, was known to be at the Duquesne Club, where Frick had left him half an hour before. He was sent for immediately, and by the time he reached the office, Dr. Buchanan was on the scene tending to the injuries. Other doctors in the area were soon on hand to assist.[23] Frick was drenched with blood, and his injuries were grave; few thought he could survive. Yet, at forty-two years old, he was hardy and strong, with a determined character. He was taken to a back room and laid on a wide leather couch, where the doctors proceeded to extract the bullets.

Frick refused to take an anesthetic, suggesting that he might be of help in locating the bullets. As the doctors probed his wounds he never flinched or complained, but pointed to the spots where he thought the metal had lodged. Both bullets were removed, the holes plugged with cotton, his neck bandaged, and leg and body wounds dressed. Through it all, Frick remained conscious and in command.[24] Before he left in an ambulance, he dictated a public statement: "This incident will not change the attitude of the Carnegie Steel Company towards the Amalgamated Association. I do not think I shall die, but whether I do or not, the Company will pursue the same policy, and it will win."[25]

At 7:45 the ambulance took Frick to his residence at Homewood. He passed a relatively comfortable night. By the following day he was in remarkably good condition, "and there seemed little doubt about his ultimate recovery." Newspapers chronicled his extraordinary, "unprecedented" progress.[26] Frick, attended around the clock by Dr. Litchfield, was "quite cheerful" and "confident" that he would get well.[27] He conducted his business as usual, propped up, reading papers and correspondence, and eating heartily.[28] He remained at home for the next ten days during a blistering heat wave. He suffered another calamity on August 3 when his month-old baby, Henry Clay Frick Jr., died. The Fricks' fourth child had been born on July 6, the day of the Pinkerton battle. On August 4 Frick attended the funeral, sat up most of the night with his distraught wife, and slept for an hour or two. Then he breakfasted, took a streetcar to his office, and arrived at eight, in time for his customary morning schedule. His friends were anxious that, in this time of great conflict, Frick should have moved freely through the streets of Pittsburgh, refusing the protection of bodyguards or police. But Frick would have it no other way. "If an honest American can't live in America in his own home without being surrounded by a guard, it's time to quit," he had said when the Homestead trouble first began.[29] His stalwart behavior after the shooting and the death of his infant son earned him some public sympathy and respect.

During this period, Berkman had been locked up in jail. On July 23, the day he attacked Frick, he was booked and placed in a cell at the central police station. Then he was searched and his belongings catalogued. His handgun was recorded as a 38-caliber revolver with five chambers. Three of the cartridges had been discharged, and twelve additional cartridges were found in a trouser pocket. His watch had been broken in the struggle. Additionally, he was carrying a purse containing a nickel coin, some sheets of paper, and a small dynamite capsule. Berkman also had two packs of cigarettes and a cigarette tin (his nicotine-stained fingers were duly noted, and newspaper reports referred to him as a "confirmed cigarette smoker," and a "cigarette fiend").[30]

After the search was concluded, Berkman was questioned by police officials, among them Assistant Superintendent Silvis, Inspector John McKelvey, and Chief Brown. Berkman said he was a Russian Jew, unmarried, and a printer and cigarmaker by trade. He claimed he had come to Pittsburgh from New York on Thursday, July 21, and checked into the Merchants' Hotel on Water Street. This part, of course, was largely untrue, but he lied about the length of his stay in Pittsburgh so as not to implicate his anarchist comrades. Why did he wish to kill Frick, he was asked by Chief Brown. "Frick is an enemy of the working man, and had to die," Berkman replied. Who were his accomplices, the chief demanded, adding, "You can be frank with me. We've got your friend Rakhmetov," unwittingly referring to Berkman's alias. Sasha suppressed a smile. He denied having accomplices, insisting he had acted alone.[31]

The initial questioning over, Superintendent Roger O'Mara, Inspector McKelvey, and Detectives Shore and Coulson brought Berkman to the gymnasium in the station yard to have his picture taken. Several photographs were made, one of which was sent to the police in New York. While Sasha was being photographed, Detective Coulson noticed an odd twitching of his mouth. "Seems to be something there," said the detective, but the remark was disregarded. Back inside, Sasha underwent a physical examination. His clothing, splattered with Frick's blood, was removed, and he was given prisoner's garments. Superintendent O'Mara issued the order to return him to his cell.

At that moment Police Surgeon Irwin J. Moyer, who had been studying Berkman, noticed that his jaws were moving vigorously again. He seemed to be chewing something. "Wait a minute," said Moyer. "What have you got in your mouth?" "Nothing," was the response. But this did not satisfy the surgeon. Thrusting in his fingers, he pried open Sasha's teeth and extracted a dynamite capsule identical to the one taken when Sasha was first searched. Sasha had concealed the second capsule in the lining of his jacket. An expert examined it and determined that "the cartridge is of the same kind as the one used by Lingg, the Chicago anarchist." Onlookers were taken aback by the discovery; the capsule had enough fulminate of mercury to "blow [Berkman's] head off" and it was "considered a miracle" that the device had not detonated. "The only reasonable conclusion that could be reached," wrote a reporter, "was that the desperate wretch had deliberately attempted to add another thrilling chapter to the tragedy, by blowing off his own head, while in front of the camera." When confronted with the dynamite cartridge, Sasha was defiant. "What's this?" he was asked. "Candy," he replied.[32]

Superintendent O'Mara sent Berkman to a cell on the first floor, and an officer was detailed to stand guard. When supper was brought to him, Berkman asked for a knife, but was refused. A few minutes later he requested a handkerchief, but this too was denied him. That evening he was allowed to speak to reporters. Accompanied by the guard, half a dozen men entered his cell, local press from Pittsburgh as well as correspondents from other cities in Pennsylvania and from New York. Berkman smoked incessantly. Though tired, he spoke "calmly and intelligently." He looked like a clerk, one of them thought, "a rather quiet commonplace one. His spectacles give him the air of studiousness and sedateness."[33]

The reporters attempted to evaluate Berkman's objective. "That he is pleased with the notoriety which he has gained is evident," wrote one journalist, "but that he is a dreamy fanatic who has gone crazy over anarchist literature is also possible." Another saw in him "the qualities of coolness and courage," while to a third, he seemed quite "an ordinary looking person, with all the characteristic features of the Russian Hebrew—the aquiline nose, the thick lips, and the deep brown eyes."[34]

In the view of the reporters, Sasha was "not very prepossessing." They seemed bemused by the proportions of his lips, the facial aspect that had earned him the nickname "Tolstogub" from his comrades. "The most remarkable part of his facial character is his mouth," wrote a journalist. "It is certainly foreboding. His lower lip and his upper lip are double, remarkably so even in the eyes of detectives who have had time to study these characteristics."[35] "His most peculiar feature," said another account, "is the mouth, which is large and sensual, and has two curious flaps of flesh, which, when it is open, still partially cover his upper teeth." His chin was deemed "strong," his forehead "excellently shaped," and his ears jutting. One reporter found fault only in "the shifty, furtive manner in which he uses his eyes."[36]

Sasha told the group that he was a Russian Jew and was "proud of his nationality." A few reports nevertheless misrepresented him as German, since he answered some questions in "good, pure German." Sasha said he switched from English because "I am not always so sure of my ground in that tongue," adding, "I speak very poor English, as I have to take it from the Latin."[37]

Berkman was asked why he had tried to kill Frick. "Do you know any person in this world who is better or happier for his ever having lived?" Berkman demanded. "I can find you thousands whom he has made miserable. Out in Homestead people will soon be suffering the pangs of hunger. Whose fault is it? Mr. Frick's. Thousands of strong, healthy men are now idle because they cannot return to work without sacrificing their self-respect. Whose fault is it? Mr. Frick's. Six workingmen were buried here last week. Who killed them? Mr. Frick. Does such a man deserve to live? Of what good is he in the world? He is a dog, and he should die. I wanted to kill him, and I am ready to die for it." Berkman was resolute. "I was only one, and my death would be nothing at all compared with the happiness of the thousands of workers who would bless my memory. The men could then win their strike and the downtrodden of this country would rejoice: Oh, how happy I would be to know that he is dead. Do you understand? I wanted to kill Frick. I came here to do so. Now I want him to die."[38]

A guard informed him that Frick would probably recover. "I suppose you are glad to hear that," remarked the guard, still convinced that Berkman would be relieved to avoid execution for murder. "I am not a bit glad," Sasha angrily replied. Berkman also refused to consider the idea that Frick had reacted with bravery during the attack, as many witnesses attested. "There is no use talking about Mr. Frick not being frightened," he told reporters while waiting for trial. "He was the worst scared man I ever saw and I don't blame him much for it. He believed I meant to kill him as I certainly did and he had a right to be scared as he certainly was."[39]

The following day, a Sunday, passed more quietly for Sasha, who was in a contemplative mood and spoke little. Eventually, however, Inspector McKelvey approached his cell. He wanted to have another set of photographs of Berkman, taken not by the police photographer but by a well-known commercial lensman. Berkman was brought to the Liberty Street studio of B. L. H. Dabbs, considered the photographer of choice among the Pittsburgh social elite. McKelvey lent Sasha his own tie for the occasion. The London-born Dabbs had taken many pictures of the strike in Homestead, the most notable an image of the July 6 clash with the Pinkertons. The photograph of Berkman was reproduced in *Harper's Weekly,* and a corresponding sketch appeared in the *Pittsburgh Post,* on July 25, 1892.

Sasha was returned to the police station. He rested on his bed and chain-smoked cigarettes until 8:15 P.M., when he was removed from his cell, placed in handcuffs, and transferred to the Allegheny County Jail. There, for several days, he was monitored around the clock. Rumors had been circulating that a confederate of his had arrived in Pittsburgh carrying dynamite. The rumors turned out to be true. The confederate was none other than Modska Aronstam, who had resolved to finish what Sasha had begun.

THE DAY AFTER THE ATTEMPT ON FRICK, Modska left Worcester for New York, taking along the explosive material that Sasha had entrusted to him. Early the next morning, Modska departed for Pittsburgh. "The pockets of his trousers were filled with dynamite," his daughter said later. "He intended to blow up Frick's house."[40] After examining Frick's well-guarded grounds, Modska took a trolley downtown, disembarking at Liberty Street. There, oddly enough, he had his picture taken in Dabbs's studio, where Sasha had been photographed the previous day.

Modska was now prepared to carry out the deed. Leaving the studio, he retraced his steps to the trolley, passing a newspaper stand on the way. His eyes fell on a headline: "WAS NOT ALONE. BERKMANN HAD ACCOMPLICES IN HIS MISSION OF MURDER. IS AARON STAMM HERE?" Modska was startled. He immediately dumped the dynamite in a nearby outhouse and hastened to the railroad station. He took the next train to Rochester, where he rendezvoused with Emma, who gave him money to go back to New York City. "Years later," said his grandson, "he told me that if I should ever visit Pittsburgh, I should watch out where I took a shit, because somewhere there was twenty pounds of dynamite under a toilet."[41]

How, wondered Modska, had his plan become known? He thought that perhaps Roman Lewis, a member of the Pioneers of Liberty who was an enemy of the Autonomists, was responsible for the leak. In this he was mistaken. The actual culprit was an informer among the Autonomists themselves, who reported to the Austrian consul in New York. Many of the Autonomists were Austrians by birth, including their leader, Josef Peukert. Some had taken part in acts of terror in Vienna during the 1880s, and their activities were carefully monitored in the Austrian capital, as well as in New York and London. In New York, a spy had been planted in the group that met in the Zum Groben Michel tavern, and he tipped off the Austrian vice-consul, who in turn sent a telegram to the Pittsburgh police alerting them to a conspiracy to assassinate Frick: if Berkman should fail, as he did, an anarchist named Aronstam was to make an attempt. The police leaked this news to the Pittsburgh press, who wrongly gave the name as "Aaron Stamm." Modska, spooked by the close call, was unable to complete the job.

At the county jail, meanwhile, Berkman remained under heavy watch. The authorities feared he would make another attempt to kill himself—they were alarmed by how close he had come with the dynamite cartridge hidden in his mouth. But by this time, Sasha had changed his mind, deciding against suicide for now. He instead wished to live long enough to justify his behavior in court, to explain "the motive and purpose of my act." He was determined, said Emma Goldman, "that the American people might know that he was not a criminal, but an idealist."[42]

A preliminary hearing was held in the jail on July 29. Frick, still recuperating from his wounds, did not make an appearance, but Leishman testified that Berkman had tried to kill him along with Frick. David Fortney, the elevator operator, said that he had seen Berkman loitering in the building on the day of the attack and for several days before. Berkman, who rejected the assistance of an attorney, denied that he had intended to kill Leishman and said that the elevator operator's testimony was false. He admitted, however, that he had planned to kill Frick. He thereupon was remanded to jail in default of $24,900 bail.

Berkman remained in the jail for fifty-eight days. He was allowed to correspond with his friends and to receive gifts of money by mail, sufficient to keep him in his requisite cigarettes. He had a few visitors, Max Metzkow among them—"a true friend and comrade," Sasha later wrote of Max's loyalty during this period. Another was Harry Gordon, a Vilnius-born machinist who lived in Pittsburgh and headed the Pittsburgh Socialist Society.[43]

Every day Sasha was granted an hour of exercise in the yard, where he could mingle with the other prisoners. Here he made a discovery that disturbed him greatly. None of his fellow inmates could understand why he had tried to kill Frick. Some thought there must have been a personal quarrel between them, a "business misunderstanding." His explanations proved a waste of effort. It was lucky, the inmates told him, that Frick had not died, for now Sasha could not be hanged for the crime. Sasha's claims of a higher purpose were rebuffed. His talk about "the welfare of the people" was met with smiles of derision. Some thought he was simply out of his mind.[44]

One prisoner, a jailed Homestead worker, rejected Sasha's rationale outright. Jack Clifford, a member of the advisory committee, had played an active part in the July 6 battle. He was now awaiting trial for throwing dynamite at the Pinkerton barges. Such a man, thought Sasha, surely would understand the motive for his attack on Frick. But when he tried to explain that he had done it for the workers, Clifford impatiently cut him off. The mill workers, he said, did not believe in killing. The violence at Homestead had been an unwelcome development. They respected the law. They had welcomed the militia to the site. The workers wanted nothing to do with anarchists. Why did Berkman want to kill Frick? Berkman was not a member of the Homestead community. The strike was none of Berkman's business, Clifford said. He had only harmed the workers with his vicious act.[45]

Clifford's reaction cut Sasha to the heart. Yet he felt it could not be typical. "The People could not fail to realize the depth of a love that will give its own life for their causes. To give a young life, full of health and vitality, to give all, without a thought of self; to give all, voluntarily, cheerfully nay—enthusiastically—could anyone fail to understand such a love?"[46] But Clifford was hardly alone. The advisory committee in Homestead was quick to condemn Sasha and extend its sympathy to Frick along with a prayer for his speedy recovery. And though cries of "Serves him right!" and "Wish he was dead!" were heard about Frick, the strikers generally were repelled by Berkman's crime.[47] Their relief was great when they learned that the assailant was an outsider and not one of their own. Some, in fact, were convinced that Berkman was a capitalist provocateur hired to kill Frick just to discredit the union.

John McLuckie of the advisory committee denounced the attack in theory, though he balked at praying for Frick. "I certainly have no reason to feel any sympathy for Frick," McLuckie said when he gave a speech in Youngstown soon after the shooting. "And I am not sorry to hear that he has been shot, as he is now suffering as some of the honest toilers did at Homestead from Pinkerton bullets fired at his declaration. Frick's name should be hated by every honest man."[48]

Frick also received scant compassion from some members of the militia sent to crush the strike. Ever since the militia had encamped at Homestead, there had been among a number of the soldiers a feeling of sympathy for the strikers and their cause. One private, William L. Iams of Company K, Tenth Regiment, who hailed from one of the most prominent families in Greene County, shouted, "Three cheers for the man who shot Frick!" when he heard the news.[49] He was overheard by regimental commander Lt. Colonel J. B. R. Streator, who ordered Iams strung up by the thumbs from a tree. After nearly a half-hour of this punishment, Iams was revived and taken to the guardhouse. Without a trial, he was found by General Snowden to have committed treason. He was dishonorably discharged from the militia, drummed out of camp in military style, and sent home.[50] The case of Private Iams made news around the country and gave Sasha much comfort when he was handed a newspaper clipping by a fellow inmate. "Glorious!" he exulted. "Who would have expected it? Such a wonderful spirit among the militia; perhaps the soldiers will fraternize with the workers."[51]

BUT THE IAMS AFFAIR WAS MERELY an isolated incident. Berkman's attack on Frick shocked the nation, and he was excoriated from all quarters. Clergymen reproached him, leaders censured him, citizens reviled him. Such condemnation was reflected in the press. The use of violence in such a case, wrote a reporter for the *New York World,* "is at once the most inexcusable and the most helpless of remedies. Nobody but a crank would have applied it. Nobody but a wretch would approve it."[52] Journalists referred to him as a Nihilist, a typical fanatic, "an anarchist of the most radical stripe."[53] They decried "the murderous policy by which anarchists propose to right the wrong of society." The *New York Times* mocked the "desperate-talking, firebrand-flinging" radicals of the Berkman type, the "hatchet-faced, pimply, sallow cheeked, rat-eyed young men of the Russian Jewish colony."[54]

That Berkman was a Jew and a foreigner exacerbated feelings against him—the charge that immigrants were perpetrators of violent acts and carried the seeds of social unrest had been commonplace since the Haymarket episode. Berkman's act gave an impetus to the popular stereotype of the foreign-born anarchist assassin. Newspapers continued to tag him as a "Russian Hebrew," a man with "an evil face."[55] The *New York Times* called him a "fanatical Anarchist," one of the "pestilent creatures . . . fostering the notion that violence and destruction are justifiable in a warfare against what they prate about as the wrongs of labor, and have been breeding possible assassins in a class that hardly knows what honest labor means. There are no worse enemies of the workingmen of this country than these same ignorant and reckless Socialists and Anarchists of foreign origin, who make so much noise about the rights and wrongs of society of which they have no intelligent comprehension."[56]

Sasha had gone to Pittsburgh hoping to trigger a social revolution. His attentat, he believed, would galvanize the workers into action, and they would be inspired to overthrow the capitalist system. But his attempt on Frick did nothing to prompt revolt or aid the workers' cause; on the contrary, it seemed to do further damage. According to one analysis, "The men [at Homestead] feel that their case is weaker than it has been at any time since the troubles commenced."[57]

In the aftermath, Frick emerged as a rather more popular figure. Before the attempt on his life, Frick had been widely criticized for his harsh and uncompromising treatment of the workers. His callous determination to break the union and his employment of Pinkertons had antagonized even those who normally sided with big business. Berkman's attack immediately reversed the situation; public sympathy shifted from the workers to Frick. The courage displayed by the wounded Frick won him grudging admiration in places where he had previously been deplored. Even his most strident critics paid tribute to his resilience.

Berkman had badly misread the mind and temper of the Homestead strikers, who were largely indifferent to radical appeals and to acts of revolutionary violence. As one paper stated it, "The feeling of the worker . . . is most bitter over the attack. They cannot feel sorry that Frick has been made to suffer but they are most sorry to think that an attempt should have been made upon his life. There are those among them who feel that this is a retribution. . . . But there is no sympathy with anarchy that sheds blood. They abhor the spectacled young man who tried so hard to become an assassin as much as any one can."[58]

Berkman's error, as Goldman admitted, stemmed from the delusion that the assassination of Frick would arouse "the dull, inert workers to overthrow the capitalist yoke." A populist at heart, Sasha sought to apply Russian tactics to American problems. America, however, was not Russia, and his act was ridiculed and rejected as a crime rather than as a social statement. Sasha was viewed, said the *New York Times,* "as a mere crank, a Nihilist, whose head was turned by the reading of the Homestead troubles, and who started forth on a mission of destruction, believing himself to be justified in his course. But . . . the affair has not only aroused intense excitement in the community, but has given a strong additional impetus to the reaction in favor of the Carnegie side of the controversy with their locked-out workmen."[59] Berkman, said one striker, was "no friend of organized labor. We know our rights, but we know we cannot vindicate them in this way." Hugh O'Donnell, chairman of the advisory committee, put it even more strongly. "The bullet from Berkman's pistol, failing in its foul attempt," he said, "went straight through the heart of the Homestead strike."[60]

There were, of course, a number of factors that contributed to the demise of the strike; as one American labor historian asserted, the machinery that ultimately thwarted the workers had been set in place before Berkman fired his shots. The company had laid its plans and made them public; the militia was in position; nonunion men were already in the mill and at work: therefore, "The struggle would have terminated in the same way, even if Berkman had never been born."[61]

Nevertheless, the defeat of the strikers weighed heavily on Sasha, as did his failure to kill Frick. "The poignancy of the disappointment pierces my heart," he wrote. "I feel it with the intensity of a catastrophe. My imprisonment, the vexations of jail life, the future—all is submerged in the flood of misery at the realization of my failure. Bitter thoughts crowd my mind; self-accusation overwhelms me. I failed. Failed!"[62]

Eventually, after much thought, Berkman arrived at a different resolution, deciding that it was his original motivation, not the outcome, that mattered. "Whether Frick was among the living or dead was a matter of comparative indifference to me," he later wrote. "It was my aim . . . to express, by my deed, my sentiment toward the existing system of legal oppression and industrial despotism; to attack the institution of wage-slavery in the person of one of its most prominent representatives; to give it a blow—rather morally than physically—this was the real purpose and signification of my act."[63] He had sacrificed himself on behalf of the common people to make a statement, "stimulate discussion," and "bring the teachings of Anarchism before the world."[64] His attentat, he concluded, had therefore been a success.

When Emma referred in a letter to his "failure to kill Frick," Sasha took umbrage. "Why do you speak of failure?" he wrote back indignantly. "You should not have your judgment obscured by the mere accident of physical results. Your lines pained and grieved me beyond words."[65]

7

JUDGMENT

After the attack on Frick, the Pittsburgh and Allegheny City police began an investigation of the anarchists in the area to determine if Berkman had accomplices. On July 25 they received an important lead. When looking over his books, the manager of the Allegheny City office of the Adams Express Company, a transport and postal service, noticed the entry "Alexander Berkman, 5 Cherry Street" on two different dates, July 14 and July 21. He immediately notified the police. That afternoon, Detective Shore of Pittsburgh went to the address and learned that Berkman had been staying with Carl Nold, who, the detective was told, was at work at Taylor & Dean's wire works on Market Street. Shore went to the company, located Nold, placed him under arrest, then took him to the central police station to be questioned by Inspector McKelvey. Meanwhile policemen searched Nold's house and found the name and address of Henry Bauer.[1]

The following morning Detective Shore, accompanied by Detective McTigue of Pittsburgh and Detective Steele of Allegheny City, arrested Bauer at his home. He, too, was taken to the central station for questioning by Inspector McKelvey. Both Nold and Bauer told essentially the same story. They had never met or heard of Berkman until he came to Pittsburgh. Berkman had claimed that he was seeking employment as a printer and that he knew Johann Most. (The *New York Times* called this tale "picturesque and weird," describing the Cherry Street address as "a miserable and squalid part of the town, which is flooded every time the river rises four or five feet, and which seems to have been especially built for the purpose of eluding and deceiving the police.")[2] Bauer and Nold said they had no knowledge whatsoever regarding the attempt on Frick's life. Nold said he had last seen Berkman on Friday, July 22, when he took him to the train station; he had pointed out the Chronicle Telegraph Building as they walked up Fifth Avenue, but did not show him Frick's office. Berkman had said his destination was Chicago, where he expected to find a job.

Bauer admitted that he had distributed leaflets at Homestead on the day after the Pinkerton battle. A wagonload of literature was seized at Bauer's residence. Weapons were discovered, including a 50-caliber bulldog revolver with cartridges to match, a rifle, and "one of the villainous looking daggers sometimes found on Italians." In Bauer's desk was uncovered a list of millionaires, along with plans for making bombs, termed infernal machines by the papers. All of this was confiscated and brought to the central station for examination.[3]

In addition to Bauer and Nold, Paul Eckert was called in for questioning, but was soon released for lack of evidence linking him to the attack.[4] Two other anarchists, both from Allegheny City, showed up at the station on July 28 to visit Bauer. They were arrested and questioned but were then allowed to go. Bauer and Nold, however, were charged with complicity in the attempt on Frick. After being locked up for nine and twenty days, respectively, they were released on $5,000 and $7,000 bail to await trial.[5]

The police were now focused on the existence of a plot. They had "new proofs," reported the *Pittsburgh Post,* "of a big, carefully laid conspiracy against the life of Chairman Frick." Declared Superintendent O'Mara, "I am now satisfied that there was an organized movement against Frick, and Berkman was only the tool of a number of conspirators."[6]

During the next few days more people were rounded up, and the anarchist group in Allegheny City was disbanded. Following up on the origin of the express letters received by Berkman at Nold's house, the police discovered that the sender was Frank Mollock, a baker from New York City, who had mailed money from Long Branch, New Jersey. The Pittsburgh authorities wired Captain James Layton of the Long Branch police, who tracked Mollock down and apprehended him at four in the afternoon on July 25. When questioned, Mollock denied he had ever known Berkman and refused to talk further; he was then locked up in a Long Branch prison cell, charged with complicity. Mollock was transferred to Pittsburgh under Superintendent O'Mara's guard for more questioning. Berkman was not alarmed—he "knew that the 'silent baker' would prove deaf and dumb." Soon Mollock was brought back to Long Branch, and eventually released for lack of evidence.[7]

The Pittsburgh police, according to the press, had been "flushing out of their holes as fine an assortment of anarchists as ever threatened life, thrown a bomb, or stabbed a victim in a dark alley." The authorities believed that "the attempt to assassinate Mr. Frick was only the initial movement of a great scheme begun by an organized band of anarchists fully as determined as the anarchists of Chicago." According to O'Mara, "There were more anarchists here than the people supposed, and they were getting ready to carry out some gigantic schemes."[8] O'Mara went to New York City to confer with local officials investigating the affair, and they all agreed with the Pittsburgh analysis that Berkman had not acted alone, but was party to an anarchist conspiracy. The attempt on Frick, the police publicly announced, "was not the act of a crazy enthusiast, but the combined effort of several Autonomists."[9]

They were right, of course; for several weeks, Emma and Modska's flat had been a nest of Autonomist militants—Timmermann, Mollock, the Oerter brothers, and the trio—engaged in a conspiracy to exterminate Frick. The *New York World* described the apartment as "the abiding place of bloodthirsty dynamiters and the hatchery of all sorts of plots."[10] Apart from Sasha himself, Emma and Modska, as the police suspected, were the main participants in the conspiracy.

Emma was pegged by the press as the "queen of the Autonomists," and gained additional attention as Berkman's apparent paramour. She was described by one newspaper as having a "very fine figure" and an "intelligent and rather pretty face, with large clear blue eyes."[11] Another publication noted her "animated expression" and her bespectacled, "studious, intellectual appearance," as well as her fluency in German, English, and Russian. The paper speculated about her relationship with Berkman, noting that she "declined to say whether he was her lover," but "whatever the precise relations between Berkman and Miss Goldman were, it is known that he was an ardent admirer of the young woman and there is reason for believing that she reciprocated his attachment."[12]

On the day of Berkman's attentat, Emma was anxious for news. Shaking off some men who seemed to be tailing her, she waited all night at Park Row to get the newspapers and read reports of Berkman's attack. When she learned that Frick was likely to recover, she was acutely disappointed. "Frick was not dead," she afterward wrote, "and Sasha's glorious youth, his life, the things he might have accomplished—all were being sacrificed."[13]

Emma's disappointment was tempered by a feeling of relief, since she knew Frick's survival meant Sasha could not be executed for the crime. The following evening, July 24, she addressed her comrades in Paul Wilzig's Hall on Division Street, where she spoke in passionate support of Sasha's act. She went to Rochester on July 25 to meet with Modska after his aborted trip to Pittsburgh, then returned to New York City and spent several nights in Mollock's apartment. When the police later raided the flat, they found pamphlets, photographs, and correspondence, but no hard evidence. After Mollock was released from custody in the Long Branch prison, he was evicted by his exasperated landlord.

Emma went to stay with her paternal grandmother, Freda Goldman. Freda operated a grocery store on East 10th Street and shared a two-room apartment with her daughter, son-in-law, and their children. There was little space, so Emma camped in the kitchen—an uncomfortable arrangement but one that afforded a measure of privacy; she was able to come and go without disturbing the rest of the family. She remained in the apartment for the next few months, using the Zum Groben Michel tavern as her mailing address to keep in touch with Sasha.[14]

As Emma went about her business, the police strained to connect her to an assassination conspiracy, but, despite her instrumental role in the plot, they could not find a way to prove her guilt. The same was true of Modska. A lack of evidence enabled him to avoid indictment or arrest. He spent several months hiding out in Detroit, where he was sheltered by German comrades, among them the anarchist writer and editor Robert Reitzel. To earn cash, Modska took a job with an engraving firm. By the time he returned to New York, in the fall of 1892, the police were no longer looking for him.[15]

The other New York–based members of the conspiracy likewise avoided prosecution. Not one of them was formally arrested, much less indicted and imprisoned—not Timmermann, nor the Oerters, nor their friends. Mollock, of course, had been briefly taken into custody, but soon after was set free. Berkman was captured and Bauer and Nold charged, but the rest escaped punishment.

For the remainder of her days Emma felt a deep sense of guilt at not having shared Sasha's fate, even as she prudently took great care to avoid indictment. She had played a major role in the affair, and her complicity was undeniable. "Who Furnished the Lazy and Poverty-Stricken Anarchist with Money?" blared a headline in the *New York Tribune.* The answer, of course, was Emma. She had been aware of every detail, and had raised the funds for Berkman's revolver, as well as for his suit and other expenses. "I had planned the *Attentat* with him; I had let him go alone," she later wrote. "I strove to shake off the consciousness of guilt, but it would give me no rest."[16]

EMMA'S CONNECTION WITH SASHA AND HIS ATTENTAT was, she said, the "leitmotif" of her life. She considered her failure to be by his side at the scene a burden she would always bear. The least that she could do, she felt, was to help mitigate his suffering. Apart from sending him letters and offering encouragement, she formed a Berkman Relief Fund to defray his expenses in jail, cigarettes naturally being the most essential item. Appeals for money, printed in *Der Anarchist,* brought contributions from various immigrant workers and groups of German, Austrian, Czech, and Jewish origin, and from American organizations, including the Knights of Labor. Fundraising picnics and other social gatherings were held, such as a well-attended concert and ball in the New Irving Hall on Broome Street.

To Goldman, most importantly, fell the task of justifying Berkman's act. If he must endure prison, she would serve as his public voice and advocate. This she accomplished through lectures, articles, and interviews with the press. She portrayed Sasha as a defender of the people, an idealist who could tolerate no injustice. "I have known Berkman for a long time," she told a host of reporters, "and have lived with him for the past two years. He is a quiet, studious, courageous fellow, who hates capitalists and tyrants."[17]

In all her interviews and speeches she stoutly denied any knowledge of a conspiracy. "The whole thing is this," Goldman said. "The capitalists are trying to trump up a conspiracy against the anarchists throughout the country because Berkman, who is one of them, tried to kill Frick. Berkman was prompted by his own feeling to do the deed."[18] She called

Sasha a "splendid man . . . of brains and courage" and said her friends were all proud of him, "as he has proved his courage and his devotion to the cause."[19] But it was not just the press and the general public that Emma hoped to convince. Her own comrades in the anarchist community were hotly divided over the crime.

To some, Berkman was a champion. Joseph Cohen, the future editor of the *Fraye Arbeter Shtime,* said that the name of Alexander Berkman became "a kind of talisman, a source of inspiration and encouragement."[20] Sergius Schewitsch, an influential and dashing Latvian immigrant of noble birth, was one of many activists who celebrated Berkman's gumption, praising Sasha in his socialist daily, the New York *Volks-Zeitung* (The People's Newspaper). "Bullets for Frick, Nemesis. A Dose of His Own Medicine," proclaimed the paper's July 24 headline.[21]

The Autonomists, naturally, were solidly behind Berkman as well, holding a series of public meetings and devoting an entire issue of *Der Anarchist* to defend his act. "The modern capitalist Caligulas and Caesars have finally found a Brutus!" they announced. "The deed of the anarchist Berkman will find its place in the history of the struggle for the emancipation of the working class from the tyranny of capital. Hail Brutus!"[22] Josef Peukert gave an interview to *Harper's Weekly,* meeting the reporter at the Zum Groben Michel tavern. "So long as there are people who are starving there will be a Berkman," Peukert said, "and these Berkmans will shoot without any conspiracy. We are proud of Berkman's act. We were associated with him, but there was no conspiracy, nor can there be among the Autonomists, where each man is responsible only to himself."[23]

At an August 1 meeting in Military Hall in the Bowery, attended by hundreds of radicals, Peukert further declared that "Berkman's heart was in the right place. It was a noble example, well worthy of imitation. We fully endorse his deed. They say that anarchists are bloodthirsty. We are not. It is the bloody barbarism of capital that we fight."[24]

Also taking the platform, which was "draped with the Stars and Stripes," was prominent American anarchist Dyer D. Lum, a fifty-three-year-old Civil War veteran and abolitionist who worked as a bookbinder and writer. A close friend of the Haymarket defendants and Albert Parsons' successor as editor of the journal *The Alarm,* Lum was an avowed advocate of violence as a tool of revolt. Lum, with Robert Reitzel, had plotted to blow up the Cook County Jail during the Haymarket trial, and it was he who had smuggled the dynamite cartridges used by Lingg to commit suicide in his cell. "If you and I want anything done," Lum told the crowd, "let us, like men, do it ourselves." Berkman had demonstrated real courage, and it was such daring, Lum said, "that will free our race from its present slavery."[25]

Emma herself addressed the hall, "an object of envy to all the women there because of the devotion and attention shown her by the sterner sex," the *New York Times* observed. "We must make the most of this deed of Berkman's," she said, "and follow it with other similar deeds until there are no more despots in America." Francesco Saverio Merlino, a brilliant Naples-born lawyer and the founder of the anarchist journal *Solidarity,* was another who stirred the assembly hall. "Revolution is inevitable in America as it is in Europe," he promised. "Law is merely the instrument with which capital stabs labor in the back."[26]

Many anarchists across the country supported Sasha. Robert Reitzel wrote in his journal *Der arme Teufel* (The Poor Devil) that Berkman was "a hero of our time." To him, Sasha was "a liberator, enabling progress to emerge from the grey stones of antiquity."[27] Lucy Parsons, the widow of hanged Haymarket martyr Albert Parsons, offered up a "fraternal handshake" from Chicago, and in her journal *Freedom* praised Sasha's "deep, sympathetic nature" and his willingness "to forget all considerations of self and sacrifice all man has to give—liberty and life—if only in doing so he was enabled to strike one blow at the source of wretchedness—a representative of the robber class. In this he has succeeded."[28]

But other leaders in the movement were concerned by the stark violence of the act, and thus unwilling to condone Berkman's crime. "Of Berkman I have little to say," wrote Joseph "Jo" Labadie, a well-known anarchist and labor leader who later founded the Labadie Collection of radical literature at the University of Michigan. "He is not insane. He is not a mad man. He is not a coward. He is not a depraved villain. He is simply a man grown degenerate from the knowledge of the industrial condition of his class."[29]

Benjamin Tucker, a Massachusetts-born, M.I.T.-educated anarchist who launched the magazine *Liberty,* had "no pity for Frick, no praise for Berkman—such is the attitude of *Liberty* in the present crisis." Wrote Tucker, "As one member of the human race, I fully confess that I am more desirous of being saved from friends like Berkman, to whom my heart goes out, than from enemies like Frick, from whom my heart withdraws. The worst enemy of the human race is folly, and men like Berkman are its incarnation. It would be comparatively easy to dispose of the Fricks, if it were not for the Berkmans. . . . The hope of humanity lies in the avoidance of that revolution by force which the Berkmans are trying to precipitate."[30]

This antiviolent sentiment was echoed by many anarchists, especially those who believed the anarchist philosophy should be entirely peaceful. A few severed all ties with the movement, repudiating terrorism of any kind. They were outraged that such a crime could take place in America, a country of hope, inspiration, and democracy.

SASHA'S MOST VIGOROUS DETRACTOR, to the astonishment of many in the movement, was Johann Most. The day after the attack on Frick, Most gave a lecture before Section One of the International Working People's Association. Emma, Modska, and a group of their Autonomist friends showed up to hear what he had to say. It was the first time Emma had seen Most in a year, since his departure for Blackwell's prison. Most spoke at length about the Homestead strike, and brought up the Frick attack, offhandedly dismissing the assailant as a nuisance, or perhaps a flunky hired by Frick himself, to generate sympathy. Emma was "dumbfounded" by the pretense and rose to her feet to object—Most knew full well what Berkman had sought to accomplish—but he ignored her.[31]

Two days later a reporter interviewed Most in his office at *Freiheit.* Most belittled Sasha, as well as the shooting itself. "It was only a mere scratch," he said of Frick's injuries, "nothing at all. What the devil is the use of making such a fuss about it!" He spoke of his former protégé in scathing terms. "Berkman! Berkman! Why, Berkman is my enemy," Most said. "He is no good. I hate him as much as I hate Frick, and Frick is the Czar of America. I took him in here and taught him to be a good printer, and then when he got so he could do some things he turned around and blackguarded me; yes sir, he blackguarded me and he joined my enemies, the Autonomists, who hate me more than the police . . . he joined the Autonomists and became a contributor to their paper *Der Anarchist,* which devotes nearly all its space to abusing me. So you see why I hate Berkman."[32]

Most denied there had been a conspiracy. "I don't think there was any plot to kill Frick. I think Berkman tried to do it himself. He thought there could be lots of glory in it, and that is what he wanted. If there was any plot it was the Autonomists, not my friends, who were in it." Most was asked about Goldman and her role, if any, in the crime. "Oh," he replied, "she is a harmless crank who couldn't do any harm if she tried. She was a friend of Berkman, but he was too sharp to trust her with any secrets."[33]

Over the next two months Most continued in this manner, publishing articles and editorials in *Freiheit,* ridiculing Berkman, and denying any connection with the attack on Frick. He mocked Berkman for using a "toy pistol," a weapon that inflicted such trivial wounds on Frick that in no time "the beast will be able to drag his carcass around again."[34]

In the *Freiheit* issue of August 27, however, Most adopted a more serious tone in an article titled "Reflections on *Attentats.*" Most acknowledged that in the past, he had emphasized the importance of terrorist acts, but observation and contemplation had brought him to question their value. Attentats, he said, might have some effect under the proper circumstances, in countries with longstanding grievances and a militant working class, but in the United States, where the anarchist movement had so far found little support, propaganda by the deed would never be understood and would only backfire. The attempt on Frick, he wrote, had proven this. Berkman might have exhibited a certain heroism, Most conceded, but in other respects the effort had been a "total failure."[35]

At the county jail in Pittsburgh, Nold managed to slip Berkman a note: "Most has repudiated your act." Sasha was dismayed. He knew Most had been upset by his association with the Autonomists, and now considered him a rival, but he wondered how Most could publicly condemn him during this crucial time. "What an awful, cruel disappointment," wrote Berkman. "My teacher—the author of *Revolutionary War Science*—he to denounce me, to repudiate propaganda by deed? It's incredible! I can't believe it! . . . He will minimize the effect of my act, perhaps paralyze its propagandistic influence altogether." Most, he lamented, was a "traitor," who had "preached propaganda by deed all his life—now he repudiates the first *Attentat* in this country."[36]

Goldman was equally enraged. That Most should denounce Berkman was nothing but hypocrisy, she felt. Most, more than anyone, had championed violence as a way to make a political statement. He had gone to prison in England for hailing the assassination of Tsar Alexander II and had showered praise on every terrorist act wherever it occurred. He had even written a manual for the making of explosive devices, the very manual that Sasha had used when he was building bombs in the apartment on East Fifth Street. Emma expressed her shock at Most's reversed position. "I could then neither understand nor forgive what seemed to me a betrayal of all that the man had so eloquently and passionately advocated for years."[37]

But on this point Emma was mistaken. The change of Most's position was not a sudden reversal. Since the Haymarket executions he had been decisively, if gradually, transforming his position on violence. During his latest imprisonment on Blackwell's Island his new stance had been cemented. "There is no greater error," he said, "than to believe that we as anarchists need only to commit any deed, no matter when, where, and against whom. To have a propagandist effect, every deed needs to be popular. . . . If that is not the case, or if it actually meets with disapproval from the very part of the population it is intended to inspire, anarchism makes itself unpopular and hated. Instead of winning new adherents, many will withdraw."[38]

Shortly after his release from Blackwell's, Most wrote an editorial in *Freiheit* stating that those in the movement who viewed violence as an end in itself were wandering down a dangerous path. To antagonize the public with irrational acts of terror and misguided sensationalism, he said, would only harm the anarchist cause.[39] Sasha shot Frick six weeks after this commentary was published, and when the crime was reviled by so many within the anarchist and labor movements, as well as widely among the general public, Most felt wholly vindicated.

Many of Most's group were shocked by the stand he had taken. More than a few never spoke to him again. Even tavern owner Justus Schwab, once one of his closest associates, snubbed him and sided with Goldman instead. *Freiheit's* circulation fell steadily, and by the end of the decade the distribution was only a fraction of what it had been in the 1880s.

Most's ongoing critique was motivated not only by a genuine philosophical dispute with his Autonomist counterparts; nor by his jealousy of Sasha and Emma's relationship, which had needled him for more than two years; nor by his anger over the trio's abandonment of his cause. Weary from his legal travails, he was greatly alarmed that the police would try to tie him to the attentat. Already he had served a total of nine years in prison, in Europe and the United States, and was still recovering from his latest stint in Blackwell's. "John Most," one anarchist posited, "is likely to be arrested again. This time in connection with the attempt upon Frick's life by Berkman. Whenever anything of this kind is committed, it seems the first thing the authorities think of is to connect Most with it and arrest him."[40]

Goldman had no patience for Most's anxiety about going back to jail, branding him a "scoundrel," a "traitor," and a "coward." Writing in *Der Anarchist,* she griped that Most was "also a liar, a dissimulator, and at the same a washrag. . . . He fears that the police are after him, and that is why he criticizes Berkman. Words can do no good with such a fellow. A good thrashing would perhaps not change this man, but it might shut up his mouth."[41]

For weeks, even months, Emma continued to fume. Most's conduct had been "outrageous, slanderous." He had derided Sasha's attentat, ridiculed his personality, cast aspersions on his character and motives. "Most," she said, "had betrayed his ideal, had betrayed us." She resolved to challenge him publicly, and seized the opportunity on December 18, when Most was slated to speak in a hall at 98 Forsyth Street on the Lower East Side. Emma attended, along with Modska and Claus Timmermann, and brazenly took a seat in the front row. When Most stood up and faced the audience, Emma rose and confronted him, demanding that he prove his accusations against Sasha. Most refused to respond, rebuffing her as an "hysterical woman." Incensed, Emma leaped to the stage, drew a horsewhip from under her cloak, and slashed him across the face and neck. When she had finished, she dramatically broke the whip over her knee and flung the pieces at him.[42]

Pandemonium erupted. Emma was instantly surrounded by a crowd of angry Most supporters, who shouted, "Throw her out! Beat her up!" Modska and Claus scooped her up and forced their way out of the hall.[43] "The ill feeling," reported a *New York Times* reporter present at the incident, "that has existed between John Most, the leader of the conservative Anarchists, and Emma Goldman, who drinks beer in Peukert's Anarchists' saloon in Fifth Street and makes incendiary speeches, developed into an assault by that woman upon Most . . . [who] stepped forward, whip in hand, flourished it in Most's face, and administered a lash accompanied by select Anarchistic billingsgate epithets."[44]

Goldman's horsewhipping of Most created a sensation, marking the climax of the battle between those who supported Berkman and those who spurned his attack on Frick. No longer was the feud merely between the followers of Most and Peukert. It engulfed the entire anarchist movement, splitting it into two irreconcilable camps, one of which advocated the use of terror, and one of which did not.

Berkman was intrigued by the dialogue about his actions, and was pleased when he heard the voices of support, but what raised his spirits the most were the words of the revered Russian anarchist Peter Kropotkin. "Berkman," Kropotkin wrote, "has done more to spread the anarchist idea among the masses who do not read our papers than all the writings that we may publish. He has shown that there are among the anarchists, men capable of being revolted by the crimes of capitalism to the point of giving their life to put an end to these crimes, or at least to open a way to such an end. And he has proved that our Chicago martyrs were not the last Mohicans of the anarchist movement in America."[45]

As the debate over his crime raged within the anarchist movement during the summer of 1892, the jailed Berkman prepared for his trial. He refused a lawyer, as at the preliminary hearing. As an anarchist he did not accept "man-made law," and an attentat, he felt, could not be measured by "the narrow standards of legality." The warden, John McAleese, warned him against this decision, citing the familiar adage that a man who acts as his own lawyer has a fool for a client. Berkman rejected the advice. "I don't believe in your laws," he said, "I don't acknowledge the authority of your courts. I am innocent morally." Sasha held this position for years. In 1915 he wrote to a friend, "If you look up the records in my case, you will find that at my trial I entirely dispensed with all legal advice and procedure. . . . My position was—and still is—that an act or deed of this nature is entirely outside the narrow limits of legal argumentation. It is too big for that. Far from being a 'crime,' it is of high moral purpose and dictated by the great stress of social necessity reflected by individuals of the finest psychology."[46]

McAleese permitted Bauer and Nold to bring their two attorneys to visit Sasha. The attorneys volunteered their services free of charge, but Sasha politely declined. And when he heard that a group of his comrades was raising funds for a legal defense, he wrote to Emma to put a stop to it. "There is no point wasting money on lawyers," he said. "That money can best be spent on revolutionary propaganda, which is so badly needed." He would act as his own counsel and use the courtroom as a forum so the whole country would hear his message and understand his actions. Afterward, with his "opportunities for propaganda . . . exhausted," he would commit suicide, "the logical conclusion."[47]

As Berkman waited for the trial to begin, he drafted a speech to deliver to the court. Written in German, as his English was still poor, it covered forty full pages of foolscap stationery, and ran two hours in length. Sasha, jittery and energized, was anxious for the trial to begin.

When, then, would the trial take place? Repeatedly Berkman attempted to learn the date, but without success; as he wrote, "the days come and go, and still my name has not appeared on the court calendar."[48] Unbeknownst to him, the date had already been set but was being kept secret by the Pittsburgh district attorney. The reason for this was that the authorities feared trouble, perhaps an attempt at liberation, or retaliation, by Sasha's comrades. And sure enough, although the Pittsburgh authorities were unaware of their plotting, Emma and Modska discussed blowing up the Allegheny County Court House just as Dyer Lum and Robert Reitzel had intended to bomb the Cook County Jail in an effort to rescue the Haymarket defendants. The wary police took every precaution to prevent such an incident.

Berkman was therefore kept in ignorance of the trial date until the very morning he was to appear in court. On Monday, September 19, 1892, he suddenly was ordered to get ready. He dressed in a brown suit, a white tie, and well-polished shoes, and assumed a deliberately impassive manner that did not go unnoticed.[49] "Berkman maintained the same indifferent demeanor," stated one report, "that has characterized his conduct since his arrest."[50] The police escorted him the short distance to the Allegheny County Court House, located on Grant Street in the heart of the city. At that time the courthouse was the grandest building in Pittsburgh. Designed by the architect Henry Hobson Richardson and built in 1884, it was impressive on a national scale, later to become a historic landmark. It was connected with the county jail by a wrought stone bridge—"The Bridge of Sighs," it was dubbed, after its Venetian counterpart.

At around ten o'clock, Sasha was brought into the courtroom by Warden McAleese, who took a seat directly behind him. Trying the case was District Attorney Clarence Burleigh. Burleigh was assisted by Philander Knox, chief attorney for Carnegie Steel; Knox would later become the attorney general under President Theodore Roosevelt. Presiding was Judge Samuel A. McClung, a wealthy Pittsburgh conservative. The judge's daughter Isabelle became an intimate friend of the writer Willa Cather, who in the early 1900s lived in the McClung house. In 1915, the year of Judge McClung's death, Isabelle married the Russian-Jewish violinist Jan Hambourg, whose own father was a London-based anarchist and a friend of Peter Kropotkin.

When Berkman entered the courtroom he found the jury already seated. This, apparently, was the work of District Attorney Burleigh. Before Berkman's arrival, Burleigh had quietly selected the jury under the guise of using it in the trial of another case. Once chosen, the jury was instead sent to Judge McClung's courtroom, and McClung made no objection to such a procedure. As a result, only the judge, the jury, and a small audience were present when Berkman's trial began. Sasha scanned the courtroom for faces of friends, but none was to be found. Instead, he recalled, "Everywhere cold eyes meet my gaze."[51]

Berkman was not allowed to examine the prospective jurors, but Judge McClung permitted him four challenges. At random he selected four names from the list, and new jurors filed into the box. The result was a jury composed of a clerk, a saddler, a broker, four farmers, a "gentleman," a manufacturer, a minister, a proprietor of a feed store, and an upholsterer. With the jury seated, the district attorney opened the proceedings by presenting six indictments, charging the prisoner with the following offenses: felonious assault with intent to kill Frick; felonious assault with intent to kill Leishman; feloniously entering the offices of the Carnegie Steel Company on three occasions, each constituting a separate indictment; and unlawfully carrying concealed weapons. Berkman pleaded not guilty to all.

Frick took the stand and related the story of the assault. The clothing he had worn that day—bloodstained and filled with holes—was exhibited before the jury. Berkman was allowed to question his victim, and asked if he had tried to kill Leishman. Frick replied that he did not know. Frick left the stand. Next came Dr. Litchfield, who testified that both of Berkman's weapons, the dagger and the pistol, could have caused death. Berkman had no questions. Leishman, the next witness, said that Berkman fired his pistol at him once and the bullet went through the ceiling. "Well," Sasha asked, "did I intend to kill you?" "I think so," was Leishman's response. "Well that's not true," asserted Berkman. "I didn't intend to do it."[52]

A number of witnesses, including the elevator operator and Frick's attendant, testified that Berkman had visited the Chronicle Telegraph Building three times. Some swore they had seen him there with Bauer and Nold. Lying to protect his friends, themselves awaiting trial, Sasha denied having accomplices and insisted that he had been inside the building only once. Then the revolver and dagger were placed in evidence, and the prosecution rested.

Judge McClung now ordered Berkman to call his witnesses. He had none but asked to read a statement. The judge consented, and a German interpreter, Frederick Luty, was provided to translate Berkman's speech from German into English. Berkman, an atheist, refused to be sworn in. Instead, he took his lengthy manuscript from his pocket and began to read. When Mr. Luty started to translate the words into English, Sasha discovered to his dismay that the interpreter was incompetent. Luty's voice, recalled Berkman, was "cracked and shrill" as he stumbled through the translation in inadequate English. A reporter present in the gallery who recorded the speech described a "flow of meaningless sentences" that "continued to the disgust of all present in the court room." The whole effect of the statement, thought Sasha frantically, was being lost. As he later wrote, "the vociferous tones pierce my ears, and my heart bleeds at his meaningless declamation."[53]

Sasha had read for about an hour, with Luty accompanying him, when Judge McClung impatiently broke in. "Mr. Berkman," he ordered, "you will have to conclude what you have to say by one P.M." Sasha protested. "I can have all the time I want for my defense and will take all the time I need," he said. "No you haven't," replied the judge, noting that Sasha had already been given more time than a defense attorney would have been allowed. "We will teach you different if you think you can dictate to us."[54]

Berkman, pleading for extra time, said he would skip the section on labor and capital and move on to church and state. He tried again to tell the court that Frick was not a man he wished to murder but a symbol of the tyranny he hoped to vanquish. "My reason for my act," he said, "was to free the earth of the oppressors of the workingmen . . . I did not assault Mr. Frick but the person who had oppressed labor."[55] At 1:10, Sasha's presentation was halted by the judge, who told him he could take up no more of the court's time. District Attorney Burleigh rose and made his final statement to the jury. He said that the defendant's guilt on every count was all too apparent. Again displaying the dagger, he asked the jurors if they had ever seen a more murderous weapon. He concluded by urging them to be "a credit to Allegheny County" and convict.[56]

Judge McClung addressed the jury and explained the different charges. He said there should be no trouble in reaching a decision, but if there was any doubt of guilt the benefit should go to the defendant. The case was then given to the jury. Without leaving the box, the twelve men found Sasha guilty on all counts. Before imposing sentence, Judge McClung asked Sasha if he had anything to say. "I did not expect justice, and I did not get it," Sasha declared.[57]

Berkman was given the maximum sentence on all six charges: for felonious assault on Frick, seven years in the penitentiary; for felonious assault on Leishman, five years; on the three charges of entering a building with felonious intent, nine years total (three years on each); and for carrying concealed weapons, one year in the county workhouse. The combined imprisonment amounted to twenty-two years, the sentences to run consecutively. The five-year sentence for assaulting Leishman was a lesser penalty, given because Leishman had not been wounded, and thus Berkman had only been "pointing fire arms." In court, Berkman had objected to the form of the indictments. He argued that he should be tried only for attacking Frick, since the other offenses were elements of the main charge of assault with intent to kill, a crime that carried a maximum punishment of seven years. The judge overruled his objection.

Sasha's trial was now over. It had lasted four hours. In this brief time he was tried, convicted, and condemned to more than two decades in prison. He was still just twenty-one years old. He was convinced Judge McClung had meted out the harshest possible sentence as an act of vengeance. "It's terrible, twenty-two years!" Berkman wrote. "Their cursed justice—they always talk of law. Yet legally I shouldn't have gotten more than seven years. Legally! As if they care about 'legality.' They wanted to make an example of me."[58]

Sasha paid dearly for refusing counsel. The date of his trial had been kept secret, from himself as well as from the public, and he had been deprived of the chance to question prospective jurors. Any competent lawyer would have raised objections, particularly about Berkman's intentions toward Leishman, which might have shortened his sentence. Additionally, a proper lawyer would have taken exceptions to the rulings of the court that were prejudicial to the accused. Sasha's own failure to take such actions limited the basis for an appeal.

———

GOLDMAN WAS GIVING A SPEECH in Baltimore when news of the verdict came. She was stunned by the harshness of the sentence, especially for one so young. "Twenty-two years!" she later wrote. "Sasha was twenty-one, at the most impressionable and vivid age. The life he had not yet lived was before him, holding out the charm and beauty his intense nature could extract. And now he was cut down like a strong young tree, robbed of sun and light. And Frick was alive, almost recovered from his wounds and now recuperating in his palatial summer house. He would go on spilling the blood of labor. Frick was alive, and Sasha doomed to twenty-two years in a living tomb. The irony, the bitter irony of the thing, struck me full in the face."[59]

Comrades shared her reaction. In Massachusetts, Ezra Heywood, an anarchist of the Individualist school, called the judgment "retaliative vengeance such as slew Nat Turner and John Brown." The October 8, 1892, issue of *Solidarity* denounced the "brutal revenge" of the sentence. Even Johann Most, for all his antipathy toward Sasha, condemned the trial as "Express-Bandit-Justice." Berkman, he said, fell victim to a "kangaroo court," designed to please Frick, the "human hyena." Kate Austin, an anarchist living in rural Missouri, did not condone the attack on Frick, but did express concern for Berkman's plight. "There are those," she wrote, "not at all sympathetic with Berkman's method or views, who hold that the judge should have considered Berkman's youth, the circumstances that led to the attempt and the great excitement of the time, and, governed by these considerations, at least stayed strictly within the limits of a lawful sentence."[60]

At the conclusion of the trial, Berkman was taken briefly to his cell in the county jail to collect his belongings. According to the press, the weapons used in Sasha's attentat were turned over to his target. "A number of relic hunter's wanted Berkman's dagger and revolver," stated one newspaper, "but they were given to H.C. Frick, who expressed a desire to have them, and who, it is thought, had the strongest claim to them."[61]

Berkman was readied for transport to the Western Penitentiary of Pennsylvania, situated near the Ohio River in Allegheny City. He was handcuffed to another prisoner, Frank Shea, dubbed the "Southside burglar," who was on his way to serve a term of eleven years in the penitentiary. It was 2:15 in the afternoon of September 19 when they boarded the patrol wagon. No friends were present to bid goodbye to either man, but Warden McAleese was on hand to see them off.

A reporter showed up to cover Berkman's departure, and Sasha took the opportunity to vent his hatred of Frick and the Carnegie Company, and of Johann Most and his associates. The reporter asked Berkman if he was sorry for what he had done to Frick. "I'm sorry I didn't kill him," Berkman replied brusquely. Just before the wagon reached the outside gate, Sasha exclaimed that he had forgotten his cigarettes. An attendant was hastily dispatched to his cell, where three packs of cigarettes were found "and returned to the overjoyed nicotine fiend." When the wagon resumed its journey, the warden was heard to remark: "That fellow made an excellent prisoner, never giving the least trouble."[62]

The same was not to be the case in his new place of residence, Riverside, as the penitentiary was commonly known. On arrival, Berkman was taken into the custody of Warden Edward S. Wright, who had him measured and dressed in a prison uniform. Sasha was entered in the books as Prisoner A7, by which he would be known for the next thirteen years.

8

BURIED ALIVE

Thus installed in the penitentiary and dressed in his prison stripes, Berkman was placed in Cell 6 of Range K, the lowest area, below the waterline. The dank, windowless cell, five by seven feet, contained a bed, a small wooden table, and a creaky chair, with a privy toilet in the corner. Near it, in the center of the wall opposite the door, hung a water spigot over a circular basin. The cell was lit by a single tallow candle, which made reading and writing difficult. Everything about the prison, thought Sasha, was cruel and coarse—the language, the guards, the sharp commands, the heavy tread of the inmates. Violence and corruption were rampant. The world outside was drifting from his horizon. "I am cast into the darkness," he said. "No ray of sunshine holds out the promise of spring."[1]

Shortly after his arrival, Sasha was assigned to work in the mat shop, a dark, low-ceilinged room with barred windows. Prisoners requiring strict discipline or close supervision were often detailed to this arduous job. The heavy dust, poor light, and rattling looms soon began to affect Sasha's health, particularly his throat and eyes. Examined by Dr. David Rankin, the prison physician, Berkman was judged unfit to continue with the assignment and was transferred to the hosiery department. There the room was "airy" and the rules less severe, although talking among the convicts was forbidden, so that Sasha had to teach himself the art of communicating by "an almost imperceptible motion of the lips." He quickly mastered his tasks, despite the limitations of his weak vision (the severity of which he exaggerated to avoid harder labor), but the hours of drudgery dragged on. His thoughts wandered—to his comrades and the movement, the injustice of his sentence, and above all his chances of committing suicide.[2]

Two weeks into his prison term, he began contemplating his options for ending his life. Back in the county jail after his trial was over, he had thought about killing himself, perhaps with a spoon honed into a blade, but he had been whisked off to the penitentiary immediately after the verdict. Now, he began to sharpen a spoon on the floor of his cell, but a guard discovered him, confiscated the crude weapon, and sent Berkman to the dungeon for the night. Once returned to his cell, he considered beating his head against the bars, yet this, he feared, might be too ghastly to undertake, or, worse, ineffective. "Oh!" he wrote, "it is such a horrible death. My skull would break, and the brains ooze out. . . . But the bars are smooth. Would my skull break with one blow? I'm afraid it might only crack, and I should be too weak to strike again."[3] Berkman was a bold man, but his instinctive will to live may have counteracted his impulse to martyr himself.

Nevertheless, desperate and lonely, Sasha resolved to write to Emma and ask her to smuggle him a dynamite capsule with which to end his life, in the dramatic manner of his Haymarket hero Louis Lingg. According to prison rules, he would not be allowed to post letters until a month into his stay, but a fellow inmate told him about an underground mail route that prisoners used for secret communication, and this he employed to contact Emma, begging her to visit as soon as possible.

New prisoners, however, could not receive visitors for the first three months of their incarceration, which for Sasha meant not until December 20, an eternity in his fraught state. Yet he found a way around this, too. Reaching out to James R. Reed, secretary of the Board of Inspectors of the Western Penitentiary, Berkman explained that his married sister had come all the way from Warsaw to see him but was unable to remain in the country very long. Could he not make an exception and allow her to visit sooner? Inspector Reed granted the request. A pass would be made available for "Sonya Niedermann," sister of Prisoner A7, for a visit to Riverside on November 26, Thanksgiving Day, 1892.

Goldman disembarked from the train in Pittsburgh on the morning of November 26, and Max Metzkow and Carl Nold were at the station to greet her.[4] Nold was still out on bail awaiting his own trial, and was being monitored by detectives, so only Metzkow accompanied her to the prison; it was imperative that Emma conceal her true identity in order to be allowed to see Sasha. She left Max outside the penitentiary gate and went in alone.[5]

Under the alias "Mrs. Niedermann," Emma greeted Deputy Warden Hugh S. McKean, who conducted her to the visitors' room. Sasha was already there, supervised by a guard who stood beside him. Berkman could see at once that Emma had not brought him the dynamite capsule. "A glance at your face," he wrote to her four days later, "and I knew my doom to terrible life." All his hopes had been focused on receiving a dynamite capsule from her, perhaps hidden in her mouth. "An embrace, a lingering kiss," he wrote wistfully, "and the gift of Lingg would have been mine."[6]

They held each other close, and Emma was startled by the dramatic change in Sasha's appearance since she had last seen him: his skin was waxen, his face drooping, his body weak. "My appearance frightens you," said Sasha in Russian. "You think that American prisons are better than those in Russia? Treatment here is more crude and brutal than in a Russian prison." Deputy Warden McKean interrupted him, and ordered them to speak only English.[7]

They conversed as best they could under the watchful eyes of Sasha's captors. Emma gave him news about a recent incident in Paris. A bomb had been placed in a mining office on the Avenue de l'Opéra. The bomb was removed from the scene, but it detonated in the police station, and five policemen were killed. The perpetrator, Emile Henry, would later go to the guillotine.[8] When their allotted twenty minutes were up, Berkman kissed Emma goodbye, offered a saucy "Greetings to the comrades," and marched off down the corridor, singing the *Carmagnole,* the unofficial anthem of the French Revolution.

It would be the last time Emma would see Sasha for nine years. Although Inspector Reed had granted Goldman a pass for a second visit, believing the fiction that she was Sasha's sister Sonya, a guard recognized her as Berkman's anarchist comrade. Reed was furious at the deception, and banned Emma from returning; moreover, he barred Sasha from having any visitors at all until further notice. It had been, as Emma described it, "a mock visit, a visit as hideous as everything else in prison life, a visit in the presence of a human beast in the form of a keeper, degrading every manifestation of feeling. The visit was a nightmare."[9]

Why Goldman did not deliver the dynamite capsule is a matter that remains unclear. Neither she nor Berkman explained it in their memoirs. Perhaps she simply could not bring herself to do it. Dyer Lum had talked about sneaking poison into the prison for Berkman, just as he had smuggled the fatal dynamite cartridges to Lingg in Chicago; but once Berkman was denied visitors, such ideas were moot. A few months afterward, Lum himself committed suicide by swallowing poison. Neither was Lum's friend, lover, and fellow anarchist, Voltairine de Cleyre, able to carry out the plan. "I told you what Lum's intentions were towards you [regarding smuggled poison]," de Cleyre wrote years later to Sasha, "but I didn't tell you that when he died I considered myself the heir of his purpose. And I thought it was my duty (I do believe in 'duties' after a sort) to see that you got his gift. But I postponed it, and it turned out for the best."[10]

In February 1893, Carl Nold and Henry Bauer were tried in Pittsburgh. Court papers described them as "evil-disposed, pernicious, and seditious persons of wicked and turbulent dispositions" who had aided Berkman and "furnished the means to shoot and stab" Frick.[11] Two charges were leveled against them: conspiring with Berkman in the assassination attempt, and inciting to riot by distributing inflammatory leaflets in Homestead. Under the guard of three policemen, Berkman was transported from the penitentiary and taken to Pittsburgh as a witness for the defense. His vigilant police escorts notwithstanding, Sasha entertained hopes for an escape, but he was brought into the courtroom for a brief appearance, and removed without delay. One news account described Berkman as "totally devoid of color," and noted that "his short-lived liberty was over, and it is probable that for fifteen years Bergman *[sic]* will never again see the outside of the penitentiary."[12]

Both Nold and Bauer were convicted and sentenced to five years' imprisonment. According to newspaper reports, "when the verdict was announced, Bauer frowned, while Nold turned pale."[13] On February 25 they were delivered in handcuffs to the Western Penitentiary. Johann Most, in *Freiheit,* was cynical. Further trials in America, he said, should take the following form: "Are you an anarchist?" "Yes, sir." "Were you born in this country?" "No, sir." "Do you believe in God?" "No, sir." "That will do. Any intelligent jury will quickly decide against you."[14]

But with the arrival at Riverside of Bauer and Nold, Sasha no longer felt so forlorn. Having fellow anarchists under the same roof lifted his spirits and gave him a curious sense of hope. "Nold and Bauer are here," he wrote to Emma and Modska. "I have not seen them yet, but their very presence, the circumstance that somewhere within these walls there are comrades, men who, like myself, suffer for an ideal—the thought holds a deep satisfaction for me."[15]

Very soon the three men began to exchange notes, written in German. Of a merely personal nature at first, their letters gradually broadened in content and scope as they set down their thoughts about social and political theories and methods of agitation. Before long they decided to transform the correspondence into an underground magazine to be circulated among their fellow prisoners. Written on wrapping paper pilfered by an inmate from the broom shop, the magazine was titled *Zuchthausbluthen* ("Prison Blossoms") and proved a source of much consolation and diversion. As a result of growing demand from the inmate community, Nold and Berkman decided to publish an English edition with a larger circulation. The German version was soon suspended and replaced by the English-language *Prison Blossoms.*

Much of the material was provided by Berkman, Bauer, and Nold, though other Riverside inmates contributed as well, recruited from what Berkman deemed "the more intelligent and trustworthy element." These included a self-described "scientist and alchemist" (in truth, a counterfeiter); a "professional gambler and confidence man"; a "sharp lawyer" known as the "Attorney General"; and burglar Frank Shea, the "philosophic 'second-story man'" who had shared Berkman's transport from the county jail to the prison after his trial.[16] The roster of contributors shifted as men entered the prison or completed their sentences and were released.

According to Berkman, the *Prison Blossoms* editorials were "short, pithy comments on local events, interspersed with humorous sketches and caricatures of the officials." Longer essays covered more serious topics of "religion and philosophy, labor and politics, with now and then a personal reminiscence by the 'second-story man,' or some sex experience by 'Magazine Alvin.'" The pages were embellished with pen-and-ink drawings. One depicted Dante visiting the Inferno; another, submitted by "Yale, a specialist in the art of safe blowing," showed a figure "with mask and dark lantern, in the act of boring a safe."[17] Nold produced a little booklet of German poems, while Sasha included a novelette about revolutionary circles in New York. A growing number of inmates welcomed the magazine's stories, anecdotes, verse, debates, prison gossip, and shared memories.

By writing for *Prison Blossoms* Sasha began to improve his English, a process that continued when he was befriended by the prison chaplain, John Lynn Milligan. A Presbyterian minister, Reverend Milligan was fifty-five years old when Sasha entered the penitentiary. Milligan had received acclaim for his services to the wounded on the front lines during the Civil War; it was uncommon for chaplains to attend to soldiers on the battlefield under fire.[18] He had joined the prison as chaplain in 1869, the same year that Edward Wright became the warden. Wright was considered a callous, imperious manager—Henry Bauer complained in *Prison Blossoms* that the warden "mainly likes to command and to invent rules (a flaw all power-hungry people have)." But Milligan exhibited an earnest, personal concern for the welfare of the inmates.[19]

One scholar called Reverend Milligan's forty-year tenure as a prison chaplain "the greatest force in the western part of [Pennsylvania] in working for the cause of prison reform," and his efforts on behalf of prisoners had a nationwide influence.[20] Empathic and thoughtful, Milligan was an industrious advocate for improving the intellectual and spiritual lot of the prisoner. He wrote about the "tomb-like limitation" of the Riverside cells upon his arrival, and stated that the "conditions served to more deeply depress [the prisoner's] mind and certainly unfit him for manful conflict in free live competition at the end of his sentence."[21]

Among other things, Milligan recognized the importance of the library. "Good books," he wrote, "have lifted many a poor prisoner out of the slough of despondency and have become the direct agent in safeguarding him against himself and determining his will power for a new effort." Largely through Milligan's efforts, the library at Riverside boasted 7,437 volumes by 1892, the year of Berkman's arrival; the number had risen to 8,200 four years later.[22] And when the use of the lockstep was eliminated soon afterward, the chaplain was the first to rejoice. "Gone!" he declared. "Yes, and it is to be sincerely hoped, gone forever. The only part it played in penal control was that of unnecessary humiliation."[23]

To Berkman, the chaplain was "a refreshing oasis of humanity" amid all the "heartlessness and cruelty" exhibited by many of the guards and encouraged by the severe system. One of Milligan's duties was to deliver the mail to the cells each day, and that was how Sasha got to know him. He asked the chaplain if he might have something to read, and the two began to talk. The chaplain, Sasha thought, was "an interesting and intelligent man," an extensive traveler who had been to Russia and was stirred by "the great possibilities of that country." Milligan, in turn, was impressed that Sasha had studied the classics and could understand Greek and Latin. Berkman was so affected by Milligan's compassion that he dismissed a fleeting notion of using the chaplain as a hostage in an escape attempt, later recalling the moment when he decided not to strike: "The deep note of sympathy, the sincerity of the trembling voice—no, no, I cannot touch him."[24] Instead, they became friendly, and thereafter, when Milligan made his rounds, he often stopped to visit at Sasha's cell. The prison, he said, had a very fine library from which an inmate might borrow one book every week. Sasha began to do so.

Hugo and Zola, Gogol and Turgenev, were available, Sasha discovered. "It is like meeting an old friend in a strange land," he wrote, "to find our own Bazarov [of Turgenev's *Fathers and Sons*] discoursing in English."[25] Among many other works, Berkman read *The Last of the Mohicans, Oliver Twist, The Captain's Daughter,* and a book of Wordsworth's poems. "Volume after volume passes through my hands," he enthused, "till my brain is steeped with the printed word. Page by page I recite the history of the Holy Church, the lives of the Fathers and the Saints, or read aloud, to hear a human voice, the mythology of Greece and India, mingling with it, for the sake of vanity, a few chapters from Mill and Spencer."[26]

Sasha read and studied, expanding and refining his command of English. He borrowed grammar books and dictionaries from the library, and pored over volumes of Shakespeare, "dissecting each word, studying origin and derivation, analyzing prefix and suffix. I find moments of exquisite pleasure in tracing some single expression through all the vicissitudes of its existence to its Latin and Greek source. In the history of the corresponding epoch I see the people's joys and tragedies, contemporary with the fortunes of the word. Philology, with the background of history, leads me into the pastures of mythology and comparative religion, through the mazes of metaphysics and warring philosophies, to nationalism and evolutionary science."[27] Emma was amazed by his intellectual progress, writing to a friend that Sasha "has used his imprisonment for active study and has accomplished great knowledge during this time."[28]

Eventually Berkman persuaded Milligan to allow him to receive anarchist journals. Most valuable to him was Robert Reitzel's *Der arme Teufel,* which had defended his attack on Frick. "The arrival of the *Teufel* is a great event," he wrote. "What joy to catch sight of the paper snugly reposing between the legs of the cell table! Tenderly I pick it up, fondling the little visitor with quickened pulse. It is an animate, living thing, a ray of warmth in the dreary evenings."[29] Another was Francesco Saverino Merlino's *Solidarity,* to which Sasha sent New Year's greetings. We may be glad, Sasha said, "that the coming of our Messiah—the Messiah of the wronged—is a year nearer." A few months later he was able to secure a copy of a new Autonomist journal, *Die Brandfachel,* edited by Claus Timmermann, with a cover sketch by Modska, proclaiming the approaching "day of vengeance." Sasha warmly welcomed this "new voice" against capitalist oppression. "My heart felt greetings to the child of revolution," he wrote.[30]

For a little while, conditions for Sasha improved. When not at work in the hosiery shop, he divided his free time into segments dedicated to exercise, reading, and study. Not long after the arrival of Bauer and Nold, he was moved to a larger cell, situated on the upper gallery with a view of the Ohio River. He had the steady companionship of his two anarchist comrades and enjoyed new friendships with men of all backgrounds and types. Though initially dubious that intimacy could occur "between those of the same sex," some of these relationships eventually took a physical turn, and Berkman later wrote explicitly about his homosexual experiences and romances. He found solace with one fellow prisoner, a man called Johnny, while the two were languishing in the dungeon. They had pet names for each other—Felipe and Sashenka—and they whispered sweetly and confidingly together. "An unaccountable sense of joy glows in my heart," Sasha later wrote, when he and Johnny admitted they longed to share a kiss.[31]

Sasha talked with his friend George, another prisoner, about the intolerance toward homosexuality inside the prison. George, a married medical practitioner sentenced to sixteen years for bank robbery, had started his term with an aversion to the homosexual activities "he considered abnormal and vicious." He also worried about the psychological implications of excessive masturbation; "mechanical self-abuse" he called it, which he feared could lead to obsessive habits and a narrow mental horizon. Berkman, too, had "known some men to masturbate four and five times a day" as an escape from the unrelenting prison gloom. Sasha felt this had a dangerous impact on the psyche, fostering isolation and delusion. "Both the physiological and psychological sexual needs of the prisoner are alike ignored by society," he wrote in *Prison Blossoms,* referring to men and women inmates. He lamented "the horrible and hair-raising results of suppressing the legitimate wants of nature."[32]

George recognized his own need for love, and began a friendship with a young inmate who reminded him of "a girl I used to court before I married." Gradually, after several years, he realized he was "wildly, madly in love" with the youth, and he said their first kiss was the most blissful moment of his life. George was aware that few would understand or respect his love for the other man. "They take everything here in such a filthy sense," George said. "Yet I knew in my heart that it was a true, honest emotion." Sasha agreed. "George, I think it a very beautiful emotion. Just as beautiful as love for a woman."[33]

But while George now considered homosexuality morally sound, and resented the prejudice against it, he loathed the sexual black market that existed within the walls, the "element," as Berkman wrote, "variously known as 'the girls,' 'Sallies,' and 'punks' who for gain traffic in sexual gratification." The warden preferred to ignore all the sexual activities going on inside the prison, consensual and otherwise. Berkman noted that incidents of rape or attempted rape occurred "almost every week, yet no one has ever been taken to court on such charges."[34]

Berkman began to clash more and more often with the administration, headed by Warden Wright and Deputy McKean. To them he was a troublemaker—a foreigner who had tried to kill a leading Pittsburgh citizen. But Berkman was incensed by the unchecked corruption within the bureaucracy and by the sadistic harassment and brutal violence from the guards. Prisoners were viciously beaten for sport, and many penalties were arbitrary and spiteful, such as days-long enforced silence; periods of starvation or extreme food rationing; capricious use of the straitjacket or chains; and the confiscation of tobacco. True to his headstrong, defiant nature, Berkman felt compelled to talk back and speak out, despite the problems he made for himself.

By 1894 Sasha was banned from reading radical publications, and his precious *Prison Blossoms* was impounded. Repeatedly, he was sent to the dungeon where he was kept on bread and water, usually for minor infractions of the rules. At times he was put in the "basket" cell, where a dense wire netting covered the barred door, allowing little light or air. He frequently was denied basic privileges, such as mail and books. Other punishments included being placed on a "Pennsylvania diet," a single slice of bread and a cup of black coffee per day, with vegetable soup twice a week. At such times he received no Sunday dinner.

"Four weeks of 'Pennsylvania diet' have reduced me almost to a skeleton," he remarked after one long period of food restriction. The poor nutrition wreaked havoc on his digestive system, a problem that prevailed throughout his sentence. When he was held at length in the basket cell, he recounted how he looked forward "the whole week" to his brief Saturday trips to the physician—the chance to glimpse other prisoners, to enjoy "the strange blue of the sky, the sweet-scented aroma of the . . . morning—[but] how quickly it is all over!"[35]

Stints in the basket cell were just one form of isolation imposed on Berkman. He was forced to withstand extended stretches of solitary confinement, one stay lasting sixteen months. After a year of this had passed, he described himself as "feeble and languid . . . my vitality ebbing . . . tortured with insomnia; my body is racked with constant pains. All my heart is dark."[36] Although he was shut away from the other prisoners, officials continued to treat him with distrust and contempt, and many of the guards indulged in unauthorized intimidation and malicious cruelty. Sometimes Chaplain Milligan (who regularly argued for lenience on his behalf) would pause at his door and speak a few words of encouragement, which helped Sasha to maintain his dignity. Occasionally he appeared in the throes of collapse. Yet he found a way to endure the isolation, and managed to preserve his self-respect and sanity.

When out of solitary, as his circumstances allowed, Sasha risked further trouble to surreptitiously gather evidence of corruption and illegal practices—reports of fierce punishments, unprovoked violence, murder, rape, clubbings of the insane, and numerous other brutalities committed by the guards; as well as convict labor covertly hired out to private manufacturers; and appropriation of prison materials and money by officers for private use. The documents he collected were carefully hidden in the wall pipes and eventually smuggled outside to investigators, resulting in a state examination of the prison.

The investigation turned out to be a whitewash. A personal friend of Warden White, J. Francis Torrance, was appointed to lead the inquiry, and the administration was promptly exonerated. From then on Wright became even more of an adversary, and consistently opposed any reduction of Berkman's term. Sasha's torments increased accordingly. Immediately after Wright's exoneration, Sasha was taken to the dungeon and placed in a straitjacket, "the 'full size' jacket that winds all around you, the arms folded. They laid me, tied in the canvas, on the bed, bound me to it feet and chest, with straps provided with padlocks." He was removed from the restraints in the morning, but was left in the dungeon for a week. He thought about journalist George Kennan's report on harsh treatment in Russian jails and, with his own attempts at reform foiled, fretted that the truth about prisons in the United States would never come out. "[Kennan] would find it almost impossible to learn the conditions in American prisons," Berkman wrote. "He would be conducted the rounds of the 'show' cells, always neat and clean for the purpose; he would not see the basket cell, nor the bull rings in the dungeon, where men are chained for days."[37]

Routinely, Sasha was made to suffer emotional, as well as physical and mental, hardship. The warden ordered the removal of Sasha's pet sparrow, a little bird he had adopted and named "Dick." He had been looking after it in his cell, petting it and feeding it bits of his bread, and was distraught when the bird was taken away from him. But, to Sasha's delight, the bird found its way back to the cell when cold weather set in. How wonderful, he thought, that it should return and recognize his "old friend and the cell," pecking "crumbs of bread and sugar" from Sasha's hand with "mute confidence and joy." But soon a fellow convict, a "third timer and notorious 'kid man' " named Bob Runyon, saw it playing near the cell and kicked it to death with his boot. Berkman rushed at Runyon and knocked him down. Runyon reported him, and Sasha was again placed in solitary.[38] Years later, when chatting with a group of children, Sasha remembered his pet. "I had a friend who was a bird," he told them. "He was my best friend when I was all alone and had no friend. And one day a very bad man came along and killed the bird."[39]

Steeped in misery, Sasha felt that his ties to life were slackening, that "the world of the living is dim and unreal with distance; its voice reaches me like the pale echo of fantasy." But he retained a thread of human connection and found strength and solace from the letters sent by sympathizers and friends. The arrival of a letter, he said, was a momentous event; "It brings a glow into the prisoner's heart to feel that he is remembered."[40] Annie Netter and her sister Rose wrote him regularly from New York, and anarchist comrades checked in with notes of support. He began a steady correspondence with Voltairine de Cleyre, whose letters with their "great charm and rebellious thought," he said, lent "color to my existence."[41]

Born in rural Michigan and educated in a Catholic convent, de Cleyre had joined the movement after the hanging of the Haymarket anarchists. In Philadelphia she founded the Ladies' Liberal League and taught English to Jewish immigrants, from whom she learned Yiddish. An inspired speaker and writer, de Cleyre published numerous poems, essays, and stories in a range of journals and anarchist publications. Goldman called her "the poet-rebel," the "liberty-loving artist, the greatest woman Anarchist in America."[42] Berkman found in her a true friend.

It was Emma herself, however, who was Sasha's unfailing lifeline. Writing as often as she could, she kept him abreast of developments in the movement and shared personal stories about their crowd. To protect themselves and their comrades from the authorities, they used a variety of aliases and codes. In private letters and in his writings, Berkman referred to Goldman as, alternately, Sister, Sonya, Musick, Sailor, E. G. Smith, and The Girl. Years later, after Sasha's release, the *New York Times* reported on the mysteries of Berkman's correspondence. "As Berkman was believed by the authorities to be a prisoner who needed to be watched, his mail was scrutinized with great care," said the paper. While his allotted monthly letters were "invariably long," they were not deemed to contain dangerous information, although once it became apparent "that the authorities did not know that the name 'E. G. Smith' was the alias" of Goldman, said the *Times,* "the authorities are in no wise sure that in the seemingly innocent phrases in which the letters were couched there were not messages of an incendiary and revolutionary character."[43]

Sasha and Emma thus managed to communicate and keep close throughout his lengthy imprisonment. Sasha marveled at Emma's intense loyalty and dedication, and believed the connection with her was essential to his survival. Receiving her letters, he told her, "I feel myself lifted across the chasm into your presence. The bars fade, the walls disappear, and the air grows sweet with the aroma of fresh air and flowers—I am again with you, walking in the bright July moonlight."[44]

9

BLACKWELL'S AND BRADY

In New York City, Goldman continued to defend Berkman's attack on Frick, often using the Autonomist meetings at the Zum Groben Michel tavern as her forum. At one such meeting, in December 1892, she met an Austrian anarchist named Edward Brady. About forty years of age and a compositor by trade, Brady was blond and blue-eyed, tall and broad, with "beautiful white teeth." Emma liked him right away. Brady told her he admired Berkman, thought him "brave," and felt great sympathy for his suffering in prison, especially considering Sasha's youth. He himself, Brady explained, had been sentenced to ten years in a Vienna prison for publishing illegal anarchist literature. Only recently was he released after serving eight years, and had subsequently emigrated to America.[1]

Within a matter of weeks Goldman and Brady became lovers. Apart from their mutual physical attraction, more passionate and intimate than any Emma had previously known, they read together, attended meetings and concerts—Beethoven and Wagner were their favorite composers—and went on outings in the country. Goldman "found Brady the most scholarly person" she had ever met, knowledgeable about a vast range of subjects. During his years in prison, he had memorized the English and French dictionaries sent to him by his sister, and read aloud to himself while in solitary confinement.[2]

Under Brady's tutelage, Emma learned the classics of English and French literature, studying Shakespeare, Voltaire, and Rousseau. When they recited *Candide,* her French pronunciation was "atrocious," but Brady "was a born teacher, and his patience was boundless." On Saturdays they frequented Justus Schwab's 50 East First Street saloon, which remained a meeting place and watering hole for revolutionists and artists from far and wide.[3]

When Goldman first met Brady, Berkman had been in the penitentiary for three months. During this time Emma had left her grandmother's home and tried to find a place of her own. Her efforts initially were hampered by constant police surveillance, which made her presence unwelcome in many rooming houses and apartments. On occasion she was forced to spend the night on the streetcar or in a park.

Eventually she secured a room on East Fourth Street, in a building she soon realized was occupied by prostitutes. While it occurred to her that her new residence might be good for her dressmaking business ("What better place could I have found than this house full of girls who must need dresses?"), Emma realized that she was not entirely comfortable with the circumstances, and that word of her new quarters might further tarnish the anarchist message. "The thought of living within sight and sound of the life around me made me feel ill," she said. "There was also the fear that the papers might find out about the nature of the place I was in. Anarchists were already outrageously misrepresented; it would be grist to the capitalistic mill if they could proclaim that Emma Goldman had been found in a house of prostitution."[4] Finally, despite being befriended by many of the women, she moved to a two-room flat in a large building known as the Bohemian Republic, and Brady became a frequent visitor.

In the spring of 1893 the United States was in the throes of an economic crisis. One of the worst depressions in the nation's history had begun in February, and before long it became a disaster for American labor. Thousands of unemployed crowded the streets of industrial cities. By midsummer it had spread throughout the land, with nearly four million workers out of jobs. As unemployment soared, trade unions and various organizations appealed to the government for relief. But other groups, who regarded such measures as futile, called instead for direct action. Among the latter, the Autonomists, and especially Goldman, played a conspicuous role. With Ed Brady's assistance, Emma threw herself into forming relief committees, collecting food, and feeding the out-of-work. In addition she organized the first female group for the Cloakmakers' Union, which was then in the midst of a strike.

Goldman's central effort lay in organizing outdoor rallies and street demonstrations, a series of which erupted on the Lower East Side. Workers and activists protested along Rivington, Allen, and Delancey Streets, and throughout Lower Manhattan. In August 1893 a gathering of the unemployed marched from Rivington Street to Union Square, with Emma and Pauline Seger, a young Goldman disciple, leading the procession. The crowd was large and exuberant, yet peaceful, monitored by dozens of policemen. Among the speakers were Adolph Ury of the Cloakmakers' Union, Meyer Schoenfeld of the United Garment Workers, and Goldman herself. She wore tinted glasses and a black straw hat decorated with artificial flowers. She blamed the existing financial crisis on the capitalist system, which she said leached the strength of the workingman for the pleasures of the rich.

On August 21 a substantial procession, perhaps 4,000 in all, marched from Convent Hall on Orchard Street to Union Square. As before, it was the women who took the lead, with Goldman, accompanied by Seger, flourishing a red banner. Eight speakers, including Claus Timmermann, addressed the crowd. Goldman gave the closing remarks, warning the audience not to expect relief from the government, the pillar of capitalism. "Do you not realize," she asked bitterly, "that the state is the worst enemy you have? It is a machine that crushes you in order to sustain the ruling class, your masters. . . . Your neighbors—they have not only stolen your bread, but they are sapping your blood. They will go on robbing you, your children, and your children's children, unless you wake up, unless you become daring enough to demand your rights. Well, then, demonstrate before the palaces of the rich. Demand work. If they do not give you work, demand bread. If they deny you both, take bread. It is your sacred right!" As Goldman recalled in her memoirs, "Uproarious applause, wild and deafening, broke from the stillness like a sudden storm."[5]

Goldman was a familiar figure in the news during this time, as her marches, speeches, and blistering rhetoric were covered in the daily papers. Members of the press often used the moniker "Queen of the Anarchists" to describe her, and they wrote about the vigorous crowd reaction to her speeches. Some articles were highly disapproving of Goldman's activities and commentary. "There was devil's work . . . in the East Side," declared one paper, "and defiance of the law was openly preached. Anarchy made hay while the sun shone." Another headlined that Goldman had become "the mouthpiece of New York Anarchists," commenting that "her speech was of a highly inflammatory character." An account of her August 21 presentation in Union Square said she was "more rabid in her utterances than ever."[6] A reporter from the *New York Times*, sent to a pre-rally gathering to "ascertain what might be at the bottom of the present Anarchist scare," found that, lest "the urgent thirst begotten by the fetid atmosphere might relax its profitable sway, a real bona-fide blood-and-thunder votary of the science had been secured on the person of Emma Goldman." Looking "rather beerthirsty than bloodthirsty . . . [she] delivered a speech which made the empty glasses outside the hall fairly ring."[7]

The next day, Tuesday, August 22, Emma left for Philadelphia to organize rallies and give speeches on behalf of the unemployed there. It was her first visit to the city, and over the next week she became acquainted with a number of anarchists she had not previously met, among them Voltairine de Cleyre. But the New York police were on her trail, and as she entered Buffalo Hall on August 31 to give a lecture, a team of detectives intervened and took her into custody.[8] De Cleyre quickly assumed Goldman's place on the platform and launched a tirade protesting the suppression of free speech.

Goldman's detention had been requested by Inspector Thomas Byrnes of New York, who had obtained a warrant for her arrest following the Union Square rally. According to the press, the police had taken "stenographic reports of all of Emma Goldman's recent speeches. Their purpose [was] to present them as evidence to the grand jury."[9] Goldman was detained for ten days in Philadelphia, incarcerated for most of that time at Moyamensing Prison, and then extradited to New York on charges of inciting to riot, even though the rally had been peaceful.

Back in New York awaiting trial, Emma was kept in the city jail familiarly known as the Tombs. While there she was interviewed by Nellie Bly, the star reporter for the *New York World,* best known for her record-breaking trip around the world in seventy-two days. Bly (born Elizabeth Jane Cochran) was struck by the contrast between Emma's fierce reputation and her girlish appearance. "You have read of her," wrote Bly, "as a property-destroying, capitalist-killing, riot-promoting agitator. You see her in your mind as a great raw-boned creature, with short hair and bloomers, a red flag in one hand, a burning torch in the other, both feet constantly off the ground and 'murder!' continually upon her lips." Bly instead found "a little bit of a girl, just 5 feet high, including her bootheels, not showing her 120 pounds; with a saucy, turned-up nose and very expressive blue-gray eyes that gazed inquiringly at me through shell-rimmed glasses."

Their conversation was wide-ranging, covering Goldman's political philosophy, background, and personal style. "I like to look well," Emma said, "but I don't like very fussy dresses. I like my dresses to be plain and quiet." She laughed at the rumor that anarchists hated soap. "Above all things, I love my bath," she told Bly. "I must be clean. Being a German, I was taught cleanliness with my youth, and I do not care how poor my room or my clothes are so long as they are clean." She also shared her passion for reading. "I kept myself in poverty buying books," she said. "I have a library of nearly three hundred volumes, and so long as I had something to read I did not mind hunger or shabby clothes." She talked of her family: her siblings who followed her exploits with interest, her father and mother, who lived "near Rochester, and, while not Anarchists, sympathize with me and do not interfere with my work."

Bly asked Emma if she approved of murder as a way to promote her cause. Any thoughts on Berkman's attentat were absent from Emma's answer; she merely said the time would come for an uprising, and until then she was "satisfied to agitate, to teach, and I only ask justice and freedom of speech."[10]

While jailed in the Tombs, Goldman learned that Claus Timmermann had also been arrested after the Union Square rally and charged with inciting to riot. He was tried and convicted and sentenced to six months on Blackwell's Island. Emma herself was formally indicted on September 6, pleaded not guilty on September 11, and was released on bail September 14. Her trial was set for October 4, in the courtroom of Judge Randolph B. Martine.

JUST AS BERKMAN HAD ENVISIONED HIS TRIAL as a forum for his radical rationale, Goldman, too, felt a trial would give her "a wonderful chance for propaganda," and she did what she could to prepare for it. "My defense in open court," she said, "should carry the message of anarchism to the whole world."[11] Unlike Sasha, however, she accepted the services of a lawyer. An attorney called Hugh O. Pentecost was first attached to the case, and then replaced by Abraham Oakey Hall, a flashy former New York mayor and district attorney nicknamed "Elegant Oakey," who took the case free of charge because he found Goldman impressive and thought her arrest unfair. As he told the jury in court, his client was an idealist at heart, the victim of police persecution. Hall refuted the charge against Emma of inciting to riot, and asserted that the August 21 meeting at Union Square was nonviolent. He argued for the right of free expression and asked that Goldman be acquitted.

The prosecutor, Assistant District Attorney John F. McIntyre, presented the case against Goldman, citing her anarchism, atheism, belief in free love, and association with Alexander Berkman and Claus Timmermann to reinforce his argument. Police Sergeant Charles Jacobs was called as a witness. He "testified that he sat directly behind the defendant on the night in question and took notes from her speech in German," then read aloud "a number of extracts from her speech."[12] When Emma took the stand, she challenged Sergeant Jacobs' testimony, and answered questions about her personal history and associates. Did she approve of Berkman's attempt to kill Frick? McIntyre asked. She said she had "sympathy and respect" for Berkman, but did not explicitly express support for his crime. Did she approve of Timmermann's speech of August 21? "Yes," she replied, "I do not believe that he spoke in violation of the law."[13]

On October 9, 1893, her trial concluded, and Goldman was found guilty; on October 16 she was given the maximum sentence of one year. A. Oakey Hall wished to file an appeal on her behalf, but, to his dismay, she refused. She heard her sentence with a "jaunty air of indifference," according to the *New York Times.* From the bench, Judge Martine deemed Goldman "an intelligent person" but warned that she was a "dangerous woman," and chastised her for unrepentantly flouting the rules of the land. "I am satisfied," he said, "that you are defiant and have no respect for law. The sentence of the court is that you be confined for the full term allowed by law." A "yellow-haired evangel of disorder," Goldman "heard her fate pronounced with a smile, almost burst out in a giggle . . . [and] marched off after sentence . . . as airily as she had entered the courtroom."[14]

On October 18 Emma was taken to Blackwell's Island to begin her term. At the prison she gave her name, occupation, and address to the head matron, a tall, stout woman "with a cruel, hard face." Emma was allowed to take a bath ("greatly refreshing," after the Tombs) and was given the standard-issue prison clothing of a blue-and-white striped dress and blue checked apron. As an experienced seamstress, Goldman was put in charge of the sewing room, where shirts, socks, and trousers were made for the male prisoners. The hours were long and the job tiring. "The sewing women have to work very hard," she said afterward. "I had to be on my feet all day."[15]

Emma's fellow seamstresses, initially wary of the controversial new inmate, warmed to her when she defied the instructions of the head matron and refused to speed up the work. After two months, however, the winter chill brought on an attack of rheumatism, and Goldman was sent to the prison hospital for treatment. She spent a month under the care of Dr. White, the prison's affable chief physician, and when she recovered, Dr. White asked if she would like to help tend to the patients in the sick ward, since the prison employed no trained nurse. Emma learned the tasks quickly and enjoyed her new assignment. Soon Dr. White, impressed by her skill, made her chief orderly of the ward, in charge of medicines and patients. For seven months she assisted the doctors on their rounds, cared for those with tuberculosis and pneumonia, looked after pregnant women, and attended at operations.

PRISON LIFE FOR GOLDMAN WAS NOT AS BAD as she had feared, and certainly nowhere near as grim as it was for Berkman. To be sure, she encountered some rough treatment by the guards, spent time in the dungeon, toiled to near-exhaustion, and witnessed the suffering of other incarcerated women. But she took comfort in the pleasant views of the surrounding water and excelled at her work. The prisoners were fed vegetable soup (albeit with "precious little meat in it") four times a week, corned beef and beans twice a week, and "a treat" on Friday: fish and potatoes.[16] To supplement this diet, Ed Brady, Modska, and other friends sent parcels of food, fruit, and "delicacies," which she shared with her fellow inmates.[17] Whereas Sasha was forbidden visitors, she was allowed guests. Modska, however, came only once. The head matron, he explained, "did not like my looks (wanted to know 'who that terrible man' was) and I discontinued my visits."[18]

Brady, by contrast, visited Emma as often as he could, and their fleeting moments together in the visitors' common room were recalled passionately in her memoirs. On one occasion he brought along Voltairine de Cleyre, and they talked of anarchism and of Sasha's imprisonment—the "things," said Emma, "nearest to our hearts." De Cleyre vowed to work with Goldman to reduce Berkman's sentence. Emma's grandmother was another who came to see her. She visited on Passover, bringing matzoh and gefilte fish.[19]

Much like Sasha, Emma found consolation in reading, broadening her knowledge and improving her English as she did so. Justus Schwab and other friends sent her books, and the prison library, run by "an educated Englishman serving a five-year sentence for forgery," had a good collection, including works by George Sand and George Eliot. Emma read many American writers, such as Walt Whitman, Ralph Waldo Emerson, Henry David Thoreau, and Mark Twain, and became familiar with the American roots of libertarian thought. Such concentrated exposure to important works had a long-term impact on her own literary career, shaping her philosophy and influencing her writing style.

During her detention, Emma also kicked her cigarette habit, something she had picked up for its shock appeal. She had become an avid smoker years earlier, "sometimes [smoking] as many as forty cigarettes a day. When we were very hard pressed for money, and it was a toss-up between bread and cigarettes," she recalled, "we would generally decide to buy the latter."[20] Although the first two months of withdrawal in prison were "torture," she claimed she never again smoked for the rest of her life.[21]

ON AUGUST 18, 1894, GOLDMAN, now twenty-five, completed her prison sentence, her one-year term commuted by good behavior to ten months. She left Blackwell's Island by boat for the East 52nd Street pier, where she was greeted by Ed Brady, as well as by a crowd of friends and fans, journalists and spectators. To a reporter who was present she seemed in good physical condition, although she had "lost five pounds in weight" during her incarceration. "Miss Goldman," he wrote, "was vivacious; her cheeks were red and her eyes were bright. She wore a new straw hat with gay flowers on it, a blue linen shirtwaist and black dress and skirt."[22]

Emma made it clear that she did not regret her imprisonment. On the contrary, she said, it had been "a school of experience for me, and my time was not altogether lost." She had learned practical skills and found greater independence. And her devotion to her cause had only grown stronger. "I am more an anarchist than ever," she wrote at the time of her release. "I am more than ever determined to use every means in my power to spread my doctrines among the people."[23]

The day after Goldman was freed from Blackwell's, a reception was held for her at the Thalia Theatre in the Bowery. More than 3,000 people attended. "The theatre was crowded from top to bottom," reported the *New York Times.* "Men, women, and children kept trooping in. Every seat was taken and the aisles were being filled until the firemen and police objected . . . about a hundred persons were turned from the doors." Revolutionary songs were sung and speeches were given in six languages by a number of Emma's comrades.

Also in attendance, to the surprise of many, was Johann Most. He had agreed to speak at the event, and some comrades viewed his presence as an opportunity for reconciliation between the two anarchist leaders. But in spite of great anticipation from the spectators, with "loud calls for Most" during the program, he did not come forward on the platform and never uttered a word. As the *Times* observed, "Many of the anarchists came on purpose to hear him speak. He came to the theatre and went so far as the wings, from where he took a peep of the audience."[24]

OUT OF BLACKWELL'S AND WELCOMED BACK in style by her comrades, Goldman moved with Ed Brady into a four-room flat on East 11th Street. Modska and Claus Timmermann came often to visit. During Emma's imprisonment, Modska had become a successful pen-and-ink artist, drawing courtroom sketches for *The World* and other leading New York papers. He had been hired at a salary of fifteen dollars a week, and regularly contributed part of his income to Goldman's needs during her stint on Blackwell's. His work was so fine that his pay was raised to twenty-five dollars a week, and he insisted that Emma take a share.

"He had remained," Goldman wrote, "the same loyal soul, more matured, with growing confidence in himself and in his art."[25] Modska, though, felt that in order to keep his job he could no longer attend anarchist meetings, let alone produce illustrations for publications such as *Solidarity* or *Die Brandfackel* as he had done in the past. Moreover, his interests had increasingly turned to the world of art and décor, and away from radical thought. But his affection for his friends continued unabated, as did his concern for Sasha, to whom he sent soap, socks, underclothes, and other necessities to improve his cousin's lot in prison.

Emma and Brady invited Modska to move in with them, and he cheerfully agreed. Emma still had tender feelings for him, which he reciprocated, but they did not resume their former sexual relations. For it was Ed, she said, "who consumed me with intense longing, Ed who turned my blood to fire, Ed whose touch intoxicated and exalted me."[26] Modska did not appear to mind a platonic relationship with Emma; he had great fondness for Ed, and they all lived together amicably. "Brady," he later said, "was a man of exceptionally clear vision, fine sense of humor and rare beauty of character."[27]

Goldman, in contrast, was moody and irritable, subject to fits of temper. Her relationship with Ed became a stormy one. "I lived with them for some years," said Modska, "and witnessed their scraps. When lacking arguments, she would become hysterical and abusive."[28] The couple clashed over the role of women in the movement, family dynamics, their romantic commitment, and many other crucial matters. Also, having shared a cramped room as a girl and lately endured nearly a year in prison, Emma "held out for her own corner" and insisted, to Brady's annoyance, that one of the rooms should be designated her personal sanctum, which she said was essential for her well-being.[29] For all Goldman's generosity and charm, many of her comrades were struck by her demanding nature. "Emma was an awful person to live with, you know," remarked one friend. "She could be quite captivating, but also difficult."[30]

With her new skills learned from Dr. White in the prison hospital, Goldman began practicing as an auxiliary nurse. Her friend Dr. Julius Hoffmann sent her his patients after he treated them in St. Mark's Hospital. She took shifts at Beth-Israel Hospital on East Broadway, and Dr. White himself employed her in his Manhattan office for several hours a day. Brady, who was earning a solid income as an insurance agent, protested that there was no need for her to work at all, but she was firm. She believed that women should hold jobs, and she enjoyed the nursing profession.

Goldman also toyed with the idea of starting a business, recalling the great success of the little lunchroom in Worcester several years before. In early 1895 she and her companions opened an ice-cream parlor in Brownsville, a growing immigrant section of Brooklyn. Brady and Modska contributed start-up money, Emma provided her services as a cook, and Claus Timmermann gave his time and labor, but the venture was a failure. Three months later and $500 poorer, they gave it up and returned to Manhattan, where Goldman decided to seek medical training so she could qualify as a fully licensed nurse. Brady suggested that she go to Vienna, his beloved native city, to study at the Allgemeines Krankenhaus, a hospital of high reputation. Modska offered to pay her passage overseas and send her twenty-five dollars a month for her expenses while she was in Austria.[31]

GOLDMAN SAILED FOR EUROPE ON AUGUST 15, 1895, traveling under the name E. G. Brady, and arrived in London on August 22. She spent three weeks in England, addressing large crowds in London at Regent's Park, Hyde Park, Whitechapel, Canning Town, Barling, and Stratford, as well as in the city of Leeds. According to James Tochatti, the editor of the radical London journal *Liberty,* Goldman "[threw] herself into the breach with all her accustomed energy, and has given a very much needed fillip to our open-air propaganda."[32]

Emma became acquainted with a number of comrades and was "enriched by personal contact with my great teachers." Among them were the revered Peter Kropotkin, the dynamic Italian Errico Malatesta, and Max Nettlau, the foremost historian of anarchism, with whom she would correspond for the rest of her life. Kropotkin invited her to his home in Bromley, a town about a dozen miles outside London. Over tea, which he prepared himself, he asked her about conditions in America, about the anarchist movement there, and about Berkman, whose case he had followed closely and for whom he expressed regard. Emma's visit with Kropotkin convinced her that "true greatness is always coupled with simplicity. He was the personification of both."[33]

Emma spoke frequently about political justice, defending Sasha's act when she did so. "What was Berkman's crime?" she demanded at a September 13 lecture at London's South Place Institute. "Had he stolen the wealth labor had created? Had he robbed mankind of the necessary means of life? Had he invested the hard earned pennies of widows and orphans in swindling schemes? Had he built factories where men, women, and half grown children were slowly tortured to death? Had he plagued, cheated, enslaved, and tyrannized humanity? No! Had he done all that, he might have remained a free man, he would have been honored and respected as a good citizen, have had a chance of being elected to Parliament, Senate, or Congress, or chosen as President of the U.S.A. Berkman was imprisoned because he hated and opposed all this, because he was strong, and let the act follow the thought, because he attempted to destroy the life of a man who had brought disaster and privation upon thousands of people."[34]

Goldman's nursing courses were scheduled to begin on October 1, so in late September, after a brief stop in Scotland, where she attended rallies in Glasgow and Edinburgh, she departed for Vienna. She fell instantly in love with the graceful city, finding it "one of the most beautiful" she had ever seen. At the Allgemeines Krankenhaus, a vast and imposing institution, she began her studies in midwifery, childhood diseases, and obstetrics. During her leisure time she took advantage of the city's culture and society and acquainted herself with the latest European literature, reading Nietzsche, Ibsen, Strindberg, and Hauptmann. This introduced her to the contemporary social theater, on which she was later to lecture and write. She attended plays starring leading performers of the era, such as Italian actress Eleonora Duse, and musical events, including the entire Ring cycle of Wagner.

She also attended talks by Sigmund Freud, joining the throngs who crowded in to hear the pathbreaking neurologist and analyst share his insights. His lectures had a dramatic effect on Emma's view of human nature and sexuality. As she later wrote, Freud's "simplicity and earnestness and the brilliance of his mind combined to give one the feeling of being led out of a dark cellar into broad daylight."[35]

Emma completed her coursework in March 1896 after five months of study. She passed her examinations and was awarded two diplomas, one in midwifery and one in nursing. She traveled to Zürich and Paris, and was pleased by the vision and vitality she discovered in Europe's radical communities. "I have made a trip through different countries on the continent," she said, "where I found our ideas marching on wonderfully."[36] She felt pangs, however, that the anarchist viewpoint had less fertile ground in America, writing to French anarchist and sociologist Augustin Hamon, "The anarchistic ideas do not seem to meet with much success in this blessed land of the 'free' and the 'brave.'"[37]

Emma prepared to leave Europe with return fare and a hundred dollars from Modska for clothes, which she instead used to buy books. She sailed for New York in April 1896, now a qualified nurse and midwife. Brady was waiting for her at the dock with a bouquet of roses, and she playfully crept up behind him and covered his eyes with her hands. He brought her to a new flat on 11th Street, decorated by Modska, with "a large kitchen" and a "beautiful garden."[38] Emma was happy to be back in America, delighted with the success of her trip, and eager to put her new skills to use. But Sasha's ongoing plight weighed heavily on her heart.

10

THE TUNNEL

SASHA MARKED THE FIFTH YEAR OF HIS SENTENCE in 1897. As he reached this milestone, his comrades increased their efforts to gain his release from the penitentiary, with Emma leading the charge. A number of legal funds had already sprung up on his behalf, such as the Berkman Defense Committee, founded in 1894 by New York Jewish anarchists, including Isidore Rudash of the Pioneers of Liberty and Jacob Adler, a well-known Jewish writer and humorist who published under the name B. Kovner.[1] Many members were not Jewish, but were invested in Sasha's fate, such as Justus Schwab and Sergius Schewitsch. Also involved were Emma and Sasha's old friend Annie Netter and her husband, Michael A. Cohn, a doctor. Cohn had been born in Vilnius and became an anarchist as a result of the Haymarket executions. A mainstay of the Jewish anarchist movement, Cohn would extend financial assistance and unwavering friendship to Emma and Sasha their whole lives.

Although Berkman had initially been opposed to legal action, considering such measures at odds with his anarchist principles, he eventually changed his mind. Both Emma and Johann Most had wrangled with the legal system, producing significant publicity; were Sasha to win a reduction of his sentence, the victory would provide a great opportunity for propaganda. And Sasha was desperate to be free of the prison. His frequent trips to the dungeon and to solitary were taking a grievous toll.

The lawyers hired by the defense committees—well-regarded in the field and committed to Sasha's case—believed the maximum penalty should not have exceeded seven years, the punishment for the assassination attempt, and that an appeal to the Pennsylvania Superior Court might result in a commutation. But Berkman had chosen to act as his own counsel. With little knowledge of the law, he had neglected to take exceptions to Judge McClung's rulings, and thus had no basis for an appeal. His only option, therefore, was a pardon, and once he had completed the first portion of his sentence—seven years, or five with good behavior—he would be eligible to apply to the Pennsylvania Board of Pardons for an early release.[2]

Since her return from Vienna, Emma's time had been consumed by her nursing duties—treating patients, delivering babies, and assisting at operations. Her clients were mostly poor women, so the job was not lucrative. But it taught her a great deal about the lives of the working class, the people she hoped the anarchist movement would one day liberate. Some pregnant women, worn down by destitution, struggling to care for the children they already had, asked her to perform abortions. The procedure was illegal, and she had been warned about the dangers to the patient when she was studying in Vienna. Each time she was asked, she refused.

"It was not any moral consideration for the sanctity of life," she wrote later. "A life unwanted and forced into abject poverty did not seem sacred to me. But my interests embraced the entire social problem, not merely a single aspect of it, and I would not jeopardize my freedom for that one part of the human struggle."[3] Neither had she any contraception, also illegal, to provide. She asked the doctors she knew—White, Hoffmann, and Solotaroff—for their thoughts about the situation, but they had no insights that were useful to her. They merely found fault with the women themselves, asserted that all children were a blessing, or expressed hope for a change in the future.

Much of Emma's free time was devoted to anarchist meetings and lectures, which did not sit well with Ed Brady. He complained that her "interest in the movement . . . is nothing but vanity, nothing but your craving for applause and glory and the limelight." Piercingly, he told her that she was "simply incapable of a deep feeling," and demanded that she make a choice between her anarchist activity and her life with him. After a brief separation, Goldman temporarily scaled back her "public interests" to accommodate Brady's wishes, but privately she feared she would never be able to experience a lasting romantic relationship.[4]

Despite the professional and personal demands on her time, Goldman kept a keen focus on Sasha. A series of her lecture tours had raised money for the ongoing defense, and when it came time for Berkman's pardon petition, she reached out to leaders of organized labor to enlist their support and strengthen the impact of the plea. She made contact with the secretary of the Central Labor Union of Boston, Harry Kelly, who had recently become an anarchist activist. Kelly, a man with thoughtful eyes and a pale moustache, was often assumed to be Irish, but had been born in Missouri in 1871, the son of Richard Kelly, a prospector and mine operator from Cornwall, England, and Nancy Jane Stevens, a member of the Calvert family of Baltimore. Kelly was described by his friends and comrades as a grave, gentle man with a strong spiritual sensibility.[5]

Kelly listened to Emma's request and obligingly brought his union on board; her letter of thanks led to an enduring friendship. Emma convinced local union representatives to present a similar resolution to the Central Labor Union of New York City, and she asked Max Metzkow, who was now living in Buffalo, to approach his city's Central Labor Union as well. "It is sad," she wrote to Max, "that so few people show an interest in poor Berkman, and if I were not constantly speaking, writing, and pressing the matter, Berkman would spend the rest of his life in prison."[6]

Other labor organizations supported Berkman's pardon campaign, such as the Bakers' International Union; the United Labor League of Pennsylvania, which represented more than 100,000 workers; and, as a result of the backing of Samuel Gompers, the American Federation of Labor, which agreed to assist the cause at its annual meeting in December in Cincinnati. A decade earlier, Gompers had requested clemency for the Haymarket anarchists from the governor of Illinois, although he did not approve of Berkman's attack on Frick. When asked about the crime during a visit to Homestead in August 1892, Gompers said that it "certainly did our cause no good." Still, he declined to criticize Sasha publicly. "I don't know why I should be asked to go out of my way," he said, "to give Berkman another kick."[7]

In May 1897, shortly before Sasha marked his fifth full year in prison, Henry Bauer and Carl Nold completed their sentences and were freed from the Western Penitentiary. They wasted no time in joining the effort to help their comrade obtain release. But when Berkman's case came before the Board of Pardons in October 1897, it was rejected. His lawyers submitted a second petition, for review on December 21, 1898.

For this endeavor, members of his defense fund discussed an unusual approach—soliciting the assistance of none other than steel magnate

Andrew Carnegie, owner of the Homestead plant. Emma thought the idea was absurd, but Ed Brady and Justus Schwab were in favor; Carnegie was said to consider himself an enlightened person, and had even invited Peter Kropotkin to his home on Fifth Avenue when the Russian anarchist toured the United States several months earlier, his first visit to the country. Kropotkin had refused Carnegie's invitation, coldly replying, "Because of your power and influence, my comrade Alexander Berkman was given twenty-two years in prison for an act which in the State of Pennsylvania calls for seven years as the highest penalty. I cannot accept the hospitality of a man who has helped to doom a human being to twenty-two years of misery."[8]

In the end, the anarchists could not devise a plausible strategy for contacting Carnegie, and the second hearing with the Board of Pardons, now with new members, was delayed, then, finally, rejected. The whole campaign, years in planning, so costly in money and effort, had come to nothing.

WITH THE LAST HOPE OF A PARDON GONE, a prison breakout seemed to Sasha the only solution. He had been contemplating this dramatic move since his earliest days in the penitentiary, and was always on the lookout for opportunities, vowing that he "would make use of any means, however terrible, to escape from this hell to regain liberty."[9]

Sasha had conceived a getaway scheme in early 1897, not long before Bauer and Nold were released from prison. The plan was to rent a house across the street from Riverside and dig an underground passage leading from the house to the prison, below the eastern wall. Sasha was entranced by the idea. "Who knows? It may prove the symbol and precursor of Russian idealism on American soil," he said. "And what tremendous impression the consummation of the bold plan will make! What a stimulus to our propaganda, as a demonstration of anarchist initiative and ability!"[10]

As soon as Bauer and Nold were freed in May 1897, they went to New York and told Emma and their other comrades about Sasha's idea to dig a tunnel; at the time, the scheme was deemed both risky and implausible, especially with legal measures pending. But by 1899, once all the options for a pardon were exhausted, Berkman resolved to put his plan into action. The time seemed right. Warden Wright had released him from solitary shortly after the Board of Pardons closed the door on legal appeal, and had made him an assistant rangeman, which gave him access to a wide section of the prison and increased his familiarity with the institution's landscape. Sasha was optimistic. "These things have been accomplished in Russia," he thought. "Why not in America?" He thrilled at the idea of freedom. "The wine of sunshine and liberty," he said, "tingles in every fiber."[11]

Berkman engaged the help of a fellow prisoner called "Tony," an Alsatian whom he described as "small and wiry," "intelligent and daring," with a "quick wit" and "a considerable dash of the Frenchman about him." Berkman had dared to solicit his aid after weeks of agonizing internal debate, and was relieved when Tony greeted the prospect with confident good humor. As Sasha later wrote, "Serene and self-possessed, he listens gravely to my plan, smiles with apparent satisfaction, and briefly announces that it shall be done."[12]

Tony, imprisoned for sodomy, was due to finish his term in several weeks, and would smuggle out diagrams, blueprints, and measurements when he left the prison.[13] Sasha's comrades would arrange the excavation of the tunnel, while Tony would serve as Sasha's contact, using a cipher code known only to them. An anarchist, but not a member of the New York or Pennsylvania circles, Tony had "more nerve than a regiment and also good judgment."[14] He was, said Berkman, "a very unusual type, rare among Germans, more like the Russian conspirators of old."[15]

Emma did not take a lead role in the operation. During a March 1899 trip to Detroit, Robert Reitzel had introduced her to two successful businessmen, both supporters of his journal *Der arme Teufel.* Herman Miller was president of the Cleveland Brewing Company, and Carl Schmidt, a millionaire who went by the name Carl Stone, was the owner of a leather factory. The two men learned that Emma entertained hopes of becoming a doctor, and they offered to fund her education at a medical school in Switzerland, with a stipend of forty dollars a month for five years, plus $500 for passage across the Atlantic, and full tuition. They showered Goldman with compliments and gifts, including a blue cape and a gold clamshell watch. Emma, who also had anarchist business to conduct in Great Britain and France, was due to depart for Europe in November 1899.[16] It was just as well, she thought. The authorities were less likely to suspect mischief if she was out of the country.

Emma promised Sasha that before she left, she would find him comrades to aide with the escape plan, and get money to finance it. She collected contributions under the pretense of launching new legal appeals, and handed over $200 from her $500 medical fund.[17] To direct the operation, Emma chose Eric B. Morton.

Morton, a carpenter, was a Norwegian-born anarchist nicknamed "Ibsen," and "Eric the Red," after the hero of a medieval Icelandic saga. He was tall, strong, and imposing, highly literate, and very resourceful. Goldman described him as "a veritable Viking, in spirit and physique, a man of intelligence, daring, and will-power." With Morton in charge, the plan was set. When Tony handed over the blueprints, the excavation process would begin. Once Sasha was through the tunnel and clear of the prison grounds, he would be spirited to Mexico or Canada, and then on to Europe. Morton assured Emma that soon they all would be celebrating with Berkman in Paris.[18]

THE ESCAPE PLOT WAS LAUNCHED IN APRIL 1900, when a man and woman, identifying themselves as Mr. and Mrs. Thomas Brown, rented a house at 28 Sterling Street, directly opposite the southeastern corner of the penitentiary. John C. Langfitt, the rental agent, who also worked as a guard at the prison, was told that Mr. Brown was an inventor of electrical mining equipment.[19] Mr. Brown was in fact Eric B. Morton himself; his "wife" was Vella Kinsella, an anarchist comrade from Chicago whom Goldman had met at a Haymarket meeting.

Morton was to dig a tunnel about 300 feet in length, starting in the cellar of the house, running under the eastern wall of the prison, and ending up inside the yard by the stable. Italian miners from the Pittsburgh coal region had been hired to assist with the digging. When the tunnel was finished, Berkman was to sneak out of the cellblock, make his way to the stable, rip up the wooden flooring, enter the tunnel, and crawl back along it to the house. There he would find civilian clothes, money, and directions to a designated meeting place.[20]

The digging, which began in May 1900, proved more difficult than expected. Morton and his coworkers encountered rocky soil beneath the eastern wall that stymied their advance. As a result, they were forced to dig underneath the foundations, and there they were nearly asphyxiated by poisonous fumes leaking into the tunnel from a gas main. This caused considerable delay and required the installation of machinery to pump fresh air to the men, who were "toiling prostrate in the narrow passage deep in the bowels of the earth." Additionally, Tony's competence as a go-between was called into question, provoking frustration on all sides. And the constraints on time and money necessitated a very narrow tunnel, which could be constructed only by stretching out "flat on the stomach," as Morton described it. The process "was so exhausting it was impossible to keep at it more than half an hour at a time. Naturally progress was slow."[21]

Morton feared the sounds of all the digging would attract attention from neighbors and the prison guards. On May 12 he bought a piano from William M. Crump, who ran a music store on Smithfield Street. Kinsella was a trained pianist with a superior singing voice. In the early morning, and late at night, she would sing and play, muffling the noises from below. The unsuspecting prison staff found the music pleasant, according to a variety of sources, including Goldman, who said that "the guards on the wall greatly enjoyed the fine performances."[22] Neighbors also could hear the relentless playing. "The shades were always down," they reported, "but the house was rarely silent. During the intervals when there was no music," they "heard a grinding, whirring noise, which gave them the impression that the Browns were always grinding coffee."[23]

Kinsella had a clear view of the street, so, as an additional precaution, the anarchists installed an electric buzzer system next to the piano that Kinsella would press to alert diggers to approaching trouble, warning them to cease operations if she saw someone come near the house. The house would fall into silence, above and below, until the danger had passed. Then Kinsella would resume her piano playing, the signal that the drilling could resume.[24]

Later in May the Browns were joined at the house by another couple, a man and woman. The foursome rarely ventured outside and never mingled with the neighbors. This odd behavior, along with the endless singing and loud piano playing, made the neighbors more and more curious. As one newspaper account noted after, "The Misses Letitia and Jennie McCarthy, who live just opposite, had their suspicions aroused because of the small quantity of furniture going into the supposed home of the new family, and by the fact that the principal article taken in was a piano."[25] The strange goings-on continued through June. In early July the music suddenly stopped and the occupants disappeared, leaving the house on Sterling Street vacant. The tunnel was complete.

It was time for Berkman to make his move. As a rangeman, he had access to large sections of the prison grounds. Additionally, he now kept two starlings, fledglings he had adopted, trained, and named Sis and Dick (the latter in memory of his first pet bird). He convinced the warden to allow him to take the delicate birds into the yard for a daily ten minutes of fresh air and sunshine. On July 5, with this errand as a cover, he made his way to the concealed tunnel opening, through which he planned to crawl his way to freedom. There he suffered a shock. The entrance to the hole was unexpectedly blocked, covered with a big load of bricks and stone that had only recently been dumped during a prison construction project. The hole into the tunnel was impassable.[26] Sasha was devastated by this bad luck. He sent a letter to Tony, later published in his memoirs. "It's terrible. It's all over. Couldn't make it."[27]

The tunnel was not discovered until July 26. (Berkman's *Prison Memoirs* gives the date as July 16). That day, some children playing in the street wandered into the yard of the now unoccupied house. The piles of freshly dug soil attracted their attention. A boy, stumbling into the cellar, located the secret passage and ran home and told his mother. She informed the sales agent, John Langfitt, who immediately notified Warden Wright. After the warden examined the tunnel, he called in a crew, who traced its path to the point inside the prison wall. In the house the police found an uneaten meal and a pot of coffee in the kitchen, a suit of clothes with money in one of the pockets, and a note in cipher code which could not be understood, all presumably intended for an escapee who had never arrived. They also found the torn end of an envelope bearing the abbreviation "Ill," apparently for Illinois (Vella Kinsella was from Chicago).[28]

"One of the boldest and most systematic plans for the release of one or more prisoners from Riverside penitentiary was thwarted yesterday by accident," blared the newspapers. Berkman was among those instantly suspected. "The first theory advanced when the matter was discovered," read the press report, "seemed to point to the release of Alexander Berkman, the anarchist, who is serving a twenty-two years' sentence for the shooting of H. C. Frick; but the conclusion reached now by Director Muth, of the Allegheny police department, is that the real object of the rescuers was to secure the freedom of the notorious real estate swindler J. C. Boyd."[29]

The revelation of the tunnel confounded the prison authorities. There were scant clues as to the identity of the diggers or the inmate who planned to escape. They narrowed the suspects to a few, including Berkman; Boyd; James Riley, a diamond thief; Paddy Cronin, leader of a gang of train robbers; George "Snake" Wilson, a safecracker; and Paddy McGraw, who had attempted a previous escape. Berkman, however, was their prime suspect. Yet they could find no proof against him, and some inspectors "argued that Berkman's friends could not afford" such an expensive, "remarkable" undertaking.[30]

On August 5, 1900, after almost two weeks of probing, the Board of Inspectors, led by George A. Kelly, declared that it had "abandoned hopes of discovering either who dug the tunnel or for whom it was intended." On October 5 the board made a further announcement: "The Board of Inspectors, after a patient and careful investigation of the tunnel mystery, failed to find anything indicating any complicity on the part of the prison officials or employees in the matter, and further, that no prisoners escaped. As to the convicts for whom the tunnel was intended, that is still a matter of conjecture, and various opinions exist."[31]

Although no evidence was found to implicate Berkman in the plot, he nevertheless was locked up in the most restrictive solitary confinement. (He managed to get out a communiqué to Tony before he was restrained: "Tunnel discovered. Lose no time. Leave the city immediately. I am locked up on suspicion.") He was allowed no contact with any other prisoner, and even the guards were forbidden to speak with him, merely pausing briefly on their rounds in silence. He was placed under constant observation, with an officer assigned to watch his door. His privileges were revoked, and he was denied access to mail and reading material. His birds, Sis and Dick, were taken from him. So it was, without work, exercise, or companionship, that he passed his next days in solitary confinement, unbearable, "monotonous, interminable."[32]

Berkman was kept in solitary for nearly a year. During this time, two of his closest friends in the prison died. One was a man named Russell, who was given a tainted injection in the hospital ward, became paralyzed as a result, and died in great pain, covered in bedsores. Sasha had "loved him with all my heart," and his "death was a most terrible shock."[33] Sasha was gravely depressed. When he demanded to be moved from solitary, the warden put him in a straitjacket. "They bound my body in canvas, strapped my arms to the bed, and chained my feet to the posts," Sasha said. "I was kept that way eight days, unable to move, rotting in my own excrement."

Then a new inspector visited the prison, saw his dreadful condition, and ordered him released from the straitjacket. "I am in pretty bad shape," he wrote to Emma on July 10, 1901, "but they put me in the general ward now, and I am glad of a chance to send you this note."[34]

Eight days later, on July 18, Sasha tried to end his life. At around midnight the guards were making their rounds and saw him hanging from the top of his cell from a strip of his blanket, torn and fashioned as a rope. Though they hastened to cut him down, he was almost dead when he arrived at the hospital, where the doctors managed to revive him. Berkman had been driven to the attempt, determined a leading anarchist paper, "because he could not endure the solitary confinement and absolute physical and mental illness in which he was kept. Tyranny dies hard, but all things have an end, even the patience of the people!"[35]

Kate Austin echoed this view, and demanded a halt to his suffering. Berkman had been "thrust into a dark cell, in solitary confinement," she wrote in a letter to the *Boston Traveler.* "Reading matter, which had been his chief consolation, was denied." He was banned from all activity, and left to stifle in the July heat. "How can those who can condemn the inhumanity of old world governments in their treatment of regicides or political criminals," asked Austin, "remain silent concerning the well-known facts of Berkman's excessive sentence, and special official dispensation in the shape of torture? Yes, how can they?"[36]

SASHA FOUGHT BACK FROM THIS, his lowest point. He was eventually reassigned to a regular cell and returned to his work on the range. He also got word that a new commutation law reduced his sentence by two and a half years, and he had already served nine. "It still leaves me a long time, of course," he wrote to Emma, "almost four years here, and another year to the workhouse. However, it is a considerable gain, and if I should not get into solitary again, I may—I am almost afraid to utter the thought—I may live to come out."[37] In addition, all his privileges were restored, including the right to receive visitors.

On August 5, 1901, Sasha was summoned to greet his first visitor in nine years, since the disastrous incident with Emma. It was Harry Gordon, who also had been to see him at the Pittsburgh jail in 1892. "I was so overcome by the sight of the dear friend, I could hardly speak," he later wrote to Max Metzkow. "You can realize with what feelings I beheld the first comrade to come to see me and with what emotions I pressed his hand."[38]

On September 2 Emma, again using the alias Sonya Niedermann, returned to the prison. It was an emotional, painful reunion. Goldman was shocked by Sasha's appearance; he was thin, gray-faced and cowering, practically mute. Sasha wrote to her several days after her visit. "The sight of your face after all these years completely unnerved me," he explained. "I could not think, I could not speak. And all the time I felt how nervous you were at my silence, and I couldn't utter a word." He also said that it was fortunate her true identity was not exposed instantly, although he believed the staff was suspicious once she left. Warden Wright, he thought, surely would have barred her, but Wright was ill and absent from the compound. Wright resigned soon afterward, on November 1, 1901, following more than thirty years of service. "The prisoners have been praying for it for years," Berkman wrote, "and some of the boys on the range celebrated the event by getting drunk on wood alcohol."[39]

Wright's successor, William McC. Johnston, was a physician by profession with the rank of major in the Pennsylvania militia. Under his management, conditions at the prison rapidly improved. The food got better, as did medical treatment, and greater efforts were made to keep the prison clean.[40] Sasha was grateful for these developments, and steadied himself for his remaining term. Years later Emma paid tribute to his strength. Berkman was, she wrote, "a living proof of what perseverance, courage, and determination can accomplish, in spite of odds."[41]

11

RED EMMA

As Sasha battled his way through his first decade behind bars, Emma was making a name for herself around the country as an orator. By the mid-1890s her English had dramatically improved (thanks in part to her stint on Blackwell's Island), and she was able to lecture to a far larger audience, although she still gave speeches in German, Yiddish, and Russian. She retained a slight European inflection, which some took as German, others as Russian, still others as a mixture of the two. "She had an odd voice with a peculiar accent," a friend of hers recalled, "but she was a good speaker and made an impression."[1] A reporter from the *Cleveland Plain Dealer* described Emma's "wonderful vigor," her "strong and resonant voice," and her "fine vocabulary."[2]

With time and practice, Emma honed and polished the natural oratorical talents Johann Most had first recognized when she was twenty. She was forceful, fluent, and witty, and her speeches were prepared with care. Fellow radicals, members of the press, workers, scholars, and the merely curious who came out to see her often commented on her power and her passion, her ability to hold a crowd. "She always spoke with great inner conviction," an anarchist comrade recalled, "and one felt that she really meant what she said."[3] Another friend said that she was "very good at repartee" and knew how to handle hecklers, a particularly important skill given the content of her lectures.[4] "Emma had a lot of charisma," remarked a comrade. "Even her political enemies respected her."[5]

Emma was able to impress, despite her harsh words. A *Chicago Tribune* reporter who heard her address a Haymarket memorial meeting called

Goldman a "strong and vigorous speaker," although "irony, sarcasm, invective, and denunciation [rolled] in a steady volume from her lips."[6] A California-based writer who attended one of Emma's lectures on the Spanish-American War found her "fierce, scornful," and "highly quotable." "This little Russian woman," said the writer, "with her thickened speech, her good rolling R's, her disdain of rhetorical rules, her vehemence of expression, her potent unstudied postures, is the most interesting woman I have met. She has life, she has courage, she has brains. She is fiercely consistent, unwaveringly true and, though I can't agree with her, I believe her to be absolutely sincere."[7]

And yet, for all her eloquence and charisma, Emma suffered from stage fright. "She was extremely nervous before the lectures," remembered Millie Grobstein, who later served as Goldman's secretary. She "ate very little, and before mounting the platform took a drink of whiskey and paced up and down. Yet the moment she got on the platform she was herself in full command. She was at home. All her fears and anxieties seemed to disappear."[8]

Goldman's frequent lecture tours carried her all over the country, from Boston to Chicago, Detroit and Denver, St. Louis and Salt Lake City. She took a liking to San Francisco, finding the city a lively, social place, where "the California wines were cheap and stimulating" and her comrades "took their tasks very seriously; but they could also love, drink, and play."[9] There she met the writer Jack London and his friends Anna and Rose Strunsky, and debated a prominent local socialist, Emil Liess. Emma also became close with Abe Isaak and his family. Isaak, an anarchist formerly based in Portland, where he edited the anarchist journal *The Firebrand,* had been arrested the previous year for publishing and sending in the mail an "obscene poem." The poem in question was Walt Whitman's "A Woman Waits for Me," and all three editors of *The Firebrand*—Isaak, Henry Addis, and Abner J. Pope—were tried and convicted. After his release, Isaak moved to San Francisco, where he and his family resumed publication of the paper, renamed *Free Society.*[10]

Goldman swept up and down the West Coast, from Los Angeles to Portland, and in Washington State visited the principal anarchist community in the region, the Home Colony. Situated on a bay near Tacoma, Home was remote and rustic, and its members followed a libertarian philosophy created in a natural atmosphere unspoiled by industrial and urban blight.[11] Emma won the colonists' admiration as a "jolly comrade, a good looking, sensible girl, who is even not averse to a little flirtation, and a sympathetic woman with a heart so large that it embraces the whole world."[12] Goldman returned often to Home, a place, she said, "where the colonists are showing to the world that society can exist without the trammels of law and authority." Her speeches there, however, attracted negative attention from residents of nearby communities; to them, her presence was a "nettling reminder of the rampant anarchism in their midst."[13]

Emma's connection to her adopted country grew stronger as her tours grew lengthier, and she loved the experience of bringing her views to people across America. She also enjoyed the perks of travel and was prone to spending quite a bit of money on her comforts, to the dismay of her more frugal comrades.[14] Because so many different types of people came to hear her speak—students, socialists, Tolstoyans, academics, local leaders—she was able to spread anarchist ideas to new audiences.

"I cannot tell you," she wrote in *Solidarity,* "how many people are now interested in the philosophy of Anarchy. Even the most conservative clubs and organizations that only a few years ago would have refused to listen to a professed Anarchist are now inviting Anarchist lecturers . . . [who are] listened to with enthusiasm by people who a few years ago joined in the plutocratic cry 'Hang the Anarchists!' "[15] After returning from one trip that lasted nearly half a year, she wrote, "I have made friends for the cause of liberty, have done away with a good deal of prejudice formerly entertained by different people against Anarchy and Anarchists, and have won a number of personal friends."[16]

Many prominent writers and reformers sought her out. Journalist John Swinton, onetime editor of the *New York Sun,* was a labor rights advocate and a former abolitionist who had fought in the Civil War. Swinton became interested in Goldman early on, wrote favorably of her in his paper, and, with his wife, Orsena, spent time with Emma socially. Goldman also formed friendships with music critic James Gibbons Huneker, journalist and satirist Ambrose Bierce, and British author Frank Harris, who considered Emma, with George Eliot and Olive Schreiner, one of the three greatest women he had known. Goldman was the greatest of all, he said, because her idealism, integrity, and love of truth placed her "among the heroic leaders and guides of humanity forever."[17]

Goldman allied with some leading New York social workers, notably Lillian Wald, who, like Emma, was from a Jewish family in Rochester, and Lavinia Dock. These women, Goldman wrote, were "genuinely concerned" about the immigrants on the Lower East Side and took a personal interest in the economic condition of the workers. "Like some of the Russian revolutionists" whom Emma had admired in her youth, "they too had come from wealthy homes and had completely consecrated themselves" to a lofty cause.[18]

NOT ONLY DID GOLDMAN ATTRACT influential friends and a wider audience, but she now had a vast range of topics in her repertoire, including sexual freedom and women's rights, patriotism, religion, and war. Her talks on sexuality included commentary on marriage, to which Emma was strongly opposed. Drawing on ideas from Ibsen and Freud, and from anarchist comrades Ezra Heywood, a suffragist and feminist, and Moses Harman, the editor of the journal *Lucifer,* she challenged monogamy in favor of free love, arguing that since most men were "varietists," women should feel comfortable with the concept as well.[19]

Herself a lusty young woman, often flirty and provocative, she demanded freedom in sexual relations as in other areas of life, despite the disapproval (and jealousy) of lovers such as Johann Most and Ed Brady. "I believe in the marriage of affection," she had said to Nellie Bly in 1893. "That is the only true marriage. If two people care for each other, they have a right to live together so long as love exists. When it is dead what base immorality for them still to keep together!"[20] Goldman believed that sex was a necessary part of life, something that should be natural rather than shameful. "I knew from my own experience," she said, "that sex expression is as vital a factor in human life as food and air." She said that she felt comfortable discussing "sex as frankly as I did other topics," and believed that prudishness and misplaced societal judgment were problems facing many American women. The "tragedy of the self-supporting or economically free woman," she declared, "does not lie in too many but in too few experiences."[21]

She had her limits, though. One night in Washington, D.C., after she spoke about free love to the Friends of *Der Arme Teufel,* Robert Reitzel's journal, an elderly member of the group, married with grown children but nevertheless looking for some "free love" for himself, knocked at the door of her room. She shouted in an effort to scare him away, warning she would "wake the whole house." "Not so loud," he pleaded, "someone may hear us.

Excuse me. I was looking for the chambermaid." Emma thought he and others were missing the point of free love, viewing the concept as "only a means for clandestine affairs [while] their heads and hearts have remained as sterile as the Sahara."[22]

Goldman was against all forms of sexual intolerance. She voiced concern about the exploitation of prostitutes and the prejudice against homosexuals. By addressing such subjects with candor and compassion she became a hero to many young women and men. The homosexual community in particular was grateful for her openness and lack of judgment—Goldman thought it outrageous that anyone should be condemned or blamed for his or her sexual orientation. Crowding up to talk with her after her lectures, they expressed their appreciation to her for reinforcing, or helping them reclaim, their self-respect. "The men and women who used to come to see me after my lectures on homosexuality," she later wrote, "and who confided in me their anguish and their isolation were often of finer grain than those who had cast them out."[23]

Many of her own friends and associates in the movement were wary of her discussion of such "unnatural" subjects, but, she said, "censorship from comrades had the same effect on me as police persecution—it made me surer of myself, more determined to plead for every victim, be it one of social wrong or moral prejudice."[24]

As Emma moved into new rhetorical territory, the Autonomist group she and Sasha had once embraced was vanishing. A major anarchist conference, meant to bring together comrades from around the world, unify the various factions, and hammer out an overarching manifesto, was held in Chicago in October 1893, during the World's Fair.[25] The watchful Chicago police intended to ban any anarchist gatherings, but the delegates managed to meet secretly in a room in the Chicago Times Building. Nothing was accomplished. Some feuding leaders, including Johann Most and Josef Peukert, did not attend on principle; the disagreement over violence could not be resolved; and the factions could find no common platform.[26]

Berkman's attack on Frick had altered the entire movement profoundly, not only dividing anarchists over the use of violence, but sounding the death knell for the Autonomists. Hounded by the police, a number of the conspirators disappeared from sight, Frank Mollock being an example. Two others, Fritz and Sepp Oerter, were back in their native Germany by the end of 1892, where they resumed their anarchist activities. Sepp was detained by the police, and when Fritz tried to intercede, he, too, was arrested and sentenced to eighteen months at hard labor. Following his release, Fritz became an anarcho-syndicalist, focusing on the labor element of anarchism, and published articles and pamphlets on such subjects as "The Woman Question," "Free Love," "Nudity and Anarchism," and "What Do the Syndicalists Want?" Fritz remained an anarchist for the rest of his life, dying in 1935. Sepp, however, abandoned the movement, and converted to Nazism during the 1920s. Turning to politics, he became prime minister of the state of Brunswick, where he died in 1928.[27]

In 1894, after Claus Timmermann finished serving his sentence on Blackwell's Island for his role in the Union Square demonstration, he closed his journal *Die Brandfackel. Der Anarchist* ceased publication in 1895. The following year, in St. Louis, Otto Rinke started *Der Kampher,* of which only four issues appeared. Timmermann then introduced *Sturmvogel* in 1897, which he personally wrote, printed, and even hand delivered. It continued only until 1899, the last of the Autonomist journals. In London, *Die Autonomie* had suspended publication in 1893. Correspondingly, the number of Autonomist groups had been declining, in England as well as in the United States. By the end of the nineteenth century, the Autonomists as a movement had all but ceased to exist.

As for Josef Peukert, the main figure of the organization, he moved to Chicago in 1893, in part to avoid police harassment in New York following Berkman's attack on Frick. He maintained his Autonomist convictions and continued to praise Berkman's daring and gumption. Berkman's "revolver shots," he said, "tore a hole in the armory of wage-slavery. They awakened in thousands of proletarians their class consciousness. The effect of this awakening cannot be long in coming. Sasha's shots were a thousand times more effective than all the shots that killed the workers in Homestead."[28] Peukert faded from prominence, dying impoverished in Chicago in 1910 at the age of fifty-five.

One more Autonomist member remains to be accounted for. This was none other than Modska Aronstam. On Emma's return from Europe in 1896, she found him decidedly altered. Though he furnished her new apartment and continued to provide her with money, anarchism seemed to have "lost its former meaning" for him. He had long ago stopped attending meetings at the Zum Groben Michel tavern, and rarely wrote to Berkman in prison. As Sasha noted, "The Twin has gradually withdrawn from our New York circles, and is now obscured from my horizon."[29]

Modska mingled with a different crowd, and his interests had changed. Nearly all his new friends worked in the newspaper and art worlds. Frequenting studios and galleries became his principal passion, his considerable income allowed him to indulge his tastes for beauty and finery, and his leisure time was "spent at sales." Sasha grumbled about his cousin's increasing focus on his art and life outside of radical circles. "Even Modska, my constant chum," he wrote, "has been swirled into the vortex of narrow ambition and self-indulgence, the plaything of commonplace fate."[30]

By the end of the 1890s Modska had abandoned the movement entirely. In 1899 he married Marcia Mishkin, a professional photographer. They had one child, a daughter, Luba, born in 1902, who would become an interior decorator. In 1904 he took his wife and daughter to Russia to visit his family in Kovno. Later that year he was sent to the Far East to produce illustrations about the Russo-Japanese War for the *New York World.* Not long after his return, he legally changed his name to Modest Stein, so as not to be connected with the events of the past, above all with the attempt on Frick. His daughter later explained that this was done in part to protect his family.[31]

Berkman in his prison memoirs, which were published in 1912, was careful not to implicate Modska, and gave him the pseudonym "Fedya." Many years later, when Goldman was writing her autobiography, Modska discouraged her from referring to him even by a pseudonym. "I don't think the experiences of Fedya have any place in your book," he told her. "As you know, Fedya has long ago retired to private life. This had at times made him useful in a certain way—so better let him stay where he is."[32]

As Modska receded from the movement, Emma was becoming a hugely controversial public figure, and even some of her natural allies from other radical groups found her unnecessarily severe and immoderate. She rejected democracy and the use of the vote, claiming it merely rendered people subservient to corrupt politicians. Because of this view, she refused to align herself with the women's suffrage movement. She rarely wrote or spoke publicly about race in America, or about racism in general. Although she occasionally expressed disgust at blatant racial discrimination, and upheld a view that people of all classes and ethnicities should be equal, she appeared somewhat ignorant of the African American experience. Her radical focus remained persistently on those concerns formed early in her life: labor injustice, freedom of speech, sexism, the perils of political power, and economic inequity. Goldman stubbornly insisted that capitalism and government existed only to protect the private property of the rich and called on members of the working class to overthrow the current system. "The ruling classes," she declared, "have never granted privileges to the oppressed until forced to do so by the latter. The struggling masses of the present century can expect nothing from their masters, and if they want to challenge their conditions and bring about a state of society in which no one shall enjoy the toil of his fellow man, they will only succeed through the social revolution, never through peaceful methods."[33]

Goldman, like Berkman, harbored a violent streak. At the age of eight she had dreamed of becoming the Old Testament's Judith, who slew Holofernes to avenge the wrongs against her people.[34] Goldman's list of hostile impulses was long: she advocated propaganda by the deed; had contemplated blowing up the office of the newspaper that had humiliated her then-mentor Johann Most; conspired with Berkman to assassinate Frick; talked of bombing the Pittsburgh courthouse where Berkman was put on trial; celebrated attentats across the globe; and was a strenuous believer in revenge. But after the Frick episode she maintained that she would no longer participate in active plots of violence, and toward the end of her life she asserted to Scottish anarchist Tom Bell, "I hope you know me well enough to know that I do not glory in violence. If ever I believed in taking a human life, no matter how dangerous that life and how evil, I was entirely cured of it after Sasha's act."[35]

This avowal notwithstanding, she offered vigorous defenses of the radicals who carried out the rash of assassination attempts across Europe in the 1890s, the "era of dynamite," as it was known. Almost invariably the crimes were the work of isolated individuals on the fringe of the anarchist movement rather than of organized terrorist groups. Yet they fostered the image of an international conspiracy bent on undermining civilized society. Goldman considered the perpetrators of these acts "brave heroes," praising their motives as noble and rationalizing their desperate measures against despots. She placed all the blame on the rulers who perpetuated greater violence—war, torture, execution—believing they had brought about their own destruction, and she sympathized with the assailants no matter the circumstance. Behind every attentat, she felt, was "an impressionable, highly sensitized personality and a gentle spirit [whose] reactions to the cruelty and injustice of the world must inevitably express themselves in some violent act, in supreme rending of their tortured soul."[36]

As examples she cited the "admirable acts" of Emile Henry, French bombers Ravachol and Auguste Vaillant, and Italian assassin Sante Caserio, who murdered President Marie François Sadi Carnot of France. All were anarchists who used bombs and other weapons as tools of protest.[37] These men, she said, "so finely attuned to the injustice of the world, so high-minded, [were] driven by social forces to do the very thing they abhorred most, to destroy human life." She even defended Italian anarchist Luigi Luccheni, who fatally stabbed Elisabeth of Austria, wife of Emperor Franz Josef, in Geneva on September 10, 1898, although Goldman regarded the Empress Elisabeth as a victim of "the ruthless social struggle."[38] Goldman stated her bias without apology: "I am on the side of every rebel, whether his act has been beneficial or detrimental to our cause; for I do not judge an act by its result but by its cause. . . . I am a revolutionist by nature and temperament, and as such I claim the right for myself, and all those who feel with me, to rebel and resist invasion by all means, force included."[39]

Goldman's refusal to condemn terrorist acts, combined with her outspoken advocacy of atheism and free love, made her a notorious figure to many respectable elements of society. Newspapers depicted her as a wild-eyed fanatic, a menace to peace and order, a hideous she-devil, the embodiment of everything that threatened contemporary life. She was charged as an enemy of God, law, marriage and government, and slapped with the monikers "Red Emma" and "High Priestess of the Anarchists." The writer S. N. Behrman recalled that when he was a boy in Worcester in the 1890s, parents cited her name as a bogey "to frighten and admonish" their children.[40]

Goldman was more muted about America's leader, President William McKinley, the Ohio Republican, former congressman, and two-term governor who had been elected president in 1896. At a speech in St. Louis in October 1897, Goldman was asked, "Do you think that Mr. McKinley should be removed—or as you call it, executed?" "McKinley—pooh," she replied. "He is only a tool, a mouthpiece for Mark Hanna, the Republican Party leader. I don't consider McKinley."[41]

During her lecture tours, Emma often found herself a target of the police, who deemed her a high-profile carrier of unrest and division. Sometimes when arriving in a city, she was intercepted by officials at the train station and forced to proceed to the next stop, or denied access to halls where she was scheduled to speak. She was repeatedly arrested, detained without a warrant, and even, on occasion, subjected to physical abuse by the authorities, although she would serve only three terms in prison.

In the fall of 1897 Emma went to Providence, Rhode Island, to give a series of open-air addresses, using a packing-box as a platform. She was introduced by John H. Cook, a leading anarchist in the city, and a union man. Well versed in Shakespeare and the Bible, Cook was an able speaker who had campaigned on behalf of the Haymarket anarchists a decade earlier, and Emma thought him "one of our most sincere and courageous comrades."[42] While Emma was giving her lecture, a policeman hurried over and ordered her to "stop her jabbering." After a heated exchange with the officer over freedom of speech, she was pulled off the platform and "literally thrown into" the patrol wagon. An angry sergeant told her, "Anarchists have no rights in this community," and she spent the night in jail.[43]

Goldman was passionately protective about freedom of speech, and fierce about fundamental American liberties. "It is Emma Goldman today," she wrote in *Free Society,* "but it may be you tomorrow and somebody else the next day."[44] She considered herself an easy scapegoat for a far greater threat to civil rights. "It is not Emma Goldman, it is not anarchy," that was being assailed, she warned. "It is liberty of speech. Let the newspapers take care. The next thing attacked will be the freedom of the press."[45]

Emma's relationship with Ed Brady ended in 1899, just before she departed on an eight-month lecture tour. They clashed constantly over basic views of convention and conduct, and over the parameters of their affair. She was tired of the strain. The tour was a welcome escape, and she visited sixty cities and towns, delivering 210 lectures to more than 50,000 people. She began in Barre, Vermont, which had an active anarchist group made up of stone and marble cutters from Carrara and other northern Italian towns who had transplanted their occupations and customs from Italy to New England. She moved briskly from city to city, then spent an entire month in Chicago, much of it in the company of Max Baginski. Emma had first met Baginski in Philadelphia in 1893, and when they saw each again in Chicago in the fall of 1897 they became good friends. In 1899 they became lovers.

Five years older than Goldman, Baginski had been born in East Prussia, not far from Koenigsberg, where Emma had lived as a child. His father was a shoemaker who had socialist leanings, and Max followed his father in both trade and political philosophy. Baginski was drawn to radical thought and began contributing to an activist paper, which got him two and a half years in Schweidnitz prison. Upon his release he went to Zürich, where he spent time with a number of well-regarded libertarian socialists, most notably Gustav Landauer and Alfred G. Sanftleben, who influenced his political and social views. He moved to Paris and gradually drifted from socialism to anarchism.

Baginski went on to London and then to America, where his older brother, Richard, also a socialist turned anarchist, had preceded him. Once in New York City, Max befriended some of Johann Most's disciples and began writing articles for *Freiheit.* In 1894 he went to Chicago to head the *Arbeiter–Zeitung,* the paper formerly edited by Haymarket anarchist August Spies. Goldman found Max a tremendously impressive person, intellectual and inspiring. Berkman would later call him one of the more estimable "personalities in our circle, understanding, clear minded, and most deeply intelligent."[46]

Renting a room near Lincoln Park, which Max christened their *Zauberschloss* (fairy-castle), the two were lovers for the duration of her stay. As Emma recalled, "The month in Chicago was filled with interesting work, the fine comradeship of new friends, and exquisite hours of joy and harmony with Max."[47] The relationship would come to naught; after Emma's visit, Max fell in love with Emilie Schumm, a sister of George Schumm, who was the assistant editor of Benjamin Tucker's *Liberty.* Max wrote to Emma to tell her that he and Millie were about to go abroad on an extended trip to celebrate their union. Emma was disappointed and hurt. "I laughed aloud at the folly of my hopes," she later wrote. "After the failure with Ed, how could I have dreamed of love and understanding with anyone else?"

But, she consoled herself, she still had her ideals to keep her stimulated, and the goals she had set out to accomplish. Ruefully, she said, "I would live and work without love."[48]

Emma traveled to Caplinger Mills, Missouri, invited to speak by anarchist writer Kate Austin, who had defended Berkman's attack on Frick in letters to mainstream newspapers and in the anarchist press, and continued to support his cause.[49] Goldman spent a week on the Austin farm with Kate, her husband, Sam, and their five children. Sam picked Emma up from the train station, situated twenty-two miles from the farm, and drove along a rough, bumpy road, first warning that he would have to tie her to the seat of the wagon, to prevent her from being "shaken out." Once at the farm, Sam instructed Kate to "Put her to bed right away and give her a hot drink else she'll hate us for the rest of her life for having taken her over that road."[50] Emma was treated to a hot bath and a massage; a passionate rebel she may have been, but she always enjoyed her luxuries.

During her visit with the Austins, Goldman's eyes were opened to the ways of the "small American farmer's life." As she later wrote, "they were at the mercy of the bankers and the railroads, not to speak of their natural enemies, storm and drought."[51] In Emma, Kate found a woman of "infinite sympathy and compassion." Neither a coward nor a hypocrite, wrote Austin, Goldman "is the incarnation of all the forces that have combated tyranny since the dawn of history, and that have paved the way for the little liberty we boast of today, and that some fools are satisfied with."[52]

Emma returned to Europe in November 1899, just as Berkman was plotting his prison breakout, intending to go to medical school in Switzerland with the funds provided by Herman Miller and Carl Schmidt. She stopped first in London, where she stayed with Harry Kelly and his companion Mary Krimont.[53] She paid another visit to Peter Kropotkin at his house in Bromley (the two squabbled pleasantly over her explicit approach to matters of sexuality, then decided their disagreement was a generational issue), and she went to Kropotkin's Russian New Year's party, attended by prominent members of London's radical Russian colony.

There she met Nicholas Chaikovsky, the leader of the Russian revolutionary youth in the 1870s; V. N. Cherkezov, a Georgian anarchist of princely blood; and L. B. Goldenberg, an old friend of the late Michael Bakunin, the celebrated anarchist and revolutionary. Also present at Kropotkin's house was Michael Hambourg, whose son, Jan, already a promising musician, would later marry Judge McClung's daughter Isabelle. Kropotkin played the piano while Cherkezov swung his twelve-year-old daughter around the floor and Emma danced happily with Chaikovsky. She relished speaking Russian with Kropotkin and his guests, later remarking, "I do not know of another language I like so well as Russian."[54]

While addressing several meetings in London's East End, Goldman became friendly with Rudolf Rocker, who edited a Yiddish anarchist paper, the *Arbayter Fraynd* (Workers' Friend). A German gentile by birth and upbringing, Rocker had never met a Jewish person until he moved to London at age eighteen, settled among the Jews, fell in love with a Jewish woman, learned to speak, read, and write Yiddish, and adopted Jewish customs. Berkman, who became close with him years later, thought Rocker "one of our very finest men and comrades." Rocker's companion, Milly Witkop, was also "a beautiful character," and the couple's abiding affection was, according to comrades, one of the great love stories in the history of the anarchist movement.[55]

One evening, while lecturing at the London Autonomie Club, Goldman met Hippolyte Havel, who would become her next serious companion.[56] Havel was a short, quirky man, with "large eyes gleaming in his pale face" and a fastidious appearance. He was, said Emma, "a veritable encyclopedia," well read in literature and history, and fluent in several languages.[57]

Havel had been born in 1869 in Bohemia, then part of the Austrian Empire, to a Czech father and a gypsy mother. He moved to Vienna for his education, where he became a journalist for the anarchist press. He was arrested in 1893 after delivering an incendiary May Day speech, for which he served eighteen months in prison, followed by deportation to his native town. He did not remain home for long, and soon was arrested again for taking part in a demonstration in Prague. Once freed, he wandered through Germany, lecturing and writing about anarchism. In the meantime his family moved to Vienna, but when he paid them a visit, he was discovered by the authorities and jailed for violating the terms of his deportation.[58]

Havel's situation took a worrisome turn when he was transferred from the jail to an insane asylum on the grounds that only a lunatic could reject the idea of government. He might have languished indefinitely in the asylum, but he had the good fortune to encounter Professor Richard von Krafft-Ebing, the famous psychologist, who happened to be touring the institution. Krafft-Ebing interviewed Havel during his rounds, and immediately informed the directors that they had made a mistake in committing Havel, telling them their patient "knows more about psychology than I do." The doctors protested that Havel was an anarchist, and therefore a deeply troubled individual. "He is saner than any of us," was the professor's reply, and he demanded that Havel be released.[59]

Out of the asylum but ejected from Vienna once again, Havel traveled to Zürich and Paris, where he continued his anarchist activity. He adopted an unusual approach, using performance art to spread his ideas. He would stand on a street corner holding up the bare, stretched ribs of an umbrella without a covering. When a sufficient number of spectators had gathered, he would begin to speak: "You may think I am crazy to be holding this open umbrella over my head, but I tell you I am no more ridiculous than is the society you live in." And then he would launch into his discourse on the evils of the world.[60]

Havel moved to London, supporting himself with odd jobs such as shining shoes and sweeping floors. At the time he met Goldman he was working in a boardinghouse, a job he despised. Although he had not been in London long, he already knew the city well and took Emma to see the sights. Soon they were an item. "Love," as Emma put it, "was making its claims again, daily growing more insistent."[61] Hippolyte agreed to go with her to Paris, where she was due to attend a number of events, including an International Anarchist Congress, and then accompany her to Switzerland for her medical training, although Emma's interest in becoming a doctor was fading rapidly.[62] The couple planned to live frugally on thirty dollars a month from the forty-dollar stipend Emma was still receiving from her sponsors Herman Miller and Carl Schmidt. The remaining ten dollars she sent to her younger brother Morris, known as "Moe," who himself was preparing to study medicine in New York.[63]

Goldman and Havel stayed in Paris for the next ten months. Their first weeks were particularly magical, as the couple was "completely engrossed in the wonders of the city and in each other." Paris, wrote Emma, was a "world of beauty . . . created by the genius of man. . . . Every street, every stone almost, had its revolutionary story, every district its heroic legend."[64] They became acquainted with eminent European anarchists such as Victor

Dave, and spent time with Max Baginski, who was visiting with Millie. Goldman and Havel attended a number of conventions, including two organized by Paul Robin, a pioneer of population control. When Emma eventually returned to New York, her luggage was stuffed with great quantities of contraceptives and related birth control literature provided by her European friends.[65]

Goldman's chief business in Paris, the International Anarchist Congress, scheduled for September 1900, did not take place. On July 29, 1900, Italian anarchist Gaetano Bresci assassinated King Umberto I of Italy. In response, the French authorities cracked down on all anarchist gatherings, although Emma and some of her comrades met secretly in private homes outside Paris.[66]

Bresci had been born in Tuscany in 1869 and emigrated to Paterson, New Jersey, where he worked in the silk mills as a weaver and helped found an Italian-language paper. Emma had known him as an active member of the Diritto all' Esistenza (Right to Existence) Group. Angered by the firing of cannons on demonstrators protesting the high price of bread in Milan, Bresci returned to Italy, tracked down the king in Monza, and shot at him with a revolver, hitting him multiple times. At his trial, Bresci was represented by Emma's comrade, the anarchist lawyer Francesco Saverio Merlino, and was sentenced to hard labor at Santo Stefano prison on Ventotene Island. To Goldman it was Bresci's "overflowing sympathy with human suffering" that made him "strike down one of the world's tyrants," and she eulogized his act as that of a hero.[67] "King Umberto," she said, "was justly put to death by a brave man who dared to act for the good of his fellow men, among whom he considered himself but a unit in a universe."[68]

Goldman and Havel remained in Paris for a few more months. During that time Emma's benefactors at last realized that she showed no signs of going to Switzerland to begin her medical education. She received an angry letter from Carl Schmidt in Detroit. "I thought it was understood when you left for Europe," he wrote, "that you were to go to Switzerland to study medicine. It was solely for that purpose that Herman and I offered to give you an allowance. I now learn that you are at your old propaganda and with a new lover. Surely you do not expect us to support you with either." Goldman replied, perhaps ungraciously, "Emma Goldman the woman and her ideas are inseparable. She does not exist for the amusement of upstarts, nor will she permit anybody to dictate to her. Keep your money." To add insult to injury, she soon thereafter hocked his gift, the clamshell gold watch, for ten dollars.[69]

In December 1900, as the French authorities were looking askance at her presence, Goldman went home to New York, and brought Havel with her. She rented a room at 195 Clinton Street on the Lower East Side and returned to her nursing duties, with patients recommended by Doctors Hoffmann and Solotaroff. Havel had difficulty finding work. He had hoped to get a job with a Czech newspaper, but it paid no wages, and eventually he went to Chicago to assist with Max Baginski's journal *Arbeiter-Zeitung.* There he remained for the next few years.

For the time being, Emma was single again. She had not been in contact with Ed Brady since breaking off their affair, but friends had informed her that he was now married and had a daughter (although he had once expressed a pronounced aversion to children). She ran into him again while visiting Justus Schwab, who had fallen ill with tuberculosis. The fifty-three-year-old Schwab was in grave condition, and it was clear that he did not have long to live. While Emma was paying her respects at Schwab's home, Ed Brady arrived, and, after some awkward moments, they talked about his child. This topic, said Emma, sent Brady "launching into a poem over his little daughter and enlarging upon her charm and remarkable intelligence." As Goldman later wrote, "I was amused to see that baby-hater waxing so enthusiastic."[70]

When the time came to leave, she and Brady parted as friends. Schwab died four days later, on December 17, 1900. At his funeral, John Swinton and an emotional Johann Most delivered the eulogies.[71] The gathering, held at the Labor Lyceum on East Fourth Street, was attended by 2,000 mourners who afterward followed the hearse down Second Avenue. "The procession passed the saloon where Schwab had lived," reported the *New York Times,* and "along the route the windows of the tenements were filled with people."[72]

Schwab was not the only friend Emma lost during this period. While she was in Paris, she learned that prominent architect and anarchist John Edelmann had died of a heart attack at the age of forty-eight. Swinton would die one year after Schwab. And several years earlier, Robert Reitzel had been stricken with spinal tuberculosis, which had paralyzed his lower limbs. After months of pain and physical deterioration, two of his close friends, aware that all hope was gone, had relieved him of his suffering by injecting him with poison. He died on March 31, 1898, at the age of forty-nine. "Ein Stern ist erloschen," wrote *Sturmvogel* of his passing; a star has been extinguished.[73]

12

THE ASSASSINATION OF McKINLEY

ON MAY 5, 1901, Emma was in Cleveland, speaking in Memorial Hall on the "Modern Phases of Anarchism." She had set off on another national tour several months after returning to the States, in part to earn some money. "I am as poor as a churchmouse," she wrote a friend.[1] In Memorial Hall, Goldman told the crowd that anarchists "demand the fullest and most complete liberty for each and every person to work out his own salvation upon any line that he pleases so long as he does not interfere with the happiness of others." She denied that anarchists favored violence, but nonetheless defended Sante Caserio, who assassinated French president Carnot; Michele Angiolillo who, incensed by the arbitrary imprisonment and brutal torture of hundreds of Spanish anarchists in Montjuich Fortress in retaliation for a bomb thrown anonymously into a Barcelona procession, shot and killed Spanish prime minister Antonio Canovas del Castillo; and Gaetano Bresci, who murdered King Umberto.[2]

Goldman broke for a brief intermission before taking questions from the floor. During the recess, she noticed a young man looking over the books and pamphlets on sale near the platform. He approached her and asked if she would suggest something for him to read. As she made a selection, she was struck by his winsome appearance and his "large blue eyes," later writing, "it was his face that held me, a most sensitive face . . . his striking face remained in my memory." It was not the last time she would encounter him.[3]

Emma went on to Chicago, staying nearly two months with Abe and Mary Isaak, who had moved from San Francisco to a place on Carroll Avenue, "a large house which was the center of anarchist activities" in the city.[4] While she was there, word arrived that Gaetano Bresci had died in prison, apparently a suicide, and Emma wrote a eulogy in *Free Society*. "He has lived and died, true to himself," she said, "and the world will have to learn that while one Bresci is killed, hundreds are born ready to lay down their lives to free mankind from tyranny, power, ignorance, and poverty."[5]

On July 12 Emma was preparing to leave Chicago for New York. She planned to go to the Pan-American Exposition in Buffalo, and then to Rochester to see her siblings and other members of her family. She had invited young Mary, the Isaaks's teenaged daughter, to join her. As the two were packing for the trip, the doorbell rang, a visitor for Emma. He identified himself as Fred Nieman, and Goldman recognized him as the blue-eyed man from Memorial Hall. They chatted pleasantly, and he accompanied her on the elevated train to the railway station where Max Baginski, Hippolyte Havel, and Abe Isaak waited to say farewell to her and Mary. Before she boarded, Emma asked them to look after Nieman and introduce him around. Her friends, though, did not find Nieman quite so appealing, and Baginski grumbled over Goldman's new acquaintance. "There is a fellow from Cleveland here who asks very peculiar questions," he said. "If we do not wish to be bored by him, we must make our escape."[6]

Abe Isaak was friendlier. After Mary and Emma departed, he chatted with Nieman for forty minutes or so. Nieman addressed Isaak as "comrade," saying that he had been a socialist in Cleveland and had learned about anarchism from Goldman's May 5 speech. He had come to Chicago, he explained, to uncover the anarchist "secret societies." Isaak was perplexed. "But we have no secret societies," he said. "We have nothing to hide and don't fear the light."[7]

Despite Nieman's odd demeanor, Isaak offered to help him find a job and lodgings, and invited him to his house for dinner the following evening. Nieman accepted but did not show up, and Isaak soon heard that he had left the city. Other anarchists had encountered Nieman during his stay in Chicago. Anarchist cobbler Clemens Pfuetzner told his friend, the social worker Jane Addams, that Nieman had visited every anarchist he could find in Chicago, asking them for "the password." Of course, no password existed, and they turned him away, some with disgust and all with a certain degree of impatience, viewing Nieman as the type of ill-balanced man who was always "hanging around the movement, without the slightest conception of its meaning."[8]

Nieman had behaved in a similar way in Cleveland, seeking out anarchists and asking peculiar and intrusive questions. Emil Schilling, the treasurer of the Cleveland Liberty Association, had met Nieman on May 19 and treated him kindly, giving him a book about the Haymarket anarchists and some issues of *Free Society,* and asking him to dinner. But when they met again, Schilling became alarmed. Nieman showed an obsessive interest in anarchist secret societies, and kept asking if the American anarchists were planning any acts such as Bresci's assassination of King Umberto of Italy. Schilling conferred with his friends, who told him that Nieman was not an anarchist, but had briefly belonged to the Socialist Labor Party. When Nieman approached Shilling a week later, seeking a letter of introduction to Goldman, Shilling refused to give him one, but informed Nieman that Goldman had gone to Chicago.[9]

In August, back in Cleveland after his trip to Chicago, Nieman visited Schilling for the fourth and final time. As before, he seemed unstable, preoccupied with violence and assassination. Something in his behavior caused Schilling to write to Abe Isaak, suggesting that Nieman might be a spy. Eventually, at Schilling's request, Isaak printed a warning in the September issue of *Free Society.* "Attention," it read. "The attention of the comrades is called to another spy. He is well dressed, of medium height, rather narrow shouldered, blond, and about twenty-five years of age. Up to the present he has made his appearance in Chicago and Cleveland. In the former place he remained but a short time, while in Cleveland he disappeared when the comrades had confirmed themselves of his identity, and were on the point of exposing him. His demeanor is of the usual sort, pretending to be greatly interested in the cause, asking for names or soliciting aid for acts of contemplated violence. If this same individual makes his appearance elsewhere, the comrades are warned in advance, and can act accordingly."[10]

GOLDMAN, MEANWHILE, HAD BEEN HAVING a lovely holiday. She had visited the Pan-American Exposition grounds in Buffalo, and was spending time in Rochester with Mary Isaak; her brother Morris and his college friends, one of whom, a nineteen-year-old named Dan, became her lover; her sisters Helena and Lena; and her nieces and nephews.[11] At home in Manhattan and on the road, Emma rarely interacted with children. She had once contemplated having a baby, writing in her memoir, "I had loved children madly, ever since I could remember," and imagined "the mystery and wonder of motherhood." But her father's gross violence and animosity toward his children had scarred her, and she worried about the "thousands of children born unwanted, marred and maimed by poverty and still more by ignorant misunderstanding."[12]

She also was aware that her work as an activist left little room for parenting, and she was "determined to serve [her ideal] completely . . . unhampered and untied." A medical condition similar to endometriosis was also a deterrent. Ultimately, she decided to "find an outlet for my mother-need in the love of *all* children."[13] In Rochester with her nieces and nephews, she relished the "new and exhilarating experience" of playing their games and enjoying their fresh perspectives. "The roof of Helena's house became our garden and gathering place," she wrote, "where my youthful friends confided to me their dreams and aspirations."[14]

As the summer came to an end, and Mary was getting ready to return home to Chicago, Goldman received the September issue of *Free Society* and saw Abe Isaak's warning about Nieman. Fuming—she had been quite taken with the ingratiating young man—Emma wrote to Abe Isaak demanding more proof that Nieman was a spy or troublemaker. Isaak replied that Nieman was untrustworthy "because he constantly talked about acts of violence," but eventually he agreed to print a retraction.[15]

At the start of September 1901 Emma received word that Sasha was again allowed visitors after nine years, and she went straight to Allegheny City for their bittersweet reunion. Afterward she traveled to St. Louis, where Carl Nold picked her up at the train station. Emma had not seen Carl for three years, and they caught up as he brought her to the house where she would be staying in the city. He was living in St. Louis, working as a machinist, and was active in the anarchist movement. She confided in Carl about the "ghastly visit" at the prison, when Sasha had been so strained and silent, and Nold explained the effects of prolonged solitary confinement. "A whole year of enforced isolation," Nold said, "never a chance to exchange a word with another human being, or to hear a kindly voice. You grow numb and incapable of giving expression to your longing for human contact."[16]

A few days later, on the afternoon of September 6, 1901, Emma was about to board a streetcar when she heard the news that President McKinley had been shot. The president's condition was serious. She jumped aboard the car and met up with Nold to discuss the development. McKinley, they discovered, had been attacked in Buffalo at the Pan-American Exposition by a man called Leon Czolgosz. Neither Goldman nor Nold had ever heard the name. Czolgosz was said to be an anarchist. It was fortunate, remarked Carl, that Emma was in St. Louis and not in Buffalo; otherwise the press and the authorities would undoubtedly try to connect her with the crime.[17]

LEON CZOLGOSZ, TWENTY-EIGHT YEARS OLD, was born in Michigan in 1873 to Polish immigrant parents. For some time he had worked at a Cleveland wire mill as a machinist. In 1898 he left the mill and went to live on the family farm near Warrensville, Ohio, twelve miles from Cleveland. In August he traveled to Buffalo, where he purchased a short-barreled 32-caliber revolver. On the afternoon of September 6, a hot and sunny day, McKinley was holding a public reception in the Temple of Music on the Pan-American Exposition grounds. McKinley had been reelected the previous year, with Theodore Roosevelt now serving as his vice president. Czolgosz entered the long line of people waiting to shake hands with the president. He was carrying the revolver, wrapped in a handkerchief, which was made to look like a bandage covering his hand. His soft features and mild bearing helped camouflage his purpose.

Shortly after four o'clock, Czolgosz reached the head of the line and McKinley held out his hand. Czolgosz raised the revolver and fired twice in rapid succession. Immediately a group of soldiers and secret service agents flung themselves on the assailant and knocked him to the ground. Before an irate crowd, Czolgosz was quickly restrained and removed to police headquarters.[18] McKinley, bleeding profusely from the abdomen, was rushed to nearby doctor Matthew D. Mann, trained in obstetrics and gynecology, who soon received assistance from several other physicians in the area.[19] At 5:20 the president underwent surgery.

Headlines blared the news that the president had been shot. The next day the *New York Times* published a lengthy account of the wounded McKinley's "illustrious career" and "brilliant record." The paper detailed the president's Scottish ancestry, his childhood in Ohio, his service in the Civil War, and his record as a congressman and governor. It recounted his two campaign battles against William Jennings Bryan, and his accomplishments and challenges in the White House, among them the acquisition of Hawaii, the Spanish-American War, his tariff policies, and his fight for the gold standard. "A gallant soldier, himself," said the *Times*, "his disposition has always been toward peace."[20]

Immediately after the shooting, Czolgosz was formally arrested and interrogated by the police. Asked to explain his act, he made the following written statement: "I killed President McKinley because I done my duty. I didn't believe one man should have so much service and another man should have none." "What was your motive?" asked Erie County District Attorney Thomas Penney. "I am an anarchist," Czolgosz replied, "a disciple of Emma Goldman. Her words set me on fire."[21]

Czolgosz had met Goldman twice, he said, once at a lecture she gave in Cleveland and once while escorting her to the train station in Chicago. He insisted, however, that he had acted alone and had no accomplices. "I had no confidants—no one to help me. I was alone absolutely," he said. "I knew Emma Goldman and some others in Chicago, and I heard Emma Goldman speak in Cleveland. None of these people ever told me to kill anybody. Nobody told me that. I done it all myself. Emma Goldman, in her lecture, did not say that rulers should be assassinated. She did not mention Presidents but only government—that she did not believe in it. She did not tell me to kill McKinley. I had decided to do it . . . [because] McKinley was going around the country shouting prosperity when there was no prosperity for the poor man."[22]

Gaetano Bresci, it appeared, had been Czolgosz's chief inspiration; he had become fascinated with the assassination of King Umberto after seeing a newspaper account of the crime. Keeping the clipping in his pocket, he read it over and over again, captivated by the boldness with which Bresci had stalked and shot his quarry. It was this incident that pushed him to become an anarchist.

"I don't believe in a Republican form of government and I don't believe we should have any rulers," Czolgosz told the police. "It is right to kill them. I had that idea when I shot the President, and that is why I was there. I planned to kill the President three or four days after I came to Buffalo. Something I read in *Free Society* suggested the idea. I thought it would be a good thing for the country to kill the President. I don't believe in voting; it is against my principles. I am an anarchist; I don't believe in marriage. I believe in free love. I fully understand what I was doing when I shot the President. I realize that I was sacrificing my life. I am willing to take the consequences."[23]

In spite of Czolgosz's insistence that he acted alone, many blamed anarchists as a group for instigating the assassination. Rumors were soon afloat that an anarchist plot had been hatched by Peter Kropotkin and Emma Goldman with Czolgosz as their chosen agent. Hull House in Chicago, where Kropotkin had stayed in April 1901 during his second American tour, was alleged to have been the scene of their "secret, murderous meetings."[24] Kropotkin was greatly disturbed by the accusation, in large part because of the repressions suffered by his Chicago comrades.

On the night of September 6, several hours after McKinley was shot, a group of Chicago detectives raided the Isaak house at 515 Carroll Street. Correspondence and issues of *Free Society* were collected, along with private letters, photographs, and other personal items. As the *New York Times* reported, "a quantity of Anarchistic literature, pictures of Emma Goldman and others, and copies of 'red' newspapers were seized."[25] The detectives smashed Isaak's printing press and confiscated his books, including his volumes of Shakespeare. Isaak was then arrested, along with his son, Abe Jr., a chief contributor to the journal.

Police also arrested and jailed Hippolyte Havel and several other Chicago anarchists, including Irish-born labor activist Jay Fox, Enrico Travaglio, Clemens Pfuetzner, and Alfred Schneider. The men were placed in a paddy wagon and taken to the Harrison Street Station. Abe's wife and daughter initially were left in the house, but shortly afterward were brought to the station along with a woman called Julia Mechanic who lived with the Isaaks, and all three were detained overnight. They were released the next day on $3,000 bail each. The men were booked and charged with conspiracy to kill the president. They were denied counsel and held without bail for seventeen days until Jane Addams intervened on their behalf.[26]

But Emma Goldman was the main target. The authorities were convinced that she had compelled Czolgosz to commit the crime—he had, after all, identified himself as her disciple in his confession—and they launched a nationwide search in an effort to track her down. The state of New York alone employed 200 detectives and spent $30,000 in its determination to link her with the murder. Her Rochester relatives were placed under surveillance, and her favorite spots in New York were carefully watched, but there was no sign of her. She was said to be in the Midwest, possibly in Chicago or St. Louis. But in neither of these cities were the police able to locate her, although she had been in St. Louis since September 2.[27]

On September 7, while running an errand in a stationery store, Goldman caught sight of a newspaper headline: "ASSASSIN of PRESIDENT McKINLEY an ANARCHIST. CONFESSES TO HAVING BEEN INCITED by EMMA GOLDMAN. WOMAN ANARCHIST WANTED." Buying a bunch of papers, she went to a restaurant to study them. As she read, she came across a picture of the assassin, the man she had met in Cleveland and Chicago. "Why that's Nieman," she exclaimed.[28] "Nieman," or "niemand," Emma might have realized, translated from German as "Nobody."

The press, as well as the police, was ready to connect her to the assassination attempt. A "wrinkled, ugly Russian woman," the *New York World* described her, she was determined to "kill all the rulers" that she could. "It was she who inspired McKinley's assassination, working in secret with slayers who are singled out from her body of anarchists. She has been in more than one plot to kill."[29] Citizens in cities and towns formed watch groups and organized searches to assist in Goldman's capture, and many angry letters were posted to the authorities. A Philadelphia lawyer wrote to Philander C. Knox, the U.S. attorney general and former counsel of Carnegie Steel, urging him to arrest Goldman as an accessory to Czolgosz's crime, for it was she who "sowed the diabolic seed" that led to the assassination. A doctor in Indiana suggested to his congressman that someone be sent to the Western Penitentiary to "Get the right side of Berkman" and determine if Emma Goldman had played a role in the conspiracy.[30]

Goldman had become the most wanted person in the country. To many, she was America's "most dangerous woman," a purveyor of immorality, murder, and revolution. Still, she remained at large, undetected as she moved about St. Louis. But when she learned of the raid on the Isaaks' home and the multiple arrests, she decided to go to Chicago in an effort to help her comrades. The police, she felt, were using her friends as pawns to reach her.[31]

The next day Emma boarded a train to Chicago. Tucked away in her berth, she could hear nearby passengers talking about her situation, describing her as "a beast, a bloodthirsty monster!" She thought about leaping forward and surprising her fellow travelers, but later wrote, "I did not have the heart to cause them such a shock and I remained behind my curtain."[32] Arriving in Chicago on September 8, she stayed briefly with Max and Millie Baginski, who were concerned about her safety. She then moved to the apartment of Charles G. Norris, the son of a well-to-do minister, at 303 Sheffield Avenue. Neither Norris nor his wife were known to be anarchists, and they were not at home when Goldman arrived, but they had left her a key, and she spent the night in peace.

The next morning the apartment was raided by policemen under the command of Captain Herman Schuettler, "a famous anarchist-hunter" who had arrested Louis Lingg during the Haymarket days. When he tried to question Goldman, she pretended to be a Swedish maid unable to speak English. The police searched the apartment as she watched, until one of the detectives discovered a fountain pen embossed with the name "Emma Goldman." Emma stepped forward. "The game is up," she said. "Well, I'll be damned," said the captain. "You're the shrewdest crook I ever met!"[33]

Goldman was arrested and brought to the Harrison Street Station, where she was questioned for eight hours. She admitted that Czolgosz had attended her lecture in Cleveland, but insisted, "I never advocated violence. I never knew the man." And while she acknowledged she had met him again in Chicago, she said that a half-hour was all the time they had spent together. Emma, moreover, vehemently denied that she had inspired Czolgosz or that she had played any part in the attack on the president. "I am an anarchist—a student of socialism, but nothing in anything I ever said to Leon Czolgosz knowingly would have led him to do the act," she said. "Am I accountable because some crack-brained person put a wrong construction on my words? Leon Czolgosz, I am convinced, planned the deed unaided and entirely alone. There is no anarchist ring which would help him." When asked her opinion of the crime, she waved her hands and replied, "I thought, 'Oh, the fool.'"[34]

Goldman, however, displayed little pity for the dying president. She told reporters massing at the police station that she would be willing to nurse the wounded McKinley if she were called upon to do so, though her sympathies were with Czolgosz, who had committed his act for an ideal, the good of the people. She dismissed President McKinley as "the most insignificant ruler that this country has ever had," one who possessed "neither wit nor intelligence, but has been a tool in the hands of Mark Hanna," the Republican Ohio senator and McKinley's influential one-time campaign manager. Of Czolgosz, she said, "I feel very deeply with him as an individual who suffers. If I had the means I would help him as far as I could. I would see that he had counsel and that justice was done him."[35]

Emma's expression of sympathy for Czolgosz, as McKinley struggled for life, outraged the American public. Once behind bars Emma, or "Beast Goldman," as she was often addressed, received a flood of unsigned hate letters accusing her of attacking "our beloved president." "You damn bitch of an anarchist," one of them read. "I wish I could get at you. I would tear your heart out and feed it to my dog." Another declared, "We will cut your tongue out, soak your carcass in oil, and burn you alive." The descriptions of what some writers said they would do to her sexually, said Emma, "offered studies in perversion that would have astounded authorities on the subject."[36]

In the meantime, District Attorney Penney attempted to extradite Emma to Buffalo to be tried for conspiracy. The Chicago authorities refused to comply. Instead she was placed under $20,000 bail. Added to the $15,000 for the Isaak group, it was too large a sum for their friends to raise for her freedom, and Emma was transferred to the Cook County Jail, where the Haymarket anarchists had once been confined. On her way to the jail in a patrol wagon, a policeman who was holding her arm made some insulting remarks. Goldman reprimanded the officer and demanded the release of her arm. In return he struck her in the mouth, knocking out one of her teeth and covering her face with blood.[37]

On September 14, McKinley died. The whole country had been anxiously monitoring every change in his condition, and for a while it seemed he would recover. But infection led to gangrene, and he took a turn for the worse on September 12. He died at the age of fifty-eight, in the home of Exposition head John Milburn. With McKinley's passing, Theodore Roosevelt was sworn in as president. Ten days later, Czolgosz was tried and convicted for murder and condemned to death. On the morning of October 29, 1901, he was electrocuted in Auburn Prison.

Goldman was released from the Cook County Jail on September 24, no evidence having been found to connect her with Czolgosz's act.

Charges against the other anarchists, including the Isaaks, also were dismissed. "We have just had a taste of howling reaction here," wrote Abe Isaak Jr. to Max Nettlau on October 7. "A number of us served seventeen days in jail, being held on the absurd charge of conspiracy to kill the president. As you know Emma was in it too. She is now staying with us. She asked me to send you her regards."[38]

But the "howling reaction" had not yet ended. The assassination of McKinley touched off a fierce reaction, a "stamping out craze," a "Saint Bartholomew of the Anarchists."[39] Public outrage and fear reached a far greater intensity than it had after the Haymarket affair or the attack on Frick. Anarchists were hunted, arrested, and persecuted throughout the country. Homes and clubrooms were raided and possessions confiscated. Many anarchists lost their jobs and lodgings and were subjected to violence and abuse. Bresci and Czolgosz, one clergyman noted, "have revealed the existence of secret forces of a terrifyingly destructive nature."[40]

In New York the offices of the *Fraye Arbeter Shtime* on Henry Street were wrecked by an angry mob, although its editor, Saul Yanovsky, who was afterward cornered and beaten in a neighborhood restaurant, had repudiated the assassination. In Pittsburgh, Harry Gordon was dragged out into the street and almost lynched but was saved when someone shouted, "He's a union man. Let him go!"[41] Bands of vigilantes invaded the mining and mill towns of western Pennsylvania and southern Illinois, including Spring Valley, where Goldman had once spoken at a Labor Day picnic, standing on a barrel to deliver her speech and later baptizing the babies of French, Belgian, and Italian comrades in the "true anarchist fashion," with names not of religious saints but of rebels and popular heroes.[42] Now the mobs drove out all suspected anarchists and their families. In Philadelphia, anarchists faced persistent harassment, and many suspended their activities or left the movement altogether as a result. Voltairine de Cleyre declared herself sickened by the hysteria, and denounced the repressions at a Haymarket commemoration when the remaining stalwarts, forbidden to rent a hall in Philadelphia, gathered in a private home.[43] "Steadily, steadily, the light [toward freedom] has grown," said de Cleyre. "And I saw it boldly, notwithstanding the recent outburst of condemnation, notwithstanding the cry of lynch, burn, shoot, imprison, deport, and the Scarlet Letter A to be branded low down upon the forehead."[44]

The West Coast also had its share of persecution. In Tacoma, a day after McKinley died, a Loyal League was formed by members of the Grand Army of the Republic, pledging "to accomplish the utter annihilation of anarchists and anarchistic teachings within the borders of North America, and to prevent disloyalty to the existing form of government." Its immediate objective was to storm the nearby Home Colony and burn it down. Captain Ed Lorenz, however, owner of the steamer *Typhoon,* which carried passengers and freight to the colony, refused to charter his boat to the League and convinced the would-be vigilantes that he knew Home as a quiet community of good and peaceful folk.[45]

In Rochester, Emma's family suffered some unpleasant consequences. Her father was shunned by his neighbors and at his synagogue, and he lost customers at his furniture store. Her niece Stella, the daughter of her sister Lena, was summoned to the police station for a day of questioning about "Aunt Emma." Stella told the police she had faith in her aunt and was proud of her. (Throughout her adult life, Stella was one of Emma's closest confidantes.) Lena's sons, Harry and Saxe, were teased at school by classmates and teachers, who told them, "Your aunt Emma Goldman is a murderess." Harry, a Republican who had idolized McKinley, was profoundly upset by the president's violent death, and was humiliated by his family's perceived connection to it, while Saxe expressed feelings of fear and confusion.[46]

The retaliation even reached inside the Western Penitentiary. On the day McKinley was shot, the president of the Board of Inspectors ordered Berkman locked up in solitary confinement, although the warden soon intervened and sent him back to work on the range. Sasha was greatly relieved. He had little strength left for solitary, and wrote to Emma, "It is almost like liberty to have the freedom of the cell-house." He wished to serve the rest of his time without trouble, and had no plans for another breakout. As he told Emma, "my weakened condition and the unexpected shortening of my sentence have at last decided me to abandon the idea of escape."[47]

Back in New York, Johann Most, too, felt the impact. On September 5, the day before McKinley was shot, Most's latest edition of *Freiheit* had featured "Mord contra Mord" (Murder against Murder), an essay on political violence written in 1849 by German radical Karl Heinzen. "Despots are outlaws," Heinzen stated. "We say murder the murderers. Save humanity through blood, poison, and iron. If you have to blow up half a continent and pour out a sea of blood in order to destroy the party of the barbarians, have no scruple of conscience." Most noted parenthetically that Heinzen's views "are still true today."[48]

The next day, when Most heard of the attack on McKinley, he immediately ordered the paper withdrawn from circulation, but a copy had fallen into the hands of the New York police. Although there was no discernible connection between the Heinzen article and Czolgosz, Most was arrested and brought to trial on charges of "disturbing the public peace" and "outraging public decency." Anarchists in New York appealed to labor unions for assistance and formed a committee called the Workingmen's Defense Association, with Ed Brady serving as treasurer. Morris Hillquit, the prominent labor lawyer and socialist leader, served as Most's attorney, and pointed out that Heinzen had been dead for twenty years; that his article had been directed against the crowned heads of Europe a half-century ago; that it had been reprinted several times since its initial publication; and that only one copy of Most's paper had been sold—to the policeman who had made the arrest.

The court nevertheless sentenced Most to a year in prison on Blackwell's Island, his third term there. Though fifty-five and in ill health, he was put to work in the blacksmith shop, where he turned the wheel of a drill press. Papers and books were prohibited him and visitors allowed only once a month. He emerged from Blackwell's, wrote Hillquit, "a broken man, sluggish, cynical, and indifferent," no longer the former "spirited and impetuous Johann Most" known to the anarchist crowd.[49]

For months the country remained in the grip of frenzy, set off by the trauma of losing the president and compounded by long-brewing hostilities toward radical movements and immigrants in general. "After the death of McKinley," said Goldman, "the campaign against anarchism and its adherents continued with increased venom. The press, the pulpit, and other public mouthpieces were frantically vying with each other in their fury against the common enemy."[50]

As the suppression continued unabated, many anarchists felt that Czolgosz had done their cause much harm. "So some fool has shot the president," wrote J. William Lloyd, a poet and doctor, to his comrade, businessman Henry Bool, "and given another excuse to the repression of liberty."[51] At Home Colony, James F. Morton, the editor of *Discontent,* had been opposed to McKinley's policies, but deplored the assassination and denied that it was the logical result of anarchist teaching. "If I thought that Anarchy led to assassination, I would not be an Anarchist," he said.[52] Czolgosz's act, wrote Moses Harman in *Lucifer,* was "that of an insane man," a "stupid, idiotic crime." Harman, however, condemned Czolgosz's "slaughter at Auburn [Prison]," calling Czolgosz "a victim of civilized vengeance."[53]

GOLDMAN REMAINED STAUNCHLY SUPPORTIVE of Czolgosz, despite the preponderance of criticism in her community, and despite the reprisals against her comrades. She was distressed by the enmity she saw from anarchists, and she defended the young killer with unflagging passion. "Czolgosz," she wrote, "was a man with the beautiful soul of a child and the energy of a giant," one who acted out of "a strong social instinct . . . and an overflow of sympathy with the pain and sorrow around us" rather than with "cruelty, or a thirst for blood." She expressed regret that "so many even in the radical ranks have lost their manhood and womanhood at the sight of Government and Power let loose." McKinley, she said, was "president of the money kings and trust magnates," a "modern Caesar" struck down by a Brutus.[54]

A few anarchist journals published by French, Italian, Spanish, and Czech immigrants also defended Czolgosz.[55] American-born Kate Austin identified Czolgosz's act "as the supreme protest of a brave and generous heart against the curse of government." Voltairine de Cleyre showed tolerance for Czolgosz, although she admitted comprehending little about his beliefs or motivation. And Abe Isaak Jr. retracted the charge in *Free Society* that Czolgosz was a spy. "No matter what opinion one may have of Czolgosz," he wrote, "it will be admitted that he was not a spy. For that note, I offer to Leon F. Czolgosz, hated and despised as he is by all the world, an apology."[56]

But most of Goldman's comrades were appalled by the crime, and were growing increasingly irritated and impatient with Emma's fervid, unchecked praise for the killer. As anarchist writer and publisher Ross Winn told Jo

Labadie, "I most heartily agree with you that we should condemn all violence, except when clearly in self-defense, and on this point I think Emma Goldman's position perfectly absurd."[57]

Much to Emma's surprise, Sasha, typically her most steadfast ally, disapproved of the crime. Up until now he had continued to glorify attentats on principle, remaining a firm believer in the effectiveness of individual acts of violence, and had endorsed Bresci's assassination of King Umberto. "He did well," was Berkman's reaction to Bresci, "and the agitation resulting from his act may advance the Cause."[58] But in the case of Czolgosz, he saw the murder as futile, differentiating it from his own attack on Frick.

"I do not believe that this deed was terroristic," Sasha wrote to Emma, "and I doubt whether it was educational, because the social necessity for its performance was not manifest." McKinley, Sasha felt, was not a "direct and immediate enemy of the people." Drastic methods such as violence and assassination, Sasha wrote, should be sought "only as a last extremity," and "the battle should be waged in the economic rather than the political field. It is therefore that I regard my own act as far more significant and educational than Leon's. It was directed against a tangible, real oppressor, visualized as such by the people."[59]

Emma was shocked by this argument—and sobbed when she received Sasha's letter—since to her, both the attack on Frick and the assassination of McKinley were inspired by the same ideals and spirit of self-sacrifice. Sasha's criticism, she thought, resembled what Johann Most had leveled against Berkman in the Frick affair. Emma remained profoundly troubled, and the Czolgosz case, like those of Haymarket and of Homestead, would torment her for the rest of her days.[60]

Emma Goldman and Alexander Berkman in New York City, February 1918, awaiting their return to prison for obstructing the draft. International Film Service.

The teenaged Emma Goldman in 1886. Emma Goldman Collection, International Institute of Social History, Amsterdam.

Alexander Berkman on March 23, 1892, four months before the assassination attempt on Henry Clay Frick. Courtesy of Magda Boris Schoenwetter, Paul Avrich Private Collection.

Modest Stein in New York City, circa 1900. In his youth, the artist and anarchist Modska Aronstam made up a third of the trio with his cousin Alexander Berkman and Emma Goldman. Goldman admired the "dreamy expression" in his eyes. Courtesy of Luba Stein Benenson, Paul Avrich Private Collection.

The Haymarket anarchist Louis Lingg shortly before his suicide by dynamite capsule in the Cook County jail on November 10, 1887. ICHi-03693, Chicago History Museum.

Carl Nold. The affable, German-born anarchist, who was sentenced to five years in prison for the Frick conspiracy, was known to wear "the truly Anarchistic style of hair, pompadour, dark mustache." Labadie Collection, University of Michigan.

The Attentat. Alexander Berkman's attempt to assassinate Frick, as depicted in *Harper's Weekly*, August 6, 1892.

Alexander Berkman on July 24, 1892, the day after his arrest, photographed by noted Pittsburgh photographer B. L. H. Dabbs. Library of Congress.

Emma Goldman in 1892. Emma Goldman Collection, International Institute of Social History, Amsterdam.

Chicago doctor Ben Reitman, longtime lover of Goldman, circa 1912. Library of Congress.

Emma Goldman in St. Louis, 1912. Courtesy of Hilda Adel, Paul Avrich Private Collection.

Alexander Berkman addresses a crowd in Union Square, April 11, 1914. Library of Congress.

Young anarchist Becky Edelsohn, taken to the Tarrytown jail on June 6, 1914. Library of Congress.

Charles Plunkett in 1914. After a youth spent in radical activity, Plunkett became a distinguished academic in the field of biology. Library of Congress.

Arthur Caron in 1914. Caron, a conspirator in the plot against John D. Rockefeller Jr., died in the Lexington Avenue explosion on July 4, 1914. Library of Congress.

Scene of the Lexington Avenue explosion, July 4, 1914. Library of Congress.

Alexander Berkman and Marie Ganz (center) preside over a mass meeting in Manhattan's Mulberry Park, May 1, 1914. Library of Congress.

Alexander Berkman (with cane), Charles Plunkett (at left) Becky Edelsohn (center, in white hat), Louise Berger (no hat), and their comrades attend the service for those killed in the Lexington Avenue explosion, July 1914. Library of Congress.

David Caplan and Matthew Schmidt, comrades on the run. Courtesy of Pauline Turkel, Paul Avrich Private Collection.

Emma Goldman's rustic retreat in Ossining, New York. A gift from benefactor Bolton Hall, the cottage was used as a vacation home and safe house. Courtesy of Ingrid and Kurt Fetz, Paul Avrich Private Collection.

Emma Goldman and Alexander Berkman on the day of their conviction, July 9, 1917. Department of Defense, National Archives.

Alexander Berkman on Ellis Island, facing deportation to Russia, December 1919. Library of Congress.

Emma Goldman on Ellis Island, facing deportation to Russia, December 1919. National Park Service, Ellis Island Immigration Museum.

The *Buford,* the ship that carried deportees Emma Goldman and Alexander Berkman to Russia. Library of Congress.

13

E. G. SMITH

Shortly after President McKinley was shot, his vice president, Theodore Roosevelt, composed a letter to Henry Cabot Lodge. "We should war with relentless efficiency," he wrote, "not only against Anarchists, but against all active and passive sympathizers with Anarchists."[1] Several months later, during his first message to Congress on December 3, 1901, President Roosevelt offered a stern denunciation of anarchism. McKinley, he said, had been killed "by an utterly depraved criminal belonging to that body of criminals who object to all governments, good and bad alike."[2]

Czolgosz, in the eyes of Roosevelt, was typical of the pattern. "This criminal," the new president stated, "was a professed Anarchist, inflamed by the teachings of professed Anarchists and probably also by the reckless utterances of those who on the stump and in the public press appeal to the dark and evil spirits of malice and greed, envy, and sullen hatred. The wind is sowed by the men who preach such doctrines, and they cannot escape their share of responsibility for the whirlwind that is reaped. They and those like themselves should be kept out of this country, and if found there they should be promptly deported to the country whence they came, and far-reaching provisions should be made for the punishment of those who stay."[3]

"Our present immigration laws are unsatisfactory," Roosevelt went on. "We should aim to exclude absolutely not only all persons who are known to be believers in anarchistic principles or members of anarchistic societies, but also persons who are of a low moral tendency or of unsavory reputation." Linking anarchism with criminality, he was echoing a view widely expressed since the Haymarket episode: "The anarchist is the enemy of humanity, the enemy of all mankind, and his is a deeper degree of criminality than any other."[4]

Six days later Goldman gave a caustic response, speaking out against President Roosevelt at a meeting of the Social Science Club in Civic Hall on East 28th Street, her first public appearance in New York since she had returned from Chicago.[5] She also rebutted the president's words in print, writing that Roosevelt's message to Congress, "intended largely to strike at anarchism, was in reality a death-blow to social and political freedom in the United States." She dubbed the President "Teddy the Terrible," a reference to the notorious Russian tsar "Ivan the Terrible."[6]

Goldman was now, more than ever, an unpopular presence in New York. She was heckled and insulted when spotted at public events; she was monitored intently by the police; she had trouble finding work and lodgings; and she heard rumblings that she might be subject to abduction or attack. Many of her comrades openly turned on her. At one event at the Manhattan Liberal Club, where she had attended meetings regularly since 1894, she detected "an atmosphere of antagonism" and soon heard shouts from the crowd, labeling her a killer. One man called out, "Emma Goldman, you are a murderess, and fifty million people know it!" She stood on a chair and replied, "The population of the United States being considerably more than that, there must be a greater number willing to inform themselves before making irresponsible accusations."[7]

Yet her characteristic bravery and bluster soon left her. Emma found herself feeling "spiritually dead," gripped by weariness and ennui in the aftermath of her dealings with Czolgosz, his execution, and her widespread notoriety. "Dejection was upon me," she later wrote, "the feeling that my existence had lost its meaning and was bereft of content."[8] From the penitentiary, Sasha was concerned about both her physical welfare and her mental health. "In your letters I feel how terribly torn you are by the events of the recent months," he wrote. "I followed the newspapers with great anxiety. The whole country seemed to be swept with the fury of revenge. There were moments when I was in mortal dread for your very life, and for the safety of the other arrested comrades."[9]

Emma dropped out of active participation in the anarchist movement. She went into seclusion, and for months neither gave speeches nor wrote for the anarchist press. She adopted the pseudonym "E. G. Smith," and in this way was able to earn money as a nurse, tending to patients, often on the night shift. She also worked at home making dresses on her sewing machine. Landlords were unwilling to have the infamous anarchist Emma Goldman in their buildings, but under her alias she managed to rent a series of flats, the first on East First Street, which she shared for a while with her brother Morris and his friend Dan.

She and Dan were still lovers, in spite of their thirteen-year age gap. She later recalled that "he had laughed at my misgivings over the differences in our ages; he did not care for young girls, he said; they were generally stupid and could give him nothing. I was younger than they, he thought, and much wiser." Dan and Emma would continue their hapless romance for several years, until they eventually broke off the relationship for good in the spring of 1906. "Too great differences in age, in conception and attitude, had gradually loosened our ties," she observed. Dismissively, she remembered Dan as "a college boy of the average American level," and added, "Our life lacked the inspiration of mutuality in aim and purpose." Neither Emma nor Dan seemed particularly sorry when they parted ways. "The end came abruptly one night," she wrote, after a fight.[10]

To add to Goldman's melancholy following the Czolgosz uproar, a number of tragedies occurred within the movement. On October 28, 1902, Kate Austin died from consumption at the age of thirty-eight. Kate "loved life," said a grief-stricken Emma, "and her soul was aflame for the oppressed, the suffering, and the poor."[11] She paid tribute in *Free Society.* "Kate to me was not the anarchist, the rebel, the thinker, the writer, she was all those things, but to me, first and foremost, she was a mother, a friend, one to whom I could go to rest in peace when tired and weary of life and hard battles."[12]

Six weeks after Austin's death, on December 19, Voltairine de Cleyre was shot by a deranged former student. In accordance with the teachings of Leo Tolstoy, who promoted the doctrine of countering evil with good, de Cleyre refused to name her assailant or to press charges against him. When he was brought to her bedside for identification the day after the incident, she said that she knew him as a pupil but claimed she could not recognize him as the man who had shot her. She expressed only sympathy for her mentally ill assailant, whom she described as "sick, poor, and friendless."[13] He nonetheless was found guilty and sentenced to seven years in prison. Emma and Ed Brady raised money for Voltairine's hospital expenses, and she improved, although she suffered from chronic pain afterward.

In April 1903, Ed himself died suddenly in New York. While drinking in a saloon he fell and hit his head against the bar. He was taken home in a taxi, but suffered a heart attack from which he did not recover. Claus

Timmermann delivered the news to Emma, who believed that Ed's death was the result of his alcoholism and his unhappy marriage. Brady's wife, by contrast, blamed Emma. She accused Emma of draining Ed's time and affection, and had her barred from the funeral.[14]

AFTER NEARLY A YEAR OF SELF-ENFORCED ISOLATION from the movement, Goldman began a gradual return to anarchist activity. "I emerged," she wrote, "from my tortuous introspection as from a long illness."[15] She was invited to Providence to address a November 11, 1902, memorial meeting in honor of the Haymarket anarchists, a suitable occasion for her reemergence. But the authorities there had been vigilant against anarchist activities since McKinley's death, and when Goldman attempted to enter the hall for her speech, the police blocked her access, escorted her to the train station, and forced her to go back to New York.[16]

Subsequent lectures were more successful. She spoke on behalf of striking coal miners in Pennsylvania. She made a bold return to Chicago, where a phalanx of police followed her from hall to hall as she gave a series of talks on the social struggles and impending revolution in Russia. At a November 16 gathering in Brand's Hall on North Clark Street, she was threatened with arrest and warned, "Say what you please about Russia, but you must not attack our institutions."[17] When a Chicago official, Captain Wheeler, banned her outright from speaking in his ward, she griped, "America is fast becoming Russianized," trapped in a "pleasant dream into which [citizens] have been lulled by the strains of 'My Country tis of Thee.' We shall soon be obliged to meet in cellars, or in darkened back rooms with closed doors, and speak in whispers lest our next door neighbors should hear that free-born American citizens dare not speak in the open; that they have sold their birthright to the Russian Tzar disguised by the coat of the American policeman."[18] Her full-throated defiance restored, Emma resumed her busy routine, giving speeches, writing articles, and involving herself in every aspect of the movement.

AT THE END OF 1902 EMMA FOUND a permanent place to live. After moving from tenement to tenement, from lower Manhattan to Harlem to

Gramercy, she finally settled in an apartment at 210 East 13th Street, where she would remain for nine years. The building, now numbered 208, still stands, bearing a bronze plaque with Goldman's name. The apartment was large enough for Emma to host many visitors, including her niece Stella, Lena's daughter from Rochester; Max and Millie Baginski from Chicago with their baby girl Peepsie; and Tom Bell from Great Britain, with his wife Lizzie and daughter Marion, called Maisie. "Mother thought Emma a good cook and a very accomplished person," recalled Maisie years later. "Mother had been sick on the boat coming across and said that there was nobody like Emma, who took care of her and me."[19]

Goldman had met Lizzie Bell during her visit to London in 1895. At that time she had also been introduced to Lizzie's brother, John Turner. As a young man Turner had been a member of William Morris's Socialist League but joined the anarchist movement as a reaction to the Haymarket affair. The general secretary of the Shop Assistants' Union, which he himself had organized, Turner was regarded, said Goldman, "as one of the ablest of the English anarchists and one of the best informed men in the labor movement."[20]

Turner had toured the United States for seven months in 1896, talking to workers about trade unions and "arousing the heartiest feelings of comradeship amongst American friends."[21] He was scheduled to begin another tour in October 1903, with Emma providing housing, introductions, and logistics. His first event was held on October 23 at the Murray Hill Lyceum before a crowd of 500. As the *New York Times* reported, "Turner made a stirring address, which was received with tumultuous applause." But as he concluded his remarks, federal marshals mounted the platform and placed him under arrest.Goldman calmed the crowd, telling them, "I know this is a crying outrage and shame, but what can we do? Take things easy and everything will come out all right. . . . I command every one of you to keep your mouth shut, and I don't want to hear a word from a single person in the hall." Turner asked the police why he was being detained, but he "manifested no surprise," reported the *Times,* "and submitted to his arrest quietly."[22]

Turner had been arrested for violating the Alien Immigration Act—also known as the antianarchist law—passed by Congress on March 3 of that year. One of its chief goals was to bar from the country "anarchists or persons who believe in or advocate the overthrow by force or violence of the Government of the United States or of all governments or of all forms of law, or the assassination of public officials." It further provided: "No person who disbelieves in or who is opposed to all organized governments, or who is a member of or affiliated with any organization entertaining or teaching such disbelief in or is opposed to all organized governments shall be permitted to enter the United States."[23]

Turner was the first person to be held under the antianarchist law. According to the *New York Evening Post,* Turner had made "no incendiary utterance in this country," nor had he "advocated the overthrow by force or violence" of any organized government. He had identified himself as an anarchist, but had not disseminated any "anarchist propaganda work." The meeting at the Lyceum, moreover, was "quiet and orderly." But the authorities believed Turner met the standards for arrest, and searched him and removed him for deportation to Ellis Island. There he was denied rights of due process, confined in an iron cage designed for insane immigrants, and "treated like a convicted felon."[24]

Goldman quickly helped establish Turner's legal defense. She and her comrades retained the services of attorney Hugh O. Pentecost, who had been peripherally involved in Emma's own trial a decade earlier. A Baptist minister before he shifted to labor reform and the law, Pentecost felt the importance of the Turner case acutely, saying, "If you do not want the government overthrown by force and violence then let the people think and speak, because it surely will be so overthrown in time if they do not have this right of free thought and free speech."[25]

Pentecost began legal proceedings while Goldman sought the aid of the Free Speech League, organized in the wake of McKinley's assassination. An early forerunner of the American Civil Liberties Union, the League was founded on May 1, 1902, its members consisting chiefly of liberals, radicals, socialists, anarchists, single-taxers, freethinkers, and a number of well-known figures in progressive circles. It also boasted several prominent lawyers, most notably Goldman's friends Gilbert Roe, Theodore Schroeder, and Bolton Hall.

Roe, a former law partner of Wisconsin Senator Robert La Follette, was "an anarchist by feeling," said Goldman, "and one of the kindest of men it has been my good fortune to know."[26] Schroeder, Roe's law school classmate at the University of Wisconsin, had met Goldman at the Manhattan Liberal Club. A leading legal expert on free speech and a notoriously colorful character, Schroeder was fascinated by many aspects of anthropology, psychology, and sociology, especially as they pertained to religion and sex. He wrote and spoke incessantly on these subjects, often in a scandalous manner, and was a practitioner of the freedoms he advocated. His "wild, swooning desire to talk, in season and out," caused his fellow League member the journalist Lincoln Steffens to remark, "I believe in Free Speech for everybody except Schroeder."[27]

Bolton Hall, whom Emma had befriended several years earlier, was "one of the most charming and gracious personalities" of her acquaintance.[28] A highly regarded figure in New York legal circles, he was the foremost disciple of the politician and economist Henry George, and later founded the single-tax colony of Free Acres, New Jersey. He also published a number of books on land reform, and was intrigued by the theoretical benefits of anarchism.[29] The Irish-born Hall was a graduate of Princeton and Columbia Law School, instinctively generous, and very wealthy; as such, he was one of Emma's most reliable and lavish benefactors. "His frock-coat, high silk hat, gloves and cane made him a conspicuous figure in our ranks," said Emma, "particularly so when he visited trade unions in behalf of Turner, or when he appeared before the American Longshoremen's Union, whose organizer and treasurer he was."[30]

The League waged a strong campaign to free Turner from detention and prevent his deportation, with fundraisers, leaflets, and protests. The radical press took up the cry, denouncing the antianarchist law as anti-American and a "hysterical" reaction by Congress to the assassination of McKinley, and criticizing President Roosevelt for championing the bill. Carl Nold lamented in *Lucifer,* "It looks as if free press and free speech will receive many a blow yet before that sleepy mule, Labor, will wake up and do some kicking."[31] Kropotkin, in London, was disgusted, complaining to Emma that the American government "throws its hypocritical liberties overboard, tears them to pieces—as soon as people use these liberties for fighting that cursed society."[32]

When Pentecost's efforts failed, the League decided to appeal Turner's case to the Supreme Court. It engaged Clarence Darrow, who was already nationally famous, and his assistant Edgar Lee Masters, later of *Spoon River Anthology* fame, to act as Turner's counsel. To cover legal expenses, the League's Turner Fund Committee collected several thousand dollars, a good portion of which was raised by Emma. "We do not expect a favorable ruling from the Supreme Court," she wrote to Sasha, but "we gained what we tried for, namely, publicity and agitation."[33] Indeed, the carefully organized radical reaction, and the breadth and impact of the resultant attention, led some to speculate that the entire episode had been engineered as an anarchist propaganda tool.

The case was argued in April 1904. Thanks to Pentecost's efforts and $5,000 bail furnished by Clarence Darrow and Bolton Hall, Turner had already been released, after nineteen weeks in detention, and had resumed his lecture tour in New York and through the Midwest. His last stop was St. Louis, where the police shut down his event. Carl Nold, who was in attendance and subsequently arrested, complained bitterly that the "American people don't give a damn for free speech and press."[34] In Washington, Darrow and Masters told the Court that Turner was only a philosophical anarchist who "regarded the absence of government as a political ideal," and contended that the antianarchist law was unconstitutional because it abridged the First Amendment right of free speech and free press. The Court rejected their argument, upheld the law, and sustained the order of Turner's deportation.[35]

At the end of the month, on April 30, 1904, Turner went back to England on the steamship *St. Louis.* Emma and other friends were at the dock to see him off. Before he set sail, Turner told reporters, "It seems rather strange to me that this free Government should undertake to deport a man of honest ideas whose principles and beliefs have nothing of violence in them. I came here on a peaceful mission."[36] Kropotkin, welcoming him home to London, praised his courageous behavior, and George Bernard Shaw offered Turner his "personal congratulations on having terrified the greatest democratic republic in the world into laying violent hands on him, not because of anything he said, but because of what Americans feared he might say."[37]

WITH THE TURNER CASE BEHIND HER, Goldman turned her attention to other matters, the looming revolution in Russia a chief concern. She attended rallies for Russian anarchists and hosted the eminent Russian revolutionary Catherine Breshkovskaya, a founder of the Socialist Revolutionary Party. Nicknamed the "Grandmother of the Russian Revolution," or Babushka, Breshkovskaya had come to America to collect funds for her party's war chest. "Babushka is staying with me," Emma wrote to Lillian Wald. "I gave her some champagne, a good cure for seasickness."[38]

Though born into a wealthy family, Breshkovskaya reminded Emma of "a Russian peasant woman, except for her large grey eyes, expressive of wisdom and understanding."[39] The two women lectured together at a number of venues around New York, public and private, with Emma often acting as Breshkovskaya's interpreter. "The hours with Babushka," she wrote, "were among the richest and most precious experiences of my propaganda life."[40]

On January 22, 1905, as Breshkovskaya was preparing to leave for a tour out west, a mass of peaceful demonstrators marching toward the Winter Palace in St. Petersburg were shot at and killed by members of the Imperial Guard. The event, known as Bloody Sunday, sparked the 1905 Revolution. Breshkovskaya reacted immediately, and confided to Goldman that she required a dependable person to help smuggle arms into Russia for her comrades.

Emma recommended Eric Morton, the man who had directed the digging of the tunnel during Berkman's escape attempt from the Western Penitentiary. Breshkovskaya was impressed by Emma's description, even more so since Morton was known to be a competent sailor and capable of running a launch. As Breshkovskaya observed, these skills would allow the cargo to be transported by sea via Finland and thereby "arouse less suspicion than if attempted by land." Emma put Breshkovskaya in touch with Morton, who arranged for the ship and accompanied her back to New York after her western tour. Breshkovskaya was full of praise for Morton. "Just the son needed for the job," approved Babushka. "Cool-headed, brave, and a man of action."[41]

While Breshkovskaya planned her return to Russia, a troupe of actors from St. Petersburg arrived in New York, headed by Pavel Orleneff and Alla Nazimova. The couple opened the Paul Orlenev Lyceum in a theater on East Third Street in November 1905, with a repertory of Ibsen, Chekhov, and Gorky performed in Russian. Emma, who adored the theater and regularly lectured on Strindberg, Ibsen, and Shaw, attended the early performances and found them outstanding.[42]

Before long "Emma G. Smith" became interpreter and manager of the Paul Orleneff Lyceum. She corralled leading theater critics to review the productions, and helped win the company stellar reviews. Goldman's friend the music and arts critic James Huneker described Nazimova's "splendid emotional power" in his column. "Those who care for acting as an art," proclaimed editor and poet Richard Watson Gilder, "should take a trolley car to Orlenev's Lyceum. There may be enjoyed some of the best acting ever seen in New York."[43] Luminaries of the theater world flocked to see the troupe, among them Ethel and John Barrymore, Minne Maddern Fiske, producer Henry Miller, and Margaret Anglin.[44]

The Lyceum lasted eighteen months, until financial difficulties and a run-in with the New York Fire Department brought about its demise. Orlenev and the troupe returned to Russia in the spring of 1906, but Nazimova remained in the United States, quickly learned English, and made her first appearance on Broadway in November 1906, starring in *Hedda Gabler*.[45] Eugene O'Neill, then eighteen years old, went to see the play, his first exposure to Ibsen, and attended the production no fewer than ten times. "That experience discovered an entire new world of drama for me," he later recalled. "It gave me my first conception of a modern theatre where truth might live."[46]

Nazimova, who had been born Mariam Adelaide Leventon in Yalta in 1879, continued to find success on Broadway, earning more than $5 million for her manager Lee Shubert. She eventually moved to Los Angeles, where she bought a mansion on Sunset Boulevard and began acting in films, although national fame was fleeting. Her dream to one day enact the role of Emma Goldman came to naught.[47]

AFTER MONTHS OF NONSTOP TOIL, Emma was drained. "I feel as if I were in a swamp and try as much as I may I can not get out," she told Sasha. "I am tired, tired, tired."[48] She had suspended her nursing career, with its difficult hours and emotionally taxing work at the end of 1904, and decided to take up scalp and facial massage, the practice of which she had learned in Vienna.[49] Bolton Hall offered to lend her money to set up an office, promising to be her first patient. Emma's niece Stella supported the idea of a lighter schedule, and her Russian comrades thought a massage studio would serve as an excellent cover for radical activities.

As Emma G. Smith she rented an office on the top floor of a building at 874 Broadway on 17th Street, with $300 in start-up funds. The space was small but bright, with a view of the river, and Emma established herself as a "Vienna Scalp and Facial Specialist." The business did quite well, and by June 1905 she was able to cover her expenses and repay Hall part of his loan. She kept the office open until April 1906, when, ready to move on, she paid off her debts, and announced, "the experience I had gained and the people I had met were worth much more than material returns."[50]

Bolton Hall also came to Emma's rescue when she decided she needed a quiet place to relax. He found her a two-story house adjacent to a farm outside Ossining, New York. It was easy to reach by train for summer weekends and getaways (and illicit retreats for her associates). "I can not tell you how happy I feel," she wrote to Hall, "that I will soon have a place all of my own with no landlord or janitor to worry me. My friends are eagerly awaiting the moment when they will be able to go out on the farm to do work and be useful."[51] Conditions were rustic, and there was no running water, but Emma loved "its rugged beauty and seclusion, and the gorgeous view from the hill."[52]

Emma had more cause for happiness. On July 19, 1905, Sasha was scheduled for release from the Western Penitentiary, to be followed by a year in the Allegheny County Workhouse. On the day of his transfer, he wrote a letter to Emma. "Dearest Girl," it began, "It's Wednesday morning, the 19th, at last!

Geh stiller, meines Herzens Schlag
Und schliesst euch alle meine alten Wunden,
Denn dieses is mein letzter Tag,
Und dies sind seine letzten Stunden!

My last thoughts within these walls are of you, dear friend, the Immutable."[53]

PART II

PALACES OF THE RICH

14

RESURRECTION

When Berkman was scheduled to leave the Western Penitentiary, 200 prisoners signed a request that he be allowed to pass along the tiers to bid them farewell. The warden refused. On the morning of July 19, 1905, Berkman was placed in handcuffs and taken in a horse-drawn carriage to the railway station, where he boarded a 12:25 train to the Allegheny County Workhouse. According to a news report, he told the accompanying deputy, "I hope there won't be any notoriety about me." He had been in the penitentiary for nearly thirteen years, and would now spend ten months in the workhouse, located in Aspinwall, a town on the Allegheny River north of Pittsburgh.[1]

The workhouse was a dismal place with thick stone walls and sentries patrolling the bulwarks. Despite his long, grueling experience inside the Riverside prison, Berkman found "existence in the workhouse a nightmare of cruelty, infinitely worse than the most inhuman aspects of the penitentiary." The cells were cramped and "unspeakably" foul smelling, with privy buckets instead of plumbing, and negligible access to clean water. Inmates wore striped black and gray uniforms and were made to work under conditions of "feverish exertion." The guards were "surly and brutal," and punishment was swift and severe, with objections to prisoner abuse answered by solitary confinement.[2]

"The slightest motion of the lips," wrote Berkman, "is punished with the blackjack or the dungeon, referred to with caustic satire as the 'White House.'" One sadistic guard disciplined the prisoners by shoving them down the stairs "cursing and swearing all the while." Berkman later commented angrily about the "perverse logic of the law" that sent men who had committed minor crimes to such places, when "the workhouses are notoriously more atrocious in every respect than the penitentiaries and State prisons, in which are confined men convicted of felonies."[3]

Berkman was assigned to the broom shop and served the rest of his sentence in "nervous restlessness" as freedom loomed. "The monotony of the routine, the degradation and humiliation," he said, "weigh heavier in the shadow of liberty." He worried about the friends he had left behind in the penitentiary, and was physically weak and mentally strained. But he felt a yearning optimism as "the banked fires of aspiration burst into life."[4] He experienced a range of emotions during those last months: excitement at the thought of impending freedom, sadness at the wasted years and the failed revolutionary dreams of his youth, and anxiety at what life would be like as a free man.

He also felt a mix of trepidation and eagerness at the prospect of sex with a woman for the first time in nearly a decade and a half, although he had found great comfort in relationships with men during his prison term. "The thought of affection, the love of a woman, thrills me with ecstasy," he said, "and colors my existence with emotions of strange bliss. But the solitary hours are filled with recurring dread lest my life forever remain bare of woman's love. . . . Thoughts of woman eclipse the memory of the prison affections, and the darkness of the present is threaded with the silver needle of love-hopes."[5]

Berkman was released from the workhouse on May 18, 1906. Every year thereafter he celebrated May 18 as his rebirth and resurrection, "the recovery of my life and liberty." His treatment in both the penitentiary and the workhouse had been marked by "great humanity" as well as anguish, but his "long Pennsylvania nightmare" was at last over. "I am very happy," he said, "because of the mere fact that I have survived the terrible nightmare of fourteen years' duration, the years in the strictest solitary confinement, the humiliation and torture, the foul underground dungeon, the systematic starvation, the bull ring, the strait-jacket and the blackjack."[6]

Berkman's time of incarceration had not been altogether negative. Despite the stifling brutality of life in the penitentiary, his character had developed and matured. He had been able to read the classics of history and poetry, philosophy and religion. "Berkman," noted the *New York Times,* "comes out a linguist, having spent his time in perfecting himself in English, German, French, Italian, Russian, and Yiddish."[7] Another news report said that during his term he had "mastered the Slavic, Polish and Hungarian languages, and also acquired a good general knowledge of Italian, Spanish and French."[8] Berkman, though, found this journalistic interest in his scholarship absurd, mocking the press attention as "nonsense."[9]

But, immersed in great literature, exposed to a range of language, heartened by books and letters, Sasha had developed a feel for the written word and discovered his full potential as a writer. He entered prison at twenty-one, a raw, stormy, and inexperienced youth, and came out at thirty-five a thoughtful adult. He had encountered true kindness and care, and gave much credit to the prison officials whose decency helped keep up his spirits during his long confinement. He would always admire Reverend Milligan, the chaplain of the Western Penitentiary, for the compassion he had shown. Resident physician Dr. Oliver J. Bennett and Deputy Warden J. Harry Corbett also had been notably humane, as was A. H. Leslie, the superintendent of the Allegheny Workhouse. The others, Berkman avowed, were nothing more than brutes. He sharply criticized the hospital staff in particular, noting that one doctor was "a murderer at heart."[10]

Prison had also served to harden his anarchist convictions. "My youthful ideal of a free humanity in the vague future," he wrote to Goldman about a decade into his sentence, "has become crystallized into the living truth of Anarchy, as the sustaining elemental force of my every-day existence."[11] Upon his release, he maintained that the anarchist philosophy had been the key to his endurance. "If I have survived," he said, "it is due . . . above everything else—to that great and noble ideal, whose wonderful power has given me the strength to bear, the faith to hope."[12]

Emma later observed that Sasha "emerged from his living tomb more than ever before convinced of the truth and beauty of his Ideal—Anarchism."[13] Reported the *New York Times,* "According to the Anarchistic group who have kept in touch with him while he has been in prison, he is far from repentant, and as much of an Anarchist as when he began his imprisonment fourteen years ago."[14]

The moment he walked out through the gates of the workhouse, Sasha was confronted by reporters and by police, including an Allegheny deputy and three Pittsburgh detectives, who advised him to leave the area at once. He was more than happy to comply.[15] He went to the Aspinwall railroad station and took a train to Pittsburgh with a thirty-cent ticket provided by the workhouse. Sasha was jarred by the sudden shock of noise and crowds and activity, by the elements of the modern world. "I am afraid to cross the street; the flying monsters pursue me on every side. A horseless carriage whizzes close by me; I turn to look at the first automobile I have ever seen."[16]

Sasha had originally planned to take the four o'clock train from Pittsburgh to St. Louis, where a local journal had invited him to head their labor department. But he abruptly abandoned this plan and instead went to Detroit to visit Carl Nold, who had moved there the previous year and was living quietly with a girlfriend.[17] Emma, on a lecture tour in upstate New York and Canada, traveled at once from Montreal to rendezvous with him at the Detroit station. Sasha found Emma little changed, but she was saddened by his appearance. "His face deathly white, eyes covered with large, ungainly glasses, his hat too big for him, too deep over his head—he looked pathetic, forlorn . . . I was seized by terror and pity, an irresistible desire upon me to strain him to my heart."[18]

The group went to a restaurant, where Emma watched as Sasha "sat with his hat on, silent, a haunted look in his eyes."[19] "Once or twice he smiled," she wrote, "a painful, joyless grin. I took off his hat. He shrank back embarrassed, looked about furtively, and silently put his hat on again. His head was shaved! Tears welled up into my eyes; they had added a last insult to the years of cruelty; they had shaved his head and dressed him in hideous clothes to make him smart at the gaping of the outside world." Emma held back her tears and grasped his hand.[20]

Afterward they headed to Nold's home, where they remained for the next few days. Berkman found the transition from prison to freedom overwhelming. Swarmed by sympathetic well-wishers, he felt fearful and jumpy, desperate to be away from the clamor. "A sense of suffocation possesses me within doors," he wrote, "and I dread the presence of people." He was tormented by nightmares of the past, uncertain of the value of his existence, assailed by doubts for the future, and nearly suicidal. "I could make my life and my prison experience useful to the world," he wrote. "But I am incapacitated for the struggle. I do not fit in any more, not even in the circle of my comrades."[21] Emma noted his pain. "I knew with a terrible certainty that the struggle for Sasha's liberation had only begun."[22]

On May 22 Berkman delivered an address in Detroit. It was his first speech following his release from jail. He told the crowd he was "a little out of practice" when it came to speaking after so many years of enforced silence, and he felt uncomfortable in the limelight. Yet, he said, they had failed to kill him, to break him. He was "sound in body," "sound in spirit also," and remained defiant. "Here tonight I want to declare as publicly as I can that I am an anarchist, my undying hatred toward all tyrants and oppressors of mankind, and my eternal, active enmity toward the assassins of justice and liberty."[23]

He spoke fluently, with controlled emotion, of the world he saw around him. "A prison," he declared, "is the model on the lines of which civilized society is built. Indeed, what is this so-called civilized society of ours but a large prison, a capitalistic hell as wide as the world? It is the hell of a civilization where the masses must starve because there is too much food on hand, where they must go naked because there is too much clothing produced, where they must be homeless because there have been too many houses built, and where we must all remain abject slaves for the greater glory of capitalistic liberty."[24]

Despite his delicate nerves, Berkman agreed to give a series of joint speeches with Emma around the country. They left for Chicago on May 23 and that evening spoke to a large gathering in Metropolitan Hall. It was "a splendid treat," said Sam Hammersmark, an anarchist in the crowd, "to put new life into the movement." Sasha and Emma talked about the 1905 revolution in Russia, the atrocities of prison life, and the tenets of anarchism. "[Goldman] showed to friend and foe," recalled Hammersmark, "as also did Berkman, the impossibility of a free government, even though it be called democratic."[25]

During their stay in Chicago, Sasha and Emma attended celebratory dinners and took a special trip to see the graves of the Haymarket anarchists at Waldheim Cemetery. The authorities attempted to track them wherever they went, and papers sounded the alarm when "that terrible pair of 'Reds'" slipped off the radar. A reporter came upon them as they sat on a bench in Lincoln Park, "holding hands and talking," and they "chuckled with glee as they ridiculed the blindness of the Chicago police."[26]

Sasha recounted the events at Homestead, calling Frick a "mean and cruel" man. "I'll tell you something about my visit to Frick's office that has never been published," he said to the reporter. "Frick was a coward. He played possum, or I would have got him." Berkman explained that he was opposed to violence, but "when an anarchist uses force it is from a choice of the lesser of two evils in order to benefit humanity." He complained about the unconstitutionality of his sentence but, despite his long punishment, left open the possibility of committing another attentat. "I am still an anarchist; will always be one," he said. "It would depend on circumstances."[27]

The reporter noted the closeness between Sasha and Emma, their glowing glances and clasped hands. As "Berkman smiled fondly upon her," Emma explained their "true spiritual love," one that allowed for independence and individuality. "I have known Berkman since 1889," she said, "and I love him."[28]

OUTSIDE AFTER FOURTEEN YEARS BEHIND BARS, Berkman found himself in an altered world. While he was incarcerated, friends had been writing him thrilling tales about the big changes taking place. America as a whole was evolving from old to modern, from rural to urban, from agricultural to industrial, with small companies giving place to giant corporations. Skyscrapers had risen in the larger cities; telephones, telegraphs, automobiles, and electric lights were becoming common. Sasha exclaimed, "You can ride on the ground, overground, above ground, and without any ground at all." The cars continued to startle him; "a new race of beings, a race of red devils—automobiles you call them," and the forms of instant communication were "winged children of thought flying above our heads."[29]

Yet to Berkman's disappointment, much remained unchanged. He had expected to find a new era of freedom sweeping the country, but as far as he could tell, capitalism and government were more malignant than ever. Carl Nold commented that Berkman "was not slow in discovering that he is in the same old circus as he was fourteen years ago, with the same old clowns, who have learned but a few tricks for the attraction of the weary ones."[30]

Sasha returned to his old neighborhood on the Lower East Side and moved into Emma's apartment on East 13th Street. Justus Schwab and Ed Brady were gone, as was John Edelmann. Orchard Street, the scene of the Pioneers of Liberty meetings, was filled with new shops and businesses. The lecture hall had been turned into a dancing school; a favorite café, the scene of myriad intellectual discussions, was now a countinghouse.[31]

THE YEAR 1906 MARKED NOT ONLY SASHA'S REBIRTH, but the inception of Emma's magazine, *Mother Earth.* Anarchist journals had been going through a transition, with many ceasing production entirely. Abe Isaak's *Free Society,* which had served as the principal revolutionary anarchist paper in the country, had expired in November 1904. Eleven months earlier, in February, the Isaak family had relocated from Chicago to New York, intending to keep the paper going. But funds were low, and young Abe Isaak Jr., who had worked on the paper since the age of thirteen, decided he needed more time for study and to master his printing craft, "to paddle his own canoe," as Emma put it. Without Abe Jr.'s input, *Free Society* lingered "between life and death," and it finally shut down after ten years of publication.[32] Moses Harman's *Lucifer* would be in production only another year, and Johann Most's *Freiheit* was nearing the end of its long run. Benjamin Tucker's *Liberty,* the leading individualist-anarchist magazine, would survive until 1908, when the offices were wiped out by a fire, after which Tucker moved to Europe, never to return to the United States. *Mother Earth* not only would fill the void left by these publications, but would have a resounding impact on the anarchist movement as a whole, and make its mark as a literary achievement.

Goldman conceived of creating a monthly journal based on libertarian principles and incorporating her interest in social issues, progressive ideas, and the arts. She invited half a dozen anarchists to meet at the office of Dr. Hillel Solotaroff on East Broadway to discuss the concept and help her flesh it out. The original name was to have been *The Open Road,* after Walt Whitman's poem "The Song of the Open Road," but there was another magazine by that title already being published in Griffith, Indiana, so *Mother Earth* was chosen instead. Goldman would be the publisher, and Max Baginski the editor. The group collected money for the first issue, produced out of Emma's East 13th Street apartment in March 1906.[33]

Emma and Max left for a short tour to raise funds for upcoming issues, and while they were in Buffalo they learned of the death of Johann Most. Just sixty, he had collapsed while speaking in Cincinnati and died soon after, his hopes for social revolution in America dashed, his final years stressful and grim.[34] Goldman and Most had never reconciled. "Whatever bitterness I had felt against my old teacher," said Emma, "had given way to deep sympathy long before his death."[35]

But while Goldman's attitude had softened with time, Most stayed aloof, and, despite her efforts, the breach was not repaired. Emma had long since come to regret the horsewhipping incident. "I admit," she wrote years later to anarchist historian Max Nettlau, "that nothing Most, or anyone else [could do], since 1892, would induce me to horsewhip them. Indeed, I have often regretted to have attacked the man who was my teacher, and whom I idealized for many years."[36] She spoke at Most's memorial on April 1 and castigated those who had hounded him in life. "The ruling powers may think they can now rest in peace because he is dead," she said. "But although he is dead, this great meeting shows that his ideas live."[37]

Berkman was reflective. "I cherished the hope of meeting him again," he wrote of Most's passing. "He had been unjust to me; but who is free from moments of weakness? The passage of time has mellowed the bitterness of my resentment, and I think of him, my first teacher of Anarchy, with old-time admiration."[38] Most's consciousness of the limits of his impact on American workers was "a source of deep sorrow." Yet, Berkman said, "his inspiration affected powerfully every man who during the decades of his activity came within his sphere of influence."[39]

A few months later, in October 1906, *Mother Earth* devoted an issue to Leon Czolgosz in memory of the fifth anniversary of his execution. Prompted by the edition, which included articles by Goldman and Baginski, a group of young anarchists arranged a gathering on the night of October 27 to discuss, among other things, whether Czolgosz had indeed been an anarchist. At the close of the meeting, three of the speakers—Max Moscow, Max Rubenstein, and Julius Edelsohn—were arrested by members of the police department's Anarchist Squad and held for $1,000 bail each.

The Anarchist Squad had been formed earlier that year with the purpose of intimidating and arresting anarchists, disrupting meetings, pressuring hall owners to refuse bookings, and blocking the distribution of *Mother Earth* and other radical journals. The police relied on the New York State Criminal Anarchy Law, enacted after McKinley's assassination, which prohibited people from lecturing, writing, or disseminating literature promoting the doctrine that organized government should be overthrown by force or violence.[40]

Three days later, on October 30, a group of anarchists congregated at the Manhattan Lyceum on East Fourth Street to protest the arrest of the three men and the suppression of free speech. Bolton Hall, Harry Kelly, Max Baginski, and Goldman were scheduled to address the crowd, and Julius Edelsohn, who had been released on bail provided by Hall, spoke first. He had been talking for a few minutes when Anarchist Squad detectives mounted the platform and again placed him under arrest. At the same time, twenty-five policemen began to club the audience out of the hall.

Eighteen-year-old Pauline Slotnikov was pulled off a chair and dragged across the floor; her clothes were torn off, and her body was severely bruised. Julius Edelsohn's younger sister, Rebecca Edelsohn, was handled roughly and put under arrest because she did not leave the hall immediately. Three other women, Annie Pastor, Rose Rogin, and Lena Smitt, also were arrested, having failed to reach the bottom of the stairs quickly enough upon command. Baginski was kicked down the stairs. Goldman was struck in the back by one of the policemen and arrested. The women, along with six men, were then packed into a patrol wagon and taken to the station house, where the police subjected them to vulgarities and mistreatment until the following morning. They were brought before a magistrate who set bail at $1,000 each for assault. "Fancy girls of fourteen and eighteen, of delicate physique, assaulting twenty-five two hundred-and-fifty pounders," Goldman observed tartly. A grand jury dismissed the cases a few weeks later.[41]

Living together again, Sasha and Emma briefly resumed their physical relationship. But time and circumstance had changed them both, and his romantic desire for her had faded during his years in prison. "I became conscious of the chasm between the Girl and myself," he wrote. "It seems unbridgeable; we cannot recover the intimate note of our former comradeship."[42] Emma herself was well aware that their mutual passion had deserted them. "Whatever physical appeal I had for you before you went to prison was dead when you came out," she told him later. "I know that we kept up our relationship for a time, but I know too much about such things to be deceived."[43]

Even though their sexual intimacy ended, Sasha and Emma remained the closest of friends, who, arguments and grievances notwithstanding, relied on each other utterly in their public and private lives. Sasha, meanwhile, was drawn to some of the young women in the movement, including the teenaged Rebecca Edelsohn, known as Becky, who regularly visited him and Emma at the 13th Street apartment. Becky eventually started helping out with *Mother Earth* and moved into the building. "She had dark hair and brown eyes and was a lively, free spirit," recalled Eva Brandes, one of Becky's anarchist contemporaries from New York.[44] Becky's brother, Julius, published a short-lived Yiddish anarchist paper, *Lebn un Kamf* (Life and Struggle), and started an anarchist colony in the Catskills.

Berkman also welcomed the companionship of his old friends. Claus Timmermann visited frequently, and Modska and Sasha were reunited as well, perhaps not as close as they once were, but happy to resume contact. The former "Twin," successful in his new life as Modest Stein, contributed money and furnished additional funds when his comrades needed it. "I was four when Berkman was released from prison," Modska's daughter later said. "He often came to our apartment in New York, a sweet and charming man."[45] Sasha had a way with children; they were drawn instinctively to him, and he was indulgent and affectionate in return, treating them with patience, kindness, and respect.

By this point Berkman was pondering what work he might do in New York. During the final years of his prison term, he had considered several options, including pursuing a journalism career or attending college to prepare for a medical course. By 1904, however, he had given up these ideas, and in 1905 he thought about returning to Russia to participate in the revolution. "The Revolution in Russia has stirred me to the very depths," he said. "The giant is awakening, the mute giant that has suffered so patiently."[46] While still in prison, he wrote to a friend, "The news from dear Russia are [*sic*]to me like a ray of sunshine streaming into the darkness of a foul dungeon. I feel younger and stronger, and I wish I could be with the heroic men and women, fighting for free Russia. But who knows? May be I shall not be too late to help drive the last nail into in the coffin of Russian autocracy."[47] By the time he got out of the workhouse in 1906, the revolution had been suppressed, to his deep disappointment.

Despite the support of his friends and the anarchist community, Sasha remained grave and melancholy, and increasingly talked of suicide. At loose ends, he announced a lecture tour with a notice in *Mother Earth,* and set up dates in Albany, Syracuse, Pittsburgh, Cleveland, Columbus, St. Louis, and Chicago. But in Cleveland, halfway through the tour, he did not show up for an event, and concerned comrades wired Emma in New York. She feared that Sasha had in fact killed himself, since he "had been in the throes of such depression that he had said repeatedly he did not care to live, that prison had unfitted him for life."[48]

For three days anarchists across the country searched police stations, hospitals, and morgues without result. The newspapers, too, wondered why Berkman had vanished, and printed rumors that he might have been kidnapped by Pittsburgh detectives, by members of the Secret Service, or by "agents of millionaires who . . . did not like the tone of his lectures."[49] The press also speculated that Sasha had gone off to Russia, although the *Washington Post* supposed that suicide was a possibility, as "Berkman grows very gloomy and pessimistic at times, and has often been heard to consider killing himself."[50]

Sasha finally turned up in New York and contacted Emma from a telegraph office on 14th Street. She rushed back from a speaking engagement in Elizabeth, New Jersey, and brought him home. He admitted that he had been miserable on his tour—panicked by the lectures, uncomfortable in the alien swirl of daily life, and despondent at his seemingly empty future. Prison seemed safe in comparison to the constant stress and drone of the outside world. "Is liberty sweet only in the anticipation," he wondered, "and life a bitter awakening?" He purchased a revolver in Cleveland with the thought of committing suicide someplace where no one knew him, his body to be unidentified and unclaimed. But he could not go through with it. Emma put him to bed and looked after him for several days until he began to recover, still "very weak, but with a touch of joy in life."[51]

After a few months' rest, Berkman was no longer critically depressed, but he was still troubled by his lack of employment. He loathed his financial dependence on Emma and his other comrades, and was determined to get work, for the sake of his mental state as well as his wallet. "I cannot remain idle," he said. "But what shall I turn to? I am too weak for factory work."[52] He thought about taking up his old printing craft. When he had worked as a printer for Johann Most's *Freiheit,* he had joined the Typographical Union No. 6 in New York, and had some knowledge of typesetting from his job with Paul Gephardt, editor of the *Connecticut Volks-Blatt* in New Haven; as a result, he was able to set type in German, Russian, Yiddish, and English. But the new linotype machine had rendered many of his skills obsolete, and he could not find a position. In December 1906 Berkman opened his own small printing shop at 308 East 27th Street, between First and Second Avenues, hoping to attract business from trade unions and radical societies, but he closed it four months later because he had no union labor and refused to hire an employee or accept nonunion assignments.[53]

Goldman, in an effort to stave off another bout of depression, stepped in and offered Sasha shared editorship of *Mother Earth.* She also encouraged him to write a book about his experiences, something he had been contemplating. "Your book, yes sweetheart your book," she told him effusively, "it must be written and I want to help you through my love, my devotion. Let me nestle close, close to you and in your strong passionate embrace let me drink the joy of life, the ecstasy of our love. I am all yours."[54]

When Emma and Max Baginski went on a fundraising tour in the spring of 1907, Sasha officially assumed editorship of *Mother Earth.* "In view of his crushing imprisonment," Emma later wrote, "he surprised everybody by the vigor of his style and the clarity of his thoughts."[55] He wrote articles and reviews for the magazine, often under pseudonyms such as A. B. McKenzie, James McLane, and Alexander Breckenridge. His writing was crisp, clever, and lucid, and he had an organized, methodical mind, but his management abilities were abysmal. Despite a substantial subscriber list, the paper lurched from one financial crisis to the next. Sasha ran up huge bills at neighborhood stores for printing and supplies, and mishandled production costs, leaving Emma to sort out the mess or beg rescue from generous benefactors. Nevertheless, the creative outlet kept Sasha productive and relatively cheerful, and he stayed on as editor of *Mother Earth* for the next eight years.

Sasha also began to lecture regularly, at last sloughing off the anxiety of appearing before an audience. He addressed anarchist meetings, spearheaded demonstrations, and agitated among workers and the unemployed.[56] While he did not possess Emma's dramatic flair, he was a straightforward, penetrating speaker who transfixed his listeners with his passion and impressed them with his dogged conviction. Although he often spoke at large rallies, he preferred intimate discussion. As his comrade Mollie Steimer later recalled, "he would say, 'For me there is no gathering too small to talk to. Count on me, I'll be there.' And he never failed to keep his word."[57]

The subject about which Berkman lectured most frequently during the years immediately following his release was the American prison system. Shortly before he completed his sentence, he wrote, "The day of my resurrection is approaching and I will devote my new life to the service of my fellow-sufferers. The world shall hear the tortured; it shall behold the shame it has buried within these walls, yet not eliminated. The ghost of its crimes shall rise and harrow its ears, till the social consciousness is roused to the cry of its victims."[58]

He put together a speech called "Prisons and Crime," compiled from notes he had made in the Western Penitentiary starting in 1895.[59] The results attained by penal institutions, he wrote, were "the very opposite of the ends sought. Prisons breed enemies of society. They cultivate the germs of social hatred and enmity . . . [as the prisoner is] brutalized by the treatment he receives and the revolting sights he is forced to witness in prison."[60]

Berkman was endlessly frustrated by the irrationality and inefficiency of the current system, which threw all sorts of prisoners together regardless of the severity of their crimes, and served only to harden them further with cruelty and neglect. "Prisons defeat the ends for which they are created," he wrote. "The promiscuous mingling of prisoners in the same institution, without regard to the relative criminality of the inmates, converts prisons into veritable schools of crime and immorality. There is not a single prison or reformatory in America where either flogging and clubbing, or the straitjacket, solitary confinement, and reduced diet (semi-starvation) are not practiced upon the unfortunate inmates, so that when they emerge from behind the bars they are condemned to repeat their transgressions. Prisons neither improve the prisoner nor prevent crime. They achieve none of the ends for which they are designed."[61]

Berkman did more than comment on the topic; he actively engaged in cases around the country and the world, advocating for imprisoned anarchists from Japan to Russia to England. And when Berkman at last published his lengthy account, *Prison Memoirs of an Anarchist,* he dedicated the book to his fellow sufferers: "To all those who in and out of prison fight against their bondage."[62]

15

THE WINE OF SUNSHINE AND LIBERTY

WITH BERKMAN AT THE HELM of *Mother Earth,* Emma and Max Baginski embarked on a series of domestic and international lecture tours. In the fall of 1907, Emma returned from a trip to Paris and Amsterdam, where she had attended an International Anarchist Congress, and saw that Sasha and Becky Edelsohn had grown closer, despite the two-decade age gap and Becky's conspicuous youth. Although Emma was well aware her romance with Sasha was in the past, the idea that he had fully moved on was a difficult adjustment. "It was painful to see that the new love that had come to Sasha completely excluded me," she said. "My heart rebelled against the cruel thing, but I knew that I had no right to complain. While I had experienced life in all its heights and depths, Sasha had been denied it. For fourteen years he had been starved for what youth and love could give. Now it had come to him from Becky, ardent and worshipful as only an eager girl of fifteen can be."[1] As she later told Sasha, "I simply clung to the hope that I may be able to awaken the same feeling in you . . . but when I came back from Amsterdam and saw your relation with Becky I knew the end had come."[2]

Sasha enjoyed his time with Becky, although romantic fidelity was never a consideration for him; after he left prison, he consistently had affairs even when involved in serious relationships. Despite his dour moods and vengeful impulses, he possessed an underlying sweetness, an invigorating wit, an endearing spirit. His brazen attempt to bring down Frick, the notorious symbol of industrial injustice, and his subsequent hard years in prison made him a martyr to the anarchist cause and lent him an air of heroic virility. Like Emma, he rarely wanted for lovers.

Berkman kept busy compiling his notes and letters from prison for his manuscript, delivering lectures, and editing *Mother Earth.* In the fall of 1907 he founded the Anarchist Federation in New York to unite and coordinate his radical comrades, which attracted a number of local groups and soon inspired a similar federation in Chicago. The goal was to popularize anarchism in America as an alternative to the current system, appealing, as always, to the workers. One leaflet put out a call "To the Unemployed and Homeless!!" "Shall we starve while the capitalistic thieves and idlers roll in luxury and waste the wealth we have created?" it demanded. "Shall we and our families suffer for the necessities of life while the stores and warehouses are overfilled with all the things we need and which we ourselves have created? We have fed and clothed and warmed the country; shall we now be contented to starve and freeze?"[3]

Berkman was reaching out to an anxious class. During 1907 and 1908 the United States lay in the grip of another severe economic depression. Millions were unemployed, and there were angry demonstrations in many cities, including Chicago, Philadelphia, and New York, where the Anarchist Federation held mass meetings of the jobless.

In March 1908 Emma traveled to Chicago to give a speech. Because of the recent protests, tensions were running high, and the police closed all meeting places and kept her under constant surveillance, making it impossible to secure a public hall.[4]

From a local comrade Emma learned that Ben Reitman, a young doctor dubbed the "King of the Hobos," was willing to let her use a storefront known as the Hobo College, where he often held assemblies. Emma read in the newspaper that Reitman had led a march of Chicago's unemployed, for which he was arrested and beaten by the police. Impressed that he had backed the cause of the jobless and poor, risking his safety to do so, she accepted the offer to use the Hobo College as a venue for her March 13 speech. Curiously, Reitman notified the newspapers that Goldman would be appearing, providing the date and location. The papers subsequently contacted the police, and on the afternoon of her talk, inspectors for the building and fire departments showed up at the storefront and declared it hazardous for Reitman to seat more than nine people in the hall. The event was scuttled.

As a substitute, Goldman and her associates decided to hold a concert on March 17 at Workmen's Hall; the plan was for Emma to take the stage and give an unscheduled lecture when the music ended. Reitman was the only outsider who knew about this scheme. Once again, he contacted a reporter and disclosed that Goldman would address the meeting. The police, forewarned, showed up and stormed the platform as soon as Goldman began to speak. They pulled her off the dais by force and dragged her toward the exit. Fearing for the safety of the audience, she called out to them: "The police are here to cause another Haymarket riot. Don't give them a chance. Walk out quietly and you will help our cause a thousand times more." The audience applauded and calmly left the hall, "filing out in perfect order."[5] Unable to speak in Chicago, Goldman gave up and moved on to Milwaukee, where lecture dates had previously been arranged. Before long, Reitman joined her there.

BEN LEWIS REITMAN WAS A TALL, STRIKING MAN about ten years Emma's junior with a riot of black, curly hair and a flashy, seductive allure. The first time Emma laid eyes on him, he wore a "large black cowboy hat, flowing silk tie," and carried an outsized cane. Emma found him extremely enticing, a "handsome brute," whose "eyes were brown, large, and dreamy," and whose lips "were full and passionate," even if "his fingernails, like his hair, seemed to be on strike against soap and brush." Young and virile, he was exactly Emma's type.[6]

After completing her Milwaukee meetings, Goldman returned with Reitman to Chicago, where the two became lovers. Emma later wrote, "I was caught in the torrent of an elemental passion I had never dreamed any man could rouse in me. I responded shamelessly to its primitive call, its naked beauty, its ecstatic joy." They spent time together in the city, and one night she and Reitman went with some of her comrades to a restaurant for dinner. Seated nearby was Herman Schuettler, the police official who had arrested Louis Lingg during the Haymarket affair and who often targeted anarchists for persecution, including Emma after the McKinley assassination.[7]

Goldman was aghast—Schuettler's "presence seemed . . . to pollute the very air"—but Reitman readily went over to Schuettler's table and engaged him in pleasant chat. Schuettler greeted him with a friendly "Hello, Ben." The men in Schuettler's group, apparently all members of the police force, also seemed to know Reitman. How could Ben have anything to do with them, Goldman wondered. She recalled the concert on March 17 and the treachery that had brought the police and reporters to that gathering. Was it Ben who had informed them? She suspected that it was.[8]

Hurt and confused, Goldman left Reitman in Chicago and went alone to her next speaking engagement in Minneapolis. Ben wrote letters begging for forgiveness and a chance to explain. Though wary of his apparent connections to the police and his underhanded behavior, Emma could not resist her attraction, and at last wired him to meet her in Minnesota. Ben accompanied her on a fundraising tour out west, helping her set up meetings and sell literature as she lectured in San Francisco, Los Angeles, Portland, Seattle, and other cities and towns along the coast.

In San Francisco, after giving a lecture about patriotism, Emma shook the hand of one attendee, a uniformed soldier named William Buwalda. Detectives followed Buwalda back to his army base and reported him. Buwalda was arrested, court-martialed, dishonorably discharged from the army, and sentenced to five years at hard labor in the prison on Alcatraz Island, notwithstanding the testimony of his superior officers that he had been an exemplary soldier for fifteen years. His commanding officer, General Funston, nevertheless condemned him for "shaking hands with that dangerous woman" and called his interaction with Goldman "a great military offence, infinitely worse than desertion, a serious crime, equal to treason."[9] A campaign to free Buwalda was successful; he was released after ten months and was pardoned by Theodore Roosevelt, despite the president's distaste for the anarchist movement and for Emma Goldman in particular. Buwalda eventually did become an anarchist, and gave back the medal awarded him for faithful military service in the Philippines. Two years later he invited Goldman to lecture in his home state of Michigan.[10]

When her West Coast tour was completed, Goldman headed back to New York, while Reitman returned to Chicago. He now was serving officially as Emma's manager, scheduler, and assistant. He also was siphoning money from the tour proceeds to pay off his debts and support his mother, and was having flagrant affairs with numerous other women. But toward the end of the summer, Ben moved to New York to join the Mother Earth group.

He did not receive a warm welcome. Many of Emma's Mother Earth comrades disdained and even detested Reitman. They were disgusted by his appearance, his manners, and his politics. They thought he was a liar and a thief, utterly lacking in integrity, and they worried that he was a police informer. (Emma continued to harbor similar suspicions.) They also were baffled by his religious practices—although Jewish by birth, he had converted and was now a Baptist.

The more the members of Emma's circle got to know Reitman, the less they liked him. They found him ignorant, shallow, and shrill. According to Margaret Sanger, Reitman walked the aisles at meetings, hawking copies of *Mother Earth* "in a voice that never needed a microphone."[11] His tasteless antics and crude commentary were feared to be harmful to the cause, and his routine of holding Sunday school classes in the Mother Earth office was considered absurd.[12] Sam Dolgoff, a comrade who was acquainted with Ben, observed acidly, "You couldn't possibly have too low an opinion of him. He was a cheap opportunist who took advantage of Emma Goldman. The one good thing about him was that, during Prohibition, he wrote a good prescription for whiskey."[13]

In spite of her advocacy of free love and her own rollicking personal history, Emma was pained by Ben's affairs, many of which he acknowledged openly, insisting that he had an overwhelming need for sex and variety, and reminding her that she herself espoused the concept of sexual exploration. One anarchist associate, Rebecca August, later said, "I didn't care for Ben Reitman much. He once took me home from a lecture and immediately asked me to sleep with him. I said no, and he said, 'Don't you believe in free love?' 'Yes,' I answered, 'I believe in choosing my lovers.' "[14]

Yet Emma could not resist her passion. She told her "beloved" Ben in one of many heated letters, "I love you. I love you, oh so desperately. You are light and air, beauty and glory to me. You are my precious Hobo." But her adoration was tainted by distrust. "Dearest, do you know, that creepy slimy, treacherous thing, doubt? Have you ever been seized by it? Has your soul ever suffered its sting, your brain ever experienced its horror beating force?"[15]

Again and again, she forgave and defended him, despite the overt disapproval of her friends, whose loathing for Ben did not abate even though they tolerated his presence for Goldman's sake. "My God, Emma, how can you stand Ben?" asked Voltairine de Cleyre, who complained to Sasha, "Reitman has been doing his usual stunts . . . he gets everybody by the ears, talks vulgarly at meetings, says untruths, and irritates everybody."[16] Writer Max Eastman described him as "a white-fleshed, waxy-looking doctor, who thought it radical to shock people with crude allusions to their sexual physiology."[17] Labor activist Elizabeth Gurley Flynn called him "an insufferable buffoon."[18] Art historian Carl Zigrosser judged him "a vulgar and unstable character, no asset to any movement."[19] Russian-born anarchist Kate Wolfson dismissed Reitman as "an example of [Emma's] physical desires. He looked coarse and gross, and we got the impression that he was not genuinely interested in anarchist ideals."[20] Margaret Anderson, editor of the *Little Review,* maintained that Reitman "wasn't so bad if you could hastily drop all your ideas as to how human beings should look and act."[21]

One comrade, Mary Eleanor Fitzgerald, known as Fitzi, who would eventually become Sasha's long-term lover, was curious to determine if Ben was actually a doctor, although she had been acquainted with him for some time. She wrote to Chicago for confirmation of his medical degree, and she learned that in 1900, Reitman indeed had entered the College of Physicians and Surgeons, and was admitted to the American College of Medicine and Surgery in 1903, from which he graduated the following year. "I am heartily glad that I was wrong," Fitzi told Reitman. "I want to be friends with you."[22]

Sasha himself had a particularly low opinion of Ben. He disliked and distrusted him, and found it hard to believe that Emma could be enamored with such an odious person. It was nothing but a temporary infatuation, he felt sure. Ben lacked sense and intelligence, had no rebel core, and did not belong in the movement. Berkman wrote that Ben had "neither spunk, social feeling nor stamina, nor anything else that one wanting to play a prominent role in such a movement should have."[23] Rejecting an article submitted by Reitman to *Mother Earth,* Sasha said that the whole piece was "pervaded by a spirit of entire misconception of the purpose and significance of the Anarchist propaganda."[24]

BUT THE COMRADES HAD MORE TO WORRY ABOUT than troubled romance. In 1908 President Roosevelt directed the postmaster general to exclude from the mail *La Questione Sociale,* an anarchist paper published in Paterson, New Jersey, on the ground that it was "immoral" because it opposed all government. Roosevelt declared that anarchist publishers were enemies of the country, and that "every effort should be made to hold them accountable for an offense far more infamous than that of ordinary murder."[25]

That same year, publications such as *Freiheit,* the Czech *Volne listy,* and the Italian *Sorgiamo* and *Nihil* also were barred from the mail. The postmaster general interfered with the delivery of other anarchist periodicals—among them *Mother Earth.* When C. L. James, an anarchist in Eau Claire, Wisconsin, did not receive the October edition, he wrote to Berkman to criticize the "business of making the Post Office a detective agency and a blackmailing bureau." And when the November issue likewise failed to arrive, he again notified Berkman of the government's neglect, remarking, "I shall make a resounding kick today." Berkman and Goldman did what they could to ensure delivery, but their subscription holders were often disappointed.[26]

It was not only radical journals that met with interference from the authorities. Police routinely interrupted radical-themed speeches and labor rallies. On March 28, 1908, a huge crowd of unemployed workers assembled in Union Square in New York. The organizers had failed to obtain a permit, and police were ordered to clear the area. Swinging nightsticks, policemen swarmed the square, on horse and on foot, and began clubbing men and women right and left, driving them into doorways and side streets while dozens more fled, defiantly singing the "Marseillaise."[27]

Suddenly, a bomb exploded. The bomb-thrower was an anarchist named Selig Silverstein who had come from Russia four years earlier. Beaten when the police made their initial incursion and having been subjected to previous abuse from the force, he hastened home to his apartment and fashioned a bomb from the brass ball of a bedpost, filling it with nitroglycerine, gunpowder, and broken nails. He then returned to the square and, as the police regrouped, lit the fuse. The bomb exploded prematurely, killing a bystander and blowing away Silverstein's hands, scoring his eyes, and filling his body with bits of metal.[28] Although his injuries were severe, he remained conscious. He was taken by ambulance to the police station and, when questioned by detectives, insisted that he had acted alone and had no accomplices.[29]

As always, Berkman fell under suspicion whenever anarchists made mischief or a bomb was thrown, and immediately the authorities tried to implicate him in the affair. Despite chatter that Berkman had gone into hiding, he was found at his home the day after the Union Square incident. "He was busily engaged at his desk," reported the *New York Times,* "and said he was preparing material for the next issue of *Mother Earth,* the organ of the Berkman–Emma Goldman creed." Berkman shrugged off accusations that "he had been trying to give the detectives the slip." "Why, I was here nearly all day yesterday, and the only times that I have been out today was when I went out to get something to eat," he said. "I have not seen a policeman or a detective all day." Berkman claimed he was not familiar with Silverstein and had not attended the Union Square rally. "If the police want me," he said, "they can find me here at any time."[30]

Find him they did. A search of Silverstein's belongings revealed a membership card for the Anarchist Federation, signed by its treasurer, Alexander Berkman. Also in Silverstein's apartment were solicitations from the group. Berkman was arrested and charged with conspiracy. According to the *New York Times,* "he seemed neither surprised nor perturbed by his arrest and cheerfully accompanied the detectives to Headquarters. There he submitted without protest to being photographed for the Rogues' Gallery, measured, and the imprints of his thumbs taken." Berkman was questioned by the inspector, made to face a roomful of masked detectives, and then was brought to Silverstein's bedside in Bellevue Hospital. Neither man showed recognition of the other.[31]

Berkman's lawyer, the socialist attorney Meyer London, established that nothing could be found to link his client with any plot, and Sasha was discharged for lack of evidence. Failing in their initial attempt to implicate him, the authorities accused him of "inciting to riot," but that charge too had to be dropped for lack of evidence. As Sasha remarked to the press,

"I do not believe they had any right to do this . . . I have committed no crime. I have not decided whether I shall take any legal action in the matter, but it was unjust." Still, he added lightly, "the masked detectives were very funny. It seemed just as if they were ashamed of their profession."[32]

Silverstein initially showed signs of recovery, but his injuries were too severe; by April 6 his temperature had risen to 104 and he was in severe pain. He died on April 28.[33] Berkman defended his actions in *Mother Earth.* "The bomb is the echo of your cannon, trained upon our starving brothers; it is the cry of the wounded striker . . . it is the dull thud of the policeman's club upon a defenseless head. . . . The bomb is the ghost of your past crimes."[34] To Sasha's disappointment, Saul Yanovsky, editor of the *Fraye Arbeter Shtime,* condemned the bomb-throwing in Union Square, which had resulted in the death of a bystander. Yanovsky was subsequently set upon and thrashed by Silverstein's friends.

Berkman continued to pour his energies into the organized labor movement, becoming one of its most ardent agitators, instinctively taking the side of the workers in any dispute or violent incident. As far as he was concerned, the workers were always in the right, no matter what they did, and the bosses were always wrong. "Labor can never be unjust in its demands," he wrote. "Is it not the creator of all the wealth in the world? Every weapon may be employed to return the despoiled People into its rightful ownership."[35]

Henry Alsberg, an American newspaper correspondent based in Russia, and later the director of the Federal Writers' Project, knew Sasha and Emma well. "A history of Berkman's activities of this period," he said, "would probably come near to being a history of the chief events in the struggle of the American workers against their industrial masters."[36] Harry Kelly similarly referred to Berkman's "active and vital participation in the labor movement of the day."[37] There was much to protest during this volatile era, with strikers subjected to police brutality, injunctions, Pinkertons, militia, and agents provocateurs. Illegal arrests and detentions were commonplace, and charges such as conspiracy and incitement were used as weapons to crush disturbances.[38]

On September 7, 1908, Berkman attended a Labor Day gathering of the unemployed at Cooper Union, sponsored by the International Brotherhood Welfare Association of New York. Ben Reitman had been asked to address the crowd of unemployed workers and labor groups; Becky

Edelsohn, Hippolyte Havel, and Emma Goldman (who because of her notoriety had not been invited to talk) were also there. The police's Anarchist Squad was on hand to monitor the proceedings. Reitman read a speech written for him by Goldman, who had watched Ben struggle and fail to put together a coherent lecture before the event and decided that "rather than have him make a rambling talk" she would prepare "a short paper on the meaning of Labour Day." It was an attack on American capitalism and a plea for the rights of the workers, and when Reitman finished, he announced that his speech had been composed by that "much maligned woman, the anarchist Emma Goldman." He then left the hall.[39]

A chairman of the meeting, Charles Oberwager, stood and apologized for the "unfortunate occurrence" of having the words of the controversial Goldman read aloud at the event, and lashed out at Reitman for "preaching the doctrines of anarchy." Berkman, offended, rose to protest on Ben's behalf, since Ben was no longer present to defend himself. Detectives at once leaped to restrain him, and dragged him out of the hall, an irate Becky following close behind. Both Sasha and Becky were taken to the Fifth Street Police Station and arrested.[40] When Hippolyte Havel arrived at the station and asked on what charge Sasha was being kept, an officer said, "We have that son-of-a-bitch anarchist Berkman at last. We'll fix him this time."[41]

The police, having failed to tie Berkman to Silverstein and the Union Square explosion, were anxious to charge him now. Sasha and Edelsohn (who had given her name as "Mary Smith") were held in jail overnight, and then brought to court and tried without hearing or counsel. Becky was fined ten dollars for "vagrancy" since she had refused to reveal her home address; she had been living in Goldman's apartment for two years, and did not want to drag Emma into the mess. (It was not, however, Edelsohn's first arrest; a previous run-in with the law had resulted in her expulsion from high school.) Bolton Hall arrived at the scene and paid Becky's fine.

Sasha was convicted of disorderly conduct and sentenced to the Blackwell's Island workhouse for five days. As Emma scoffed, "What were five days to a man who had served fourteen years?" She went to Blackwell's Island to visit him, and they both joked over the five-day sentence. "I can do them on one toe," Sasha laughed. Emma later wrote, "I left him with the old certainty that whatever our disagreements, our friendship was of an eternal quality. . . . I still felt the hurt caused by his attitude towards Ben, yet I knew that nothing could ever come between us."[42]

BERKMAN WAS COMMITTED TO LABOR ACTIVITY, but his primary goal was to communicate the principles and ideals of anarchism. The older he got, the more he believed that the future of the movement rested with the education of the young. "Just in the proportion that the young generation grows more enlightened and libertarian, will we approach a free society," he said. "Can we indeed expect a generation reared in the atmosphere of the suppressive authoritarian educational regime to form the cornerstone of a free, self-reliant humanity?"[43]

To this end, Berkman became involved in the Modern School movement, which sprang up in the United States in 1910 and lasted for more than fifty years. The collection of schools and the movement's philosophy of teaching were inspired by the life and death of Spanish educator and freethinker Francisco Ferrer y Guardia (January 10, 1859–October 13, 1909). In the aftermath of the so-called "Tragic Week" in Spain, a July 1909 clash between the Spanish army and workers and revolutionaries, Ferrer was accused of fomenting insurrection. He was convicted without proper evidence and executed on the grounds of Montjuich fortress in Barcelona.

The death of Ferrer stirred outrage around the world. In many countries, streets were named and statues erected in his honor. Radicals and freethinkers were motivated to create schools based on his model for libertarian education; such centers appeared in England, France, and across Europe, in Brazil and Argentina, Poland and Czechoslovakia, and China and Japan. The schools, which bore Ferrer's name and promoted his philosophy of education, emphasized the rights of the child, offered a more balanced relationship between pupil and teacher, and cultivated manual skills in a libertarian environment. Children were urged to grow and learn without the formality or discipline of a traditional classroom so that they might participate in their education with genuine enthusiasm and open minds.

The most extensive Ferrer movement arose in the United States. No fewer than twenty schools were started in different parts of the country, in cities such as New York, Philadelphia, Boston, Detroit, Chicago, Salt

Lake City, Seattle, Portland, San Francisco, and Los Angeles. Classes were conducted in English, German, Yiddish, Czech, Italian, Spanish, and, in some places, Esperanto, a language invented by Polish occultist L. L. Zamenhof to promote solidarity within a multilingual group. Most of the students were the children of workers, and the founders were mainly anarchists and radicals who hoped to dispense with all forms of authority, educational as well as political and economic.

Berkman and several other New York anarchists began a local Modern Sunday school, which was considered to be the first Ferrer establishment in America. Additionally, Sasha assisted Harry Kelly and Leonard Abbott when they and other comrades formed a Ferrer Association. Abbott, born in Liverpool, England, to wealthy parents, immigrated in his youth to New England, where he became a leading figure in the American socialist movement. Even as he moved closer to anarchism, Abbott never gave up his socialist beliefs, finding both movements compatible within a "comprehensive social philosophy."[44]

The Ferrer Association held its first meeting on June 3, 1910, at the Harlem Liberal Alliance on West 116th street. "Ferrer would wish no granite or marble shaft as a monument to perpetuate his name," Berkman assured the crowd. Instead, Ferrer's admirers would pay tribute to him with a learning environment in which children would not have "ideas crammed into their heads," but could enjoy "forming their own ideas and imbibing natural notions of everything about them."[45]

Over the next few years the Ferrer Association flourished. It provided centers in which the students, educated without rewards or punishments, were taught about working-class movements and revolutions. Instead of learning facts of history and civilization, relying on memorization and recitation, preparing for exams, or acknowledging religious rituals, they read books for pleasure, worked on crafts, and acquired practical skills. Adults were encouraged to attend evening lectures and take courses in art, literature, and science. Many Ferrer schools promoted causes such as unionism, free speech, and pacifism.

Berkman and Goldman, along with Abbott, Kelly, and the historian and philosopher Will Durant, were frequent participants at the New York Modern School, formally established in 1911. At the Ferrer Center, the anarchists organized talks and discussions on the issues of the day, as seen through the prism of their radical perspective. A number of well-known individuals (many with ties to Goldman and Berkman) lectured at the center, including Clarence Darrow, Elizabeth Gurley Flynn, Jack London, and Upton Sinclair. Plays and concerts were performed there, and it served as a hub for activist thought.[46]

ALONG WITH HIS DUTIES MANAGING the Ferrer Center and editing *Mother Earth,* Berkman was working to complete his prison memoirs. While incarcerated together in the Western Penitentiary, he and Carl Nold had discussed the idea of writing a book about their prison experiences. They collaborated on a manuscript in the penitentiary and smuggled the pages to comrades in New York. When Nold was released in 1897, the two agreed to publish the book as soon as Berkman was also free, "whenever such a miracle should happen." Its title was to be "To Hell and Back."[47]

Years later, after returning to New York and settling into Emma's apartment on East 13th Street, Sasha resumed work on the book on his own, with an autobiographical focus. Whenever possible, he went to Goldman's Ossining house to write. He loved the "wildness" of the place, its tranquility and seclusion. The pair often went there together, and while Sasha pored over his manuscript and enjoyed the open space and quiet, Emma cooked, read books, wrote letters, and tended to the garden, growing potatoes, cucumbers, beets, lettuce, beans, and radishes. Sasha took hearty advantage of her cooking skills, devouring as much as he could. "Having been starved for so many years," Emma noted, "he now ate ravenously. It was extraordinary what an amount of food he could absorb. . . . It was nothing at all for him to follow up a substantial meal with a dozen blintzes . . . or a huge apple pie."[48] Friends regularly joined them at the little house for dinners and social events, and the remote location made it a perfect place for radical comrades from around the world to hide out or meet in secret.[49]

As he drafted the book, Sasha sought assistance from Voltairine de Cleyre. They had first got to know each other in 1893, a year after his attack on Frick, when she began corresponding with him in prison. For the next dozen years, he looked forward to her letters, with their vibrant anecdotes and sensitive insights.[50] She, in turn, found comfort in his replies during her own periods of depression and pain. "Your letters from prison (especially the contraband ones) were a relief to me in my agony," she later told him. "They pulled me up towards the light and air for a while, when I was like one grasping under dark, cold water."[51]

De Cleyre had long been one of Berkman's most ardent and eloquent defenders, and she took part in the fruitless campaigns to free him during the 1890s. Later their friendship grew through their association with *Mother Earth,* to which de Cleyre was a contributor. The two also shared a more personal connection, as both suffered from depression. The buoyant, blunt Emma, in spite of her dejection following the Czolgosz debacle, was unable to fully comprehend Sasha's recurrent moods of deep despair. But de Cleyre, who had twice attempted suicide, could offer words of intimate sympathy. They met face to face for the first time in the summer of 1906, when Sasha visited her in Philadelphia. The occasion was "memorable and vivid," said Voltairine. "I like you as a spirit akin," she told him. "I like you because you are strong and because you are troubled with weakness; because you are not cocksure; because you have lost the power to be narrow—as I have."[52]

Voltairine herself was a wonderfully resonant writer, and Sasha benefited from her counsel as he crafted his book. She urged him to "strike out on an independent line. On no account write like anybody else." He followed her advice, but still had difficulty formulating his thoughts and composing a narrative, which led to bouts of writer's block. Voltairine had experienced this in her own writing as well. "Now let the book idea drop from the present," she suggested when he was at a loss, "and if what you feel most like doing is lying on the grass and watching the ants, do it. Let the sun burn into you, and the water run over you; do it day after day, and if you can get where you don't think about anything but the bugs etc. and insects so much the better. Don't worry about constructing the book, till the thoughts fill you again."[53]

Voltairine also advised Sasha to be confident. "You are a writer of some skill. . . . When the time comes for things to be said you will say them. You leave a forceful impression on people—that is the real transmigration of the soul. All there is in life for any man is still open to you; be assured your forces will return—will awaken rather. Let them sleep awhile, and do not worry about it in the least."[54]

During the years that it took Berkman to finish the book, de Cleyre could always be relied on for encouragement. She read the manuscript at every stage and corrected the proofs when it was finished, answering Sasha's queries regarding style and usage and helping him to master written

English. She also gave him many shrewd suggestions, chief among them "Dare—write things which others have been afraid to write."[55]

Sasha began to find the process cathartic, and he emerged with a greater sense of purpose and resolve, a better handle on his moods.[56] By September 1911 the manuscript was nearly finished. It was written in direct, spare prose, at once deeply personal and evocative of the common prisoner experience. Emma read his draft and was impressed. "He is doing very well," she told Ben. "In fact, what he has written so far is extraordinary. I think it will be a great work."[57]

At the end of the autumn the manuscript was complete. The title, "Autobiography of an Anarchist," had been changed to "Prison Memoirs of an Anarchist." As Goldman said later, "It was a document profoundly moving, a brilliant study of criminal psychology. I was filled with wonder to see Sasha emerge from his Calvary an artist with a rare gift of music in his words."[58] With the manuscript ready for publication, Goldman wrote to Jack London asking if he would read it. "If the book appeals to you strongly," she said, "perhaps you would feel moved to write the preface."[59]

London agreed to write an introduction, but Berkman was disappointed with the result. For one thing, London's political viewpoint did not match up with his own—London was a member of the Socialist Party. "As a socialist," London had said to a friend, "I have not the slightest sympathy for the anarchist philosophy; it is diametrically opposed to socialism."[60] For another, London dismissed the entire justification for Sasha's attack on Frick. London stated in his preface that Berkman's attempt to kill Frick seemed "solemnly silly" to his mind. "I cannot grasp the utility nor rationality of his act. Berkman, by his own confession, admits that he failed to understand the people." London asserted that Berkman was "very young, very naive, when he went forth to do propaganda by deed. Also, he was hag-ridden by ideas and ideals and without contact with the real world."[61] Berkman and Goldman discarded London's submission and turned to their friend *New York Globe* writer Hutchins Hapgood to provide the preface. Hapgood, a Harvard-educated journalist, was an anarchist and free thinker who lived a bohemian lifestyle with his wife, the author Neith Boyce. In contrast to London, Hapgood produced a far more sympathetic "Introductory" with which Sasha and Emma were satisfied.

Goldman began to canvass commercial publishers. Many of them turned down the manuscript. Some conservative houses refused even to read it once they learned the author's name. One publisher asked whether

Berkman would be willing to use a pseudonym, a suggestion Goldman rejected. Another thought it a remarkable work, but would Berkman leave out the anarchist part? Yet another insisted on eliminating the portions relating to homosexuality in prison. In the end, Emma and Sasha decided to publish the book themselves, with Gilbert Roe and Lincoln Steffens enlisted to raise the necessary money.[62]

IN THE SPRING OF 1912, Emma and Ben Reitman were on her seasonal lecture tour. That January, several months before Emma and Ben's arrival in Los Angeles, the City Council of San Diego had passed an ordinance designating the central part of town as a district in which speaking on the streets was prohibited. This new regulation was a direct effort to prevent labor groups from organizing the city's workers. The powerful Industrial Workers of the World, which had been founded in Chicago in 1905 by William D. Haywood, Daniel De Leon, Eugene V. Debs, and Haymarket widow Lucy Parsons, among others, was considered a particular nuisance, given its agenda to claim control for the workers through direct action and subversive means. The labor forces, viewing the San Diego decree as a violation of the laws of the United States and California, and as an attempt to deprive the workers of their first amendment rights, created a local branch of the Free Speech League to challenge the act.[63]

Numerous workers defied the ordinance, and many were arrested, enduring harassment, beatings, and torture in prison. Vigilance committees were brought in to further intimidate the I.W.W. members, known as Wobblies, and their supporters. Those who carried out the threats often were prominent city officials. One paper spoke to an eminent San Diego attorney, Patterson Sprigg, who classified himself as having acted in an "advisory capacity" to the vigilance committees. "The identity of the 'vigilantes' was no particular secret," Sprigg said, "many of the well known businessmen openly admitting their participation and rather glorying in it than anything else."[64]

On May 14, Goldman and Reitman took a train from Los Angeles to San Diego to join the fight. By the time they arrived at the scene, hundreds of workers, mostly Wobblies, had been arrested and assaulted by vigilantes and law enforcement officials. The previous week, moreover, the police had shot and killed an I.W.W. member named Joseph Mikolasek, sparking further controversy and anger.[65]

At the hotel where Ben and Emma were staying, a group of armed vigilantes turned on Ben and dragged him into a waiting car, driving sixteen miles out of town and into the desert. There they tore off his clothes and shouted curses at him, then kicked and brutally beat him. With a lighted cigar one of the men burned the letters I.W.W. into his buttocks. Others pulled his hair and shoved their fingers into his ears and nose, and still others poured a can of tar over his head and rubbed handfuls of sagebrush onto his battered body. One tried to shove Ben's cane into his rectum, and another twisted his testicles. Then he was forced to kiss the American flag and to sing "The Star-Spangled Banner." Finally they made Ben run the gauntlet, each man delivering a parting blow or kick as he passed through. Beaten, bruised, tarred, humiliated, and clothed only in his undergarments, Reitman dragged himself to the nearest railroad station, where he took a train to Los Angeles and rejoined Emma, whom police had escorted out of San Diego. It was a frightful experience he would never forget, one that would cause him severe emotional trauma for a long time to come.[66]

Berkman, Hippolyte Havel, and Harry Kelly issued "A Protest and a Warning" stating that "Violence Begets Violence." They denounced the bloodshed and persecution in San Diego, and the vicious suppression of free speech. "If the public sentiment of the country and the passive attitude of the press continue to encourage these outrages," they wrote, "we feel that the Anarchists and other social rebels will be forced, as a matter of self-defense, to answer violence with violence. Not because they wish it, but because driven by utmost necessity."[67]

PRISON MEMOIRS OF AN ANARCHIST WAS PUBLISHED by the Mother Earth Publishing Association in the fall of 1912. The price for the book was $1.50, and the manuscript eventually was translated into Yiddish, German, and French.[68] Sasha's friends were proud of his achievement. Jay Fox of the Home Colony wrote that "few men have the experience of prison combined with the ability and the sociological viewpoint necessary to write a great book on prison life. Berkman has all these qualifications."[69] Harry Kelly said that the memoirs "astonish us by their erudition and power of their moving prose," while other comrades considered them equal to Kropotkin's famous *Memoirs of a Revolutionist.*[70]

The book created a sensation. It was seen not only as a literary accomplishment, but as a stimulus for investigations into prisons and the penal system, in Pennsylvania and other areas of the country. It also was one of the first books—outside of medical and criminological literature—to deal explicitly with the issue of homosexuality in prison. Writer and poet Edward Carpenter, a major figure in the English homosexual rights movement and a friend of William Morris and Peter Kropotkin, wrote that the book "makes one realise how the human spirit—unquenchable in its search for love—is ever pressing outward and onward in a kind of creative activity. There are in the book cameos describing how friendships may be and are formed and sustained even in the midst of the most depressing and dispiriting conditions."[71]

Prison Memoirs of an Anarchist was widely, and for the most part favorably, reviewed. "Berkman has succeeded in making you live in his prison experiences with him," commented the *New York Evening Post,* "and his book is probably as complete a self-revelation as is humanly possible."[72] According to the *New York Tribune,* "When the writer . . . wields his pen in the manner of the Slavic realists and is compared by critics with such men as Dostoyevsky and Andreyev, his work must possess a tremendous fascination as well as a social value."[73] "Berkman is a staccato realist," said the *St. Louis Mirror.* "He is an odd rationalist and emotionalist. But he gets himself over into your comprehension and does it completely. . . . His exposition of himself and his cause is a rare piece of psychology. Reading him, taking his point of view, you cannot call him a murderer."[74] The *New York Times* said that the book "must remain as a moving presentation of misery for the most part avoidable, an arraignment of a system in which we have much to be bettered even though the system itself is not to be swept away." The *Times* further praised the book as "vivid, candid, honest. Here and there, too, are touches of sweetness, flowers of human fineness not altogether lost in the prison air."[75]

To thank Emma for all her help with the editing, publishing, and promotion, Sasha gave the very first book to her. "First Copy off the press," he inscribed. "October 14, 1912, 4.P.M. To you dear Emma, who helped me to live this book and to write it, Sasha."[76] De Cleyre, who had provided such instrumental support, did not survive to see the book's publication, which came several months after her death from meningitis at the age of forty-five.

Voltairine was buried in the Waldheim Cemetery in Chicago on June 23, 1912. Her anarchist comrades in New York held a service for her on the Lower East Side, attended by a grief-stricken crowd.[77] Goldman had been on a lecture tour out west during the funeral, and afterward went to Chicago to visit Voltairine's grave.

"There she lies," wrote Emma, "whose body had never known respite from pain, whose soul had never tasted peace, and who yet never relaxed, until the end, in her zeal, her wonderful zeal, for the ideal she loved so well—Anarchism, the redeemer of the human race."[78] Despite some friction between the two women, de Cleyre's death affected Goldman profoundly. "As I stood beside Voltairine's grave, in the shadow of the monument dedicated to the memory of our comrades," she said, "I felt that another martyr had been added to them."[79]

16

THE INSIDE STORY OF SOME EXPLOSIONS

As Sasha was achieving catharsis through the pages of his memoirs, Emma was seeking new inspiration in the arts. After years of lecturing on playwrights and the theater, she began to hone her interpretation and analysis. In January 1913 she launched a series of Sunday night talks on modern drama, featuring works by Ibsen, Strindberg, Mirabeau, Shaw, Tolstoy, and Chekhov. The lectures were held at the Lenox Casino in Harlem, not far from the Ferrer Center. During her annual spring tour, she also found that her run of six talks on Nietzsche, presented at the Women's Club of Denver, was a particular success. When Goldman returned to New York, she arranged to give more lectures about Nietzsche at the Harlem Masonic Temple on Lexington Avenue and 125th Street.

At this time Goldman decided to vacate her apartment at 210 East 13th Street, as well as the Mother Earth office on West 28th Street, which she had opened in January 1910. The East 13th Street apartment had been a natural gathering spot for nearly a decade, a "home of lost dogs," as Hutchins Hapgood called it, and "one of the lively centers of thinking of New York," according to historian and literary critic Van Wyck Brooks.[1]

While Emma had affectionate, sentimental feelings for 210—the "entire kaleidoscope of human tragedy and comedy had been reflected in colourful variegation within the walls"—it was cramped and poorly heated, often noisy with the clangs of the *Mother Earth* presses and the clamors of unexpected visitors. Neighbors regularly came to them for assistance, most frequently the gamblers. As Emma recalled, "Expecting a raid, they would run up the fire-escape to ask us to hide their paraphernalia. 'In your place,' they once told me, 'the police may look for bombs, but never for chips.'"[2]

She decided she needed more space and a change of scene, and soon found a suitable new home: a ten-room brownstone at 74 East 119th Street in Harlem. Not only did it have rooms enough on the upper floors for everyone in her circle to have privacy, but it boasted a parlor that could seat 100 people ("the very thing we needed for small sessions and social gatherings") and a large basement with enough light to serve as the office and bookshop. Too busy to look after the place herself, Emma hired a housekeeper, Rhoda Smith, a capable French woman with a sharp tongue and a taste for alcohol. Emma also needed a secretary to handle the office work, and Ben Reitman recommended his friend Fitzi, whom Goldman had met in Chicago during her 1908 free speech campaign.[3]

MARY ELEANOR FITZGERALD, no-nonsense and piercingly intelligent, had been born in 1877 to James and Ada Fitzgerald, and raised in the town of Deerfield, Wisconsin. She was then called Mamie, a name she dropped when she got older. She was tall, fair-skinned, blue-eyed, and attractive; Ben nicknamed her "Lioness" because of her mane of red hair. Tom Bell's daughter, Maisie, remembered Fitzi as "so lovely," and many comrades admired her integrity and mettle.[4] "She had soul!" recalled anarchist Hilda Adel. "She was a wonderful person."[5]

Fitzi's father, a conscientious objector during the Civil War, was Irish, but her mother came from American pioneer stock, and her ancestors were among the earliest settlers in Wisconsin. "From them," said Goldman, "she inherited her independence and self-reliance. I grew to love Fitzi for her inherent idealism and understanding spirit, and we gradually came very close to each other."[6] She and Fitzi developed a strong friendship, a special one for Emma, who had a tendency to clash with the women in her orbit.

At the age of fifteen Fitzi renounced her father's Roman Catholicism and joined the Seventh Day Adventists, her mother's faith. At sixteen she taught school in Hancock, Wisconsin, then, in 1898, went to Battle Creek, Michigan, to work in the sanitarium at the headquarters of the Adventist sect and prepare for missionary work. Shortly after, however, she gave up the church and became a nurse in a North Dakota clinic. "I joined the Seventh Day Adventist Church when I was fifteen years old," she wrote to anarchist activist Lucy Robins, "but no one could ever catch me again and stick me into the narrow creeds of any church, social, political, and religious."[7] Instead, she became attracted to free thought and radical activities, especially labor causes and anarchist ideas. When Goldman offered her a position, Fitzi was more than intrigued. "She was interested in our work," Goldman said, "and she would be glad to give up her job and join us in New York."[8]

Fitzi arrived in New York in September 1913 to begin her life with Mother Earth. She and Reitman took charge of the office and bookstore, Rhoda Smith did the cleaning and cooking, and Goldman and Berkman ran the magazine. Becky Edelsohn was still in residence, and Ben Reitman invited his mother to join them in the apartment, although he soon left with her to live in a small flat. Emma and Ben had been having particular difficulties; as Emma later wrote, "He was thirty-five and I nearing forty-four. That was a tragic difference in age. I felt lonely and unutterably sad."[9]

Ben continued to antagonize her friends, to have affairs, and to behave in a disruptive manner. He moved back to Chicago for a while, with the thought of practicing medicine. Emma missed him terribly, recalling mournfully, "To be away from Ben meant sleepless nights, restless days, sickening yearning." Berkman was supportive of Emma during this time. "Sasha," she said, "had never been more thoughtful and considerate than during the months of my struggle to free myself from Ben." Ben and Emma did not break for good for several more years; and in any case, they continued to correspond, tour, and work together long after their love affair had come to an end.[10]

Emma, meanwhile, had been working on a book called *The Social Significance of the Modern Drama,* which was largely based on her recent series of lectures. She "had long since become convinced that the modern drama is a fruitful disseminator of new ideas," and had always had a great appreciation of the theater, artistic as well as intellectual.[11] She dictated the manuscript to Fitzi, and it was published in Boston in 1914.

Apart from her work on Emma's book, many of Fitzi's tasks involved helping Sasha edit *Mother Earth.* Within a few months the two fell in love. With Berkman otherwise involved, Becky Edelsohn, "a tremendously fiery person," in the words of a comrade, and "one of the strongest persons in the group of agitators" according to the *New York Times,* found other lovers, ultimately taking up with Charles Robert Plunkett, a young activist at the Ferrer Center.[12] The two were later married, and the union lasted nearly a decade, producing a son. Plunkett, many years afterward, remembered Becky as "five feet four inches tall, moderately plump, with black hair; she was very pretty—beautiful, I should say—and very generous."[13] Emma was pleased with the romantic shuffle. "Sasha is now going to Fitzi," Emma wrote to Ben, "which is a godsend, for it takes Becky Edelsohn out of my intimate life."[14]

Becky continued to spend time at the Ferrer Center, where she was a speaker as well as a model in the art classes conducted by Robert Henri and George Bellows, both Ohio-born painters of some renown. Becky, Emma, and Sasha all took part together in free speech fights, labor protests, antimilitarist events, and support for the jobless, and scarcely allowed personal entanglements to interfere with the cause.

DURING THE WINTER OF 1913–14 the United States was in the midst of yet another severe depression, and millions were out of work. As before, demonstrations broke out across the country to protest the dire circumstances of the poor, their paltry wages, and the slow response to the crisis. On February 27, 1914, in New York City, a twenty-one-year-old anarchist named Frank Tannenbaum took matters into his own hands. He called together about 1,000 unemployed people and led them to the Old Baptist Tabernacle at 164 Second Avenue, demanding shelter. The evening service had just begun, reported the *New York Times,* when "the tramping of many feet down the church aisle brought it to a sudden close." After an exchange of words between Tannenbaum and church officials, the police appeared. When a patrolman asked the group to identify its leader, "Several of the crowd pointed to a tall man wearing a flowing tie. No one seemed to know who he was." The throng soon dispersed.[15]

The following night Tannenbaum led 600 men to the Labor Temple on East 14th Street, and on March 1 he assembled a group of homeless people in Rutgers Square and guided them through the snowy streets to the First Presbyterian Church on lower Fifth Avenue. The pastor there gave them money for food and shelter. On March 2 they went to the parish house of St. Mark's Episcopal Church at Second Avenue and Tenth Street, and received bean sandwiches, coffee, and a place to stay overnight, while Tannenbaum decried the squalid conditions and "red tape" of the Municipal Lodging House, where the homeless were expected to find refuge.[16]

On March 3 the "church invaders" tramped down the Bowery, then west to Broadway, singing the "hoboes' marching song" as they passed Worth Street ("Hallelujah, on the bum, bum; Hallelujah, amen; Hallelujah, give us a handout, Revive us again").[17] They arrived at the parish house of St. Paul's Protestant Episcopal Chapel at Broadway and Vesey Street, where George Washington once worshipped. There they were given tongue and corned beef sandwiches, and were invited to spend the night and have breakfast the following morning.

Tannenbaum told the crowd, "The capitalistic papers call us hoboes, tramps, and bums, but I hurl the accusation back at them as a lie. We are willing to go to work if we get union wages. . . . What we are getting here is no charity. If I felt for a moment that it was I wouldn't come here. We are here because our friends have bread that they don't need and we can use it. We are here to demand what we deserve, and what rightfully belongs to us because we are starving. Until a few days ago New York didn't have an unemployed movement. Then we decided to show the city what it meant. . . . The papers say we aren't willing to work. That I brand as a lie. We will work if we can get $3 a day for an eight-hour day."[18]

As it happened, the young agitator was well acquainted with Emma and Sasha, and both were aware of Frank's plan to march to churches as a way to enact nonviolent propaganda by the deed. Tannenbaum was a frequent visitor to the Ferrer Center, where he attended meetings and evening classes, and from time to time helped out at the Mother Earth offices.

"Emma Goldman and Alexander Berkman," stated the *New York Times,* "did not suddenly sweep upon [the church invasion effort] after they saw its progress and the opportunities it afforded. They were privy to it from the beginning."[19] Tannenbaum, an immigrant from Austria-Hungary, had come to America at the age of nine, run away from his home on a Massachusetts farm at thirteen, and by twenty was working at a restaurant in New York. There he became a labor activist and began to associate with anarchists and I.W.W. members.[20] Goldman described Tannenbaum as "a vivid youth. . . . We had all loved Frank for his wide-awakeness and his unassuming ways."[21]

Three men assisted Tannenbaum in organizing the demonstrations: Frank Hamilton, Arthur Caron, and Charles Plunkett. Frank Hamilton was a friend of Jack London's, and had served as a model for a character in one of London's novels. As he explained the marches, "Our object is to put it up to the City of New York. This city won't deal with the problem of the unemployed unless it is compelled to, to save the nuisance of looking after us from day to day."[22]

Arthur Caron was a handsome, high-cheekboned man with an "erect, dignified bearing."[23] Born and raised in Fall River, Massachusetts, he worked in a cotton mill, and then as a machinist and engineer. He was a wandering spirit who had traveled throughout the United States, the West Indies, and France, a "vibrant fellow with boundless energy and great physical courage," according to Ferrer School student Maurice Hollod. One friend described him as "an extremely fine person, charming and a gentleman in every sense of the word."[24] Of Scottish and Native American descent, Caron was proud of his native heritage, speaking often about the tribe of his ancestors.[25]

Charles Plunkett, Becky Edelsohn's lover, was a bright, dynamic New Yorker who had been an avid fan of radical literature and ideology from an early age. "I never did anything by halves," Plunkett said later. He won a scholarship to Cornell University, but left college in 1912 to become an organizer for the I.W.W. after being fired from a summer job at Thomas Edison's New Jersey laboratory, where he recorded the life histories of insects. (Plunkett went on to an academic life, earning his doctorate from Columbia and becoming the chairman of the Biology Department at New York University.)[26]

The marches received a great deal of attention from the community and the press. "At last we have a chance to let the city know what we want," Tannenbaum told a crowd of demonstrators. "I am glad the reporters are here to tell the city our demands. We are members of the working class. Everything in this city was created by our hands or the hands of our brothers and sisters."[27] Both Berkman and Leonard Abbott helped lead some of the marches. Abbott said the "adventurous" tactic advertised "the issue of the unemployed in a way that is compelling and that makes everybody think."[28]

John Haynes Holmes, minister of the Church of the Messiah in New York and a future leader of the American Civil Liberties Union and the

National Association for the Advancement of Colored People, was among those church officials who believed that it was their duty to provide food, shelter, or money to the people who sought assistance, although some of his colleagues cancelled evening services or requested police protection to avoid the mass visits. The marches, said Holmes, forced "ninety million people in the United States to acknowledge that there is a question of the unemployed and to ask what can be done about it."[29]

The church invasions soon came to an end. On March 4 Tannenbaum, Caron, Plunkett, and Hamilton brought several hundred unemployed people to St. Alphonsus on West Broadway, and were denied permission to spend the night. The police were sent for, and as the protesters began to leave, a faulty flash bulb exploded with a pop when a photographer from the *New York World* tried to take their pictures. The sound was mistaken for a gunshot, and police and demonstrators panicked, creating a minor riot. The police locked down the church and arrested 189 men and one woman, Gussie Miller, of the Ferrer Center.[30]

Tannenbaum was charged with inciting to riot, and was tried, convicted, and sentenced to the maximum penalty of one year in prison. He also was ordered to pay a $500 fine, which was covered by funds generated by the Ferrer Association, the *Fraye Arbeter Shtime,* and the Labor Defense Committee. Caron and Plunkett each got a month on Blackwell's. Six others received minor sentences and the rest were released.[31]

"If we are kept in prison, other men will take our places," warned Tannenbaum.[32] Society, he said, had condemned him for challenging its conventions. "That's my crime. I was going about telling people that the jobless must be housed and fed, and for that I got locked up."[33] According to the *Modern School* magazine, Tannenbaum served his term on Blackwell's engaged in active study so he could leave prison "better equipped than before to play his part in the social struggle."[34] He went on to attend Columbia University, earn his doctorate in economics, and teach at Cornell University. He returned to Columbia as a distinguished professor, one of the nation's leading authorities on Latin America.

After Tannenbaum's incarceration, his church invasions ended but the open-air demonstrations continued, with then-unprecedented numbers assembling in Lower Manhattan to protest their plight and listen to radical speeches.[35] Sasha coordinated and advised the many groups that formed on behalf of the demonstrators; Emma called him the "active spirit of the movement," its "organizing and directing influence."[36]

ON SATURDAY, MARCH 21, Goldman was the key speaker at the first of a series of mass meetings in Union Square, arranged by the Conference of the Unemployed, one of the groups inspired by the Tannenbaum protests. Her words were reminiscent of those she had delivered in the same place two decades earlier when she told a crowd to "demonstrate before the palaces of the rich," to demand work and bread, and to seize both, if necessary.[37] It was the events surrounding that speech that had led to her imprisonment on Blackwell's Island, and she herself remarked on the evolving social landscape. "Times have changed," she said. "Even the courts would not send a person to jail for a year for such an utterance, if made today, as I served a year for making then." The workers had changed as well. "Then it was just simply a blind groping and now it is a consciousness that they are entitled to a share of the good things of life."[38] She instructed her audience to "go to the churches. Go to the hotels and restaurants, go to the bakeshops and tell them that they must give you something to keep you from starving."[39]

A parade up Fifth Avenue followed, "a march of the disinherited," said Sasha, "whose very appearance was a challenge to the guilty conscience of the exploiters and well-fed idlers."[40] A thousand people advanced from 14th street all the way to the Ferrer Center on 107th street; a large black banner waved before them, embroidered in red with the Italian word "Demolizione" (Demolition). According to the *New York Times,* "Alexander Berkman . . . led the march with a woman on each arm" as the demonstrators "defied the traffic regulations at important crosstown streets" and sang revolutionary songs, "punctuated with maledictions upon the homes of the rich that they passed," including those of Andrew Carnegie and former Montana senator W. A. Clark. At the corner of 84th Street, a motorcar found itself blocked by the procession, and a female marcher—none other than Becky Edelsohn—spat at the passengers within its tonneau.[41]

Two weeks later, on Saturday, April 4, the Conference of the Unemployed staged a second major rally in Union Square. People gathered for speeches and a march, and brandished banners and black flags carrying slogans such as "Hunger," "Bread or Revolution," and "Tannenbaum Shall Be Free." Berkman ascended the platform and gave a brief speech, then "quietly slipped out of the crowd and disappeared."[42] But the police, who had arrived in the hundreds, on horse and foot, were intent on shutting down the demonstration, and used their clubs without restraint.

Journalist Lincoln Steffens wrote the next day, "I was sick at heart last night. I was in Union Square yesterday, and saw the unemployed clubbed. I've seen such things for twenty years now, but I can't get used to it. It lifts my stomach every time I see a policeman take his night stick in both his hands and bring it down with all his might on a human being's skull. And then, when he does it, the crowd come about me and asks me if I won't make a complaint against the cop and have him fired! As if I could!"[43]

Many demonstrators were injured, and a number arrested as well. Arthur Caron was among those brutally clubbed, and a well-known I.W.W. leader, Dublin-born Joe O'Carroll, called "Wild Joe" by the police, was targeted for attack. Detectives followed him from the square and set upon him, beating him around his head and nearly killing him. "The police swung their clubs right and left," reported the *New York Times*, "and in the scuffle O'Carroll received a blow on the head that split his scalp open." Becky Edelsohn threw her body on his to protect him from the strikes, and probably saved his life, although he never fully recovered from his injuries. As one witness recalled, "I saw O'Carroll covered with blood. Police and plain clothes men were all around him clubbing and blackjacking him. I saw Becky Edelsohn standing over Joe trying to shield him. I tried to get to her but the police pushed me back."[44]

When O'Carroll and Caron were taken to the police station, said Caron afterward, "The plain clothes men then discussed what charges they should bring against us." After bandying about options for indictment, the officers made the two men wash the blood from their "faces and necks and hands" and "took away O'Carroll's collar which was soaked with blood." Then the police charged them with disorderly conduct and police interference, in part to justify O'Carroll and Caron's pronounced injuries.[45] Several other demonstrators were arrested for various offenses. Sculptor and poet Adolf Wolff, who was hit by an officer, was charged with threatening the police. Joseph Gans, a printer, was charged with carrying a banner without a permit. Student Samuel Rapoport was charged with uttering threatening language.[46]

But when the magistrate caught sight of the battered Caron and O'Carroll, not only did he release them on the grounds that they had been unjustly arrested, but he condemned the police officers for interfering with their right to free speech. He further suggested that the defendants sue the officers for assault. Both were taken to the hospital. Caron suffered a broken nose, among other wounds, but was discharged soon after, and was back among his fellow demonstrators in no time. O'Carroll, in far worse condition, remained in the hospital for several weeks with operations on his scalp and jaw expected in the future.[47]

As the unemployed were protesting in New York with violent consequences, trouble had been brewing in Colorado, leading to a terrible incident that would become known as the Ludlow massacre. Workers at the Colorado Fuel and Iron Company had been demonstrating since the summer of 1913. The miners, many of them immigrants from Greece and Italy, were demanding appropriate safety precautions, eight-hour workdays, cash wages rather than scrip, and the freedom to organize—all rights to which they were entitled under existing Colorado law. Mine operators, who had been ignoring the Colorado statutes for years and had refused to meet with union representatives, eventually hired private guards who were deputized by local sheriffs and given official authority. In September 1913 striking miners were evicted from their company-owned homes and were forced to relocate to a tent colony at Ludlow provided by the union.

The conflict between the guards and workers began in earnest. On October 7, 1913, guards invaded the tent colony and killed a miner and a child. Several days later they fired upon a meeting and killed three. Workers responded, shooting at an elaborate armored car known as the "Death Special," and killing one guard. On October 28 the Colorado governor called in the National Guard to control the fighting, a move the miners initially welcomed. Yet it soon became clear that the National Guard troops favored the side of the company, bullying and arresting workers, harassing and assaulting their families, and displaying hostility to the strike itself.[48]

John D. Rockefeller Jr., who held a controlling interest in the mining company, refused to negotiate with the strikers. "We would rather that the unfortunate conditions should continue and that we should lose all the millions invested," he said, "than that American workmen should be deprived of their right, under the Constitution, to work for whom they please. That is the great principle at stake. It is a national issue."[49] President Woodrow Wilson, who had taken office in March 1913, said that he was "deeply disappointed" by the ongoing situation, but Rockefeller defended his position before a congressional committee. "We have gotten the best men obtainable and are relying on their judgment," he said. He was opposing organized labor on principle. "And you will do that if it costs all your property and kills all your employees?" one Congressman asked. "It is a great principle," Rockefeller replied.[50]

The conflict concluded with tragic results. On April 20, 1914, a unit of National Guard troops attacked the tent colony with rifles and machine guns, killing five miners and a boy. They poured oil on the tents and set them on fire. One witness later said, "Some of the soldiers carried torches which looked like brooms on fire. Others carried cans which I supposed contained oil. They went about setting the tents on fire and shooting at every person they saw."[51]

Another survivor fled with her three small children from their burning tent and hid with others in a cellar. All three of her children died when the tent above the cellar was set on fire; a total of eleven children and two women suffocated.[52] Three men, including a leader of the strike, were savagely beaten and murdered. The strikers retaliated by attacking mines throughout the area. By April 29, when President Wilson sent in federal troops, seventy-four had been killed on both sides. The strike ended in December 1914, when, out of money, the miners surrendered.[53]

The Ludlow massacre had a resounding effect on the reputation of the Rockefeller family. "Mr. Rockefeller," said the *New York World* on April 27, 1914, "recently testified that he was willing to sink his entire investment in Colorado rather than yield to the demand of his employees that they be permitted to organize. He has not sunk and he does not intend to sink his entire investment, but he has debauched an American commonwealth, and the blood of women and children is on the hands of his barbarous agents, private and public."

Peaceful demonstrations took place, many focused on Rockefeller himself, with protestors holding silent vigils outside his New York City home and office. Berkman, Leonard Abbott, and muckraking writer Upton Sinclair were among the chief organizers of the Free Silence Movement, headquartered at 3 Trinity Place. As Abbott explained, "We have been fighting to establish the right of free speech. Now you give us a new fight. It is the fight to establish the right of Free Silence."[54] Upon the office wall was scrawled a directive to recruits: "If you want to brawl or fight, go to Colorado, but don't hurt our movement by trying it here. We want only men who will pledge themselves to speak to no one and go quietly with the police if arrested."[55]

On April 30 Berkman, Becky Edelsohn, and militant activist "Beautiful Marie" Ganz brought nearly 1,000 people to gather outside Rockefeller's office in the Standard Oil building at 26 Broadway. There, Ganz dispensed with silent protest. She made it inside the building and up to Rockefeller's outer office on the fourteenth floor, where, in loud tones, she promised to "wake this town up" and "shoot [Rockefeller] down like a dog." She was later arrested and sentenced to sixty days in jail for her threats. The rest marched up and down the block until five in the afternoon.[56]

Elsewhere, Upton Sinclair turned himself in for a three-day stint in the Tombs on a charge of disorderly conduct, and proceeded to undertake a hunger strike. Leonard Abbott held a conference with Police Commissioner Arthur Woods, at the commissioner's invitation, afterward reporting that the city administration was braced for "a period of intense public feeling, due to the killing of men, women, and children in Colorado" and expected a display of emotion through "free speech, free assemblage, and free passage through the streets." Abbott also told reporters that prominent and well-known citizens had telephoned the headquarters of the Free Silence Movement offering money and support "to send the social chill" to Rockefeller, whose "conduct is not approved by the moral sense of the community." Later that evening, Arthur Caron and several Ferrer Center comrades attracted a crowd by standing mutely outside the homes of both John D. Rockefeller and John D. Rockefeller Jr., at 4 and 10 West 54th street.[57]

The mass protests in front of Rockefeller's office and home continued daily. At a vigil in May, organized by Berkman and led by Upton Sinclair, demonstrators presented a passive display of "silent mourning" outside 26 Broadway. Participants, including Caron and Abbott, dressed in black or wore black armbands. Upton Sinclair drafted a "solemn warning" to Rockefeller. "I intend this night," he wrote, "to indict you upon a charge of murder before the people of this country."[58]

The Commission on Industrial Relations, in a report released the following year, placed the blame for the conflict on the younger Rockefeller, who "wrote letter after letter in enthusiastic praise of men whose acts, during this period, had precipitated a reign of terror and bloodshed. It was only when the Ludlow massacre filled the press of the nation with editorial denunciation, when mourners in black silently paraded in front of his New York office, when cartoons in the conservative press pilloried him and his father before an angry public, that at last complacency gives way to concern."[59]

FOR PERHAPS THE FIRST TIME, Berkman was not hovering at the fringe of society, dangerous and undesirable, but was united with mainstream leaders and thinkers on the side of righteousness. The Ludlow massacre reverberated within the labor movement and around the country. In New York, Berkman relentlessly organized the nightly demonstrations and Saturday afternoon rallies in Union Square, with Rockefeller the symbol of their outrage. At one rally, the charismatic Italian-born anarchist and I.W.W. organizer Carlo Tresca prompted his listeners to chant the name of the person responsible for the Ludlow deaths. As Tresca later wrote, "A roar of angry voices answered: 'Rockefeller! Rockefeller!' "[60] Throughout the spring, many labor and anarchist publications, including *Mother Earth,* demanded vengeance. "This is no time for theorizing, for fine spun argument and phrases," said one editorial. "With machine guns trained upon the strikers, the best answer is—dynamite."[61]

Rockefeller, fearing for his safety, removed himself to the heavily secured family estate in Pocantico Hills near Tarrytown, New York, thirty miles north of Manhattan. This ploy did not deter Berkman. On May 30 he sent to Tarrytown a number of Ferrer Center members, including Caron, Plunkett, Jack Isaacson, and Becky Edelsohn. There they held a meeting in the town's Fountain Square.[62] One by one they tried to speak, and all were arrested, charged with disorderly conduct, blocking traffic, and endangering the public health.

The next day Sasha returned in person with another group of comrades in tow. The police in Tarrytown, wrote the *New York Times,* "decided to 'play football' with [the anarchists] instead of locking them up, and under this policy the agitators were simply pushed and shoved about and not permitted to linger in one place long enough to make a speech or attract a crowd." Alexander Berkman "was [the] leader," the *Times* continued, but when "he mounted a barrel and sought to harangue a crowd of curious persons," he was driven off by police and by a jeering mass of spectators. Sasha then climbed onto a chair to "call upon the people to help him in his fight for free speech 'as guaranteed by the Constitution, but as suppressed by Mr. Rockefeller, the real owner of the Tarrytown police.'" An officer "grabbed him and threw him from the improvised rostrum." He landed on the ground and was "dragged by the policeman and pushed backward to the Tarrytown line," while his comrades "did their best to keep Berkman on his feet."[63]

The police arrested several more protesters. Although Sasha was not detained, he went to check on the "boisterous" scene at police headquarters. Edelsohn, Caron, and those locked up the previous day had been kept "six to a cell" and "were singing I.W.W. songs in chorus and banging at the cell doors." Brought before the judge after twenty-four hours of detention and a self-enforced hunger strike, Becky Edelsohn called the charges against herself, Caron, and their comrades "fictitious and a gross lie" and protested the cramped, dirty conditions of the jail. "You ought to build your hen coops for your chickens and not for those who come to speak at the place dedicated to public speaking," she said. By ten that night Sasha and those not under arrest were driven out of town, with angry villagers urging the exhausted police to "beat them up."[64]

Undaunted, Berkman vowed to continue the struggle. "We are going to defy Rockefeller, the mayor, and the city magistrate," he declared, "and will carry on our agitation and hold meetings no matter who is opposed to us or what machinery is used against us." On June 22 Caron, Plunkett, and Edelsohn, all out on bail for their May 30 arrest, returned with Berkman to the village to stage another protest. This time the "demonstration was far fiercer than anything that had occurred before."[65]

Gathering at the city-owned Croton Aqueduct, they were confronted by hostile locals who yelled insults, threw "showers of rotten eggs," and hurled rocks. Sasha jumped on a soapbox and tried to speak about freedom of speech, but was jerked from the platform by the Chief of Police. Becky took Sasha's place and cried that she was "here on American soil." A clod of dirt was flung at her and landed on her shoes. "That is American soil. Take that," shouted a man in the crowd. Sasha tried to climb back onto the box, but was "downed with an avalanche of missiles" consisting of eggs, stones, vegetables, dirt, sticks, and clumps of sod.[66]

When Arthur Caron stepped onto the soapbox and attempted to speak, he was struck hard in the mouth by a rock and began bleeding heavily. "He faltered, dazed [and] his comrades caught him as he fell from the box."[67] At the railroad station, policemen who had stood by when the villagers made mischief now actively joined the attack on the anarchists, clubbing them as they boarded the train. This assault enraged Berkman and his comrades, who afterward abandoned the attempt to protest peacefully in Tarrytown.

It may have been this incident that shifted their focus from passive demonstration to violent expression, and spurred Sasha, in the summer of 1914, to revisit the idea of attentat. Any principled ground and positive attention he might have achieved with his peaceful protests against Rockefeller would now be relinquished with the hatching of a new lethal intrigue. As Leonard Abbott wrote, "Some cherished thoughts of revenge, and some may have decided to take revenge."[68]

A PLOT WAS DEVISED AT THE FERRER CENTER to blow up Rockefeller's Pocantico Hills mansion. Between June 22 and July 4, conspirators including Arthur Caron, Becky Edelsohn, Charles Plunkett, and young Latvian immigrants Carl Hanson and Charles Berg met to discuss how to do it. Caron in particular had been growing more and more incensed: twice imprisoned, repeatedly beaten, constantly insulted, he was seething with outrage at the treatment of the unemployed and the murders of the men, women, and children at Ludlow. "It ran through his consciousness like a flame," said Leonard Abbott.[69] On June 22, after being injured yet again, Caron shouted, "I shall avenge myself!" "I knew Caron well," Carlo Tresca later wrote. "I already suspected what he was up to and what the consequences might be."[70]

Carl Hanson and Charles Berg, both former sailors, were young revolutionaries and close friends.[71] They met while working on the same ship, came to New York together in 1911, got work as carpenters, and joined the local Latvian Anarchist Group. In December 1913 they helped found a

Latvian branch of the Anarchist Red Cross, along with Hanson's half-sister Louise Berger, another participant in the Rockefeller plan, whose apartment on Lexington Avenue in Manhattan would become the site of the fatal climax. Berg, a "quiet, reserved man" with a "distinct and strong personality," had been arrested at Tarrytown on May 30, and also was present at the demonstration there on June 22. Hanson, meanwhile, had been fired from his job as a construction worker on a Long Island bridge for distributing anarchist literature among his workmates.[72]

Emma was away on a lecture tour and not involved in the Rockefeller plot. But Sasha was at the very center of the conspiracy. For all his ordeals and hard-earned insights, he still considered terrorism a valid form of protest, especially when enacted upon a single symbol of repression and persecution. Such a crime, he felt, was more moral than the acts perpetrated by corrupt government institutions and greedy captains of industry such as Frick and Rockefeller. Although these men led lives of civic honor, sitting on boards of charitable organizations, teaching at Sunday schools, accepting honorary degrees from universities, belonging to fashionable clubs, and attending church services, Berkman thought of them as criminals.

"I am sick of appeals to legality, sick of the hope for class justice," he wrote in *Mother Earth*. "It is high time to begin to fight Satan with his own hell fire. An eye for an eye; a tooth for a tooth!"[73] In Berkman's mind, Ludlow, with its oppression, unchecked militia, and slaughter of workers, was another Homestead, and Rockefeller another Frick. Twenty-two years after his attentat, his indignation and impulse to retaliate came flooding back in full force.[74]

Berkman's role in the Rockefeller plot was much different from his role in the Frick attack. He was not involved with the construction of the bombs, having proven in 1892 that he was ill-equipped for such a task. He did not intend to take public credit for the crime to make headlines, but was vague and enigmatic about the conspiracy, although the outline of his formal autobiography, drafted two decades later, promised "the inside story of some explosions."[75] Even close comrades were kept in the dark. They knew that since Sasha was older, experienced, and methodical, he was a natural fit to guide the Rockefeller operation, but they remained unsure of the contours of his complicity.

"Was Berkman involved?" mused Moritz Jagendorf, director of the Free Theatre at the Ferrer Center, when the question was put to him years later. "Well, he was very straightforward, practical, a man of action and organizing strength. I honestly feel that Berkman was involved, that he helped, at least with the planning."[76] Will Durant, who met Sasha at the Ferrer School in 1912, later wrote that when it came to aggressive acts, Berkman "was unrepentant and still believed that when other avenues of social protest were blocked by the power of wealth, the oppressed were justified in resorting to violence."[77] Some Ferrer Center and Mother Earth members were certain of Sasha's guilt. "Berkman," Jack Issacson's wife flatly declared, "was the mastermind of the plot."[78]

Charles Plunkett knew the full story, but even six decades later was cagey. "I'm the only one still alive who knows about Lexington Avenue, but I'm not going to tell you or anyone else. Why should I? After all, it was murder." Eventually the details spilled out. "Only a few people were involved," Plunkett said. "Caron, Hanson, and Berg, of course. Louise Berger, Hanson's half-sister, knew about it. Becky Edelsohn knew about it. And Alexander Berkman. It was Berkman who organized it, though the others were to carry it out. Berkman still believed in the necessity of violence."[79]

THE GROUP OF CONSPIRATORS MET a number of times between June 22 and July 3. The plan, apparently, was for Caron, Hanson, and Berg to deliver a bomb they had constructed to Rockefeller's home at Pocantico Hills. The three men had been accumulating a supply of dynamite over the past several months, even before the plot was formulated, either to be smuggled into Russia for use by revolutionary groups or to be used in connection with the demonstrations in New York. Some of the dynamite had been stolen from the site of the Lexington Avenue subway, at the time still under construction, and stockpiled in Louise Berger's apartment at 1626 Lexington Avenue between 103rd and 104th Streets, a thickly populated immigrant district of Harlem five blocks from the Ferrer Center.

On July 3 the three men made their move, traveling upstate with the bomb, unaware that Rockefeller had already left Tarrytown for his summer home at Seal Harbor, Maine. Plunkett later suggested that the conspirators only planned to set off an explosion nearby Rockefeller's home as a warning, without intending to injure anyone. In any case, had the house been successfully attacked, the victims would have been the mansion's servants and staff, yet another indication that the plot was ill-conceived as well as morally misguided.

Ferrer student Maurice Hollod was among those who stood guard at the Center on July 3. "Berkman was upstairs," Hollod recalled, "with Caron, Hanson, and Berg. In fact, he was the central figure. There had been a number of earlier meetings, and Berkman had attended them all. He hadn't gotten rid of his 'propaganda by the deed' mentality. Around 1 A.M., the men came downstairs. I was wearing a button that said 'GENERAL STRIKE.' Berg saw the button and asked me if he could wear it at a meeting the following day. That was the last I saw of them."[80]

The Rockefeller domain remained untouched. The conspirators' efforts were frustrated, either because the explosive failed to detonate or because the three anarchists were unable to penetrate the heavily guarded estate. With their mission thwarted, they returned to Louise Berger's apartment to regroup.[81] Perhaps intending to store it temporarily until they could make another try at Rockefeller, they took the bomb with them to the apartment, which was still filled with stolen dynamite.

The next morning, July 4, a bright and sunny Independence Day, Louise Berger left her apartment and went to see Berkman at the Mother Earth office on 119th Street. She was speaking with him, possibly about the bomb and the plot itself, when, at 9:16 A.M., the explosion occurred. "It was the bomb for Rockefeller that set [all the dynamite] off," said Plunkett. "I'll never know why they brought the damn thing back!"[82]

Meanwhile the whole Ferrer Center crowd had been planning to celebrate the Independence Day festivities with a large picnic at Leonard Abbott's cottage in Westfield, New Jersey. Many comrades were preparing to depart for the event just as the bomb went off. Jack Isaacson left his apartment on East 103d Street to buy the morning paper, and as he approached the corner of Lexington Avenue, there was a terrific explosion, "a crash like that of a broadside from a battleship." He saw a piece of a body, a man's arm, fly through the air and fall to the street.[83]

Moritz Jagendorf, who lived with his parents on East 109th Street, was getting ready to go to Abbott's picnic. "Suddenly," he recalled, "there was a great crash. I rushed out and ran down Lexington Avenue about five or six blocks and saw rubble and smoke. A crowd had gathered, and the police were hustling everyone away. I started home but saw detectives questioning my father—they wanted to talk to me—so I went straight to Abbott's place. He served us corned beef and tongue sandwiches and beer. Everyone was hushed. There was an undercurrent of excitement. No one knew what to say."[84] Abbott informed his guests of the misfortune, but carried on with the picnic, and even entertained the crowd with a fireworks display in the evening.[85]

The explosion, which could be heard clearly from the Ferrer Center, destroyed the three upper floors of the six-story tenement. The roof splintered into fragments. Brick and mortar showered into the street and over neighborhood roofs. The fire escape and ironwork in front of the building were twisted and torn out of place, and ceilings, walls, and stairways of the apartments on the upper floors collapsed. Furniture was blown hundreds of feet into the air, "some of the wreckage landing on the tops of houses more than a block away." The upper portion of the excavation site for the subway caved in, leaving a fifty-foot-long trench. "Of the hundreds of windows in the tenements on both sides of Lexington Avenue," reported the *New York Times,* "all but a dozen were shattered by the shock."[86] A rain of glass crashed to the street. Panicked residents rushed onto the pavement, and crowds gathered to behold the wreckage.[87]

Four people died in the explosion, three men and a woman, all in the apartment where the blast originated: Arthur Caron, Charles Berg, Carl Hanson, and Marie Chavez, who had not been involved in the conspiracy but had rented a room and occasionally attended Ferrer Center lectures. Berg was torn to pieces ("blown to atoms," as the *New York Times* put it), and it was his arm that Jack Isaacson saw fall to the street. The mutilated bodies of Hanson and Mrs. Chavez were found inside the apartment; Berkman was asked to identify Hanson's "mangled remains" at the East 104th street police station.[88] Caron was thrown out onto a fire escape. His body was still intact, and death was probably due to a fractured skull.

Twenty other people were injured, including seven who required hospitalization. Fortunately, many of the building's tenants had already left for July Fourth celebrations, and only about a third were inside when the detonation occurred; survivors described the reverberating blast, caving ceilings, tumbling plaster, and clouds of dust. A four-month-old baby, flung from his aunt's arms, escaped injury when he landed in a padded dog basket.[89]

One other person was inside Louise Berger's apartment when the bomb exploded. Michael Murphy, a young I.W.W. member, was in bed, sleeping. Amazingly, his bed was blown downward two floors, leaving him dazed but unhurt. He staggered into the street, half dressed, and a policeman kindly gave him his coat. Murphy, unrecognized, slipped away and went to the office of Mother Earth, where Berkman directed him to Leonard Abbott's picnic in New Jersey. Plunkett accompanied him there, and Murphy was subsequently spirited away to Philadelphia by members of the Radical Library who had been summoned on the telephone by Joseph J. Cohen, smart and stalwart, one of the leading figures in the movement.

A reporter went to the Westfield picnic, and Abbott told him that Murphy was not in attendance; the police were given the same story.[90] The police continued to search for Murphy, but were unable to find any sign of him. Murphy remained in hiding for a while, and then went to England by way of Canada. More than twenty years later, he wrote a letter to Joseph Cohen asking if it was safe to come back. "Dad gave a double-take when he read that," remembered his daughter Emma Cohen, a Modern School student who was ten at the time of the explosion, "and figured that if he had to ask such a question after all that time he had better stay put. So he answered no."[91]

Berkman, meanwhile, was taken to the police station for questioning. "Cool and suave," wrote the *New York Times,* "he smilingly answered all questions asked him . . . and appeared hurt when asked if he knew of any plan to make a bomb to be used to injure any person who had incurred the enmity of the organization of which he is a leader."[92] Berkman said he was acquainted with Caron, Hanson, and Berg, but denied any knowledge of a conspiracy, and stated that the July 3 meeting had been held to discuss the upcoming trial for those arrested at the May 30 Tarrytown demonstration. He expressed ignorance about explosives stored in the Lexington Avenue apartment, and said he had learned of the blast from Mike Murphy.[93]

The police let him go but put him under twenty-four-hour surveillance; when young Maurice Hollod approached him on the street soon after, Berkman at once instructed him to hurry along.[94] "Berkman was a lovable character," Hollod reminisced. "He loved children. He was an impeccable dresser in a light gray suit with Panama hat and cane, mustache and glasses. I ran instinctively to him. He stopped me and quietly told me to go home. I was crushed. But he later explained that he was being followed and didn't want me hurt."[95]

A number of anarchists likewise were questioned, including Louise Berger, Marie Ganz, and other Ferrer Center militants. Female police detectives offered little Emma Cohen ice cream, she recalled, and "tried to wheedle information out of me," but she, too, remained silent.[96] The Ferrer School and Mother Earth offices were put under surveillance, and other radical organizations were investigated, raided, and threatened. Yet police could find no evidence of a conspiracy, and were unable to implicate anyone else in the explosion.

Members of the Ferrer Center worried for its reputation, and the entire Modern School project suffered repercussions. Police agents infiltrated lectures and meetings, and the schools were seen as pushing subversive and violent doctrines and representing a haven for bombmakers and terrorists.[97] The Ferrer Center's day school moved to Stelton, New Jersey, in the spring of 1915 and the Center itself remained open for only four more years.[98] Meanwhile many radicals, including several I.W.W. spokesmen, attempted to distance themselves from the controversy, and renounced the use of explosives and criminal retaliation in their activism. Even a few of the Tarrytown demonstrators were "horrified when the explosion occurred." Said one observer, "They did not approve of such methods. What they wanted was protesting—a lot of protesting—but not bombing."[99]

Some anarchists, however, maintained solidarity with the three lost conspirators. Mike Gold and Adolf Wolff dedicated poems to their memory, and tributes appeared from the Anarchist Red Cross and a number of publications.[100] On July 6 Berkman, abandoning caution despite the police scrutiny, demanded a public funeral for the men, with a procession through the city streets and a display of their coffins in Union Square. This idea was met with ringing scorn. The city was up in arms over the bombing, and editors, writers, businesspeople, politicians, citizens of all stripes, were disgusted by the notion of equating terrorism with martyrdom.

Many of Sasha's comrades feared such a public spectacle would invite riots or worse, and even Emma, absent from New York for the whole episode, was alarmed by Berkman's zeal. She found his blatant defiance during this delicate time damaging both to the anarchist movement and to *Mother Earth,* which she had always tried to keep free of gratuitous incendiary jargon and to protect its standing as a substantive paper with a broad appeal. (Berkman, hotheaded as always, published the entire July issue as a moral defense of the bombing.) The police banned the public funeral, and on July 8 the bodies of Caron, Hanson, and Berg were quietly cremated in Queens in the presence of a small group of mourners, including Berg's brother; Hanson's half-sister Louise Berger; and Caron's mother and sister, who came from Fall River for the ceremony.

Berkman, however, was intent on a conspicuous commemoration. He organized a mass memorial held in Union Square on the afternoon of Saturday, July 11, 1914. Eight hundred police officers stood by as more than 10,000 people assembled, the men wearing red roses in their lapels and the women wearing red ribbons on their hats and clothing.[101] Placards and banners that carried pronouncements such as "We Mourn Our Comrades," "You Did Not Die in Vain," and "Capitalism Is the Evil, Anarchism Is the Remedy" were unfurled as Berkman, decked in a "brilliant red" tie, a black and blue ribbon around his sleeve, ascended the platform and began to speak.[102]

"Fellow mourners," shouted Berkman, "we are gathered here to honor the memories of murdered soldiers who died in the cause of humanity . . . I want to go on record as saying that I hope that our comrades were manufacturing the bomb that caused their death and that they had hoped to use it against our enemies." When he finished, "perspiration streamed from his face," and "his bald head shone in the sunlight as the cheers he called for ended."[103] Leonard Abbott and Carlo Tresca spoke, as did a belligerent Charles Plunkett, who threatened "not only defensive vigilance, but offensive violence. I don't believe in waiting until we are attacked."[104]

Becky Edelsohn was irate when she took the stage. "Why is it," she demanded, "that in the twentieth century, men, sensitive men and women can be so goaded by oppression that they are forced to retaliate with violence? Every day that the capitalist system is in existence, it is perpetuated by violence, and that is the only way that it manages to hold its own. They talk about violence! What about the massacre in Ludlow? What about the Triangle fire? What about the thousands and thousands of victims in the factories who are daily crippled and maimed or killed in explosions in the subway, railways and mines?

"Talk about violence!" Edelsohn continued. "What about the thousands of boys who are enlisted in the armies, sent to murder or be murdered before they realize the significance of joining the army? Talk about violence! . . . Oh, don't let us hear any more twaddle about violence. All the violence that has been committed by the labor movement since the dawn of history wouldn't equal one day of violence committed by the capitalist class in power."[105]

The rally closed without disruption. Berkman presented an urn containing the ashes of the three men, which bore the inscription "Killed, July 4, 1914, Caron, Hanson, Berg." A band played Chopin's Funeral March, the "Marseillaise," the "Internationale," and selections from the late poet David Edelstadt's revolutionary songs. The crowd joined in, and strains of music carried far across the square. The following day, the urn was put on display on a draped pedestal in the garden of the Mother Earth office on East 119th Street, surrounded with wreaths, flowers, and banners from the Union Square rally. Designed by sculptor Adolf Wolff, it formed the shape of a pyramid symbolic of the class system, with a clenched fist bursting from the apex. Thousands of visitors filed through the offices and into the garden to pay their respects. The urn, said to exert a hypnotic effect, was remembered vividly decades later by those who had seen it.[106]

17

TROUBLE IN PARADISE

After the Lexington Avenue affair, Berkman decided to embark upon a lecture tour—getting out of town seemed a wise move, especially given the spate of small bombs that exploded around New York in the wake of the July 4 disaster. Although the bombs caused relatively little damage, they heightened the pressure on radicals in the city, and were making life difficult for Emma, now home from her travels, and for her friends. Sasha chose Pittsburgh as his first stop, in commemoration of the completion of his prison sentence, and planned an itinerary that would take him on to Cleveland, Detroit, Chicago, Madison, and across the country to California. He published a notice of his tour in *Mother Earth* to alert his comrades nationwide, and set his departure date as November 9, 1914. In October Goldman relocated her base of operations to a smaller, less expensive apartment at 20 East 125th Street. She needed to tighten her budget, since money went out as quickly as it came in, despite ongoing assistance from wealthy benefactors and various fundraising efforts. Then she left for another circuit, lecturing often about the war in Europe, which had broken out in August.

Emma and Sasha were staunchly against American military engagement, and opposed the Great War from its very beginning. Sending soldiers to fight was, in their opinion, just another form of domination and oppression by the government. During the early months of 1914, as war clouds were gathering in Europe, the pair initiated the Anti-Militarist League of Greater New York. Berkman, who acted as secretary-treasurer of the League, organized some of the first antimilitarist rallies in New York, as well as open-air meetings and a wide distribution of related literature. The League held a number of events, including a ball and bazaar at the Lenox Casino in Harlem, where a one-act play by Adolf Wolff was presented as a highlight.[1] Both Emma and Sasha rejected so-called American military preparedness and the readying of the country for combat, fearing such activity would set the United States inexorably on a path to war.

"Almost the whole of Europe," Sasha wrote in *Mother Earth,* "is involved in a murderous struggle that would be impossible if the workers were class-conscious or enlightened in an anti-militant sense."[2] In August, when the conflict began, *Mother Earth* printed an antiwar issue, for which the artist Man Ray created a compelling cover. "We proclaim the INSURRECTION AGAINST THE WAR," blared the lead editorial. "No lie more heinous than the jingo motto that 'preparedness for war is the best guarantee for peace.' War will last as long as capitalism and government last. . . . Down With Militarism! Up With the Rights of Man! Insurrection Rather Than War!"[3]

On November 8 a dinner party was held to bid Sasha farewell. A group of more than twenty, including Harry Kelly, Hippolyte Havel, Leonard Abbott, and Russian-born anarchist Bill Shatoff (whose given name was Vladimir Sergeyevich Shatoff), gathered at a Romanian restaurant on the Lower East Side. Also present were two sisters, Helen and Lillian Goldblatt, who frequented the Ferrer Center and had taken part in the free-speech demonstrations at Tarrytown. The friends ate, drank, talked, and sang, and had a fine time until midnight, when they took their leave. As they walked toward the elevated train at Houston Street, some of them again started singing revolutionary songs, until several policemen approached to complain of too much noise and ordered them to be quiet.

A disagreement followed, and the officers said that the comrades were being excessively rowdy and impertinent. One of the policemen seized Helen Goldblatt, who cried out in pain. Another lifted his nightstick to strike Shatoff, who was walking with Sasha; Berkman grabbed the policeman's arm, causing him to drop the nightstick. More officers arrived, surrounding them, and arrested Shatoff, the Goldblatt sisters, and one other comrade. Berkman was not initially recognized, but when he accompanied his friends to the police station to make sure they had enough money for bail, Shatoff called out to him, "Comrade Berkman, give me your cigarettes." Sasha's identity was revealed. "Just the man we wanted," said an officer with satisfaction.[4]

The hearing was held the next day. The two women and two men were charged with disorderly conduct, and the magistrate fined each of them $10. Shatoff paid his fine—a linotype operator, he was due to print the next issue of the Russian anarchist paper *Golos Truda* (The Voice of Labor) and could not afford to be detained. The remaining three, however, refused to pay the fine, and were sent to Blackwell's prison for ten days. When the arresting officers testified that Berkman had interfered during the arrests and had snatched a police stick, the magistrate recommended that he be charged with felonious assault. Sasha hired lawyer Gilbert Roe to handle his case and was released on $1,000 bail supplied by the father of an Italian comrade; he then went off on his lecture tour as scheduled. But Roe advised Berkman to go no farther than Denver so that he would be available to return to New York within forty-eight hours if indicted and remanded for trial.[5]

In Pittsburgh, Berkman gave speeches in remembrance of the November 11 anniversary of the Haymarket affair, and on the necessity of violent acts. While in the city he sent a sympathetic letter to Helen Goldblatt, jailed on Blackwell's Island with her sister. "My dear little Helen," he said, "I am far away from you but my spirit is with you both. I hope you are not treated inhumanely. You should never be there in the first place, of course. Well, we know what justice amounts to and we must take things as they come. A pinch of philosophy in these matters helps a great deal, and I know both of you girls are sensible enough to profit by this little experience. It's an education to have a taste of all sides of life. I know you'll agree with me. Only I'm sorry I'm not there to keep you company—time might not seem to drag so much for you."[6]

Sasha reached St. Louis in December; there, with Fitzi's help, he set up a Ferrer Association branch to raise funds to start a day school, and delivered a speech on modern education. Fitzi wrote to comrade Jacques Rudome about Berkman's performance, which was intellectually stimulating if not lucrative. "He is the greatest of them all, Jack," said Fitzi. "It is really a joy to work up meetings for him even if they are not of such financial success. Spiritually and morally they are a great success."[7]

By February 1915 Berkman was in Denver, where he remained until he received a wire from Gilbert Roe: "Case against you dismissed. You are free to go where you please. Congratulations." The grand jury dropped the case after Roe exerted his influence with the new district attorney in New York. "Roe was an unusual man," Berkman later observed, "clear thinking, logical, cool, and with a strong sense of justice and wide sympathies."[8]

Berkman wrote again to Helen and Lillian Goldblatt, their brief sentences on Blackwell's Island long completed. "Denver is an overgrown village," he said, "very much spread out. Cowboys, Westerners, Mexicans—every type is on the streets. A small circle of radicals here, and they are pretty intelligent." He concluded the letter affectionately. "You are both splendid, sweet girls, and I love you both. And when I get to see you again, I'll kiss you till your head will swim and you'll holler 'murder, stop thief!!' But I'll not consider it robbery for you'll have plenty of kisses left, see?!" Berkman also asked the Goldblatts about another matter. "What's this I hear about some arrest in New York of a man called Schmidt? Write me all about it, because I saw some papers mention my name in connection with this, and I have been wondering what the police are up to now."[9]

Schmidt was anarchist Matthew A. Schmidt, who, with comrade David Caplan, would draw both Sasha and Emma into a coast-to-coast manhunt and a sensational bombing trial.

Several years earlier, brothers John J. and James B. McNamara of the International Association of Bridge and Structural Iron Workers Union were arrested and charged with conceiving a bombing plot targeting the Los Angeles Times Building and the newspaper's editor, Harrison Gray Otis, whom the radical community considered a major enemy of labor. The deeply conservative Otis was strongly antiunion, and for years had maneuvered to ban unions from the city, although many Los Angeles workers had been successfully unionized by organizers from San Francisco.

On October 1, 1910, in the midst of an iron workers' strike, the Los Angeles Times Building was dynamited; at least twenty were killed and two dozen injured, some severely. It was a scene, said witnesses, of "terrific violence" and horror.[10] The massive explosion, set off by a bomb planted in the adjacent alleyway, led to a raging fire that engulfed the building within minutes, and some of the terrified employees died when they leapt from windows to escape the blaze.[11] "Editors and Printers Meet Awful Death in Flames Following Big Explosion," ran the headlines.[12]

Otis (whose home was one of several other targets around Los Angeles) accused the unions of resorting to murder and terror to achieve their goals. In response, labor representatives argued that the bombing was a conspiracy to impede unionizing in Los Angeles. After the McNamara brothers were apprehended for the crime—seized on the run in Indianapolis and brought to Los Angeles—it was suggested that Otis and his agents had framed them, particularly given the number of irregularities surrounding their capture, arrest, and prosecution.

Samuel Gompers of the American Federation of Labor engaged Clarence Darrow as lead defense counsel for the brothers. Initially they pleaded not guilty, but Darrow was unhappy with the progress of the case and foresaw a guilty verdict. Anxious to remove the threat of the death penalty, he advised them to change their plea to guilty. In December 1911, J. B. McNamara was sentenced to life and J. J. McNamara to fifteen years at hard labor. The sudden admissions of guilt came as a shock to their defenders, who were convinced the brothers had been framed, were pawns in a broader conspiracy, or were unfairly prosecuted. It was a severe setback to the organized labor movement that union workers could be convicted of such a horrific crime. Darrow, meanwhile, would consider the McNamara case one of the great failures of his career. It resulted not only in guilty verdicts for his clients, but in personal and professional humiliation for himself: he was put on trial for jury tampering, for which he was acquitted.

Berkman and Goldman continued to support the brothers long after they confessed to the crime, lashing out at Gompers and other labor leaders such as Morris Hillquit, who advocated harsh punishment for the bombings—a betrayal, the anarchists felt, of labor solidarity. Shortly after the McNamaras entered their guilty pleas, Berkman wrote a scathing editorial in *Mother Earth* placing the blame for the murders on Otis and those who had curtailed the rights of the workers.[13]

Three other men were accused in the plot. Ortie McManigal, another member of the Bridge and Structural Iron Workers Union, testified that he had helped plant the dynamite, and gave evidence against the McNamara brothers in exchange for a reduced sentence. He also implicated two anarchists in the conspiracy: David Caplan and Matthew A. Schmidt.

Caplan, short, dark-haired, and free-spirited, was a Russian Jewish immigrant who lived with his wife, Flora, and their two children in San Francisco, where he ran a grocery store. Wisconsin-raised Schmidt was a former member of the Chicago Woodworkers' Union, a carpenter and machinist by trade. Blind in one eye and tough looking, he was witty and bright, considered "quite a philosopher" by his comrades, with an "almost mystical affection for machines."[14] Schmidt had moved from Chicago to San Francisco, where he became acquainted with J. B. McNamara. He also became friendly with several local anarchists, including Sasha and Emma's trusty comrade Eric Morton, who was living in San Francisco and editing the journal *Freedom.*

In September 1910, a month before the bombing, Schmidt and Caplan were said to have gone with J. B. McNamara to purchase some dynamite from the Giant Powder Company near San Francisco, posing as commercial explosives buyers and claiming the dynamite would be used to demolish tree stumps near Auburn.[15] By the time Caplan and Schmidt were pegged by McManigal and indicted for conspiring with the McNamaras, they had disappeared.[16]

Given the magnitude of the bombing disaster, Los Angeles mayor George Alexander hired the Burns Detective Agency, headed by William J. Burns, to help investigate the crime. William Burns personally directed the effort to track down Caplan and Schmidt, and the search brought his team to the Home Colony, the anarchist community near Tacoma, Washington. Agents infiltrated Home, renting rooms, disguising themselves as engineers and surveyors, and spending their days searching for the two fugitives.[17] They placed some members, including Jay Fox, the editor of Home Colony's paper *The Agitator,* under surveillance.

Burns managed operations from Tacoma "with the tenacity of a bulldog," but he failed to pick up the trail.[18] Occasionally he visited the Home Colony himself, posing as a bookseller, although his efforts at masquerade fooled no one: his photograph had been circulated to all the residents.[19] "He came to the door one day," said a local woman, the wife of a Tacoma barber, "and he had a book under one arm and another in his hand. I knew him at once."[20]

In his account of the investigation, Burns wrote with expansive disdain about the community. "Home Colony," he said, "is the nest of Anarchy in the United States. There are about 1,200 of them living there without any regard for a single decent thing in life. They exist in a state of free love, are notoriously unfaithful to the mates thus chosen and are so crooked that even in this class of rogues there does not seem to be any hint of honor."[21]

Burns was incorrect about the number of colonists; there were actually 213 inhabitants, including 75 children. The social activities, while undoubtedly bohemian and nonconformist, were perhaps somewhat less wanton than Burns described. Much fuss, for instance, was made over photos taken of colonists bathing nude in the water—a fairly common practice for those who lived along the sound. Many other residents opposed the nudity, however, sparking considerable conflict within the society. The images, when published by a newspaper, "created a scandal and 'free love' accusations," according to one colonist.[22]

For a while Caplan and Schmidt hid in a cabin deep in a timber area bordering the colony. Before long Caplan moved to Bainbridge Island on Puget Sound, and found work on a chicken farm. Schmidt went to Seattle, then to Butte, Montana, and on to New York, arriving in the city on October 23, 1910. He changed his name and pretended to be a German immigrant, a disguise that came easily because his boyhood had been spent among German-speaking people in Wisconsin.[23]

Schmidt became acquainted with the New York anarchists, and frequented the Ferrer Center, getting to know Hutchins Hapgood and Lincoln Steffens, among others. Steffens called him "a quiet, observant, able man, philosophic, thoughtful, and, above all, an artist. He was a highly skilled mechanic, who really loved to make and handle fine machinery."[24] Hapgood believed that Schmidt may have turned to violence because he felt "human society had become crystallized to the point of inertia . . . just as it was sometimes useful to employ dynamite to break up rocks in a field, that the field might bear crops, so it was also necessary at times to dynamite the rockbound crust of organized human society."[25]

Schmidt kept a low profile in New York, but did not go into hiding by any means. Under his assumed name, he lived openly, mingling with friends, dining in restaurants, attending the theater, romancing women, and taking odd jobs, including carpentry work at the Mother Earth office.

As Burns and his men continued their search at Home Colony, they came upon a young colonist named Donald Vose. Born in 1892, he was a descendant of freethinkers who traced their lineage back to the earliest settlers of Massachusetts. His mother, Gertie Vose, was strong-willed, feisty, and eccentric, and a prominent member of the Home community. An ardent advocate of women's rights, she openly flouted the conventional morality of the era, particularly in her relationships with men. When Donald was still very young, Gertie left her husband, Joseph Meserve, whom she had married in 1888, and lived as a single mother and free-lover.[26]

After a brief attempt at homesteading in Montana in the 1890s, Gertie relocated to Portland, Oregon, where she befriended Abe Isaak and his family, then settled with a new lover in the small lumber town of Scio, Oregon, in 1897.[27] The following year, Gertie invited Goldman to lecture in Scio and stay at her house. Emma had heard about Gertie from comrades including the Isaaks, and "was eager to meet the woman, who, in those days, was one of the few unusual American characters in the radical movement." The visit went well, and the two formed a solid friendship. "Gertie," Emma said, was "even more than I had expected—a fighter, a defiant, strong personality, a tender hostess and a devoted mother." Emma met Donald then, too, who at the time was a child of six.[28]

In the summer of 1901 Gertie visited the Home Colony and decided to put down permanent roots there, inviting her father, O. B. Vose, her daughter, Bessie Gray, and Gray's child to join her. She became an active, energetic member of the colony, serving as its treasurer. She contributed articles to the local journals *Discontent* and *The Demonstrator,* and wrote for other anarchist publications such as Isaak's *Free Society* and Moses Harman's *Lucifer.* Her tone was that of a revolutionary. "Every foot of advance ground," Gertie said, "has been bought with the blood of martyrs."[29]

Donald Vose was very different from his mother. To Gertie's great disappointment, he had no interest in anarchism or in radicalism of any kind. He far preferred iconic American leaders such as George Washington and Theodore Roosevelt to the heroes of his community—Karl Marx, Peter Kropotkin, Michael Bakunin, and other celebrated radicals of the world.[30]

Beyond his choice of idols, he was widely regarded by his neighbors as untrustworthy and a troublemaker. William Z. Foster, the future American Communist leader who lived at Home Colony for a time, remembered Vose as "generally unreliable," "a dull-wit, a sneak" who "grew up in the midst of radical teachings but remained impervious to them."[31]

Shortly after the Burns agents infiltrated Home Colony in 1910, the teenaged Vose was caught in an act of petty theft on a passenger boat in Puget Sound. A Burns detective happened to be on board and intervened, saving Donald from arrest. He recognized how useful Vose could be and engaged him as a spy to help the Burns team locate Caplan and Schmidt. Many people at Home Colony were perfectly aware that Caplan was hiding nearby on a chicken farm, and Vose had no trouble finding the site. Vose promptly reported Caplan's whereabouts to the Burns agency. From then on, Caplan was kept under surveillance until Schmidt could be located as well.[32]

Snaring Schmidt proved more difficult. Despite numerous wanted posters and offers of substantial rewards, Schmidt managed to elude capture for several years. Donald continued to pay regular visits to Caplan, and ingratiated himself with the lonely man, who trusted Gertie's son as a comrade. Eventually Caplan confided that "Schmitty" was hiding in New York, and asked Donald to deliver a letter to his friend should he happen to go there. Donald reported this development to the Burns detectives, who sent him to New York straightaway to attempt contact with Schmidt.[33] He arrived in New York in May 1914, just as the Rockefeller drama was heating up. He went to the headquarters of Mother Earth with a note of introduction from his mother, and Sasha welcomed him warmly. Gertie was well known in anarchist circles, a dear friend of Emma's, and Donald was a child of Home Colony. Vose therefore had easy, almost unquestioned access to the New York radical set, and soon was a regular at the Ferrer Center and the Mother Earth office.[34]

Now twenty-two years old, Donald was tall and lanky with a blond crew cut. "He looked like a real westerner, with his western-style hat," Ferrer School student Eva Brandes recalled.[35] He visited Tarrytown, and was among those who attended the July 4 picnic at Leonard Abbott's cottage in New Jersey, the day of the Lexington Avenue explosion. A group photograph taken at the picnic shows Donald in the background. Emma, out west on tour through the entire summer, went to Home in August, where

Gertie confided her pleasure at Donald's sudden interest in the movement and his newfound embrace of her causes.[36]

Goldman returned to New York on September 15, 1914, and found Donald in her home. She had not seen him since he was a child. "When I met him again," she wrote in hindsight, "he produced on me a very disagreeable effect, which was probably due to his high-pitched voice or to his shifting look, which seemed to avoid my eyes."[37] But he was Gertie's son, out of work, wretchedly clad, and she was inclined to help him. He told her he planned to return to Home Colony as soon as he had enough money, and mentioned that he was carrying a letter for Matthew Schmidt from someone in Washington State. A few of the anarchists in Goldman's circle later claimed it was at the Mother Earth offices that Vose overheard Goldman addressing a man she called "Schmitty," and thus was able to pinpoint the fugitive at last.[38]

Vose met Schmidt face to face on a Saturday in late September when Goldman invited some friends to the house. Schmidt was chatting with Sasha, Hutchins Hapgood, and Lincoln Steffens, when Donald arrived in the company of Terry Carlin, an Irishman and a former disciple of *Liberty's* Benjamin Tucker. Carlin, an alcoholic, was stooped and gaunt, with yellowing teeth and disheveled hair, but he was an engaging and charming fellow, a natural storyteller. He had once worked as a leather tanner but was now a drifter who survived on handouts, although he socialized with Eugene O'Neill, Theodore Dreiser, and other luminaries.[39] Carlin knew Schmidt from Chicago, and introduced Vose, who handed over Caplan's letter. Now personally acquainted with the fugitive and aware of his alias, Donald was able to provide the Burns operatives with detailed information about Schmidt's comings and goings.

Emma took off for her lecture tour in October 1914 (Sasha departed for his own tour in November, after his police dustup with the Goldblatt sisters), and when she returned on December 24, she was surprised to see Vose still in New York. He told her that he was awaiting money from Washington so he could return to the Home Colony. At the same time, rumors reached her that he was spending large sums on drink, although he did not appear to have a job.[40] At the Ferrer Center, Eva Brandes' mother suspected Donald of being a spy because he seemed to have "too much money."[41] Jack Isaacson and Hippolyte Havel also were concerned about where Vose's loyalties might rest. Seeing the bulge of a gun in Vose's pocket, Jack said, "He is a hunter and he's going hunting."[42]

Emma, increasingly suspicious, contacted friends on the West Coast, who told her that no one was sending Donald pocket money. Before Emma's concerns took shape, Vose abruptly announced that funds for his ticket had arrived, and he would be heading back to Washington State. Emma was relieved and "a little ashamed" of her distrust.[43] In February 1915 Vose at last departed for Home Colony. Immediately afterward detectives carried out coordinated arrests of Caplan and Schmidt, separated by thousands of miles.

On February 13, 1915, Schmidt was captured on Broadway and 64th Street, two blocks from his apartment. The *New York Times* reported that Schmidt had been shadowed while "fraternizing with Alexander Berkman and his followers."[44] Caplan was apprehended in his cabin on Bainbridge Island, "asleep when the detectives swooped down on him."[45] According to reports, he had been living under the alias Frank Moller, working on the chicken ranch, and managing a barbershop in Rolling Bay. Both men were transported to Los Angeles for trial.[46]

Following the arrests, Vose received a large reward, $2,500, and was promised a similar amount if he would take the witness stand against the two men. Goldman called Donald's betrayal "a staggering blow, one of the worst I had received in my twenty-five years of public life."[47] Devastated, she later wrote to a comrade, "I came nearly ending my life over the horrible shock that a child of an old friend of mine, who moreover lived in my house, should have betrayed Schmidt and Caplan."[48]

In Denver, soon after he read about Schmidt's arrest in the newspaper, Berkman was approached by police and quizzed by the Colorado authorities. He denied having met Schmidt, who, he pointed out, would be particularly memorable because of his one eye. "I have been in New York for twenty-eight years, off and on," Sasha said, "and I know every anarchist, Socialist, and I.W.W. member in the city." Schmidt, he insisted, was not among them. William Burns scoffed at this statement, explaining that Berkman had known Schmidt under the name Hoffman. "Schmidt, alias Hoffman, did some work at Mr. Berkman's house recently," Burns said. "He had one eye then and he has one eye now." Burns suggested that Schmidt had been privy to the Lexington Avenue plot and added,

"Mr. Berkman knows all about the circumstances leading up to the bomb explosion on Lexington Avenue July 4 last."[49]

Berkman shrugged off the accusations and continued west with Fitzi, ending up in Los Angeles, where they joined the Caplan-Schmidt Defense League formed on behalf of the two men. Aided by Eric Morton, San Francisco–based anarchist activist Lucy Robins, and other comrades and workers, Berkman rallied support with a series of speeches to labor groups in major industrial cities including Kansas City, Buffalo, and Philadelphia. Then Sasha went back to Los Angeles to offer his service before the trials.

Schmidt, the first to be tried, was charged with abetting J. B. McNamara in blowing up the Los Angeles Times Building. Donald Vose (identified in press accounts as Donald Meserve, his father's last name) was a witness for the prosecution at both trials, testifying that Schmidt had personally confessed his guilt.[50] When Berkman and his comrades first became aware of Vose's betrayal, some considered kidnapping him, or even shooting him (Sasha's idea), until Schmidt himself objected to such a rash deed.[51] But their anger blazed. At one point during the trial, Joe O'Carroll, the New York Wobbly, jumped Vose and had to be removed from the courtroom.[52]

Schmidt was convicted of murder on December 30, 1915, and was sentenced to life imprisonment. On January 12, 1916, he calmly addressed the court, condemning the "vassals of capital" whom he blamed for the crime. "I feel very deeply the suffering of those who lost relatives and friends in the Times disaster," he said, telling the prosecutors that he had grieved for the victims of "Ludlow, Lawrence, Bayonne, Couer d'Alene, and hundreds of other places where workers have been slaughtered." He challenged Vose's statement on the stand. "Let me ask you—do you believe in Donald Vose? You would not whip your dog on the testimony of a creature like Vose. No honest man would. Any man who would believe Vose would not deserve to have a dog."[53]

David Caplan was charged with complicity in the Los Angeles Times Building bombing, and his trial began on April 3, 1916. The jurors could not reach an agreement, seven voting for conviction and five for acquittal. At a retrial, held in October, he was convicted of voluntary manslaughter and sentenced to ten years in San Quentin prison, where Schmidt already was serving his life sentence. Caplan was released after seven and a half years, but by then he had little to return to. Since the bombing, his wife Flora had remarried and then died; his children had run away from home. Scorned as a convict, Caplan went first to Russia, his homeland, and then to Europe. Lucy Robins met him in Paris, a ruined beggar in ragged clothes, and gave him some money. That same day, she said, Caplan bought a pistol and committed suicide. Other comrades, however, claimed that Caplan died alone and unknown, in a London rooming house.[54]

Schmidt, an industrious machinist even in prison, eventually was put in charge of the penitentiary's technical and mechanical section, including the lighting and machine shop. He was said to be an exemplary prisoner, one who gained the admiration of both the prison administrators and his fellow inmates. In August 1939, after twenty-three years in San Quentin, he was paroled, and in 1942 his sentence was commuted to time served. He fell in love with Beth Livermore, a member of an illustrious San Francisco family, who worked for the board of education and was active in social causes. They married in Nevada in 1946.[55]

The couple, by every account, had a happy union. In 1954, after a Memorial Day weekend spent at their ranch in Big Sur, Beth was driving them home to San Francisco. Blinded by the late afternoon sun, she veered the car over an embankment, crashed forty feet below, and was killed.[56] Schmidt sustained only minor injuries and was hospitalized for shock after trying to save his wife.[57] Obituaries noted the "story book romance, she being a socially prominent sister of a millionaire industrialist and he, a parolee" convicted for the Los Angeles Times bombing.[58] The bereaved Schmidt remained active in the anarchist and labor movements until he died in 1955 after a fall.[59]

DONALD VOSE RETURNED TO THE HOME COLONY, where he was ostracized as a traitor by many members of the community. "He was a shyster, that guy," recalled a colonist many years later. "He did his darndest to get these people into trouble. He was the cause of several of them being arrested. He was no damn good. Nobody had any use for him."[60] "We had a baseball team," recalled another colonist, "that played with all the teams around Tacoma and gave a good accounting of itself. One Sunday most of Home was up on the hill watching a game, and off by himself along the sidelines between third base and home plate stood the stool pigeon Vose. When one of the older French colonists, Gaston Lance, spied him standing there, he ran over to where he stood, faced him, let out a stream of words in French . . . spat squarely in his face, then walked away. Donald didn't make a move in return. He just took it."[61]

Not long after this incident, Donald left Home and drifted into odd jobs along the Pacific Coast, working at Seattle shipyards and serving in the merchant marine. He was said to lead a rather lonely existence, and was a heavy drinker. Over the years he occasionally showed up at Home, asking for money from Gertie, who dreaded his visits. There was little forgiveness from the anarchist community. "Donald Vose you are a liar, traitor, spy," wrote Goldman. "You have lied away the liberty and life of our comrades. Yet not they but you will suffer the penalty. You will roam the earth accursed, shunned and hated; a burden unto yourself, with the shadow of M. A. Schmidt and David Caplan ever at your heels unto the last."[62]

In December 1945 the S.S. *Whirlwind,* on which Vose was employed, was docked in San Francisco. Donald was seen staggering up the gangplank carrying a case of beer on his shoulder. As he reached the top he stumbled, lost his balance, and plunged twenty-six feet to his death on the dock below. He was fifty-three years old.[63]

Vose was not forgotten, however. He appears as a character in Eugene O'Neill's *The Iceman Cometh,* which O'Neill considered "one of [the] best plays I've ever written."[64] O'Neill, a Princeton University dropout, had become interested in anarchism in 1907, when he was introduced to Benjamin Tucker and spent time in Tucker's Sixth Avenue bookshop in New York. There O'Neill read a range of writers—literary, philosophical, and radical—including Tolstoy, Kropotkin, Nietzsche, and Shaw. He studied Tucker's works, learning about the philosophy of individualist anarchism, which influenced O'Neill's "inner self." He also read Goldman's *Mother Earth,* much to his father's chagrin, and was swayed by her views. According to O'Neill biographer Louis Sheaffer, Goldman became "one of O'Neill's idols," and an early O'Neill poem was published in the May 1911 issue of *Mother Earth.*[65]

When O'Neill joined the New York bohemian scene, he came to know Emma personally, and met Berkman and other anarchists, including Hippolyte Havel, whom he would depict as Hugo Kalmar ("one-time editor of Anarchist periodicals") in *The Iceman Cometh.* Another of O'Neill's friends, Terry Carlin, was immortalized as Larry Slade, *Iceman's* "old foolosopher." Not only did Carlin inspire the Slade character, but he gave O'Neill the idea for one of the main themes of the play, telling him the inside story of the McNamara case and how Donald Vose had infiltrated Mother Earth and the Ferrer Center and double-crossed David Caplan and Matthew Schmidt. Vose is represented as Don Parritt (branded in the play by Hugo Kalmar as a "stool pigeon"), a guilt-racked soul who betrays his anarchist mother and her friends for their involvement in a bombing on the West Coast.[66]

18

THE BLAST

FROM THE TIME BERKMAN ASSUMED the editorship of *Mother Earth* in 1907, he had harbored a desire to begin his own weekly paper with a rebel theme, "a practical weekly, a fighting champion of revolutionary labor." Goldman was wholeheartedly in favor of the idea. *Mother Earth,* well established as a significant journal in cultural and activist spheres, was "theoretical, literary, and educational" rather than purely radical, and it reflected Emma's sensibilities and style.[1] It had burnished her reputation as a major player in contemporary life, and was a source of personal pride. She recognized that Berkman "longed for something of his own making, something that would express his own self."[2] For many years, Sasha had been regarded as Goldman's "satellite," as Lucy Robins put it, and he craved the chance to assert his independence and put forth his own ideas.[3]

It was not until the end of 1915 that Sasha realized his dream. After many failed attempts to raise money for such a project, he finally seized upon Eric Morton's suggestion that he establish a journal in San Francisco.[4] "I find that no time could possibly be more appropriate for a revolutionary labor paper than the present," Berkman told Upton Sinclair. "There is a great deal of rebellious discontent, especially among the organized labor element, which is now seeking some definite expression."[5]

"You see my new letter head?" Sasha wrote to Helen Goldblatt on December 18, 1915. "Like it? I suppose you have already heard that I am to publish and edit a new revolutionary labor weekly on the Coast. Now, Helen dear, I am sure that with the cooperation of our friends we can make *The Blast* a power in this country. And I want you to help me with it; you and Lilly and our other good friends in New York. I want you to line them up for me." Sasha was equally enthusiastic about his new home base in San Francisco. "The climate is great, the country beautiful. The bay and the ocean and the mountains—all around you, and the great red woods with their giant trees—out of the stump of one a whole house can be built."[6]

In San Francisco, Berkman and Fitzi rented an apartment at 569 Dolores Street in the Mission District, which served as both their residence and *The Blast* headquarters. With Sasha as editor and Fitzi as manager, they brought in Carl Newlander, a young Swedish anarchist, as an assistant, and asked Eric Morton to be associate editor. "Let the voice of rebellion be heard!" Berkman announced in the December *Mother Earth.* "THE BLAST is to be such a voice. It will propagate no *isms.* It will speak frankly and unafraid the language of revolutionary labor. It will deal with all the vital problems facing labor and the people at large . . . and may it thus blaze the path for the coming greater blast, the Social Revolution."[7]

Anarchists in New York, Chicago, St. Louis, and Los Angeles held a series of dinners and fundraisers to finance the effort, while the staff of *The Blast* raffled off the works of Nietzsche and other writers. On Christmas Eve 1915, San Francisco anarchists gave a party to celebrate the new journal. The launch of *The Blast* was planned for January 1916, with departments devoted to labor news, prisoners' issues, children's education, antimilitary activities, and the world war raging overseas.[8] Friends sent their congratulations, and Goldman's wired missive was published in the first issue. "Birthday greetings!" she declared. "Let THE BLAST re-echo from coast to coast, inspiring strength and courage in the disinherited, and striking terror into the hearts of the craven enemy. . . . May THE BLAST tear up the solidified ignorance and cruelty of our social structure. Blast away! To the daring belongs the future."[9] From the Home Colony, Jay Fox wrote a cheerful letter that closed with a little poem: "Here's to THE BLAST; may it blow, / Till the flame of Freedom envelops the earth, / And the last limb of tyranny's laid low."[10]

At Berkman's request, Robert Minor, an artist and political writer, came to San Francisco to contribute to the paper. Minor was a well-known cartoonist in his early thirties who had worked for such publications as the *San Antonio Gazette,* the *St. Louis Post Dispatch,* and the *New York World,* as well as a number of radical journals including *Mother Earth.*[11] Minor's future wife, Lydia Gibson, designed the masthead for *The Blast,* and drew covers and wrote poetry. Eric Morton submitted reports, poems, and limericks under the pen name "Eric the Red," while Berkman sometimes signed his own articles with the pseudonym "R. E. Bell."

The result was a visually striking journal with an incendiary tone, sharp commentary, and a snappy flourish. The price per issue was five cents, with a yearly subscription rate of one dollar, and subscriptions came in from labor organizations, Workmen's Circle branches, anarchist groups, and Wobblies.[12] "The paper is paying its way," said Sasha to the journalist Louise Bryant, "and we are trying to enlarge our circle of subscribers."[13]

Berkman used *The Blast* as a platform for further radical dialogue and activity. He organized a Current Events Club and coordinated with San Francisco–based organizations such as the Freedom Group, the Blast Group, the local Union of Russian Workers, and the Gruppo Anarchico Volonta, which was made up of Italian men and women who admired Luigi Galleani, a militant Italian anarchist who lived in Massachusetts. Gruppo members met Saturdays in a club on Stockton Street, where they celebrated their fierce hero, promoting Galleani's ideology with lectures, picnics, and a well-maintained library.

In the summer of 1916 Emma came to visit Sasha and Fitzi in San Francisco after a tumultuous few months. In February she had been arrested for giving a speech on birth control (openly discussing or distributing contraception was illegal), and beginning in late April spent two weeks in prison for the offense. Emma had first publicly broached the issue of contraception in 1900, although back then, she said, "I did not discuss methods, because the question of limiting offspring represented in my estimation only one aspect of the social struggle and I did not care to risk arrest for it. . . . I was so continually on the brink of prison because of my general activities that it seemed unjustifiable to court extra trouble. Information on methods I gave only when privately requested for it." Eventually, she decided, "the time had come when I must either stop lecturing on the subject or do it practical justice."[14] Her arrest and trial had caused a stir, and, as an act of protest, she had opted for the jail sentence rather than pay the small fine.

Emma planned to stay for a while in San Francisco, and took her own apartment in the hope that Ben Reitman would join her there. Their tempestuous relationship continued its erratic path as they grappled with Ben's recent prison stints, his desire to have another child (he had a daughter from a liaison in his youth, but was ready to experience hands-on fatherhood), and his latest love affairs, including with a young girl who attended his Sunday school classes at Mother Earth. Emma had encouraged his interest in teaching a Sunday school course, believing that "Ben's religious emotionalism was stronger than his anarchistic convictions, and I could not deny him his right of expression." As she noted sardonically after learning of his unorthodox teaching style, "it was indeed the height of tragicomedy that my stand in favour of Ben's Sunday-school in the Mother Earth office should result in an affair with one of his girl pupils. . . . It was all so absurd and grotesque."[15]

On July 22, 1916, Emma was lunching with Sasha and Fitzi at their home on Dolores Street. Goldman was scheduled to lecture that night about America's role in the war in Europe and the prospect of U.S. military action. The telephone rang, and the three were alerted to the news that an explosion had occurred during the Preparedness Parade, a massive event staged by the city of San Francisco to demonstrate America's readiness for war. Tens of thousands of people had gathered to watch 50,000 marchers and dozens of bands pass in a three-and-a-half-hour procession. A large explosion occurred shortly after the parade began. A suitcase bomb had been placed against a saloon wall near the corner of Steuart and Market Streets. Ten people had been killed, and forty more wounded.

The newspapers ran headlines about "Anarchist Bombs" and attributed the crime to "anarchist elements." That evening Goldman went ahead with her lecture, titled "Preparedness: The Road to Universal Slaughter," and observed that in the hall were "more detectives than people."[16] "As usual in such cases," wrote Berkman in *The Blast,* "the local authorities immediately raised the cry of 'Anarchist.' The enemy is athirst for blood; it is planning to transplant to San Francisco the [Haymarket] gallows of 1887 when five of Labor's best and truest friends were strangled to death in Chicago."[17]

Within days after the explosion, five suspects had been arrested: Thomas J. Mooney, his wife, Rena Mooney, his friend Warren K. Billings, Israel Weinberg, and Edward D. Nolan. Their status as anarchists was unproven, although all five were acquainted with Berkman, and were familiar with *The Blast.* Mooney, a thirty-four-year-old organizer for the International Molders' Union, had written an article for the April 1 issue of *The Blast* and helped collect subscriptions for the paper.[18] A week before the Preparedness Day Parade, he had attempted unsuccessfully to lead a strike of streetcar workers. Rena Mooney, a music teacher, was involved in her husband's labor activity, including the streetcar strike. Billings, twenty-three, had raised funds for *The Blast,* and was a member of the Boot and Shoe Workers' Union; Weinberg was a leader of the Jitney Bus Drivers' Union; and Nolan belonged to the Machinists' Union.

Berkman and his comrades were among those who were convinced Mooney and Billings were being framed. Immediately after the explosion, the authorities dangled a substantial reward, which soon grew to about $17,000, for information leading to the bombers; the *New York Times* called the amount a "sweepstake for perjurers."[19] The shock and horror of the bombing—the shrapnel released by the dynamite caused great human damage, including lost limbs and terrible mutilation—propelled some citizens into vigilante mode while law enforcement officials worked frantically to solve the crime.

A special bomb bureau was formed, and a glut of tips and conflicting stories was sorted and sifted by the detectives assigned to the case, including the person in charge, San Francisco district attorney Charles M. Fickert. Anarchists often were the default culprits in the city, not without reason, and Martin Swanson, a former Pinkerton agent and private detective employed by PG&E, the Pacific Gas and Electric Company, came forward to offer up a list of possible suspects within the radical community. Swanson named Mooney and Billings in particular. Both men were known as labor agitators, Mooney was pegged as a special enemy of PG&E and other local companies, and Billings had previously been convicted for using dynamite during protests.

The Mooney-Billings trials became notorious. While the bombing itself was a ghastly act of terrorism and a great tragedy in San Francisco, the investigation of the crime, detailed by Richard H. Frost in his book on the case, was a travesty of justice. After the explosion, police failed to rope off the scene or systematically collect evidence. The inquiry throughout was shoddy and haphazard. There were stark indications of witness tampering, and much dubious data were presented at the trial by the prosecution. Some jurors later were deemed incompetent or unreliable.

Martin Swanson was described in the press as a "private detective, who has hovered as a dark figure in the ranks of the prosecution."[20] Concern sharpened that Fickert had encouraged perjury, fabricated evidence, and, with the help of others, including Swanson, deliberately framed the suspects. Although a few in the anarchist community suspected that Mooney and Billings might have been involved in some way, all were certain they had been unfairly prosecuted in the interest of expediency and retribution. Mooney, Billings, and the others were the casualties of a desperate and cold-blooded compulsion to resolve the case.[21]

BERKMAN HIMSELF SOON FELL UNDER SUSPICION. His rumored involvement in the Lexington Avenue bombing was duly recalled by authorities, and, to them, his presence in San Francisco seemed fishy. That he had named his journal "The Blast" did not help matters. "Berkman's Hand Seen in Dynamiting," declared a local newspaper. A week after the explosion, the offices of *The Blast* were visited by a squad of detectives from the bomb bureau. "A raid, b'gosh!" Berkman mocked in his paper. Assistant District Attorney Edward A. Cunha, accompanied by three agents, including Martin Swanson, spent four hours searching for explosives. Berkman made his contempt clear. "The degree of intelligence the raiders showed convinced us that they couldn't detect the trail of an elephant on a muddy cowpath. They actually asked me whether I had explosives in the house! Of course I had." Berkman made a show of handing his 38-caliber weapon over to Cunha, which Cunha declined, although, Berkman recounted, "I noticed that he had very cautiously removed the bullets from the revolver. Safety first!"[22]

The squad departed, taking with it copies of the journal's California subscription list, and several days later Berkman and Fitzi were summoned to police headquarters. They were questioned for five hours. Berkman fielded queries about anarchist philosophy, while Fitzi had to explain why "such a nice sweet lady with such a good Irish name" would associate with anarchists. Their responses provoked only frustration. "Every Anarchist is a criminal," cried Assistant District Attorney James Brennan. "We'll hang you all, every one of you!"[23]

"Five of our friends are now facing trial on charges of murder in connection with the bombing affair of July 22nd," wrote Sasha to anarchist editor and writer Warren Starr Van Valkenburgh in New York. "Our offices have been raided. There is no doubt that they are planning to suppress the paper."[24] In addition to the raid on the offices of *The Blast,* the federal government excluded several issues of the journal from second-class mail delivery. Berkman regarded this sort of move as "postal tyranny."[25] When he and Fitzi were prevented from sending out *The Blast* from San Francisco, they forwarded copies to friends outside the state for distribution. Maisie Bell, the daughter of Thomas Bell, recalled carrying out the task from her home in Arizona. "We kids," said Bell, "went around on bicycles mailing batches in different post boxes."[26]

But such measures of distribution were impractical at best, and circulation of *The Blast* soon became nearly impossible. Nor was *The Blast* the only anarchist paper to be barred from the mail. During the same period, in 1916 and 1917, a number of anarchist periodicals again were suppressed or withheld from shipment, including *Revolt* of New York, which was published by the Ferrer Center; *The Alarm* of Chicago; *L'Era Nuova* of Paterson, New Jersey; *Volne listy* of New York; and *Regeneración* of Los Angeles. Additionally, some editors were arrested and intimidated. Following the disaster at the Preparedness Parade, and with war looming, the authorities began shutting down revolutionary papers altogether. "Invasion of personal liberty, suppression of free speech and free press, silencing non-conformists and protestants [*sic*], shooting down rebellious workers," wrote a furious Berkman, "all this is the very essence of government."[27]

ONCE THE PREPAREDNESS PARADE BOMBING TRIALS were under way, Berkman devoted himself to the defense effort, as he had done the previous year for Caplan and Schmidt. District Attorney Fickert described Berkman as "the real power behind the defense."[28] Sasha worked with the Mooney-Billings Defense Committee, which was sponsored by the International Workers' Defense League of San Francisco and consisted of socialists, anarchists, syndicalists, labor groups, and unions who agitated for the release of "class-war prisoners."[29]

Leaving Fitzi to get out *The Blast,* Sasha traveled around the country to arouse interest in the case, visiting large labor unions in major industrial cities and prevailing upon the members to get involved.[30] Emma gave speeches, collected funds, and sought support from her powerful friends and acquaintances. Fitzi and Robert Minor also worked for the cause, and Minor wrote the first pro-Mooney pamphlet to help spur those in the labor movement to action.[31] In September 1916, when Warren Billings went on trial, Sasha was present in court every day to observe the proceedings. He was greatly disappointed when Billings was convicted of second-degree murder and, in October, sentenced to life in prison.[32]

After the Billings verdict, Sasha went back to New York, where he focused on Mooney's upcoming trial.[33] His first step was to secure an attorney willing to take charge of Mooney's defense. Several prominent people declined; Goldman had personally appealed to Frank P. Walsh, a noted liberal lawyer, but he had refused. (Walsh did, however, speak out unofficially in favor of the plaintiffs, and personally contributed $250 to the defense.)[34] Sasha contacted W. Bourke Cochran, a distinguished attorney and orator, who agreed to take the Mooney case without compensation. Berkman then lobbied New York radicals and large labor unions for their support, formed a publicity committee, and arranged rallies to generate positive press as well as funds. In December 1916 a mass meeting was held in Carnegie Hall, which was decorated with the flags and banners of numerous unions and radical societies.[35]

In January 1917, as Mooney's trial was about to commence, Sasha began another lecture tour to spread the word about this latest threat to the labor movement. He spoke at the Old Masonic Temple in Washington, D.C., held a meeting at the Arch Street Theatre in Philadelphia, and appeared at the Trades Assembly Hall in Ann Arbor, Michigan, where he befriended anarchist scholar Agnes Inglis.[36] He proceeded westward, although he had no intention of going as far as California, since he knew that Fickert and his team were intent on linking him to the crime. Sasha's friends recalled that the McNamara brothers had been seized in Indiana and taken to California against their will after the Los Angeles Times Building explosion; to prevent a similar occurrence, Bill Shatoff was brought in to serve as Berkman's bodyguard throughout the tour.[37]

In February 1917, Mooney's trial came to a close. He fared worse than Billings, despite having Bourke Cochran in charge of his defense. The jury found him guilty of first-degree murder, and he was sentenced to death. Mooney's defense put forth the alibi that he and his wife, Rena, had observed the parade from the roof of the Eilers Building, at Sixth and Market Streets, 1.15 miles from the explosion site. Not only did a dozen eyewitnesses place the couple there, but Tom Mooney could be seen in a series of photographs taken during the event, a clock in the frame indicating his presence on the roof between 1:58 and 2:04, the last photo captured just two minutes before the bomb went off at 2:06 P.M. While this detail in itself could not exonerate Mooney (and as the photographic negative was not submitted in court some doubted its authenticity), it cast yet another shadow on the soundness of the prosecution's case. The theory that the prosecution had presented false evidence during both trials, including putting fraudulent witnesses on the stand, continued to gain traction throughout the country.[38]

Berkman was devastated by the outcome of the Billings-Mooney trials and by Mooney's death sentence. "Already the voice of Labor is being heard in protest against the heaven-crying outrage," he mourned. "Every labor and labor-friendly organization must at once go on record in behalf of Mooney from the Pacific to the Atlantic in a storm of protest that shall terminate the masters' conspiracy to legally murder these labor men."[39] Billings was serving his life sentence at Folsom prison, and Mooney, in San Quentin, was scheduled to hang on May 17, 1917.

During this difficult period, Berkman received an additional blow. Fitzi, who had remained in San Francisco to edit *The Blast,* sent a telegram informing him that their office had again been raided by Assistant District Attorney Cunha and a team of detectives. The police confiscated manuscripts, subscription lists, files, cartoons, and three of Sasha's personal letters, which they removed forcibly. Fitzi, who was roughly handled, "fought like a tigress," and her arm was almost broken.[40]

Berkman decided that it was no longer feasible to continue publication in San Francisco, and he asked Fitzi to relocate the paper. "I have decided to bring *The Blast* to New York," he told W. S. Van Valkenburgh, "as its publication in San Francisco has become absolutely impossible now. I have given the last six months exclusively to the San Francisco cases and have entirely neglected *The Blast.*" Moreover, with the Mooney-Billings trials wrapping up, *The Blast* would now concentrate particularly on antiwar themes. On April 6 the United States formally entered the conflict in Europe, declaring war against Germany, and both Sasha and Emma were increasingly absorbed in protesting America's military activities. "I feel that a strong antimilitaristic agitation is of the utmost importance just now," Berkman told Van Valkenburgh. "Miss Fitzgerald will soon join me in this city."[41]

Fitzi arrived in New York at the end of April 1917, and she and Sasha set up *The Blast* at 20 East 125th Street in Harlem, where it shared offices with *Mother Earth.* "Do You Want *The Blast?*" demanded Berkman and Fitzgerald in the first issue published in New York. "We feel that our work on the Coast, in connection with the cases of the imprisoned labor men, has been accomplished. We came to New York to devote most of our time and energy to anti-militaristic work. If you believe that the work we are doing is important, give us your aid. If you want *The Blast* to continue, you must help us."[42]

THE MOONEY-BILLINGS CONVICTIONS became not only a cause célèbre for the American labor movement, but an issue in countries around the world. The Russian tsarist regime had been overthrown by revolutionaries in March 1917, an event that thrilled Emma and Sasha to the core and made them consider abandoning their commitments in America to join the fight. As Goldman later wrote, "The hated Romanovs were at last hurled from their throne, the Tsar and his cohorts shorn of power. It was not the result of a political coup d'état; the great achievement was accomplished by the rebellion of the entire people." She and Berkman pondered the idea of returning to their homeland. "Our own old yearning, Sasha's and mine, began to stir again in our hearts," she said. "All through the years we had been close to the pulse of Russia, close to her spirit and her superhuman struggle for liberation."[43]

But for many years, Emma had thought of America as her true home, a place of excitement, hope, and promise. "Our lives," she said, "were rooted in our adopted land. We had learned to love her physical grandeur and her beauty and to admire the men and women who were fighting for freedom, the Americans of the best calibre. I felt myself one of them, an American in the truest sense, spiritually rather than by the grace of a mere scrap of paper. For twenty-eight years I had lived, dreamed, and worked for that America. Sasha, too, was torn between the urge to return to Russia and the necessity of continuing his campaign to save the life of Mooney, whose fatal hour was fast approaching. . . . Russia had great need of her revolutionary exiles, but Sasha and I now felt that America needed us more. We decided to remain."[44]

Emma and Sasha stayed, but other Russian-born anarchists in America, including Bill Shatoff, rushed to their native country to take part in the ongoing rebellion. They brought with them news of the recent legal events in San Francisco. Morris Ganberg was one such example. Before he departed for Russia, he stopped by the Mother Earth office on 125th Street. "Berkman was there," Ganberg recalled, "and I told him I'm going to Russia. He said he had something to give me for the Russian comrades, a declaration for Tom Mooney and instructions to the comrades to organize demonstrations to save Mooney. Fitzi typed it up and I came back for it a few days later. I went to Russia by the Pacific route via San Francisco. Berkman gave me a letter to Robert Minor, and I stayed with him in San Francisco for three days while waiting for my ship to sail. I told Minor about the declaration, and the next day he took me to visit Mooney and Billings in prison. Minor told Mooney, 'This man is going to Russia, and will do something there to help you.' Mooney shook the bars and said very loudly, 'I hope you Russian people will help me.' Once in Russia, I traveled . . . to Kiev, and gave Berkman's appeal to the Kiev anarchist group. They distributed it to Moscow, Petrograd, and Odessa, and demonstrations were organized, especially at the American Embassy in Petrograd."[45]

On April 22, 1917, an officer of the Provisional Government in Petrograd telephoned the American embassy to warn the ambassador, David R. Francis, that an anarchist crowd was gathering to attack the embassy. Francis could hear shouts of "Muni! Muni!" but was not sufficiently briefed on the Mooney case, and did not recognize the pronunciation of the defendant's name. The crowd was dispersed, but the situation remained unnervingly volatile. Russia's instability was exceptionally dangerous in the midst of world war, and the intensity of the local outcry against Mooney's death sentence prompted President Woodrow Wilson to become involved.

On May 11, 1917, just six days before Mooney was to hang, Wilson sent a telegram to Governor William D. Stephens of California, asking him to intercede for the sake of U.S. foreign relations. "I hope that in view of certain international aspects which the case has assumed," the President wrote, "you will not deem me impertinent or beyond my rights if I very warmly and earnestly urge upon you the wisdom and desirability of commuting the sentence of Mooney or at least suspending its execution until the charges of perjury lodged against the witnesses in the case are judicially probed to the bottom. Such an action on your part would I can assure you have the widest and most beneficial results and greatly relieve some critical situations outside the United States." Stephens wasted no time in arranging for Mooney's sentence to be stayed indefinitely by the appeal pending in the state supreme court. On May 14 President Wilson sent his thanks: "It relieves a rather serious anxiety."[46]

It may have been due in part to Berkman's international campaign that Mooney was spared. Back in San Francisco, District Attorney Fickert was determined to connect Berkman with the Preparedness Parade explosion. On July 13, he won a grand jury indictment against Berkman on charges of complicity in the bombing.[47] Sasha wrote to Emma, "The indictment against me in San Francisco is not simply against me, as an individual involved in the bomb affair. They know I am not involved. The indictment was asked and found against me as Alexander Berkman, the Anarchist."[48]

IN JULY BOTH RENA MOONEY AND ISRAEL WEINBERG were acquitted by juries. Edward Nolan was never brought to trial, although he was kept in jail for more than nine months until released for lack of evidence. But Sasha remained a target, and Fickert's attempts to extradite him to stand trial in San Francisco worried his comrades. Newspaper correspondent Henry Alsberg believed that it was personal hostility that prompted "a determined effort [to extradite him] on a trumped-up charge."[49] Emma and Fitzi wrote anxious letters to many of their friends, asking for help.[50] "The intention," Emma told Bolton Hall, "is to interject Berkman in the San Francisco situation thereby to obscure the entire issue and then to hang him."[51]

Goldman also contacted Catherine Breshkovskaya in Russia. "Dear Babushka," she wrote, "you know something about Berkman, so you will believe me when I tell you that he had no more to do with the Preparedness Parade explosion than the other five victims [the defendants], and that the reason for his present predicament must be traced to his undying devotion to the cause of humanity, and his particular zeal in behalf of the other five victims. . . . Give the San Francisco frame-up the widest possible publicity in the Russian newspapers . . . Use your influence in every way possible to prevent the legal murder of six human beings." Goldman also suggested that Babushka pass on her letter to Sasha's uncle, Mark Natanson, the revolutionary. "He ought to be able to do something for a worthy nephew as Sasha is."[52]

Emma's concerns were realized when Fickert successfully petitioned Governor Stephens to request Berkman's extradition as an alleged fugitive from justice from the state of California. Emma and Fitzi pressed the New York Publicity Committee to send to Albany a delegation of legal experts and labor representatives, including lawyers Morris Hillquit and Harry Weinberger, to warn Governor Charles S. Whitman of the repercussions should Berkman be removed to California.[53]

At the same time, President Wilson had been feeling intense pressure from a host of prominent people from the legal, political, and entertainment communities. They strenuously objected to the manner in which Moody and Billings had been arrested, tried, and convicted, and were clamoring for executive intercession. The president appointed a Mediation Commission, headed by Secretary of Labor William B. Wilson and legal scholar Felix Frankfurter, the future Supreme Court Justice, to conduct an investigation of the Mooney-Billings affair. The commission noted "the dubious character of the witnesses" and the shifty behavior of the prosecution, among other contraventions.[54]

By the time Fickert was ready with Berkman's extradition papers, Governor Whitman had been convinced that it was necessary to review the California grand jury minutes that resulted in Berkman's indictment, as well as the full commission report, before granting the request. Fickert, perhaps discomfited by the scrutiny, declined to send the grand jury minutes, and instead notified Governor Whitman that he would not seek extradition at present. He never again pursued his case against Berkman.[55]

The protests in Russia continued through September and October 1917, with revolutionaries decrying the manner in which America dealt with its own dissenters. In Petrograd, a rally was held in the Cirque Moderne, where thousands heard the speeches of Bill Shatoff, John Reed, Albert Rhys Williams, and other activists. Ambassador Francis remained under siege, the object of numerous threats and frequent acts of intimidation.[56] Threats also were made against the Russian Foreign Office. "If measures are not taken to save the lives of our comrades in America," read the warning, "then we, the revolutionary workers and soldiers of the city of Petrograd, will take energetic measures in the line of demonstration before the American Embassy."[57]

In March 1918 President Wilson again wrote to Governor Stephens. "With very great respect I take the liberty of saying to you that if you could see your way to commute the sentence of Mooney it would have a most helpful effect upon certain international affairs which his execution would greatly complicate." Stephens replied from Los Angeles: "You can rest assured that the Mooney case will have careful consideration." Stephens commuted Mooney's death sentence to life imprisonment. "The propaganda in his behalf, following the plan outlined by Berkman," said Governor Stevens, "has been so effective as to become world-wide."[58]

THE MOONEY-BILLINGS CASE WAS INFAMOUS for its transgressions. Both men had been convicted on the basis of perjured testimony and fabricated evidence. As in the Haymarket affair of the 1880s, the actual bomber was never brought to justice. Mooney and Billings spent more than two decades behind bars, despite the steady current of new information about the unfairness of the investigation and trials, the national and worldwide indignation, and the relentless efforts to free them.

But who was responsible for the bombing? The explosion was the work of the San Francisco members of the Gruppo Anarchico Volonta as an act of antimilitarist protest.[59] The perpetrators were disciples of Luigi Galleani, a preacher of terrorism and bombs. Galleani indicated that he had particular insight into the bombing during his November 1918 deportation hearing in Boston.

QUESTION FROM THE DEPORTATION INVESTIGATOR: Do you recollect at any time writing about the arrest of Mooney, the labor man in San Francisco?

ANSWER FROM GALLEANI: I think so; we had a special correspondent in San Francisco for this Mooney affair.

Q: I recollect seeing an article which I believe you wrote, saying that Mooney was innocent and that they had not got the right criminal; is that so?

A: Yes.

Q: Would you mind telling us how you got that impression?

A: It isn't an impression that I have that Mooney is innocent; I have the mathematical certitude that he is innocent.

Q: Do you realize that this is of vital interest to the country if you could prove that he is innocent; the Secretary of this Department has put in lots of time on that case and is vitally interested in getting the facts?

A: It is a very ticklish affair upon which I do not wish to comment; I am positively sure that it was not Mooney who threw the bomb.

Q: That is your personal conviction without evidence?

A: I believe it absolutely.[60]

19

THE GREAT WAR

From the first rumblings of world war, anarchists across the globe were divided on the issue of military involvement. The anarchist movement had a long tradition of resistance to war, and Sasha and Emma were adamantly opposed from the beginning. Yet there were occasions when leading anarchists took sides in armed conflicts between nations. Peter Kropotkin was one who staunchly supported the fight against Germany and its collaborators. Afraid of the influence of German militarism and authoritarianism, unable to tolerate the threat of an expanding German Empire, he approved of the Entente between France, Great Britain, and Russia.[1] "I consider that the duty of every one who cherishes the ideals of human progress," he wrote in 1914, "is to do everything in one's power, according to one's capacities, to crush down the invasion of the Germans into Western Europe."[2]

His daughter, Alexandra Kropotkin, said her father's hostility toward Germany was so profound that he sorely regretted being too old to join the French army. Yearning for the fight, he wrote, "the moment a conqueror would come to conquer, I would bite him like a good bull-dog."[3] By the autumn of 1914, Kropotkin had taken an unqualified prowar stand, and Berkman and Goldman were upset that their mentor had embraced the cause of the Allies. "Our old comrade and teacher," lamented Sasha, "the clear Anarchist thinker that he is, the uncompromising revolutionist and anti-governmentalist, takes sides in the European slaughter, and thereby gives aid and encouragement to this or that government? Impossible. . . . An anarchist has no country. . . . I know only one invader: the government which robs me of liberty and forces me to do things against my will."[4]

The majority of anarchists were pacifists—the ideology called for a peaceful society, even though some of its most visible adherents accepted, and committed, acts of terrorism. In March 1915 the London journal *Freedom* printed an "International Anarchist Manifesto on the War," signed by Berkman, Goldman, and a number of notable colleagues from America and Europe.[5] The manifesto stated that the role of anarchists was to urge the oppressed in all countries to actively pursue their own liberation. Government-sponsored war was a dangerous distraction. Anarchists should focus only on "cultivating the spirit of revolt, and arousing discontent in peoples and armies."[6]

Yet Kropotkin's prowar posture had its backers as well. In February 1916 Kropotkin and fourteen other anarchists issued a "Manifesto of the Sixteen" (only fifteen actually signed) in which they set forth a "defensist" position. The international anarchist community remained divided, with some upholding their antimilitarist heritage, and others switching from an antiwar to a prowar stance as the fighting progressed. Many in America, including Harry Kelly, Saul Yanovsky, and Adolf Wolff, eventually changed their position in support of the war in 1917 once the United States entered the conflict.[7]

PRESIDENT WILSON HAD BEEN REELECTED to a second term in November 1916, in part because of his slogan, "He kept us out of war." Yet by April 1917, the situation in Europe had reached such a crisis that Wilson asked Congress to declare war on the Central Powers "to make the world safe for democracy."[8] A month after the United States joined the fight on April 6, a draft act was passed requiring all men between twenty-one and thirty to register with the draft board on June 5.

The anxiety across the nation and within the government sparked a period of acute xenophobia and suppression of dissent. President Wilson addressed the country on Flag Day, June 14, 1917, and declared: "Woe to the man or group of men that seeks to stand in our way in this day of high resolution."[9] The outbreak of the Russian Revolution intensified the fear of radicalism and unrest, which precipitated the first Red Scare in America. Antiwar sentiment was quashed wherever possible, and radical activity was considered an outright obstruction of the war effort.

Not only did the authorities increase scrutiny of anarchists, socialists, Wobblies, and other militants, but private individuals and groups took up the pursuit in the name of patriotism. Vigilante activities often were sanctioned by state and local authorities, and "superpatriots" engaged in surveillance of their neighbors. Proprietors of halls and gathering places were pressured by police and civilian groups alike to deny access to radicals, and, as happened to *Mother Earth* and *The Blast,* radical publications were hindered in production or removed from the mail. The I.W.W., unable to rely on its standard methods of dissidence, saw a critical diminution of power. The Bureau of Investigation escalated its raids on the headquarters of radical organizations, and labor strikes and slowdowns now could be judged as seditious interference in the manufacture of war materials.

Immigrants and foreigners, already grappling with indifferent or hostile treatment, faced a deepened chill. A decade earlier, in 1906, the Naturalization Act had required that an applicant for American citizenship had to state that he or she was "not a believer in or opposed to organized government or a member of or affiliated with any organization or body of persons teaching disbelief in or opposed to organized government," and to swear that he or she was not an anarchist. By 1917 many immigrants were viewed with elevated suspicion and dislike, and blamed for importing such dangerous philosophies as anarchism, socialism, and syndicalism. With the mounting wave of anti-Red feeling, Congress passed legislation for the deportation of "aliens who are members of the anarchistic and similar classes."[10] Radical dissent was viewed as an insult to the American way of life. In this environment, anarchists in particular were regarded as a menace, given their professed antimilitarism, antipatriotism, and anticapitalism.[11]

ON MAY 9, 1917, SASHA, EMMA, FITZI, and Leonard Abbott established the No-Conscription League in the office of *Mother Earth* on 125th Street. Before long, chapters of the League were organized in other cities, and 100,000 copies of anticonscription manifestos were circulated around the country. A successor to the Anti-Militarist League, which they had founded three years earlier, the No-Conscription League's primary purpose was to protest against the draft.

"I for one," wrote Emma in *Mother Earth,* "will speak against war so long as my voice will last, now and during war. A thousand times rather would I die calling to the people of America to refuse to be obedient, to refuse military service, to refuse to murder their brothers, than I should ever give my voice in justification of war, except the one war of all the peoples against their despots and exploiters—the Social Revolution."[12] Goldman summarized the platform of the No-Conscription League as "opposed to all wars waged by capitalist governments. We will fight for what we choose to fight for: we will never fight simply because we are ordered to fight. . . . The militarization of America is an evil that far outweighs . . . any good that may come from America's participation in the war. We will resist conscription by every means in our power, and we will sustain those who, for similar reasons, refuse to be conscripted."[13]

On May 18, 1917, the day that President Wilson signed the conscription law, the No-Conscription League held a protest meeting in the Harlem River Casino at 127th Street and Second Avenue, with Berkman and Goldman representing the anarchists. League members Louis Fraina and Carlo Tresca spoke for the revolutionary socialists and the I.W.W, respectively. Before a crowd of 8,000, they called for a general strike against the war and denounced forced military service. Also in attendance was a hefty contingent of soldiers, policemen, and detectives.

Sasha was in some pain, having sustained an injury the week before, when he fell down the steep stairway leading from *The Blast* offices on the upper floor, and tore the ligaments in his left foot.[14] Sasha wrote to Agnes Inglis on May 17, "I had an accident last week in running down the stairs. . . . I hurt my foot so that now I am unable to walk. It's unfortunate especially now that we are going to have a mass meeting tomorrow, but I intend to be there just the same. Perhaps my speech will be more effective when I stand on crutches."[15] In the end, he rested his leg on a chair as he spoke. The event had a special poignancy for Sasha; May 18 was the twelfth anniversary of his release from the Workhouse in Pennsylvania, and he and Emma were happy to be together for the occasion.[16]

A week after the rally, Sasha wrote a memorandum complaining of the "autocratic tendencies" that allowed America to pass the Conscription Bill "without making even the slightest proviso for conscientious objectors to human slaughter. There are thousands of men who will not under any circumstances allow themselves to be conscripted." He announced a "Mothers" themed No-Conscription event on June 4, the day before official draft registration.[17]

The demonstration took place at Hunts Point Palace on Southern Boulevard in the Bronx, and Berkman and Goldman were the main presenters, with an array of women on stage to represent the mothers who opposed sending their sons to war. The meeting was "a great event," wrote Sasha to a friend, with 35,000 seeking admission. Only 2,000 were able to enter the hall; thousands more remained outside, filling the air with revolutionary songs.[18] "The audience inside was for the most part made up of young men and young women," reported the *New York Times*, "nine-tenths of whom, according to the police, were foreign-born. But not every one in the audience was an anarchist, a fact that was proved on several occasions when the speakers approached the danger line and seemed about to say something which would have resulted in the arrest of the speaker. But the great majority was friendly to the Goldman-Berkman school."[19]

Department of Justice officials, members of the federal attorney's office, U.S. marshals, hundreds of policemen, and detectives from the Anarchist Squad showed up to monitor and disrupt the rally. Soldiers and sailors whistled, stamped their feet, and heckled the speakers, and when Berkman, unsteady on his injured foot, began his lecture, he was pelted with electric bulbs and lemons. Journalist and activist John Reed, who was present, implored the police captain to intervene, but the officer refused.

Emma, as was her practice, warned the crowd against disturbance, calling out, "Friends, friends, wait! The soldiers and sailors have been sent here to cause trouble, and the police are in league with them. . . . File out in an orderly manner, intone our inspiring revolutionary songs, and leave the soldiers to their tragic fate, which at present they are too ignorant to realize." Despite the taut atmosphere, the meeting ended peacefully, although the press reported a few scuffles and arrests in the street afterward.[20]

The No-Conscription League held one final meeting, on June 14 at Forward Hall on East Broadway, a venue that belonged to the Jewish Socialist Party. While Emma and Sasha had been careful in their previous speeches to avoid any patently illegal utterance, the police swarmed the event and demanded to see the registration cards of every young man in attendance; those who could not produce one were subject to arrest. "It was apparently the intention of the federal authorities to use our meetings as a trap," observed Goldman, and she and her comrades decided to cease all public gatherings and concentrate on written propaganda for the time being.[21]

The next day, June 15, President Wilson signed the Espionage Act, which brought penalties of up to twenty years' imprisonment and fines up to $10,000 for persons aiding the enemy, interfering with the draft, or encouraging disloyalty in the armed forces. The postmaster general also was empowered to restrict printed matter urging "treason, insurrection, or forcible resistance to any law in the United States." The Espionage Act paved the way for prosecutions of radicals for treason and conspiracy against the government. Indictable offenses included policy declarations, articles, speeches, and even private correspondence. The distribution of such materials also served to establish conspiracy, the classic charge against radicals for want of hard evidence.[22] Throughout the country, anarchist meeting places were raided, men and women assaulted, equipment smashed, libraries and files seized.[23]

ON THE AFTERNOON OF JUNE 15, the day the Espionage Act was signed, U.S. Marshal Thomas McCarthy arrived with a team of officials at Emma and Sasha's headquarters at 20 East 125th Street. Emma was in the room that served both as the office of Mother Earth and of the No-Conscription League, while Sasha was upstairs in the workplace of *The Blast.* A full staff of their comrades also was in the building, including Fitzi, Carl Newlander, Walter Merchant, and their young assistant, W. P. Bales. McCarthy, flanked by an assistant U.S. attorney and officers from the Bomb Squad and Police Department, brandished a copy of the June *Mother Earth* and presented Goldman with a warrant for her arrest. Cheekily, she called up the stairs to her comrades, "Sasha, Fitzi—some visitors are here to arrest us."[24]

Both Berkman and Goldman were charged with violating the Espionage Act and "conspiracy to interfere with the draft." Emma was jaunty and defiant, but Sasha seemed anxious, alarmed. That evening they were taken to the Tombs jail. Bales, who was unable to supply a draft registration card, was arrested without a warrant.[25]

The federal agents also conducted a thorough search of the offices, seizing documents, correspondence, and mailing lists. They confiscated "a wagon load of anarchist records and propaganda material," wrote the *New York Times*, and "included in the lot is what is believed to be a complete registry of anarchy's friends in the United States. A splendidly kept card index was found." Police also removed bank and check books, and numerous copies of *Mother Earth* and *The Blast,* which had been held up on the order of Postmaster General Albert S. Burleson, as well as books and pamphlets written by Kropotkin, Errico Malatesta, Voltairine de Cleyre, Max Stirner, Maxim Gorky, Ibsen, Strindberg, William Morris, Edward Carpenter, and George Bernard Shaw. (The *New York Times* noted that "The Shaw books . . . were later ordered to be left on the shelves together with other works not of an anarchistic character.")[26]

Mother Earth and *The Blast* would not survive the summer. The June 1 issue of *The Blast,* after just eighteen months of publication, was its last. Fitzi and Newlander relocated the offices to a place on Lafayette Street, but *Mother Earth* printed its final volume in August. Goldman called the loss of the journal a "greater blow" than the prospect of prison. "A struggle of over a decade, exhausting tours for its support, much worry and grief," she wrote, "had gone into the maintenance of *Mother Earth,* and now with one blow its life had been snuffed out!" For some months, the comrades continued a version of the journal, circulating a newsletter called the *Mother Earth Bulletin,* which Emma deemed "small compared with our previous publication, but it was the best we could do in those harassing days."[27]

The morning after their arrests, Emma and Sasha appeared before U.S. Commissioner Samuel Hitchcock. Bail was set at $25,000 each, an amount that their lawyer Harry Weinberger protested as unreasonable. It was noted in court that Goldman and Berkman were not U.S. citizens, and thus could be deported upon completion of their prison sentences. Emma said she had been born in Russia, provided a bit of biographical information, and gave her age as 48. Sasha refused to reveal any personal data, and claimed to be 250 years old.[28]

A few days later a federal grand jury brought in an indictment, and the trial date was set for June 27. On June 21 their comrades had only enough money to post bail for one of them; Sasha was too "gallant" to accept the bond and remained in jail several more days despite his injured foot and Emma's assurance that she was perfectly comfortable in the Tombs, "resting and enjoying an absorbing" book Margaret Anderson had sent her—*A Portrait of the Artist as a Young Man,* by James Joyce. As Emma later remarked, "I had not read that author before and I was fascinated by his power and originality."[29] Fitzi, meanwhile, fretted over their plight, and told the press, "I can't understand it at all, for they are fine and beautiful characters, and are hundreds of years ahead of their time."[30]

20

BIG FISH

THE TRIAL BEGAN ON JUNE 27, 1917, at Foley Square in lower Manhattan with Judge Julius M. Mayer on the bench and Harold A. Content, assistant U.S. district attorney for the Southern District of New York, prosecuting the case. Harry Weinberger was on hand to give the defendants legal advice, although Emma and Sasha had decided that, as anarchists, they should "go into court without an attorney." "Our trial," Goldman said, "would have meaning only if we could turn the court-room into a forum for the presentation of the ideas we had been fighting for."[1]

They entered the packed courtroom at ten o'clock, Sasha still on crutches. A few friends had been allowed to view the proceedings, Fitzi, Emma's niece, Stella Ballantine, and Leonard Abbott among them. (Hundreds of supporters, wearing red roses, were turned away.)[2] Emma scornfully assessed Mayer and Content, "their Prussianism carefully hidden, like wrinkles on a woman's face, under the thick paint of Americanism."[3]

June 27 was Emma's forty-eighth birthday, and during the lunch hour, a group of comrades brought her a bouquet of red roses. Goldman was without the companionship of Ben Reitman, who, at the height of the anti-war effort, had left for Chicago to live with his young female pupil from the Sunday school; the girl was expecting his child. Emma was tormented by Ben's absence, and felt "deeply grieved and humiliated at the same time."[4] Yet she summoned her strength, and wrote in the penultimate issue of *Mother Earth,* "Tell all friends that we will not waver, that we will not compromise, and that if the worst comes, we shall go to prison in the proud consciousness that we have remained faithful to the spirit of Internationalism and to the solidarity of all the people of the world."[5]

The first few days were taken up with jury selection; then, on Monday morning, July 2, Harold Content opened his case. Fitzi was his first witness. Described by the papers as "six feet tall and ruddy of feature," she answered questions regarding the No-Conscription League and *The Blast*.[6] Fitzi adhered to the argument Sasha had established for the defense: that neither defendant explicitly dissuaded people from draft registration. "We have been carrying on an anti-militarist propaganda for twenty-five or thirty years," Berkman had explained. "But we did not conspire, and we did not advise people not to register. The No-Conscription League refused to commit itself to a policy of definitely advising young men not to register. We decided to leave the matter to the conscience of each individual."[7] Following in this vein, Fitzi cited a letter written by Goldman stating that she would not counsel young men against registration—and that men should have the character to decide for themselves whether to enlist or not.

During the trial, a number of comrades and acquaintances testified that Emma had never encouraged violence or nonregistration in their presence. Similarly, John Reed, Lincoln Steffens, Leonard Abbott, and Bolton Hall asserted that they had known Emma and Sasha for many years and that they did not regard either as "violent"—a claim that may have raised a few eyebrows given Berkman's criminal history and Goldman's rhetoric.[8] Content called as a rebuttal witness a stenographer who stated that, at several anarchist meetings for which he recorded notes, Goldman had professed support for the use of violence.[9]

The trial concluded on Monday, July 9. Content's closing argument ran about an hour, and then Sasha began his address. "The indictment is in regard to a conspiracy to urge people not to *register*," Berkman reminded the jury. "If you look through the indictment you will not find a single word about *conscription*. . . . Did the prosecution prove the alleged conspiracy? Did the prosecution prove that we urged people not to register? Did it prove any overt acts in furtherance of that alleged conspiracy? Did it even attempt to prove or to demonstrate that we are guilty as charged? Oh no . . . [n]either I [n]or Miss Goldman ever said in our speeches or in *Mother Earth* or in *The Blast* 'Don't register,' or 'You should not register.'

"I believe in complete free speech," Berkman went on. "I am willing to take the consequences that may follow from the expression of my opinions. That is free speech. Will you proclaim to the world that you who carry liberty and democracy to Europe have no liberty here, that you who are fighting for democracy in Germany, suppress democracy right here in New York, in the United States? Are you going to suppress free speech and liberty in this country, and still pretend that you love liberty so much that you will fight for it five thousand miles away?"[10] By the time Berkman reached his concluding words two hours later, the *New York Times* reported, he "was near collapse."[11]

When it was her turn before the jury, Goldman offered sarcastic compliments to the authorities who arrested them. "The methods employed by Marshal McCarthy and his hosts of heroic warriors," she said acidly, "were sensational enough to satisfy the famous circus men, Barnum & Bailey. A dozen or more heroes dashing up two flights of stairs . . . only to discover the two dangerous disturbers and trouble-makers, Alexander Berkman and Emma Goldman, in their separate offices, quietly at work at their desks, wielding not a sword, nor a gun or a bomb, but merely their pens! Verily, it required courage to catch such big fish."[12]

Emma also spoke with passion about her love for America. "We respect your patriotism," she told the jurors. "But may there not be different kinds of patriotism as there are different kinds of liberty? I know many people—I am one of them—who were not born here, nor have they applied for citizenship, and who yet love America with deeper passion and greater intensity than many natives whose patriotism manifests itself by pulling, kicking, and insulting those who do not rise when the national anthem is played. Our patriotism is that of the man who loves a woman with open eyes. He is enchanted by her beauty, yet he sees her faults."[13]

The case then went to the jury. The men deliberated for thirty-nine minutes. When they returned, it was clear what the outcome would be. "Miss Fitzgerald," said the *New York Times,* "leaned over and grasped her woman chief by the hand, and it was evident that she had correctly guessed the verdict that was about to be recorded." It was a unanimous verdict of guilty against both defendants.[14]

"Emma Goldman," observed the *Times,* "her face red with anger and disappointment, was immediately on her feet. She never made a more defiant picture." Tartly, Emma told the judge, "I want to thank your Honor for your marvelous fairness in this trial."[15] Judge Mayer imposed the maximum sentence of two years' imprisonment and fines of $10,000 each. Additionally, he recommended that deportation to Russia should follow their prison terms. "The defendants," he said, "have shown remarkable ability, an ability which might have been utilized for the great benefit of this country had they seen fit to employ themselves in behalf of the government rather than against it."[16]

Emma and Sasha were to be incarcerated immediately; Marshal McCarthy announced that they would be taken from New York to their respective prisons shortly after midnight. "I consider these persons a menace to the peace and safety of the United States," the marshal said, "and I believe that the sooner they are in prison the better it will be for all concerned." Berkman asked that their sentence be deferred for a few days so they might clear up their affairs. "We have been convicted simply because we are anarchists," he said, "and the proceeding has been very unjust." Judge Mayer denied the request. "Are we to be spirited away in a speedy manner?" Goldman exclaimed, reproving the judge "for refusing us the two days which are given even to the most heinous of criminals."[17]

Fitzi hastened to Sasha to say goodbye. "Twice she kissed him," witnesses observed, "and then she kissed Miss Goldman and rushed out of the room." Emma was irate. "This whole thing is cruelty added to injustice," she snapped to reporters. "They are shipping us away without giving us a chance to see friends or even to get our baggage." Just hours later, on July 10, 1917, both prisoners were transported by overnight trains, Sasha to the federal penitentiary in Atlanta, Georgia, and Emma to the state penitentiary in Jefferson City, Missouri. A crowd of comrades gathered to see them off. "Be of good cheer," Sasha called out reassuringly before he was taken away.[18]

His friends tried to follow that directive. "It is marvelous," said Leonard Abbott, "to think that Alexander Berkman, after serving fourteen years in a Pennsylvania prison with spirit unbroken, is still willing to go to jail again in behalf of the liberties of the people."[19] Wrote Fitzi to Agnes Inglis, "It was hard—terribly hard to see them taken away so suddenly—one sent to one part of the world and one to the other—but they were splendid, proud, and spirit unbroken. They are the pioneers of a new civilization and some day will be appreciated."[20]

ON THE TRAIN TO MISSOURI, Goldman pondered her life, Ben's inconstancy, and Sasha's fate—the federal penitentiary at Atlanta was said to be a brutal place, while she would be held at a more moderate state prison. She was escorted by Deputy Marshal John Whalen and his wife (sworn in specially for the trip), both of whom, much to Emma's distaste, insisted on sleeping in her compartment. Overnight, she wrote, "the watchful eyes of the law were closed in sleep, but its mouth was wide open, emitting a rattle of snores."[21]

When the train arrived in Missouri the next day, she elected to walk from the station to the prison. For all her arrests, detentions, and trials, she had served very few prison terms. First was her long-ago ten months on Blackwell's, then her two weeks' incarceration for speaking about birth control in 1916. "A disgusting record," she joked, "for one who could boast of the never-failing attention of every police department in the country."[22]

Emma was brought to the prison matron, who asked if she had any diseases. Goldman ignored the question and said she would welcome a cold drink and a bath. She was chided for impudence by the matron, who told her many convicts carried sexual illness. "Venereal disease is not particular whom it strikes," Emma replied. "The most respectable people have been known to be victims of it. I don't happen to have it, which is due perhaps much more to luck than to virtue."[23]

Goldman was not in Missouri for long. Harry Weinberger won the chance to appeal to the U.S. Supreme Court, testing the constitutionality of the Draft Act. Just a few weeks after Emma and Sasha were dispatched to Jefferson City and Atlanta they were back in New York awaiting their case against the United States, which was set for argument in the Supreme Court on December 10, 1917. After another stay in the Tombs, both were released on bail pending the appeal.[24]

"I want you and the rest of our friends to know that Harry Weinberger is not an ordinary lawyer," Emma assured Agnes Inglis. "He is above all a man of ideals and of wonderful fighting spirit, aside from the fact that he is very brilliant."[25] Born in New York City in 1886, the son of Jewish immigrants from Budapest, Weinberger was five feet four inches tall and stocky, with dark hair and eyes. He financed his New York University Law School education by working as a stenographer at night and eventually became a well-regarded attorney, one to whom Goldman, Berkman, and various radicals turned when they tangled with the law.[26]

In fact Goldman and Berkman were not the only defendants Weinberger was representing in the case. He also was arguing on behalf of Louis

Kramer and Morris Becker, young New York anarchists who were the first to be charged with conspiracy against the draft. The two had attended a peace rally in Madison Square Garden, and had distributed No-Conscription leaflets and handbills about the June 4 antidraft meeting at Hunts Point Palace. Additionally, Kramer had refused to register for the draft, calling himself a "citizen of the world."[27]

Becker and Kramer were tried in Judge Mayer's courtroom and found guilty on June 12.[28] Judge Mayer praised the verdict as "absolutely just and meets my views of this case in every way."[29] Mayer sentenced Kramer to serve two years in a federal prison and one year in a state penitentiary; to pay a fine of $10,000; and ultimately to face deportation to Russia. "You have talked bravely, but you have shown the characteristics of men like you," the judge told Kramer. "This country does not want your kind."[30] Becker was ordered to serve twenty months. Both were sent to the federal penitentiary in Atlanta, although they, too, were out on bail pending the Supreme Court verdict. After his trial Kramer declared, "Bullets cannot shatter ideals. I am an idealist and am firm in my belief. I am willing to sacrifice my life for my cause."[31]

Weinberger's appeal failed. In January 1918 the Court affirmed the verdicts of all four anarchists and declared the Draft Act constitutional; Sasha and Emma would be returned to prison the next month. Goldman had been making energetic use of her respite from Jefferson City. With the aid of comrades and usual benefactors Theodore Schroeder and Bolton Hall, she helped form the League for the Amnesty of Political Prisoners in New York, which generated public relations, support, and agitation for similarly imprisoned radicals across America. She conducted a hurried lecture tour, which she called "hectic and exciting," traveling to Chicago and Detroit and speaking about the Russian Revolution. She also spent time with San Francisco comrades Bob and Lucy Robins who were visiting New York, and befriended Helen Keller, whom she had admired for years.[32]

"I had long wanted to meet this remarkable woman who had overcome the most appalling physical disabilities," Goldman later wrote. "Helen Keller's phenomenal conquest had strengthened my faith in the almost illimitable power of the human will." When the two met in person, Goldman was further moved. "The marvelous woman, bereft of the most vital human senses, could nevertheless, by her psychic strength, see and hear and articulate. The electric current of her vibrant fingers on my lips and her sensitized hand over mine spoke more than mere tongue. It eliminated physical barriers and held one in the spell of the beauty of her inner world."[33]

Sasha devoted his time to the Mooney case during his prison hiatus, feeling melancholy and unsettled. But he was cheered whenever he contemplated his bond with Emma. "My dear, dear Sailor," he wrote to her in October 1917, "Our friendship and comradeship of a lifetime has been to me the most beautiful inspiring factor in my whole life. And after all, it is given to but few mortals to live as you and I have lived. Notwithstanding all our hardships and sorrows, all persecution and imprisonment—perhaps because of it all—we have lived the lives of our choice. What more can one expect of life! If I were really free now, I do not see how I could go on living in this country under the present conditions of the white terror from Washington. I wish I were in Russia. I wish you and I both could throw ourselves heart and soul in the great reconstruction needed there. I don't know when I shall be able to write to you in this mood again. So let me bid you farewell now, my dear, beloved friend and comrade. You have been my mate and my comrade in arms—my life's mate in the biggest sense, and your wonderful spirit and devotion have always been an inspiration to me, as I'm sure your life will prove an inspiration to others long after both you and I have gone to everlasting rest."[34]

On February 5, 1918, Emma and Sasha were sent back to Jefferson City and Atlanta, where they settled in for the duration of their sentences. Both were assigned to perform garment work. Berkman was placed at "the cotton-duck mill," he told Fitzi, "working all the time on a Singer sewing machine." The prisoners, he further reported, were granted half an hour in the yard every afternoon and as much as two hours on Saturdays and Sundays, "unless one is deprived of this as a result of punishment."[35]

Goldman, too, found herself once again before the sewing machine, making clothing for more than nine hours each day. She was permitted food from friends and a few personal belongings in her cell, but because she refused to attend chapel, she could not enjoy the outdoor recreational hour on Sundays. Berkman was not allowed any special privileges or gifts of food, and his old stomach complaint from his Pittsburgh years soon returned. Weinberger asked the prison physician, J. Calvin Weaver, if Berkman might be allowed to receive fruit to relieve his digestive troubles, but Warden Fred G. Zerbst said Berkman was in "fairly good health" and rejected the request.[36]

Zerbst, who aimed to treat all the prisoners equally, also denied Weinberger's other requests on Sasha's behalf, such as extra letter privileges and writing supplies. Nonetheless, after a two-day visit on February 18 to see Berkman, Louis Kramer, and Morris Becker, Weinberger came away liking the warden.[37] "I must say that I found [Zerbst] a man of broad and kindly views," he told Stella Ballantine. "A strict disciplinarian probably, and doing his duty as he sees it, but doing it without bitterness or personal animus, a man of forward looking ideas who really believes that it his duty not only to keep all prisoners safe, but to see that their physical and mental welfare is fully taken care of."[38]

The three prisoners were faring well in those early days, said Harry, "cheerful, healthy, interested in every current of thought and every ideal being struggled for in every part of the world." Weinberger reminded Stella that "all who are interested in them should write them as often as possible, signing their full names. Receiving letters is a prisoner's great recreation, and one of the things that break the monotony."[39]

Letters and books were vital to Sasha. "Outside you try to economize time," he said. "Here we are doing our best to kill it."[40] Whenever he could get books, he studied French and Italian, and read classic literature. "My soul," he told Fitzi, "has traveled with Dante, and Milton has been my companion."[41] He received a flood of letters from comrades around the world, and Upton Sinclair presented him with his latest novel: "I am instructing my publisher in New York to send you a copy of *Jimmie Higgins,*" Sinclair said.[42]

Sasha got love notes as well. Through the safe intermediaries of pen and paper, comrade Minna Lowensohn admitted to a years-long crush. "I never told you that ten years ago I fell in love with you as we sat and talked about books and literature," she wrote. "Yesterday I saw [Alla] Nazimova in *The Wild Duck,* a splendid performance. I thought of you all evening. I don't suppose you remember but our first conversation was on *The Wild Duck* about ten years ago. The play yesterday called forth old memories."[43]

Sasha's weekly letter often went to Emma or to Fitzi, to whom he assigned the pseudonym Vera Figner, the Russian revolutionary and member of the People's Will he had once idolized. "I'm in good health," he assured Fitzi, "getting along well and doing the best under the circumstances. You know that I can always call my philosophy to my assistance. I live mostly in my thoughts—and environment becomes a secondary matter."[44] Several weeks later he told her, "Weather rainy all day is hard on my sprained ankle and revives my rheumatism, therefore the doctor has permitted me to use a cane to aid my bad foot."[45]

Berkman made some new friends, too, getting to know fellow prisoners in the penitentiary. Among them was Ammon A. Hennacy, a socialist and pacifist from Ohio, who was serving a two-year sentence for obstructing the draft. He arrived a few days after Berkman, and in the prison yard Sasha gave him advice about enduring captivity: don't tell a lie; don't be a stoolie; draw your line about what you will do, and don't budge, even if they kill you; never crawl or you will always be crawling; if a guard hits you, don't hit back, for if one can't beat you up for good then two or ten will do it. "Berkman was obviously watched more closely than the rest of us," Hennacy noted. He later became an anarchist and a leading figure in the Catholic Worker movement, and said he admired Berkman as "the only living anarchist, other than Emma Goldman, Malatesta, and Kropotkin whom I wished to know." Sasha thought Hennacy "a splendid young fellow of fine character and idealism."[46]

Berkman also briefly encountered the socialist leader Eugene Victor Debs, transferred in June 1919 to the Atlanta penitentiary from a prison in West Virginia. Debs, who had been present at the formation of the I.W.W., had been four times a candidate for president of the United States, receiving 900,000 votes in 1912. In 1918 Debs gave a speech in opposition to the war and the draft. Called "a traitor to his country" by President Wilson, he was convicted under the Sedition Act and sentenced to ten years in prison.[47]

Debs was in poor health, sharing a cramped cell with five other men for fifteen hours each day during the heat of an Atlanta summer. Berkman told Zerbst of Debs's difficulty, and the warden took steps to improve conditions for the ailing political figure. Goldman herself had met Debs back in 1898 at the first annual Social Democracy of America convention. She thought him "the most striking figure . . . so genial and charming as a human being that one did not mind the lack of political clarity which made him reach out . . . for opposite poles."[48]

Debs and Berkman did not become well acquainted in the prison (Berkman was released four months after Debs arrived), but they expressed mutual respect and appreciation during their careers.[49] In 1920, while still incarcerated in Atlanta, Debs again ran for president representing the Socialist Party, and pulled in a considerable 913,000 votes, although Republican Warren Harding won the election in a landslide. In December 1921 President Harding commuted his sentence, and Debs was released. "I was happy to have the opportunity," Berkman later said, "before leaving the Federal Prison at Atlanta, to shake hands with the Grand Old Man of the New Day. If there ever was a martyr to liberty, Debs is that man. How stupid it is of the Government to jail men of his type! Prison cannot crush their spirit, nor iron bars and brutality change their conscience. Their love of humanity transcends the fear of punishment or death."[50]

BEFORE LONG, EVEN WITH THE SUPPORT of his comrades on the outside and his new companions on the inside, Berkman began to feel the familiar strains of prison life. To his great frustration, with no access to writing materials beyond those approved for his weekly letter, he was unable to continue with his literary work. Some public figures tried to intervene on his behalf. New York City publisher B. W. Huebsch appealed to Louis F. Post, the assistant secretary of labor; while Roger Baldwin, director of the National Civil Liberties Bureau in Washington, D.C., promised Francis H. Duehay of the Department of Justice that the authorities could inspect and retain Sasha's papers. But all requests for writing privileges were denied.[51]

Berkman was saddened to discover that aggression and abuse within prison walls remained the norm. "Very few essential changes have taken place in the administration of our prisons within the last twenty-five years," he said. "The same system of brutalizing and degrading the prisoners still prevails."[52] He clashed with the guards he deemed malicious or unnecessarily cruel and witnessed many incidents of wanton violence. He was especially troubled by the murder of "Kid" Smith, a young black prisoner who was shot by a guard. Men in the prison were "clubbed frequently, on the least provocation," Berkman said, but on February 21, 1919, Smith was "shot dead for not walking fast enough while being taken to 'the hole.' "[53]

Berkman allowed that some officers, including Warden Zerbst, were decent and "of a humane spirit"; but he reported that "the majority of the guards are vulgar, brutal, and dissipated men." The deputy warden, Charles Girardeau, was particularly harsh. Girardeau had once been in charge of a chain gang, and he encouraged the sadistic behavior of the Atlanta guards. Zerbst later defended his deputy, calling Berkman's statements "ridiculous" and "irresponsible," and describing Girardeau as "a Christian gentleman of high character, clean habits and high ideals."[54]

But after Sasha circulated a petition to protest the abuse he had seen, Girardeau called him in for questioning and accused him of subversive activity. "I explained to him the general indignation regarding the abuse of the prisoners," said Sasha. "I said that he was cruel to the men, that he lacked all sense of justice and fair play. . . . For this I was put on bread and water in 'the hole,' a dark and filthy cell hardly big enough to stretch out in. After my time in 'the hole' had expired, I was placed in solitary confinement for the rest of my [sentence]."[55]

Harry Weinberger made every effort to have Sasha released from solitary. He denied the charge that Berkman had been engaged in inflammatory plots, and asked for the return of books, paper, and especially cigarettes. "A man who is used to smoking all his life when deprived of tobacco gets into a nervous state," Weinberger wrote to Francis Duehay, "and [withholding tobacco] is a punishment not necessary for discipline." Duehay responded, "If a prisoner in punishment is to have his tobacco, writing privileges, and books, there would be very little real punishment involved, especially to men of Berkman's type."[56]

Berkman spent a total of seven and a half months in solitary. He became doubly convinced that "the criminal is made, not born. He is the product of his environment, a child of poverty and desperation, of misery, greed, and ambitions. No amount of punishment can obviate or 'cure' crime so long as prevailing conditions, in and out of prison, drive men to do it." Sasha further avowed that all political and "industrial" prisoners "should be the pride of the United States. . . . Ideals cannot be imprisoned, nor can the eternal spirit of liberty be exterminated by shutting up its champions in dungeons or deporting men and women out of the United States."[57]

Harry Kelly admired Berkman's courage. "Sasha would not keep quiet while others were ill treated," Kelly marveled. "When prison guards brutalized his fellow prisoners he protested. His interference cost him dear, and he paid just as years before he had paid in Western Penitentiary in solitary for protesting against the brutalities inflicted upon other inmates."[58]

Sasha emerged from Atlanta, Emma said, "a physical wreck, with the horrors of his experience burned into his soul." In some ways, she said, Sasha's term in Atlanta was as grievous as his ordeal in the Western Penitentiary. After they were released, Emma found him once more beset by depression and pain. "At night," she said, "he would wake up in a cold sweat, tortured by the nightmare of his recent experience," convinced he was back in the prison. It was difficult to persuade Sasha that he was free. "How strange is the human mind!" he exclaimed.[59]

EMMA'S TERM IN JEFFERSON CITY WAS SOMEWHAT less trying, although she always had been a hardy soul. The Missouri prison had its share of harassment and deprivation, and her sewing work was physically grueling, but she established for herself a relatively tolerable berth. She rose at 5:30 A.M., went to breakfast at 6:15, and was in the workshop at 6:30. She sewed until 11:30 A.M., and then had lunch in the dining hall. Always skilled as a seamstress, she expertly stitched jackets, overalls, coats, and suspenders. The official working hours were nine a day, but in order to complete the daily tasks, prisoners took away fabric and needles and continued sewing in their spare time. Emma was in her cell from 12:00 to 12:30 in the afternoon, returning to the shop until 4:30 P.M., after which she had an hour and a half outdoors. For her labor at the sewing machine, she earned twenty-eight cents a day. The work was exhausting, and she often felt sore and worn.

Emma later spoke of the stuffy darkness, the "putrid air"; the "cold indifference" to the needs of the prisoner; "the methods of breaking his will"; the particular cruelty toward black female prisoners; the restriction of food and recreation; and the rude, rough treatment by male guards of women inmates, young and old. "He bullies and terrorizes the women," she wrote, "holding the threat of the blind cell and the bread-and-water diet over them." (Jefferson City held about 80 female inmates, out of a total population of 2,600.)[60] The prison was dank and noisy, and she observed much mistreatment. To top it all off, the guards were endlessly suspicious of Red Emma, their most notorious female convict.

But unlike Sasha, Emma had access to many basic comforts of life: adequate food, regular entertainment, and steady companionship.[61] She was well looked after by her comrades on the outside; those in nearby St. Louis kept her "supplied with eatables" and arranged for a local grocer to send her whatever she liked, and "even ordered a spring mattress" for her cot. She could receive books and letters, and Ben Reitman kept in contact. She was anxious to free herself of her obsession with Reitman, hoping two years in prison would help "break the bond that had chained me so long." Yet Ben expressed his abiding love for her, described his delight in his newborn son, Brutus, and confided his most private fears and hopes. Emma's heart was caught once more.[62]

Emma welcomed a number of visitors, including Stella Ballantine, Fitzi, and Saul Yanovsky. Since Stella was Emma's niece and a blood relation, the chairman of the Prison Board, William Rock Painter, allowed them lengthy visits on successive days, including an hour spent in the yard.[63] Emma, said Stella, talked "of the privileges she enjoyed," but that "one must no longer address her as a political prisoner, because they are not recognized in this country." In a newsletter she circulated among comrades, Ballantine described her aunt's prison duties, and said Emma's seamstress labor "brings her back to her cell completely exhausted and with an aching spine at the end of the day."[64]

Emma formed close friendships at Jefferson City. In November 1918, around the time the Great War reached its close, Gabriella Antolini, a young Italian anarchist, arrived at the penitentiary to begin an eighteen-month sentence after a conviction for transporting explosives. "She was a proletarian child," said Emma, "familiar with poverty and hardship, strong, and socially conscious." For all her youth and inexperience, Ella shared Emma's "conception of life and values," and provided "intellectual comradeship with a kindred spirit."[65]

Six months later a third female radical, Kate Richards O'Hare, was brought to the Missouri prison. O'Hare, forty-three, was the most prominent female socialist in America, and a friend and political associate of Eugene V. Debs. Like Debs, she had been arrested for delivering an antiwar speech. She was convicted under the Espionage Act and sentenced to five years.

The three women, despite their differing philosophies and backgrounds, soon became close friends—"the American Revolutionary Soviet," O'Hare called it—united by similarly lively spirits, intellectual curiosity, hatred of capitalism, and opposition to the war. "It is certainly a great thing to have two women like the two politicals with me here," O'Hare wrote to her family. "Emma is very fine and sweet, and intellectually companiable, while the little girl is a darling. We have really interesting times."[66]

They ate together in the dining room and occupied adjacent cells. As O'Hare merrily observed, "Emma is on one side of me and Ella on the other, and the executive committee holds nightly conclaves to direct by wireless the affairs of the universe. Just imagine what interesting stories the historian of the future can write of this strange trio and our doings."[67] The "American Revolutionary Soviet" was dissolved, however, when Emma completed her sentence and was released from Jefferson City in September 1919.

Emma had greeted her fiftieth birthday, June 27, 1919, in the penitentiary. Her fellow prisoners celebrated the day with her, and she received birthday messages from friends and comrades—wires and notes from around the country, one letter signed by fifty people from New York, another by thirty-five people from Los Angeles—and boxes of oranges, apples, and preserves. Her elderly mother wrote her a letter in Yiddish, "filled with affection for her most wayward child."[68]

"What more fitting place for the rebel to celebrate such an occasion?" Goldman wondered. "Fifty years! I felt as if I had five hundred on my back, so replete with events had been my life."[69]

PART III

OPEN EYES

21

THE RUSSIAN DREAM

EVEN BEFORE THEY WERE FREED FROM THEIR CELLS, Sasha and Emma's fight to remain in America had begun. At the conclusion of their trial, Judge Mayer had recommended that deportation to Russia should follow their sentences, and both had been served with warrants while in prison. Berkman was visited on August 13, 1919, by an immigration inspector, Eugene Kessler, from the Jacksonville, Florida, branch office, and a hearing was scheduled in the penitentiary for the morning of September 18.[1] Berkman refused to participate.[2] "Thought is, or should be, free," he said. "The proposed hearing is an invasion of my conscience."[3]

The hearing was rescheduled for September 25. Berkman refused to answer questions, although the authorities presented an extensive inventory of his deeds. Kessler was in attendance, along with Assistant Examining Officer John W. Humphreys, who conducted the proceeding; Bureau of Investigation agent Edward Chastain; and J. Edgar Hoover, the special assistant to Attorney General A. Mitchell Palmer.[4]

Hoover, then just twenty-four, paid close attention to the Berkman case. Not only did he request a full record of the hearing, but he compiled a file filled with related documents, including a transcript of Berkman's 1892 trial in Pittsburgh and a copy of his *Prison Memoirs of an Anarchist,* which he received by special delivery.[5]

A week later, on October 1, 1919, Sasha completed his term and was released from the Atlanta penitentiary, transferred from the custody of the Department of Justice to the Department of Labor's Bureau of Immigration, under Kessler's supervision, until his $15,000 bond was paid the next day. He left for New York by train after midnight on October 3, in the company of Harry Weinberger.[6]

Sasha's freedom came at a complicated time. President Wilson suffered a massive stroke on October 2, and although the severity of his condition was concealed from the public through the remainder of his term and long afterward, his incapacitation had a great impact on the direction of postwar America. The nation already was in tumult, dealing with the aftermath of the world war, as well as with the implications of prohibition and women's suffrage.

It had also been a tense period for the radical and labor communities. There had been a rancorous general strike in Seattle in February, and in the spring a series of mail bombs had been sent to prominent government and business leaders around the country. John D. Rockefeller, Oliver Wendell Holmes, and both San Francisco District Attorney Charles Fickert and Assistant District Attorney Edward Cunha were among the intended victims; another was Attorney General Palmer, who spearheaded raids on subversives and was targeted twice. The second attempt on Palmer's residence in Washington, D.C., resulted in the death of the bomber, the anarchist Carlo Valdinoci, a follower of Luigi Galleani and an associate and lover of Emma's prisonmate, Ella Antolini. Valdinoci accidentally blew himself to pieces outside Palmer's home.[7]

Emma had been served her deportation papers at Jefferson City on September 12, and she was discharged from the penitentiary on September 27. Stella Ballantine was there to greet her, along with hordes of spectators and plenty of press. The papers were filled with news of her fate, but the publicity was hardly useful to her cause. "For many years," said one editorial, "Emma Goldman has been the most conspicuous woman anarchist and foe of the established order resident in the United States. . . . Early in life she developed nihilist tendencies of an aggressive nature, and before she was twenty she became associated with the worst anarchists in America."[8]

"The American people," stated another column, "generally will applaud the decision of the government to deport Emma Goldman as an undesirable alien. Berkman and the Goldman woman have caused a good deal of trouble in this country, by persistently pushing anarchistic propaganda and encouraging public unrest and sedition." It was, therefore, in the public interest "if this precious pair can be bundled off to some other land where they will find more congenial company." Not only did America have "no room" for people of their ilk, concluded the essay, but the country "should proceed to get rid of them as rapidly as possible."[9]

Before returning to New York, Emma stopped in Chicago to see Ben and his new baby, and then went to Rochester to visit her family. The Goldmans had endured several tragedies during her incarceration. Her brother Herman had lost his wife to heart disease, and her nephew David, the son of her sister Helena, had been killed in the war. Helena was sick with grief.

Back in New York City, Emma found her life's work in ruins. The books and writings confiscated in the raid had not been returned, and *Mother Earth* and *The Blast* could not be resuscitated because of the ongoing ban. "We had nothing left," she wrote, "neither literature, money, nor even a home." Still, she was thrilled to be reunited with Sasha, who was terribly weak and ill but "otherwise apparently his usual stoical and humorous self."[10]

"We are to be deported," Sasha told comrade Pierre Ramus (aka Rudolf Grossmann), a Vienna-based anarchist. "The first step towards repression of all social protest." But Sasha felt the winds of change. "The war," he said, "has certainly served one great purpose. It has shaken, and to some degree even destroyed the mental foundations of present day civilization. This is how I view the present situation the world over. The old branches are falling off. The very foundations of present day society are diseased. But the situation remains confused and uncertain."[11]

On October 27 a dinner was held to honor Sasha and Emma at the Hotel Brevoort on lower Fifth Avenue. Earlier that day, Emma had appeared at Ellis Island for her deportation hearing, but she was in fine spirits nonetheless. Leonard Abbott chaired the event and gave the opening speech. "No idea was ever destroyed by force, or by imprisonment, or by deportation," said Abbott. "Here were two individuals who refused to compromise, who set themselves against the psychology and hysteria of the mob, who had the courage to be themselves even in wartime. Free Speech and free press lie prostrate. The Constitution of America, so far as it relates to free speech and free press, is a dead letter." Dublin-born poet Lola Ridge read a poem titled "To Alexander Berkman on Solitary." "I know / How the days pass / The prison squats / With granite haunches on the young spring / Battened wonder with its twisting green." Harry Kelly, quoting Haymarket anarchist August Spies, called Emma and Sasha "the birds of the coming storm."[12]

A month later, on November 25, 1919, the Bureau of Immigration recommended that Berkman be deported to Russia "at the earliest practicable date."[13] Hastily, Berkman and Goldman together launched a final American lecture tour; Emma said she had "a foreboding that it would be my last opportunity to raise my voice against the shame of my adopted land."[14] She thought it would be good for Sasha to join her, to move past his Atlanta trauma and see their comrades "for perhaps the last time." Their trip was brief and bittersweet. "From New York to Detroit, and thence to Chicago, we made a whirlwind tour," recounted Emma. "Our movements were watched by local and federal agents, every utterance noted down and attempts made to silence us. Unperturbed, however, we continued, as it was our last supreme effort, and we felt our die had been cast."[15]

They were in Chicago on December 2, spending the evening with friends at a farewell dinner, when news arrived that Henry Clay Frick, at the age of sixty-nine, had suffered a heart attack. A reporter rushed up to Berkman. "Mr. Frick has just died," he said, asking for comment. "Deported by God," replied Berkman dryly. "Henry Clay Frick was but a man of the passing hour," Goldman declared. "Neither in life nor in death would he have been remembered long. It was Alexander Berkman who made him known, and Frick will live only in connection with Berkman's name. His entire fortune could not pay for such glory."[16] Sasha was nonchalant. "I'm glad he left the country before me," he shrugged.[17]

ON DECEMBER 3 WEINBERGER SENT A TELEGRAM informing them that the Department of Labor had issued their deportation orders and that they must surrender on December 5 at the immigration station on Ellis Island. "That is the end, Emma Goldman, isn't it?" asked a reporter. "It may only be the beginning," she responded.[18] She told the press that she "had great faith in the American people, especially the younger generation."[19]

Goldman's deportation order had been signed by Assistant Secretary of Labor Louis F. Post. Emma was appalled. She and Post were well-acquainted; she had been a "guest in his home and entertained by him and Mrs. Post." She admired Post's past work as a writer and editor, considered him a "champion of free speech and press," and believed him to be an ally to her cause. Post, she marveled caustically, "the man who had flayed the authorities for their brutal methods during the McKinley panic, who had defended me . . . he now a champion of deportation?"[20] She never forgave him for approving the order.

Harry Weinberger worked doggedly, pursuing every legal avenue and opportunity to prevent the deportation.[21] He petitioned for a writ of habeas corpus on behalf of Goldman, who he posited was a U.S. citizen by virtue of her marriage to Jacob Kershner in February 1887, more than thirty years earlier, although in 1909 the government had revoked Kershner's citizenship in an effort to target Goldman.[22] Emma now learned the sober news that "Jacob Kershner had been dead for years," more than a decade. Missouri-born Harry Kelly offered to marry her to provide her with citizenship, but she declined.[23]

Emma was grateful for Weinberger's persistence. "Our counsel was not one to accept defeat easily," she said. "Beaten at one place he would train his guns upon another. Harry was irrepressible, and I was glad to take advantage of every hour left me on American soil." Goldman's legal case against deportation was somewhat stronger than Berkman's, but she decided they should not be separated. "If Sasha was to be driven out of the country, I would go with him," she said. "He had come into my life with my spiritual awakening, he had grown into my very being, and his long Golgotha would forever remain our common bond. He had been my comrade, friend, and co-worker through a period of thirty years; it was unthinkable that he should join the Revolution and I remain behind."[24] In the end, Weinberger's efforts were in vain. On December 8 deportation proceedings began before Judge Mayer.

The government was represented by J. Edgar Hoover, Federal District Attorney Francis G. Caffey, and W. J. Peters, law officer of the Bureau of Immigration. Hoover, who kept an index of radicals and subversives (and eventually amassed a vast cache of files filled with intimate data on powerful figures), claimed personal credit for the expulsion of Berkman and Goldman. "[They] are, beyond doubt, two of the most dangerous anarchists in this country," he wrote in a memo. Hoover also noted that Goldman's private letters made for "spicy reading."[25]

Judge Mayer remanded Berkman and Goldman to the custody of the commissioner of immigration at Ellis Island and uttered strong words when rendering his decision. "The court," he said, "views these defendants as enemies of the United States and of the peace of this country."[26] Sasha and Emma were taken to Ellis Island, where they spent nearly two weeks in somber surroundings. As Goldman later remarked, "The condition of the emigrants on Ellis Island was nothing short of frightful. Their quarters were congested, the food was abominable, and they were treated like felons. These unfortunates had cut their moorings in the homeland and had pilgrimed to the United States as the land of promise, liberty, and opportunity. Instead they found themselves locked up, ill-treated, and kept in uncertainty for months."[27]

On December 20 Sasha and Emma were "photographed, finger-printed, and tabulated like convicted criminals."[28] It was evident that deportation was imminent, but Harry Weinberger was not permitted to see them a final time, nor was Stella Ballantine, nor Eleanor Fitzgerald, who reportedly "had expressed a desire to be deported with Miss Goldman and Berkman, whom she kissed in public when he was surrendered for deportation."[29] Late that evening, Sasha and Emma, along with 247 radicals apprehended during the postwar Red Scare, most of them rounded up in the so-called Palmer raids unleashed the previous month by the attorney general, were roused suddenly from their quarters and ordered to prepare for immediate departure. At four in the morning on December 21, 1919, they began their journey.

It was dark, frigid, and snow lay deep on the ground. The deportees, many glum and downcast, milled about, carrying "old-fashioned, foreign-looking portmanteaus, their Old World tin trunks—small affairs in weird colors." Some talked quietly; others read books or "tattered copies of newspapers." Reporters sought out Emma. "I insist that I am an American," she declared stoutly. "Incidentally, I am coming back. I am not going to stop my work as long as life remains."[30]

Sasha cut a striking figure in his high leather boots, khaki shirt and trousers, and broad sombrero hat, a symbol of the Mexican Revolution. Suffused with nervous excitement, he was, according to press accounts, "the central figure in a merry group. They played banjos and guitars and sang the 'Internationale.' "[31] Sasha hurried to finish the last lines of a pamphlet he and Emma had composed on Ellis Island, decrying their deportation as a spiteful punishment for protesting the draft. Their banishment was, they felt, a weapon of the state against the rights of the individual. "The protest of one's conscience against killing was branded by them as high treason, and even mere disagreement regarding the causes of the war, or the slightest criticism of the administration, was condemned as disloyalty," the pamphlet stated.[32]

The group was transported on a barge, past the Statue of Liberty, across New York Harbor. "Through the port-hole," wrote Emma, "I could see the great city receding into the distance, its sky-line of buildings traceable by their rearing heads. It was my beloved city, the metropolis of the New World."[33] They boarded the S. S. *Buford,* an old army transport from the Spanish-American War.[34] At 5:00 that morning J. Edgar Hoover visited the ship, eager to be present for Berkman and Goldman's expulsion. At 6:00 A.M. the deportees started on their voyage. A group of government officials and lawmakers gathered at the dock to witness the deportation, while armed soldiers manned the deck, the gangways, and the passenger quarters.[35] Sasha gazed back at the city as they headed out to sea. "The tall skyscrapers, their outlines dimmed, looked like fairy castles lit by winking stars, and then all was swallowed in the distance."[36]

On board were 246 men of various types and nationalities, as Berkman later catalogued them: "Great Russians from New York and Baltimore; Ukrainian miners from Virginia; Letts, Lithuanians, and one Tartar." Many were anarchists, some were nonpartisan, a few were socialists. "There are editors, lecturers, and manual workers of every kind among us," observed Sasha.[37] Goldman was one of only three women on board, along with Dora Lipkin and Ethel Bernstein, both arrested in a raid of the Union of Russian Workers, an anarchist group. Lipkin was "sad and very quiet," while Bernstein wept as the boat took her away, calling out, "Good bye, America." She was, reported the press, "leaving behind Samuel Lipman, her fiancé, [who was] facing a 20-year term in the Atlanta penitentiary for violating the espionage law."[38]

Robert Minor, illustrator and writer for *The Blast,* wrote about the depressing scene. Given the unexpected departure, women and children were unable to bid farewell to the husbands and fathers they might never see again. Some family members came to the dock moments too late, just as the ship was setting sail, carrying with them thick overcoats for the Russian winter, cheap gloves, and parcels of food, items that would go unused by their loved ones. Distraught, they rushed to the ferryhouse, shouting and crying, and were driven back by the soldiers.[39]

THE JOURNEY WAS ARDUOUS, WITH ROUGH SEAS, unpleasant food, minimal fresh air, and cramped conditions for the men. The deportees were often cold, wet, and seasick. Emma derided the *Buford,* known in the American press as the "Red Ark," as "unseaworthy," a "battered old tub."[40] Yet the hardships of the *Buford* were tempered by the exhilaration of their pilgrimage to the home of the revolution. "Though we were prisoners," wrote Sasha, "the journey was an inspiration . . . the thought that we were on the way to the land of revolutionary promise kept the whole company of deportees in high spirits, a-tremble with expectation of the great Day soon to come." Sasha was giddy with anticipation. "My heart was glad," he said. "I was going to the country that had swept Tsardom off the map, I was to behold the land of the Social Revolution!"[41]

Since his arrival in New York, Sasha had maintained a romanticism about the country of his birth, despite his sour childhood experiences. In Russia were the origins of his revolutionary dreams and hopes, the inspiration of his uncle Max Natanson, whose ideals, Berkman believed, had come to fruition as the civil war transitioned into social revolution. But, unbeknownst to Sasha, the situation in Russia was veering far from his imaginings. He also did not know that his Uncle Max, a leader of the Left Socialist Revolutionaries, who were already being liquidated by the Bolsheviks, had fled to Switzerland, and had died in Bern on July 29, 1919.

From afar, the Russian Revolution seemed to Sasha "unquestionably the greatest event of modern times." He hoped it would "spread to Germany and other countries bringing with it the downfall of war and tyranny everywhere and ushering in the birth of a really free and beautiful New World."[42] Emma's attitude was similar; she viewed the Bolshevik Revolution as "the beginning of the real Social Revolution." As she told Agnes Inglis in 1917 when the uprising commenced, "I really think that the Russian situation under the guidance of the Boylsheviki is the most gigantic thing in history. Long live the Boylsheviki! May their flames spread over the world and redeem humanity from its bondage."[43] The following year, Goldman exclaimed to Helen Keller, "Is not Russia the great miracle? I feel as if I walked on air when I think of what is being carried out in Russia now. I have always lived in her revolutionary traditions, all the 33 years of my life in America. And now all our young dreams for Russia are being realized. How long must we wait until Boylshevism comes to pass in America?"[44]

During the first years of the revolution, Goldman and Berkman were fully supportive of the conflict, tolerating even its most malevolent manifestations and hailing it as a landmark event in the struggle between workers and the state. Bolshevism, they imagined, had been transformed from an authoritarian philosophy into a libertarian one, and they accepted the "dictatorship of the proletariat" as a temporary necessity rather than as a worrisome step toward repression.

The pair had met Leon Trotsky in New York after attending a speech he delivered on March 26, 1917.[45] Emma found him "powerful and electrifying." Trotsky's "analysis of the causes of the war was brilliant," she said, "his denunciation of the Provisional Government in Russia illuminating. We fully shared his profound faith in the future of Russia."[46] Trotsky was friendly and encouraging, and asked if they would meet again in Russia.

Berkman, too, was lenient toward Trotsky and his tactics, seeing the leader's actions as unavoidable during revolution. "We anarchists," he said in January 1918, "would be first to oppose Bolsheviks should they attempt to establish themselves as a PERMANENT Government with the power to impose its authority upon the people. . . . As for present activities, I can only say that an extraordinary situation may demand extraordinary measures. All revolutions involve force and violence."[47] Later he would describe Trotsky as "a character strong by nature rather than by conviction, one who could remain unbending even if he felt himself in the wrong."[48]

Sasha and Emma's friends were divided on the shadowy progression of the Russian Revolution. Some were wholeheartedly supportive. In 1918 Harry Weinberger commented to Goldman, "The Bolsheviki are still the hope of the world and are doing more at the present moment to educate the world and give it a new hope and a new vision . . . [not seen] since the American and French revolutions. Things are always darkest before the dawn, and my hope is, and my work will be, for a hurrying of that dawn."[49] Lincoln Steffens visited Soviet Russia in 1919 and announced that he had "been over into the future and it works."[50]

But Saul Yanovsky criticized the Bolshevik regime as merely a new era of dictators. With the return of Lenin to Russia in April 1917, Yanovsky condemned him as a "Mephistopheles" and warned, "There'll be no happiness in Russia in our lifetime."[51] In early 1919, Catherine Breshkovskaya was in New York to give a lecture in Carnegie Hall, and "her bitter denunciation of the Bolsheviki came as a fearful shock" to Goldman.[52] "Dear Babushka," Emma asked plaintively, "Whither are you going? I am not doubting what you say about the Bolsheviki. As an American I am naturally opposed to their dictatorship, their centralization, their bureaucracy. But whatever their faults and shortcomings, the mistakes of the Bolsheviki, they are flesh of our flesh, blood of our blood. They have with them, if not a majority, surely a large percentage of the Russian people for whom you have given fifty glorious years of your life. Yes, they are all your children, even if they are not all you hoped and wanted them to be. . . . Come back to your children, beloved Babushka. Your heart broken child, Emma."[53]

In the fall of 1919, Goldman and Berkman met Russian-born anarchist Mollie Steimer. Steimer had immigrated to New York as a teenager and was active in the American antiwar movement; she had been arrested multiple times, and was alongside Jacob Abrams when he was charged with violating the Espionage Act, a case that received national attention. Emma, Sasha, and Mollie had discussed with concern the mounting persecution of anarchists and socialists in Russia who disagreed with the Bolshevik government. But they decided to wait and see. "Let us give them a chance," said Sasha. "It is too early for criticism."[54] In 1922 Steimer, too, would be deported to Russia.

THE *BUFORD* PASSED THROUGH THE ENGLISH CHANNEL on January 5, 1920, and on January 8 anchored in the Kiel Canal in Germany. During the voyage Berkman, irrepressible and assertive as always, befriended fellow deportees, crew, and soldiers and spoke out vigorously to improve the conditions on board. He sent word to the commander of the ship, a colonel of the U.S. Army, that the men, who were almost suffocating, needed daily exercise. That afternoon the hatches were opened, and they were permitted out on deck. The colonel nevertheless regarded Berkman with distrust. He had been informed that Berkman was "inciting mutiny" among officers and prisoners alike. "You've been fraternizing with the soldiers and weakening the discipline," the colonel accused Berkman. Below deck, several soldiers had been arrested for insubordination and drunkenness, and the number of guards on duty was doubled.[55]

The ship headed out for the Baltic on January 13, sailing through water made especially dangerous by the presence of mines left over from the war, and reached the Finnish port of Hango on January 16. The passengers were exhausted after almost a month at sea. The following morning the ship radioed Georgy Chicherin, the commissar for foreign affairs in Moscow, to notify him that the first group of political deportees from America had arrived.

Journalists waited at the dock to observe the moment. "Berkman and Miss Goldman," reported the press, "led a procession of radicals down the gangplank, a large number of persons assembled on the wharf, gazing curiously at the landing. The reds made up of a motley throng, their faces being full of curiosity as to what their future might be, while there were traces of anxiety lest they might be attacked after they had left the protection of their American guardians."[56]

Emma spoke to the reporters, protesting her deportation as an "injustice," and offering a summary of world bolshevism and anarchy. When asked if she wished to overthrow the American government, she replied, "You need a new government, and I hope the [upcoming 1920 presidential] election will provide it." She also took a moment to complain about the conditions on the ship, particularly annoyed that she had been "compelled to eat her meals in the Buford's dining room 'of which she was an object for all eyes.' " When Berkman was interviewed, he said that once in Russia, he would "form a League of Russian Friends of America," just as there was a League of American Friends of Russia, which, he added wryly, "has grown so eminently respectable that even former President Taft is a member." Goldman and Berkman also promised to one day "return to America to save it."[57]

The soldiers and crew bade Berkman and his company a cordial farewell, and the deportees were taken in sealed cars through Finland to the Russian border, carrying with them rations for three days. By the time they reached Viborg, however, they were nearly out of supplies, for the Finnish guards had pilfered most of their provisions. There was still no word from Chicherin. Representatives of the Finnish Foreign Office agreed to permit a committee of deportees to go to the frontier to make contact, and the exiles selected three people to represent them. The Finnish military, however, would allow only one representative to make the trek: Sasha. He set off, walking "in deep snow, through the sparse forest west of the destroyed frontier railroad bridge," accompanied by a Finnish officer, a soldier, and an interpreter. Trailing him, Berkman wrote, were "several correspondents (among them, needless to say, an American press man)."[58]

They reached the border after a quarter of an hour. Sasha shouted *"Tovarishch"* (Comrade) to the Bolshevik guards across the frozen creek. According to the press account, "There was a slight delay in getting in touch with the bolsheviki, whose lines were about a mile distant from the brook marking the frontier of soviet territory. When finally a conference had been arranged, Berkman . . . went out on the ice, meeting the bolsheviki in the middle of the stream."[59] With white flags raised on both sides, Sasha succinctly explained their predicament. "The Soviet Committee has just arrived," the Russian officer told him.[60]

A delegation of the committee, including Secretary Zorin of the Communist Party and Maria Andreyeva Gorky, wife of the political figure and writer Maxim Gorky, was sent across the border to greet them. "There is no question but that they will be welcomed in Russia," Zorin assured the press. "We will give them work according to their professions and trades, but first we must provide them with comfortable homes and feed them well." Added Madame Gorky, "Russia opens her arms to all who are politically persecuted."[61]

On January 19, 1920, Sasha and Emma at last crossed the border of revolutionary Russia. Their arrival was celebrated with a mass meeting of soldiers and peasants in the town of Belo-Ostrov. "We who had been driven out of America as felons," said Goldman, "were welcomed on Soviet soil as brothers by their sons and daughters who had helped to set her free. Workers, soldiers, and peasants surrounded us, took us by the hand, and made us feel akin to them."[62] Amid clouds of tobacco, the revelers enjoyed speeches, songs, strong drink, and lively conversation. "It was," Berkman later wrote, "the most sublime day of my life."[63]

22

THE BOLSHEVIK MYTH

Sasha's joy at touching "the soil of Soviet Russia" was threatened almost at once. At the Belo-Ostrov reception, a Russian anarchist of Italian descent, Peter Bianchi, gave a speech, saying, "We anarchists are willing to work with the Bolsheviki if they will treat us right. But I warn you that we won't stand for suppression. If you attempt it, it will mean war between us." Berkman interrupted him to protest. "Let not this great hour be debased by unworthy thoughts."[1]

The group was taken to Petrograd. A demonstration was held in the vast Tauride Palace, and then the deportees were given rooms in the Smolny, the grand building used as the headquarters of the Communist Party. Goldman and Berkman met up with their old friend Bill Shatoff, formerly a Ferrer Center leader, who had gone to Russia to join in the revolution and had lately been serving as chief of police in Petrograd. Shatoff was known in both countries for his oratorical gifts; American anarchist Manuel Komroff, an artist, reporter, and later a successful novelist, described Shatoff as "the Danton of the Russian Revolution, a very powerful speaker."[2]

An avowed anarchist who refused to join the Communist Party, Shatoff had clashed often with the Bolsheviks, even while acquiescing in some of their more distasteful practices, and he was to be relocated to Siberia in a matter of weeks. Yet he was still, Sasha noted, "the jovial good fellow I knew in America." Shatoff told Sasha and Emma that Russia was now "passing through the difficult stage of violent social revolution." Of course, he said, "the Bolsheviki have committed many errors; that's because they are human. We live in the period of transition, of much confusion, constant danger, and anxiety. . . . We anarchists should remain true to our ideals, but we should not criticize at this time. We must work and help to build."[3]

Shatoff did not seem concerned by the apparent lack of freedoms in post-tsarist Russia; instead, he explained, "the Communist State in action is exactly what we anarchists have always claimed it would be—a tightly centralized power, still more strengthened by the dangers to the Revolution. Under such conditions, one cannot do as one wills. One does not just hop on a train and go, or even ride the bumpers, as I used to do in the United States. One needs permission. But don't get the idea that I miss my American 'blessings.' Me for Russia, the Revolution, and its glorious future!"[4]

Goldman also was reunited with John Reed, who "burst into [her] room like a sudden ray of light." Reed's eyewitness account of the start of the revolution, *Ten Days That Shook the World,* had been published the previous year, and now Emma found him "buoyant" and "adventurous" as always, although she was shocked by his disquieting reports about conditions in Russia. "You are a little confused by the Revolution in action because you have dealt with it only in theory," he told her breezily. "You'll get over that, clear-sighted rebel that you are, and you'll come to see in its true light everything that seems so puzzling now. Cheer up, and make me a cup of the good old American coffee you have brought with you. Not much to give you in return for all my country has taken from you, but greatly appreciated in starving Russia by her native son."[5]

As the weeks and months passed, Emma grew increasingly uneasy, and also homesick. She missed America, the country she cherished and, as far as she was concerned, had fought to improve. In her room in Petrograd, according to *Chicago Tribune* reporter John Clayton, who interviewed her there, she proudly and unapologetically displayed the American flag, declaring, "I'm going back there some day, for I love America as I love no other land."[6] (Goldman later scoffed at the quote as "sheer nonsense.")[7] The longer Emma was in Russia, the more discontented she became. "I felt lost in the labyrinth of Soviet Russia," she later wrote, "stumbling constantly over the many obstacles, vainly groping for the revolutionary light."[8]

Berkman and Goldman went to Moscow, the capital of Soviet Russia, where they became acquainted with British philosopher Bertrand Russell, who was touring as a member of a British Labour delegation. Russell had initially been supportive of the idea of a revolution in Russia, but after visiting the country himself, he determined that the government had become "a Bonapartist military autocracy."[9] Russell told the French writer Colette, "I loathed the Bolsheviks and their regime . . . I think there is less liberty in modern Russia than has ever existed anywhere before."[10]

Russell's time with the anarchists was fleeting, but he observed that he and Berkman "both deplored the strangling of the Russian Revolution in a cruel bureaucracy," and later called Sasha "a man of rare single-mindedness and consistency, one of those whom it is a happiness to have known."[11] Goldman respected Russell, with his "reserved nature" and "gracious and simple personality." She also had some affectionate words for her old friend journalist Henry Alsberg, who was covering the British delegation's visit for the New York *Nation* and the London *Daily Herald.* Henry, she said, "brought with him a whiff of the best that was in America—sincerity and easy joviality, directness and camaraderie."[12]

Sasha and Emma's enthusiasm for the Soviet Revolution continued to cool. What they learned from trusted sources and observed firsthand did not match up with the idealistic vision they had nurtured while in the United States. Danger signals piled up: the restrictions on basic activities, the strong military presence, the encroachments on free speech, the ominous secrecy, the repression of dissenters, the widespread poverty and disease, the lack of food and medicine, the callous control by the ruling party. After four months in Russia, Goldman had come to a grim conclusion. "There is no health in it," she said. The state "has taken away even the little freedom the man has under individual capitalism and has made him entirely subject to the whims of a bureaucracy which excuses its tyranny on the ground it all is done for the welfare of the workers."[13]

Emma was aghast at the treatment of the citizens. "People raided, imprisoned, and shot for their ideas!" she cried. "The old and the young held as hostages, every protest gagged, iniquity and favouritism rampant, the best human values betrayed, the very spirit of revolution daily crucified. . . . I felt chilled to the marrow of my bones."[14] According to reporter John Clayton, Goldman agreed that the situation was "rotten." "But it is what we should have expected," she said. "We always knew the Marxian theory was impossible, a breeder of tyranny. We blinded ourselves to the faults in America because we believed it might accomplish something."[15]

Goldman and Berkman's disenchantment was increased by their isolation. "We both feel very lonesome and forlorn here," wrote Emma to Fitzi at the end of February 1920. To Stella Ballantine, she admitted, "I cannot tell you in words how torn away I feel from all that was dear and precious to me during a lifetime. You must exert every possible effort to get in touch with me—it is almost enough to drive one insane not to know what has happened to one's beloved ones all this time."[16] On March 8 Emma reached out to Ben Reitman. "I miss America. I lived there thirty years, you know," she told him. "It is very difficult for one of my age to acclimatize one's self in a new country, even in the best conditions in normal times. . . . But Russia, bled white by over four years of war and starved by the [Allied] blockade, is not a place where one may hope to take root easily."[17]

Harry Kelly was concerned about his dejected comrades. "Emma and Berkman write rather sad letters from Russia," he said to Max Nettlau on May 10. "Things are pretty bad there and they are finding it difficult to adjust themselves. I expected this of Emma but not of Berkman."[18] Lincoln Steffens noticed this too. "Emma Goldman doesn't like Bolshevism in action, and wants to get back to free America," he remarked to a libertarian associate. "[But the] important thing is that Bolshevik Russia shall go through its tyranny patiently and arrive at liberty for the whole Russian people and perhaps for the world."[19]

Adding to Emma's melancholy, she learned that her sister, Helena, had died in February 1920, having never recovered from the loss of her son. And Peter Kropotkin, who had left London and returned to Russia in 1917, also was showing signs of decline. In the summer of 1918 he had been compelled to relocate to a modest wooden house in the village of Dmitrov, forty miles north of the capital, after his ancestral home in Moscow was requisitioned by the government. In Dmitrov, Kropotkin spent much of his time writing a book on ethics. He and his family were living under hard conditions. They had little heat and were forced to rely on handouts and what was produced by their garden and their cow.[20]

Kropotkin's position on the revolution was knotty. He was greatly disturbed by the authoritarian methods of the Soviet government, and he opposed the dissolution of the Constituent Assembly and the aggressive practices of the Communist secret police, the Cheka, forerunners of the KGB. But he nevertheless urged the workers of western Europe to prevail upon their governments to end the blockade of Russia and cease their interference in the civil war.[21]

When the Bolsheviks seized power, Kropotkin was despondent. "This buries the revolution," he remarked to a friend. His repeated warnings against conspiratorial parties and revolutionary dictatorships had gone unheeded. In March 1920 Kropotkin wrote to Lenin that Russia had become "a Soviet Republic only in name. . . . At present it is not the [elected] soviets which rule in Russia, but party committees. . . . The very word 'socialism' will become a curse, as happened in France with the idea of equality for forty years after the rule of the Jacobins."[22]

Berkman and Goldman visited him at Dmitrov in May 1920. It was Sasha's first encounter with Kropotkin in person, and he was entranced. "Meeting 'celebrities,'" he wrote, "is generally disappointing: rarely does reality tally with the picture of our imagination. But it was not so in the case of Kropotkin; both physically and spiritually he corresponds almost exactly to the mental portrait I had made of him. . . . Every time Kropotkin entered the room it seemed to light up by his presence. The stamp of the idealist is so strikingly upon him, the spirituality of his personality can almost be sensed. But," Sasha added, "I was shocked at the sight of his emaciation and feebleness."[23]

"We found Peter ill and worn-looking," Goldman said, "a mere shadow of the sturdy man I had known in Paris and London in 1907." Kropotkin's wife, Sophie, and their daughter, Alexandra, were at the house as well. Alexandra presented Emma with a sailor hat, and Kropotkin directed her to "send special love to Harry Kelly." (Kropotkin and Kelly had been close associates and friends during their years in London.) Berkman was eager to learn his idol's views on the situation in Russia, and his opinion of the Bolsheviks. Kropotkin was somber. "They have shown how the Revolution is not to be made."[24]

AFTER RETURNING FROM DMITROV, Goldman and Berkman were invited to the Kremlin to meet with Lenin. They were escorted with stern spectacle, Emma later recalled, to "one of the ancient buildings" in the imposing complex, and ushered into Lenin's office. He was sitting "behind a huge desk, everything on it arranged with the strictest precision, the rest of the room giving the impression of the same exactitude. A board with numerous telephone switches and a map of the world covered the entire wall behind the man; glass cases filled with heavy tomes lined the sides. A large oblong table hung with red; twelve straight-backed chairs, and several armchairs at the windows. Nothing else to relieve the orderly monotony, except the bit of flaming red. The background seemed most fitting for one reputed for his rigid habits of life and matter-of-factness. Lenin, the man most idolized in the world and equally hated and feared, would have been out of place in surroundings of less severe simplicity."[25]

Lenin had read the speeches the anarchists had presented in Judge Mayer's courtroom, which had been published as a pamphlet, and he greeted them with enthusiastic appraisals of their work. "Great stuff! Clear-cut analysis of the capitalist system, splendid propaganda!" he remarked. "And you, *Tovarishtch* Berkman, what an organizer you must be, like your comrade Shatoff, who shrinks from nothing and can work like a dozen men. He is now in Siberia as commissioner of railroads in the Far Eastern Republic. You, Berkman, will soon find your place."[26]

He turned to Emma. "And you, Comrade Goldman? Have you thought of the work you want to do?"[27] Both Emma and Sasha had made clear they wished for no role in the government, and would not work for it in any capacity except for purely humanitarian projects.[28] Goldman therefore suggested that they lead a public relations thrust for the United States and set up a League of Russian Friends of American Freedom, to encourage a similar uprising in America and repay the American Friends of Russian Freedom for their longtime support. Lenin proclaimed this "a brilliant idea . . . a fine practical proposal. You must proceed to carry it out at once." He promised to provide them with supplies, funds, couriers, and an office. "Don't forget to send me the prospectus," he called to them as they left.[29]

Lenin was a commanding character, thought Sasha. A person of "logic and cold reasoning," the Soviet leader was "free and confident," and gave "the impression of a man so convinced of the justice of his cause that doubt can find no place in his reactions." He was "a fighter," said Sasha, and "revolutionary leaders must be such. In this sense Lenin is great—in his oneness with himself, in his single-mindedness; in his psychic positiveness that is as self-sacrificial as it is ruthless to others, in the full assurance that only his plan can save mankind."[30]

Charged with their duty for the Soviet state, Berkman and Goldman embarked on an expedition across Russia to collect documents and material about the revolutionary movement, which would be preserved in the new Museum of the Revolution in Petrograd and used for future study of the events surrounding the "great upheaval." They would witness daily life throughout the country and observe the results of the new system.[31] As Goldman told John Clayton before she left, "We are studying conditions in Russia. We want to make a trip through the country districts and talk to the peasants. Then we will be ready to speak. We probably will go to jail when we start criticizing, but that doesn't matter. We've been in jail before. We cannot be true to our principles and not speak."[32]

In July 1920 Sasha and Emma began their journey, traveling from Odessa in the south to Archangel in the north. They were furnished with a special railroad car and were accompanied by a small group, including Henry Alsberg. Their findings were alarming. Conditions in factories and institutions were bad. Jails were filled with political prisoners, many of them anarchists, Mensheviks, and Socialist Revolutionaries. Goldman and Berkman heard stories of mass arrests, the aggressive disbanding of anarchist insurrectionist Nestor Makhno's guerrilla army, and the consolidation of the soviet councils under government control.[33]

In the Ukraine they went to Kiev, Poltava, Kharkov, and smaller towns where anti-Jewish pogroms had taken place, collecting a vast array of documents and data.[34] "Our trip south was very successful," wrote Berkman to Fitzi, "both in point of the quality and quantity of the material we brought for the Museum of the Revolution, as well as in the wealth of impressions we gathered." But Sasha was robbed while in Kiev. "Completely cleaned out at night in our own car, while everyone slept," he said. "Lost my three American suits, money, gun, gold watch and Ingersoll, and other things. Have only that new suit left, the dark grey. A suit would come in handy, as it is almost impossible to buy one here." He mentioned, too, the funeral of John Reed. "Poor Louise and how hard she takes it."[35]

In October 1920 Emma and Sasha had learned of the death of Reed from a Soviet newspaper. Goldman had last seen him in Petrograd in June, when he was already in a delicate state after a harrowing experience in detention. In Baku, Reed was stricken with typhus. Mortally ill, he was brought back to Moscow by his wife, Louise Bryant, where he died on October 17. His funeral was held on October 23, and he was buried in the Kremlin wall. "Sasha and I had been very fond of Jack," Emma said, "and we felt his demise as a personal loss."[36]

Several months later, in January 1921, Peter Kropotkin, nearly eighty, fell sick with pneumonia. Emma had met with him a final time in July 1920, when they had shared hopes that the revolution might find its way back to its idealistic foundations, ushered by the workers' committees and peasant cooperatives. She had been greatly comforted by their conversation, "by the warmth and light which the beautiful personality of Peter Kropotkin radiated."[37] Learning of his grave condition, Emma traveled again to Dmitrov, accompanied by anarcho-syndicalist Alexander Schapiro, the editor of *Golos Truda,* and Nikolai Ivanovich Pavlov, a comrade from the Bakers' Union. But their train was delayed, and on February 8, 1921, Kropotkin died, an hour before they reached his home.[38]

Kropotkin's family declined Lenin's offer of a state burial, and a committee of anarchists, with Berkman as secretary, arranged a dignified funeral that took place on February 13. A number of imprisoned anarchists were granted their freedom for one day so that they might participate in the procession. Tens of thousands of people marched through the frigid Moscow winter to the elegantly sumptuous Novodevichi Monastery, the burial place of Kropotkin's princely ancestors. Members of the procession bore the black flag of anarchy and carried signs and banners reading, "Where there is authority, there is no freedom" and "The liberation of the working class is the task of the workers themselves." Goldman was among the speakers at the flower-strewn graveside. Kropotkin's home in Moscow, the grand old place of his birth, was returned to his widow and was dedicated as a museum for his books, papers, research, and theory. The museum was closed in 1938, and the house later became an embassy school for American and British children.[39]

THREE WEEKS AFTER KROPOTKIN'S FUNERAL, the Kronstadt rebellion broke out. In March 1921 the sailors at the Kronstadt naval base in the Gulf of Finland near Petrograd rose in revolt against the Bolshevik government to which they had once been loyal and which they had steadfastly backed with military force. The sailors demanded the right to choose their own representatives to the Kronstadt soviet; in retaliation, Lenin and Trotsky declared Kronstadt outlawed and prepared an attack.[40] According to Berkman, the slaughter of 10,000 Kronstadt sailors, soldiers, and workers was "the greatest crime committed by the soviet government against the Revolution and Russia, symbolizing the beginning of a new tyranny."[41]

The rebels at Kronstadt, as self-proclaimed "free soviets," created a commune that lasted for sixteen days, until armed forces stormed across the ice to extinguish the insubordinate community. The Kronstadt uprising united radicals, socialists, Mensheviks, anarchists, and rank-and-file Communists, who possessed no organized ideology. Rather than following a formal credo, they were motivated by a sense of grievance, protesting instinctively against deprivation, oppression, and totalitarianism.

Anarchists hailed Kronstadt as "the Second Paris Commune," denounced the government for its violent revenge, and circulated leaflets in Petrograd in support of the rebels. Berkman and Goldman had initially sought to mediate the conflict and avert a bloodbath; together with two comrades, on March 5 they sent a letter to Petrograd Soviet Chairman Zinoviev proposing an impartial commission to settle the conflict peacefully. But on March 7 the attack against Kronstadt began. The sounds of cannons and gunfire could be heard clearly all the way to Petrograd.[42]

Sasha was devastated. "Days of anguish and cannonading," he recorded in his diary. "My heart is numb with despair; something has died within me. The people on the streets look bowed with grief, bewildered. No one trusts himself to speak. The thunder of heavy guns rends the air." The battle, savage and bloody, continued for days, with heavy losses on both sides. Finally, on March 17, 1921, it ended. "Kronstadt has fallen today," Berkman wrote. "Thousands of sailors and workers lie dead in its streets. Summary execution of prisoners and hostages continues." Emma saw his torment. "The last thread of [Sasha's] faith in the Bolsheviki [is] broken," she said. When silence fell in Petrograd after days of carnage, Emma remained in the hotel, "unutterable weariness in every nerve," while Sasha, desolate, "desperately roamed the streets."[43]

The Kronstadt rebellion set off a wave of political arrests. Anarchist bookstores, clubs, printing shops, and periodicals were shut down. The pacifist followers of Tolstoy who were still alive—many of their brethren had been shot during the civil war for refusing to serve in the Red Army—were imprisoned or exiled.[44] Across the country, in cities such as Petrograd, Moscow, Kiev, and Kharkov, anarchists were rounded up and arrested by the Cheka, and taken to the Taganka and Butyrki prisons in Moscow. To the horror of Goldman and Berkman, a number of their close comrades were apprehended, including V. M. Volin, Senya Fleshin, Mark Mratchny, and married revolutionaries Aron and Fanya Baron.[45] In September 1921, without formal charges or a trial, the Cheka executed Fanya Baron, whom Sasha and Emma had known in Chicago, and the poet Lev Cherny.[46]

Berkman and Goldman were now certain that the Bolsheviks had fully despoiled the Revolution, corrupting its ideals and exploiting its principles. The goals of 1917—proletarian democracy, social equality, workers' self-management—were shoved aside. Soviets, trade unions, and factory committees were appropriated as tools of the state apparatus, while authority was concentrated in the hands of a party elite.[47] Berkman's dreams for a new society were shattered. "Before Kronstadt," he wrote to Harry Kelly, "I myself was still hopeful that the Bolsheviks would change their policies and methods. Emma Goldman was more against them than I then. It was Kronstadt that turned us both completely and irrevocably against the Bolsheviks. It was the beginning of the Kronstadt situation that turned the scales."[48]

Outrage burned within Goldman over the Kronstadt massacre. And the execution of Fanya Baron and other comrades so incensed her that she considered chaining herself to a bench in the hall where the Third International was in session, to shout her protest. Emma realized that she had no place in Russia, that she must "escape from the horrible revolutionary sham and pretense."[49]

Sasha came to the same conclusion. As he wrote in his diary, "Grey are the passing days. One by one the embers of hope have died out. Terror and despotism have crushed the life born in October. The slogans of the

Revolution are foresworn, its ideals stifled in the blood of the people. The breath of yesterday is dooming millions to death; the shadow of today hangs like a black pall over the country. Dictatorship is trampling the masses under foot. The Revolution is dead; its spirit cries in the wilderness. High time the truth about the Bolsheviki were told. The white sepulcher must be unmasked, the clay feet of the fetish beguiling the international proletariat to fatal will o' the wisps exposed. The Bolshevik myth must be destroyed. I have decided to leave Russia."[50]

23

CHARLOTTENGRAD

EMMA AND SASHA BEGAN TO PLOT their departure from Soviet Russia. "I am desperately trying to get out now that I have come to the conclusion that the situation here is utterly hopeless as far as anarchist activities are concerned," wrote Emma to their friend and benefactor Dr. Michael Cohn, who over the years had been a reliable source of personal and financial support. "Yet it is not the Russian Revolution which is to blame for the general debacle. It is the regime. But about that when we meet again, or when I am somewhere where I can again raise my voice. As I said before, we are trying desperately to get out. I do not know whether we will succeed. I only know it is beyond me to stay here another winter. I manage to go on only by sheer force of will. Most people who came here like me were in the grip of the great delusion. They go away heart broken."[1]

Near the end of 1921, Goldman applied to the Soviet commissioner of foreign affairs for permission to attend the International Anarchist Congress, scheduled to be held in Berlin from December 25, 1921, to January 2, 1922. The request was granted on December 1, and, along with equally disillusioned *Golos Truda* editor Alexander Schapiro, Emma and Sasha took their leave. Despite her relief at escaping Russia, Goldman was mournful. "In the train. . . . My dreams crushed, my faith broken, my heart like a stone. *Matushka Rossiya* [Mother Russia] bleeding from a thousand wounds, her soil strewn with the dead. I clutch the bar at the frozen window-pane and grit my teeth to suppress my sobs."[2]

Their getaway was not without hurdles; the three were detained by Latvian officials in Riga, and as a result missed the Anarchist Congress and were left without a fixed destination. Goldman told the Associated Press in an interview at the Bolshevik Consulate Building in Riga, "My stay in Russia has only served to convince me that I have always been right, and that anarchy is the only sound system." Appearing "thin and aged" by the past two years, she said she was "not going back to Russia," because "America is my country."[3]

They found a haven in Sweden, under the Socialist government of Hjalmar Branting, who allowed them temporary residence. Arriving in Stockholm on January 5, 1922, they boarded with their comrades Albert and Elise Jensen. As Sasha and Emma adjusted to their new surroundings, they struggled to comprehend what they had witnessed in Russia, and to process their shock that the Bolshevik regime was "a phantom . . . a nightmare of repression and bureaucracy." Emma realized how naive she had been. "Poor Babushka, how we all criticized her," she wrote to feminist writer Alice Stone Blackwell. "Yet every word she said two years ago was based on facts. How little we understood what the crushing machine the Bolshevik State must have meant to her. Now I know, after I myself have fought against the truth, that Babushka spoke the truth."[4]

Sasha and Emma remained in Sweden for several months, tolerated by the government, if not entirely welcome. Goldman, always keen for romance regardless of circumstance, immediately took up with young Swedish anarchist Arthur Svensson. As one of Emma's friends later observed, "She liked men, especially young men. She really liked the boys!"[5] Svensson was not yet thirty.

Emma began to spread the word about her experiences in Russia, contributing articles to a variety of journals, most notably a series of seven reports for the *New York World,* which ran from March 26 to April 4, 1922.[6] The editorials, with titles such as "The Crushing of the Russian Revolution," "Bolsheviks Shooting Anarchists," and "Persecution of Russian Anarchists," caused a stir among her comrades in America and were denounced by Communists, liberals, and radicals who supported the Soviet undertaking. Many discounted her reports as erroneous; others accused her of deliberately betraying the working class.

In New York, writer and *Daily Freiheit* editor Moissaye J. Olgin, a staunch supporter of the revolution and a communist leader, told an audience at Arlington Hall in St. Mark's Place, "Emma Goldman does not seem to have understood the Russian language. Hasn't she read any history, and what has she been doing over there these last two years? She may have been conspicuous in America, but she is not conspicuous at all in Russia."[7] Perhaps, it was suggested, Goldman was irked that her role within the Soviet system was insignificant, that she was not treated with proper deference, or that she had grown used to a "comfortably bourgeois" life in America and was too soft for the daily hardships of Russia.[8]

"Such criticism," Goldman said, "was meant to silence uncomfortable truths." But her detractors remained strident and angry. One former ally, communist advocate Rose Paster Stokes, demanded that Emma be burned in effigy. "Since my articles were written," Emma said to Max Nettlau, who was based in Vienna, "I have been quartered, burned in oil, lynched, and what not. It would amuse you to read the awful stuff that appeared in the communist press in America."[9]

Nor did Emma find consolation from Sasha, who opposed her decision to publish her reports in commercial newspapers. "His attitude hurt me very much and we argued for days," said Emma. "Was it not more important how and what one said than where? Sasha insisted that it did not apply in this case. Anything I might write in the capitalist press would inevitably be used by the reactionaries against Russia and I would justly be censured for it by our own comrades."[10]

Berkman, for his part, shunned the mainstream press, and would only publish his pieces in anarchist journals and pamphlets. "I won't have articles in capitalist papers," he informed Michael Cohn from Stockholm. "Stella [Ballantine] sold my article on the journey from Russia to Stockholm to the *New York World,* but I asked her to withdraw it."[11] Still, he had much to say about his years in Russia, and contributed plenty of articles to the journals that met his strict standards. Additionally, Emma and Sasha together submitted appeals to local radical publications about political prisoners in Russia, including the Stockholm *Arbetaren* (*the Worker*), a daily syndicalist paper, and the *Brand,* an anarchist weekly.[12]

Before long, Sasha was asked to leave Sweden. On March 14, 1922, he wrote to Michael Cohn, thanking him for the latest supply of cash and telling him of his most recent expulsion. "Today we were informed that we must get out of this country," Sasha said. "Ordered to leave tomorrow. I have decided to cut the Gordian knot by going as a stowaway to Germany. To hell with all those legalities, I am sick of it all, we've been at it two months or more. I am bound for Germany."[13]

Sasha was impatient to get "a bit of quiet" and write all about "the experiment in Russia" once he reached Berlin. "As soon as I get there I mean to start in at full speed," he said. "For I am just choked up with the subjects I want to write about, and I am experiencing a veritable passion for writing." Sasha was in particularly good spirits, as the meticulous journal he had used to chronicle his deportation voyage and daily life in Russia had been located, after a long disappearance. Goldman had hidden "the precious diary" in her room in Russia while the Cheka "ransacked" Sasha's quarters, until friends smuggled the notebook out of the country. It then went missing for some time, but turned up just before Sasha left for Germany. "Glory, hallelujah," he told Cohn.[14]

Berkman stowed away on a tramp steamer and entered Germany illegally, while Goldman went through the regular channels to obtain a visa from the German consul before joining Sasha in Berlin. Weary from her travels, she rented an apartment at 3 Rudesheimerstrasse under the name Mrs. E. G. Kershner. At first she missed Svensson, her Swedish lover, longing for the "tender devotion" of her "flaxen-haired, blue-eyed Swedish boy." But when Svensson came to Berlin four weeks later in May, her interest cooled and she was acutely conscious "that he was twenty-nine and I fifty-three."[15] The relationship nevertheless would last for eight strained months until it disintegrated when he fell in love with her secretary.

Berlin had opened its doors to tens of thousands of refugees, many of them Russian exiles, and when Goldman and Berkman arrived, they joined a thriving community. The center of this society formed in the borough of Charlottenburg, known colloquially as Charlottengrad because of its bursting new Russian population. The city boasted fifty-eight Russian dailies and periodicals; by the mid-1920s some 200,000 Russians lived in Berlin, ranging from governmental and military officers to creative writers and artists such as Boris Pasternak, Vladimir Nabokov, and Mark Chagall, who passed through briefly or remained for years.[16]

Goldman enjoyed the stimulating environment and was pleased to speak German, her "mother tongue." She devoted her time to editorializing about Russia, and spent a few months in the spring of 1923 making a study of German experimental schools in Stuttgart, Frankfort, Fulda, Leipzig, Hamburg, and Dresden, where she visited A. S. Neill's international school at Hellerau. The Ferrer School model, however, remained of particular interest to her, and she kept up with some of the New York students, including former pupil Benjamin Greenstein, who had since become a well-regarded artist, known as Benjamin Benno. "I am glad and proud," she wrote to a Ferrer School leader, "that the New York Ferrer School was the first place to give him his initiation."[17]

Emma and Sasha socialized with local comrades in Berlin and reunited with some of their old friends. They both became close to Rudolf and Milly Rocker, whom Emma had not seen since 1907, and she now "came to appreciate and love their beautiful spirit." Rudolf, she wrote, was "a force in the German anarchist movement and an inspiration to everyone who came in contact with him," while "Milly was also sensitively attuned to human suffering and unstinted in her sympathy and affection."[18]

Emma and Sasha's dear friend Hutchins Hapgood, in the midst of an excursion through Italy, took a detour to Germany and spent five weeks with them in Berlin. Fitzi, although no longer Berkman's romantic partner, visited in July and August 1923. Max Nettlau stopped in from Vienna to attend a Beethoven concert with Emma and the Rockers.[19] Michael Cohn made the trip from America with his second wife (Annie Netter had died in 1920) and joined Emma and Sasha on sightseeing jaunts around the country.[20] Stella, along with her husband Teddy Ballantine, a stage actor, and their six-year-old son, Ian, came for an extended visit, staying in Emma's "lively 4-room apartment." In his adulthood, Ian Ballantine worked in the publishing industry, and in 1952 founded the publishing house Ballantine Books.[21]

In the summer of 1923, Emma, Stella, and a group including Fitzi took a trip to Munich, where foreign visitors were required to register with the Bavarian police.[22] "I discovered," wrote Emma, "that the police had my full record with photos of thirty years ago. After hours of grilling, I was ordered to leave Bavaria within two hours. We then went to see the town and attend a Wagner festival." The police came to the hotel the next morning and took everyone in Emma's party to the police station, where they questioned them, and told Stella to leave Bavaria at once because she was Emma's niece. As Goldman joked to her longtime friend Leon Malmed, "You see dear, I am still considered dangerous, even though my life is so devoid of interest and purpose that it sometimes seems so useless to go on."[23]

Minna Lowensohn, Sasha's admiring fan, visited him in Berlin in 1924. He took her sightseeing, on walks and rides, and to famous cafés and restaurants. They went on an outing to Wannsee to enjoy the lakes and scenery, bringing along sandwiches for a picnic. On the way Sasha bought a bag of peanuts. "To me," wrote Minna in her memoirs, "the whole trip just seemed like a fairy land, especially the boat ride with the houses on the shore and the flowers in the window boxes to grow out of the sea. We just fed each other with peanuts and closed our eyes and laughed. Of course such behavior seems silly in retrospect, but it was certainly one of the happiest days of my life."[24]

Sasha and Emma continued to make noise about postrevolution conditions in Bolshevik Russia. Emma's *New York World* series was extensively reproduced; and Sasha's pamphlets were funded by Michael Cohn, printed in *Der Syndikalist* in Berlin, and circulated by Agnes Inglis in America.[25] Their work reached a wide audience. "In France, Norway, Sweden, in South America, even in China, the word is spreading now, for we are supplying all those countries with information on conditions in Russia, especially with regard to political prisoners," Berkman told a friend. "Recently a comrade, whom I met in Russia, and who is now in Shanghai, translated all my pamphlets into Chinese. He published a whole pamphlet containing all the information for the instruction of the Chinese workers. In this way the light breaks through."[26]

With the attention brought by their articles, both Emma and Sasha decided to publish books about their travails in Russia, the logical next step professionally and monetarily. An expansive accounting of the journey seemed potentially cathartic, and Emma was still grappling with lingering trauma. "My two years in Russia meant a daily and hourly Golgotha," she wrote. "Like an iron ring around my heart and mind I see the ghastly thing in my waking hours, and try as I may, I cannot escape it."[27]

In December 1922 she completed her manuscript, which she titled, simply, *My Two Years in Russia.* Doubleday, Page bought it in May 1923, and it reached bookstores on October 26, 1923. When Emma received an early copy of her book she was shocked to discover that it had been retitled *My Disillusionment in Russia,* and that the last thirteen chapters had been omitted. "As printed," she fumed, "the volume was an unfinished work, because the last chapters and particularly my Afterword, which represented the culminating essence of the whole, were left out. The unauthorized name was fearfully misleading: My Disillusionment in Russia was sure to convey to the reader that it was the Revolution that had disillusioned me rather than the pseudo-revolutionary methods of the Communist State."[28] She was angry enough to consult Harry Weinberger about legal recourse, but the volume was released in its abbreviated form over her protests.

"A number of reviews have appeared," Emma wrote to Leon Malmed after the book's publication. "Only one man in a Cleveland paper had sense enough to see that the book ended too abruptly and was not finished. The rest noted nothing."[29] Michael Cohn again came to her rescue, and put up the funds to produce the remaining thirteen chapters in a second volume.[30] The restored portion was published in November 1924 as *My Further Disillusionment in Russia.* The *Washington Post* called the combined works "a complete and sweeping indictment of bolshevism. Miss Goldman displays a feminine acuteness of observation and womanlike clings to her point that had the Russians made the revolution à la Bakunin instead of à la Marx the result would have been different and more satisfactory."[31] In October 1925 the British publishing house C. W. Daniel published both of Goldman's books in a single volume. An appraisal of the book appeared in the *Times Literary Supplement* of London. "No more scathing attack upon the Soviet tyranny and its leaders has been written," it said, "than this sincere and authoritative statement."[32]

In January 1923 Sasha began work on his own manuscript, compiled from his detailed diary, and he finished it in August 1924. "In general," he told a friend, "the book is written in the style of my *Prison Memoirs*—written objectively."[33] *The Bolshevik Myth,* as the book was called, was published in 1925 by Boni & Liveright of New York, although the concluding chapter was rejected as an "anti-climax," and excluded.[34] "Anxious to place [the] book before the public," Berkman consented to the cut, publishing the conclusion separately in Berlin at the cost of "$200 to pay the printer." "Bolshevism is of the past," Sasha wrote in the final pages. "The future belongs to man and his liberty."[35]

Fitzi did what she could to promote Sasha's book. She was living in New York City, serving as the business manager for the Provincetown Players, an acting troupe established in Provincetown on Cape Cod in 1915 at the home of Hutchins Hapgood. A number of friends and acquaintances had been involved with the group over the years, including Hapgood's wife, Neith Boyce, Mary Heaton Vorse, Floyd Dell, Max Eastman, John Reed and Louise Bryant, and Eugene O'Neill. The daring plays and experimental style had a marked influence on modern theater.

After Sasha and Emma were deported, Fitzi devoted much of her attention to the theater company. Yet she always made time for Sasha, and did her best to encourage sales of *The Bolshevik Myth.* In an advertisement, she described the book as "the first day-by-day record that any one has succeeded in getting out of Russia since the revolution." Berkman, she said, presented his experiences "with great simplicity, but at the same time with terrible realism," introducing the reader to the leaders Lenin, Trotsky, Zinoviev, as well as to "the humble, the work-a-day people."[36]

Fitzi continued, "You see through his eyes the terrible bourgeoisie; the starving intelligentsia; you hear the factory worker speak; and the Red army man; and the Tchekist, frankly cynical; you get an insight into the psychology of the sincere Communists, now persecuted for their opposition to the prevailing party; he takes you into the huts of the Ukrainian peasant; into the Soviet prisons; he gives you a glimpse of the impending famine."[37]

Goldman's and Berkman's books on Russia were reviewed simultaneously by H. L. Mencken, the influential journalist and critic, who commented that the volumes were perhaps "the best books that the Russian debacle has yet produced."[38] In his appraisal, Mencken overlooked Emma and Sasha's violent histories and focused on their intellectual gifts and descriptive testimony. "One commonly hears of such persons as Emma Goldman and Alexander Berkman only as remote and horrendous malefactors, half human and half reptilian," he wrote. "Editorial writers on dull days exhume ancient bits of complaint against them. . . . They are denounced by orators before the American Legion, by suburban pastors, and by brave Congressmen. . . . All this indignation, unfortunately, conceals the somewhat disconcerting fact that both are extremely intelligent—that once their aberrant political ideas are set aside they are seen to have very sharp wits. They think clearly, unsentimentally, and even a bit brilliantly. . . . In the United States," Mencken wrote, "where such criticism is needed quite as sorely as in Russia and where it could be turned to use ten times as well here the only thing we can think of doing to such a man as Berkman is to lock him up in jail. Because his fulminations alarm a few profiteers we hunt him as if he were a mad dog—and finally kick him out of the country. And with him goes a shrewder head and a braver spirit than has been seen in public among us since the Civil War."[39]

Sales of both books were sluggish, and the proceeds were barely sufficient to offer even a brief respite from Sasha and Emma's cash-strapped anxiety. "I can't tell you how the uncertainty of a living worries me," wrote Emma to Sasha. "It's getting to be an obsession."[40]

IN THE AFTERMATH OF THE RUSSIAN REVOLUTION, Sasha and Emma were active in a number of organizations devoted to helping political captives detained in Soviet jails and camps. The files accumulated by these advocacy groups bulged with letters and dossiers of incarcerated anarchists, their names followed by such grim annotations as "beaten in Butyrki," "repeated hunger strikes," "killed in prison," "shot by Kiev Cheka," "beaten for resisting forced feeding," and "fate unknown."[41] In October 1924 Michael Cohn wrote to Berkman, "The appalling condition of our martyrs in Russia prisons actually haunts me day and night. . . . When will the horrible nightmare end?"[42]

Sasha had taken a leading role in Soviet prisoner advocacy since December 1922, when he attended the founding congress of the International Working Men's Association and became secretary-treasurer of its Relief Fund Committee, as well as editor of the fund's *Bulletin,* which was published in German, Russian, and English.[43] He was aided by Mark Mratchny and V. M. Volin, both of whom had survived imprisonment in Russia, and by Mollie Steimer and her partner Senya Fleshin, who had together left Russia in 1923 and met up with their comrades in Berlin.

Sasha collected documents for a book called *Letters from Russian Prisons,* which included testimonials from Russian political prisoners; affidavits about political persecution; official statements by Soviet authorities; excerpts from Soviet laws pertaining to civil liberties; and letters of protest by illustrious intellectuals including Albert Einstein, Knut Hamsun, Thomas Mann, Romain Rolland, and H. G. Wells.[44] *Letters from Russian Prisons* served as an early documentation of the Gulag Archipelago and Communist oppression.[45]

Emma and Sasha also arranged a fund for aging and needy anarchist exiles, soliciting their wealthiest and most faithful patrons for contributions. "Often I think that we revolutionists are like the capitalist system," observed Goldman. "We drain men and women of the best that is in them and then stand quietly by to see them end their last days in destitution and loneliness."[46] The pair continued to struggle financially themselves, and the overhead of their advocacy organizations—the printed bulletins and protest meetings, the steady stream of parcels, letters, food, and supplies they sent to prisoners in Russia and around the world—exhausted their meager personal funds. Nevertheless, they considered the outreach a priority.

Sasha, perpetually haunted by his own prison nightmares, had a particular concern for those comrades in captivity. He never lost interest in the plight of Tom Mooney, still in San Quentin, for whom he had worked tirelessly during his last years in America. Sasha contacted friends in the States for updates, and he and Mooney corresponded regularly.[47] "Alex," Mooney wrote, "I hope that Fate deals kindly with you—you have known only the rough hard road so far—it has made you what you are—a wonderful fellow."[48]

"I can well realize how hard those long years of prison have been on you," Berkman replied. "Greetings to Billings, Matt [Schmidt], and Jim McNamara. Tell them, and be assured yourself, that I don't forget friends and that I am always not only willing but also anxious to help, if it be in my power."[49] Sasha repeated this promise in subsequent letters. "Whenever I can," he told Tom, "my help can be counted on in the right cause."[50]

For all the efforts on his behalf, Mooney remained in his San Quentin cell. In December 1931 Sasha wrote to Mooney, "There is no more crying injustice today in the whole U.S. than your and Billings' continued imprisonment. Your case has literally gone around the world, and every decent man and woman knows of your martyrdom, of your courageous stand in the face of years-long persecution and suffering. May the coming holidays see the triumph of justice the world over. But that is only a pious wish, too much to expect. Yet it is not too much to expect that you, at least, should see justice triumph in your individual case, and that you may soon breathe the air outside prison walls. That is my deepest wish for the New Year."[51]

24

GLOBE-TROTTERS AND COLONIZERS

Still longing for America, Emma grew weary of Berlin, where the atmosphere made her "gloomy" and the cost of living stressed her pocketbook. "Poor thing," said Stella Ballantine of her aunt, "she wants to come home but sees no way to do it. Having a limited means of earning a living, she decided to go to Paris and then move to London."[1] In July 1924, while Berkman remained in Berlin to finish writing *The Bolshevik Myth,* Goldman left Germany in search of a freer political culture and better professional opportunities. After a stop in the Netherlands, where she was hustled out after a mere twenty-four hours, she arrived in Paris, registering as E. G. Kershner at the Hotel Terrasse on the rue Maitre.

"I finally got out of Germany," Goldman wrote to Agnes Inglis at the beginning of September. "I could barely stand being there another minute. Not that it was not interesting, but it got so expensive to live I just could not support it. I had to leave. I am [in France] five weeks and feel 15 years younger. Paris is like sparkling wine, it gets in one's blood and takes hold of one's being beyond redemption."[2]

Emma was ecstatic to be back in the French capital. "Paris is more fascinating, virile, reckless, and alive than seventeen years ago," she told Stella. "The city is never asleep. It is dance, drink, and joy. I never saw such abandon. Never at any time did I see so many Americans abroad. Like the Dome on the Montparnasse, where only Americans come, the place is jammed every evening. There you meet everybody. People from my part of the U.S.

are there and have recognized me. And there are any number of such places in Paris."[3]

Emma mingled with Harry Weinberger, Louise Bryant, and British writer Frank Harris and his companion Nellie, who encouraged her to visit Nice in the south of France. She met Marie Curie and got to know Paris-based American expats, including the owner of the iconic English-language bookstore Shakespeare and Company. "There is an awfully fine woman here, Sylvia Beach, who published [James] Joyce's last book," Emma told Stella. "She has a lovely bookshop and is going to put my books on sale." Emma attended many events, and was introduced to Ernest Hemingway at a party given by Ford Madox Ford. Hemingway, she said, reminded her "of both Jack London and John Reed because of his simplicity and exuberance of spirit." When Hemingway invited her for dinner, she found that "Ernest, in his role as proud father of a buxom baby, looked younger and was gayer in his home setting."[4]

Much though she adored Paris, Goldman took steps to arrange entry to England. She sought help from John Turner, Bertrand Russell, and Frank Harris, and soon procured a visa. In the autumn of 1924 she arrived in London.

Emma had been dreading the London weather, recalling the persistent mist and chill of her visit in 1900. She found the "monster fog" as relentless as ever, despite her cheery new quarters near Regent's Park, on the third floor of a boardinghouse run by her friend Doris Zhook. Her English acquaintances were amused by her complaints about the weather. "I had been in Archangel when the temperature was fifty below zero and I had not felt so chilly," she told them. "Poetic fancy, they teased. If the damp makes one miserable, it produces good complexions, rich foliage, and the strength of the British Empire. Delicate skins, the luscious green lawns and meadows, are due to the weather, and the need to escape from his own climate has made the Englishman foremost among globe-trotters and colonizers."[5]

Once settled, Emma went about finding an audience for her speeches and editorials, mobilizing local anarchists, and decrying the Soviet system from her British base. She approached London native Rebecca West, born

Cicely Isabel Fairfield in 1892, who was an established writer and journalist and a well-connected member of the British cultural scene. West had been introduced to Stella Ballantine in New York and said Stella was "one of the most interesting people" she had met.[6] She offered to be of assistance to Goldman. Emma told Stella that Rebecca reminded her of "the early Russian revolutionists who would give their last skirt for their friends."[7]

West and Goldman soon became close. At their first meeting, Emma went to lunch at West's home, and found her "vivacious, eager, charming, direct. . . . I left my hostess with the comforting feeling that I had found a friend, an oasis in the desert London seemed to me."[8] After their second visit, she wrote to Sasha about her intriguing new acquaintance, noting that West had read his *Prison Memoirs* and wanted to know all about him. "I am sure your ears must have burned."[9] Goldman reported to her New York legal advisers, Harry Weinberger and his colleague Arthur Leonard Ross, that she had found a gracious and gifted London ally who was keen to help her cause.[10]

West did indeed provide an entrée for Goldman. She contacted George Bernard Shaw, H. G. Wells (the father of her son), and others in political and literary circles. She supplied her own staunch support, although a number of people, including Bertrand Russell and West herself, refused to endorse Emma's all-out attack on the Soviet Union.[11] She introduced Goldman to her sisters and intimates, gave luncheons and tea parties in Emma's honor, and presided at her lectures.

Another active English supporter was Colonel Josiah Wedgwood of the renowned pottery firm, a member of Parliament who had previously held a Cabinet seat in the Labour Party. On November 12, 1924, Wedgwood chaired a dinner of 250 people at Anderton's Hotel to launch Goldman's crusade. West organized the dinner and presented Emma to the crowd. "We are very grateful to America," she said, "for the loan of Emma Goldman." When Goldman took the podium, her words were abrasive and uncompromising. "To call the present Soviet Government a workers' experiment is the most preposterous lie ever told," she pronounced. "The time has come when silence on the Russian situation makes you a party to the crimes which are being committed there."[12]

The event drew considerable publicity and alerted the media to Goldman's presence in England. "Rebecca West, distinguished novelist, and Bertrand Russell, well-known socialist of a rather respectable shade, were hosts recently in London to Emma Goldman, militant anarchist," reported the *Atlanta Constitution,* adding that Goldman was "a hunted little woman in a hostile world."[13] Still, Emma was delighted with the dinner's outcome, "a much greater success than I had anticipated," she told Alexander Schapiro. "But more important was the spirit."[14]

Two of the dinner guests were Havelock Ellis and Edward Carpenter, both social reformers in the field of sexuality, and Emma contacted them afterward to thank them for their attendance. "I have known you for many years by your great work," Goldman wrote to Havelock Ellis. "It will interest you to learn that I have carried your ideas and your pleas for human rights all over the United States, into the Industrial Centers and wherever I came to lecture. You see therefore that you are not a stranger to me although I am a stranger to you." She said she wished to meet him personally, so she could thank him for all he had done for her "development," and Ellis invited Emma to his house.[15]

Socialist and homosexual activist Edward Carpenter also was happy to make Emma's acquaintance, asking her to visit him and his lover in Guildford, Surrey. Emma described Carpenter, nearly eighty, as "frail and feeble. Alongside of his dapper companion, whom everybody addressed as George, his clothes looked shabby. But there was distinction in his carriage, and grace in every gesture."[16] Carpenter had read *Prison Memoirs of an Anarchist* and "raved" about Sasha and the book, so Goldman suggested that he provide an introduction to the British edition, soon to be published by C. W. Daniel.[17] Carpenter wrote to Berkman shortly thereafter, praising Sasha for his forthright and sensitive approach to the topic of homosexuality. "I want to thank you for the good work you have done in the old and sacred cause," Carpenter said. "The ultimate success is certain of your gospel of human love and solidarity."[18] Emma was happy to have met both Ellis and Carpenter. "My summer was indeed enriched by these two grand seigneurs of intellect and heart," she said.[19]

In spite of the vigorous efforts of Goldman, the backing of West, and the interest of some prominent British citizens, Goldman's Russia crusade never gained traction in Great Britain. Her notoriety as an anarchist and proponent of violence was unsettling to those who might have sympathized with her anti-Soviet view, while many radicals thought she was a traitor to the ideals of the Russian Revolution and wanted nothing to do with her. Furthermore, the political climate in England was inhospitable to her message. A British trade union delegation had just returned from the Soviet Union with glowing reports on conditions in the country. As Emma later wrote angrily, the delegation was "on fire with the wonders they had seen—rather, had been shown! They waxed enthusiastic in the *Daily Herald* and at meetings about the splendid Soviet achievements." Goldman was profoundly disheartened by the cool reception to her ideas and the collapse of her campaign.[20]

The friendship between West and Goldman endured, however. After nearly a year in England, Emma declared, "Rebecca continues to be my joy. I always feel rested when I am with her."[21] West remained a loyal advocate and contributed the introduction to the British edition of *My Disillusionment in Russia,* published in full in October 1925. Rebecca later described Emma as "a solid thickset woman with heavy glasses and no vestige of sexual attraction, but great warmth and charm. She had a rollicking sense of fun, but for the most part she was sad because she had no outlet for her gifts." West's admiration for Goldman's character was boundless. "Emma Goldman is one of the great people of the world," she said. "She is a mountain of integrity. She has a proven genius for honesty and courage."[22]

TOWARD THE END OF 1925, with her political effort against Soviet Russia in tatters, Emma once again turned her attention to the arts. The British Drama League sponsored a series of her lectures, and she received requests to appear all over England, from Manchester to Liverpool to Bath. She informed the league's secretary, Walter Peacock, that she would be discussing Strindberg, Ibsen, a variety of Russian dramatists, and Eugene O'Neill. "I know O'Neill personally, and of course also know and love his work," she told Peacock. "I would be so glad to speak about both and perhaps thereby help to create sufficient public interest . . . [and] a better understanding of the man and his creative genius."[23]

Goldman had been lecturing on British dramatists for years, but to prepare for her course of talks on Russian playwrights, she immersed herself in research at the British Museum. "Six hours every day was the very least I needed to cope with the historic treasures I discovered in the British Museum on the Russian theatre and drama," she later wrote. "The longer I worked in the museum, the more information I unearthed on stage arrangement, old plays, scenery, and costumes. This led to wider fields, embracing the political and social backgrounds of the dramatists of different periods, and their correspondence that reflected their feelings and reaction to Russian life. It was a fascinating study and so absorbing as to make me forget the closing-hour."[24]

She told Sasha about her industry, and the mounting pressure to succeed. "In the British Museum," she said, "I have been busy as a bee . . . working about eight hours a day. By the way, I was told today that Bernard Shaw has sent his check for two subscription tickets to the Russian courses. That means I must work doubly hard not to disgrace my American friends and those here who vouch for me."[25]

To balance her study with practical exposure, Goldman took full advantage of London's theater scene, and attended many contemporary productions. She was enchanted by Paul Robeson, whom she saw in *The Emperor Jones.* "Robeson also sang," she wrote to Sasha. "My God what a voice. . . . No wonder Stella, Fitzi, and everybody else in New York rave about him. Really he is simply marvelous."[26]

DURING HER MONTHS IN LONDON, Goldman befriended a young student, Gabriel Javsicas, who had been born in Russia in 1906 and raised in Germany, graduating from secondary school in Frankfurt am Main. The eighteen-year-old Javsicas arrived in England in November 1924 to study at the London School of Economics, despite his father's wishes that he join the prosperous family lumber business. Through a student agency, he rented a room at Doris Zhook's home near Regent's Park.[27]

When he arrived at the door, he later recalled, "It was opened by a woman who spoke excellent German, a very forceful personality. She told us that Mrs. Zhook was away and that she too was a lodger in the building. She showed us our rooms, and we took them. This woman became our great friend. She cooked us breakfast—an excellent breakfast. We began to discuss things: politics, art, and the like. Can you imagine my surprise when, about three weeks after taking my lodgings at Titchfield Terrace, I opened the newspaper and saw a picture of my new friend. 'Red Emma,' it was captioned, 'Living in London.' I knew very little about anarchism, but I knew that she was a remarkable woman, and I liked her!"

Javsicas read the story about the Wedgwood dinner. "Everybody had been invited," Gabriel learned from the paper. "Bertrand Russell was there, and so was Harold Laski, my teacher at the London School of Economics. . . . When Emma got up to speak, the article said, she was wildly applauded. When she sat down there was absolute silence. She had criticized the regime in Soviet Russia as a dictatorship, not of the proletariat but over the proletariat, a very unpopular stand to take at that time among liberals and socialists. I heard her speak soon afterwards in a hall in the East End. . . . Her words had the ring of truth. She was a forceful, convincing speaker. I was deeply impressed. She repeated what she said at the previous meeting: that the Bolsheviks had betrayed the revolution and established a dictatorship over the proletariat. I accepted this implicitly. Emma and I became close friends. We talked a lot, went places together, and afterwards wrote to one another. I took her often to the theater—she especially loved that! Emma loved young men. At one point she suggested that we sleep together, but I demurred."

Javsicas also became acquainted with Sasha. "During my Christmas vacation in 1924," he remembered, "I went to Berlin, and there I met Alexander Berkman. Emma had given me his address. I told him how much I admired his book, *Prison Memoirs of an Anarchist,* and he was pleased. I fell in love with both of them instantly. Berkman had a sharp wit, a kind of graveyard humor."[28]

Berkman liked Gabriel, too, and Emma was delighted the two had hit it off. "Yes, Javsicas is an awfully nice kid," she said to Sasha. "He has a wonderful humor and is remarkably unspoiled for a child of immensely wealthy parents. I think his father is a millionaire, owns forests, mills, and what not in Memel. I am glad he went to see you. Since he read your *Memoirs* he has not stopped raving about you."[29]

Emma's friendship with Gaby remained close, and it was further cemented by his frequent, freehanded gifts of cash. Emma may have experienced bouts of self-consciousness about her small income, but for much of her adult life she was willing to be kept in relative comfort by the munificence of her wealthier contacts. All her benefactors were delighted to provide support while Emma pursued her causes. "The whole time I was in London I spent much time with [Gaby]," she said to Sasha. "He lent me a good deal of money to do with as I saw fit. Is a generous person."[30]

GOLDMAN, MEANWHILE, HAD GROWN TIRED of her tenuous position as a perennial tourist—and exile. Her passport was due to expire in June 1925, and she needed to solidify her legal status in Europe and make decisions about her future, even if that meant retreating "to some quiet little place in France where," she said, "I might sit down to the task of writing my autobiography." Around the same time, she became reacquainted with James Colton, a Scottish anarchist coal miner employed in the mines of southern Wales. "Jim Colton," she wrote to W. S. Van Valkenburgh in April 1925, "has settled in Wales, but who is himself of Irish and Scotch mixture, is an old comrade I first met in Glasgow in 1895. It is amazing to see his fire and enthusiasm. I assure you he has more than I. One of the few of the old guard—perfectly unspoiled and absolutely sincere."[31] She realized Colton could provide a special service to her and to the movement, by giving her citizenship.

On June 27, 1925, when Goldman turned fifty-eight, she married Colton and became a British subject. Colton, having happily done his duty, promptly returned to his home alone. "I am very fortunate in the man," said Emma to Stella of her new husband. "He is an old comrade who understands the situation perfectly and went into it with great zeal, it was for the 'cause' you see. To him it is a great honor. He went back to South Wales, and that is the end of his obligations. Thus the scope of my activities has been enlarged. Canada and Australia and New Zealand are now open to me, and I can easily get to France, Belgium, and Switzerland if need be. It means a terrible lot to me after years of cramped uncertainty, so you may congratulate me."[32]

Emma retained her own last name. She used Colton on occasion as a convenient shelter and alternate alias, but whenever possible went by Goldman, saying she could see no sense in losing her identity.[33] With the new autonomy of citizenship, Emma was able to move effortlessly between Great Britain and the Continent, a welcome respite as the London weather continued to plague her. "The fogs and wet remained faithful and wandered through my system at their own sweet will," she sighed.[34]

Throughout Emma's stay in London, Sasha was often in her thoughts. She wrote him a special letter on May 18, 1925, the anniversary of his release from the Pennsylvania prison. "19 years ago," said Emma, "I left Montreal for Detroit to meet you. What terrible 19 years they have been. Terrible and fascinating, full of struggle and disappointment, but also of much joy and many rich experiences. The greatest of joys, however, is the fact that you have remained in my life, and that our friendship is as fresh and intense as it was many years ago, more mellow and understanding than when we were both young and unreasonable. My heart goes out to you on this our day with deep love and devotion."[35]

Alexander Berkman in Russia, circa 1920. To Fitzi: "This is the way I'd look in the Caucasus. S." Courtesy of Pauline Turkel, Paul Avrich Private Collection.

Lawyer Harry Weinberger with his friend and client Emma Goldman, in France, mid-1920s. Courtesy of Pauline Turkel, Paul Avrich Private Collection.

M. Eleanor Fitzgerald, known as "Fitzi," beloved for her loyalty and strong spirit, with Alexander Berkman, circa 1923. Courtesy of Hilda Adel, Paul Avrich Private Collection.

Bon Esprit, Emma Goldman's cheerful little house in St. Tropez. Courtesy of Pauline Turkel, Paul Avrich Private Collection.

Alexander Berkman, "On the seashore, Nice, Jan. 21 1926," sent "To Darling Fitzie, S." Courtesy of Pauline Turkel, Paul Avrich Private Collection.

Emma Goldman photographed by Senya Fleshin in Berlin, 1932. Courtesy of Federico Arcos, Paul Avrich Private Collection.

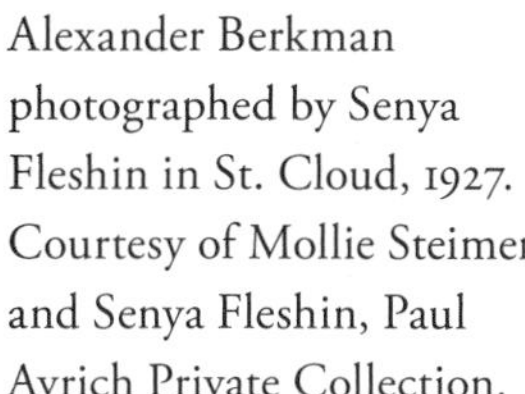

Alexander Berkman photographed by Senya Fleshin in St. Cloud, 1927. Courtesy of Mollie Steimer and Senya Fleshin, Paul Avrich Private Collection.

Alexander Berkman and his devoted lover Emmy Eckstein in France, 1930. Courtesy of Pauline Turkel, Paul Avrich Private Collection.

Emma Goldman, Senya Fleshin, Modest Stein, and Alexander Berkman at Bon Esprit, St. Tropez, 1935. Senya Flechin Collection, International Institute of Social History, Amsterdam.

The Trio: Modest Stein, Emma Goldman, and Alexander Berkman at Bon Esprit, St. Tropez, 1935. International Institute of Social History, Amsterdam.

Emma Goldman in Spain, 1938, in the fight against General Francisco Franco, surrounded by her Spanish anarchist comrades. Courtesy of Proudhon Carbo and Mollie Steimer, Paul Avrich Private Collection.

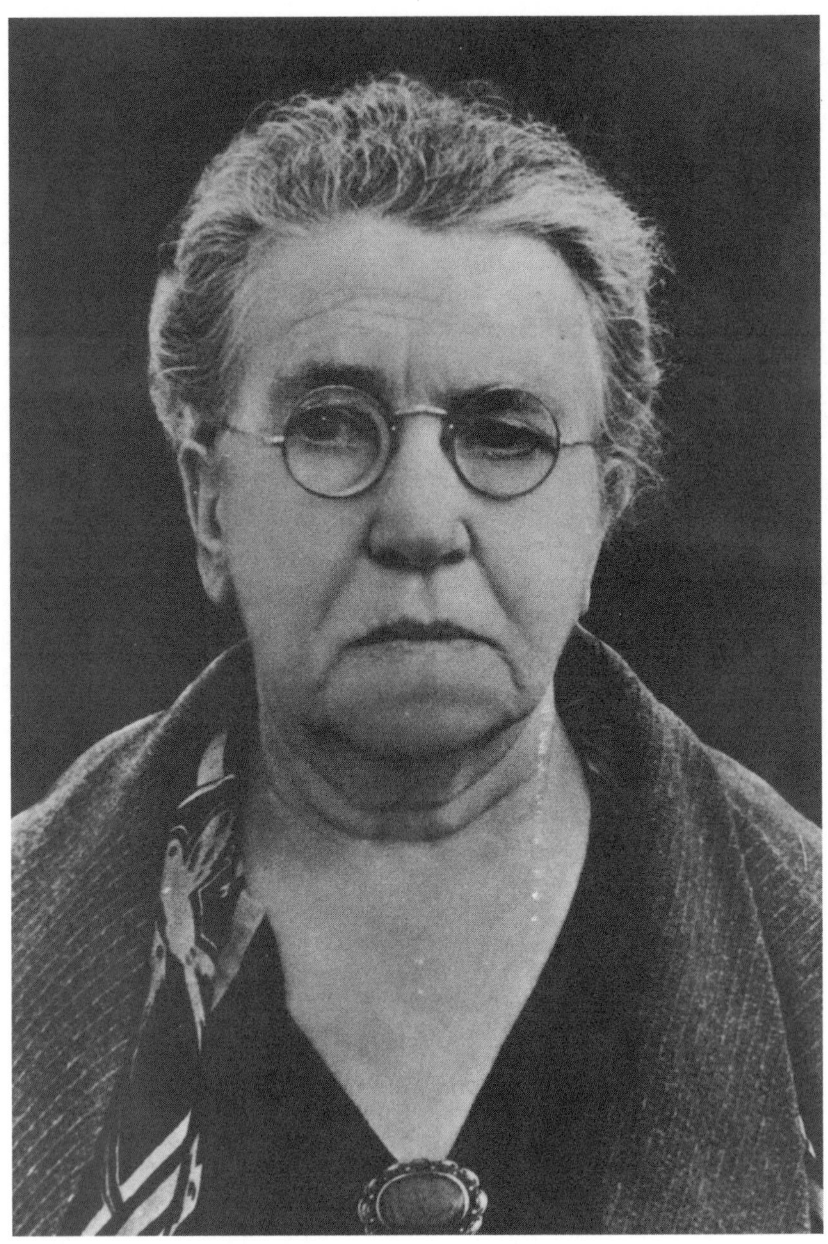

A portrait of Emma Goldman, 1938. Courtesy of Mollie Steimer, Paul Avrich Private Collection.

25

NOW AND AFTER

After Goldman departed for London in July 1924, Berkman remained in Berlin for another year. He corresponded with Joseph Ishill, a printer from New Jersey, who sent him some books on anarchism. "As an old printer myself," Sasha wrote, "I admire your beautiful work, both in the social and literary sense, as well as typographically, and I love a book well done in every way." In October 1925, after securing traveling papers with some difficulty, Berkman went to Paris, where he took a room in a hotel on the rue de la Voie Verte in the suburb Clamart. When he decided to remain in France, he informed Ishill of his relocation. "I went to Paris for a three-weeks vacation, and now I have spent two months in France and seem fated to remain here for an indefinite time."[1] Paris, he told Harry Kelly, had "a freer atmosphere than in Berlin. It is very nice and clean and orderly and without losing interest."[2]

After an eight-month stay in the hotel, Berkman decided to move to more permanent quarters, and found a home in St. Cloud, a quiet suburb across the Seine from Paris. For the next five years, he lived at 120 rue Tahère, a two-story house with a red tile roof, located on a narrow street in a hilly section of the town.[3] The neighborhood was inhabited largely by Russian émigrés, and there were a bakery and small grocery on the street. Sasha rented two sitting rooms, a dining room, and a kitchen on the second floor of the house. A Russian couple occupied the bottom floor with their son Valyla.[4] From a railroad station at the bottom of the hill, Sasha could take a train to the St. Lazare station in central Paris, a mere fifteen-minute journey.

In Berlin in 1922, Sasha had met a young woman, Emmy Eckstein, on the terrace of a café. He was then fifty-two, and she only twenty-two, but they took to each other at once. Emmy had been born in Berlin on October 10, 1900, to Jules, a Hungarian, since deceased, and Paula, a former singer in the Vienna theater. Emmy's mother and stepfather heartily disapproved of her relationship with the notorious older man. But Sasha and Emmy continued to correspond, and eventually she went to live with him in St. Cloud.[5] Adoring and possessive, Emmy was utterly smitten with Sasha, and treated him with something like reverence.

Michael Cohn, always generous, had sent a substantial amount of money to finance the move, and Berkman told him about the pleasant setup. "I have a little furnished apartment here with two living rooms, a dining room, a kitchen, hallway, and stairs," he wrote. "My apartment is now shared with me by a young woman I had known and was a friend with in Berlin for four years, and who joined me here last October 1926. She is a very fine type . . . and is very fond of me and devoted to me. Last, but not least, she is also a very good cook—and that is important, as you no doubt know yourself. I have just trimmed the little garden in front of the house, and I expect a few nice red roses to climb in the summertime right into my front window."[6]

Sasha felt affection for his young lover, if not an overwhelming passion, and he appreciated her modest habits. In February 1927, after several months of cohabitation, he remarked to Goldman, "I must say that Emmy is a good sort, really very good and economical, and she herself never goes even to a theater or concert, though she loves music—costs too much and she is satisfied to stay home."[7] By October 1927 his feelings were ambivalent. "Emmy has not read or learned much, does not much care for books," he told Emma. "In most things she is naive and babyish even sometimes. But somehow she feels the meaning of life. She is conservative at heart and does not at all take a radical viewpoint in any matter whatever. But I prefer that she have her own views than she ape and repeat the opinions of 'her man,' as is the case with only too many women. And she has courage, for she is at constant war with her people over her being with me. And she does not even believe that it is right to live free with a man, only that she submits to her love. A funny combination she is."[8]

Berkman's sympathetic view of Eckstein was not shared by his friends. "Sasha's companion," said Gaby Javsicas, was "a package of poison if there ever was one, an absolute disaster. She came from the lowest kind of middle-class bourgeoisie in Hungary. Her dream was to be Frau Berkman, and she nagged him day after night to marry her. She was a fool and a hypochondriac."[9] Nor was Goldman impressed with Sasha's choice of a lover. When she came to know Emmy, she found the young woman vexing and shallow, a jejune provincial with no strong social conscience. Emma had never felt much jealousy or resentment toward Fitzi, whom she respected as a comrade, but she considered Emmy an irritant and an intruder. "Am trying to get her to go home to Berlin," she wrote to a friend in Los Angeles in late 1927. "She is a nuisance."[10]

But, Emma told Minna Lowensohn (who naturally despised Eckstein as a rival), "The more I live the more I learn that in any intimate choice no outsider can understand the motives which bring two people together. . . . The most important thing after all is that he is not lonely; that he has somebody who really cares for him; and that he is getting the necessary comfort which protects his health and makes it possible for him to devote himself to his work."[11]

Emmy grew increasingly needy, however, and discouraged Sasha from socializing with both his friends and the luminaries he met in Paris, such as Paul Robeson, who visited St. Cloud several times after Berkman attended one of his concerts.[12] "France had many tourists, and among them were many comrades who went to see Sasha," recalled Mollie Steimer. "Here is where trouble started. One day Emmy said to me: 'Mollie, I wish Sasha were a miner, a shoemaker, or a carpenter, but not an international figure! I want him to belong to me, and not to the world!' I was very much surprised at this outburst and replied: but Emmy, you knew who Sasha was when you fell in love with him! 'No,' she said, 'in Berlin I had him to myself.' "[13]

Soon Sasha was receiving fewer people at home. Harry Kelly mused that Berkman was "living as quietly as that restless soul could live. I think he is lonely."[14] Complained Javsicas, "One couldn't simply drop in for a visit, as I liked to do. [Emmy] got terribly upset."[15] Still, Berkman went regularly to central Paris, and to St. Tropez and Nice on the French Riviera, where he encountered a number of notable figures. Among them was Laurence Vail, an artist and writer, prominent in literary Paris during the 1920s.[16] Vail's first wife, the American heiress and art collector Peggy Guggenheim, became friendly with both Sasha and Emma.

"[In France] I met Emma Goldman and Alexander (Sasha) Berkman," Guggenheim wrote later. "They were glamorous revolutionary figures, and one expected them to be quite different."[17] In both creative and political circles, Sasha impressed with his brilliance and his biting humor, while Emma continued to attract celebrated figures with her notoriety, her vision, her gusto.

———

IN THE SPRING OF 1926, during a holiday in St. Tropez, Goldman saw a small cottage that charmed her immediately. "An enchanted place it was," she wrote. "A little villa of three rooms from which one caught a view of the snow-covered Maritime Alps, with a garden of magnificent roses, pink and red geraniums, fruit-trees, and a large vineyard."[18] The cottage, which was situated twelve minutes from the town, rented for about fifteen dollars a month and offered a vista of the harbor and the sea.

Goldman spent the summer in St. Tropez and completed the manuscript "Foremost Russian Dramatists: Their Life and Work," which she had started earlier that year. She welcomed such guests as writers Theodore Dreiser and Howard Young, and Peggy Guggenheim, who pressed her to begin an autobiography, something Emma had talked about doing for years.

In October 1926 Goldman left for Canada on an extended lecture tour, still her best method of earning money and spreading her ideas. She spoke on a wide range of topics, many controversial, including birth control, sexuality, feminism, free speech, the repression of Russian political prisoners, and the dramatic arts. Though advancing through middle age, Goldman retained her spirited gift for oratory, which continued until nearly the end of her life. One comrade recalled his wonder at her facility with language, "her energy . . . the beauty of her sentences. She was nothing to look at—short, fat, unattractive—but when she spoke, with that fire in her, you forgot everything. In front of you was something that transcended looks."[19]

Goldman went first to Montreal, where she met up with old comrade Carl Newlander, who had worked on *The Blast* in San Francisco and *Mother Earth* in New York. Newlander had been deported from the United States to Sweden in 1919, but after spending several years in his native country, he brought his family to Canada.[20] He took Emma to dinner and a movie, and subsequently accompanied her to Toronto, where he assisted with her lecture and travel arrangements.

In Toronto, Emma stayed with her friend and supporter Esther Laddon in an apartment on Lytton Boulevard. Laddon looked after Emma, who had been suffering from sciatica and lumbago, and also had some minor problems with her teeth. "The dear woman, Esther Laddon," wrote Emma in her memoirs, "was about my own age, but she mothered me as if I were a child. She fretted about my health and worried about my meals, and buttonholed everybody to warn them not to dare miss hearing the great orator Emma Goldman."[21] As Laddon's daughter, Ora, an aspiring actress, later recalled, "Emma took over the house, dominated the place. She stayed up all night talking on the phone. She drank a good deal of whisky and she woke up late in the morning. . . . I thought Emma was wonderful. She was a brilliant woman and a marvelous speaker, full of original ideas."[22]

As always, Emma was a busy social bee. Toronto was close to Rochester, and her siblings came up with their families.[23] Comrades visited often from New York City, and Ben Reitman made the trip from Chicago. Emma began an affair with her frequent correspondent Leon Malmed—although he was married—when he traveled from Albany to see her. She also spent time with Freda Diamond, the daughter of her good friend Ida Diamond, Morris Goldman's former lover. Freda, who viewed Moe as a surrogate father, had grown into "a very beautiful looking creature" with a "fine nature."[24] "[Emma] didn't have time for small talk," Freda later said. "And yet she wasn't pompous. We soon became friends, young as I was, though at first she was a little frightening. Not that she actually was. But she looked important, she acted important. She was an imposing figure."[25]

It was difficult for Goldman to be so close to her beloved America without the right to return; all her efforts to gain a temporary reentry to the United States had thus far failed. Some of her friends and associates suggested she might try to cross the border surreptitiously, but she rejected the idea as artificial and unfeasible. "With my picture in every rogues' gallery in the United States, I could not have remained there long without being recognized, and there was no object in hiding," she reasoned. "I never liked sensation for its own sake. There still was a large place in my heart for my erstwhile country, regardless of her shabby treatment. My love for all that is ideal, creative, and humane in her would not die. But I should rather never see America again if I could do so only by compromising my ideas."[26]

FROM HIS QUIET PERCH WITH EMMY in St. Cloud, Sasha carried on an extensive correspondence in English, French, German, Russian, and Yiddish with anarchists and friends around the world. He remained a powerful force in the radical underground, keeping a hand in political intrigues and prisoners' rights, and working hard on the Relief Fund *Bulletin.* He granted the occasional interview, and submitted to a questionnaire in Margaret Anderson's Paris-based *Little Review,* in which he described himself as "a reasonable being in a crazy scheme" and said his greatest goal was "a chance to tell the truth."[27]

He also reconnected with his brother Boris, who was living in Baku.[28] It was the first contact between the two in the forty years since Sasha had left Russia for America; they had not seen each other when Sasha had toured Russia in 1920 and 1921. Sasha's other two siblings had died long before; the spirited Max had been stricken with fatal consumption while studying at medical school in Russia, and Sonya had died shortly after marrying and moving to Warsaw, still a young woman.[29]

Berkman grew closer to the anarchist couple Mollie Steimer and Senya Fleshin. Fleshin had been an ardent and militant anarchist in the United States and Russia, and continued his involvement from the Continent. Steimer, petite and apple-cheeked, was as energetic an activist as anyone in radical circles, possessing a ferocity that belied her delicate appearance. "Diminutive and quaint-looking," said Emma, Mollie had "an iron will and a tender heart." Emma joked to Stella Ballantine that Steimer was "a sort of Alexander Berkman in skirts."[30]

Fleshin, a naturally gifted photographer, was learning the technique and not yet established as a professional. Berkman was friendly with both the famed surrealist Man Ray and his onetime assistant, the photographer Berenice Abbott. Abbott was an intimate of Hippolyte Havel's, whom she had met in New York City in 1918 before moving to Paris. She opened her own studio in 1926 and, as an American pioneer of modern photography, soon achieved fame with her portraits of writers and artists such as James Joyce, Janet Flanner, and Jean Cocteau. Berkman, too, was one of her subjects. As for Man Ray, Emma suggested vaguely to Sasha, "you ought to see [Abbott], then that chap she worked with, his name has escaped me, you know, he used to paint and be at the Ferrer School often."[31] Sasha and Emma had been introduced to Man Ray at the New York Ferrer Center.

With such illustrious advisers, Senya's photographs began to show signs of improvement. Sasha sent Emma some examples of Senya's work. "You will see what wonderful progress he has made in the short time he has been studying it," he wrote. "I am glad for his sake, for I am sure he will be a very fine photographer, and as such he can always and everywhere earn good money."[32] Senya photographed Berkman in St. Cloud, sitting at his desk and standing against his bookcase. Fleshin's sensitive images of Berkman, Goldman, and V. M. Volin, among others, graced the pages of many radical biographies and histories.

Sasha himself found it a constant struggle to get employment. He managed to earn a modest income translating essays, novels, and plays or typing and reading proofs, and he received supplemental financial support from organizations such as the New York *Fraye Arbeter Shtime* and longtime benefactors including Michael Cohn and Ben Capes. He contributed essays to international activist publications, writing often about the Bolshevik debacle.[33] He gave speeches in France, and saw *Prison Memoirs of an Anarchist* translated into Dutch, as well as French, German, and Yiddish.[34]

Friends threw work his way. Roger Baldwin collaborated with him on a Kropotkin anthology, and Fitzi, still acting as the business manager for the Provincetown Players (she would continue in this role until 1929, when the company closed), got him some assignments translating German plays for the group.[35] Fitzi also prevailed upon Eugene O'Neill to hire Sasha to translate his play *Lazarus Laughed* into Russian for the Moscow Art Theater, collaborating with Volin.[36]

"My dear Berkman," wrote O'Neill. "I have been immensely pleased ever since I talked with Fitzi about your doing the translation. Most of the stuff, I believe, has not been very well done into foreign languages, and as I have a very meager knowledge of them myself, I have been in no position to check up. It has been all a gamble. But with you I feel secure, naturally . . . I have a very clear picture of you in my mind to this day. I had had a very deep admiration for you for years, and that meeting was sort of an unexpected wish fulfillment. As for my fame (God help us!) and your infame, I would be willing to exchange a good deal of mine for a bit of yours. It is not so hard to write what one feels as truth. But it is damned hard to live it!"[37] The resulting Russian production was a success, and the Moscow Art Theater was "extremely pleased with it," as Berkman told Upton Sinclair, although in the end there were no royalties to be had.[38]

IN 1928 BERKMAN REFOCUSED, IN A FASHION, on his anarchist roots. Prompted two years earlier by the Anarchist Federation of New York, Berkman decided to write a primer on anarchism. With the rapidly changing configurations of twentieth-century governments and the letdown following the Russian Revolution, Berkman thought it was time to update and consolidate anarchist ideas for a contemporary audience. "To most people our ideas are entirely un-understandable," he told Max Nettlau. "It is also necessary to revalue them, reexamine many of the views held by Bakunin, Kropotkin, and others—all in view of the practical issues of the Russian Revolution, and the Bolshevik regime."[39] Berkman felt that "the chief lesson" of the failures of the Russian Revolution was that "authoritarian methods cannot lead to liberty."[40]

Goldman loved the idea of the primer. "It is [of] the utmost importance that you should consent to do it," she told him. "We have absolutely nothing that is of any value on Anarchism in the light of modern events. I agree with you absolutely that we need an ABC of Anarchism."[41] Berkman hoped to make the book accessible to a wide audience, a rather tricky objective. He was "convinced," as he told Emma, "that the book must be written for the common reader in plainest language. I want the book to be of such a character that the average man could read and understand it, and at the same time that our people could learn something from it."[42] But it was hard going, although he put in eight to ten hours of work each day. "Even the average intelligent man knows nothing of anarchism," Sasha said to Nettlau. "And way down deep in his sub-conscious anarchism is still identified in some vague or even more or less conscious manner with bomb throwing and personal violence."[43]

Berkman's manuscript, ultimately titled *Now and After,* with the subtitle *The ABC of Communist Anarchism,* incorporated and explained the philosophies and models of Kropotkin and other founding fathers of the movement. By illuminating the basic principles of anarchism, Sasha tried to encourage readers to break their preconceived notions of what freedom and government could mean, opening them up to the promise of cooperation, mutual aid, and peace.

He received a $500 stipend for his living expenses from the Anarchist Federation, and the book was published jointly with the Vanguard Press of New York in May 1929. When Berkman received his copy he declared himself very pleased with it.[44] Members of the anarchist community were excited to read it. *Freedom* editor Thomas Keell told Minna Lowensohn, who served as secretary and treasurer of the Anarchist Federation, that "new books on Anarchism in English are like angels' visits—few and far between."[45]

Despite his relationship with Emmy, Sasha remained close to Lowensohn, and considered her his "main source of information about things going on in the States, in the movement." He pressed flowers inside his letters and thanked Minna for being "one of [his] truest and most devoted friends."[46] Minna's adoration did not wane; observed Emma, "Sasha is her great passion."[47] Minna visited Berkman in Paris, as did Henry Alsberg and Gaby Javsicas.[48] Fitzi also came to Paris and took long walks with Sasha on the beautiful streets and in the parks.

But it was always Emma who was the center of Sasha's world. "Such a friendship as ours is exceptional under such circumstances, of that there can be no doubt," he told her. "It is a lifetime friendship, cemented by mutual ideas and interests, and strengthened by mutual joy and suffering. One begins to feel the weight of the days. But . . . I think both you as well as I have reason to be satisfied with some things, namely we have kept our health and not lost our heads, either. That at least is something. . . . The passing years only make our friendship and understanding deeper, and that is the highest achievement."[49]

WHILE ALL THIS WAS TAKING PLACE IN PARIS, a long-brewing crisis was culminating in Massachusetts. On April 15, 1920, a paymaster and his guard had been shot to death during a robbery of a shoe factory in the town of South Braintree. Weeks later, Nicola Sacco, a shoe worker, and Bartolomeo Vanzetti, a fish peddler, both Italian immigrants and anarchists, were charged with the crime. The following year they were brought to trial. The methods of the district attorney involved coaching and badgering witnesses, withholding exculpatory evidence from the defense, exploiting the prejudices of the jury, and possibly tampering with physical evidence. The judge in the case, Webster Thayer, made comments revealing a conspicuous bias against the defendants. ("Did you see what I did with those anarchistic bastards the other day?" he chortled at one point.)[50] On July 14, 1921, Sacco and Vanzetti were found guilty of robbery and murder, setting off years of appeals and legal petitions.

Many observers, even those without radical sympathies of any kind, became convinced that the two had been convicted because of their foreign birth and anarchist beliefs, rather than on solid evidence of criminal guilt. In the aftermath of the trial, there was mounting evidence that the men had been unfairly targeted and indicted. Key prosecution testimony was retracted, and new evidence was produced that was favorable to the defense. Judge Thayer's overt bias and the conviction on inconclusive evidence provoked outrage; sympathy for the two men blossomed. Eventually, in June 1927, Massachusetts governor Alvan T. Fuller appointed an advisory committee, which found that Judge Thayer had been guilty of a "grave breach of official decorum" in his derogatory references to the defendants. The committee nevertheless concluded that justice had been done, and the convictions stood.[51]

While the case was being appealed, a number of personalities spoke out in support of Sacco and Vanzetti, several of Emma and Sasha's intimates among them. (Advocates included Bertrand Russell, George Bernard Shaw, Upton Sinclair, Dorothy Parker, Katherine Anne Porter, Edna St. Vincent Millay, and H. G. Wells.) Berkman and Goldman were in Russia when the trial began, and they learned more when they reached Germany. The case recalled acutely the Haymarket affair, with all its prejudices, emotion, and divisive import. But to Sasha and Emma, the fate of Sacco and Vanzetti furthermore served to gauge the vitality of the anarchist movement, and the successes and failures of their own decades-long fight.

Berkman took up the cause and worked tenaciously to aid the two men. He published articles about the case and dedicated a Relief Fund *Bulletin* to the matter.[52] "The conscience of humanity," he wrote, "is outraged by a terrible wrong the whole world protests, yet one single person, an American Governor, has the power to defy the enlightened and human sentiment of the entire world and to send two innocent men to their death! If this be the true spirit and meaning of Americanism, then all its industrial and financial achievements are but so many instruments of inhuman brutality and fiendish torture."[53]

Berkman contacted many leading figures about the case, including aviator Charles A. Lindbergh, whom he begged for assistance. "Dear Captain Lindbergh," he wrote. "I congratulate you most heartily on your wonderful feat of pluck and self-reliance. Only the future will be able to estimate fully the far-reaching effects of your phenomenal achievement. But in the hour of your triumph do not forget the two innocent men facing death in your country. You have added to the glory of the United States. Do not unprotestingly permit Uncle Sam to commit judicial murder. Speak up in behalf of Sacco and Vanzetti. You are their spirit brother: they, like yourself, are inspired by idealism. The only difference is that they—their social aspirations still misunderstood—are persecuted, while you—having succeeded—are hailed as a hero. Speak up in behalf of Sacco and Vanzetti. Remember, the cause of Justice is even more important than aerial navigation. Sincerely, Alexander Berkman."[54] Lindbergh did not respond.

Berkman followed every twist and turn of the proceedings, perusing the public documents and assessing their significance. He grew certain that there would be no legal salvation. "I have just received from Boston the complete statement of Governor Fuller in the case of Sacco and Vanzetti," he wrote to Max Nettlau, "and it is clear from it that he will refuse even a commutation of sentence to life imprisonment. Not that it would be preferable to execution, but it shows how bitterly class conscious the Governor and his clique are. . . . I fear the men will be executed, in spite of the whole world protesting. The capitalist class of America demands it, and theirs is the final word. . . . And that after almost a hundred years of liberal, progressive, radical and anarchist work! It is terrible and paralysing! . . . We are a long way from the light."[55]

Sasha thought Sacco and Vanzetti should consider a prison escape, just as he had attempted to break out of the Western Penitentiary in 1900. Vanzetti did indeed have such a plan before his execution, but it failed. "Myself, if I were in Sacco and Vanzetti's place, I should prefer to die rather than receive a commutation," wrote Berkman to Goldman. "Because neither of them will survive even ten years in prison, and there would be no hope for them to get free before 20 years or so."[56]

But Emma became distraught once it became clear to her that Governor Fuller would not commute the sentences and the executions would take place as scheduled. She felt as hopeless as she had when the Haymarket anarchists were hanged. "I am in such a terrible turmoil over the verdict of the Sacco and Vanzetti case that I have not been able to work," she wrote to Senya Fleshin. "My heart is heavy with horror over the approach of the murder that is to be committed by the State of Massachusetts. . . . How little progress we have made in the last forty years when the crime which was committed then in the State of Illinois can be repeated in the State of Massachusetts, when such heroic men as Sacco and Vanzetti must pay the price even as their comrades died on the black Friday of 1887."[57]

On August 23, 1927, after seven years of imprisonment, the men were electrocuted. By the time of the executions, millions around the globe were convinced of their innocence, and millions more were convinced that, guilty or innocent, they had not received impartial justice. Both Goldman and Berkman were devastated, for the loss of the men, for their disappointment in the American justice system, and for what the outcome signified regarding their lifetime of labor on behalf of the anarchist movement. As Berkman wrote to Michael Cohn, "The more I think of it, the more I realize that it is the heaviest blow we have had to suffer, greater even than the Chicago tragedy—because, after all, 40 years have passed since then, 40 years of hard work and effort on our part, and yet we were powerless to prevent the judicial murder of two of the noblest men."[58]

Sasha further believed that the outcome of the Sacco and Vanzetti case was "the most heinous crime America has committed." He told Leonard Abbott he longed for a display of revenge. "Not that I think that an act of vengeance in this case would do any good," he added; "But merely as a purely human expression of an outraged individual and social conscience."[59] As it happened, Leonard Abbott was not a great fan of Berkman's darker side, later writing, "I never accepted his violent doctrines. I liked him in spite of his violence, rather than because of it."[60] For all his misery, Sasha clung to the notion that perhaps the executions would inspire new young revolutionaries to the cause. "And in that there is hope," he wrote.[61]

Berkman shared his sadness with Tom Mooney, who was following the events from his prison cell in San Quentin. "Need I comment upon the terrible tragedy?" wrote Sasha. "I am sure you know how we all feel here about it. The conscience of the entire civilized world has been outraged—

the voice of humanity has found no sympathetic echo in the hearts bent upon class verdicts. It is time that you, as well as Billings, were out. More than high time. You should never have been in were there any justice in the world."[62]

Mooney and Billings, after decades in prison, were meted a measure of justice in the end. Over the years, they had been refused new trials even though witnesses came forward shortly after the convictions, and again in the 1920s, to insist that Fickert had influenced their statements. Still more witnesses renounced their testimony in July 1930, without consequence to the two prisoners.[63] In 1939 both at last were set free by Governor Culbert Olson, who pardoned Mooney in January and commuted Billings' sentence in October.[64]

When Mooney was released, he appeared with Governor Olson at "a dramatic and perhaps unprecedented hearing." Spectators cheered and applauded the signing of the pardon, while Rena Mooney watched and wept. "Governor Olson," said Mooney, "I shall dedicate the rest of my life to work for the common good in the bond of democracy. Dark and sinister forces of Fascist reactionism are threatening the world." Reported the *New York Times*, "Although Mooney spoke smoothly and with apparent calm, his voice broke as he promised also to seek freedom for his convicted associate, Warren K. Billings." Mooney's first order of business was to visit Billings at Folsom prison, and then he addressed a crowd of 3,000 gathered in Sacramento's Southside Park. "We want a unity movement that will look to the future, not one based on the past," he said.[65] But Mooney struggled to adjust to his freedom and unwelcome fame, and died in 1942 at the age of fifty-nine. Warren Billings, a decade younger and somewhat less physically affected by the hardships of prison life, returned to San Francisco after his commutation. He married in 1940 and opened a jeweler's shop; in 1961 he was finally pardoned. He died in 1972.[66]

GOLDMAN WAS IN TORONTO WHEN THE EXECUTIONS of Sacco and Vanzetti took place. Freda Diamond was with her at the time. "That night I shall never forget," recalled Diamond. "[Emma] had a phone in her room and it rang all evening long. There were calls from all over the world, but especially from Boston, pleading with her to do something. But there was nothing she could do, and she knew it. For someone as positive as Emma, she was quite modest, not at all like the commander-in-chief many took her to be. 'What can I do, what can I do,' she murmured very quietly, anxiously. Then came the call that they had been electrocuted. We were devastated."[67]

Emma had been desolate all through the summer, culminating in her despair over the executions. She sent a letter to Vanzetti before his death, praising his unflinching courage. "You and Sacco are both in my mind and heart," she said. "America cannot boast of many such rebels as you and your comrade—for few indeed, since our martyred comrades in Chicago proclaimed the justice and beauty of anarchism. The greater the value of your struggle, the more admirable your courage. Accept my fraternal greetings and my fervent hope that the truth will conquer."[68]

A week after the executions, Emma spoke at a memorial meeting in Toronto, delivering a talk called "The Heroic Struggle of Sacco and Vanzetti." Afterward she sent a note to Sacco's widow, Rosina Sacco. "We had a beautiful memorial meeting last night attended by a large audience," she wrote. "If our loss were not so great you would have reasons to feel that the death of our two friends will not have been in vain. Their memory will be a shining star in the social and economic darkness of our life, and will, I am sure, inspire many to throw themselves into the gap left by their death."[69]

Several years after the executions, Sasha and Emma coauthored an essay on Sacco and Vanzetti for Hippolyte Havel's *The Road to Freedom.* "Throughout the civilized world Sacco and Vanzetti have become a symbol, the shibboleth of Justice crushed by Might," they wrote. "[But] we should rejoice that in this time of debasement and degradation, in the hysteria of conquest and gain, there are still MEN that dare defy the dominant spirit and raise their voices against inhumanity and reaction: that there are still men who keep the spark of reason and liberty alive and have the courage to die, and die triumphantly, for their daring."[70]

26

BON ESPRIT

In late January 1928, after nearly sixteen months in Canada, Goldman began to prepare for her return to France. She received farewell visits from family and friends and gave final speeches in Toronto and Montreal. On February 18 Goldman set sail on the R.M.S. *Antonia,* for Halifax, Nova Scotia, and continued the journey across the Atlantic. "I'll meet you in Havre," Berkman promised, and he was there to greet her.[1] He told the printer Joseph Ishill that when he picked Emma up at the port, she looked "fresher and younger than two years ago. She seems to thrive on difficulties and obstacles."[2]

Goldman spent the spring in Paris and, in June 1928, went back to the cottage near St. Tropez to write her autobiography. With funds supplied by a group of her faithful supporters, including Peggy Guggenheim, Theodore Dreiser, W. S. Van Valkenburgh, and her lawyer Arthur Leonard Ross, she was eventually able to purchase the little house. Sasha named the cottage "Bon Esprit" and helped Emma plant and tend to grapes, an orange tree, a lemon tree, and several additional fruit trees bearing peaches and plums, figs, cherries, and almonds. He also prepared the ground for vegetables. The soil was very fertile, and the southern climate allowed three plantings each year.

"Sasha kept the grounds blooming," recalled Irene Schneiderman, the daughter of American anarchists who visited Bon Esprit. "When I walked there on my morning missions delivering fresh eggs or whatever, I could feel a surge of anticipation as I left the main road, rounded the curved driveway and caught sight of the house. It seemed to have a life of its own."[3] According to Emma's friend Ida Gershoy, nearby St. Tropez was "not a very fashionable place at that time [but] it was a charming town then. A number of artists lived there, and when you bought fish or vegetables the shopkeeper would ask, 'Is it for eating or painting?' "[4]

Goldman received many visitors at the cottage. Friends came from around the world to see her, and new acquaintances dropped in to meet the famous anarchist in her home. A surprise party was thrown on the occasion of her fifty-ninth birthday.[5] Sasha came down from St. Cloud, and brought Emmy Eckstein with him, much to the chagrin of his comrades. "The presence of Emmy caused considerable friction," said Mollie Steimer. "Emma was right nearby, whom Sasha loved, even if not physically, but [for] a longer time and with a deeper love than anyone else."[6] Ida Gershoy, introduced to the anarchists by Emma's nephew Saxe Commins, attended the party with her husband, Leo, an American historian of France. "Emmy was an absolute idiot, a perfect dope, a very uninteresting girl," said Ida. "She was sort of pretty in a way, but never said very much and was very much under Sasha's thumb. She had no personality."[7]

But Gershoy and her husband adored Sasha, and thought he was "a really wonderful man. We didn't think we would like him, but developed a great affection for him—and we weren't anarchists and weren't accustomed to such people. . . . [He] was intelligent, he was kind, and he was sweet; and after a while I came to love him. He never said anything nasty about anybody, where Emma constantly did." To be sure, Ida was fond of Goldman, too, although she sometimes found her brusque and overbearing. She noticed the "great bond" between Sasha and Emma. "They had a deep understanding of one another, and a strong rapport," said Gershoy. "They were constantly in communication, and every little thing that happened to Sasha was very important to Emma."[8]

All this made Eckstein a bit of an outsider, and in addition to enduring rampant unpopularity within Berkman's circle, she was frequently ill, suffering from a variety of digestive ailments. "Emmy is not well and it seems impossible to find out what is wrong," Sasha informed Saxe Commins.[9] Sasha suspected her physical troubles were partly psychological. "You and Fitzi are normal persons," he wrote to Emma. "Emmy is not. She is terribly nervous, even neurotic, certainly not a well woman. She is compulsive by nature." But Sasha had genuine affection for Emmy, regardless of the scorn of his friends. "I am thinking myself of marrying [her] some day," he told Emma. "Before I die I want to realize for Emmy her highest ideal—

which is to be married. It may be foolish to us, and so it is, but to her it means life itself."[10]

IN THE 1920S THE ANARCHIST MOVEMENT was struggling to redefine itself—or to achieve some traction in a changing society. Much to Sasha and Emma's dismay, anarchism's basic tenets were challenged during this time by a group of Paris-based Russian radicals who launched a campaign to redirect the movement. The effort was led by Ukrainian anarchist and former Bolshevik Peter Andreevich Arshinov, who promoted a modified, structured version of anarchism. "The only hope for a revival of the movement," he wrote in his magazine *Dielo Truda* (Labor's Cause) "is the formation of a General Union of Anarchists with a central executive committee to coordinate policy and action."[11]

Arshinov published an accompanying booklet, called the *Organizational Platform,* to further communicate his ideas. Berkman was concerned that Arshinov was infecting the fundamentals of anarchism with the oppressive aspects of his original Bolshevik creed. Sasha also disliked the resulting discord among his comrades, which was bitter and acute. "I consider it terrible," he wrote to Fleshin and Steimer in 1928, "that our movement, everywhere, is degenerating into a swamp of petty personal quarrels, accusations, and recriminations. . . . It shows that the movement is rotting from within, and I am convinced that everything must be done to stop this process of degeneracy."[12]

Other anarchists were similarly concerned by the new threat to their ideal, and they felt vindicated when Arshinov eventually defected to the Soviet Union under Stalin and rejoined the Bolshevik Party he had abandoned for anarchism a quarter-century before. Soon afterward he was executed.[13]

Berkman and Goldman remained loyal to the unadulterated anarchist philosophy that had consumed them since their youth, even though they had long ago grown out of their impetuous, impatient fervor for immediate social transformation. "Don't be pessimistic," wrote Sasha to comrade and benefactor Ben Capes. "We stand for a new civilization, not only for a new form of government, and that is why our work is necessarily slow. Yet there is nothing in the world that can disprove this fact: our ideal is the very finest and biggest thing that humanity has ever thought of that can give one liberty and well-being and peace and joy to the world. And I think it is a glory to work for such a thing, even if the thing itself is never realized."[14]

Goldman also seemed resigned to the improbability of achieving the anarchist dream anytime soon. "Don't think I have lost my faith in the beauty and ultimate success of Anarchism," she told her friend Stewart Kerr, "but I have drawn nearer to the idea . . . that Emma Goldman is 8,000 years ahead of her time."[15] To Emma, anarchism remained a pure vision, unlike the destructive forces that raged in Russia. She coldly dismissed Leon Trotsky, who had been expelled from the Communist Party in November 1927, and was banished from the Soviet Union a little over a year later. "The collapse of Trotsky," Emma observed to Kerr, "is only a repetition of similar events in past revolutions. I cannot muster up much concern for his fate. . . . Nothing that has happened to him could possibly atone for the inhumanity which he practiced on the defenseless people of his country, and I am quite sure that he would do it again if he got the chance."[16]

While Goldman focused on writing her autobiography, she called upon her affluent cohorts to "raise enough money to secure [her] for two years."[17] Her longtime patron Bolton Hall organized a fund to keep her supplied with cash and comforts, and Peggy Guggenheim kicked off the endowment with $500.[18] "[Peggy] belongs to the Guggenheim family," Emma told her lawyer Arthur Leonard Ross, "but is one of the most generous persons among the wealthy I know. We are great friends [and] Peggy also agreed to make it a sustaining fund and will continue to add to it whenever necessary."[19]

Theodore Dreiser was among those who contributed to Emma's account. "You are—and will remain—a real force," he told her fondly.[20] The fund grew to several thousand dollars, with donations flowing in from the usual suspects, as well as from a few surprise supporters. Emma received a $10 gift from a man called Arthur Garfield, whom she knew to be "the grandson of Moses Garson, who was the largest clothing manufacturer in Rochester." Emma had worked in his factory in her youth. Moses Garson was, wrote

Goldman in disgust, "the man who exploited me for a number of months on $2.50 a week."[21]

Emma spent months gathering material for her autobiography, contacting friends in America and other countries to ask for old letters and copies of periodicals, photos, newspaper clippings, and personal memorabilia.[22] The help flooded in. Michael Cohn shared stories about his early years with first wife Annie Netter, Emma's friend and comrade, who had died of cancer in 1920. Annie's death was "the greatest calamity of my life," Cohn said.[23] Arthur Leonard Ross sent Emma as many books as she wanted, and Agnes Inglis granted her access to the treasure trove of the Labadie Collection at the University of Michigan, which documented radicalism in America.[24]

H. L. Mencken attempted to recover Goldman's papers, confiscated by the Department of Justice during its raids on *Mother Earth* and *The Blast.* His request was denied; he was informed that the entire collection, along with all of Berkman's records, had been destroyed. Mencken also tried to help Emma in her quest to return to America—she was as homesick as ever, and there was much research she wanted to do on the ground. But Mencken had no luck. "The Commissioner General of Immigration informs me that there is absolutely no legal means of getting around the law which forbids the Secretary of Labor to rescind his order for your deportation. Not even the President could do it," he said.[25]

Mencken and Goldman had a curious relationship. "[Mencken] is not at all like his writing," Emma observed after they were introduced briefly in Paris. "He is a man of the world, jovial, very kind, and exceedingly mild . . . I liked him immensely."[26] Mencken, for his part, had from afar thought Goldman an impressive person, describing her in 1924 as "one of the most notable women now extant upon this planet . . . a woman of wide and deep culture, a graceful and urbane writer, an idealist of a rare and often singularly winning sort." Less flatteringly, he called her a "monomaniac" and "a naïve believer in human perfectibility, an enthusiast carried far beyond common sense, a kind of mad mullah or whirling dervish."[27]

IN MAY 1929, IN THE MIDST of putting together her life story, Goldman invited Mollie Steimer to join her at Bon Esprit. "Emma liked to write at night—sometimes from eleven until three or four in the morning," said Steimer. Sasha was staying at Bon Esprit to help with the project, "working intensely on the manuscript." *Now and After* had been published, and he had largely abandoned his translation work to assist Emma with her memoir and her other literary pursuits.[28] "[Sasha] appeared happy," Steimer recalled, and "arranged himself a small shack in the garden to be by himself when he felt like it, as there were always comrades, friends, and journalists around. When he did not work on the manuscript, he read, worked in the garden, went shopping, and was always in good spirits. The name 'Bon Esprit' was his idea, and he lived up to it."[29]

Sasha painstakingly revised and corrected every line of Emma's text, and he praised the book as a "great work, fascinating from first page to last, powerful, dramatic, and gripping as her life was."[30] Emma was grateful for his effort. "At first I was rather a little dubious about having him help," she confided to Danish writer Karin Michaelis. "His life is so intimately connected with mine and was like a thread through the entire book, that I was a little afraid he may not have the necessary detachment and aloofness. But I must say that he has shown both to a most beautiful extent. No doubt it has often been difficult for him to see himself [through] my eyes. You will admit it requires strength of character and a large sense of justice not to impose one's own views of one's self on the work of another. Well Sasha has done that admirably and has relieved me of all anxiety." She said that Sasha had come up with the title: *Living My Life*. "I am very happy," Emma said, "because it symbolizes my story."[31]

It was not all work for Emma. To break from her writing, she took a trip to London, enjoyed an extensive tour of Spain, and indulged in her vigorous social life. She "had a steady stream of visitors and quite a few dinners and parties," recalled Ida Gershoy. "Emma was fond of drinking—especially wine—and was very proud of her cooking. 'Have some of E. G.'s coffee,' she would say. 'Have some of E. G.'s pudding'—or whatever she was making that day." After Emma served her guests supper, they would all go to a café near the harbor where they drank and danced to an accordion. "Emma loved to dance!" exclaimed Gershoy. "She was very funny to watch, so short and squat and having such a time of it." Sasha was less dynamic. "He couldn't relax enough to be fun," Ida said. "He laughed, of course, and told amusing stories, but deep down he was very serious."[32]

With the help of A. L. Ross, who served as her literary lawyer, and Saxe Commins, formerly a Rochester dentist who had joined the publishing industry, Goldman sought out a publisher willing to give her a sizable advance.[33] She eventually signed with Alfred A. Knopf.[34] Emma met Knopf himself in Paris, where they discussed a Yiddish edition of her memoirs, and the two formed a lasting friendship. In January 1930 Goldman sent 288 pages to Knopf, less than one-quarter of the book. In February she sent another batch, and a year later she mailed the final installment. The full manuscript resulted in 1,019 typeset pages (and would be sold in two volumes for a substantial $7.50).[35]

In July 1931, several months before the release date, a reporter from the United Press went to interview her at Bon Esprit, described as "a little white cottage near St. Tropez, with a garden running down to the blue Mediterranean." Goldman, who had "spent 10 hours a day over many months to complete the [lengthy] autobiography. . . . still considers herself an American, despite her British citizenship by marriage and her British passport." The reporter added that "Mrs. Goldman-Colton" enjoyed a "daily plunge in the Mediterranean" and, except for rheumatism, was "in perfect health."[36]

With *Living My Life* out of her hands, Goldman went to Berlin, where she stayed with Mollie Steimer and Senya Fleshin, and acquired new glasses from the famed doctor Graf Wiser to correct the eyestrain brought on by toiling over her book. She gave lecture tours in Germany and across Scandinavia, stopping in Copenhagen, Stockholm, and Oslo, and treated herself to a brief vacation. When she returned to St. Tropez, she found the cottage greatly improved. "Sasha and Emmy have worked there like beavers to make our little house attractive," she wrote to a friend. "My room was newly painted, etc. For the present all is peaceful."[37]

Berkman, meanwhile, was considering writing his own autobiography, something that covered his life beyond his confinement in the Western Penitentiary. He began to compose a summary of its contents in July 1930. The book initially was to be called "I Had to Leave." As Berkman explained the title, "I had to leave because of a disagreement with my rich uncle and also to avoid forced military service. I had, later on, to leave on many occasions."[38] He produced a seven-page rough outline with a proposed title *An Enemy of Society,* which he sent to Fitzi. Several publishers expressed interest, but Berkman never wrote the book.[39]

THE MASSIVE *LIVING MY LIFE* WAS RELEASED in October 1931 and was regarded as a significant work. It landed on lists of the year's most notable books and received attention in academic circles and the press. "Everybody admires a fighter who has heart," wrote *Time* magazine in its review. "Now that Emma Goldman's fighting Red career is finished, you may even find it possible to add a kind of warmth to your disapproving admiration of her. That is, after you have read her own story of her stormy life. To look at her as she appears now, with that hard, defiant old face, that grim and challenging eye, it is easy to see how hateful, what a nuisance society found her; you would never guess how many lovers she has had, how many friends."[40]

The *New York Times* called Goldman's story a "great human narrative" and the autobiography "one of the great books of its kind."[41] But it tweaked her romantic exploits, labeling her "a feminine Casanova" and jabbed at her uncompromising nature. Goldman, the review stated, showed "a genius for friendship, yet she never understands human nature well enough to see that its golden and leaden strains are mingled in capitalists as well as in anarchists and in anarchists as well as in capitalists. For those who differ with her she has little tolerance, and her book is full of what may be called brutal judgments . . . [yet] she also can be magnificent." Berkman, the *Times* said, was "the most influential of all upon the course of her life."[42]

Many of Emma's friends wrote to tell her how much they appreciated her story. In November 1931, halfway through reading her "monumental work," Upton Sinclair offered congratulations. "You have provided me with many entertaining hours," he said. "There are many points on which you and I would fight vehemently, but at least we agree in our belief in the usefulness and frankness of truth-telling."[43] The writer Kay Boyle, who would soon become Laurence Vail's second wife, praised the book as "very beautiful, very heartbreaking," written "so simply and well."[44] Pa Chin, a Chinese anarchist who had befriended Sasha and Emma in Paris, said the memoir made his "soul tremble fiercely. Throughout the whole book your roaring of forty years, like spring thunder, knocked at the door of my living grave. . . . The fire of my life was lit."[45]

"The book is great, I think," wrote Sasha to Fitzi. "It is well done in every respect. Some details could have well been left out, but you know Emma—she fought me on every passage and page that I cut out." Despite all the acclaim from critics and friends, the autobiography was not a financial success. "The sales seem to be very poor so far," Sasha told Fitzi, "and Emma has been very miserable about it. But the price is prohibitive, especially these days."[46]

27

PILLAR TO POST

Modest Stein, formerly Modska Aronstam, had not seen Sasha or Emma for fifteen years. He enjoyed a successful career as an artist, lived in an elegant apartment on Gramercy Park in New York City, and had long since abandoned anarchism. But he was rather lonely. His beloved wife had died, and his only child, Luba, was grown. In June 1929 he went to France to seek out his old friends, "the friends of his youth," according to Gabriel Javsicas.[1]

"Modska is in Paris," wrote Sasha to Emma. "I've been around with him. You are too enthusiastic about him, my dear. There is no depth to him and never was. But I like him in spite of all that, possibly because of the old days."[2] Stein traveled south to visit Emma in St. Tropez for her sixtieth birthday. Her neighbors Robert and Eugenie Sandstrom agreed to put him up in a room. Sasha arrived for the celebration, and the trio was briefly reunited.

Comrades came to meet the famous "Fedya." "He was, as I saw him, a distinguished personality," Mollie Steimer recalled, "but completely absorbed by some personal grief [over the death of his wife]. At any rate, he was very reserved and kept mostly to himself. As far as I can remember, there were no discussions whatsoever about the past, nor about [the Frick plot in] 1892. As by a gentleman's agreement, all of us present respected his silence, never disturbed him nor questioned him. The nicest part of the day was lunch hour, when Sasha entertained everybody with his countless jokes. Then, even Fedya had a smile!"[3] Shortly after returning to New York, Modest wrote to Emma reminding her that, despite his affection for her and Sasha, he preferred to keep a low profile and maintain his privacy.[4]

In November 1930 Stein received an invitation to Sasha's sixtieth birthday party, to be held in New York City, even though the guest of honor was barred from entering the United States. Stein declined to attend with a dismissive air, telling Sasha he had no interest in "all that after dinner drivel that is going to be perpetrated by all those bastards that like to hear themselves talk on the occasion of your having entered your seventh decade. And to quote the invitation literally, it will be a treat as well as a tribute to a rare and beautiful soul! So your rare and beautiful soul will ascend heavenwards on the wings of cold storage chicken washed down by 'bootleg' gin; and the speeches of . . . numerous others, will be the sweet music speeding you on your way. I shall not attend but leave a vacant chair—a vacant chair in the midst of vacant minds!"[5]

Sasha was deeply hurt by Modska's attitude toward the birthday banquet, pronouncing their friendship at an end. Emma was saddened by the rupture, and contacted Eckstein to see what could be done. "My dear Emmy," she wrote, "I am just as sure as I can be that Stein had no intention of hurting Sasha with the harsh and cruel things his letter contained."[6] But Berkman was unyielding. Too many miles, long years, and differing views had taken their toll on the cousins; the "Twins" for the time being were estranged once more.

Stein's absence notwithstanding, hundreds of comrades and friends gathered on November 20, 1930, in the Central Opera House of New York to memorialize Sasha's sixtieth birthday. Harry Kelly presided, music was played, and affectionate speeches delivered.[7] A smaller event was held in Los Angeles, where Tom Bell and others shared a cake and discussed Berkman's life.[8] To mark the occasion, a booklet of tributes, letters, and poems was published, with messages sent from all over the world, including ones from Errico Malatesta in Rome, Augustin Souchy in Berlin, Bertrand Russell in London, and Max Nettlau in Vienna. "Men like Alexander Berkman never grow old," wrote Nettlau. "They have the highest ideal to live and strive for." Max Metzkow, now seventy-seven, called Sasha "one of the best and truest hearts in our circle."[9] Erich Mühsam, a Jewish poet and performer based in Berlin, contributed a poem:

Alexander Berkman was forced to leave his native Russia because he loved Liberty;

> Alexander Berkman was forced to leave his adopted America because he loved Liberty;
> Alexander Berkman was hunted down, persecuted, driven from pillar to post in many countries because of his love for Liberty.
> But Alexander Berkman not only loves Liberty; Liberty also loves him.
> His home is in the hearts of all the peoples everywhere, although he is not persona grata with the rulers and governors of the states.
> Every human who loves Liberty loves him.
> We celebrate Alexander Berkman's sixtieth birthday because we are the comrades of his ideology and the admirers of his work and his great soul.
> There will come a time when humanity will celebrate this brave man,
> Alexander Berkman, as the pioneer and great champion of its happiness;
> A time in which all mankind will come to admire and love him.
> That time will be when Liberty has become Truth, the time of Anarchy.[10]

ALTHOUGH SASHA HAD REACHED AN AUSPICIOUS AGE and now lived a comparatively mellow existence (his radical activity was ongoing and intense, but largely below the radar), the French authorities viewed him as an unwelcome presence and a potential threat. Unlike Emma, who had acquired a British passport when she married the Scot James Colton, Berkman's residence in Europe was tenuous. His identity card was confiscated, and he received a succession of expulsion orders and challenges to his visa, resulting in arrest.

Berkman first was seized for "conducting anarchist propaganda" on May 1, 1930, "arrested at 6:30 A.M. while still in bed and compelled to leave the country the very same day," he wrote. "I was put on an express train going to Belgium and which did not stop until it reached Brusselles [*sic*]. There I was taken off the train, as I entered the country without a visa, perforce." He was held up in Belgium for several weeks, although a directive from the Belgian police required that he remove himself at once. Goldman and other friends worked to secure his reentry to France while he traveled through Belgium, going from Brussels to Antwerp.[11] He met a Dutch diamond dealer who personally drove Berkman across the French border in his car.

Once Berkman was back in France, he and Eckstein moved out of the house in St. Cloud and went south to the Riviera. They stayed with Emma in St. Tropez for a number of months before relocating to Nice, where they rented an apartment about sixty miles from Bon Esprit.[12] While Berkman was stuck in Belgium, Goldman looked after Emmy and, for once, found her sympathetic and pleasant. "I know you did not like [Emmy]," she wrote to Henry Alsberg. "Neither did I. But during the [visa] trouble Sasha had . . . I learned to care for her a great deal. She is as reactionary as they make them and middle-class to boot. But with that she has many fine qualities. She is genuine for one thing. There is no guile whatever in her, she is very kind. And her devotion to Sasha is simply extraordinary."[13]

This harmony did not last long. Eventually Emmy's fractious nature and Emma's innate abrasiveness got the better of them. Eckstein wrote a letter to Sasha detailing her grievances. "Emma is malicious, so terribly hurting [and] malicious," she wrote. "Sweetheart, my own, my Darling, I can't bear that character. I tried, I tried, I tried. I feel she is my enemy, she brings me flowers, and each flower has a knife with which she cuts into my happiest moments of my whole life . . . life is so strange, so difficult, so complicated—why look for such exhausting problems???"[14]

Sasha was perplexed, uncertain how to balance the two women in his life. "I am sorry you are so miserable," he told Emmy. He attributed Emma's sharp tongue and acerbic manner to "her character. . . . But it has nothing to do with you in particular," he said. "She is that way with all people." He made it clear to Emmy that nothing could come between him and Goldman: she was tied to his work, his past, his life. "Emma belongs to it, she is part of it," he said.[15]

Sasha continued to be hassled by the French government, receiving a second notice of expulsion in November 1930 ("a little surprise for my birthday"), and a third on July 28, 1931. He prevailed upon his contacts within the government, and managed to procure a temporary visa, to be reassessed every three months. But the regular trips from Nice to Paris to renew his visa were stressful and expensive, and comrades were obliged to call in favors and offer bribes on his behalf.[16]

"I live under the constant menace of being expelled without reason or prior notice," he complained to lawyer Morris Hillquit, "and this state of affairs is entirely unbearable. Nor can I financially afford the luxury of constant travel between Nice and Paris. Expelled again and again, I must get off the earth, but I am still here. Nowhere to go, but awaiting the next order. If expelled from France I have no place whatever to go. No country is willing to give me a visa."[17]

Sasha worked all the angles. He applied for status as a political refugee, and he and Emma appealed to as many influential people as they could round up to vouch for him.[18] The "galaxy of names" from across Great Britain, the Continent, Scandinavia, and America included Albert Einstein, Thomas and Heinrich Mann, Nobel Prize–winning Swedish writer Selma Lagerlöf, and a number of prominent political leaders.[19]

Theodore Dreiser sent a plea to French prime minister Pierre Laval. "Berkman is old, he is weary," Dreiser wrote. "For his one crime, the wounding of Henry Clay Frick, one of the most savage of our many savage American individualists and money-mad fortune hunters, who warred upon labor throughout his life, he spent eighteen years in the Western Penitentiary of Pennsylvania and came out broken, his great crime sympathy for the little people of the world whom, after all, he could not aid. Let me ask your understanding: Has he not paid enough? And may I not ask of you consideration of his wish, now that he is old, for a place of rest? Cannot France let him have that?"[20] After reviewing the letter, Goldman told Dreiser, "Alexander Berkman was imprisoned fourteen not eighteen years. . . . Your reference to him as 'old and weary' made me laugh. I assure you he is the most alive, most spirited youngster of sixty-one I know."[21]

Emma and Sasha developed a number of theories to explain the continued aggravation over his residency. They suspected that his circulation of anarchist propaganda, including the publication of *Now and After,* was raising flags within the French government; that his fund for Russian political prisoners and work on the related *Bulletin* were provoking the "Moscow outfit"; or that J. Edgar Hoover continued from across the Atlantic to target him for persecution—they had heard rumors that Hoover was monitoring them from afar.[22]

To lower his political profile, Berkman scaled back his involvement with the anarchist movement (at least publicly) and focused on his blander duties as an editor and translator. He gave up the *Bulletin* and spread the word that his controversial activities had been reduced, telling friends it was "vital" that everyone believed he no longer distributed radical material, a condition of maintaining his residency in France.[23]

But although Sasha adopted these prudent measures, he wasn't happy about it. "Dear Friends," he wrote in a dispatch published in the *Road to Freedom,* "My case certainly illustrates most strikingly the brutality and stupidity of government. The situation is actually such that I have no right to exist anywhere on this earth. . . . I cannot remain in France and I cannot enter any other country! The only thing that remains is to get off the earth, but the earth being round, that is also not practical."[24]

Neither was Goldman immune to harrying from the French government. On April 29, 1930, she was served with an expulsion notice for conducting anarchist propaganda, although the order, decades old, was the result of a bureaucratic error, and her trouble was quickly resolved. "I have been expelled from France—or at least I was given a copy of the order of expulsion," she wrote to Henry Alsberg. "The order was issued in 1901 by a man dead fifteen years. I was taken to police headquarters and told I may be shipped out the same day. But I had a British passport and they gave me ten days."[25] The order was withdrawn once her lawyer, Henri Torres, illuminated the situation—the request for her expulsion had come during Goldman's ten-month stay in Paris with Hippolyte Havel thirty years earlier; at that time, she had sailed back to New York before the authorities could take action. Emma gaily recounted the latest drama to Lincoln Steffens: "Taken to police headquarters, photographed, finger-printed, measured and weighed, everything in dear good old-style. . . . You can see, dear man, I am still considered a dangerous person, regardless of all my ex-friends who have given me up as a real bourgeoisie."[26]

BERKMAN'S BATTLE FOR PERMANENT RESIDENCY weakened his health. "Oh, what a contrast!" exclaimed Mollie Steimer after a visit. "Sasha had changed completely, walked with difficulty, looked worn, thin, and was seriously ill.[27] Emmy was dominating, absorbing, and both were desperately unhappy." The pressures were mounting, said Mollie. Sasha's "struggles with Emmy, constant harassment by French police, daily struggle for existence; though he worked hard he earned little."[28]

Jobs were tough to come by. The worldwide economic depression, which had begun around the time the stock market crashed in 1929, had not struck France as severely as it had Germany, Great Britain, or the United States, but its effects were felt nonetheless. "The season has been bad for the last two years," Sasha told Fitzi. "We live from day to day."[29]

He and Emmy had to hustle to find even small assignments. Berkman did translations and ghost writing, while Emmy took in typing. Berkman printed cards to advertise their work, and Emmy went around to shops and hotels to hand them out. Occasionally Berkman was hired as an assistant by writers who were passing through the south of France.[30] Some proposals that came his way were not to his liking. A man called Paul E. Sann expressed an interest in writing a book about Berkman's experiences. Sasha was first intrigued, then affronted. Put off by the manner in which Sann made contact ("Dear Alex," Sann began, "How are you and how is Anarchism?"), Sasha asked Minna Lowensohn to investigate. Deciding that Sann was an "idiot" and an "ignoramus" who understood little about the anarchist philosophy, he instructed his friends to refuse to cooperate. To Sann, he snapped, "If you will pardon my frankness, I want to tell you that you are a fool. . . . And your cheek beats even your stupidity." Paul Sann eventually became the executive editor of the *New York Post*.[31]

Emma, meanwhile, was still strong and dynamic, able to earn a living with lecture tours and paid appearances, but Sasha was tired. "[Emma's] energy is as vital today as it was thirty years ago," Sasha remarked to a friend. "But Emma is full of life and the need to be active. I confess I have neither energy nor strength enough to do such things any more under such conditions."[32]

IT WAS MODEST STEIN WHO KEPT Sasha afloat. Despite the falling-out with his cousin in November 1930, Stein again began to visit his comrades in the summer of 1931.[33] He gave both Sasha and Emma substantial contributions of cash, bought gifts for Emmy, and paid Sasha's rent. "We talked some things over," Sasha told Emma. "He is generous." Stein also offered to help Berkman get jobs writing for the movie business; Sasha was playing around with script ideas and film scenarios, and Modska, who had contacts in the entertainment community, was planning a trip to California in the fall. Sasha told Emma that "Mods" was going "to Hollywood and that he knows one of the very big men well, the main man of Fox Film Co. Fox is one of the biggest houses of course."[34]

Harry Kelly, a frequent visitor to the south of France, dined at Bon Esprit with "the old romantic trio of forty years ago," as he fondly described them.[35] Before Stein left St. Tropez, Emma threw an all-night farewell party, inviting the acquaintances he had made in France. It was a jolly affair.[36] After a stop in Paris, Modska was home in New York by mid-September 1931, and almost immediately supplied his friends with more funds. "I've sent a check to A. L. Ross," Modska wrote Emma from New York. "I am mailing some money to you to give to Sasha."[37]

A year later, in August 1932, Stein made another visit to Paris, Nice, and St. Tropez. He gave Emma a large sum for the purchase of a plot of land near Bon Esprit, pressed on Sasha a total of 3,000 francs, and again paid the rent on Sasha's apartment. Sasha and Emmy had moved a number of times since relocating to Nice, seeking housing that fitted with their ever-shrinking budget. They first lived in a flat at 8 rue Trachel, then found cheaper quarters in a neighborhood largely populated by Russian exiles at 22 avenue Monplaisir, a fifth-floor apartment that offered some sunshine for Sasha and a view for Emmy, "in the distance," said Sasha, "of the mountains which she prefers to the sea."[38]

In May 1933, mortified by his financial dependence, Sasha found an even less expensive place at 101 boulevard de Cessole, away from the center of town. "We sold the desk, some clothes, and other items to raise needed cash," he told Goldman, and announced that he would no longer accept support from Stein.[39] Emma begged him to reconsider. "Sasha dear . . . I assure you it means nothing whatever to him. He lives like a lord and has absolutely nothing in life except his affection for you. He really loves you and it is a great satisfaction to him to help you. Why then deprive him of the only worthwhile pleasure he has. I hope you will not do it again."[40]

Modska may have been, in the eyes of his hardened comrades, indulgent, conventional, and soft, but he had not entirely forgotten his own anarchist past. On November 10, 1933, with the Haymarket anniversary in his thoughts, he composed a letter to Sasha. "Tomorrow is November 11, forty-six years since the Chicago hanging," he wrote. "[August] Spies's prophecy still unfulfilled—the voice of the dead is being heard less than ever. I am being more firmly convinced that the only obligation one has is the obligation to himself. I mean that one should live his own life according to the truth that he sees and not deviate from it. In other words, I believe in the proposition of one's own example, one's own life."[41]

MODSKA WAS BACK IN THEIR LIVES, but Sasha and Emma mourned the deaths of some of their most beloved anarchist comrades. Pathbreaking Italian anarchist Errico Malatesta, whom they both revered, died in Rome in 1932. John Cook of Providence passed away in a home for the aged in 1931. "He was active till the last and corresponded with me regularly," wrote W. S. Van Valkenburgh to Goldman. "He never failed to ask for you and Sasha."[42] "I expected to hear of John Cook's death almost any moment because he wrote in the last letter how feeble he was," Emma replied. "The dear old soul, he was a true comrade and rebel faithful until the end."[43]

The death that disturbed the comrades the most was that of Eric B. Morton, loyal and dependable, who had so long ago assisted in Berkman's attempted prison break, and always came through in a pinch. After Morton suffered a great family tragedy, marital woes, and other setbacks, he drifted into depression and despair. "Eric Morton lost his daughter Anita," Emma told Ben Capes in 1926. "She died of cancer after prolonged illness. Eric had written me with great pride that Anita, who had belonged to a circle of the Young Communist League, left the organization because the idiotic Communists called him a counter-Revolutionist. She was evidently a clever girl. It is all so sad."[44]

Nearly four years later, Morton was in bad shape. His personal life was in a shambles, and his health was poor. "I have recently learned that Eric Morton has gone to some kind of home because he is ill and incapacitated for work," Emma told Harry Kelly.[45] Morton attempted suicide, and died in 1931. "I heard of the death of Eric Morton," Emma afterward wrote to a friend in San Francisco. "Knowing how dreadful the last years of his life were, I did not regret his going. . . . He was a great boy and had a large part in my heart. He was brave and heroic in everything he understood."[46]

"The old guard is passing away," Sasha wrote forlornly to Pierre Ramus, "and there are almost none of the younger generation to take its place, or at least to do the work that must be done if the world is ever to see a better day."[47]

28

OLD GLORY

MUCH AS GOLDMAN ENJOYED LIVING in St. Tropez, she yearned to return to the United States, the country in which she had first become an anarchist. The months she had spent in Canada, so close to her former home, only sharpened her longing. She often expressed this desire to her comrades, and viewed the United States as the ripest earth in which to plant her anarchist ideas. "Oh, Sasha dearest, if only I could be in America now," she wrote in 1931. "For another five years intensive activity I would gladly give the balance of years still left me."[1]

To Emma, America was "the land of the Walt Whitmans, the Lloyd Garrisons, the Thoreaus, the Wendell Phillipses, the country of Young Americans of life and thought, or of art and letters; the America of the new generation knocking at the door, of men and women with ideals, with aspirations for a better day; the America of social rebellion and spiritual promise, of the glorious 'undesirables' against whom all the exile, expropriation and deportation laws are aimed. It is to THAT America," she declared passionately, "that I am proud to belong."[2]

Over an extended period she pursued her quest to return, seeking the help of powerful friends, including American Civil Liberties Union founder Roger Baldwin. Previous efforts had failed; indeed, she had been told that return would be impossible. But toward the end of 1933, as she prepared for another junket in Canada, it appeared she might get her wish. In December she went to Montreal and filed an application to the U.S. government for a reentry permit and a three-month visa to carry out a lecture tour in America.

Franklin Delano Roosevelt had been inaugurated in March 1933, in the midst of the Depression. The United States had far bigger problems than a visit from an aging radical, and *Living My Life* even had found a fan in first lady Eleanor Roosevelt. The authority to grant permission for an anarchist deportee to reenter the country rested with the secretary of labor, Frances Perkins, and on December 27, 1933, Baldwin informed Emma that he had opened channels with Colonel Daniel W. MacCormack, the commissioner general of the Immigration and Naturalization Service. "One will do whatever he directs, because he is really speaking for Miss Perkins and the President. As a matter of fact," Baldwin added, "I happen to know that Mrs. Roosevelt read your book with great interest. She spoke highly of it to a friend of mine."[3]

Emma wanted Sasha to apply for a visa and come with her, but he would have none of it. He did not share her confidence that America now would be more open to their ideas. Berkman had never felt the pure, sentimental tug of a homeland or missed his adopted nation—he cared about his anarchist creed, not any one country. His experience in Russia and his passport problems in Europe had only made him more hostile to government bureaucracy. Moreover, a significant portion of his years in America had been spent suffering in prison, the resulting trauma a lifelong burden, whereas Emma, despite dealing with persecution and frustrating obstacles in the States, had enjoyed decades of lectures and laurels, travels and revelry, comforts and kindnesses.

"If you get in to America," wrote Sasha to Emma, "I shall be pleased on YOUR account, since you are so keen about it. But, dear, do not forget what I told you on previous occasions. You said then, as you often say, that I would change my mind. No, dear, I have not and will not. As a matter of fact, I feel even stronger about it than even before. I DON'T WANT to go to the U.S. on any considerations. Please remember it. . . . I hate America now and don't want even to see it again. So, please do not give the impression that I want to come back."[4]

Roger Baldwin was aided in his efforts on Goldman's behalf by "a committee," said Emma proudly, "consisting of the best known people in art, letters, and the liberal movement," including Sherwood Anderson, John Dewey, Sinclair Lewis, Margaret Sanger, and John Haynes Holmes. It was organized by activist Mabel Carver Crouch, who had admired Emma's memoir and tracked her down in St. Tropez the previous summer, promising to help her return to America.[5]

The group directed a flurry of personal letters to Secretary Perkins pleading for Emma's homecoming. "I am very sure, Miss Perkins," said

Sherwood Anderson, "that you know about the case of Miss Goldman's great hunger to get back into America. . . . I am sure we both look upon her as a great old-warrior and I hope there will be some way—without too much noise—of letting her come back into America." Education reformer Dorothy Canfield Fisher noted that Goldman wanted to return "for the purpose of giving some public lectures. The cause of freedom of speech could not be, I feel, better served than by allowing this serious woman to address American audiences," she said. Eugene O'Neill assured Perkins that "Miss Goldman has the admiration and respect of many of the leading citizens of this country, and thousands would welcome her re-entry to this country."[6]

Along with this glittering deluge of entreaties, Baldwin negotiated the delicate details of the agreement. The government issued a rigid requirement that Goldman offer no lecture or remarks of a political nature, should she be permitted admittance, yet the parameters of this directive were hazy. Emma's standard repertoire included speeches on drama, the arts, and her autobiography; also anarchism, Communism, and, lately, conditions in Germany, the rise of Nazism, the threat of Adolf Hitler, and fascism in Europe. But even her tamest topics could veer into the controversial, and there was some debate about whether *Living My Life* should be characterized as literature or politics.[7]

Baldwin advised Emma to engage A. L. Ross to argue on her behalf, and Ross went to Washington, D.C., to handle the legal aspects while Baldwin dealt directly with the administration.[8] Shortly thereafter, Ross cabled Goldman from Washington with the good news. Her application had been approved; she would be allowed to remain in the country for ninety days, beginning February 1, 1934.[9]

Berkman warned Emma just a few weeks before her visa was granted that she should not get her hopes up. "I am sorry, dear, but I fear disappointment is awaiting you," he said. "It stands to reason that even if Perkins is favorably inclined, they cannot afford to let you in. There would be too much criticism of the administration for it—and the Roosevelt administration has enough trouble on its hands. I hope, for your sake, that you still get a chance to lecture in the U.S. I don't mean to discourage you, but it does not look promising."[10] When he learned the visa had been approved, he was astounded. "Emma has gotten a visa to the U.S.," he wrote to Fitzi's companion Pauline Turkel. "I confess I did not believe it possible. Seems things have changed in the U.S. Hope she won't be disappointed with the visit. As to myself, I don't hanker after the U.S. at all."[11]

EMMA'S RETURN WAS MET WITH CURIOSITY but little outcry; President Roosevelt's America was a rather different place from the country Goldman had left behind in 1919. Lecture agencies immediately offered to represent her, and a number of groups signed up to hear her speak. Many in the public now regarded her as a bold woman with a complicated past, rather than as a chilling specter of chaos. Even so, not everyone was pleased with "Red Emma's" reappearance. Editorials objecting to the visit ran in newspapers around the country, and some irate citizens took pains to make their sentiments known.

Maude Murray Miller, a writer retired from the Columbus, Ohio, *Dispatch,* contacted Eleanor Roosevelt expressing her dismay that Goldman had been granted a visa. "I believe her to be a grave menace to this country," wrote Murray Miller. "The assassin of President McKinley said it was her influence which induced him to commit that atrocious crime. I am afraid that she may have designs upon the life of our beloved President Roosevelt. He is accomplishing so much wonderful work that anarchists do not want this country to regain its former prosperity. It would be her first thought, I suggest, to remove him, or have it done."[12]

"Thank you very much for your solicitude and interest in the President," replied Mrs. Roosevelt. "He is very carefully protected and, in any case, Emma Goldman is now a very old woman. I really think that this country can stand the shock of her presence for ninety days. I appreciate your writing, however, and hope you have not been unduly alarmed."[13]

When the day came, Emma took a train from Toronto to Niagara Falls, and continued on to Rochester, arriving as scheduled on February 1, where she was reunited with her extended family of siblings and their children, and greeted by a crowd of friends, admirers, reporters, and photographers.[14] For the occasion, she wore "a black felt hat and a fur-trimmed coat of a mild shade of red." Her "thick glasses" were round-framed, and her hair was cut in a simple bob. Whereas once "'Red Emma' was a name to frighten little children," said one reporter, she now looked "like a motherly housewife or perhaps the president of the library committee of the local women's club."[15]

Her modest appearance aside, Goldman was as blunt as ever. "My views have not changed," she announced in Rochester. "I am still an anarchist. I am the same. The world has changed—that's why I haven't had to. Everyone is an anarchist who loves liberty and hates oppression. But not everyone wants it for the other fellow. That is my task; I want to extend it to the other fellow."[16]

Emma flatly denied that while on tour she would avoid topics of politics or the economy—"I promised nothing"—and pronounced herself free of resentment for all that had befallen her. "I believe in the principle of letting people think for themselves," she explained, "so why should I be bitter?"[17] "The fires have cooled somewhat in the years," wrote a reporter who accompanied her from Toronto to Rochester, "but they still burn."[18]

Goldman's first major public appearance was on February 11 in Manhattan, hosted by pastor John Haynes Holmes.[19] According to the *New York Times,* "2000 persons stormed the Community Church services in the Town Hall in the hope of hearing her old fiery oratory. They heard instead a calmly delivered eulogy of the Russian anarchist Peter Kropotkin. . . . Only once, when she denounced Hitler, did her voice ring with the indignation that formerly provoked her sympathizers and opponents to stormy demonstrations." Except for this outburst, Goldman came across as a "mild, gray-haired woman" in a black dress and red and gold shawl.[20]

Arthur Leonard Ross later recalled Emma's Town Hall speech, which, as far as he was concerned, pushed the boundaries of her visa agreement. "I personally vouched that Emma would make no political speeches during her stay here. And the first thing she did was to make a political speech! It was about Kropotkin, and it was quite an occasion. . . . Town Hall was packed, and people were hanging from the chandeliers. I thought the upper gallery would collapse, it was so heavy with people."[21]

Over the next few nights, Emma spoke at a number of New York venues, including the Brooklyn Academy of Music. Her lecture tour then took her to more than a dozen cities, from Washington to Kansas City. At times she traveled by plane, telling her lecture agent, James B. Pond, "If the weather is good and the cost of flying not much more I shall fly. My friends have always charged me with living too much in the air. I might as well be guilty of their charges."[22]

While in Pittsburgh, she paid solemn visits to Homestead and the Western Penitentiary—Sasha's "living grave," as she called it. "The memories of your trip to Pittsburgh," she wrote to Sasha, "your act, your Calvary and my own desperate struggle during the years of your imprisonment settled like a stone on my heart and spirit. . . . Homestead looks as hideous as ever. So does the Western Penitentiary, except that there seems to be a new addition, a new wall. The friends that took me in their car suggested that we go in. But I could not face that. The sight of the ghastly place was enough to bring a lump to my throat."[23]

In Philadelphia, members of Emma's welcoming committee told the *New York Times* that Goldman "had the appearance of a quiet housewife, considerably younger than her years." She warned the crowd about the threat in Germany. "Financial and military interests are deliberately planning a war in Europe," she said. "Hitler will last a long time. It is not just the man who stands out in Germany, but it is a mass movement, just as it is in Italy and Austria."[24]

Emma spent a good deal of time in Chicago, where comrades Jay and Jeanne Levey helped coordinate her lectures. "They are the most marvelous workers, the most beautiful people I have met in many years," she told Rudolf Rocker. "It is entirely due to their help, and especially Jeanne's splendid organizing abilities that many [Chicago] meetings were so successful."[25] In the city, Emma found time for romance when she met Frank Heiner, a sociologist at the University of Chicago. Heiner was in his mid-thirties, and had been blind since the age of three months. He was a knowledgeable anarchist scholar, as well as a skilled writer and speaker. He also had a wife and two children. But for Emma, his marital status was not a deterrent.

"Heiner is the greatest event in the last seventeen years," she confided to Sasha. "He combines all that I had longed for and dreamed about all my life and never achieved."[26] Her bliss, however, was bittersweet. "Here, I had longed for so many years for fulfillment of love with someone who would share my ideas and ideals, blend harmoniously with my tastes and desire," she said six months after meeting him. "And now at sixty-five, when all this riches is laid at my feet, it is only for a fleeting moment."[27]

After the pair consummated their relationship, they exchanged heated love letters. "Oh, my Frank, if only I could make you understand how completely you have fulfilled me," Emma wrote. "No, not only physically, but intellectually, and spiritually as well. Frank, my Frank I long for you with every fiber of my being."[28] Emma, in turn, was Heiner's "Goddess." "I could not love you more," he told her. "You are my true love, my own supreme, complete love, the love of my life."[29]

Emma was thrilled to be back on American soil, delighted to reconnect with her old friends and revisit her favorite haunts.[30] Although she took issue with the president's policies—neither she nor Sasha had any faith in the New Deal—the nation's energy excited her. "True, America remains naive, childish in many respects in comparison to the sophistication of Europe," she said to Sasha. "But I prefer its naivety, there is youth in it, there is still the spirit of adventure, there is something refreshing and stimulating in the air."[31]

From a financial standpoint, Emma's lecture tour was a failure. Some segments of the circuit were inefficiently managed, and while anarchist followers showed up with enthusiasm, many of her speeches drew small crowds and she had difficulty filling the halls. In March, Stella Ballantine wrote a note to the tour organizer to apologize for the disappointing turnout: "I do hope your other business is so booming that you are not completely in the red with the others as you are with Miss Goldman."[32]

Goldman was routinely observed by the authorities. Recalled one comrade who attended a speech near the end of Goldman's tour, "reporters and detectives sat in the front row, writing down everything she said."[33] At times Emma was uncharacteristically circumspect with her words; during an April event in New York, she would allow only that Roosevelt "has a very pleasant voice on the radio. Beyond that, I really wouldn't want to say anything." Hitler and Mussolini, meanwhile, were dismissed jointly as a "nuisance."[34]

But Bureau of Investigation Director J. Edgar Hoover considered the tone of her lectures grounds to prohibit future visits, and prospects for another return seemed dim. A gloomy Berkman wrote to Pauline Turkel, "Emma's tour was a disappointment in various ways, I believe, also financially."[35] To Pierre Ramus, he noted that she "even had to borrow money for her return ticket."[36] Emma herself described the tour to W. S. Van Valkenburgh as "a complete flop."[37]

Nevertheless, Goldman was gratified by the respectful reception she had received. Her life was deemed "amazing" by a host of journalists and elites, and she was recognized by some as a true admirer of the United States after years of being branded a traitor. "America is where I had my spiritual growth," she said in New York. "I am loyal to all that is cultural and fine in America." She enjoyed the attention of the throngs of reporters, and joked with them about her relationship with James Colton, the anarchist coal miner she had wed in 1925. "Was your marriage with Colton a real marriage, or just for the sake of becoming a British subject?" she was asked. "What do you mean by 'real'?" she queried. "Well, did you marry him because you loved him?" Emma responded with "a peal of laughter."[38]

Emma also chatted comfortably about her long-ago smoking habit. During a train trip, while she was seated with a group of interviewers in a Pullman dining car, it was pointed out that "Miss Goldman was the only woman present not smoking." She had once smoked, she explained, but was forced to quit. "Back in 1890 I smoked forty cigarettes a day," she said. "I think I started just to be different and shock people. Often I was thrown out of restaurants. Then in 1893 I was sent to Blackwell's Island prison for a year. By that time smoking had become a habit and for two months I suffered torture for want of a cigarette. Finally, I overcame the pangs of appetite. When I was discharged, I decided never to smoke again. I knew I would be in jail often and never wanted to suffer so again."[39]

At the end of April 1934, Goldman's three months in America came to a close, and she departed with great reluctance. "The trip to the United States has revived my spirit more than my fifteen years in exile," she wrote to Joseph Ishill before she left. "If ever I had any doubts about my having roots in the United States my short visit has dispelled them completely. . . . I don't know what it is in America, but I felt years younger and full of vigor and enthusiasm. . . . I felt a changed woman from the moment I arrived in New York. And my departure will be more painful than it was when Sasha and I were deported."[40]

But the experience was well worth the heartache, and Emma was optimistic about the country's future. "This is the age of youth," she told reporters during her tour. "Youth now has the controls. Let's see what youth can do. The old ones made a mess of things."[41]

Goldman was back in Canada in May 1934. In Hamilton and Montreal, she continued her lectures on literature, drama, birth control, and the menaces of Nazism and fascism. In Toronto she organized an anarchist meeting called the Libertarian Group, with Dutch, Italian, and Jewish comrades participating; Carl Newlander served as secretary, and her friends Dien Meelis and Tom Meelis, a printer, were members. She also formed close friendships with two young men: Attilio Bortolotti, also known as Tilio or Arthur Bartell; and Ahrne Thornberg, later known as Ahrne Thorne, who would become the final editor of the *Fraye Arbeter Shtime.*[42]

Goldman remained in Canada for a year, clinging to the hope that she would be granted another visa to America. Her friends and family came across the border to visit her, and she remained active socially and professionally. But the environment was comparatively dull, her prospects limited, and eventually she made plans to go back to France.

Berkman, in Nice, was looking forward to her return. He had enjoyed a short period of relative contentment, despite his depressive nature. Emmy had been in fair health for a change, and his passport problem had stabilized; he was allowed, he said, "to go to places without notifying the authorities or registering everywhere. That is good as long as I have a permanent residence in Nice." Writing to Pauline Turkel, he said, "I feel in general that life is a silly tragicomedy, and that perhaps I have lived too long already. But otherwise everything is OK, as the old Jewish woman said, after recounting her dozen fatal maladies."[43]

On May 3, 1935, Goldman sailed from Montreal on the Cunard steamer *Ascania,* and arrived in Paris on May 15. In St. Tropez, she was reunited with Berkman, who looked reasonably well but rather thin. She resumed her hostess activities at Bon Esprit, and the cottage was again filled with visitors, which Sasha thought was good for her temperament. "Emma has plenty of company which she constitutionally needs," he wrote to Frank Heiner, with whom he had established a friendly correspondence. "She needs an outlet for her tremendous energy, and when she is not lecturing she must have other interests to occupy her mind and time."[44]

Modest Stein came again to see them, bringing memories and more money.[45] Sasha could no longer resist his cousin's generosity. He now accepted a monthly stipend from Stein, coordinated by Stella Ballantine and occasionally supplemented by other friends including Claus Timmermann. Emma thanked Claus warmly on Sasha's behalf and told him affectionately, "I am sure you are the same happy go lucky irrepressible Claus, still laughing at the world and all its follies."[46]

For all Modska's constancy and bounty, Goldman continued to disparage his affluent lifestyle in New York. "Had a lot of visitors this month, among them an old friend whom you will know from the book as Fedya," she wrote to Dorothy Rogers, a member of the Toronto Libertarian Group. "How rich is Sasha's and my life in comparison to his. True the price we paid was terrific, but we'd gladly do it all over again rather than to be so empty as his life is. He began with very considerable artistic talents and sacrificed it on the altar of commercialism. He began with a great ideal and believes in nothing now. He still has the same kind heart, ready to help those he knows. But he has nothing, not even friendship in his life except Sasha and me. It is sad."[47]

Still, Emma was sorry she and the "Twins" did not get a chance to spend quality time together on this occasion, as the simple trio of old. "I would have enjoyed having you and Sasha here, just the three of us in memory of our common life when we were so young, so naive, and so full of ardent hopes," she wrote to Modska after he left. "Let us hope we will still have 'Bon Esprit' next year."[48]

EUROPE WAS BECOMING A FORBIDDING PLACE. Berkman and Goldman had been following the political situation in Germany for years, and were concerned about its fearsome path. They were appalled as well by the continued display of power in Communist Russia, and what they viewed as a cruel and criminal regime that threatened every element of society. Berkman judged fascism and Communism to be mirror images—ideologically contrary yet identical in result: despotism, a police state, corrupt bureaucracy, and mass murder. Nazi Germany and Bolshevik Russia were, to Berkman, the representations of everything he had always opposed, everything offensive to a valuable and rightful human existence.

In 1932 Goldman predicted that with Hitler and the Nazis in power a dictatorship would ensue. As she wrote to Joseph Ishill, "Already, the military hordes of Hitler have been given carte blanche. I dread to think of the butchery that is bound to begin. The Jews and the Radical movement will be the first to suffer. It is horrible to contemplate, yet I too feel that there is nothing to be done about it. We are in for a large dose of dictatorship—black this time. It is a modern religious hysteria, and like all such movements, spreads like wildfire."[49] "The world is just crazy," Berkman wrote to

Max Nettlau in January the following year, "and we can only hope that 1933 will bring a little more sense to mankind."[50]

Berkman's hopes were not realized. As the months passed, he became more and more alarmed by what was occurring across Europe. "I am sorry I cannot tell you anything encouraging, but we must face facts," he wrote in August 1933 to Mollie Steimer, who had left Germany with Senya Fleshin after escaping Nazi persecution, eventually relocating to Mexico City, where they opened SEMO, a photography studio. "Fascism is growing. It is coming to Austria, England, and even Ireland. It is everywhere already, even if in some places still underground. And do not forget that this Fascism, whether in black skirts, brown shirts, blue or red shirts is supported by the masses. Else it could not exist. . . . It is the masses themselves who consciously support Mussolini, Hitler, etc. I meet a good many people here in Nice—Italians, Germans, and even some French and Americans who admire Mussolini and Hitler. So there you are. There is a wave of reaction throughout the world. That wave will have to pass, but we are too powerless to stem against it. Maybe it will soon begin another war. And against that we are also powerless."[51]

Anarchism, Sasha fretted, was a foundering ideal, and his comrades were helpless against the onslaught of evil. "The truth is," he said to Mollie, "our movement has accomplished nothing, anywhere. I cannot fool myself with any belief that we can do something for our people in the prisons of Germany. No more than we could free our people from the Russian prisons. But for the latter we could at least arouse some little sympathy and get some financial help. But now for German prisoners we cannot even do this. I have tried, so I know."[52]

Berkman was no longer a frenetic, impassioned youth, and his lifelong dream that the anarchist movement would someday bring freedom and truth to countries across the world gave way to a more immediate fear. "The Nazis are dangerous maniacs, more dangerous than any other party, perhaps with the exception of the Communists," he told Goldman. "I think that a war there will be, maybe in a year or two, and I am afraid the damned masses will again go to slaughter."[53] He felt that the governments of Europe and America were failing to prevent a global catastrophe from occurring, instead rushing headlong into another world war. "The world," he said to Max Nettlau, "is certainly not learning anything from experience, and today we seem to be in the same position as in 1914. In fact, even in a worse and more dangerous situation."[54]

Goldman, too, was convinced of imminent disaster. "I fear we are in for a period of black reaction for which I hold Russia entirely responsible," she wrote to the labor activist Rose Pesotta. "It was the Bolshevik regime that introduced fascism and taught Mussolini as well as Hitler the way to exterminate liberty and libertarians. It did more. It made the masses drunk with the desire for the strong armed man, the bully who can save them from having to think or do anything for themselves. And not only the masses, but the entire intelligentsia in every country as well. Except that the intelligentsia sees in dictatorship and fascism a way to play its part at good and comfortable jobs. Don't for a moment think I am pessimistic. I only face facts. Not for a moment do I believe either fascism or bolshevism has come to stay for good, or even for a long time. But it will remain longer than I have to live. It is like a terrific storm. It's got to spend itself, and it will. But that it may go for all times it is necessary for us Anarchists to hold our banner high, and to let our voices be heard in the present political wilderness. It is all we can do. And it is by no means little."[55]

When Hitler came to power, becoming chancellor in January 1933, Rudolf and Milly Rocker knew it would be dangerous for them to remain in Germany because of their anarchist ideology and pro-Jewish activities, as well as Milly's Jewish heritage. In March 1933, shortly after the arson at the Reichstag, they took the last train out of Berlin for Switzerland, just before the Nazis sealed the border. Rocker, who had recently turned sixty, carried with him the manuscript of his major work, *Nationalism and Culture,* on which he had labored for twenty years. His personal library of 10,000 volumes, one of the last private anarchist collections in Europe, was burned and his property confiscated. The Rockers went to Paris and London before settling permanently in the United States.

"I'm glad you're out of Germany," Sasha wrote them. "Knowing what these scoundrels are, and knowing the experiences of Russia in similar matters, I expect the WORST. . . . One has to look facts and possibilities in the face, and one should learn from the past. Health and happiness to you both in spite of the dark clouds. One day the sun MUST come out and bring its warmth and light."[56] Had he not escaped, Rocker certainly would have shared the fate of fellow German anarchist and writer Erich Mühsam, who was arrested in February 1933, beaten and mutilated while in captivity, and finally brutalized and strangled to death in a Nazi prison camp in July of the following year.

Berkman, who had known Mühsam in Berlin in the 1920s and had corresponded with him during the past decade, was horrified by his arrest and torture. After Mühsam was first captured, Sasha expressed his anguish to Michael Cohn. "As to Germany, things there beggar all description. . . . Fortunately some of our comrades—notably Rudolf and Milly Rocker—have succeeded in escaping alive, but many others are still in Germany and unable to get out. Some of them are in prison, and not a few of them have been tortured, like Erich Mühsam, for instance. He was beaten, compelled to submit to every indignity and his hair was pulled out by the handful and a swastika cut on his scalp with a knife. Surely we are again in the Dark Ages. First the Bolsheviks, now the Fascists and Nazis."[57]

Later, when Goldman learned about Mühsam's death, she was aghast. "Thinkers, poets, writers, and musicians were sunk deep into savagery, all their achievements thrust into the gutter, besmirched with blood," she lamented to a friend. "Erich Mühsam, who wrote a poem about Sasha for his sixtieth anniversary, was among the finest poets and writers, was beaten repeatedly and tortured. The fact is that the Communists are the forerunners of fascism. Neither Mussolini nor Hitler have made a single original step. All they had to do is to follow and copy faithfully the steps taken by Lenin and Stalin."[58]

Berkman was convinced the worst was coming. "The world is getting too rotten to live in," he wrote to Pauline Turkel in September 1934. "Fascism is spreading throughout Europe, and it looks like a fight between Fascism and Communism before very long. I only hope that may prove a final lesson to the world."[59] In October 1935 he told the Rockers, "there is bound to be another holocaust, for all the governments are prepared for it, the militarists itch for it, and the Mussolinis and Hitlers really NEED it badly to keep up their regimes. There is no end to this insanity. I must admit, it is a mighty poor showing after half a century of anti-militarist work and general education of the masses."[60]

Goldman traveled to England in November 1935 to lecture about Mussolini, Hitler, and Stalin. She felt her decade-long anti-Russia stance had been validated, writing to Carlo Tresca that the "crimes and horrors" occurring in Russia under Stalin had merely grown from "the evil legacy left him by Lenin, Trotsky, and the other unfortunates who have been done to death at Stalin's behest."[61]

Nonetheless, Goldman again received a hostile reception from the British radical community. "The Communists came out in full force," she told Berkman after one disorderly event. "They did everything except break up the meeting. But that was only due to my presence of mind and my self control on the platform. But I came away with frightful pain in my lungs and chest. And today I feel as if I had been gone over with a steam roller. I have not met with such a wild, ignorant, and fanatical group of people in a long while."[62]

"The time is past when Russia was to be treated differently from Italy or Germany," Berkman responded. "I would expose Stalin in the New York Times, the same as I should expose Hitler, if they would give me a chance."[63]

ON NOVEMBER 21, 1935, SASHA TURNED SIXTY-FIVE. His comrades in America, from New York to Los Angeles, celebrated his life and raised money for his personal support.[64] Emma wrote him a special letter that ended, "Goodbye my dear, dear *tolstogub,* with all my heart I wish you a grand birthday, very much improved health and some interesting and vital work that would relieve you of economic stress and anxiety."[65]

29

NOTHING BUT DEATH CAN END

BY THE EARLY 1930S SASHA'S HEALTH had begun to fail, and in his letters he often complained of depression and fatigue. His lifelong cigarette habit, poor nutrition during his years of incarceration, and stress from his residency problems had taken their toll. His old ligament injury from his 1917 fall down a flight of stairs at *The Blast* and Mother Earth offices flared up in 1930, and his teeth were in terrible shape.[1] Emma related his ailments to Minna Lowensohn. "Sasha has rheumatism in his leg, and neuralgia in his face, which finally forced him to go to the dentist and have teeth removed."[2] Eventually ten of Sasha's teeth were pulled and replaced, and loose bone was removed from his gums.[3]

In 1932 he was still suffering from an assortment of disorders, and the local doctors were having a difficult time diagnosing him. "He is frightfully run-down and has been ill all winter," wrote Emma to Arthur Leonard Ross, noting that Sasha had, as usual, been smoking heavily. "The doctors he consulted had different opinions: one said the heart, another the liver, and a third, hardening of the arteries."[4] His problems with his teeth persisted, and in 1935 Goldman summarized Sasha's dental ordeal in a letter to Henry Alsberg. "Some five years ago Sasha had rotten dentistry in Paris, an American dentist at that. . . . Since that time he has known nothing but pain in the jaw."[5] Berkman, meanwhile, kept two black notebooks with a list of remedies for his sundry afflictions, along with aphrodisiacs, hair restorers, and other tonics as his inventory of maladies expanded.

Sasha was further taxed by a project he took on for Rudolf Rocker translating Rocker's opus *Nationalism and Culture,* from the original German into English. "I have to work long and steady hours in order to get through in about eight months as promised," Sasha wrote to Pauline Turkel in May 1934.[6] He soon ran into trouble. "It is a difficult work, written in a heavy style," he told Emma. "It is too long. I have not as much energy for writing as I used to have. It tires me out."[7] By August, Sasha's energy was sapped, and although he still was physically active, he felt "a general lassitude" and was able to work only a few hours a day.[8] He nevertheless continued to pore over the immense book, preparing hundreds of pages of typescript and numerous penciled corrections. In November, six months after he began the project, he warned Rocker that the translation was going slowly, that because of "illness, Emmy's and my own," the work was delayed, and he had so far completed only half of what was promised.

Adding strain to the painstaking process, Sasha and Rudolf differed over the length and content. "The Work is entirely too big," Sasha advised Rocker. "It could amount to about 1,000 printed pages. No publisher could sell it for less than $5 a copy, more likely more. Who is going to buy a book these days at such a price? Hardly any workingman could afford to buy it." He also cautioned that the book was too abstract and inaccessible to the average reader.[9] Rocker disagreed, and was dissatisfied with Sasha's translation style overall. He eventually dispatched his wife, Milly, to cancel Berkman's contract.[10] Berkman was distraught and offered to return his fee so that the English translation might proceed. "The book is of such great value, and so vitally necessary particularly these days, that nothing must be permitted to stand in the way of its publication," he said.[11]

Sasha's friends carped privately about the clumsy turn of events, and thought it unnecessary that he refuse payment for his months of work. ("It is sheer nonsense for Sasha to return the money to Rocker," Modska complained to Emma. "He has no kick coming and no leg to stand on.")[12] Rocker found another translator, and the book was published in English; Sasha, initially mortified, later decided that his own version passed muster.[13] "A translation, in my estimation, must use judgment and also have some imagination—which of course I did—at least to my own satisfaction if not to Rudolf's!!"[14]

By the time Sasha ceased work on the Rocker manuscript, his health and mental state were worse than ever. Emmy was scarcely in better shape; she continued to be plagued by various illnesses, including attacks of stomach pain, and she periodically needed to travel to Paris for appointments with her doctors. Goldman had lately been abroad for extended stretches, and Sasha missed her company. He maintained contact with his friends—Max Metzkow, Claus Timmermann, and Carl Nold among them—but many comrades were aware of his low spirits, which by early 1935 were sinking noticeably. "I had a postcard from Sasha in Nice the other day," wrote Tom Bell to Joseph Ishill. "Rather melancholy, I think it. A lonely exile, I am afraid."[15]

In the course of her lifetime, Goldman had her own share of physical complaints; she had long been beleaguered by foot problems and, more recently, with varicose veins and a few minor ailments associated with age. But she was made of sturdier stuff than Sasha. While dining in a restaurant on August 11, 1931, she fell down a flight of stone steps, landed on her head, and came away with a gash on the forehead and extensive bruises, but no serious injuries. "As my friends always used to say," she told Agnes Inglis, " 'Emma is like a cat, throw her down from the highest point and she will land on her paws.' I assure you the end has no terror for me. I should dread however being crippled or incapacitated in my old age."[16] Goldman's leg problems abated in 1934 when an Italian anarchist shoemaker in New York fashioned her special footwear. Her gratitude when he presented the finished pair was overflowing—she put them on, cried with happiness, and kissed him with relief.[17]

While Emma's health was relatively stable as she aged, Berkman's continued to deteriorate, and by the fall of 1935 he was suffering with prostate disease. Stein, during his visit to France earlier that summer, noticed his cousin's developing condition, and after beseeching Sasha to have it checked out, cabled Emma to express his concern. Berkman was annoyed by the interference. "When [Modska] was in Nice he noticed [my urination] trouble and I told him about it," he explained to an anxious Goldman. "He thought it was a dangerous thing and insisted I should see a doctor. . . . But the matter is not very serious, so don't worry about it. Modska was a fool for cabling you about it."[18]

At last Berkman consulted a local physician, Dr. Rosanoff, who referred him to a urologist at the nearby St. Roche clinic. Berkman was not satisfied with the clinic, and moved to the Pasteur Hospital in Nice, where he was treated by well-regarded urological surgeon Dr. Adolphe Tourtou. On February 11, 1936, Berkman had his first operation for his prostate condition.

"Sasha is well, operation went OK," wrote Eckstein to Goldman, who now was in the middle of a five-month lecture tour in England, away from the medical crisis at home.[19] "He must stay in hospital for ten days and must get a truss for his rupture."[20]

Eckstein's affliction at this time also was worrying, and she underwent X-rays and a series of operations for her acute stomach trouble. Berkman told Goldman that, after Emmy's latest surgery, she was experiencing "a severe pressure of the stomach on the bowels, and pain and fainting spells, getting thin, suffers a great deal . . . Emmy's operation was very serious, the surgeon told her, part of her stomach will have to be removed. And the world goes on as crazy as ever, and worse, and now the clouds of war hang heavy upon us all."[21]

In March 1936 both Sasha and Emmy required additional surgery. Berkman worked to preserve his strength for his next procedure, eating "certain kinds of food, vegetables, and light things."[22] His second operation was scheduled for March 24, and he was feeling philosophical about life and death.

"Dearest Sailor Mine, staunchest chum of a lifetime," he wrote to Goldman, "In case anything happens, don't grieve too much, dearest. I have lived my life and I am really of the opinion that when one has neither health nor means and cannot work for his ideas, it is time to clear out. . . . But it is not of this I want to speak now. I just want you to know that my thoughts are with you, and I consider our life of work and comradeship and friendship, covering a period of about forty-five years, one of the most beautiful and rarest things in the world. In this spirit I greet you now, dear, immutable Sailor Girl, and may your work continue to bring light and understanding in this topsy-turvy world of ours. I embrace you with all my heart, you bravest, strongest, and truest woman and comrade I have known in my life."[23]

Berkman came through the operation but began a prolonged convalescence. In April, Goldman, back in France after the conclusion of her British tour, relocated temporarily to Nice so she could make daily trips to the hospital, and moved into Sasha and Emmy's apartment on the boulevard de Cessole.[24] "Our Emma has arrived, and we both are living in our little flat," Emmy wrote to a friend. "She visits Sasha every day. I bet you she will do her utmost to get Sashenka strong again as well as myself. You know by now what a wonderful cook she is!"[25]

Berkman remained in the hospital for several more months and went back to the flat in Nice still in considerable pain. "Am now home, with a drain in my abdomen," he told Stella in June. "During ten days I was in convalescence and kept shouting almost continuously. . . . I don't remember any previous occasion when I had yelled with pain but those ten days I certainly did, and it seemed that the whole ward, patients and visitors alike, were hushed in awe."[26] He resumed a deceptively upbeat correspondence with his friends, many of whom he had neglected during his hospital stay, and acknowledged to Fitzi that for too long he had willfully disregarded his symptoms. "I hate to bother the doctors," he admitted, "so I ignored the matter."[27]

Sasha now suspected cancer, although he told his intimates that his doctors had not made that diagnosis.[28] Weak and pensive, Sasha was able to muster some fond words for Fitzi. "Dearest old chum," he wrote, "I know what a beautiful and understanding spirit you are. Even at the risk of repetition, for I have said it so often before, I must permit myself the real joy of telling you again that you are one of the most beautiful and great women it has been my good fortune to know in life."[29] Sasha also received some unexpected pleasant news: his French residency had been renewed for a full year.

ON JUNE 27, 1936, EMMA CELEBRATED her sixty-seventh birthday at Bon Esprit. Michael Cohn and his family visited her at the cottage for the occasion, and she received greetings from many of her friends. But Sasha, along with Emmy, was too unwell to join in the festivities. He and Cohn together had been planning a surprise party for Emma, but now his surgical wound was inflamed, and he was confined to his bed.

Sasha wrote Emma to apologize ahead of time for his absence. "I'm sorry I can't come for it was all arranged and I meant this surprise for you," he said. "Well, such is life. The best laid plans often go awry as the old saying has it. . . . I embrace you heartily and hope that this birthday may bring you some joy and brighten the days that will follow."[30] On the morning of June 27 he sent her another letter. "Sorry I can't be with you," it read. "Both feeling somewhat better. Will call you up late in the day. I hope you have a nice day there. Affectionately, Sasha." That evening he telephoned her with his good wishes.[31]

By the early hours of the following day, Berkman's condition had taken a turn for the worse, and he was in great physical distress. The pain, his poverty, fear of illness, and his general misery apparently became too much for him, and he decided once and for all to end his life. He wrote a short farewell note: *"I do not want to live a sick man and dependent. Forgive me darling Emmy and you too Emma. Love to all. Help Emmy."* Then he took his pistol and tried to shoot himself in the heart. The bullet pierced a lung and lodged in his stomach. He was taken from his apartment in Nice to the St. Roche clinic, and an emergency operation was performed to extract the bullet.

Emma was summoned by Emmy immediately after the shooting, "torn out of sleep by the ringing of the telephone." She and Michael Cohn, who was staying at a hotel in St. Tropez, set off together before dawn, but "not until 5:30 Sunday could [they] get the bus to St. Raphael and then to Nice." They "found Emmy in an incoherent state," Emma later recounted to Stella Ballantine. "But we could get out of her that Sasha had had a violent attack, and while she was on the street trying to get a doctor Sasha had fired a bullet into his side. She found him in bed covered with a blanket. The doctor on arrival found the revolver on the floor. He notified the police and Sasha was taken to the hospital. There he was operated on but it was too late. The bullet had perforated the stomach and the lower part of his lungs. It landed in his spinal column and paralyzed his legs. When Michael and I arrived Sasha was conscious but in frightful agony."[32]

Sasha was in excruciating pain for hours. He was able to recognize Emma and Cohn, but could not speak.[33] Emma left his room at three in the afternoon, and when she returned at four, he was unconscious.[34] He never woke up. On the evening of June 28, with Emma at his bedside, he died. "I remained," she wrote to Modska, "alone with my precious until the last."[35]

THE NEWS SOON REACHED THEIR COMRADES. "Sasha, our teacher, our comrade, our best friend and brother, our dearest pal has disappeared. Is it possible that we will not hear from him any more?" wondered Mollie Steimer. "How did it happen that he left us just when we thought he was improving?"[36] "How can one know what goes on in the human mind," replied Emma. "He did what . . . he had tried several times to do while we were still in America."[37] Fitzi was "heartbroken."[38] Jeanne Levey was shocked. "Only yesterday, I received such a cheerful letter from him," she said to Emma. "I was so elated because I felt assured that he was on the road to recovery. . . . I am terribly unhappy about our great loss."[39]

"A rare person has left us," wrote Rudolf Rocker in a tribute, "a great and noble character, and a real man. We bow quietly before his grave and swear to work for the ideal which he served faithfully for so many years."[40] Minna Lowensohn was bereft, and Emma tried to soothe her. "My dear girl, your devotion to Sasha was very rare indeed. . . . You gave without asking anything in return. . . . Keep up the fight which is so necessary with the horrible flood of fascism coming from all sides."[41] Emma's erstwhile husband, James Colton, himself seriously ill, sent his sympathies. "To loose such a brave comrade as Alexander Berkman is a calamity and again [I] extend to you my deepest sympathy in your terrible predicament," he wrote, signing the letter "Yours in deepest sorrow, Jim."[42] Shortly after Colton died of cancer, on August 5, 1936.

Emma was charged with explaining Berkman's final deed, although to her his death "was a bolt from a clear sky." She told Max Nettlau that Sasha "had always maintained that if he ever would be stricken with suffering beyond his endurance, he will go out of life by his own hand."[43] "Sasha's fixation with revolvers dates back to the [1892] act," she said to Pauline Turkel. "I do not believe Sasha ever got over his failure to end Frick's life. Once more he drew a pistol, as he had done forty-four years before. This time he turned it on himself."[44] Many of Sasha's friends were well aware of his preoccupation with weapons and his hunger for a rebel's defiant demise. "He was fascinated by guns and always wanted to have them," said Ida Gershoy. "I think he felt guilty that he wasn't able to kill Frick. And when he committed suicide he was still a bad shot!"[45]

Some thought suicide a fitting end. "I believe [his death] was as brave as his life," said lawyer C. E. S. Wood, "and I have always felt with the old Romans that a man has a perfect right to make his own decision."[46] "No need to ask what made him do it," said Harry Kelly to Emma, "for it was not like Sasha to give up if there was any hope, but no doubt he felt it was the beginning of the end and it was foolish to suffer so he took the first train out."[47] Gaby Javsicas later observed that Sasha's operations had "transformed him from a powerful individual into a doddering old man," convinced "that there wasn't any sense in living any longer."[48]

Ammon Hennacy, whom Berkman had befriended in the Atlanta penitentiary in 1917, admired the example Sasha set both in prison and in life. "My memory of his time in solitary in Allegheny helped me to do my time in a courageous manner," said Hennacy. "He chose the hard life, and he chose the hard death. To me he is a friend, a comrade, a hero."[49] Tom Bell thought that Sasha, "lonely, condemned to inactivity, largely isolated from the anarchist movement, ill . . . showed himself once more a brave man by taking his own life." But Bell also remembered Berkman's gentleness. "As a man, as a personality, Sasha was a splendid fellow, the most beloved man in the movement," he wrote to a confidant. "My children will never forget him."[50]

"What a strange man!" exclaimed Roger Baldwin. "He, unlike Emma, was just full of despair. He never gave up completely his belief in violence, to which desperate men are prone. He took his own life, finally. While he held anarchist views and professed to be an idealist, and therefore an optimist, he really at heart had no faith in himself. That's why he had all those mistresses. He couldn't be faithful. He had a very disorderly life. But he was a very nice person. His *Prison Memoirs* showed the same contradictions as his life: compassion for his fellow inmates combined with fatalism and cynicism."[51]

EMMY ECKSTEIN WAS CRUSHED BY SASHA'S DEATH. Not only did she have to contend with her profound grief, but she also found herself in trouble with the law. Suspecting her of foul play, the police placed her under arrest for the crime of "shooting her husband," although they released her when the facts emerged. As Emma told Max Nettlau, "Fortunately a woman neighbor, Mme. Tournayre, had seen Emmy distractedly pacing up and down the sidewalk near their flat waiting for the doctor to come, and . . . testified that at that time she had heard a shot in M. Berkman's apartment, so that Emmy was not held as Sasha's murderer."[52] The official police report of July 3, 1936 read: "Shot self June 28, 1936. Suicide. Nationality Russian. Driven to his act by poor health, having undergone a serious operation without being cured."[53]

About seven months before his death, just after his sixty-fifth birthday, Sasha composed a handwritten will. He left all his money and personal effects "to my beloved companion Emmy Eckstein. And to my life-long friend and co-worker Emma Goldman Colton I leave whatever books she may want from my little library, as well as my unpublished sketches, stories, translations, manuscripts, and other similar documents, including my note books and diaries, as well as my correspondence. . . . P.S. In case of Emmy Eckstein's death, everything I own belongs to Emma Goldman Colton."[54]

Goldman tried to make certain that Emmy was well settled. She arranged for Eckstein to spend several months with her family in Brno, Czechoslovakia, and then helped her move to Paris. Emma contacted Michael Cohn for medical advice about Emmy's heath problems, and attempted to get her a visa so that she might travel to the United States for treatment. Supplementing financial support from Emmy's sister in Chicago, Goldman and Modska sent her a monthly allowance, and the treasury of the *Fraye Arbeter Shtime* contributed another ten dollars to the collection. Emmy also had a small salary from her job doing typing work for a local theater in Paris.

Yet Emmy's stomach trouble continued. She returned to Nice, and on February 1938 had an operation that, as she told Goldman, "took away a large piece of intestines and [appendix]."[55] She had another operation on December 18, 1938, and then a fifth in which her large intestine was removed. "I only know that the obsessed creature is being operated into the grave without having gained any relief," wrote Emma to Fitzi.[56] Gabriel Javsicas, too, cast a dubious eye on the medical diagnoses. "[Eckstein] found a quack in Nice who tried to cure her stomach trouble by shortening her intestine. Instead, he shortened her life."[57] On June 8, 1939, after a sixth operation, Eckstein died.[58] Goldman learned the news from Nellie Harris. "Poor Emmy's whole life consisted of deception and such self-centeredness as I have never met before," Emma said to Fitzi. "I hope she is at peace. She was the strangest critter I have ever met."[59]

BERKMAN'S PASSING WAS NOTED IN AMERICA. "Every time a bomb exploded he was suspected," said the *New York Times*.[60] *Time* magazine called Sasha and Emma "unwelcome world wanderers," writing that "Emma Goldman was fifty miles away in her villa at St. Tropez last week when, in his mean, fifth-floor flat in Nice, Alexander Berkman, obscure, outmoded, sixty-five, wracked by uremia and with only $80 to his name, once more drew a pistol, this time used it to kill himself."[61] When Ben Reitman received a cablegram from Emma informing him of Berkman's death, he contacted the Chicago papers with the news.[62]

Goldman handled the funeral arrangements, and Sasha was buried on June 30 in Nice. Sasha had always dreamed of being interred in the Waldheim Cemetery in Chicago, where the Haymarket anarchists rested, but Emma was unable to fulfill this desire. "I had planned to have Sasha cremated carrying out his lifelong wish," she told Stella, "and to send his ashes to Chicago to have him buried in Waldheim near the graves of the men who had given us spiritual birth. But it could not be done. A grave there was too expensive. We put Sasha in what they call in France a communal grave. Last Monday at eleven a few friends we had in this part of France went to the cemetery . . . and put our beloved to rest."[63]

Although Emma was unable to afford a private plot, she asked her comrade Nonore Teissier to order a simple tablet with a personalized inscription to be placed in the cemetery, and the stone was carved with the following words: "ALEXANDER BERKMAN, Born November 21, 1870, Laid to rest June 30, 1936. HIS DREAM WAS A NEW FREE AND BEAUTIFUL WORLD. HIS WHOLE LIFE A CEASELESS STRUGGLE. FOR THE ULTIMATE TRIUMPH OF HIS IDEAL." Goldman's St. Tropez neighbor, Robert Sandstrom, provided a French translation.[64]

"Sasha's end has been the most devastating blow life has dealt me," Emma said to Stella, and a month after his death she was still in turmoil.[65] "I am gritting my teeth and showing a bold front. But the nights with Sasha's vision ever before me, his life, his suffering, his last painful years. But I must, I must, I will be strong."[66] To her good friend, the writer John Cowper Powys, Emma said, "forty-seven years of ordinary lives make it hard to continue when one of the two departs. How much more painful is it to see ties broken of two lives like Berkman's and mine have been, lives of dreams, of ideals, of struggle, lives of friendship that have never wavered, that gave without stint and always understood? In the Romantic age poets sang of such friendship. In our own few can boast of it, nor does it enrich the lives of many."[67]

EMMA DECIDED TO SELL BON ESPRIT. "The place has lost its meaning to me now that Sasha is gone," she informed Max Nettlau. "I will sell it if I can. After that I will go to London."[68] Meanwhile, anarchists in America remembered Berkman's life at memorial meetings in Webster Hall in New York City on July 9; at the anarchist colony on Lake Mohegan on July 24; in Philadelphia on August 7; and in the Music-Arts Hall in Los Angeles on August 14.[69] Goldman released a general statement. "Let us gather strength to remain true to the flaming spirit of Alexander Berkman. Let us continue the struggle for a new and beautiful world. Let us work for the ultimate triumph of Anarchism—the ideal Sasha loved passionately and in which he believed with every fiber of his being. In this way alone can we honor the memory of one of the grandest and bravest comrades in our ranks."[70]

While Emma mourned the loss of Sasha, the Spanish Civil War broke out. "The one thing which has kept me from utter despair," she told a comrade, "is the marvelous courage and heroism of our comrades in Spain."[71] "Ah, if only Sasha had lived a little longer," she wrote to Gwyneth King Roe, the wife of her old friend and benefactor, the lawyer Gilbert Roe. "He would have been inspired to overcome his own great suffering so as to help our comrades with his pen. And he would have felt as I do now the deep urge to go to Spain and take our place in the very thicket of the fight. For what more glorious end for him and for me than that?"[72]

But she would have to carry on alone. During her American lecture tour, when a reporter asked about her connection to Sasha, she was absolute. "My friendship with Berkman," Emma said then, "is one which nothing but death can end."[73]

30

WALDHEIM

As Emma struggled to cope with Sasha's death, the opportunity to go to Spain presented itself. The Spanish Civil War had begun in mid-July, and many of her comrades were transfixed—the uprising initially seemed an opportunity for ideological revolution, as well as resistance against the fascist elements sweeping across Europe. On August 18, 1936, anarchist and journalist Augustin Souchy, who had fled Germany three years earlier, just days before the capture of his friend Erich Mühsam, invited Goldman to work with the foreign-language press office of the Confederación Nacional del Trabajo-Federación Anarquista Ibérica (CNT-FAI), the anarcho-syndicalist union that defied General Francisco Franco. Emma jumped at the chance. "I have been thinking day and night about going to Spain," Goldman replied to Souchy. "What do you and the comrades consider most important and where I can be of great help?"[1]

Goldman believed the new battle would lift her morale. "Spain is going to be my salvation for myself and from the utter futility of my life," she wrote to comrade Joe Desser in Toronto. "They have no one who knows English and could help them with the English *Bulletin,* papers, and radio talks." She would be able to travel the country and broadcast her firsthand observations to Great Britain, Canada, and America.[2] The CNT-FAI sent Goldman a credential that enabled her, as a certified representative, to approach Spanish labor organizations and liberal and radical groups. She soon received another credential for use in England, where, after her Spanish tour, she would continue the publicity campaign and raise money for the cause.

Soon Emma assured her friends she was feeling herself again. "You will be glad to know that the awful pall that hung over me since Sasha's untimely death has been broken," she told Arthur Leonard Ross. "It was due to the call I have received from my Spanish comrades to help them in their heroic struggle against the black forces in their own country as well as those outside."[3] She confided to Stella Ballantine, "I know that my life can still be useful and that it still has meaning and purpose."[4]

As Goldman prepared to leave St. Tropez in September 1936, she composed an open letter to her friends and associates, explaining her excitement over her new mission and its influence on her grieving process. "It came as a golden ray from a black sky," she wrote. "For the untimely death of my old chum and life-long comrade Alexander Berkman had well nigh broken my spirit. The more I tried to overcome the pain of his loss the worse it grew, the more paralyzing the blow his death dealt me.

"I can say with absolute truth that the call of anarchist comrades in Spain saved me from utter despair. It fairly electrified me. For what grander chance than to join whatever force still at my command, and whatever ability I still have to give with our people in Spain. Nothing more wonderful could have come to me in my hour of need. The first time in history our comrades while fighting back the enemies are yet doing constructive work. They are giving a shining example to the oppressed all over the world HOW REVOLUTION SHOULD BE MADE."[5]

Goldman left St. Tropez for Barcelona on September 15, 1936. She got to work at once, delivering her first radio address and giving a speech before an audience of 10,000. "I have come to you as to my own," she declared. "For your ideal has been my ideal for forty-five years and it will remain to my last breath." The thousands of eager Spanish workers who greeted her in Barcelona moved her with their enthusiasm and appreciation. "I cannot begin to tell you the feeling aroused in my old revolutionary heart by the marvelous events here," she wrote to Mark Mratchny on September 23. "At last, at last our comrades are trying to articulate our ideas. I am walking on air. I feel so inspired and so roused that I am fortunate enough to be here and to be able to render some service to our brave and beautiful comrades."[6]

Yet despite her ebullient words, Goldman had real doubts about the prospects for her Spanish anarchist comrades. They had plenty of spirit but were at the center of a complex and vicious tug-of-war. After giving another radio talk on September 24, she wrote to Fitzi of her concerns. "I confess I am not too optimistic about the outcome of the struggle," she said. "The odds against the CNT-FAI are too strong. They are not only from the Fascists but also from the Socialists and Communists. But our people in Catalonia are set on winning or going down. I hope fervently they may win. Their experiment is the first, grandest, and most inspiring in history because it is entirely an out and out Anarchist experience."[7]

Goldman toured peasant villages, factories, railroads, oil and gas works, and clothing workshops. She went to the Aragon front and to Madrid, continued to speak on the radio, and composed copy for the English *Bulletin*. She met with old friends and fellow revolutionaries, many of whom she had encountered on her first trip to Spain in 1928, among them Federica Montseny (now the minister of health and the first woman to serve in a Spanish cabinet); author and anarchist leader Diego de Santillán; and anarcho-syndicalist Arthur Lehning.[8] According to press reports, Goldman's journeys to the front were useful in "encouraging the government troops during her tour."[9]

At the Aragon front, Emma visited Spanish rebel Buenaventura Durruti's anarchist brigade. "I found Durruti an outstanding personality," she said, "perhaps the most outstanding I have met during my stay here. His people adore him. One can well understand it. He leads them by the charm of his personality, by his fraternal spirit of solidarity, and by his immense energy."[10] In November, Goldman was still in Spain when Durruti was killed, and she narrated a film about his epic memorial service in Barcelona.[11] Durruti became a legend among those who supported his cause, and, according to the Associated Press, "his funeral in Barcelona called forth one of the largest demonstrations since the outbreak of the war," with hundreds of thousands participating in the memorial procession.[12]

In December Goldman wrapped up her tour of Spain and, after a brief stop in Paris, went to London to set up CNT-FAI's press service and propaganda bureau. She submitted a steady stream of letters and editorials to newspapers around the world, and assured her readers that the goals of her Spanish brethren were honorable. "I have never justified the notion that wrong acts committed by one's own comrades should be ignored more than when committed by our opponents," she claimed. She said that she had made an impact in her limited time despite, or because of, her notoriety. "My name in Spain having opened all doors," she said, "continues to affect capitalist countries like a red cloth does a bull."[13]

But retreating to London bothered her. "It was very painful indeed to leave our brave comrades in danger knowing that I would be in safety in 'His Majesty's' country," she said. She wasn't even sure she would be able to adequately disseminate the message in England, a country she had never found particularly hospitable to her views. She observed that the holiday season also proved a barrier to gearing up her new project. "I arrived the 23rd December, rather an unfortunate time to begin a publicity campaign. If anything the English make more fuss about Christmas than people do in the States."[14]

In mid-January 1937, after several weeks of flurried activity, Emma was interviewed by the American press in her "small flat in West Kensington." A reporter noted the many dangers of her Spanish tour, which included "trips to places where shot and shell were flying." Emma explained that she had "found a cause worth living for—and worth dying for as well." She felt energized rather than frightened, elated that she was able to see real anarchism in action. "Myself, I'm not afraid to die," she said. "Not any more than those brave Spanish people are afraid to die for what they believe in. And what's glorious about Spain for me is seeing the very things I've worked for and believed in all my life. I'm seeing my ideas put into practice by a people who are building while they fight; doing something constructive while they keep the enemy back." The reporter noted that Goldman avoided the word "government," instead crediting the "people" for holding off Franco's army. "The Spaniards will never accept any form of dictatorship," Emma vowed. "Not after fighting the way they are for liberty."[15]

During her stay in Great Britain, Goldman helped organize exhibitions of Catalonian art and literature to be displayed in London and Paris. The shows consisted of photos, posters, and other printed propaganda, presented with an artistic flair. Emma arranged a large meeting on February 19, 1937, speaking alongside her friend the British activist and writer Ethel Mannin, and lectured around Great Britain, in southern Wales, Bristol, Glasgow, and Plymouth.

Goldman and her comrades took part in a sprawling 1937 May Day demonstration in London, waving signs; posters of the CNT-FAI; images of Francisco Ascaso, an anarcho-syndicalist who had been killed in Barcelona at the very start of the civil war; and photos of Buenaventura Durruti. They brought a wagon to Hyde Park, from which they made speeches, and 60,000 workers participated in the rally. "No one could have missed our banners and slogans," said Goldman proudly.[16]

Goldman continued her efforts for her Spanish comrades, sending packages and supplies to headquarters in Barcelona and penning editorials. "I have abiding faith in the resiliency of the Spanish people," she wrote in the *New York Times.* Still, she expressed her fears about global conflict and lamented the fate of her fellow revolutionaries. "The present reaction in Spain denotes the danger of dictatorship once more," she said. "But also it demonstrates that my comrades were babes in the political woods; that they naively underestimated the perfidy of their enemies."[17]

In August 1937 Emma went one last time to southern France. She traveled to Nice, where she visited Sasha's grave, and then made a farewell trip to Bon Esprit, which she arranged to sell to a Belgian family. Before she departed, she compiled eighteen boxes of Berkman's writings and material, to which she added two boxes of his work that she had taken from Nice. After another tour in Spain, she returned to her London base, and for the next ten months lectured across Great Britain, decrying fascism as Europe careened into world war and Franco's forces intensified their onslaught.

Around the time of the Anschluss in March 1938, when Austria was annexed to Germany, Emma began to consider moving permanently to Canada. As always, she longed for readmittance to America, but her friends' efforts to help her obtain another U.S. visa met with no success. During this period, Emma endured some more personal blows. Her faithful correspondent W. S. Van Valkenburgh died of a heart attack in May 1938, and Stella Ballantine was hospitalized after suffering an emotional breakdown from which her recovery would be arduous.

In September 1938 Goldman returned to Spain for six weeks, her final journey to the country. She reunited in Barcelona with Gabriel Javsicas, who was serving as an economic adviser to the CNT-FAI and writing about the war for *The Nation, Atlantic Monthly, Harper's,* and other magazines. In late December she went to Amsterdam to establish Berkman's papers, as well as her own, at the International Institute of Social History, an organization she admired and trusted. Her life and Berkman's, she told Teddy Ballantine, had "been so interwoven it is impossible to separate one from the other."[18]

A weary Goldman was back in London by January 20, 1939. She wrote to Max Nettlau about her "mental anguish" over the fall of Barcelona on January 26, and prepared to leave Europe, its atmosphere grim with the haze of war.[19] On April 1, 1939, shortly after Madrid and Valencia surrendered, General Franco declared victory, announcing that the Spanish Civil War had come to an end.

THE FOLLOWING WEEK, APRIL 8, 1939, Emma set sail for Canada. In Toronto she organized public meetings to raise funds for Spanish Civil War refugees and aligned with groups including the Solidarité Internationale Antifasciste. She settled into new quarters, a small apartment in a house owned by Dutch comrades Dien and Tom Meelis at 295 Vaughan Road. On May 19 she gave a lecture in Windsor, Ontario, a border city situated on the Detroit River. "The Spanish people are defeated but not conquered," she said. "In the end they will emerge triumphant. As long as one Spaniard has the revolutionary spirit, there is no security for Franco. Spain will be free." She was asked by reporters if she would try to enter the United States just across the river. "No," she replied. "I have not applied. . . . I doubt if they would let me in. But the United States is still my country, as much as an anarchist can have a country."[20]

Her proximity to America, though, made Emma as wistful as ever. Thwarted in her efforts to return home, she visited the Canadian border simply to stare across at the United States, weeping as she took in its silhouette. Italian anarchist Attilio Bortolotti, whom she had first met in Canada in 1934 when he joined the Libertarian Group, recalled driving her along the Detroit River and the international border. "She was enthralled just to be near the United States," Bortolotti said. "She looked at Detroit as though through the eyes of a lover. It was then that I understood how much America meant to her."[21]

On June 27, 1939, Emma celebrated her seventieth birthday in Toronto. She received calls, cables, and letters from all over the world, and a deluge of flower bouquets and gifts. "As you see," she wrote to her comrades in

America, "I am now very near to you in the United States, yet still very far away. Fortunately, there are no spiritual boundaries or [boundaries] to the all-embracing force of comradeship and solidarity. I, therefore, feel very close to all of you regardless of the arbitrary frontier divisions."[22]

That summer, Ben Reitman came to visit. Emma and Ben had fallen out of touch for several years, but he contacted her again in the spring of 1939, and she responded with a warm letter. Ben was grateful for her goodwill. "It's the letter I've been waiting for for years," he said. "To know that you feel kindly and somewhat appreciative of our work together and that you are sharing your troubles and your confidences . . . is all that I ever asked for." She assured him that despite the pain he had caused her, "I would not have missed knowing such an exotic and primitive creature as you."[23] In October 1939, several months after their reunion in Canada, Reitman suffered a mild stroke; he would die in 1942 of a heart attack at the age of sixty-three.

Also in October 1939, Emma launched a campaign for the legal defense of Bortolotti and three of his anarchist comrades. On October 4 police raided Bortolotti's home, arrested him and his housemates, and confiscated books, periodicals, pamphlets, and a large quantity of anarchist literature, including Kropotkin's *Memoirs of a Revolutionist* and *Modern Science and Anarchism,* Berkman's *ABC of Communist Anarchism,* and *Evolution and Revolution* by Elisée Reclus. Bortolotti's entire collection of 1,500 volumes, save for half a dozen pamphlets returned to him by a sympathetic Mountie, were destroyed.[24] Officers found a printing press, which the court claimed Bortolotti used to print and distribute subversive literature. The police also discovered two rusty revolvers, and Bortolotti was charged with being in possession of the weapons without a permit.

The men were brought to court on October 5 and were held without bail or counsel until October 12. Those who did not have Canadian citizenship were subject to deportation if convicted. With Bortolotti threatened with deportation to Italy, and certain death at the hands of Mussolini, Goldman entered the fray, securing prominent attorney J. L. Cohen and raising funds for the defense.[25] Emma focused her appeals for help on Bortolotti's case, since he was most at risk for deportation because of the charge of weapons possession, and because he had stepped up to assume most of the blame.[26]

Emma was determined to save her young friend. "Bortolotti," Goldman told a comrade, "is one of the biggest men we have in our movement, intellectually and morally, besides being a tremendous worker. . . . He lives for nothing else but for his ideal . . . [and] has carried on relentless anti-fascist work."[27] Her campaign was successful, and Bortolotti was set free; legal proceedings against all the men were dropped. Bortolotti later credited Goldman with doing "more than anyone else to prevent the deportation."[28]

As Ahrne Thorne recalled, "My wife Paula and I went to visit [the men] in jail. . . . We spoke to them through a barred window, with a guard listening to every word. In court they were found not guilty and were immediately released. Emma had worked hard to achieve that result. She made speeches, wrote letters, organized teas and gatherings to raise money."[29] The Bortolotti case would be Goldman's last battle against the state.

AT SEVENTY, EMMA'S MIND WAS AS SHARP as ever, and she retained much of her old spirit. But her energy was not what it had been, and she had bouts of melancholy. On December 31, 1939, she spent the evening with her core group of Toronto friends. "Dorothy Rogers was there, the Meelises, Bortolotti, and a few others," recalled Ahrne Thorne, who was also present. "[Emma] was again in a pessimistic mood. She reminisced about New Year's parties of the past, including one in Spain, when she was in the CNT headquarters and an air-raid alert was sounded. Everyone rushed downstairs to the shelter. But she refused to go. 'It was not heroism,' she told us. 'If a bomb hit me, I didn't care. I was ready to die.' Then she spoke about Alexander Berkman's death—the call she got from Emmy early in the morning to come at once, that a tragedy had happened."[30]

Six weeks later, on February 17, 1940, Emma suffered a stroke.[31] She collapsed in the Meelis home during a game of bridge with her hosts and a neighbor. "Emma had been active all day," Dien Meelis explained, "dictating letters in the afternoon, and after supper helping with the dishes. About eight o'clock she came downstairs and had been talking and laughing with us when suddenly, without a sound, she slumped down in her chair."[32] Dorothy Rogers summoned Attilio Bortolotti. "Come right away! Emma has had a stroke!" she told him. "I jumped in my car and raced over there," Bortolotti recalled. "I found [Emma] lying on the sofa. . . . She couldn't talk. But her eyes talked a lot, and her handshake was firm."[33]

"I had just come home from work," said Thorne, "when I got a call from Tilio Bortolotti that Emma had a stroke at the Meelises' home that paralyzed the right side of her body. 'Come as quickly as possible.' I grabbed a streetcar. When I got there, she was lying on a couch with her eyes closed. They had been playing bridge—Emma, the Meelises, and a neighbor. Suddenly they noticed that she was bending over on her side. They thought she had dropped a card. But she remained like that. She didn't get up. They saw that she was ill. When she didn't respond, they called an ambulance. The ambulance arrived shortly after I did. By then she was again conscious. As the attendants lifted her onto a stretcher, her dress rolled up over her knees, and with one hand she pulled it down to cover her exposed knees."[34]

Emma was in the Toronto General Hospital for six weeks. Her condition stabilized, but she remained unable to speak. Two weeks after the attack she showed slight progress. "She seems fully conscious now," Dien Meelis wrote to Leon Malmed, "understands what is said to her and recognizes those who go to see her, but she cannot speak. Besides being unable to speak, her right side is completely paralyzed."[35] Millie Grobstein, the daughter of Toronto comrades Joseph and Sophie Desser, had been doing secretarial work for Emma, and had spent the afternoon of February 17 taking dictation. After Goldman was hospitalized, Grobstein "went to visit her every day. Her speech was gone, yet her mental faculties were all there. . . . To see such a vital woman one minute, immobilized the next, was profoundly disturbing. . . . Yet she was still communicating."[36]

Ahrne Thorne also spent a good deal of time in the hospital with Goldman. "I visited her often and tried to cheer her up," he said. "She was fully conscious. She could hear and understand. But she couldn't talk. What worse punishment for Emma could there be? I thought. Speaking was her life. She was always talking. But there she lay, unable to utter a word. She never recovered the power of speech."[37]

Eventually Goldman was able to read again. In New York a Friends of Emma Goldman Committee was established by Stella Ballantine—now recovered from her two-year struggle with depression—to raise funds for Goldman's treatment; members included John Hayes Holmes, Roger Baldwin, Eleanor Fitzgerald, and Modest Stein.[38] On April 1, stabilized but still without speech, Emma was discharged from the hospital and sent home to her apartment, under the care of her physicians and nurses.

"The hospital could do nothing more for her, so . . . she returned to her apartment in the Meelises' place," Thorne recalled. "I suggested to Tom Meelis getting a set of movable letters for Emma to enable her to form words. They got it but she refused to use it. And she couldn't write because her right hand was paralyzed from the stroke. She wanted to die. After Spain and the outbreak of the [Second World] war she had grown increasingly pessimistic. She had said that if the First World War had been 'a war to end all wars,' this was a war to end the world."[39]

Emma showed some signs of improvement, but then grew weaker toward the end of April. On May 6 she suffered a second stroke. Relatives, including Stella Ballantine and Goldman's brother Morris, hurried to Toronto to see her one last time. On May 14 she died.

"SHE HAD LOST HER WILL TO LIVE," said Thorne. "I saw her the day before she died. She was a pitiful sight, speechless and forlorn. It was a tragic end."[40] In her obituary, the *New York Times* described her as "an incorrigible revolutionist to the end. . . . In the social history of the United States she wrote a chapter all her own." The *Times* called her a "writer of distinction and an able critic of the drama" and noted her passion for America, evident during her tour in 1934. At that time, "She did not conceal her happiness at having been permitted to return to this country, if only for a brief span. She was warmly received here by old friends and left with deep regret and some hope that she might yet be permitted to return to the United States permanently."[41]

A service was held in Toronto in the Labor Lyceum on Spadina Avenue. But Emma's remains were not buried in Canada. Instead, the U.S. government granted her final wish, and she was at last allowed to come home to America. Her body was brought by train to Chicago, where a number of her friends, including Ben Reitman and Harry Weinberger, gathered to meet it. "Emma came back to America today in a baggage car," said Reitman bitterly. "She gave 50 years of her precious life trying to make America a better place to live in and to stop wars. And the only way she could get back to America was in a steel casket."[42] Years later Arthur Leonard Ross made a similar point. "She loved America deeply, in spite of what it did to her. She could talk and breathe relatively freely here. Yet the only way she could return permanently was in a coffin."[43]

On the afternoon of May 17, Emma was interred in the Waldheim Cemetery, the resting place of the Haymarket anarchists.[44] Comrades collected at her gravesite to make speeches and pay her tribute, and Modest Stein created a likeness for the bronze plaque at her monument.[45] Modska was still a successful artist, drawing magazine covers and painting portraits. He spent a few years in Hollywood as a graphic artist, then moved back to New York. He died in Flushing, Queens, in February 1958 at the age of eighty-seven, two days after winning a prize for his artwork. The *New York Times* obituary described him simply as an "old-time pen-and-ink newspaper artist" who, as a young man, had done courtroom sketches for papers in the city.[46]

"So Emma finally got back to America," Ahrne Thorne said. "She had loved America. She considered it her country. She had been born there spiritually and intellectually. The greatest moments of her life had been spent there. Outside America she felt without a home. How she wanted to return! She always blamed J. Edgar Hoover for keeping her out. He had won his spurs in her deportation case, she said. And now he was blocking her from coming home."[47]

Despite her exile, many of her comrades believed Emma's influence knew no borders. "She opened your mind and made you think about things you never thought about before," Freda Diamond said. "That was her outstanding characteristic. *She made people think!*"[48]

On May 31, 1940, a memorial was held at New York's Town Hall on 123 West 43d Street. Speakers included many of Goldman's faithful associates, such as Rudolf Rocker, Leonard Abbott, Roger Baldwin, and Harry Kelly. Pictures of Goldman in Spain and Canada were displayed, alongside photographs of her burial site in the Waldheim Cemetery. Harry Weinberger addressed the assembled crowd.

"For more than thirty years I have known Emma Goldman, as her lawyer and her friend," said Weinberger. "Never in all those thirty years have I known her except as a battler for freedom and justice. She was tireless; she was fearless; she never compromised. Liberty was always her theme; liberty was always her dream; liberty was always her goal. . . . Emma Goldman is gone, gone to a dreamless sleep, gone to join that army of men and women of the past to whom liberty was more important than life itself.

Emma Goldman in her lifetime had been ostracized, jailed, mobbed, and deported from these shores for advocating that which all the world now admits should be brought about—a world without war, a world without poverty, a world with hope and the brotherhood of man.

"Emma Goldman, we welcome you back to America, where you wanted to end your days with friends and comrades. We had hoped to welcome you back in life—but we welcome you back in death. You will live forever in the hearts of your friends, and the story of your life will live as long as the stories are told of women and men of courage and idealism."[49]

SASHA AND EMMA WERE SEPARATED IN DEATH, he buried in southern France, she in America. But their friendship endures in their writing and in their legacy. In the letter Emma composed on the occasion of Sasha's sixty-fifth birthday, she reminded him of their everlasting bond. "It is fitting that I should tell you the secret of my life," she said. "It is that the one treasure I have rescued from my long and bitter struggle is my friendship for you. Believe it or not dear Sasha. But I know of no other value whether in people or achievements than your presence in my life and the love and affection you have roused.

"True, I loved other men. But it is not an exaggeration when I say that no one ever was so rooted in my being, so ingrained in every fiber as you have been and are to this day. Men have come and gone in my long life. But you my dearest will remain for ever. I do not know why this should be so. Our common struggle and all it has brought us in travail and disappointments hardly explains what I feel for you. Indeed, I know that the only loss that would matter would be to lose you, or our friendship."[50]

Sasha was moved. "Of all the letters I received yours is the most beautiful," he said. "Naturally so, everything considered."[51]

NOTES

ACKNOWLEDGMENTS

INDEX

Notes

Prologue

1. Alexander Berkman, *Prison Memoirs of an Anarchist* (New York: Mother Earth Publishing, 1912), 59.

2. Alexander Berkman to Ben Capes, April 25, 1927, Berkman Archive, International Institute of Social History, Amsterdam; Paul Avrich, *Anarchist Portraits* (Princeton: Princeton University Press, 1988), 200.

3. Berkman, *Prison Memoirs*, 59.

4. Mollie Steimer, "Alexander Berkman—The Unforgettable Friend and Comrade," *Fraye Arbeter Shtime*, 1966.

5. Henry Alsberg, "Alexander Berkman's Sixtieth Birthday Celebration," Central Opera House, New York City, pamphlet (New York: n.p., November 20, 1930), Joseph A. Labadie Collection, Harlan Hatcher Library, University of Michigan.

6. Emma Goldman, *Living My Life* (New York: A. A. Knopf, 1931), 986.

7. Voltairine de Cleyre, *In Defense of Emma Goldmann* [sic] *and the Right of Expropriation* (Philadelphia: The Author, 1894).

1. Mother Russia

1. Lithuania became a part of the Russian Empire in the eighteenth century. Some sources erroneously give Berkman's birthplace as Kovno, Lithuania's second-largest city, to which his family moved when he was twelve. Berkman himself clarified the point: "I know that some writers have written that I was born in Kovno. That is not correct. . . . I was born in Vilna, then belonging to Russia." Alexander Berkman to Zalman Reisen, February 1931, Berkman Archive, International Institute of Social History, Amsterdam.

2. Alexander Berkman, *Prison Memoirs of an Anarchist* (New York: Mother Earth Publishing, 1912), 13.

3. Howard M. Sachar, *A History of the Jews in the Modern World* (New York: Vintage Books, 2006), 183.

4. Ibid. As a result, the percentage of Jewish students in Vilnius more than tripled during the 1860s and 1870s, and the percentage of Jews in Russian universities more than doubled.

5. Louis Greenberg, *The Jews in Russia: The Struggle for Emancipation* (New Haven: Yale University Press, 1944), 73.

6. Emma Goldman, "A Sketch of Alexander Berkman," Alexander Berkman, *The Russian Tragedy (A Review and An Outlook)* (Berlin: Der Syndikalist, 1922).

7. Vladimir Weidle, *Russia: Absent and Present* (New York: Vintage Books, 1961), 88; David Footman, *The Russian Revolutions* (London: Faber and Faber, 1962), 19.

8. Alexander Berkman, *An Enemy of Society*, Autobiography outline, unpublished, Berkman Archive.

9. Stephen M. Berk, *Year of Crisis, Year of Hope: Russian Jewry and the Pogroms of 1881–1882* (Westport: Connecticut Press, 1985); I. Michael Aronson, *Troubled Waters: The Origins of the 1881 Anti-Jewish Pogroms in Russia* (Pittsburgh: University of Pittsburgh Press, 1990); John D. Klier and Shlomo Lambroza, *Pogroms: Anti-Jewish Violence in Modern Russian History* (New York: Cambridge University Press, 1992); Michael T. Florinsky, *Russian History and Interpretation* (New York: Macmillan, 1953).

10. Berkman, *Prison Memoirs,* 14.

11. Alexander Berkman, "Looking Backward and Forward," *Mother Earth,* December 1912; Alexander Berkman, *The Russian Tragedy,* comp. William G. Nowlin Jr. (Sanday, Orkney Islands, Scotland: Cienfuegos Press, 1976).

12. Alexander Berkman to Hudson Hawley, June 12, 1932, Berkman Archive; Vera Figner, "Mark Andreevich Natanson," *Katorga i Ssylka* (Hard Labor and Exile), no. 56 (1929), 142.

13. Berkman to Hudson Hawley, June 12, 1932, Berkman Archive; Emma Goldman, *Living My Life* (New York: A. A. Knopf, 1931), 28–29.

14. Berkman, *An Enemy of Society,* Autobiography outline; Berkman, *Prison Memoirs,* 104, 205, 239.

15. Nikolai Chernyshevsky, *What Is to Be Done?,* trans. Benjamin R. Tucker (Boston: B. R. Tucker, 1886).

16. Berkman, *Prison Memoirs,* 73–74.

17. Gene Sharp and Marina Finkelstein, *The Politics of Nonviolent Action* (Berkeley: University of California Press, 1973), 368; Franco Venturi, *Roots of Revolution: A History of the Populist and Socialist Movements in Nineteenth-Century Russia* (London: Weidenfeld and Nicolson, 1960), 69–70.

18. Alexander Berkman, "Looking Backward and Forward."

19. *Worcester Daily Telegram* (Massachusetts), July 27, 1892; *New York World,* July 29, 1892.

20. Berkman, *Prison Memoirs,* 14–16. A classmate of Berkman's, later living in New York, recalled him as "an avowed disbeliever in God." *The World,* July 29, 1892.

21. *The World,* July 29, 1892.

22. Berkman to Emma Goldman, November 23, 1931, Goldman Archive, International Institute of Social History, Amsterdam.

23. Emma Goldman, Introduction to Berkman, *The Russian Tragedy* (Berlin: Der Syndikalist, 1922).

24. Emma Goldman, *Living My Life,* 11.

25. Ibid., 23.

26. Ibid., 28.

27. Ibid., 11.

28. Ibid.

29. Floyd Dell, *Women as World Builders: Studies in Modern Feminism* (Chicago: Forbes, 1913), 55–56; Margaret S. Marsh, *Anarchist Women, 1870–1920* (Philadelphia: Temple University Press, 1981).

30. Goldman, *Living My Life,* 20.

31. Ibid., 25.

32. Berkman to Hudson Hawley, June 12, 1932, Berkman Archive.

33. Berkman, *An Enemy of Society,* Autobiography outline.

34. Berkman, *Prison Memoirs,* 20, 56.

35. Quotas prevented many Jews from attending schools in Russia; those who could afford it went abroad for their education. Maxim would later transfer to Kazan University in Russia. Sonya finished the gymnasium at the top of her class, but because she was Jewish was denied a gold medal at graduation and received the silver instead.

36. Berkman, *An Enemy of Society,* Autobiography outline.

37. "Russians to America Passenger Data File, 1834–1897," U.S. National Archives. Also see Ira A. Glazier, ed., *Migration from the Russian Empire: Lists of Passengers Arriving at the Port of New York* (Baltimore: Genealogical Publication, 1995).

38. Berkman to Hudson Hawley, June 12, 1932, Berkman Archive.

2. Pioneers of Liberty

1. Alexander Berkman, *Prison Memoirs of an Anarchist* (New York: Mother Earth Publishing, 1912), 206.

2. Alexander Berkman to Milly Rocker, March 22, 1929, Berkman Archive, International Institute of Social History, Amsterdam; Richard Drinnon and Anna Maria Drinnon, eds., *Nowhere at Home: Letters from Exile of Emma Goldman and Alexander Berkman* (New York: Schocken Books, 1975), xxvi; *New York World,* July 25, 1892.

3. Berkman, *Prison Memoirs,* 20, 206; Berkman to Milly Rocker, March 22, 1929, Berkman Archive.

4. Berkman, *Prison Memoirs,* 206.

5. Ibid.

6. Seven police officers died soon after the event; the eighth police officer died two years later, apparently as a result of his injuries.

7. A ninth anarchist, Rudolph Schnaubelt, was indicted but fled to Argentina; his absence prompted some to peg him as the bomb thrower. Schnaubelt was Michael

Schwab's brother-in-law. A likelier suspect was anarchist George Schwab (no relation to Michael Schwab). Some in the anarchist community claimed Schwab had escaped Chicago after the riot, fled to California, and later admitted his guilt privately to several comrades.

8. Paul Avrich, *The Haymarket Tragedy* (Princeton: Princeton University Press, 1984), xi.

9. Berkman, *Prison Memoirs,* 56; Paul Avrich, *Sacco and Vanzetti: The Anarchist Background* (Princeton: Princeton University Press, 1991), 46.

10. Emma Goldman, *Living My Life* (New York: A. A. Knopf, 1931), 9–10.

11. Frank Harris, *Contemporary Portraits* (New York: Brentano's, 1923), 224.

12. Alexander Berkman, *What Is Anarchism?* (Oakland, Calif.: AK Press, 2003), 50–51; Berkman, *Now and After: The ABC of Communism and Anarchism* (New York: Vanguard Press, 1929), 60.

13. Alexander Berkman, "The Causes of the Chicago Martyrdom," *Mother Earth,* November 1912; Berkman to Hudson Hawley, June 12, 1932, Berkman Archive.

14. Albert Fried, *Socialism in America: From the Shakers to the Third International* (Garden City, N.Y.: Doubleday, 1970), 237.

15. Berkman, *Prison Memoirs,* 67.

16. Alexander Berkman, *The Bolshevik Myth* (New York: Boni and Liveright, 1925), 72–73.

17. Berkman to Dear Comrade, December 6, 1933, Berkman Archive; Goldman, *Living My Life,* 5–6.

18. Emma Goldman to Augustin Harmon, June 25, 1897, Harmon Archive, International Institute of Social History, Amsterdam; Berkman to Zalman Reisen, February 1931, Berkman Archive; Mollie Steimer to Ahrne Thorne, October 18, 1979, Paul Avrich Collection, Library of Congress.

19. Stanley Nadel, *Little Germany: Ethnicity, Religion, and Class in New York City, 1845–80* (Urbana: University of Illinois Press, 1990).

20. Israel Kopeloff, *Amol in Amerike* (Warsaw: Ch. Brzoza, 1928), 113–114; Elias Tcherikower, *The Early Jewish Labor Movement in the United States* (New York: YIVO, 1961), 220–221.

21. Berkman, *Prison Memoirs,* 79.

22. Modest's last name was often spelled Aronstamm, especially in German sources, and his uncle Elias, a New York pharmacist, used the double *m.*

23. Paul Avrich interview with Luba Stein Benenson, New York City, December 4, 1973.

24. *New York World,* July 25, 1892; *The World,* July 25, 1892.

25. Berkman, *Prison Memoirs,* 207; Fritz Fuhse, quoted in *Pittsburgh Commercial Gazette,* July 25, 1892.

3. The Trio

1. Alexander Berkman, *Prison Memoirs of an Anarchist* (New York: Mother Earth Publishing, 1912), 236.

2. Ibid.

3. Emma Goldman, *Living My Life* (New York: A. A. Knopf, 1931), 5–6; Berkman, *Prison Memoirs,* 235–237.

4. Goldman, *Living My Life,* 6.

5. Emma Goldman, *Anarchism and Other Essays* (New York: Mother Earth Publishing, 1911), 41.

6. Goldman, *Living My Life,* 36.

7. Ibid., 26–30, 55.

8. Alexander Berkman, February 1931, Berkman Archive, International Institute of Social History, Amsterdam; Goldman, *Living My Life,* 55.

9. Emma Goldman to Morris Finestone, July 30, 1939, Goldman Archive, International Institute of Social History, Amsterdam; Goldman, *Living My Life,* 3.

10. Goldman, *Living My Life,* 43; Richard Drinnon, *Rebel in Paradise: A Biography of Emma Goldman* (Chicago: University of Chicago Press, 1961), 41; Alix Kates Shulman, ed., *Red Emma Speaks: An Emma Goldman Reader* (New York: Schocken Books, 1983), 71–72.

11. Goldman, *Living My Life,* 26, 36, 46; Berkman, *Prison Memoirs,* 83.

12. Goldman, *Living My Life,* 44.

13. Ibid.

14. Goldman, *Living My Life,* 32, 44–45; Paul Avrich interview with Luba Stein Benenson, New York City, December 4, 1973.

15. Goldman, *Living My Life,* 31–32, 44–45; Berkman, *Prison Memoirs,* 72–73.

16. Goldman to Michael Cohn, August 12, 1931, Goldman Archive. The anarchist journalist Hutchins Hapgood stated that Berkman belonged to "that very rare species of human being, a genuine fanatic!" Hutchins Hapgood, *A Victorian in the Modern World* (New York: Harcourt, Brace and Co., 1939), 204.

17. Berkman, *Prison Memoirs,* 9–10.

18. Nikolai G. Chernyshevsky, *What Is to Be Done?* (Ann Arbor: Ardis, 1986); Berkman, *Prison Memoirs,* 7–8.

19. *Freiheit,* September 18, 1880, and March 18, 1883. Nechaev's *Catechism,* excerpts from which were published in Most's *Freiheit,* laid down all the qualities to be expected of a radical conspirator. "The revolutionary is a doomed man," the *Catechism* began. "He has no personal interests, no affairs, no sentiments, attachments, property, not even a name of his own. Everything in him is absorbed by one exclusive interest, one thought, one passion—the revolution. . . . Day and night he must have one thought, one aim—inexorable destruction."

20. Berkman, *Prison Memoirs,* 73. Berkman later discovered his uncle's dislike of Nechaev.

21. *Fraye Arbeter Shtime,* October 30, 1891; *Solidarity,* November 5, 1892; Berkman to Goldman, February 5, 1933, Goldman Archive; Berkman, *Prison Memoirs,* 8–9.

22. Goldman to Thelma Koldofsky, February 1, 1936, Nettlau Archive, International Institute of Social History, Amsterdam; Goldman, *Living My Life,* 76.

23. Miriam Michelson, "A Character Study of Emma Goldman," *Philadelphia North American,* April 11, 1901; Paul Avrich interview with Kate Wolfson, New York City, October 16, 1972.

24. Goldman, *Living My Life,* 56.

25. Ibid., 31.

26. Paul Avrich interview with Luba Stein Benenson.

27. Goldman, *Living My Life,* 48, 61.

28. Berkman, *Prison Memoirs,* 415; Goldman, *Living My Life,* 62.

29. *The Famous Speeches of the Eight Chicago Anarchists in Court* (Chicago: Lucy E. Parsons, 1910), 35–36. Also reissued as *Famous Speeches of the Eight Chicago Anarchists in Court* (New York: Arno Press, 1969).

30. Paul Avrich, *The Haymarket Tragedy* (Princeton: Princeton University Press, 1984), 159.

31. Goldman, *Living My Life,* 42.

32. Goldman, "On the Road," *Mother Earth,* May 1907, 3.

33. Berkman, *Prison Memoirs,* 73.

34. Goldman, *Living My Life,* 38.

35. Ibid., 31, 40.

36. Richard Drinnon and Anna Maria Drinnon, eds., *Nowhere at Home: Letters from Exile of Emma Goldman and Alexander Berkman* (New York: Schocken Books, 1975), 100.

37. Paul Avrich, *Anarchist Voices: An Oral History of Anarchism in America* (Princeton: Princeton University Press, 1995), 46.

38. Frank Harris, *Contemporary Portraits* (New York: Brentano's, 1923), 223.

39. *Baltimore Critic,* October 25, 1890, Paul Avrich Collection.

40. Melech Epstein, *Jewish Labor in U.S.A.: An Industrial, Political and Cultural History of the Jewish Labor Movement* (New York: Ktav Publishing House, 1969), 119.

41. *Free Society,* January 24, 1904.

42. Paul Avrich interview with Johann Most Jr., Boston, October 28, 1979.

43. Goldman, *Living My Life,* 35, 54.

44. George Kennan, "The Latest Siberian Tragedy," *Century Magazine,* April 1890, 246–253. An explorer and war correspondent, Kennan was a distant cousin of George F. Kennan, the diplomat and historian.

45. Goldman, *Living My Life,* 70. Berkman and Aronstam had trouble raising funds for the trip. Requests to borrow money were refused, including by Modska's uncle Elias, who worked as a pharmacist at 1904 Third Avenue. *New York World,* July 25 and 27, 1892.

46. *New York World,* July 25, 1892.

47. Berkman, *Prison Memoirs,* 202.

48. *Pittsburgh Commercial Gazette,* July 25, 1892.

49. Goldman, *Living My Life,* 71. The dress shop was modeled after one started by the character Vera Pavlovna in Chernyshevsky's *What Is to Be Done?*

50. Goldman, *Living My Life,* 173.

51. Berkman, *Prison Memoirs,* 203. Both plays were performed in New Haven in 1891, *Tosca* on February 5–14 and *Fédora* on March 2–4.

52. *New York World,* July 27, 1892. A. Cohen, "Di almone fun Barrintes Johann Most," *Forverts,* August 27, 1932. Most's first wife, Clara, had died in 1882.

53. Paul Avrich interview with Johann Most Jr.

54. Berkman, *Prison Memoirs,* 101.

4. Autonomists

1. Emma Goldman, *Living My Life* (New York: A. A. Knopf, 1931), 75.

2. *New York World,* July 28, 1892.

3. Goldman, *Living My Life,* 75; Rudolf Rocker, *Johann Most: The Life of a Rebel* (Berlin: Verlag Syndikalist, F. Kater, 1924), 250–292.

4. Neve was a carpenter from Holstein and a popular member of the movement. In February 1887, while smuggling literature and arms into Germany from a town on the Belgian frontier, he was detained and handed over to the German police. In October 1887 Neve was sentenced to fifteen years behind bars and was locked up in a prison at Halle. The following year he was transferred to Moabit prison in Berlin. Neve would never leave Moabit; he died of tuberculosis in 1896. *Freiheit,* December 31, 1896; Heiner Becker, "Johann Neve (1844–1896)," *The Raven,* August 1987, 99–114; Heiner Becker, "Johann Most in Europe," *The Raven,* March 1988, 291–321.

5. *Anarchist,* January 10, April 1, 1886.

6. *Der Anarchist,* February 1, 1890.

7. Ibid., August 1, 1889.

8. Alexander Berkman, *Prison Memoirs of an Anarchist* (New York: Mother Earth Publishing, 1912), 83.

9. *New York World,* July 28, 1892.

10. Peukert transformed *Der Anarchist* from a fortnightly into a weekly and resumed publication in September 1891. No editor's name, however, was listed in the paper, not only to keep such information from the police but because of the Autonomist rejection of designated leaders. All told, there were to be five Autonomist periodicals in the United States, three of which were edited by Timmermann: *Anarchist,* Chicago, 1886, edited by George Engel and Adolph Fischer; *Der Anarchist,* St. Louis, then New York, 1889–1895, edited first by Claus Timmermann, then by Joseph Peukert; *Die Brandfackel,* New York, 1893–1894, edited by Claus Timmermann; *Der Kampfer,* St. Louis, 1896, edited by Otto Rinke; and *Sturmvogel,* New York, 1897–1899, edited by Claus Timmermann.

11. Goldman, *Living My Life,* 86.

12. Paul Avrich interview with Luba Stein Benenson, New York City, December 4, 1973.

13. Paul Avrich interview with Johann Most Jr., Boston, October 28, 1979.

14. Emma Goldman, "Johann Most," *American Mercury,* June 1926, 158–166.

15. Alexander Berkman, "Kropotkin," *Freedom,* March 1922; Berkman, *The Bolshevik Myth* (New York: Boni and Liveright, 1925), 72–73; Berkman, "Some Reminiscences of Kropotkin," Berkman Archive, International Institute of Social History, Amsterdam.

16. Goldman, *Living My Life,* 81.

17. *Worcester Daily Telegram,* July 27, 1892.

18. Goldman, *Living My Life,* 81, 431.

19. *Worcester Evening Gazette,* July 27, 1892.
20. Ibid.; Goldman, *Living My Life,* 82.
21. *Worcester Evening Gazette,* July 27, 1892.
22. Goldman, *Living My Life,* 84–85.
23. Berkman, *Prison Memoirs,* 477.

5. Homestead

1. George Brinton McClellan Harvey, *Henry Clay Frick, the Man* (New York: C. Scribner Sons, 1928), 151.

2. Andrew Carnegie, *The Gospel of Wealth and Other Timely Essays* (New York: Century, 1901), 115.

3. Leon Wolff, *Lockout: The Story of the Homestead Strike of 1892* (New York: Harper and Row, 1965), 81.

4. Harvey O'Connor, *Steel Dictator* (New York: John Day, 1935), 93.

5. *Report of Mr. Gallinger, from the Select Committee to Investigate and Report to the Senate the Facts in Relation to the Employment for Private Purposes of Armed Bodies of Men, or Detectives, in Connection with Differences between Workmen and Employers,* U.S. Senate (Washington, D.C.: Government Printing Office, 1893). The Secret Service agent was Robert Bruce.

6. Harvey, *Henry Clay Frick, the Man*, 114.

7. Arthur G. Burgoyne, *The Homestead Strike of 1892* (Pittsburgh: University of Pittsburgh Press, 1979), 54.

8. Ibid., 92.

9. "A Bloody Flight: Strikers and Pinkertons Do Battle at Homestead, Sixteen Men are Killed," *Pittsburgh Commercial Gazette*, July 7, 1892.

10. "Quiet Day at Homestead," *New York Times,* July 8, 1892.

11. "A Truce, but under Arms," *New York Times,* July 8, 1892.

12. William W. Delaney, "Father Was Killed by the Pinkerton Men," *Violations of Free Speech and Rights of Labor*, U.S. Congress (Washington, D.C.: Government Printing Office, 1939), 14.

13. *New York World*, July 19, 1892.

14. "Carnegie's Regret," *St. Louis Post-Dispatch*, August 1892.

15. Harvey, *Henry Clay Frick, the Man*, 166.

16. Jeremy Brecher, *Strike!* (Cambridge, Mass.: South End Press, 1997), 76.

17. *Topeka Advocate*, July 1892.

18. "Both Sides Are Defiant: Homestead Still Held in a State of Siege," *New York Times,* July 9, 1892.

19. Frick telegram to Carnegie, November 21, 1892; Carnegie telegram to Frick, November 22, 1892, Henry Clay Frick Foundation Archives, New York City.

20. Emma Goldman, *Living My Life* (New York: A. A. Knopf, 1931), 85.

21. Alexander Berkman, *Prison Memoirs of an Anarchist* (New York: Mother Earth Publishing, 1912), 4; Goldman, *Living My Life,* 85–86.

22. Berkman, *Prison Memoirs,* 2.

23. Goldman, *Living My Life,* 87; Berkman, *Prison Memoirs,* 10. Attentat, from the French, for murder attempt, attack.

24. Goldman, *Living My Life,* 87–88.

25. Berkman, *Prison Memoirs,* 7.

26. Ibid., 55.

27. Goldman, *Living My Life,* 88.

28. Ibid., 84–90; Richard Drinnon, *Rebel in Paradise: A Biography of Emma Goldman* (Chicago: University of Chicago Press, 1961), 44.

29. Modest Stein to Alexander Berkman, December 23, 1931, Berkman Archive, International Institute of Social History, Amsterdam; Berkman, *Prison Memoirs,* 123.

30. Paul Avrich interviews with Attilio Bortolotti, Toronto, Ontario, November 29, 1972, North Miami Beach, Florida, December 10, 1988 and January 19, 1990. Shortly before his departure, Berkman sent an article to *Der Anarchist* titled "The Tragedy at Homestead." It was published, coincidentally, on the day he shot Frick. Homestead, wrote Berkman, marked the birth of a new era in the history of American labor. "The tragedy at Homestead will serve as the beginning of a crusade by the anarchists to enlighten the works and sow the seeds of freedom." Alexander Berkman, "The Tragedy at Homestead," *Der Anarchist,* July 23, 1892.

6. Attentat

1. Alexander Berkman, *Prison Memoirs of an Anarchist* (New York: Mother Earth Publishing, 1912), 10.

2. A copy of the leaflet is preserved in the Joseph A. Labadie Collection, Joseph A. Labadie Collection, Harlan Hatcher Library, University of Michigan.

3. *Der Anarchist,* July 16, 1892; *Freiheit,* July 16 and July 23, 1892; Henry Bauer, "A Fateful Leaflet," April 17, 1892. Also in Miriam Brody and Bonnie Buettner, eds., *Prison Blossoms: Anarchist Voices from the American Past* (Cambridge, Mass.: The Belknap Press of Harvard University Press, 2011), 10.

4. "A Friend of Herr Most," *New York Times,* July 26, 1892.

5. *Pittsburgh Chronicle and Telegraph,* July 25 and 26, 1892.

6. Berkman, *Prison Memoirs,* 180.

7. Johann Most to Carl Nold, July 15, 1892, Labadie Collection.

8. "Caging the Plotters," *Trenton Times,* July 27, 1892.

9. Berkman, *Prison Memoirs,* 180.

10. Ibid., 23.

11. Emma Goldman, *Living My Life* (New York: A. A. Knopf, 1931), 91.

12. Ibid., 93.

13. Ibid., 93–94; Richard Drinnon, *Rebel in Paradise: A Biography of Emma Goldman* (Chicago: University of Chicago Press, 1961), 44–45.

14. "The Assault on Mr. Frick," *Harper's Weekly,* August 6, 1892.

15. As *Harper's Weekly* reported, "The aim had been for the brain, but the sudden turning of the chairman spoiled it, and the bullet ploughed its way into the left side of his neck." "The Assault on Mr. Frick," *Harper's Weekly*, August 6, 1892.

16. "Chairman Frick Shot: Desperate Crime of a Russian Anarchist," *New York Times*, July 24, 1892; "The Assault on Mr. Frick," *Harper's Weekly*, August 6, 1892; Berkman, *Prison Memoirs*, 34.

17. "Shot Down: An Anarchist Attempts the Life of Manager Frick," *Jackson Sentinel* (Maquoketa, Iowa), July 28, 1892; "Chairman Frick Shot: Desperate Crime of a Russian Anarchist," *New York Times*, July 24, 1892.

18. *Pittsburgh Chronicle and Telegraph*, July 25, 1892; *Pittsburgh Commercial Gazette*, July 25, 1892; *Pittsburgh Post*, July 25, 1892; *Pittsburgh Press*, July 24 and 25, 1892; *New York Herald Tribune*, July 7, 1938.

19. Berkman, *Prison Memoirs*, 35.

20. "Shot Down: An Anarchist Attempts the Life of Manager Frick," *Jackson Sentinel*, July 28, 1892.

21. "Frick Shot Down," *Hamilton Daily Democrat*, July 25, 1892; *Iowa State Reporter*, July 28, 1892; "Shot Down: An Anarchist Attempts the Life of Manager Frick," *Jackson Sentinel*, July 28, 1892; "Chairman Frick Shot: Desperate Crime of a Russian Anarchist," *New York Times*, July 24, 1892; Berkman, *Prison Memoirs*, 35.

22. Berkman, *Prison Memoirs*, 33–35; *New York Sun*, July 24, 1892; *Pittsburgh Press*, July 25, 1892; "Frick Shot Down," *Hamilton Daily Democrat*, July 25, 1892.

23. Press accounts list the doctors present as Litchfield, McClelland, Murphy, Joseph, and Dickson.

24. Frick was given sedatives once the bullets were removed and his wounds dressed. "Shot Down: An Anarchist Attempts the Life of Manager Frick," *Jackson Sentinel*, July 28, 1892.

25. "Frick Will Live," *The World*, July 25, 1892.

26. "Frick's Condition Continues to Improve," *Alton Daily Telegraph*, July 28, 1892.

27. "Shot Down: An Anarchist Attempts the Life of Manager Frick," *Jackson Sentinel*, July 28, 1892. An additional serious cut to Frick's leg, just below the calf, was discovered on Sunday, the day after the attack.

28. "Mr. Frick Nearly Well," *Boston Daily Globe*, July 29, 1892.

29. "Chairman Frick Shot: Desperate Crime of a Russian Anarchist," *New York Times*, July 24, 1892.

30. "The Shooting of Frick," *The Reading Eagle* (Reading, Pa.), July 24, 1892.

31. Berkman, *Prison Memoirs*, 41.

32. "Frick Shot Down," *Hamilton Daily Democrat*, July 25, 1892; Shot Down: An Anarchist Attempts the Life of Manager Frick," *Jackson Sentinel*, July 28, 1892; Berkman, *Prison Memoirs*, 69.

33. "Frick Will Live," *The World*, July 25, 1892; "Frick Shot Down," *Hamilton Daily Democrat*, July 25, 1892; *Iowa State Reporter*, July 28, 1892; "Shot Down: An Anarchist Attempts the Life of Manager Frick," *Jackson Sentinel*, July 28, 1892; "Chairman Frick

Shot: Desperate Crime of a Russian Anarchist," *New York Times,* July 24, 1892; *New York Sun,* July 24, 1892.

34. "Frick Shot Down," *Hamilton Daily Democrat,* July 25, 1892; *Iowa State Reporter,* July 28, 1892; "Shot Down: An Anarchist Attempts the Life of Manager Frick," *Jackson Sentinel,* July 28, 1892; "Chairman Frick Shot: Desperate Crime of a Russian Anarchist," *New York Times,* July 24, 1892.

35. "Berkman Unconcerned," *The Trenton Times* (Trenton, N.J.), July 25, 1892.

36. "Shot Down: An Anarchist Attempts the Life of Manager Frick," *Jackson Sentinel,* July 28, 1892; "Frick Shot Down," *Hamilton Daily Democrat,* July 25, 1892; *Iowa State Reporter,* July 28, 1892; "Chairman Frick Shot: Desperate Crime of a Russian Anarchist," *New York Times,* July 24, 1892; *New York Sun,* July 24, 1892.

37. *Boston Daily Globe*, July 26, 1892. Berkman's name was frequently misspelled in press accounts as Bergman, Bergmann, Burkman, and variations thereof.

38. "Bergman [*sic*] Makes Threats," *Cedar Rapids Evening Gazette* (Cedar Rapids, Iowa), September 9, 1892; "Anarchist Bergman Says He Will Not Stand More Than a Ten Years Sentence," *The Bradford Era* (Bradford, Pa.), September 10, 1892.

39. "Bergman [*sic*] Makes Threats," *Cedar Rapids Evening Gazette,* (Cedar Rapids, Iowa), September 9, 1892.

40. Paul Avrich interview with Luba Stein Benenson, New York City, December 4, 1973.

41. Paul Avrich interviews with members of the Stein family, New York City, December 4, 1973 and March 22, 1990.

42. Berkman, *Prison Memoirs,* 58; Goldman, *Living My Life,* 87.

43. Goldman later claimed that Harry Gordon visited Berkman only in 1901, not in 1892.

44. Berkman, *Prison Memoirs,* 51.

45. Ibid., 54. Berkman refers to Clifford as "Jack Tinford."

46. Ibid., 59.

47. "H. C. Frick Shot and Seriously Wounded at His Office in Pittsburgh," *Newcastle News,* July 27, 1892.

48. "Anarchy's Aim: A Foul Attempt to Assassinate Chairman Frick," *Salem Daily News* (Salem, Ohio), July 25, 1892.

49. "Drummed Out of Camp: The Punishment of a Soldier Who Cheered for Mr. Frick's Assassin," *New York Times,* July 25, 1892.

50. "A Guardsman's Treason," *Pittsburgh Commercial Gazette,* July 25, 1892. Iams also had "half the hair on his head and mustache" shaved off. "H.C. Frick Shot: A Cowardly Anarchist Attacks the Millionaire," *Indiana County Gazette* (Indiana, Pa.), July 27, 1892.

51. Berkman, *Prison Memoirs,* 60.

52. "The Shooting of Frick," *New York World,* July 24, 1892.

53. "H. C. Frick Shot and Seriously Wounded at His Office in Pittsburgh," *Newcastle News,* July 27, 1892.

54. "Anarchists Mild as Lambs," *New York Times,* August 23, 1893.

55. "H. C. Frick Shot and Seriously Wounded at His Office in Pittsburgh," *Newcastle News,* July 27, 1892.

56. "Labor and Anarchy," *New York Times,* July 25, 1892.

57. "Frick Will Live," *The World,* July 25, 1892.

58. Ibid.

59. "Chairman Frick Shot: Desperate Crime of a Russian Anarchist," *New York Times,* July 24, 1892.

60. Edward W. Bemis, "The Homestead Strike," *Journal of Political Economy,* June 1894, 369–396.

61. John Bernard Hogg, *The Homestead Strike of 1892* (Chicago: University of Chicago, 1943).

62. Berkman, *Prison Memoirs,* 66.

63. Miriam Brody and Bonnie Buettner, eds., *Prison Blossoms: Anarchist Voices from the American Past* (Cambridge, Mass.: The Belknap Press of Harvard University Press, 2011), 80.

64. Berkman, *Prison Memoirs,* 68.

65. Alexander Berkman to Emma Goldman, October 19, 1892, quoted in Berkman, *Prison Memoirs,* 136.

7. Judgment

1. *Pittsburgh Chronicle Telegraph,* July 25, 1892.

2. "A Friend of Herr Most," *New York Times,* July 26, 1892.

3. *Pittsburgh Chronicle Telegraph,* July 26, 1892; *Pittsburgh Post,* July 27, 1892; *New York World,* July 26, 1892.

4. Paul Eckert worked hard on behalf of Berkman, Bauer, and Nold, raising money for their bail and defense. Of Bauer and Nold, he said, "They are Anarchists, it is true, but that is not a crime. We will not see them suffer." "Berkman Held for Trial," *New York Times,* July 30, 1892.

5. *Worcester Daily Spy,* July 28, 1892; *New York World,* July 29, 1892; *Freedom,* September 1892.

6. *Pittsburgh Post,* July 27, 1892.

7. Alexander Berkman, *Prison Memoirs of an Anarchist* (New York: Mother Earth Publishing, 1912), 69. Mollock was released in August, although he was found with the shipping receipt and two letters, apparently from Berkman, which bore the Allegheny City postmark.

8. *Pittsburgh Post,* July 27, 1892.

9. *Pittsburgh Commercial Gazette,* July 25, 1892; *Worcester Daily Telegram,* July 27, 1892.

10. *New York World,* July 29, 1892.

11. "Emma Goldman's Statements," *Middletown Daily Press,* July 27, 1892.

12. "Frick Will Live," *The World,* July 25, 1892.

13. Emma Goldman, *Living My Life* (New York: A. A. Knopf, 1931), 97, 135.

14. *Pittsburgh Commercial Gazette,* July 25, 1892; *Worcester Daily Telegram,* July 27, 1892; *New York World,* July 29, 1892; Goldman, *Living My Life,* 99–102.

15. Modest Stein to Emma Goldman, September 20, 1929, Berkman Archive, International Institute of Social History, Amsterdam.

16. Goldman, *Living My Life,* 114.

17. *Pittsburgh Commercial Gazette,* July 25, 1892; *Worcester Daily Telegram,* July 27, 1892; *New York World,* July 29, 1892.

18. "Emma Goldman's Statements," *Middletown Daily Press,* July 27, 1892.

19. *New York World,* July 28, 1892.

20. Joseph J. Cohen, *The Jewish Anarchist Movement in the United States: A Historical Review and Personal Reminiscences* (Philadelphia: Radical Library Branch 273, 1945), 194.

21. *Volks-Zeitung,* July 24, 1892.

22. *Der Anarchist,* August 1892.

23. Peukert interview, *Harper's Weekly,* August 20, 1892.

24. "Wild Anarchist Talk: Berkmann [*sic*] Praised at Public Meeting of the Reds," *New York Times,* August 2, 1892.

25. Ibid.

26. Ibid.

27. Robert Reitzel, *Der arme Teufel,* 1892.

28. Lucy Parsons, *Freedom,* September 1892.

29. Paul Avrich Notes, Paul Avrich Collection, Library of Congress.

30. "Save Labor from Its Friends," *Liberty,* July 30, 1892.

31. Goldman, *Living My Life,* 97.

32. *New York World,* July 27, 1892.

33. Ibid.

34. Goldman, *Living My Life,* 98; "Das Untier seinen Kadaver schon wieder herumschleppen kenne," *Freiheit,* July 30 and August 6, 1892.

35. Johann Most, "Attentats-Reflexionen," *Freiheit,* August 27, 1892. See also his "Zur Propaganda der That," *Freiheit,* September 17, 1892; Rudolf Rocker, *Johann Most: The Life of a Rebel* (Berlin: Verlag Syndikalist, F. Kater, 1924), 356–357.

36. Berkman, *Prison Memoirs,* 79, 85, 101.

37. Goldman, *Living My Life,* 105.

38. Johann Most, April 23, 1892, quoted by Heiner Becker in *Haymarket Scrapbook,* (Chicago: Charles H. Kerr Publishing Company, 1986), 139.

39. Johann Most, *Freiheit,* June 1892.

40. Paul Avrich Notes, Paul Avrich Collection.

41. *Der Anarchist,* July 30, 1892.

42. "Struck by Emma Goldman: John Most Made Fun of Her and She Resented It," *New York Times,* December 20, 1892.

43. Goldman, *Living My Life,* 105–106.

44. "Struck by Emma Goldman: John Most Made Fun of Her and She Resented It," *New York Times,* December 20, 1892. According to Isidore Rudash (Rudashevsky), who

attended the meeting, Goldman lashed Most with a toy whip, not a horsewhip as she later claimed.

45. *Die Autonomie,* September 24, 1892; *Solidarity,* October 8, 1892.

46. Berkman, *Prison Memoirs,* 61, 91.

47. Ibid., 87.

48. Ibid., 77.

49. Arthur G. Burgoyne, *The Homestead Strike of 1892* (Pittsburgh: University of Pittsburgh Press, 1979), 159.

50. "Sent to Prison," *Daily Journal* (Logansport, Ind.), September 20, 1892.

51. Berkman, *Prison Memoirs,* 89. According to anarchism expert Agnes Inglis, Berkman's comrade Max Metzkow attended at least part of the trial. Paul Avrich Notes, Paul Avrich Collection.

52. *Hamilton Daily Democrat,* September 20, 1892.

53. Berkman, *Prison Memoirs,* 91.

54. "Will Wear Stripes," *Logansport Daily Reporter* (Logansport, Ind.), September 20, 1892.

55. "Sent to Prison," *Daily Journal,* September 20, 1892.

56. Berkman, *Prison Memoirs,* 91–92.

57. "Berkman, the Anarchist, Tried and Sentenced," *Reno Evening Gazette,* September 19, 1892; *Janesville Gazette,* September 20, 1892; *Oxford Mirror,* September 22, 1892; Berkman, *Prison Memoirs,* 97.

58. Berkman, *Prison Memoirs,* 107–108.

59. Goldman, *Living My Life,* 107.

60. *The Word,* January 1893; *Solidarity,* October 8, 1892.

61. "A Fool for A Client," *The Courier* (Connellsville, Pa.), September 23, 1892.

62. *The Word,* January 1893; *Oxford Mirror,* September 22, 1892.

8. Buried Alive

1. Alexander Berkman, *Prison Memoirs of an Anarchist* (New York: Mother Earth Publishing, 1912), 110, 138, 141. Berkman's prison records are no longer available, probably having been destroyed in a flood in 1936. Kostas F. Mastros, Data Supervisor, State Correctional Institution in Pittsburgh, to Paul Avrich, February 13, 1974, Paul Avrich Collection, Library of Congress.

2. Berkman, *Prison Memoirs,* 129–134, 153.

3. Ibid., 104.

4. Emma Goldman to Max Metzkow, October 8, 1892, Joseph Ishill Collection, Houghton Library, Harvard University.

5. Emma Goldman, *Living My Life* (New York: A. A. Knopf, 1931), 111.

6. Alexander Berkman to Goldman, November 30, 1892 printed in Berkman, *Prison Memoirs,* 150–151.

7. Emma Goldman, "Une Entrevue avec Berkmann," *La Revolte,* December 24–30, 1892.

8. The bomb exploded on November 2, 1892. Emile Henry later threw a bomb into the Café Terminus in Paris. Henry, who gave an impassioned speech to the jury, was found guilty and sentenced to death in Paris on April 28, 1894. "Henry Sentenced to Death: He Heard the Judgment with a Cry of Defiance," *New York Times,* April 29, 1894.

9. Emma Goldman, "Une Entrevue avec Berkmann," *La Revolte,* December 24–30, 1892.

10. Voltairine de Cleyre to Berkman, July 10, 1906, Berkman Archive.

11. Court documents from the trials of Henry Bauer and Carl Nold, Joseph A. Labadie Collection, Harlan Hatcher Library, University of Michigan.

12. *Tyrone Daily Herald,* February 10, 1893.

13. "Guilty as Charged: Anarchists Accessories to Frick's Attempted Murder Will Go to Jail," *Daily Citizen* (Iowa City), February 13, 1893.

14. Johann Most, *Freiheit,* February 18, 1893.

15. Berkman to Goldman and Modest Aronstam, March 4, 1893, Berkman Archive.

16. Berkman spells Frank Shea's name "Shay" in *Prison Memoirs*, 284.

17. Berkman, *Prison Memoirs,* 284.

18. According to Milligan's obituary, he was present at "the battles of Spottsylvania, the Wilderness, Cold Harbor, Appomattox and the siege of Petersburg, and many other minor engagements. At the battle of Gettysburg he was a member of the army sanitary commission." Milligan died in 1909 at his sister's home in Newport, Pennsylvania. *Pittsburgh Gazette Times,* July 13, 1909.

19. Miriam Brody and Bonnie Buettner, eds., *Prison Blossoms: Anarchist Voices from the American Past* (Cambridge, Mass.: The Belknap Press of Harvard University Press, 2011), 113.

20. Harry Elmer Barnes, "Progress of American Penology as Exemplified by the Experience of the State of Pennsylvania 1830–1920," *Journal of the American Institute of Criminal Law and Criminology,* May 1922–February 1923.

21. Charles William Dahlinger, *Western Pennsylvania Historical Magazine,* Historical Society of Western Pennsylvania, vol. 3, January 1920.

22. Chaplain's Report," *Biennial Report of the Inspectors of the State Penitentiary for the Western District of Pennsylvania* (Pittsburgh: A.A. Anderson & Son, 1895–1896), 107.

23. "Chaplain's Report," *Biennial Report of the Inspectors of the State Penitentiary for the Western District of Pennsylvania* (Pittsburgh: A.A. Anderson & Son, 1897–1898), 92.

24. Berkman, *Prison Memoirs,* 117–118, 463.

25. Ibid., 221.

26. Ibid., 229.

27. Ibid., 234.

28. Goldman to Augustin Hamon, December 17, 1896, Augustin Hamon Archive, International Institute of Social History, Amsterdam.

29. Berkman, *Prison Memoirs,* 166.

30. Paul Avrich Notes, Paul Avrich Collection.

31. Ibid., 172, 234.

32. Ibid., 425; Brody and Buettner, eds., *Prison Blossoms,* 166.

33. Berkman, *Prison Memoirs,* 440.

34. Ibid., 321–322, 433–434.

35. Ibid., 219.

36. Ibid., 342.

37. Ibid., 299, 328, 342.

38. Ibid., 325, 361–363.

39. Paul Avrich interview with Freda Diamond, New York City, May 13, 1983. The killer of Dick was alternately named as the warden.

40. Berkman to Goldman, April 12, 1896, quoted in *Prison Memoirs,* 297–298.

41. Berkman, *Prison Memoirs,* 350.

42. Emma Goldman, *Voltairine De Cleyre* (Berkeley Heights, N.J.: Oriole Press, 1932).

43. "Alexander Berkman's First Speech after His Release from Jail," *The Demonstrator,* June 6, 1906.

44. Berkman to Goldman, November 18, 1892, quoted in *Prison Memoirs,* 148–149.

9. Blackwell's and Brady

1. Emma Goldman, *Living My Life* (New York: A. A. Knopf, 1931), 115–116.

2. Ibid., 115.

3. Ibid., 118–119.

4. Ibid., 104.

5. Ibid., 122–123.

6. *Lowell Daily Sun,* August 19, 1893; *Marion Daily Star,* August 21, 1893; *Lowell Daily Sun,* August 22, 1893.

7. "Anarchy's Dingy Stronghold," *New York Times,* August 22, 1893.

8. "Emma Goldman Held without Bail," *New York Times,* September 2, 1893.

9. "Anarchy Feared by the Police Officials of New York City," *Ohio Democrat,* August 24, 1893.

10. Nellie Bly interview with Emma Goldman, *New York World,* September 17, 1893.

11. Goldman, *Living My Life,* 127.

12. "Emma Goldman on Trial," *Olean Democrat* (Olean, N.Y.), October 6, 1893.

13. *People of New York v. Emma Goldman,* 28, 31, 29 (Court of General Sessions of the Peace, City and County of New York), October 4, 1893.

14. "One Year for Emma Goldman: The Anarchist Receives Her Sentence with Smiles," *New York Times,* October 17, 1893.

15. Emma Goldman, "My Year in Stripes," *New York World,* August 18, 1894.

16. Ibid.

17. Goldman, *Living My Life,* 137.

18. Paul Avrich interviews with members of the Stein family, New York City, December 4, 1973 and March 22, 1990.

19. Goldman, *Living My Life,* 140.

20. Ibid., 142.

21. "Still an Anarchist, But—Red Flame Is Only a Glow When Emma Goldman Returns at 68 [*sic*]," *Burlington Daily Times-News,* February 9, 1934.

22. *New York World,* August 20, 1894.

23. Goldman, "My Year in Stripes," *New York World,* August 18, 1894.

24. "Howls For Emma Goldman: Thalia Theatre Filled with Enthusiastic Anarchists," *New York Times,* August 20, 1894.

25. Goldman, *Living My Life,* 156.

26. Ibid., 183.

27. Paul Avrich interviews with members of the Stein family, New York City, December 4, 1973 and March 22, 1990.

28. Ibid.

29. Goldman, *Living My Life,* 156.

30. Paul Avrich interview with Ida Gershoy, New York City, June 8, 1983.

31. Goldman, *Living My Life,* 162.

32. James Tochatti, *Liberty,* August 1895.

33. Goldman, *Living My Life,* 168–169.

34. Emma Goldman, "Political Justice in England and America," September 13, 1895. See Candace Falk, ed., *Emma Goldman: A Documentary History of the American Years, Vol. 1: Made for America* (Berkeley: University of California Press, 2003), 223.

35. Goldman, *Living My Life,* 170, 173.

36. Candace Falk, ed., *Emma Goldman: A Documentary History of the American Years,* 237.

37. Emma Goldman to Augustin Hamon, April 25, 1896, and April 13, 1897, Augustin Hamon Archive, International Institute of Social History, Amsterdam.

38. Goldman, *Living My Life,* 174.

10. The Tunnel

1. In addition to the Berkman Defense Committee, a number of similar groups sprang up to raise money for Sasha's support and legal needs, including the Berkman Rescue Fund and the Berkman Defense Association.

2. Alexander Berkman, *Prison Memoirs of an Anarchist* (New York: Mother Earth Publishing, 1912), 288–290.

3. Emma Goldman, *Living My Life* (New York: A. A. Knopf, 1931), 186.

4. Ibid., 183.

5. Paul Avrich, *The Modern School Movement: Anarchism and Education in the United States* (Princeton: Princeton University Press, 1980); "Joy at the Death of Canovas," *New York Times,* August 17, 1897. Kelly's full name was Henry May Kelly.

6. Emma Goldman to Max Metzkow, December 2, 1896, Goldman Archive, International Institute of Social History, Amsterdam.

7. Stuart B. Kaufman, Peter J. Albert, eds., *The Samuel Gompers Papers* (Urbana: University of Illinois Press, 1986), 209.

8. Roger N. Baldwin, ed., *Kropotkin's Revolutionary Pamphlets: A Collection of Writings by Peter Kropotkin* (New York: Dover Publications, 1970), 25–26.

9. Berkman, *Prison Memoirs,* 111, 115–116.

10. Ibid., 332–333.

11. Ibid., 356, 334.

12. Ibid., 357–358.

13. G. L. Doebler indentifies "Tony" as Charles Snyder, imprisoned in 1894 for sodomy. " 'Tony' Revealed," *Fifth Estate,* Spring 2008, 26.

14. Berkman, *Prison Memoirs,* 372; Goldman, *Living My Life,* 246; Gary Doebler, "Berkman's Tunnel to Freedom," *The Fifth Estate,* Spring 1992.

15. Alexander Berkman to Goldman, February 17, 1929, Goldman Archive.

16. Goldman, *Living My Life,* 245–246, 268.

17. Berkman, *Prison Memoirs,* 379; Goldman, *Living My Life,* 249, 268; Goldman to Berkman, November 23, 1928, Goldman Archive; Richard Drinnon and Anna Maria Drinnon, eds., *Nowhere at Home: Letters from Exile of Emma Goldman and Alexander Berkman* (New York: Schocken Books, 1975), 96.

18. Goldman, *Living My Life,* 247–248, 367. Berkman ultimately planned to go to Russia if the escape attempt was successful.

19. Thomas Brown was also said to be a solicitor. "Regardless of Cost," *Logansport Pharos,* July 27, 1900.

20. *Pittsburgh Press,* August 7, 1983; *Biennial Report of the Inspectors of the State Penitentiary for the Western District of Pennsylvania* (Pittsburgh: A.A. Anderson & Son, 1899–1900), 10–11.

21. Goldman, *Living My Life,* 276.

22. Ibid., 275.

23. "Regardless of Cost: Friends of a Prisoner in the Allegheny Prison Work for His Release," *Logansport Pharos,* July 27, 1900.

24. Goldman, *Living My Life,* 275–276; *Pittsburgh Press,* August 7, 1983; *Fraye Arbeter Shtime,* December 5, 1897; *Pittsburgh Post-Gazette,* January 20, 1997.

25. "Regardless of Cost," *Logansport Pharos,* July 27, 1900.

26. Berkman, *Prison Memoirs,* 372, 380; Goldman, *Living My Life,* 276–277.

27. Berkman, *Prison Memoirs,* 380.

28. Ibid., 382; *Pittsburgh Press,* August 7, 1983.

29. "Regardless of Cost," *Logansport Pharos,* July 27, 1900.

30. Ibid.

31. Berkman, *Prison Memoirs,* 384–385; *Pittsburgh Press,* August 7, 1983; *Biennial Report of the Inspectors of the State Penitentiary for the Western District of Pennsylvania* (Pittsburgh: A.A. Anderson & Son, 1899–1900), 10–11. The mystery remained unsolved until 1912, when Berkman revealed the truth in *Prison Memoirs of an Anarchist.*

32. Berkman, *Prison Memoirs,* 381, 390.

33. Ibid., 405–408.

34. Berkman to Goldman, July 10, 1901, quoted in *Prison Memoirs,* 409–410; Goldman, *Living My Life,* 292.

35. *Fraye Arbeter Shtime,* July 28 and August 4, 1901.

36. Kate Austin, letter to *Boston Traveler,* August 23, 1901.

37. Berkman to Goldman, July 25, 1901, quoted in Berkman, *Prison Memoirs,* 410; *Fraye Arbeter Shtime,* January 10, 1904.

38. Berkman to Max Metzkow, October 19 and December 3, 1930, Joseph Ishill Collection, Houghton Library, Harvard University.

39. Berkman to Goldman, December 20, 1901, quoted in Berkman, *Prison Memoirs,* 412.

40. *Biennial Report of the Inspectors of the State Penitentiary for the Western District of Pennsylvania* (Pittsburgh: A.A. Anderson & Son, 1899–1900), 10–11; Berkman, *Prison Memoirs,* 412.

41. Emma Goldman, "Light and Shadows in the Life of an Avant-Guard," *Mother Earth,* April 1910.

11. Red Emma

1. *Solidarity,* July 15, 1898; Paul Avrich interview with Freda Diamond, New York City, May 13, 1983.

2. *Cleveland Plain Dealer,* May 6, 1901.

3. Rudolf Rocker to Richard Drinnon, August 29, 1954, Rocker Archive, International Institute of Social History, Amsterdam.

4. Paul Avrich interview with Ahrne Thorne, Bronx, N.Y., October 2, 1979.

5. Paul Avrich interview with Attilio Bortolotti, Toronto, Ont., November 29, 1972; Miami Beach, December 10, 1988, and January 19, 1990.

6. *Chicago Tribune,* November 12, 1897.

7. *San Francisco Call,* April 27, 1898. The writer concluded: "And you should hear her talk! You can better afford to miss hearing Melba or even Bernhardt than listening to this genuine creature."

8. Paul Avrich interview with Millie Grobstein, Brooklyn, N.Y., April 20, 1975.

9. Emma Goldman, *Living My Life* (New York: A. A. Knopf, 1931), 225.

10. *Lucifer,* October 13, 1897; Paul Avrich, *Anarchist Voices: An Oral History of Anarchism in America* (Princeton: Princeton University Press, 1995), 24, 483. Pope, seventy-four, served three months in prison, while Isaak and Addis were released on appeal.

11. Paul Avrich, *The Modern School Movement: Anarchism and Education in the United States* (Princeton: Princeton University Press, 1980), 195. *The Firebrand* editors Henry Addis and Abner J. Pope moved to the Home Colony after their arrest.

12. *Discontent,* June 8, 1898.

13. Goldman, *Living My Life,* 245; *Discontent,* June 7 and 14, 1899; Charles Pierre Le Warne, *Utopias on Puget Sound, 1885–1915* (Seattle: University of Washington Press, 1975), 411.

14. Goldman, *Living My Life,* 230.

15. *Solidarity,* March 15, 1898.

16. Emma Goldman, "A Short Account of My Late Tour," *Free Society,* July 31, 1898, 2.

17. Frank Harris, *Contemporary Portraits* (New York: Brentano's, 1923), 223–224.

18. Goldman, *Living My Life,* 160.

19. Emma Goldman, "Marriage," *The Firebrand,* July 18, 1897.

20. *New York World,* September 17, 1893.

21. Goldman, *Living My Life,* 225; Emma Goldman, "Anarchism and the Sex Question," *The Anarchist* (London), September 27 and October 4, 1896.

22. Emma Goldman, "Reise-Briefe," *Sturmvogel,* January 15, 1898; Goldman, *Living My Life,* 196–197.

23. Goldman, *Living My Life,* 287.

24. Ibid.

25. *Solidarity,* December 31, 1892; *Freedom,* September 1893. The Chicago World's Fair was officially known as the World's Fair: Columbian Exposition.

26. *Freedom,* January–February 1894; *Fraye Arbeter Shtime,* November 13, 1904.

27. Fritz Oerter, "Zur Frauenfrage," *Der Pionier,* 1912, no. 2; Oerter, "Die freie Liebe" and "Der freie Arbeiter," ibid., no. 9, 1912; Oerter, *Nacktheit und Anarchismus* (Berlin: Verlag Freier Arbeiter); Oerter, *Was wollen die Syndikalistn?* (Berlin: Der Syndikalist, 1920); Goldman, *Living My Life,* 565; Richard Drinnon and Anna Maria Drinnon, eds., *Nowhere at Home: Letters from Exile of Emma Goldman and Alexander Berkman* (New York: Schocken Books, 1975), 145–146; Alexander Berkman, *Prison Memoirs of an Anarchist* (New York: Mother Earth Publishing, 1912), 139.

28. Josef Peukert, *Erinnerungen eines Proletariers aus der revolutionären Arbeiterbewegung* (Berlin: Verlag des Sozialistischen Bundes, 1913), 300–310.

29. Berkman, *Prison Memoirs,* 349.

30. Goldman, *Living My Life,* 182–83; Berkman, *Prison Memoirs,* 331.

31. Paul Avrich interview with Luba Stein Benenson, New York City, December 4, 1973.

32. Modest Stein to Emma Goldman, September 20, 1929, Berkman Archive, International Institute of Social History, Amsterdam.

33. *Detroit Sentinel,* July 30, 1898.

34. Goldman, *Living My Life,* 370.

35. Goldman to Tom Bell, July 1, 1937, Goldman Archive.

36. Goldman, *Living My Life,* 152, 190.

37. Ravachol was born François Claudius Koenigstein. Sentenced to death for a chain of murders, burglaries, and bombings targeting prominent members of the French judiciary, he was guillotined on July 11, 1892, twelve days before Berkman's attentat.

38. Goldman, *Living My Life,* 231, 272.

39. *Liberty* (London), October 1895; Goldman to Max Nettlau, January 24, 1932, Nettlau Archive, International Institute of Social History, Amsterdam; Emma Goldman, "An Open Letter," *Fraye Arbeter Shtime,* February 17, 1901.

40. S. N. Behrman, *The Worcester Account* (New York: Random House, 1954), 181, quoted in Drinnon and Drinnon, *Nowhere at Home,* 89.

41. *St. Louis Post-Dispatch,* October 17, 1897.

42. *Boston Daily Globe,* September 6, 1897; *Providence Evening Bulletin,* September 7, 1897; *Road to Freedom,* August 1931; Emma Goldman, *Cronaca Sovversiva,* June 1, 1903.

43. Goldman, *Living My Life,* 191.

44. *Free Society,* April 21, 1901.

45. Miriam Michelson, "A Character Study of Emma Goldman," *Philadelphia North American,* April 11, 1901; Candace Falk, ed., *Emma Goldman: A Documentary History of the American Years* (Berkeley: University of California Press, 2003), 440–445.

46. Rudolf Rocker, "Max Baginski," *Die Freie Gesellschaft* (Darmstadt), September 1951; Dirk Hoerder, ed., *Plutokraten und Sozialisten: Berichte deutscher Diplomaten und Agenten über die amerikanische Arbeiterbewegung, 1878–1917* (Munich: K. G. Saur, 1981), 320; *Mother Earth,* May 1906.

47. *Sturmglocken,* February 15, 1899; *Fraye Arbeter Shtime,* March 5, 1899, and April 8, 1900; Goldman to Augustin Hamon, September 27, 1899, Hamon Archive, International Institute of Social History, Amsterdam; Goldman, *Living My Life,* 238–239; *Fraye Arbeter Shtime,* February 2 and June 4, 1899; *Lucifer,* April 22, 1899; Goldman, *Living My Life,* 239.

48. Goldman, *Living My Life,* 244.

49. *Rocky Mountain News,* August 19, 1899; Agnes Inglis notes, Joseph A. Labadie Collection, Harlan Hatcher Library, University of Michigan; *The Firebrand,* October 4, 1896.

50. Goldman, *Living My Life,* 240–241.

51. Ibid., 241.

52. *Fraye Arbeter Shtime,* September 16, 1899.

53. *Free Society,* April 22, 1900; *Freedom,* March–April 1900. Speeches included "The Aim of Humanity," "Woman," "The Foundations of Morality," "The Effect of the War on the Workers."

54. Goldman, *Living My Life,* 261–262; Goldman to Max Nettlau, July 15, 1900, Nettlau Archive.

55. Alexander Berkman to Michael Cohn, February 13, 1933, Berkman Archive.

56. Goldman said elsewhere that she first met Hippolyte Havel in Harry Kelly's house in London.

57. Goldman, *Living My Life,* 259–261.

58. *L'Adunata dei Refrattari,* May 13, 1950.

59. Avrich, *The Modern School Movement,* 132.

60. Harry Kelly, "Roll Back the Years," 175, Tamiment Library, New York University; Carl Zigrosser, *My Own Shall Come to Me: A Personal Memoir and Picture Chronicle* (Haarlem: J. Enshede en Zonen, 1971), 74.

61. Goldman, *Living My Life,* 261.

62. Emma Goldman, "The Propaganda and the Congress," statement read before the organizing committee of the Anarchist Congress, Paris, March 1900. Transcript printed in *Free Society,* April 8, 1900.

63. Morris Goldman, with Emma's help, attended the College of Physicians and Surgeons of Columbia University.

64. Goldman, *Living My Life,* 265. Goldman had visited Paris in 1896 after finishing her nursing studies in Vienna.

65. *Itinéraire,* no. 8, 70; Goldman, *Living My Life,* 272–275.

66. *Fraye Arbeter Shtime,* October 21, 1900. Reports from abroad were collected and published in *Les Temps Nouveaux,* Paris' leading anarchist journal. "True," wrote Goldman, "the Congress was prohibited . . . but [the event took place] in spite of all and every order, on a small scale, that is true, but by no means less important."

67. Emma Goldman, "Gaetano Bresci," *Free Society,* June 2, 1901.

68. "Rented by Emma Goldman," *New York Times,* December 12, 1900; *New York Tribune,* December 12, 1900.

69. Goldman, *Living My Life,* 281.

70. Ibid., 282.

71. Harry Kelly, "American Notes," *Freedom,* February 1901.

72. "Justus Schwab Mourned: Anarchists Forget Their Differences at His Funeral. The Tribute of John Swinton—Most in Tears—Emma Goldman Looks Calmly On," *New York Times,* December 21, 1900.

73. Carl Nold, "Robert Reitzel on His Sick Bed," Labadie Collection; *Sturmvogel,* April 1, 1898; Voltairine de Cleyre, "American Notes," *Freedom,* June 1898; Goldman to Berkman, February 1904, Goldman Archive.

12. The Assassination of McKinley

1. Emma Goldman to James B. Elliott, March 15, 1901, Joseph A. Labadie Collection, Harlan Hatcher Library, University of Michigan.

2. On June 7, 1896, a bomb exploded during a religious procession in Barcelona, killing at least six people and injuring many others. In retaliation, hundreds of anarchists were arrested and subjected to savage tortures in Montjuich fortress outside Barcelona. Many died of their injuries. After the assassination, which occurred in August 1897, Angiolillo was sentenced to death for the crime.

3. *Chicago Daily Tribune,* September 8, 1901; Emma Goldman, *Living My Life* (New York: A. A. Knopf, 1931), 290–291.

4. Goldman, *Living My Life,* 291.

5. Emma Goldman, "Gaetano Bresci," *Free Society,* June 2, 1901. Bresci was found hanging in his cell; many believed he had been murdered by the guards.

6. Max Baginski, "Leon Czolgosz," *Mother Earth,* October 1906.

7. *Free Society,* October 6, 1901.

8. Ibid., Jane Addams, *Twenty Years at Hull House* (New York: Macmillan, 1911), 409–412.

9. A. Wesley Johns, *The Man Who Shot McKinley* (South Brunswick, N.J.: A. S. Barnes, 1970), 40–41.

10. Abe Isaak Jr., *Free Society,* September 1, 1901.

11. Among them were Lena's children, Stella, Harry, and Saxe Commins, and Helena's son, David Hochstein.

12. Goldman, *Living My Life,* 58–59.

13. Ibid. Solotaroff told Goldman an operation would correct the problem. She decided against the treatment.

14. Goldman, *Living My Life,* 291.

15. Ibid.

16. Ibid., 295–296.

17. Ibid., Johns, *The Man Who Shot McKinley,* 137–138.

18. Charles S. Olcott, *The Life of William McKinley* (New York: Houghton Mifflin, 1916), 315–316; Margaret Leech, *In the Days of McKinley* (New York: Harper, 1959), 594–595.

19. Doctors in attendance included Herman Mynter and John Parmenter of the University of Buffalo; E. Wallace Lee of St. Louis, who was visiting the Exposition; Eugene Wasdin of the Marine-Hospital Service; and Presley M. Rixley, the president's physician, who arrived after the operation had begun. Dr. Matthew Mann later requested remuneration from Congress for the surgery. "Surgeons Who Attended Mr. McKinley Ask for Pay," *New York Times,* December 18, 1901.

20. "President M'Kinley's Illustrious Career," *New York Times,* September 7, 1901.

21. Statement in Czolgosz's writing, September 6, 1901, Erie and Buffalo Historical Society.

22. Ibid.; Johns, *The Man Who Shot McKinley,* 122–123.

23. Statement in Czolgosz's writing, September 6, 1901, Erie and Buffalo Historical Society; *Philadelphia Medical Journal of 1901.*

24. "Chicago Anarchists Raided," *New York Times,* September 8, 1901.

25. Ibid.

26. Paul Avrich, *Anarchist Voices: An Oral History of Anarchism in America* (Princeton: Princeton University Press, 1995), 103, 251; *Free Society,* October 6, 1901.

27. Goldman, *Living My Life,* 296; Johns, *The Man Who Shot McKinley,* 137.

28. Goldman, *Living My Life,* 296.

29. *New York World,* September 14, 1901.

30. Thomas W. Bacot to Philander C. Knox, September 10, 1901; B. Rubin, M.D., to E. D. Crumpacker, September 11, 1901.

31. Goldman, *Living My Life,* 296; Johns, *The Man Who Shot McKinley,* 138.

32. Goldman, *Living My Life,* 297.

33. Ibid., 296–300; "Emma Goldman Abuses President," *Massillon Independent,* (Massillon, Ohio), September 12, 1901; Johns, *The Man Who Shot McKinley,* 148–149; *New York World,* September 11, 1901.

34. "Emma Goldman Abuses President," *Massillon Independent* (Massillon, Ohio), September 12, 1901.

35. Goldman, *Living My Life,* 299–306; Johns, *The Man Who Shot McKinley,* 148–149; *New York World,* September 11, 1901; *Chicago Daily Tribune,* September 11, 1901; "Emma Goldman Abuses President," *Massillon Independent* (Massillon, Ohio), September 12, 1901.

36. *New York Times,* November 1, 1959; *Free Society,* October 6, 1901; Goldman, *Living My Life,* 301.

37. Johns, *The Man Who Shot McKinley,* 252; *Free Society,* October 6, 1901; Goldman, *Living My Life,* 307. These sources give somewhat different versions of the incident.

38. Abe Isaak Jr. to Max Nettlau, October 7, 1901, Nettlau Archive, International Institute of Social History, Amsterdam.

39. *Free Society,* October 27, 1901; *Fraye Arbeter Shtime,* September 20, 1901.

40. *Pittsburgh Leader,* September 15, 1901.

41. Avrich, *Anarchist Voices,* 275.

42. Goldman, *Living My Life,* 245; *Fraye Arbeter Shtime,* September 24, 1899; *Freedom,* November 1899.

43. Voltairine de Cleyre to Harriet E. de Claire, September 22, 1901, Joseph Ishill Collection, Houghton Library, Harvard University.

44. Voltairine de Cleyre, *The Selected Works of Voltairine de Cleyre,* ed. Alexander Berkman, ed. (New York: Mother Earth Publishing, 1914), 171; *Free Society,* December 15, 1901.

45. Charles Pierre Le Warne, *Utopias on Puget Sound, 1885–1915* (Seattle: University of Washington Press, 1975), 180–181; Avrich, *Anarchist Voices,* 292–293.

46. Goldman, *Living My Life,* 291, 314. Her sister Lena, had six children: Saxe Commins (whose given name was Isidore Cominsky) and Stella (whose married last name was Ballantine) were especially close to their aunt. In 1893 Goldman had told journalist Nellie Bly that she had "a married brother, who does not bother about anything, and only reads the papers when there is something in them about me. My sister is also married and, while not actively engaged in our cause, is bringing up her children to our principles." Nellie Bly interview with Emma Goldman, *New York World,* September 17, 1893. Goldman's other sister, Helena, had three children, including David, who was killed in 1918. Her brothers were Herman and Morris; Louis did not live to adulthood.

47. Alexander Berkman to Goldman, December 29, 1901, quoted in Berkman, *Prison Memoirs of an Anarchist* (New York: Mother Earth Publishing, 1912), 412–413.

48. Morris Hillquit, *Loose Leaves from a Busy Life* (New York: Macmillan, 1934), 124; Rudolf Rocker, *Johann Most: The Life of a Rebel* (Berlin: Verlag Syndikalist, F. Kater, 1924), 401–403.

49. Hillquit, *Loose Leaves from a Busy Life,* 28.

50. Goldman, *Living My Life,* 325.

51. John William Lloyd to Henry Bool, September 13, 1901, Labadie Collection.

52. *Discontent,* September 18, 1901.

53. *Lucifer,* November 7, 1901.

54. *Lucifer,* November 21, 1901; Emma Goldman, "The Tragedy of Buffalo," *Free Society,* October 6, 1901.

55. The *Fraye Arbeter Shtime* was a notable exception.

56. Voltairine de Cleyre, "McKinley's Assassination from the Anarchist Point of View," *Mother Earth,* October 1907; *Free Society,* October 13, 1901; January and February 14, 1903.

57. *Discontent,* September 18, 1901; *Lucifer,* November 7, 1901.

58. Berkman, *Prison Memoirs,* 398–399.

59. Berkman to Goldman, December 20, 1901, quoted in Berkman, *Prison Memoirs,* 416–417.

60. Goldman, *Living My Life,* 324.

13. E. G. Smith

1. Theodore Roosevelt to Henry Cabot Lodge, September 1901, Theodore Roosevelt Papers, Manuscripts division, Library of Congress.

2. Presidential message, first session Fifty-seventh Congress, December 3, 1901, Washington, D.C.

3. Ibid.

4. Ibid.; Roy L. Garis, *Immigration Restriction: A Study of the Opposition to and Regulation of Immigration into the United States* (New York: Macmillan, 1927), 102; Theodore Albert Schroeder, *Free Speech for Radicals* (New York: Free Speech League, 1916), 78.

5. "Emma Goldman Speaks," *New York Times,* December 10, 1901.

6. Emma Goldman, *Living My Life* (New York: A. A. Knopf, 1931), 325; *Cronaca Sovversiva,* June 1, 1903.

7. Goldman, *Living My Life,* 320.

8. Alice Wexler, *Emma Goldman: An Intimate Life* (New York: Pantheon Books, 1984), 15; Goldman, *Living My Life,* 320–321, 330.

9. Alexander Berkman to Emma Goldman, December 20, 1901, quoted in Alexander Berkman, *Prison Memoirs of an Anarchist* (New York: Mother Earth Publishing, 1912), 413.

10. Goldman, *Living My Life,* 321, 382.

11. Ibid., 331; *Free Society,* November 9, 1902.

12. *Free Society,* December 14, 1902.

13. Goldman, *Living My Life,* 334.

14. *Free Society,* April 12, 1903; *Freedom,* May 1903; Goldman, *Living My Life,* 341.

15. Goldman, *Living My Life,* 329–330.

16. *Free Society,* July 6 and November 23, 1902.

17. *Chicago Tribune,* November 17, 1902; *Free Society,* November 23, 1902; *Lucifer,* December 11, 1902.

18. Emma Goldman letter, November 30, 1902, in *Lucifer,* December 11, 1902.

19. Paul Avrich interview with Marion Bell, Los Angeles, June 21, 1974.

20. Emma Goldman in *Lucifer,* October 22, 1903.

21. Goldman, *Living My Life,* 178–179; *The Firebrand,* May 24 and December 20, 1896; *Freedom,* January 1898.

22. "Anarchists Are Raided: Murray Hill Lyceum Meeting Goes Wild with Rage," *New York Times,* October 24, 1903.

23. David M. Rabban, *Free Speech in Its Forgotten Years* (New York: Cambridge University Press, 1997), 135.

24. *Liberty,* November 1903; E. H. Crosby, "How the United States Curtails Freedom of Thought," The North American Review, Vol. 178, No. 569, April 1904.

25. *Lucifer,* February 18, 1904.

26. Goldman, *Living My Life,* 484.

27. Hutchins Hapgood, *A Victorian in the Modern World* (New York: Harcourt, Brace, 1939), 279; *The Syndicalist,* March 1, 1913; Rabban, *Free Speech in Its Forgotten Years,* 54.

28. Goldman, *Living My Life,* 348.

29. Bolton Hall to Joseph J. Cohen, October 20, 1931, Sunrise Colony Archives, Bentley Historical Library, University of Michigan. Hall wrote, "Of course I am an anarchist; and a Land Rent man, only as the best method of getting anarchy."

30. Goldman, *Living My Life,* 348; *Lucifer,* February 25, 1904.

31. *Lucifer,* January 7, 1904.

32. Peter Kropotkin to Goldman, December 16, 1903, Jeanne Levey Papers, Tamiment Library, New York University.

33. Goldman to Berkman, January 18 and February 1904, Goldman Archive, International Institute of Social History, Amsterdam. Max Metzkow, now living in Brooklyn, was among those who aided in collecting funds. Goldman to Max Metzkow, February 9, 1904, Joseph Ishill Collection, Houghton Library, Harvard University.

34. *Free Society,* April 3, April 10, May 10, 1904; *Lucifer,* February 2, 1905; John Turner to Goldman, April 10, 1929, Goldman Archive.

35. U.S. Supreme Court, U.S. ex rel Turner v. Williams, 194 U.S. 279 (1904), United States ex rel. John Turner, Appt. v. William Williams, United States Commissioner of Immigration for the Port of New York, No. 561. Argued April 6 and 7, 1904. The case was decided May 16 after Turner had returned to England.

36. "Anarchist Turner Sails: Thinks That His Detention Has Caused Spread of Anarchistic Feeling," *New York Times,* May 1, 1904.

37. Richard Drinnon, *Rebel in Paradise: A Biography of Emma Goldman* (Chicago: University of Chicago Press, 1961), 94; Goldman, *Living My Life,* 357; *Free Society,* June 26, 1904.

38. Goldman to Lillian D. Wald, November 1904, Lillian Wald Papers, New York Public Library.

39. Goldman, *Living My Life,* 362.

40. Goldman to Lillian D. Wald, November 1904, Lillian Wald Papers, New York Public Library; Goldman, *Living My Life,* 362–363.

41. Goldman, *Living My Life,* 364; Thomas H. Bell, "Catherine Breshkovsky," 1934, Bell Papers, Los Angeles, Private collection.

42. See Goldman's speech "The Unpleasant Side of George Bernard Shaw," May 25, 1904, for her thoughts on Shaw.

43. Gavin Lambert, *Nazimova: A Biography* (New York: A. A. Knopf, 1997), 119, 126; Goldman, *Living My Life,* 366–370.

44. Goldman, *Living My Life,* 373.

45. Goldman to unknown, November 21, 1905; Goldman to James Gibbons Huneker, November 23, 1905, both in Goldman Papers, Northwestern University Library; Lambert, *Nazimova,* 3–4, 119, 126, 138, 321–322.

46. Eugene O'Neill to Hans Olav, May 13, 1938, *Eugene O'Neill Review,* 18 (Spring/Fall 1994); Lambert, *Nazimova,* 3–4.

47. Lambert, *Nazimova,* 331; S. N. Behrman, *The Worcester Account* (New York: Random House, 1954), 178.

48. Goldman to Berkman, January and February 1904, Goldman Archive.

49. Goldman to Lillian Wald, November 12, 1904, Lillian Wald Papers.

50. Goldman, *Living My Life,* 365, 382.

51. Goldman to Bolton Hall, 1905, Goldman Archive.

52. Goldman, *Living My Life,* 371.

53. Ibid., 368. The lines translate as "Go slower, beating heart of mine—and close, ye bleeding wounds—this is my final day—and these its waning hours!"

14. Resurrection

1. "From Prison to Workhouse: Anarchist Berkman Finishes One Stint and Begins Another," *Fort Wayne Daily,* July 19, 1905.

2. Alexander Berkman, *Prison Memoirs of an Anarchist* (New York: Mother Earth Publishing, 1912), 474–476.

3. Ibid., 474–476; Alexander Berkman to Emma Goldman, April 15, 1905, Berkman Archive, International Institute of Social History, Amsterdam; *Pittsburgh Press,* May 18, 1906.

4. Berkman, *Prison Memoirs,* 477.

5. Ibid., 478.

6. *Pittsburgh Press,* May 17, 1906; Max Nettlau, "Alexander Berkman's Sixtieth Birthday Celebration," pamphlet (New York: n.p., November 1930), Joseph A. Labadie Collection, Harlan Hatcher Library, University of Michigan.

7. "Berkman Will Lead New York Anarchists," *New York Times,* May 20, 1906.

8. "Learns Languages in Jail," *Evening Times* (Cumberland, Md.), August 4, 1906.

9. "Alexander Berkman's First Speech after His Release from Jail," *The Demonstrator,* June 6, 1906.

10. *Pittsburgh Press,* May 18, 1906. The hospital death rate was very high.

11. Berkman to Goldman, December 20, 1901, quoted in Berkman, *Prison Memoirs,* 415.

12. *Pittsburgh Press,* May 17, 1906. "Alexander Berkman's First Speech after His Release from Jail," *The Demonstrator,* June 6, 1906.

13. Emma Goldman, "A Sketch of Alexander Berkman," *The Russian Tragedy: A Review and An Outlook* (Berlin: Der Syndikalist, 1922), 2.

14. "Berkman Will Lead New York Anarchists," *New York Times,* May 20, 1906.

15. "Berkman out of Prison: Man Who Tried to Kill Frick Ordered to Leave Pittsburgh," *New York Times,* May 19, 1906.

16. Berkman, *Prison Memoirs,* 485–486.

17. Goldman, *Living My Life* (New York: A.A. Knopf, 1931) 393. Carl Nold remained in Detroit, working as a tool and dye maker, contributing to anarchist periodicals, and collecting material in German for the Labadie Collection at the University of Michigan. He died in 1934. Paul Avrich, *Anarchist Voices: An Oral History of Anarchism in America* (Princeton, N.J.: Princeton University Press, 1995), 386, 522.

18. Emma Goldman, *Living My Life,* 384.

19. Ibid.

20. Ibid.; Berkman, *Prison Memoirs,* 489.

21. Berkman, *Prison Memoirs,* 490, 495.

22. Goldman, *Living My Life,* 383–384.

23. "Alexander Berkman's First Speech after His Release from Jail," *The Demonstrator,* June 6, 1906.

24. Ibid.

25. *The Demonstrator,* June 20, 1906.

26. "Anarchist Honeymoon," *New York World,* June 8, 1906.

27. Ibid.

28. "An Anarchist Honeymoon: Emma Goldman and Berkman Hold Hands on a Park Bench," *New York Times,* May 26, 1906.

29. Alexander Berkman, "A Greeting," *Mother Earth,* June 1906.

30. *The Demonstrator,* July 4, 1906.

31. Berkman, *Prison Memoirs,* 492.

32. Goldman to Berkman, January 1904, Goldman Archive, International Institute of Social History, Amsterdam; *Free Society,* June 19, 1904.

33. Orlenev and Nazimova, still performing in New York at this time, staged a benefit and raised enough money to publish the first issue.

34. Johann Most to Max Nettlau, October 24, 1890, Nettlau Archive, International Institute of Social History, Amsterdam.

35. Goldman, *Living My Life,* 379.

36. Goldman to Max Nettlau, January 24, 1932, Nettlau Archive; Richard Drinnon, *Rebel in Paradise: A Biography of Emma Goldman* (Chicago: University of Chicago Press, 1961), 82.

37. "Woman Anarchist Calls Our Flag a Sham: Violent Speeches Made to Reds in Memory of Johann Most," *New York Times,* April 2, 1906.

38. Berkman, *Prison Memoirs,* 492.

39. Alexander Berkman, "Vorwort" to Rudolf Rocker; Rudolf Rocker, *Johann Most: The Life of a Rebel* (Berlin: Verlag Syndikalist, F. Kater, 1924), 7–8.

40. Harry Kelly, *The Voice of Labour,* February 2, 1907.

41. Emma Goldman, "Police Brutality," *Mother Earth,* November 1906; Goldman, *Living My Life,* 390–391.

42. Berkman, *Prison Memoirs,* 493.

43. Goldman to Berkman, May 14, 1929, Goldman Archive.

44. Paul Avrich interview with Eva Brandes, New York City, June 13, 1972.

45. Paul Avrich interview with Luba Stein Benenson, New York City, December 4, 1973.

46. Berkman, *Prison Memoirs,* 467.

47. Berkman to Nikolaev-Korn, March 5, 1905, Berkman Archive, International Institute of Social History, Amsterdam.

48. Goldman, *Living My Life,* 387.

49. "Berkman: Anarchists Allege a Plot of Millionaires," *Washington Sunday Post,* October 27, 1906.

50. Ibid.

51. Goldman, *Living My Life,* 386–390; Berkman, *Prison Memoirs,* 506–508.

52. Berkman, *Prison Memoirs,* 496.

53. *Mother Earth,* December 1906; *Fraye Arbeter Shtime,* December 29, 1906.

54. Goldman to Berkman, March 19, 1907, Goldman Archive.

55. Goldman, *Living My Life,* 398.

56. *Mother Earth,* December 1907 and May 1908.

57. Mollie Steimer, *Fraye Arbeter Shtime,* July 1, 1966.

58. Berkman, *Prison Memoirs,* 451–452.

59. Miriam Brody and Bonnie Buettner, eds., *Prison Blossoms: Anarchist Voices from the American Past* (Cambridge, Mass.: The Belknap Press of Harvard University Press, 2011), 155.

60. Alexander Berkman, "Prisons and Crime," *Mother Earth,* August 1906.

61. Ibid; Berkman, "The Confession of a Convict," *Mother Earth,* January 1914.

62. Berkman, *Prison Memoirs,* dedication; Hippolyte Havel, "The Kotoku Case," *Mother Earth,* December 1910; Robert A. Scalapino and George T. Yu, *The Chinese Anarchist Movement* (Berkeley: Center for Chinese Studies, 1961), 31–32; F. G. Notehelfer, *Kotoku Shusui: Portrait of a Japanese Radical* (Cambridge: University Press, 1971), 186; Paul Avrich interview with Morris Ganberg, Bronx, N.Y., February 2, 1974; M. Weitzman (Morris Ganberg), *Fraye Arbeter Shtime,* February 1 and March 1, 1971; *Freedom* (San Francisco), December 1910; *The Agitator,* December 15, 1910; *Mother Earth,* November 1910.

15. The Wine of Sunshine and Liberty

1. Emma Goldman, *Living My Life* (New York: A. A. Knopf, 1931), 411–412.

2. Emma Goldman to Alexander Berkman, May 14, 1929, Goldman Archive, International Institute of Social History, Amsterdam.

3. Anarchist Federation of America, "To the Unemployed and Homeless!!" 1908, copy in Tamiment Library, New York University.

4. "Police Chief Kills Anarchist in Fight," *New York Times,* March 3, 1908; *Mother Earth,* March 1908; Goldman, *Living My Life,* 413–415; Roger Bruns, *Knights of the Road: A Hobo History* (New York: Methuen, 1980), 62.

5. Goldman, *Living My Life,* 415–418; Richard Drinnon, *Rebel in Paradise: A Biography of Emma Goldman* (Chicago: University of Chicago Press, 1961), 122–123; Alix Kates

Shulman, ed., *Red Emma Speaks: An Emma Goldman Reader* (New York: Schocken Books, 1983), 147.

6. Goldman, *Living My Life,* 415–416.

7. Ibid., 420.

8. Ibid., 421; Bruns, *Knights of the Road,* 65–67.

9. Goldman, *Living My Life,* 431; Emma Goldman, "Patriotism: A Menace to Liberty," *Mother Earth,* June 1908 and May 1909; Drinnon, *Rebel in Paradise,* 138; Leon Whipple, *The Story of Civil Liberty in the United States* (New York: Vanguard Press, 1927), 306.

10. *American Journal of Eugenics,* July 1908; *Mother Earth,* May 1909 and March 1911.

11. Margaret Sanger, *Margaret Sanger: An Autobiography* (New York: Cooper Square Press, 1938), 207.

12. Drinnon, *Rebel in Paradise,* 125–126.

13. Paul Avrich interviews with Sam Dolgoff, New York City, 1971–1972.

14. Paul Avrich interview with Rebecca August, Los Angeles, June 20, 1974.

15. Goldman to Ben Reitman, August 15, 1909, The Emma Goldman Papers, Richard J. Daley Library, University of Illinois at Chicago.

16. Voltairine de Cleyre to Berkman, December 31, 1910, Berkman Archive, International Institute of Social History, Amsterdam; Ben Reitman to Leonard D. Abbott, June 15, 1940, Abbott Papers, Private Collection; de Cleyre to Joseph J. Cohen, February 1, 1912, Joseph A. Labadie Collection, Harlan Hatcher Library, University of Michigan. "We had a month's siege of Reitman, but are now relieved of him."

17. Max Eastman, *Enjoyment of Living* (New York: Harper, 1948), 424.

18. Elizabeth Gurley Flynn, *The Rebel Girl: An Autobiography, My First Life, 1906–1926* (New York: International Publishers, 1973), 50.

19. Carl Zigrosser, *My Own Shall Come to Me: A Personal Memoir and Picture Chronicle* (Haarlem: J. Enschede en Zonen, 1971), 73.

20. Paul Avrich interview with Kate Wolfson, New York City, October 16, 1972.

21. Margaret Anderson, *My Thirty Years' War: An Autobiography of Margaret Anderson* (New York: Covici, Friede Publishers, 1939), 70.

22. Mary Eleanor Fitzgerald to Ben Reitman, no date, Ben Lewis Reitman Papers, Richard J. Daley Library, University of Illinois at Chicago.

23. Berkman to Pauline Turkel, April 26, no year, Private collection.

24. Goldman, *Living My Life,* 435; Berkman to Ben Reitman, April 7, 1913, Reitman Papers.

25. "Rout Out Anarchy, Says the President," *New York Times,* March 24, 1908.

26. *Current Literature,* May 1908; Paul T. Ringenbach, *Tramps and Reformers, 1873–1916: The Discovery of Unemployment in New York* (Westport, Conn.: Greenwood Press, 1973), 67; *Mother Earth,* April 1908; Bruns, *Knights of the Road,* 71; C. L. James to Berkman, November 20, 1908, Berkman Archive.

27. *New York Times,* March 29–31, 1908; Ringenbach, *Tramps and Reformers,* 67–68; *Mother Earth,* April and May 1908; *Current Literature,* May 1908.

28. "Bomb Thrower Tells All: Silverstein Says He Set Off the Explosion with a Cigarette," *New York Times,* April 7, 1908. Selig Silverstein also went by the name of Selig Cohen. The bystander was said to be Silverstein's friend and co-worker.

29. Goldman, *Living My Life,* 424; Berkman to Goldman, April 16, 1929, Goldman Archive.

30. "No 'Red' Plot, Say the Police," *New York Times,* March 30, 1908.

31. "Police Find 'Reds' Are in Federation," *New York Times,* March 31, 1908.

32. Ibid.

33. "Death of Bomb Thrower," *Racine Daily Journal* (Racine, Wis.), April 28, 1908.

34. Alexander Berkman, "Violence and Anarchism," *Mother Earth,* April 1908.

35. Alexander Berkman, *Prison Memoirs of an Anarchist* (New York: Mother Earth Publishing, 1912), 183.

36. Henry G. Alsberg was a foreign correspondent who had written editorials for the *New York Evening Post* and had worked for *The Nation* and *The Call,* a socialist daily in New York. Henry G. Alsberg, "Alexander Berkman's Sixtieth Birthday Celebration," Central Opera House, New York City, pamphlet (New York: n.p., November 20, 1930), Joseph A. Labadie Collection, Harlan Hatcher Library, University of Michigan.

37. Harry Kelly, "A Tribute to Berkman," *Alexander Berkman: Rebel and Anarchist* Alexander Berkman Memorial Committee and Jewish Anarchist Federation (New York, July 1936).

38. Whipple, *Civil Liberty in the United States,* 228.

39. Goldman, *Living My Life,* 437.

40. "Berkman Gets Five Days," *New York Times,* September 8, 1908.

41. Goldman, *Living My Life,* 438.

42. Emma Goldman, "The Latest Police Outrage," *Mother Earth,* September 1908; Goldman, *Living My Life,* 437–438; Bruns, *Knights of the Road,* 88–89.

43. *Mother Earth,* November 1910.

44. Paul Avrich, *The Modern School Movement: Anarchism and Education in the United States* (Princeton: Princeton University Press, 1980), 186.

45. "The Organization of the American Ferrer Association," Francisco Ferrer Association leaflet, June 1910, Ramus Archive, International Institute of Social History, Amsterdam; Avrich, *The Modern School Movement,* 36.

46. *Mother Earth,* January, February, and April 1913.

47. *Pittsburgh Press,* May 17, 1906; *The Demonstrator,* June 6, 1906.

48. Goldman, *Living My Life,* 385.

49. Goldman to Ben Reitman, July 18, 1912, Goldman Papers, New York Public Library.

50. Berkman, *Prison Memoirs,* 350.

51. Voltairine de Cleyre to Berkman, August 7, 1906, Berkman Archive.

52. De Cleyre to Berkman, August 24, 1906, Berkman Archive.

53. De Cleyre to Berkman, July 10, 1906, Berkman Archive.

54. De Cleyre to Berkman, August 7, 1906, Berkman Archive.

55. De Cleyre to Berkman, June 24, 1910. Her comments and corrections, always careful and to the point, are preserved in the Berkman Archive.

56. *Freedom,* February 1913.

57. Goldman to Ben Reitman, September 13, 1911.

58. Goldman, *Living My Life,* 483.

59. Goldman to Jack London, September 26, 1911.

60. Jack London to Elwyn Hoffman, September 18, 1901, in *The Letters of Jack London,* ed. Earle Labor, Robert C. Leitz, and I. Milo Shepard, 3 vols. (Stanford: Stanford University Press, 1988), 253.

61. "Jack London on Alexander Berkman: An Unpublished Introduction," *American Literature,* 61 (1989), 447–456.

62. Goldman, *Living My Life,* 506–507.

63. *Mother Earth,* April 1912.

64. "Tells of Tarring of Anarchist Reitman," *San Antonio Light,* May 23, 1912.

65. Goldman, *Living My Life,* 494–501.

66. *Mother Earth,* June 1912 and May 1913; Goldman, *Living My Life,* 494–501; Drinnon, *Rebel in Paradise,* 135–136; Shulman, *Red Emma Speaks,* 152–157.

67. *Mother Earth,* June 1912; *The Agitator,* June 15, 1912.

68. "An Anarchist's Story," *New York Times,* November 17, 1912.

69. *The Syndicalist,* March 15, 1913.

70. Harry Kelly, "A Tribute to Berkman," *Alexander Berkman: Rebel and Anarchist.*

71. Introduction to British edition of Berkman, *Prison Memoirs* (London: C. W. Daniel, 1926).

72. "Prison Memoirs of An Anarchist by Alexander Berkman: What the Reviews Say of this Book," advertisement in *Mother Earth,* Mother Earth Publishing Association,

73. Ibid.

74. Ibid.

75. "An Anarchist's Story," *New York Times,* November 17, 1912.

76. Paul Avrich interview with Freda Diamond, New York City, May 13, 1983.

77. Paul Avrich, *An American Anarchist: the Life of Voltairine de Cleyre* (Princeton: Princeton University Press, 1978), 236.

78. *Mother Earth,* July 1912. De Cleyre was saluted by *Mother Earth* with a memorial issue. The Mother Earth Publishing Association, with a committee of Voltairine's friends and comrades, printed a collection of her work, "an arsenal of knowledge for the student and soldier of freedom." Avrich, *Voltairine de Cleyre,* 237–238; *Mother Earth,* July 1912; Berkman to Upton Sinclair, July 27, 1925, Berkman Archive.

79. Goldman, *Living My Life,* 504–505.

16. The Inside Story of Some Explosions

1. Harry Kelly, "Mother Earth, 1905–1915," *Mother Earth,* March 1915; Van Wyck Brooks, *The Confident Years* (London: J. M. Dent and Sons, 1955), 376.

2. Emma Goldman, *Living My Life* (New York: A. A. Knopf, 1931), 516.

3. Ibid., 515–517.

4. Paul Avrich interview with Marion Bell, Los Angeles, June 21, 1974.

5. Paul Avrich interview with Hilda Adel, a member of the Frayhayt Group, Croton-on-Hudson, New York, April 14, 1973 and September 18, 1979.

6. Goldman, *Living My Life*, 520.

7. M. Eleanor Fitzgerald to Lucy Robins, July 14, 1919, Lucy Robins Lang Papers, Joseph A. Labadie Collection, Harlan Hatcher Library, University of Michigan; Lucy Robins Lang, *Tomorrow Is Beautiful* (New York: Macmillan, 1948), 87–88.

8. *Hancock-Coloma Wisconsin News,* April 7, 1955; Goldman, *Living My Life,* 515–520.

9. Goldman, *Living My Life,* 521.

10. Ibid., 527–528. Goldman and Reitman ended their relationship in 1917. Ben Reitman was married a total of three times, had a daughter with his first wife, had a son with his second wife while still involved with Goldman and, later, had four daughters with a girlfriend.

11. Goldman, *Living My Life,* 493.

12. Paul Avrich interview with Maurice Hollod, North Miami, Fla., December 20, 1972; "Fast Hasn't Hurt Becky Edelson Yet," *New York Times,* July 23, 1914.

13. Paul Avrich interview with Charles Plunkett, Long Valley, N.J., June 4, 1975.

14. Emma Goldman to Ben Reitman, Ben Lewis Reitman Papers, Richard J. Daley Library, University of Illinois at Chicago.

15. "1,000 Jobless Seek Shelter in Church," *New York Times,* February 28, 1914.

16. "Urges Workless On to Anarchy," *New York Times,* March 3, 1914.

17. "Tells Unemployed to Adopt Force," *New York Times,* March 4, 1914.

18. Ibid.

19. Charles Willis Thompson, "So-Called I.W.W. Raids Really Hatched by Schoolboys," *New York Times,* March 29, 1914.

20. Alexander Berkman, "Tannenbaum before Pilate," *Mother Earth,* April 1914.

21. Goldman, *Living My Life,* 523.

22. "Tells Unemployed to Adopt Force," *New York Times,* March 4, 1914.

23. Paul Avrich interview with Maurice Hollod, North Miami, Fla., December 20, 1972.

24. Paul Avrich interview with Rose Goldblatt, New York City, October 20, 1975.

25. Marie Ganz, *Rebels: Into Anarchy—and Out Again* (New York: Dodd, Mead, 1919), 167. Paul Avrich interview with Maurice Hollod. Hollod mentioned that one of Caron's grandfathers was a Native American chieftain. As the *New York Times* described it, "The grandmother of Arthur Caron was a New York State Indian squaw, while his grandfather was a Scotchman. He was proud of his Indian blood and shouted the fact that it ran through his veins." "Caron's Career in Anarchy," *New York Times,* July 5, 1914.

26. Paul Avrich interview with Charles Plunkett.

27. "Urges Workless on to Anarchy," *New York Times,* March 3, 1914.

28. *New York World,* March 23, 1914. Thompson, "So-Called I.W.W. Raids Really Hatched by Schoolboys."

29. Alexander Berkman, "The Movement of the Unemployed," *Mother Earth,* March 1914; Paul T. Ringenbach, *Tramps and Reformers, 1873–1916* (Westport, Conn.: Greenwood Press, 1973), 163; "Urges Workless on to Anarchy," *New York Times,* March 3, 1914.

30. Paul Avrich, *The Modern School Movement: Anarchism and Education in the United States* (Princeton: Princeton University Press, 1980), 186–187; Avrich, *Anarchist Voices: An Oral History of Anarchism in America* (Princeton: Princeton University Press, 1995), 216; *Retort,* June 1944; *New York Times,* March 5, 1914; "Police Drive I.W.W. Crowd from Park," *New York Times,* March 6, 1914.

31. City Magistrate John A. L. Campbell sentenced Tannenbaum. Once finished with their prison terms, Arthur Caron, Charles Plunkett, and Frank Strawn Hamilton became leading activists; Mary Heaton Vorse called them three young men "of education and attainment who had thrown their lot with the workers." Mary Heaton Vorse, *A Footnote to Folly: Reminiscences of Mary Heaton Vorse* (New York: Farrar & Rinehart, 1935), 5.

32. "Police Drive I.W.W. Crowd from Park," *New York Times,* March 6, 1914.

33. *New York Call,* March 28, 1914.

34. *Modern School,* January 1915.

35. *Mother Earth,* July 1914. Charles Plunkett wrote, "Hunger had become articulate. Misery had found its voice!"

36. Goldman, *Living My Life,* 523, 525. The groups included the Labor Defense Committee; the I.W.W. Unemployed Union of New York, with headquarters on East Fourth Street, and the Conference of the Unemployed, based at the Ferrer Center. The Labor Defense Committee was founded by companions Elizabeth Gurley Flynn and Carlo Tresca, and Bill Haywood and others at Mary Heaton Vorse's apartment on East 11th Street.

37. Goldman, *Living My Life,* 231.

38. Thompson, "So-Called I.W.W. Raids Really Hatched by Schoolboys."

39. *New York Times,* March 22, 1914.

40. Berkman, "The Movement of the Unemployed."

41. "Anarchists Spread Alarm in 5th Ave," *New York Times,* March 22, 1914.

42. Ibid.

43. *Mother Earth,* April 1914.

44. "Police Use Clubs on I.W.W. Rioters," *New York Times,* April 5, 1914; Vorse, *A Footnote to Folly,* 71.

45. Vorse, *A Footnote to Folly,* 71–72. See Avrich, "Lexington Avenue," in *The Modern School Movement,* 183–216.

46. "Police Use Clubs on I.W.W. Rioters," *New York Times,* April 5, 1914.

47. Joe O'Carroll to Mary Heaton Vorse, May 6, 1914, Mary Heaton Vorse Papers, Walter P. Reuther Library of Labor and Urban Affairs, Wayne State University, Detroit, Michigan; Avrich, "Lexington Avenue," 183–216.

48. Howard Zinn, "The Ludlow Massacre," in *The Politics of History* (Boston: Beacon Press, 1970), 79–105; Richard Hofstadter and Michael Wallace, eds., *American Violence*

(New York: A. A. Knopf, 1970); Harry Kelly, "The Miners' War in Colorado," *Freedom* (London), June 1914.

49. Avrich, *The Modern School Movement,* 212.

50. *Conditions in the Coal Mines of Colorado: Hearings before a Subcommittee of the Committee of Mines and Mining,* U.S. Congress (Washington, D.C: GPO, February 25–27, 1914), 2874.

51. George McGovern and Leonard F. Guttridge, *The Great Coalfield War* (Boston: Houghton Mifflin, 1972), 135; Zinn, "The Ludlow Massacre," 100–101; Samuel Yellen, *American Labor Struggles* (New York: Harcourt, Brace, 1936), 221.

52. "Two Women Depict Battle of Ludlow," *New York Times,* February 4, 1915.

53. Zinn, "The Ludlow Massacre," 79; Avrich, "Lexington Avenue."

54. "Rockefeller Balks Sinclair Mourners," *New York Times,* April 30, 1914.

55. "Night Picketing at Rockefeller's," *New York Times,* May 1, 1914.

56. Ibid. Ganz served thirty days in the Queens County Jail. "Exploded in Apartment Occupied by Tarrytown Disturbers," *New York Times,* July 5, 1914.

57. "Night Picketing at Rockefeller's," *New York Times,* May 1, 1914; "Mourners Growing Glum," *New York Times,* May 9, 1914.

58. Avrich, *The Modern School Movement,* 213.

59. "Hold Rockefeller at Fault in Strike," *New York Times,* August 28, 1915.

60. Tresca, unpublished autobiography, 302–306, Tamiment Library, New York University, 296.

61. *Mother Earth,* May 1914; The following month *Mother Earth* again demanded militant action, including a general strike of all American workers, because the Ludlow murders were "so far unavenged." *Mother Earth,* June 1914.

62. According to Leonard Abbott, "Berkman inspired the entire fight and was in the thick of it." Leonard D. Abbott, "The Courage and Faith of Alexander Berkman," *Road to Freedom,* December 1930.

63. "Tarrytown Police Rout I.W.W. Forces," *New York Times,* June 1, 1914.

64. Ibid.

65. "Anarchists Egged in Tarrytown Riot," *New York Times,* June 23, 1914. Also arrested was David Sullivan, who spent thirty days in jail. Sullivan was an undercover New York City police detective who had infiltrated the I.W.W. and Berkman's circle.

66. Ibid.

67. Ibid.

68. Leonard D. Abbott, "The Fight in Tarrytown and Its Tragic Outcome," *Mother Earth,* July 1914.

69. Ibid.

70. Tresca, unpublished autobiography, 302–306. Avrich, "Lexington Avenue."

71. Paul Avrich, *The Russian Anarchists* (Princeton: Princeton University Press, 1967), 63.

72. *Mother Earth,* July 1914.

73. *Mother Earth,* August 1914.

74. Avrich, *The Modern School Movement,* 219.

75. Richard Drinnon and Anna Maria Drinnon, eds., *Nowhere at Home: Letters from Exile of Emma Goldman and Alexander Berkman* (New York: Schocken Books, 1975), xxvii.

76. Paul Avrich interview with Moritz Jagendorf, New York City, May 28, 1973. Avrich, *The Modern School Movement;* Avrich, *Anarchist Voices.*

77. Will Durant and Ariel Durant, *A Dual Autobiography* (New York: Simon and Schuster, 1977), 25.

78. Paul Avrich interview with Gussie Denenberg, Washington, D.C., March 20, 1973. Denenberg was Jack Isaacson's wife.

79. Paul Avrich interview with Charles Plunkett. Plunkett said: "Emma Goldman was not involved—in fact she was away on a lecture tour at the time." In the July 1914 issue of *Mother Earth,* Plunkett wrote, "We replaced [Rockefeller's] conscience; we became his Nemesis. His well-oiled conscience acquitted him; but we, the militant workers, have convicted him and passed judgment from his own Bible–'A life for a life.' "

80. Paul Avrich interview with Maurice Hollod.

81. Paul Avrich interview with Charles Plunkett; Paul Avrich interview with Gussie Denenberg.

82. Paul Avrich interview with Charles Plunkett; Paul Avrich interview with Gussie Denenberg; Paul Avrich interview with Jacques Rudome, New York City, February 10, 1972.

83. "Exploded in Apartment Occupied by Tarrytown Disturbers," *New York Times,* July 5, 1914; Paul Avrich interview with Gussie Denenberg.

84. Paul Avrich interview with Moritz Jagendorf.

85. "Caron's Death Won't End It," *New York Times,* July 5, 1914.

86. "Exploded in Apartment Occupied by Tarrytown Disturbers," *New York Times,* July 5, 1914; Avrich, "Lexington Avenue."

87. "The Lexington Avenue Explosion," *Mother Earth,* July 1914; "Exploded in Apartment Occupied by Tarrytown Disturbers," *New York Times,* July 5, 1914.

88. "Exploded in Apartment Occupied by Tarrytown Disturbers."

89. Ibid.

90. "Caron's Death Won't End It," *New York Times,* July 5, 1914.

91. Paul Avrich interview with Emma Cohen Gilbert, White Plains, N.Y., September 23, 1974.

92. "Exploded in Apartment Occupied by Tarrytown Disturbers."

93. "Berkman Reveals Anarchists' Plot," *New York Times,* February 16, 1915.

94. *Mother Earth,* July 1914.

95. Paul Avrich interview with Maurice Hollod.

96. Paul Avrich interview with Emma Cohen Gilbert.

97. Joseph J. Cohen and Alexis C. Ferm, *The Modern School of Stelton: A Sketch* (Stelton, N.J.: Modern School Association of North America, 1925), 121.

98. The commemorative urn was brought to Stelton, where the ashes were scattered in a ceremony led by Leonard Abbott; the urn was then used as a bell to summon colonists

to classes and meetings. The Ferrer Center closed in 1918 as a result of strife over the war. See Avrich, *The Modern School Movement.*

99. Paul Avrich interview with Rose Goldblatt, New York City, October 20, 1975. Rose Goldblatt's sisters, Lillian and Helen Goldblatt, participated in the Tarrytown demonstrations. Rose Goldblatt said "the horror over the whole [bombing incident] for them cannot be exaggerated."

100. Irwin Granich and Mike Gold, "Three Whose Hatred Killed Them," *The Masses,* August 1914; Adolf Wolff, "To Our Martyred Dead: Arthur Caron, Charles Berg, and Carl Hanson," *Mother Earth,* July 1914; *Golos Ssylnykh I Zakliuchennykh Russkikh Anarkhistov,* October 1914; *Woman Rebel,* July 1914.

101. According to *Mother Earth,* it was "the most impressive of its kind ever held in America." *Mother Earth,* July 1914.

102. "5,000 at Memorial to Anarchist Dead," *New York Times,* July 12, 1914.

103. Ibid.

104. Ibid.

105. *Mother Earth,* July 1914; "5,000 at Memorial to Anarchist Dead," *New York Times,* July 12, 1914.

106. *Mother Earth,* July 1914. Avrich, "Lexington Avenue."

17. Trouble in Paradise

1. *Mother Earth,* May 1914; Alexander Berkman, "Anti-Militarist Propaganda," *Mother Earth,* September 1914; *Mother Earth,* October 1914.

2. Berkman, "Anti-Militarist Propaganda."

3. *Mother Earth,* August 1914.

4. Isadore Wisotsky, "Such a Life," Tamiment Library, New York University, 147; Alexander Berkman to Leonard Abbott, February 2, 1930, Abbott Papers, Private collection, New York City.

5. *Mother Earth,* January 1915; Emma Goldman, *Living My Life* (New York: A. A. Knopf, 1931), 562–563.

6. Berkman to Helen Goldblatt, November 16, 1914, Rudome Papers, Paul Avrich Collection, Library of Congress.

7. *Mother Earth,* February 1915; M. Eleanor Fitzgerald to Jack Rudome, December 14, 1914, Rudome Papers.

8. Berkman to Lucy Robins Lang, February 2, 1930, Lucy Robins Lang Papers, Joseph A. Labadie Collection, Harlan Hatcher Library, University of Michigan.

9. Berkman to Helen and Lillian Goldblatt, February 18, 1915, Rudome Papers.

10. "Los Angeles Times Plant Is Demolished by Explosion," *Oakland Tribune,* October 1, 1910.

11. "Many Killed in Newspaper Fire," *Marion Daily Star,* October 1, 1910.

12. *Oakland Tribune,* October 1, 1910.

13. *Mother Earth,* December 1911.

14. Paul Avrich interview with Jeanne Levey, Miami, Fla., December 19, 1972; Lucy Robins Lang, *Tomorrow Is Beautiful* (New York: Macmillan, 1948), 45–46.

15. Lang, *Tomorrow Is Beautiful,* 76; William J. Burns, *The Masked War* (New York: George H. Doran, 1913), 55–56.

16. Lang, *Tomorrow Is Beautiful,* 51–54.

17. Burns, *The Masked War,* 91–92.

18. Grace Heilman Stimson, *Rise of the Labor Movement in Los Angeles* (Berkeley: University of California Press, 1955), 413.

19. *Seattle Post-Intelligencer Northwest,* August 24, 1975.

20. Charles Pierre Le Warne, *Utopias on Puget Sound, 1885–1915* (Seattle: University of Washington Press, 1975), 203–204.

21. Burns, *The Masked War,* 65.

22. Paul Avrich interview with Radium La Vene, Los Angeles, June 22, 1974.

23. Ibid.

24. Lincoln Steffens, *The Autobiography of Lincoln Steffens* (New York: Harcourt, Brace, 1931), 697.

25. Hutchins Hapgood, *A Victorian in the Modern World* (New York: Harcourt, Brace, 1939), 197, 291.

26. According to records from Columbia County, Oregon, Gertrude E. Vose married Joseph B. Meserve on November 18, 1888.

27. Carlos A. Schwantes, "Free Love and Free Speech on the Pacific Northeast Frontier," *Pacific Northwest Frontier Quarterly.*

28. Emma Goldman, "Donald Vose: The Accursed," *Mother Earth,* January 1916.

29. *Discontent,* August 7, 1901; *The Demonstrator,* June 7, 1905; *Free Society,* May 10, 1903; May 15, 1904.

30. Lang, *Tomorrow Is Beautiful,* 50.

31. William Z. Foster, *Pages of a Worker's Life* (New York: International Publishers, 1939), 208–209.

32. Lang, *Tomorrow Is Beautiful,* 76, 80; Foster, *Pages of a Worker's Life,* 208.

33. Anitra Balzer, "Donald Vose: Home Grown Traitor," *Communal Societies,* 8 (1988), 90–103.

34. Foster, *Pages of a Worker's Life,* 208–209; *Mother Earth,* December 1915; Lang, *Tomorrow Is Beautiful,* 76–80; Goldman, *Living My Life,* 550–551; Le Warne, *Utopias on Puget Sound,* 204–205.

35. Paul Avrich interview with Eva Brandes, New York City, September 9, 1974.

36. Goldman, "Donald Vose: The Accursed."

37. Goldman, *Living My Life,* 545.

38. Paul Avrich, *Anarchist Voices: An Oral History of Anarchism in America* (Princeton: Princeton University Press, 1995), 213, 278.

39. Hapgood, *A Victorian in the Modern World,* 200.

40. Goldman, "Donald Vose: The Accursed"; Goldman, *Living My Life,* 550–551.

41. Paul Avrich interview with Eva Brandes.

42. Paul Avrich interview with Gussie Denenberg, Washington, D.C., 1973, 1976.

43. Goldman, *Living My Life,* 551.

44. "4-Year Chase Lands Alleged Dynamiter," *New York Times,* February 14, 1915.

45. "Last of Alleged Dynamiters Taken," *La Crosse Tribune,* February 19, 1915. Caplan was arrested on February 18, five days after Schmidt.

46. "Charged with Complicity in Dynamite Case," *Newark Daily Advocate,* February 19, 1915.

47. Goldman, *Living My Life,* 551.

48. Goldman, "Donald Vose: The Accursed"; Emma Goldman to Reb Raney, October 23, 1929, Goldman Archive, International Institute of Social History, Amsterdam.

49. "Berkman Reveals Anarchists' Plot," *New York Times,* February 16, 1915.

50. "Typist Testifies in Favor of Schmidt," *Ogden Standard,* December 28, 1915.

51. Balzer, "Donald Vose: Home Grown Stool Pigeon," 11–12; Lang, *Tomorrow Is Beautiful,* 81–82.

52. *The Blast,* January 15, 1916; "Address of Matthew A. Schmidt before his Executioner in the Court of Los Angeles, January 12, 1916," *Mother Earth,* February 1916; Balzer, "Donald Vose: Home Grown Stool Pigeon." Lincoln Steffens also was involved in the defense efforts.

53. *Bridgeman's Magazine,* February 1916, 90.

54. *Mother Earth,* March–June 1916, January 1917; *The Blast,* October 15, 1916; Lang, *Tomorrow Is Beautiful,* 229, 270–271; Wisotsky, "Such a Life," 150.

55. "Sister of Millionaire Marries Former Convict," *Tucson Daily Citizen,* January 13, 1947. Livermore, the daughter of an electrical power tycoon, was friendly with Matthew Schmidt's sister, Katherine Schmidt. After his release, Schmidt spent some time in Wisconsin and Chicago, where he was offered work at the Chicago Federation of Labor newspaper and radio station. Schmidt and Livermore announced news of their marriage in January 1947, and some accounts list their marriage year as 1947.

56. "Socialite Dies in Car Plunge," *Oakland Tribune,* June 3, 1954.

57. "Plunge Kills SF Socialite," *Fresno Bee,* June 3, 1954.

58. "Socialite Dies in Car Plunge."

59. Steffens, *Autobiography,* 697; Lang, *Tomorrow Is Beautiful,* 289; Matthew Schmidt to Senya Fleshin and Mollie Steimer, April 26, 1953, Fleshin Archive, International Institute of Social History, Amsterdam.

60. Balzer, "Donald Vose: Home Grown Stool Pigeon," 1–2; Goldman, *Living My Life,* 573.

61. Paul Avrich interview with Radium La Vene.

62. Goldman, "Donald Vose: The Accursed."

63. Balzer, "Donald Vose: Home Grown Stool Pigeon."

64. "Diary of Eugene O'Neill," Eugene O'Neill Papers, Yale Collection of American Literature, Beinecke Rare Book and Manuscript Library.

65. Winifred L. Frazer, *Emma Goldman and The Iceman Cometh* (Gainesville: University Press of Florida, 1974); Frazer in *Eugene O'Neill Newsletter,* May 1979; Louis Sheaffer, *O'Neill, Son and Playwright* (Boston: Little, Brown, 1968), 102, 106, 122–123.

66. Sheaffer, *O'Neill,* 335–336, 427–428, 491; Terry Carlin letter, *Revolt,* January 22, 1916; Hutchins Hapgood, "The Case of Terry," *Revolt,* February 19, 1916; Arthur and

Barbara Gelb, *O'Neill* (New York: Harper, 1962), 286–294, 309; Hapgood, *A Victorian in the Modern World,* 396–397; S. E. Parker letter, January 18, 1978, Paul Avrich Collection, Library of Congress; Paul Avrich interview with Eva Brandes.

18. The Blast

1. *Mother Earth,* September 1907; *The Demonstrator,* October 2, 1907.
2. Emma Goldman, *Living My Life* (New York: A. A. Knopf, 1931), 399–400.
3. Lucy Robins Lang, *Tomorrow Is Beautiful* (New York: Macmillan, 1948), 89.
4. Goldman, *Living My Life,* 399–400; Emma Goldman to John Fitzpatrick, August 20, 1917, B. W. Huebsch Papers, Library of Congress. Berkman liked the idea of relocating to California, but setting up shop in Los Angeles, he believed, might have interfered with the ongoing Caplan and Schmidt trials.
5. Alexander Berkman to Upton Sinclair, December 31, 1915, Upton Sinclair Papers, Lilly Library, Indiana University, Bloomington.
6. Berkman to Helen Goldblatt, December 18, 1915, Rudome Papers, Paul Avrich Collection, Library of Congress.
7. Alexander Berkman, "An Intimate Word to the Social Rebels of America," *Mother Earth,* December 1915.
8. Alexander Berkman, "THE BLAST," *Mother Earth,* January 1916.
9. *The Blast,* January 15, 1916.
10. Jay Fox to Berkman, Eric Morton, and Eleanor Fitzgerald, January 19, 1916, Paul Avrich Collection. The paper was soon considered one of the most influential anarchist publications in America, second only to *Mother Earth.*
11. *The Blast,* February 19 and May 1, 1916.
12. *The Blast,* January 15, 1916. One could subscribe for half a year at the price of sixty cents.
13. Berkman to Louise Bryant, July 20, 1916, Louise Bryant Papers, Manuscripts and Archives, Yale University Library.
14. Goldman, *Living My Life,* 313. Goldman makes a similar comment on 125.
15. Ibid., 552–553, 582.
16. *Mother Earth,* September 1916; Goldman, *Living My Life,* 577–578.
17. *The Blast,* August 15, 1916.
18. Tom Mooney, "Will Organized Labor Help?" *The Blast,* April 1, 1916.
19. Richard H. Frost, *The Mooney Case* (Stanford: Stanford University Press, 1968), 95. This comment was attributed to the editor of the *New York Times.*
20. "Doctor Saw Bomb Hurled into Preparedness Parade," *Oakland Tribune,* September 20, 1916.
21. Paul Avrich interview with Grace Umrath, New York City, September 24, 1974, and October 27, 1975.
22. Alexander Berkman, "A Raid and a Visit," *The Blast,* August 15, 1916.
23. Ibid.

24. Berkman to Warren Van Valkenburgh, August 23, 1916, Emma Goldman's Papers Project, University of California, Berkeley. Van Valkenburgh often went by the pseudonym Walter Starrett.

25. Alexander Berkman, "To Hell with the Government," *The Blast,* May 1, 1916.

26. Paul Avrich interview with Marion Bell, Los Angeles, June 21, 1974; Thomas H. Bell to Frank Scully, December 6, 1936, Paul Avrich Collection, Library of Congress.

27. *The Blast,* March 4 and July 1, 1916; *Mother Earth,* June and July 1916.

28. Richard Drinnon, "The Blast: An Introduction and an Appraisal," *Labor History* 11 (1970), 2; *Mother Earth,* January 1917.

29. Ibid.

30. Paul Avrich interview with Joseph Spivak, Bronx, N.Y., October 5, 1971.

31. *Mother Earth,* November 1916; Berkman to Harry Weinberger, December 13, 1916, Harry Weinberger Papers, Yale University.

32. Berkman to Weinberger, August 12, 1917, Weinberger Papers.

33. Paul Avrich interview with Art Shields, New York City, December 23, 1986.

34. "Frank Walsh Gives to Bomb Defense," *Fresno Morning Republican,* September 9, 1916.

35. *Mother Earth,* December 1916; Berkman to Weinberger, December 13, 1916.

36. Goldman to Agnes Inglis, February 27, 1917, Joseph A. Labadie Collection, Harlan Hatcher Library, University of Michigan; Agnes A. Inglis notes, Labadie Collection, Harlan Hatcher Library, University of Michigan.

37. Goldman to Ellen Kennan, February 5, 1917, Goldman Papers, Tamiment Library, New York University; Agnes A. Inglis notes, Labadie Collection.

38. Paul Avrich interview with Grace Umrath, New York City, September 24, 1974, and October 27, 1975. Some anarchists, though, doubted the authenticity of the photos—even those who were certain Mooney had been framed. Grace Umrath, the granddaughter of Abe and Mary Isaak, later recalled, "I used to take piano lessons from Rena Mooney. She had a large copy of that photograph—with the clock—on the piano leaning against the wall. It was a phony picture, you know, a composite with the clock superimposed. The defense could never produce the negative in court . . . everybody used to look at the picture and laugh at it. They all knew it was a fake."

39. *Mother Earth,* February and April 1917; *The Blast,* March 15, 1917.

40. Eleanor Fitzgerald to Ellen Kennan, October 28, 1916, Paul Avrich Collection; *Mother Earth,* January 1917; *The Blast,* January 1, 1917; Alexander Berkman in *Cronaca Sovversiva,* January 4, 1917.

41. Berkman to Warren Van Valkenburgh, April 21, 1917, Berkman Archive, International Institute of Social History, Amsterdam.

42. *Mother Earth,* May 1917; *The Blast,* May 1, 1917. After all this, however, only two issues appeared, on May 1 and June 1, not for lack of funds but because the paper was suppressed by the federal government.

43. Goldman, *Living My Life,* 594.

44. Ibid., 593.

45. Paul Avrich interview with Morris Ganberg, Bronx, N.Y., February 2, 1974; Goldman, *Living My Life,* 599.

46. Frost, *The Mooney Case,* 284–286.

47. "Berkman Indicted Again," *New York Times,* July 15, 1917; Berkman to Weinberger, August 12, 1917.

48. Drinnon, "The Blast: An Introduction and an Appraisal," 2–3; Frost, *The Mooney Case,* 252; Berkman to Goldman, 1917, Berkman Archive.

49. Henry Alsberg, "Alexander Berkman's Sixtieth Birthday Celebration," Central Opera House, New York City, pamphlet (New York: n.p., November 20, 1930), Joseph A. Labadie Collection, Harlan Hatcher Library, University of Michigan.

50. Eleanor Fitzgerald to Lucy and Bob Robins, July 14, 1917, Lucy Robins Lang Papers, Joseph A. Labadie Collection, Harlan Hatcher Library, University of Michigan. Goldman contacted Lillian Wald and Bolton Hall, seeking aid. Goldman to Lillian D. Wald, August 22, 1917, Lillian Wald Papers, Columbia University.

51. Goldman to Bolton Hall, August 26, 1917, Goldman Archive.

52. Goldman to Catherine Breshkovskaya, October 4, 1917, Goldman Archive.

53. Emma Goldman, *Mother Earth,* August 1917.

54. *The Papers of Woodrow Wilson, Volume 46: January 16–March 12, 1918*, ed. Arthur S. Link (Princeton: Princeton University Press, 1984), 71.

55. Goldman, *Living My Life,* 637–639; Frost, *The Mooney Case,* 253; *Mother Earth Bulletin,* October 1917.

56. George F. Kennan, *Russia Leaves the War* (Princeton: Princeton University Press, 1956), 356–403.

57. Frost, *The Mooney Case,* 295–297; Kennan, *Russia Leaves the War,* 356–403.

58. Frost, *The Mooney Case,* 297–298; Drinnon, "*The Blast*: An Introduction and an Appraisal," 3.

59. Paul Avrich interviews with undisclosed sources.

60. Paul Avrich, *Sacco and Vanzetti: The Anarchist Background* (Princeton: Princeton University Press, 1991), 138, 142–145.

19. The Great War

1. Kropotkin was particularly concerned about France, the home of the great revolution and the influential if short-lived Paris Commune, which he viewed as a potential haven for social enlightenment.

2. Peter Kropotkin, "A Letter on the Present War," *Freedom* (London), October 1914; *Mother Earth,* November 1914. Kropotkin addressed the remark to Norwegian chemist Gustave Steffen.

3. Paul Avrich interview with Alexandra Kropotkin, New York City, March 10, 1965; Paul Avrich, *The Russian Anarchists* (Princeton: Princeton University Press, 1967), 116; Peter Kropotkin to Luigi Bertoni, August 27, 1913, *Le Reveil,* Joseph Ishill Collection, Houghton Library, Harvard University.

4. *Mother Earth,* November 1914; *The Blast,* February 19, 1916.

5. These included U.S.-based Errico Malatesta, Leonard Abbott, Hippolyte Havel, Harry Kelly, Bill Shatoff, Saul Yanovsky, and Joseph Cohen, as well as such European anarchists as Luigi Bertoni, Thomas Keell, F. Domela Nieuwenhuis, and Alexander Schapiro.

6. *Freedom* (London), March 1915.

7. *Mother Earth,* December 1914. Among those who signed were Jean Grave, Paul Reclus, V. N. Cherkezov, Christian Cornelissen, Thomas Bell, John Turner, and William C. Owen. For a critique see Errico Malatesta, "Pro-Government Anarchists," *The Blast,* May 15, 1916. Kropotkin's attitude against Germany had its antithesis in Max Nettlau and Dr. Michael Cohn, who took a strongly pro-German stance.

8. Woodrow Wilson statement to joint session of Congress, April 2, 1917, Washington, D.C.

9. Horace C. Peterson and Gilbert C. Fite, *Opponents of War, 1917–1918* (Madison: University of Wisconsin Press, 1957), 14.

10. Paul Avrich, *Sacco and Vanzetti: The Anarchist Background* (Princeton: Princeton University Press, 1991), 133.

11. William Preston, *Aliens and Dissenters: Federal Suppression of Radicals, 1903–1933* (Champaign: University of Illinois Press, 1994), 67–76.

12. *Mother Earth,* March 1917.

13. Emma Goldman, "The No-Conscription League," *Mother Earth,* June 1917.

14. Emma Goldman, *Living My Life* (New York: A. A. Knopf, 1931), 599; Paul Avrich interview with Morris Ganberg, Bronx, N.Y., February 2, 1974.

15. Berkman to Agnes Inglis, May 17, 1917, Joseph A. Labadie Collection, Harlan Hatcher Library, University of Michigan.

16. Goldman, "The No-Conscription League"; Goldman, *Living My Life,* 598–603.

17. Berkman to Dear Friend, May 25, 1917, Berkman Papers, Tamiment Library, New York University.

18. Leonard Abbott to Emma Goldman, December 28, 1929, Goldman Archive, International Institute of Social History, Amsterdam; *The Blast,* June 1, 1917; Berkman to Dear Friend, June 1917, Berkman Papers, Tamiment Library.

19. "Anarchists Awed by Police Clubs," *New York Times,* June 5, 1917.

20. *Mother Earth,* July 1917; "Anarchists Awed by Police Clubs," *New York Times,* June 5, 1917.

21. Goldman, *Living My Life,* 607–609; Richard Drinnon, *Rebel in Paradise: A Biography of Emma Goldman* (Chicago: University of Chicago Press, 1961), 186–187.

22. Zechariah Chafee, *Free Speech in the United States* (Cambridge, Mass.: Harvard University Press, 1948), 3.

23. Paul Avrich, *Sacco and Vanzetti: The Anarchist Background,* 94. The following year, on May 16, 1918, the Sedition Act extended penalties to anyone who discouraged recruitment or uttered, printed, wrote, or published any "disloyal, profane, scurrilous, or abusive language" against the government, constitution, flag, or uniform of the United States. Altogether some 1,500 prosecutions were carried out under the Espionage and Sedition Acts, resulting in more than 1,000 convictions.

24. Goldman, *Living My Life,* 610. The raiding party included Assistant U. S. Attorney E. M. Stanton; Lieutenant Barnitz of the Bomb Squad; Deputy Marshals Doran, Hearne, and Meade; and Detectives Murphy and Kiely of the Police Department.

25. Telegram to Agnes Inglis, June 15, 1917, Labadie Collection; *Mother Earth,* July 1917; Goldman, *Living My Life,* 610–613.

26. "Emma Goldman and A. Berkman behind the Bars," *New York Times,* June 16, 1917.

27. Goldman, *Living My Life,* 642, 644. The *Mother Earth Bulletin* lasted until April 1918. Stella Ballantine and M. Eleanor Fitzgerald also ran the Mother Earth Book Shop in Greenwich Village, where they sold radical literature and distributed pamphlets and information; this, too, closed in 1918.

28. "Emma Goldman and A. Berkman behind the Bars," *New York Times,* June 16, 1917.

29. Goldman, *Living My Life,* 612.

30. "Emma Goldman and A. Berkman behind the Bars," *New York Times,* June 16, 1917.

20. Big Fish

1. Emma Goldman, *Living My Life* (New York: A. A. Knopf, 1931), 613–614.

2. "Reds Are Defiant, Can Get No Delay," *New York Times,* June 28, 1917.

3. Goldman, *Living My Life,* 615.

4. Ibid., 613.

5. *Mother Earth,* July 1917.

6. "Convict Berkman and Miss Goldman; Both Off to Prison," *New York Times,* July 10, 1917.

7. Leonard Abbott, "The Trial and Conviction of Emma Goldman and Alexander Berkman," *Trial and Speech of Alexander Berkman and Emma Goldman in the United States District Court, in the City of New York, July, 1917* (New York: Mother Earth Publishing Association, 1917).

8. Ella Winter and Granville Hicks, eds., *The Letters of Lincoln Steffens,* 2 vols. (New York: Harcourt, Brace, 1938); Justin Kaplan, *Lincoln Steffens: A Biography* (New York: Simon & Schuster, 1974), 234; Abbott, "Trial and Conviction of Goldman and Berkman." The prosecutor asked Abbott a number of questions about his own anarchist activity.

9. "Anarchists Close Their Defense," *New York Times,* July 7, 1917.

10. "Alexander Berkman's Address to the Jury," *Trial and Speech of Alexander Berkman and Emma Goldman in the United States District Court, in the City of New York, July, 1917* (New York: Mother Earth Publishing Association, 1917).

11. "Convict Berkman and Miss Goldman; Both Off to Prison," *New York Times,* July 10, 1917. Berkman spoke for about two hours, Goldman for about one hour.

12. "Emma Goldman's Address to the Jury," *Trial and Speech of Alexander Berkman and Emma Goldman in the United States District Court, in the City of New York, July, 1917* (New York: Mother Earth Publishing Association, 1917).

13. Ibid.

14. "Convict Berkman and Miss Goldman; Both Off to Prison," *New York Times,* July 10, 1917.

15. Ibid.

16. *Mother Earth Bulletin,* October 1917.

17. "Convict Berkman and Miss Goldman; Both Off to Prison," *New York Times,* July 10, 1917.

18. Ibid.

19. Abbott, "Trial and Conviction of Goldman and Berkman."

20. Eleanor Fitzgerald to Agnes Inglis, July 12, 1917, Joseph A. Labadie Collection, Harlan Hatcher Library, University of Michigan; Harry Weinberger to Frank P. Walsh, July 10, 1917, Harry Weinberger Papers, Yale University.

21. Goldman, *Living My Life,* 624.

22. Ibid., 626.

23. Ibid.; "Convict Berkman and Miss Goldman; Both Off to Prison," *New York Times,* July 10, 1917.

24. It was in the Tombs that Berkman learned of his indictment in California for conspiracy in the Mooney-Billings case.

25. Emma Goldman to Agnes Inglis, July 29, 1917, Labadie Collection.

26. Harry Weinberger, "A Rebel's Interrupted Autobiography," *American Journal of Economics and Sociology,* October 1942, 112–113.

27. "More Anti-Draft Agitators in Jail, Anarchists Held," *New York Times,* June 3, 1917.

28. Two others, Joseph Walker and Louis Sternberg, were acquitted.

29. "Anarchists Convicted of Obstructing Draft," *New York Times,* June 13, 1917.

30. "To Recommend that Kramer Be Deported," *Lewiston Daily Sun* (Lewiston, Maine), June 12, 1917.

31. *Mother Earth,* July 1917.

32. *Mother Earth Bulletin,* November 1917, March and April 1918; Goldman to Helen Keller, February 3, 1918, Goldman Papers, Tamiment Library, New York University.

33. Goldman, *Living My Life,* 648–649.

34. Berkman to Goldman, October 1, 1917, Labadie Collection.

35. Berkman to Eleanor Fitzgerald, March 31, 1918, Berkman Archives, International Institute of Social History, Amsterdam; Richard Polenberg, *Fighting Faiths: The Abrams Case, the Supreme Court, and Free Speech* (New York: Viking Books, 1987), 302.

36. *Mother Earth Bulletin,* March 1918; Harry Weinberger to Dr. J. Calvin Weaver, April 17, 1918; Fred G. Zerbst to Harry Weinberger, April 20, 1918, both in Harry Weinberger Papers.

37. Harry Weinberger to Berkman, February 15, 1918, Harry Weinberger Papers.

38. Weinberger to Stella Ballantine, March 6, 1918, Harry Weinberger Papers; *Mother Earth Bulletin,* March 1918.

39. Weinberger to Ballantine, March 6, 1918, Harry Weinberger Papers.

40. Polenberg, *Fighting Faiths,* 302.

41. Berkman to Eleanor Fitzgerald, June 3, 1919, Berkman Archive.

42. Upton Sinclair to Berkman, October 28, 1924, Lilly Library, Indiana University, Bloomington; Hutchins Hapgood to Berkman, March 5, 1918, Berkman Papers, Tamiment Library, New York University; Rebekah Raney to Berkman, March 9, 1918, Berkman Papers; Berkman to Eleanor Fitzgerald, April 21, 1918, Berkman Papers; Goldman, *Living My Life,* 220–222.

43. Minna Lowensohn to Berkman, March 8 and March 15, 1918, Berkman Papers.

44. Berkman to Eleanor Fitzgerald, via Fitzgerald to Harry Weinberger, March 20, 1918, Harry Weinberger Papers.

45. Berkman to "Vera Figner" (Fitzgerald), April 7, 1918, Berkman Archive.

46. Ammon A. Hennacy, *The One-Man Revolution in America* (Salt Lake City: Ammon Hennacy Publications, 1970), 99, 105, 110; Hennacy, "In Prison with Alexander Berkman," *Road to Freedom,* December 1930; Ammon A. Hennacy to Agnes Inglis, September 8, 1940, Labadie Collection.

47. Joseph Patrick Tumulty, *Woodrow Wilson as I Know Him* (Garden City, N.J.: Doubleday, Page & Company, 1921), 505.

48. Goldman, *Living My Life,* 220–222; *Solidarity,* June 15, 1898.

49. Ray Ginger, *Eugene V. Debs: A Biography* (New York: Collier Books, 1965), 412–413; J. Robert Constantine, ed., *Letters of Eugene V. Debs* (Urbana: University of Illinois Press, 1990), 531.

50. "Statement by Alexander Berkman," October 1, 1919.

51. B. W. Huebsch to Louis F. Post, February 12, 1918, National Archives Record Group 60, Department of Justice, Central File #186233-13, section 3, Washington, D.C.; Post to Huebsch, February 14, 1918; Francis H. Duehay to B. W. Huebsch, February 16, 1918; C. H. McGlasson, Acting Superintendent of Prisons, to Frank G. Zerbst, March 8, 1918; Francis H. Duehay to Roger Baldwin, March 18, 1918; Harry Weinberger to C. H. McGlasson, June 20, 1918; Samuel J. Graham to Harry Weinberger, June 24, 1918, all in ibid., file 186233-13. Graham copied Warden Fred Zerbst on this exchange.

52. Berkman to Rudolf Grossmann, November 7, 1919, Berkman Archive, International Institute of Social History, Amsterdam.

53. "A Fragment of the Prison Experiences of Emma Goldman and Alexander Berkman in the State Prison at Jefferson City, Mo., and the U.S. Penitentiary at Atlanta, Ga., February, 1918–October, 1919," Stella Ballantine, ed. (Mother Earth Publishing, 1919).

54. "Reply of Fred G. Zerbst, Warden," *Atlanta Constitution,* October 4, 1919.

55. "Statement by Alexander Berkman," *Atlanta Constitution,* October 1, 1919.

56. Harry Weinberger to Francis H. Duehay, March 5, 1919, Department of Justice, Record Group 60, file 186233-13, National Archives; Duehay to Weinberger, March 14, 1919, Harry Weinberger Papers; Harry Weinberger to Frank G. Zerbst, March 27, 1919, Department of Justice, Record Group 60, file 186233-13; Weinberger to Zerbst, April 7, 1919; Zerbst to Weinberger, March 29, 1919, both in Harry Weinberger Papers. Zerbst to Duehay, March 12 and 18, 1919, Department of Justice, Record Group 60, file 186233-13, National Archives.

57. Alexander Berkman and Emma Goldman, "A Fragment of the Prison Experiences," 3, 13, 25.

58. Harry Kelly, "A Tribute to Berkman," *Alexander Berkman: Rebel and Anarchist,* Alexander Berkman Memorial Committee and Jewish Anarchist Federation (New York, July 1936).

59. Goldman, *Living My Life,* 698–700.

60. Emma Goldman, "The State Prison at Jefferson City, Mo.," "A Fragment of the Prison Experiences." As noted earlier, Goldman seldom discussed the subjects of race and racism, although racial discrimination of the kind she witnessed in the prison disturbed her greatly.

61. *Mother Earth Bulletin,* March 1918.

62. Goldman, *Living My Life,* 659.

63. Stella Ballantine was allowed visits of two hours, twice a day, for three successive days, plus an hour in the yard. According to Ballantine, Painter was "an open minded liberal individual." Stella Ballantine, "My Visit to Emma Goldman," *Instead of a Magazine,* June 29, 1918.

64. Polenberg, *Fighting Faiths,* 319; Sally M. Miller, *The Life of Socialist Activist Kate Richards O'Hare*; Goldman to Harry Kelly, July 27, 1919; Berkman and Goldman, "A Fragment of the Prison Experiences"; Ballantine, "My Visit to Emma Goldman."

65. Emma Goldman, *Living My Life,* 671; Paul Avrich, *Sacco and Vanzetti: The Anarchist Background* (Princeton: Princeton University Press, 1991), 114.

66. Philip S. Foner and Sally M. Miller, eds., *Kate Richards O'Hare: Selected Writings and Speeches* (Baton Rouge: Louisiana State University Publisher, 1982), 206–209, 219; Kate Richards O'Hare to Dear Sweethearts, October 2, 1919, in "Letters of Kate Richards O'Hare to Her Family," typescript, Bowling Green State University Library (also in the Schlesinger Library, Radcliffe College).

67. Kate Richards O'Hare, June 6, 1919, ibid.

68. Goldman, *Living My Life,* 687.

69. Ibid., 686.

21. The Russian Dream

1. Alexander Berkman to Harry Weinberger, August 13, 1919, Harry Weinberger Papers, Yale University.

2. Berkman to M. Eleanor Fitzgerald, September 17, 1919, M. Eleanor Fitzgerald Papers, Archives Department, University of Wisconsin-Milwaukee.

3. "Statement of Alexander Berkman," September 18, 1919, in Emma Goldman, *Living My Life* (New York: A. A. Knopf, 1931), 703.

4. Berkman was represented by Samuel Castleton, filling in for Weinberger, who was unable to attend.

5. J. Edgar Hoover file, National Archives Record Group 60, Department of Justice, Central File #186233-13, section 3, Washington, D.C.

6. Report of Agent Edward Chastain on October 1, 1919; Report of Agent A. E. Farland, Atlanta, October 4, 1919, both in ibid.

7. Paul Avrich, *Sacco and Vanzetti: The Anarchist Background* (Princeton: Princeton University Press, 1991). The incident occurred June 2, 1919.

8. "Emma Goldman to Be Deported When Released," *Clearfield Progress,* September 27, 1919.

9. "Time to Get Rid of Them," *Daily Northwestern,* September 19, 1919.

10. Goldman, *Living My Life*, 698.

11. Berkman to Rudolf Grossmann, November 7, 1919, Berkman Archive, International Institute of Social History, Amsterdam.

12. Speeches were given by Harry Weinberger, Michael Cohn, activist writer Ella Reeve Bloor, Dr. A. L. Goldwater, and art critic Sadakichi Hartmann. Both Goldman and Berkman took the stage. *Modern School,* June–July 1919; *Freedom* (Stelton, N.J.), August 1919.

13. Approved by Anthony Caminetti, commissioner general of immigration, and John W. Abercrombie, acting secretary of labor. "Decide to Deport Emma Goldman," *New York Times*, November 30, 1919.

14. Emma Goldman to Agnes Inglis, November 21, 1917, Joseph A. Labadie Collection, Harlan Hatcher Library, University of Michigan.

15. Goldman, *Living My Life,* 708–709.

16. Ibid., 709. According to John K. Winkler, upon hearing of Frick's death Berkman said, "Well anyway Frick left the country before I did." John K. Winkler, *Incredible Carnegie: The Life of Andrew Carnegie* (New York: Vanguard Press, 1931), 210.

17. Paul Avrich interview with Gabriel Javsicas, New York City, May 27, 1980.

18. Goldman, *Living My Life,* 710.

19. "Two Notorious 'Reds' Await Deportation," *Oneonta Daily Star,* December 6, 1919.

20. Goldman, *Living My Life,* 711.

21. Harry Weinberger to Anthony Caminetti, November 26, 1919, Harry Weinberger Papers, Yale University.

22. Candace Falk, ed., *Emma Goldman: A Documentary History of the American Years, Vol. 2: Made for America* (Berkeley: University of California Press, 2003), 68–69.

23. Lucy Robins Lang, *Tomorrow Is Beautiful* (New York: Macmillan, 1948), 161; Richard Drinnon, *Rebel in Paradise: A Biography of Emma Goldman* (Chicago: University of Chicago Press, 1961), 217–218.

24. Goldman, *Living My Life,* 712, 714.

25. Richard Polenberg, *Fighting Faiths: The Abrams Case, the Supreme Court, and Free Speech* (New York: Viking Press, 1987), 167.

26. "Alien Radicals Must Get Out," *Star and Sentinel* (Gettysburg, Pa.), December 13, 1919.

27. Goldman, *Living My Life,* 713.

28. Ibid., 715.

29. "Army Transport under Secret Orders," *Fort Wayne Journal Gazette,* December 22, 1919.

30. "249 Reds Sail, Exiled to Soviet Russia; Berkman Threatens to Come Back; Second Shipload May Leave This Week," *New York Times,* December 22, 1919.

31. "Army Transport under Secret Orders," *Fort Wayne Journal Gazette,* December 22, 1919.

32. Alexander Berkman and Emma Goldman, "Deportation–Its Meaning and Menace: Last Message to the People of America," Ellis Island, New York City, December 1919.

33. Goldman, *Living My Life,* 717.

34. Alexander Berkman, *The Bolshevik Myth* (New York: Boni and Liveright, 1925), 14. Buster Keaton's film *The Navigator* made use of the *Buford,* the filmmakers having bought it when the government was going to scrap it. *New York Times,* December 27, 1991.

35. Among the viewing party were Congressmen Isaac Siegel of New York, William Vayle of Colorado, and J. E. Raker of California, and Commissioner General Anthony Caminetti. "249 Reds Sail, Exiled to Soviet Russia," *New York Times,* December 22, 1919.

36. Berkman, *The Bolshevik Myth,* 13.

37. Ibid., 14–15.

38. "Army Transport under Secret Orders," *Fort Wayne Journal Gazette,* December 22, 1919. Lipman, a socialist and participant in the Abrams case, was eventually deported to Russia and executed by Joseph Stalin during the purges.

39. Robert Minor, Introduction to Berkman and Goldman, *Deportation—Its Meaning and Menace,* 3–4.

40. Goldman, *Living My Life,* 723.

41. Alexander Berkman, *The Russian Tragedy* (Berlin: "Der Syndikalist," 1922), 10–11.

42. Berkman, *The Bolshevik Myth,* 21; *The Blast,* May 1, 1917; *Mother Earth Bulletin,* October and November 1917.

43. Goldman to Agnes Inglis, November 21, 1917; *Mother Earth Bulletin,* February and December 1917, January 1918.

44. Goldman to Helen Keller, February 3, 1918, Goldman Papers, Tamiment Library, New York University.

45. "Berkman Sponsor for Trotzky [*sic*] Here," *New York Times,* January 22, 1919.

46. Goldman, *Living My Life,* 596–597.

47. Alexander Berkman, "The Surgeon's Duty," *Mother Earth Bulletin,* January 1918.

48. Berkman, *The Bolshevik Myth,* 90.

49. Harry Weinberger to Goldman, January 15, 1918, Emma Goldman Papers Project, University of California, Berkeley.

50. Lincoln Steffens, *The Autobiography of Lincoln Steffens* (New York: The Literary Guild, 1931), xvi.

51. Lang, *Tomorrow Is Beautiful,* 112; *Fraye Arbeter Shtime,* April 17, 1917.

52. Goldman, *Living My Life,* 661.

53. Goldman to "Babushka," March 19, 1919, Goldman Papers, Tamiment Library, New York University.

54. Berkman, *The Bolshevik Myth,* 30; Mollie Steimer, "Alexander Berkman–The Unforgettable Friend and Comrade," *Fraye Arbeter Shtime,* 1966.

55. Berkman, *The Bolshevik Myth,* 22.

56. "Anarchists Would 'Save United States,'" *Kingsport Times,* January 20, 1920.

57. Ibid.

58. Berkman, *The Bolshevik Myth,* 27.

59. "Russ Welcome Reds from U.S.," *The Pointer,* January 23, 1920.

60. Berkman, *The Bolshevik Myth,* 27.

61. "Russ Welcome Reds from U.S.," *The Pointer,* January 23, 1920.

62. Goldman, *Living My Life,* 726.

63. Berkman, *The Bolshevik Myth,* 28.

22. The Bolshevik Myth

1. Alexander Berkman, *The Bolshevik Myth* (New York: Boni and Liveright, 1925), 28.

2. Paul Avrich interview with Manuel Komroff, Woodstock, N.Y., September 29, 1972.

3. Berkman, *The Bolshevik Myth,* 33.

4. Emma Goldman, *Living My Life* (New York: A. A. Knopf, 1931), 729.

5. Ibid., 739–740.

6. John Clayton for the *Chicago Tribune,* "Anarchist Has Flag in Hotel Room," *San Antonio Evening News* (San Antonio, Tex.), June 18, 1920.

7. Emma Goldman, "Emma Goldman in the Herald Tells How Bolshevism Killed the Real Russian Revolution," *Syracuse Herald,* March 26, 1922.

8. Goldman, *Living My Life,* 738.

9. Theodore Draper, *The Roots of American Communism* (New York: Octagon Books, 1977), 128.

10. Caroline Moorhead, *Bertrand Russell: A Life* (New York: Viking, 1993), 142; Bertrand Russell to Ottoline Morrell, June 25, 1920, Ottoline Morrell Papers, University of Texas, Austin.

11. Bertrand Russell, "Alexander Berkman's Sixtieth Birthday Celebration," Central Opera House, New York City, pamphlet (New York: n.p., November 20, 1930), Joseph A. Labadie Collection, Harlan Hatcher Library, University of Michigan.

12. Goldman, *Living My Life,* 794.

13. Clayton, "Anarchist Has Flag in Hotel Room."

14. Goldman, *Living My Life,* 757.

15. Clayton, "Anarchist Has Flag in Hotel Room."

16. Emma Goldman to Fitzi and Stella, February 28, 1920, Goldman Archive, International Institute of Social History, Amsterdam.

17. Goldman to Dr. Ben L. Reitman, March 8, 1920, Goldman Archive.

18. Harry Kelly to Max Nettlau, May 10, 1920, Nettlau Archive, International Institute of Social History, Amsterdam.

19. Lincoln Steffens to Daniel Kiefer, June 21, 1920, in *The Letters of Lincoln Steffens, 1920–1936,* ed. Ella Winter and Granville Hicks (New York: Harcourt, Brace, 1938), 545.

20. Kropotkin had been receiving rations from the Dmitrov co-op, but it had ceased operation. Goldman, *Living My Life*, 769.

21. Paul Avrich, *The Russian Anarchists* (Princeton: Princeton University Press, 1967), 226. Paul Avrich, *Kropotkin i Ego Uchenie*, ed. G. P. Maximoff (Chicago, 1931), 196–200; Peter Kropotkin, *Kropotkin's Revolutionary Pamphlets* (New York: Vanguard Press, 1927), 24.

22. Berkman, *The Bolshevik Myth*, 75; Paul Avrich, ed., *The Anarchists in the Russian Revolution* (Ithaca: Cornell University Press, 1973), 147–148.

23. Berkman, *The Bolshevik Myth*, 74.

24. Goldman to Lillian Wald, 1920, Lillian D. Wald Papers, Columbia University; Goldman, *Living My Life*, 768–771; Berkman, *The Bolshevik Myth*, 75.

25. Goldman, *Living My Life*, 764.

26. Ibid., 766.

27. Ibid.; Berkman, *The Bolshevik Myth*, 91–92.

28. Clayton, "Anarchist Has Flag in Hotel Room."

29. Goldman, *Living My Life*, 767.

30. Berkman, *The Bolshevik Myth*, 91–92.

31. Goldman, *Living My Life*, 782.

32. Clayton, "Anarchist Has Flag in Hotel Room."

33. Alix Kates Shulman, ed., *Red Emma Speaks: An Emma Goldman Reader* (New York: Schocken Books, 1983), 203–210.

34. Goldman, *Living My Life*, 822.

35. Alexander Berkman to Fitzi and Stella, November 3 and November 22, 1920, Joseph A. Labadie Collection, Harlan Hatcher Library, University of Michigan.

36. Goldman, *Living My Life*, 849.

37. Emma Goldman, *My Disillusionment in Russia* (Garden City, N.Y.: Doubleday, Page, 1923), 100.

38. Ibid.

39. Avrich, *The Russian Anarchists*, 227–228; Avrich, *The Anarchists in the Russian Revolution*, 26.

40. Paul Avrich, *Kronstadt 1921* (Princeton: Princeton University Press, 1970).

41. Berkman to Hudson Hawley, June 12, 1932, Berkman Archive, International Institute of Social History, Amsterdam.

42. Berkman, *The Bolshevik Myth*, 301–302; Avrich, *Kronstadt 1921*, 147, 170.

43. Avrich, *Kronstadt 1921*, 212–213; Berkman, *The Bolshevik Myth*, 303; Goldman, *Living My Life*, 886.

44. Avrich, *The Anarchists in the Russian Revolution*, 138.

45. V. M. Volin's given name was Vsevolod Mikhailovich Eikhenbaum; he generally went by "Volin." Avrich, *Anarchist Portraits* (Princeton, N.J.: Princeton University Press, 1988), 126.

46. Alexander Berkman, ed., *Letters from Russian Prisons* (New York: Albert and Charles Boni, 1925), 253–255. After eighteen years in prison and exile, Aron Baron, Fanya's husband, was unexpectedly set free in 1938, but after settling in Kharkov was seized by the police and never heard from again. Avrich, *The Russian Anarchists*, 245.

47. Paul Avrich, "Bolshevik Opposition to Lenin: G. T. Miasnikov and the Workers' Group," *Russian Review,* 43 (1984), 1–29.

48. Berkman to Harry Kelly, February 13, 1933, Berkman Archive.

49. Goldman, *Living My Life,* 885.

50. Berkman, *The Bolshevik Myth,* 303, 318–319.

23. Charlottengrad

1. Emma Goldman to Michael Cohn, July 23, 1921, Michael Cohn Papers, YIVO Institute for Jewish Research, New York.

2. Emma Goldman, *Living My Life* (New York: A. A. Knopf, 1931), 927.

3. "Not Yet Repentant, Says Emma Goldman," *New York Times,* December 11, 1921.

4. Goldman to Alice Stone Blackwell, 1922, Tamiment Library, New York University.

5. Paul Avrich interview with Ida Gershoy, New York City, June 8, 1983.

6. Goldman, *Living My Life,* 938.

7. "Says Emma Goldman Misjudges the Soviet," *New York Times,* April 17, 1922.

8. "Confirms Discontent of Emma Goldman," *New York Times,* October 23, 1920.

9. Goldman to Max Nettlau, August 7, 1922, Nettlau Archive, International Institute of Social History, Amsterdam.

10. Goldman, *Living My Life,* 928–934, 937.

11. Alexander Berkman to Michael Cohn, March 14, 1922, Michael Cohn Papers.

12. Alexander Berkman, *The Russian Tragedy* (Berlin: Der Syndikalist, 1922).

13. Berkman to Cohn, March 14, 1922.

14. Ibid.

15. Goldman, *Living My Life,* 944.

16. Richard Pipes, *Russia under the Bolshevik Regime* (New York: A. A. Knopf, 1994), 139–140.

17. Goldman to Stewart Kerr, February 12, 1923, Goldman Papers, New York Public Library.

18. Goldman, *Living My Life,* 944.

19. Goldman to Max Nettlau, September 8, 1922, Nettlau Archive.

20. Goldman, *Living My Life,* 950.

21. Teddy and Stella's younger child, David Ballantine, born in 1926, became a writer.

22. Pauline Turkel and Ellen Kennan were among those in the group. Pauline Turkel and M. Eleanor Fitzgerald lived together in Greenwich Village from 1918 to 1923, and then shared a home in Sherman, Connecticut. Paul Avrich interview with Pauline H. Turkel, New York City, January 21, 1972.

23. Goldman to Leon Malmed, August 28, 1923, Leon Malmed and Emma Goldman Papers, Arthur and Elizabeth Schlesinger Library, Radcliffe College.

24. Minna Lowensohn, "Memoirs," Paul Avrich Collection, Library of Congress.

25. Berkman to Agnes A. Inglis, July 10, 1922, Joseph A. Labadie Collection, Harlan Hatcher Library, University of Michigan.

26. Berkman to Joseph Spivak, June 19, 1924, Spivak Papers, Paul Avrich Collection; Bao-Puo, "The Anarchist Movement in China," *Freedom* (London), January 1925.

27. Goldman to Bayard Boyesen, August 23, 1922, Goldman Papers, New York Public Library.

28. Goldman, *Living My Life,* 953.

29. Goldman to Leon Malmed, January 16, 1924, Emma Goldman and Leon Malmed Papers; Goldman to Joseph Ishill, February 25, 1924, Joseph Ishill Papers, Houghton Library, Harvard University.

30. Goldman to Harry Weinberger, June 5, 1924, Harry Weinberger Papers, Yale University.

31. "More about Russia Told by Goldman," *Washington Post,* December 21, 1924.

32. *Times Literary Supplement,* 1925, 159–659.

33. Berkman to Ben Capes, August 11, 1924, Berkman Archive. The complete handwritten diary is in the Berkman Archive, International Institute of Social History, Amsterdam.

34. *New York Times,* April 26, 1925.

35. Alexander Berkman, *The Anti-Climax* (Berlin: Maurer & Dimmick, 1925), 3.

36. M. Eleanor Fitzgerald, printed advertisement, New York City, 1925.

37. Ibid. Fitzgerald sold copies of the book herself, for three dollars a copy, plus fifteen cents for postage, from 45 Grove Street in New York.

38. H. L. Mencken, "Two Wasted Lives," *New York World,* April 26, 1925. Syndicated in papers including the *Syracuse Herald.*

39. Ibid.

40. Goldman to Berkman, June 2 and 6, 1926, Berkman Archive.

41. Fleshin and Berkman Archives, International Institute of Social History, Amsterdam.

42. Michael Cohn to Berkman, October 31, 1924, Berkman Archive.

43. *Bulletin of the Relief Fund of the International Working Men's Association for Anarchists and Anarcho-Syndicalists Imprisoned or Exiled in Russia.*

44. Nicholas Walter, *The Raven: Anarchist Quarterly,* July 1989.

45. Berkman to Max Nettlau, March 21, 1925, Nettlau Archive.

46. Paul Avrich, *The Russian Anarchists* (Princeton: Princeton University Press, 1967), 233–236.

47. Berkman to Theo L. Miles, October 28, 1929, Berkman Archive.

48. Tom Mooney to Berkman, March 18, 1927, Mooney Papers, University of California, Berkeley.

49. Berkman to Mooney, June 24, 1927, Mooney Papers. Matthew Schmidt and Tom Mooney were in San Quentin at the same time, their sentences overlapping for more than two decades.

50. Berkman to Mooney, September 5, 1927, Mooney Papers.

51. Berkman to Mooney, December 2, 1931, Mooney Papers.

24. Globe-Trotters and Colonizers

1. Paul Avrich interview with Freda Diamond, New York City, May 13, 1983.

2. Emma Goldman to Agnes Inglis, September 4, 1924, Joseph A. Labadie Collection, Harlan Hatcher Library, University of Michigan.

3. Goldman to Stella Ballantine, August 20, 1924, Goldman Papers, New York Public Library.

4. Ibid.; Emma Goldman, *Living My Life* (New York: A. A. Knopf, 1931), 959, 961.

5. Goldman, *Living My Life,* 962.

6. Victoria Glendinning, *Rebecca West: A Life* (New York: A. A. Knopf, 1987), 106.

7. Goldman to Stella Ballantine, December 19 and 26, 1924, Goldman Papers, New York Public Library.

8. Goldman, *Living My Life,* 964.

9. Goldman to Alexander Berkman, October 25, 1924, Goldman Archive, International Institute of Social History, Amsterdam.

10. Goldman to Harry Weinberger, October 1924, Harry Weinberger Papers, Yale University; Goldman to Arthur Leonard Ross, October 1, 1924, Goldman Papers, Tamiment Library, New York University.

11. Bertrand Russell to Goldman, October 25, 1924, Goldman Archive.

12. "Emma Goldman in Her New Role," *New York Times,* November 13, 1924.

13. "The World's Window," *Atlanta Constitution,* November 27, 1924.

14. Goldman to Alexander Schapiro, November 1924, Goldman Archive; Goldman, *Living My Life,* 964.

15. Goldman to Havelock Ellis, December 1, 1924, Goldman Archive.

16. Goldman, *Living My Life,* 979.

17. Goldman to Berkman, August 27, 1925, Berkman Archive, International Institute of Social History, Amsterdam.

18. Edward Carpenter to Berkman, October 30, 1925, Berkman Archive; Carpenter to Goldman, December 3, 1924, Goldman Archive.

19. Goldman, *Living My Life,* 980.

20. Ibid.

21. Goldman to Stella Ballantine, June 2, 1925, Goldman Archive.

22. Glendenning, *Rebecca West,* 106–107.

23. Goldman to Walter Peacock, September 2, 1925, Goldman Archive.

24. Goldman, *Living My Life,* 979.

25. Goldman to Berkman, August 13, September 23, and September 27, 1925, Berkman Archive.

26. Goldman to Berkman, August 23, 1925, Berkman Archive.

27. Gabriel Javsicas went on to study economics at Columbia University, wrote about Spain for magazines such as *The Nation,* the *Atlantic Monthly,* and *Harper's,* and later was a supporter of Amnesty International.

28. Paul Avrich interview with Gabriel Javsicas, New York City, May 27, 1980.

29. Goldman to Berkman, July 13, 1925, Berkman Archive.

30. Goldman to Berkman, April 11–12, 1925, Berkman Archive.

31. Goldman to W. S. Van Valkenburgh, April 2, 1925, Goldman Archive.

32. Goldman to Stella Ballantine, June 30, 1925, Goldman Papers, New York Public Library.

33. "Flame Only Glow When Emma Goldman Returns," *Ironwood Daily Globe,* February 3, 1934.

34. Goldman, *Living My Life,* 981.

35. Goldman to Berkman, May 18, 1925, Berkman Archive.

25. Now and After

1. Alexander Berkman to Joseph Ishill, February 25 and March 3, 1926, Joseph Ishill Papers, Houghton Library, Harvard University; Joseph Ishill, *The Oriole Press: A Bibliography* (Berkeley Heights, N.J.: Oriole Press, 1953).

2. Berkman to Harry Kelly, March 5, 1926, Berkman Archive.

3. Paul Avrich visited the house and neighborhood in March 1992. Karen Avrich visited in December 2008.

4. While in St. Cloud Paul Avrich spoke with a Mr. Cost, a retired businessman who had lived at 139 rue Tahère for thirty-five years. Cost explained that M. Tahère had been a prominent physician during the Franco-Prussian War and the First World War. Mr. Cost introduced Paul Avrich to Merion Hanson of 107 rue Tahère, a house located diagonally from number 120. Hanson was originally from Minnesota and had served in France in the Second World War. He married a French woman, Gisèle, who was born at 107 rue Tahère during the 1920s, as was her older brother. Hanson ran the American Diaper Service from his house until his retirement. These residents of St. Cloud described the neighborhood at the time Berkman lived there.

5. Kay Boyle, "Alexander Berkman: A Memory," *The Phoenix,* 6 (1939), 158–171; Emma Goldman to Modest Stein, August 18, 1936, Goldman Archive, International Institute of Social History, Amsterdam.

6. Berkman to Michael Cohn, January 11, 1927, Michael Cohn Papers, YIVO Institute for Jewish Research, New York City.

7. Berkman to Goldman, February 4, 1927, Goldman Archive.

8. Berkman to Goldman, October 24, 1927, Goldman Archive.

9. Paul Avrich interview with Gabriel Javsicas, New York City, May 27, 1980.

10. Goldman to Bessie Kimmelman, December 29, 1927, Goldman Archive.

11. Goldman to Minna Lowensohn, November 11, 1927, Paul Avrich Collection, Library of Congress.

12. Berkman to Goldman, November 15, 1927, Goldman Archive.

13. Paul Avrich correspondence with Mollie Steimer, 1972 to 1980, Paul Avrich Collection.

14. Harry Kelly to Jim and Nellie Dick, January 24, 1928, James and Nellie Dick Papers, Private Collection, Oyster Bay, Long Island.

15. Paul Avrich interview with Gabriel Javsicas.

16. Vail was married first to Peggy Guggenheim, and then to the writer Kay Boyle. Peggy Guggenheim served as matron of honor at the Vail-Boyle marriage. "Laurence Vail Weds Writer in Nice, France," *New York Times,* April 3, 1932.

17. Peggy Guggenheim, *Out of This Century* (New York: Universe Books, 1979), 92.

18. Emma Goldman, *Living My Life* (New York: A. A. Knopf, 1931), 985.

19. Paul Avrich interview with Attilio Bortolotti, Toronto, 1972, and Miami Beach, 1988 and January 19, 1990.

20. Newlander was born in Sweden in 1890 and arrived in America in October 1906. He went to Stockholm after his deportation in 1919, then to the Swedish town of Hjorkvara, then traveled with his family to Canada in 1922.

21. Goldman, *Living My Life,* 991.

22. Paul Avrich interview with Ora Robbins, Flushing, N.Y., December 5, 1985.

23. Goldman wrote: "My sister and nephew Saxe [Commins, aka Comyns, altered from Cominsky] are already here, and [my brother] Moe is now with me, and Stella [Ballantine] and Ian will arrive to stay over Christmas." Goldman to Ellen Kennan, December 18, 1926, Goldman Archive. Moe was Morris, Emma Goldman's younger brother. Saxe was the son of her sister Lena. Emma's other brother, Herman, brought his wife and child for a holiday.

24. Goldman to Berkman, September 19, 1927, Berkman Archive, International Institute of Social History, Amsterdam.

25. Paul Avrich interview with Freda Diamond, New York City, May 13, 1983.

26. Goldman, *Living My Life,* 988.

27. Alexander Berkman, "Confessions-Questionnaire," *Little Review,* 12, no. 5 (Spring–Summer 1926), 13–15, accompanied by a photo of him.

28. Sasha and Boris exchanged letters in 1926 and 1927, Berkman Archive.

29. Berkman to Milly Rocker, March 21, 1929, Berkman Archive. Boris had worked as a clerk in a pharmacy in Kovno and Moscow before moving to Baku.

30. Goldman, *Living My Life,* 701–702.

31. Goldman to Berkman, May 17, 1927, Berkman Archive.

32. Berkman to Goldman, September 17, 1927, Goldman Archive.

33. Berkman to Goldman, February 4, 1927, Goldman Archive.

34. French translation by Professor Leon Laurent, German translation by Rudolf Rocker, and Dutch translation by Karin Michaelis.

35. M. Eleanor Fitzgerald to Berkman, April 9, 1929, Provincetown Papers, Lincoln Center Library, New York; Berkman to Goldman, April 24, 1929, Goldman Archive. Berkman's royalty payment was $121.44. Berkman to Goldman, March 1927, Berkman Archive; Berkman to Tom Mooney, September 5, 1927, Mooney Papers, University of California, Berkeley.

36. Berkman to Michael Cohn, April 11, 1927, Michael Cohn Papers.

37. Eugene O'Neill to Berkman, January 29, 1927, in *Selected Letters of Eugene O'Neill,* ed. Travis Bogard and Jackson R. Bryer (New Haven: Yale University Press, 1988), 232–233.

38. Berkman to Upton Sinclair, February 6, 1929, Upton Sinclair Papers, Lilly Library, Indiana University; Berkman to Goldman, April 19, 1927, Berkman Archive.

39. Berkman to Max Nettlau, December 17, 1926, Nettlau Archive, International Institute of Social History, Amsterdam.

40. Emma Goldman, preface to Alexander Berkman, *Now and After* (New York: Vanguard Press, Jewish Anarchist Federation, 1929); Berkman to Max Nettlau, June 28, 1927, Berkman Archive.

41. Goldman to Berkman, January 31 and June 29, 1927, Berkman Archive.

42. Berkman to Goldman, June 13 and 18, 1927, Berkman Archive.

43. Berkman to Max Nettlau, June 28, 1927, Nettlau Archive.

44. Michael Cohn contributed funds for the book's production costs, as did Minna Lowensohn, who also helped distribute it. A cheaper edition was printed simultaneously in a smaller format under the title *What Is Communist Anarchism?* as part of Vanguard's "What Is" series about the outlines of social philosophy.

45. Thomas H. Keell to Minna Lowensohn, October 28, 1929, Minna Lowensohn Papers, Paul Avrich Collection, Library of Congress.

46. Berkman to Minna Lowensohn, November 11, 1932, and June 10, 1934, Minna Lowensohn Papers, Paul Avrich Collection.

47. Goldman to Henry Alsberg, June 2, 1935, Goldman Archive.

48. Berkman to Goldman, July 21 and 17, 1927, Goldman Archive. Javsicas brought his girlfriend Erma Rockhill, later to become his wife.

49. Berkman to Goldman, May 12, 1927, Goldman Archive; Berkman to Goldman, June 11, 1927, Berkman Archive.

50. *The Sacco-Vanzetti Case: Transcript of the Record of the Trial of Nicola Sacco and Bartolomeo Vanzetti in the Courts of Massachusetts and Subsequent Proceedings, 1920–7*, 6 vols. (New York: Henry Holt, 1928–1929), vol. 5, 5065.

51. Paul Avrich, *Sacco and Vanzetti: The Anarchist Background* (Princeton: Princeton University Press, 1991), 3–4.

52. Louis Joughin and Edmund M. Morgan, *The Legacy of Sacco and Vanzetti* (Princeton: Princeton University Press, 1978), 323.

53. Alexander Berkman, "About American Justice," *International Review*, 1927, 330.

54. Berkman to Charles A. Lindbergh, May 25, 1927, Berkman Archive.

55. Berkman to Max Nettlau, August 20, 1927, Nettlau Archive.

56. Berkman to Goldman, August 20, 1927, Goldman Archive.

57. Goldman to Senya Fleshin, August 10, 1927; Goldman to Joseph Ishill, August 10, 1927, both in Goldman Archive.

58. Berkman to Michael Cohn, September 23 and October 4, 1927, Berkman Archive.

59. Berkman to Leonard Abbott, October 12, 1927, Berkman Archive.

60. Leonard Abbott to Anna Strunsky Walling, July 3, 1936, Leonard Abbott Papers, Private Collection, New York City.

61. Berkman to Michael Cohn, September 23 and October 4, 1927, Berkman Archive.

62. Berkman to Tom Mooney, September 5, 1927, Mooney Papers.

63. "Mooney 'Framed' Witness Insists," *New York Times*, February 9, 1921; "National Affairs: California's Case," *Time*, December 8, 1930.

64. "Mooney is 'Glad,'" *Arizona Republic* (Phoenix, Ariz.), October 16, 1939. Mooney told the *Associated Press* that he was "glad" Billings had received a commutation, but was "genuinely sorry" he had not been pardoned. "Billings was just as innocent as I and just as deserving of freedom as I."

65. "Mooney Pardoned," *New York Times*, January 8, 1939.

66. "Billings, Convicted with Mooney in 1916 Bombing, Is Pardoned," *New York Times*, December 22, 1961.

67. Paul Avrich interview with Freda Diamond, New York City, May 13, 1983.

68. Goldman to Bartolomeo Vanzetti, July 19, 1927, Emma Goldman Papers, Schlesinger Library, Radcliffe.

69. Goldman to Rosina Sacco, September 3, 1927, Emma Goldman Papers, Schlesinger Library. Emma also sent her sympathies to Ella Antolini, the young Italian anarchist who had been imprisoned with her at the Jefferson City prison. Goldman to Ella Antolini, October 28, 1927, Goldman Archive.

70. Alexander Berkman and Emma Goldman, *Road to Freedom,* August 1929.

26. Bon Esprit

1. Alexander Berkman to Emma Goldman, January 27, 1928, Goldman Archive, International Institute of Social History, Amsterdam.

2. Berkman to Joseph Ishill, February 28, 1928, and September 20, 1932, Joseph Ishill Papers, Houghton Library, Harvard University.

3. Irene Schneiderman to Paul Avrich, December 11, 1992, Paul Avrich Collection, Library of Congress.

4. Paul Avrich interview with Ida Gershoy, New York City, June 8, 1983.

5. The party was organized by Goldman's secretary Emily Holmes Coleman. Ibid.

6. Paul Avrich correspondence with Mollie Steimer, 1972–1980, Paul Avrich Collection.

7. Paul Avrich interview with Ida Gershoy, New York City, June 8, 1983.

8. Ibid.

9. Berkman to Saxe Commins, December 18, 1929, Berkman Archive, International Institute of Social History, Amsterdam.

10. Berkman to Goldman, August 7, 1929, Goldman Archive; Berkman to Goldman, November 14, 1931, and October 29, 1932, Berkman Archive.

11. Peter Arshinov, *Dielo Truda,* 1926.

12. Berkman to Senya Fleshin and Mollie Steimer, September 28, 1928, Fleshin Archive, International Institute of Social History, Amsterdam.

13. *Le Reveil,* October 1 and 15, 1927; Mollie Steimer to Comrade Ginev, November 30, 1927, Fleshin Archive.

14. Berkman to Ben Capes, April 25, 1927, Berkman Archive.

15. Goldman to Stewart Kerr, May 31, 1926, Goldman Papers, New York Public Library. Goldman was quoting William Marion Reedy, a former newspaper editor.

16. Goldman to Stewart Kerr, May 31, 1926, Goldman Papers. Trotsky was expelled to Turkey in February 1929.

17. Goldman to W. S. Van Valkenburgh, May 5, 1927, Goldman Archive; Van Valkenburgh to Floyd Dell, July 6, 1927, Dell Papers, Newberry Library, Chicago.

18. Goldman to Bolton Hall, June 17, 1928, Bolton Hall Papers, New York Public Library.

19. Goldman to A. L. Ross, May 26, 1927, Ross Papers, Tamiment Library, New York University.

20. Theodore Dreiser to W. S. Van Valkenburgh, June 19, 1927, Goldman Archive; Goldman to Dreiser, June 16, 1927, Goldman Archive; Dreiser to Goldman, February 29, 1926, Goldman Archive.

21. Goldman to W. S. Van Valkenburgh, June 17, 1927, Goldman Archive.

22. Goldman went through three secretaries during the writing process; Demi Coleman left St. Tropez for New York, after which Miriam Lerner, the daughter of a comrade from California, took over; she was replaced by Emma's former landlady from London, Doris Zhook, who served as Goldman's assistant for the duration.

23. Michael Cohn to Goldman, November 1, 1929, Goldman Archive.

24. Charles Joseph Antoine ("Jo") Labadie launched the collection with the donation of his papers and library.

25. H. L. Mencken to Goldman, March 27 and May 3, 1930, Goldman Archive; Goldman to Lincoln Steffens, May 30, 1930. Steffens Papers, Rare Book and Manuscript Library, Columbia University.

26. Goldman to Hutchins Hapgood, January 16, 1930, Goldman Archive.

27. H. L. Mencken, "Two Views of Russia," *American Mercury,* May 1924, 122–123.

28. Berkman to Saxe Commins, December 18, 1929, Berkman Archive.

29. Paul Avrich correspondence with Mollie Steimer, 1972–1980, Paul Avrich Collection, Library of Congress.

30. Berkman to Minna Lowensohn, December 2, 1931, Minna Lowensohn Papers, Paul Avrich Collection.

31. Goldman to Karin Michaelis, February 20, 1930, Goldman Archive; Goldman to A. L. Ross, March 21, 1930, Ross Papers, Tamiment Library, New York University.

32. Paul Avrich interview with Ida Gershoy, New York City, June 8, 1983.

33. Paul Avrich interview with Freda Diamond, New York City, May 13, 1983. According to Diamond, "Saxe had charm, but was an opportunist. He used Emma and he used Fitzi—that's how he came to the Provincetown Players and got to know Eugene O'Neill. Through O'Neill he got a job at Covici-Friede, O'Neill's publisher, before moving to Random House." Commins then became an editor at Random House.

34. Paul Avrich interview with Arthur Leonard Ross, New York City, February 3, 1974.

35. R. L. Duffue, "An Anarchist Explains Herself," *New York Times,* October 25, 1931.

36. "Emma Goldman Takes Life Easy along the Mediterranean Sea," United Press, *Daily Courier* (Connellsville, Pa.), July 21, 1931.

37. Goldman to Karin Michaelis, July 21, 1930, Goldman Archive.

38. Richard Drinnon and Anna Maria Drinnon, eds., *Nowhere at Home: Letters from Exile of Emma Goldman and Alexander Berkman* (New York: Schocken Books, 1975), xxv–xxviii.

39. Berkman to M. Eleanor Fitzgerald, November 14, 1932, Fitzgerald Papers, Tamiment Library, New York University. The original outline is in her papers; there is a copy in the Berkman Archive. Printed in full in Drinnon and Drinnon, *Nowhere at Home,* xxv–xxiii.

40. "Living My Life by Emma Goldman," *Time,* November 9, 1931.

41. A decade later the *New York Times* repeated this sentiment, calling the work "one of the important books of its kind." "Emma Goldman, Anarchist, Dead," *New York Times,* May 14, 1940.

42. R. L. Duffue, "An Anarchist Explains Her Life," *New York Times,* October 25, 1931.

43. Upton Sinclair to Goldman, November 10, 1931, Goldman Archive.

44. Kay Boyle to Goldman, January 17, 1932, Goldman Archive.

45. Pa Chin to Goldman, September 1933, Goldman Archive.

46. Berkman to M. Eleanor Fitzgerald, February 9, 1932, Fitzgerald Papers.

27. Pillar to Post

1. Paul Avrich interview with Gabriel Javsicas, New York City, May 27, 1980.

2. Alexander Berkman to Emma Goldman, July 27, 1929, Goldman Archive, International Institute of Social History, Amsterdam.

3. Paul Avrich correspondence with Mollie Steimer, 1972–1980, Paul Avrich Collection, Library of Congress.

4. Modest Stein to Goldman, September 20, 1929, Berkman Archive, International Institute of Social History, Amsterdam.

5. Modest Stein to Berkman, November 13, 1930, Berkman Archive.

6. Goldman to Emmy Eckstein, June 10, 1930, Goldman Archive.

7. Michael Cohn to Goldman, November 25, 1930, Goldman Archive.

8. Harry Kelly to Berkman, December 11, 1930, Berkman Archive. Stephanus Fabrijanovic, a Yugoslav anarchist and pastry baker, provided the cake.

9. "Alexander Berkman's Sixtieth Birthday Celebration," Central Opera House, New York City, pamphlet (New York: n.p., November 20, 1930), Joseph A. Labadie Collection, Harlan Hatcher Library, University of Michigan. Berkman to Max Metzkow, October, 19, 1930, Metzkow Papers, Joseph A. Labadie Collection, Harlan Hatcher Library, University of Michigan.

10. "Alexander Berkman's Sixtieth Birthday Celebration," Central Opera House, New York City.

11. Goldman to A. L. Ross, May 2, 1930, Ross Papers, Tamiment Library, New York University; Daniele Stewart to Paul Avrich, October 1994, Paul Avrich Collection, Library of Congress.

12. Berkman to Agnes Inglis, June 15, 1930, Labadie Collection.

13. Goldman to Henry Alsberg, June 27, 1930, Goldman Archive.

14. Emmy Eckstein to Berkman, October 1931, Berkman Archive.

15. Berkman to Eckstein, October 16, 1931, Berkman Archive.

16. Goldman to Leonard Abbott, August 21, 1931, Goldman Archive; Richard Drinnon and Anna Maria Drinnon, eds., *Nowhere at Home: Letters from Exile of Emma Goldman and Alexander Berkman* (New York: Schocken Books, 1975), 208.

17. Berkman to Morris Hillquit, July 17, 1931, Berkman Archive.

18. Berkman to Pierre Renaudel, July 18, 1931, Berkman Archive; Goldman to Karin Michaelis, June 30, 1931, Goldman Archive.

19. Goldman to Ellen Kennan, October 4, 1931, Goldman Archive.

20. Theodore Dreiser to Pierre Laval, September 21, 1931, in *Letters of Theodore Dreiser: A Selection,* ed. Robert H. Elias (Philadelphia: University of Pennsylvania Press, 1959), vol. 2, 562–564.

21. Goldman to Theodore Dreiser, October 4, 1931, Goldman Archive.

22. "Berkman to Be Deported," *Fairbanks Daily News-Miner,* July 6, 1931; Drinnon and Drinnon, *Nowhere at Home,* 208.

23. Goldman to Leon Malmed, July 2, 1931, Schlesinger Library, Radcliffe College; Berkman to Hudson Hawley, June 12, 1932, Berkman Archive.

24. *Road to Freedom,* September 1931.

25. Goldman to Henry Alsberg, March 4, 1930, Goldman Archive.

26. Goldman to Lincoln Steffens, March 10, 1930, Goldman Archive.

27. Avrich and Steimer correspondence, Paul Avrich Collection.

28. Mollie Steimer, "Alexander Berkman—The Unforgettable Friend and Comrade," *Fraye Arbeter Shtime,* 1966.

29. Berkman to M. Eleanor Fitzgerald, February 9, 1932, Fitzgerald Papers, Tamiment Library, New York University. In his letter, Berkman asked after Fitzgerald's companion, Pauline Turkel, who had been working at the American consulate in Rome. Turkel returned to New York, worked with the Provincetown Players, took a job as a secretary to a psychiatrist, Gregory Zilboorg, then served as managing editor of the *Psychoanalytical Quarterly* from 1937 until her retirement in 1964. Turkel lived with Fitzi at her farm in Gaylordsville, Connecticut, for about two decades until Fitzi's death in 1955. Turkel died in 1987. Paul Avrich interview with Pauline Turkel, New York City, January 21, 1972.

30. Goldman to Gwyneth King Roe, May 14, 1931, State Historical Society of Wisconsin, Madison.

31. Paul E. Sann to Berkman, July 12, 1934, Berkman Archive; Berkman to Sann, December 17, 1934, Berkman Archive; Berkman to Minna Lowensohn, December 17, 1934, Minna Lowensohn Papers, Paul Avrich Collection, Library of Congress.

32. Berkman to J. Edward Morgan, April 2, 1932, Berkman Archive.

33. Modest Stein to Goldman, April 29, 1931, Berkman Archive.

34. Berkman to Goldman, August 1, 1931, Goldman Archive.

35. Berkman to Goldman, August 7, 1931, Berkman Archive.

36. Goldman to Berkman, August 18, 1931, Goldman Archive.

37. Modest Stein to Goldman, September 30, 1931, Berkman Archive.

38. Berkman to Goldman, August 24, 1932, Goldman Archive; Modest Stein to Goldman, September 21 and December 4, 1932, Berkman Archive; Berkman to M. Eleanor Fitzgerald, February 9, 1932.

39. Berkman to Goldman, May 1933, Goldman Archive. Berkman also wrote: "Emmy's mother sends her some money from time to time, a couple hundred francs. Occasionally her sister in Chicago sent five or ten dollars. Her brother escaped from Berlin.

Her mother's [art publishing] business in Berlin is entirely gone up in smoke, and her sister in Chicago complains that 'times are hard.' "

40. Goldman to Berkman, April 12, 1934, Berkman Archive.

41. Modest Stein to Berkman, November 10, 1933, Berkman Archive.

42. W. S. Van Valkenburgh to Goldman, July 14, 1931, Goldman Archive.

43. Goldman to Van Valkenburgh, August 2, 1931, Goldman Archive.

44. Goldman to Ben Capes, February 16, 1926, Goldman Archive.

45. Goldman to Harry Kelly, December 1929, Goldman Archive.

46. Goldman to John Kassel, February 25, 1931, Schlesinger Library.

47. Berkman to Pierre Ramus, August 21, 1935, Berkman Archive.

28. Old Glory

1. Emma Goldman to Alexander Berkman, December 23, 1931, Goldman Archive, International Institute of Social History, Amsterdam.

2. Emma Goldman, "A Woman without a Country," *Free Vistas,* ed. Joseph Ishill (Berkeley Heights, N.J.: Oriole Press, 1933), 134–135. An early version was published in *Mother Earth* in May 1909.

3. Roger Baldwin to Goldman, December 27, 1933, Goldman Archive.

4. Berkman to Goldman, December 31, 1933, Berkman Archive, International Institute of Social History, Amsterdam.

5. Goldman to Thomas H. Bell, January 19, 1934, Goldman Archive.

6. Emma Goldman Papers, New York Public Library.

7. Telegram from Roger Baldwin to Goldman, January 2, 1934, Goldman Archive.

8. Paul Avrich interview with Arthur Leonard Ross, New York City, February 3, 1974.

9. Roger Baldwin to Goldman, January 4, 1934, Baldwin Papers, Princeton University; Baldwin to Goldman, January 5, 1934, Goldman Archive.

10. Berkman to Goldman, January 10, 1934, Berkman Archive.

11. Berkman to Pauline Turkel, January 18, 1934, Paul Avrich Collection, Library of Congress.

12. Maude Murray Miller to Eleanor Roosevelt, January 19, 1934, Eleanor Roosevelt Collection, Clifton Waller Barrett Library, University of Virginia.

13. Eleanor Roosevelt to Maude Murray Miller, January 31, 1934, Eleanor Roosevelt Collection.

14. Those who met Goldman in Rochester included her brother Morris and his wife; her brother Herman; her sister Lena; and Lena's children Stella Ballantine and Saxe Commins.

15. "Still an Anarchist, But—Red Flame Is Only a Glow When Emma Goldman Returns at 68 [*sic*]," *Burlington Daily Times-News,* February 9, 1934.

16. "Rochester Visited by Emma Goldman," *New York Times,* February 2, 1934.

17. Ibid.

18. "Still an Anarchist, But—Red Flame Is Only a Glow When Emma Goldman Returns at 68 [*sic*]," *Burlington Daily Times-News,* February 9, 1934.

19. Holmes attended a private dinner with Goldman on February 6 and wrote to Stella Ballantine, "Wasn't last night's dinner grand?" He added that he was "particularly pleased to see Miss Goldman looking so fresh and vigorous." John Haynes Holmes to Stella Ballantine, February 7, 1934, Paul Avrich Private Collection, New York City.

20. "Emma Goldman Extols Anarchist," *New York Times,* February 12, 1934.

21. Paul Avrich interview with Arthur Leonard Ross.

22. Emma Goldman to James B. Pond, March 15, 1934, Paul Avrich Private Collection.

23. Goldman to Berkman, April 12, 1934, Berkman Archive.

24. "Says 'Money' Plans War," *New York Times,* February 27, 1934.

25. Goldman to Rudolf Rocker, April 12, 1934, Rudolf Rocker Archive, International Institute of Social History, Amsterdam.

26. Goldman to Berkman, June 7, 1934, Berkman Archive.

27. Goldman to Emmy Eckstein, September 9, 1934, Berkman Archive.

28. Goldman to Frank Heiner, July 7, 1935, Goldman Archive. The couple consummated their romance when he visited her in Canada after her American tour ended.

29. Heiner to Goldman, October 1934, Goldman Archive.

30. Agnes Inglis' notes at the Joseph A. Labadie Collection, of which she was the curator, Harlan Hatcher Library, University of Michigan; Goldman to Berkman, March 9, 1934, Berkman Archive.

31. Goldman to Berkman, May 27 and June 30, 1934, Berkman Archive.

32. Stella Ballantine to James B. Pond, March 2, 1934, Paul Avrich Private Collection.

33. Paul Avrich interview with Sarah Taback, Bronx, New York, November 11, 1976.

34. "Emma Goldman Returns," *New York Times,* April 22, 1934.

35. Berkman to Pauline Turkel, May 13, 1934, Tamiment Library, New York University.

36. Berkman to Pierre Ramus, August 21, 1934, Berkman Archive.

37. Goldman to W. S. Van Valkenburgh, April 7, 1934, Goldman Archive.

38. "Still an Anarchist, But—Red Flame Is Only a Glow When Emma Goldman Returns at 68 [*sic*]," *Burlington Daily Times-News,* February 9, 1934.

39. Ibid.

40. Goldman to Joseph Ishill, April 19, 1934, Joseph Ishill Papers, Houghton Library, Harvard University.

41. "Still an Anarchist, But—Red Flame Is Only a Glow When Emma Goldman Returns at 68 [*sic*]," *Burlington Daily Times-News,* February 9, 1934.

42. The journal ceased publication in 1977 after eighty-seven years.

43. Berkman to Pauline Turkel, January 18, 1934, Tamiment Library, New York University.

44. Berkman to Frank Heiner, August 22, 1935, Berkman Archive.

45. Goldman to Berkman, April 1, 1935, Berkman Archive.

46. Goldman to Claus Timmermann, March 1935, Goldman Archive; Goldman to Modest Stein, March 23, 1935, Berkman Archive. Timmerman, who had developed a serious alcohol problem, continued to work as a carpenter and handyman. He died in Massachusetts in 1941.

47. Goldman to Dorothy Rogers, September 18, 1935, Goldman Archive.
48. Goldman to Modest Stein, September 28, 1935, Berkman Archive.
49. Goldman to Joseph Ishill, June 15, 1932, Goldman Archive.
50. Berkman to Max Nettlau, January 4, 1933, Berkman Archive.
51. Berkman to Mollie Steimer, August 16, 1933, Berkman Archive.
52. Ibid.
53. Berkman to Goldman, February 12, 1933, Goldman Archive; Berkman to Goldman, July 27, 1934, Berkman Archive.
54. Berkman to Max Nettlau, August 21, 1935, Nettlau Archive, International Institute of Social History, Amsterdam.
55. Goldman to Rose Pesotta, May 27, 1935, Goldman Papers, New York Public Library.
56. Berkman to Rudolf and Milly Rocker, March 23, 1933, Rudolf Rocker Archive.
57. Berkman to Michael Cohn, May 24, 1933, Berkman Archive.
58. Goldman to Mildred Mesirow, February 10, 1936, Goldman Archive.
59. Berkman to Pauline Turkel, September 1, 1934, Paul Avrich Collection.
60. Berkman to Rudolf and Milly Rocker, October 24, 1935, Berkman Archive.
61. Goldman to Carlo Tresca, April 28, 1938, Solo Linder Archive, International Institute of Social History, Amsterdam.
62. Goldman to Berkman, November 26, 1935, Berkman Archive.
63. Berkman to Goldman, January 9, 1936, Berkman Archive.
64. Samuel Polinow to Berkman, January 13, 1936, Berkman Archive.
65. Goldman to Berkman, November 19, 1935, Berkman Archive.

29. Nothing but Death Can End

1. Emma Goldman to Modest Stein, March 10, 1930, Berkman Archive, International Institute of Social History, Amsterdam.
2. Goldman to Minna Lowensohn, May 6, 1930, Goldman Archive, International Institute of Social History, Amsterdam.
3. Alexander Berkman to Goldman, April 18, 1931, Goldman Archive.
4. Goldman to A. L. Ross, May 25, 1932, Goldman Archive.
5. Goldman to Henry G. Alsberg, June 2, 1935, Goldman Archive. Berkman was subsequently treated locally in Nice throughout that five-year period.
6. Berkman to Pauline Turkel, May 13, 1934, Paul Avrich Collection, Library of Congress.
7. Berkman to Goldman, May 12–13, 1934, Berkman Archive.
8. Berkman to Goldman, August 5, 1934, Berkman Archive.
9. Berkman to Rudolf Rocker, November 16, 1934, Rudolf Rocker Archive, International Institute of Social History, Amsterdam; Berkman to Michael Cohn, December 12, 1934, and June 24, 1935, Berkman Archive.
10. Milly Rocker to Berkman, May 30, 1935, Berkman Archive; Rudolf Rocker to Goldman, June 2, 1935, Goldman Archive; Goldman to Rudolf Rocker, June 16, 1935, Schlesinger Library, Radcliffe College.

11. Berkman to Rudolf Rocker, June 16, 1935, Rudolf Rocker Archive.

12. Modest Stein to Goldman, July 1935, Goldman Archive.

13. Berkman's translation is available at the International Institute of Social History, Amsterdam; he seemed to be on his way to making a readable version.

14. Berkman to Stella Ballantine, August 14, 1935, Goldman Papers, New York Public Library.

15. Thomas H. Bell to Joseph Ishill, February 9, 1935, Joseph Ishill Papers, Houghton Library, Harvard University.

16. Goldman to Agnes Inglis, August 21, 1931, Joseph A. Labadie Collection, Harlan Hatcher Library, University of Michigan. Goldman was also diagnosed with diabetes at the end of her life.

17. Paul Avrich interview with Ahrne Thorne, Bronx, N.Y., October 2, 1979.

18. Berkman to Goldman, October 23, 1935, Berkman Archive.

19. Emmy Eckstein to Goldman, February 11, 1936, Goldman Archive. Goldman left for her lecture tour of England in mid-November 1935; she returned to France in April 1936.

20. Eckstein and Berkman to Goldman, February 14, 1936, Goldman Archive.

21. Berkman to Goldman, January 11, 1936, Berkman Archive.

22. Berkman to Goldman, March 5, 1936, Berkman Archive.

23. Berkman to Goldman, March 1936, Joseph A. Labadie Collection and copy in Berkman Archive.

24. Goldman to Modest Stein, April 10, 1936, Berkman Archive.

25. Emmy Eckstein to Liza Koldofsky, April 1936, Berkman Archive.

26. Berkman to Stella Ballantine, June 10, 1936, Berkman Archive.

27. Berkman to Dorothy Rogers, June 20, 1936, Arcos Collection, Joseph A. Labadie Collection; Berkman to M. Eleanor Fitzgerald, March 10, 1936, Tamiment Library, New York University.

28. Paul Avrich interview with Gabriel Javsicas at Sam Dolgoff's New York City apartment, April 17, 1980; Paul Avrich interview with Luba Stein Benenson, New York City, December 4, 1973.

29. Berkman to M. Eleanor Fitzgerald, June 13, 1936, Tamiment Library.

30. Berkman to Goldman, June 22 and 24, 1936, Berkman Archive.

31. Berkman to Goldman, June 27, 1936, Berkman Archive.

32. Goldman to Stella Ballantine, July 6, 1936, Rudolf Rocker Archive.

33. Goldman to Mollie Steimer, July 11, 1936, Goldman Archive.

34. Goldman to Stella Ballantine, July 6, 1936, Rudolf Rocker Archive. His comrades reported different times of death.

35. Goldman to Modest Stein, July 6, 1936, Goldman Archive.

36. Mollie Steimer to Goldman, July 1, 1936, Goldman Archive.

37. Goldman to Steimer, July 11, 1936, Goldman Archive.

38. M. Eleanor Fitzgerald to Goldman, July 3, 1936, Goldman Archive.

39. Jeanne Levey to Goldman, July 1, 1936, Goldman Archive.

40. *Vanguard,* August–September 1936.

41. Goldman to Minna Lowensohn, August 12, 1936, Paul Avrich Collection, Library of Congress.

42. James Colton to Goldman, July 1936, Goldman Archive.

43. Goldman to Harry Kelly, August 1936, Goldman Archive; Goldman to Max Nettlau, July 12, 1936, Nettlau Archive, International Institute of Social History, Amsterdam.

44. Goldman to Pauline Turkel, July 19, 1936, Paul Avrich Collection.

45. Paul Avrich interview with Ida Gershoy, New York City, June 8, 1983.

46. C. E. S. Wood to Thomas H. Bell, July 19, 1936, T. H. Bell Papers, Private Collection, Los Angeles.

47. Harry Kelly to Goldman, July 24, 1936, Goldman Archive.

48. Paul Avrich interview with Gabriel Javsicas, April 17, 1980.

49. Alexander Berkman Memorial Meeting held at the I. W. W. Hall, Friday, July 3, 1936. Hennacy served as speaker and chairman. Ammon Hennacy, *The One-Man Revolution in America* (Salt Lake City: Ammon Hennacy Publications, 1970), 111.

50. Thomas H. Bell in "A Meeting in Commemoration of Alexander Berkman," Thomas H. Bell Papers, Private Collection, Los Angeles; Tom Bell to Frank Scully, December 1936, Paul Avrich Collection.

51. Paul Avrich interview with Roger N. Baldwin, New York City, January 29, 1974.

52. Goldman to Max Nettlau, July 12, 1936, Nettlau Archive.

53. "Alexander Schmidt-Bergmann, 101 Boulevard de Cessole, shot self June 28, 1936. Suicide. Nationality Russian. Driven to his act by poor health, having undergone a serious operation without being cured. Born 21 November 1870 in Vilnius, Russia. Expelled from France on April 29, 1930, for conducting anarchist propaganda." Daniele Stewart to Paul Avrich, October 1994, Paul Avrich Collection, Library of Congress.

54. The will was signed: "In witness, whereof, I sign Alexander Berkman (Alexander Schmidt-Bergmann), Nice, November 22, 1935." Berkman Archive.

55. Emmy Eckstein to Goldman, March 28, 1938, Goldman Archive.

56. Goldman to M. Eleanor Fitzgerald, February 15, 1939, Tamiment Library.

57. Paul Avrich interview with Gabriel Javsicas, New York City, May 27, 1980.

58. "Hotel du Dome. Born in Berlin on October 10, 1900. No profession. Daughter of Jules Eckstein and Paula Silberknopf. Unmarried. Rumanian subject. City Register, Nice." According to her death certificate, Emmy died on June 8, 1939, at the age of thirty-nine at the Clinique Belvedere. Her last address had been 19 avenue Auber, Nice, which was a hotel. Daniele Stewart to Paul Avrich, October 1994, Paul Avrich Collection, Library of Congress.

59. Goldman to M. Eleanor Fitzgerald, June 30, 1939, Tamiment Library.

60. "Exiled Berkman Commits Suicide," *New York Times,* July 2, 1936.

61. "Labor: Home to Homestead," *Time,* July 13, 1936.

62. "Deported Radical Dies in France," *Huntington Daily News,* July 1, 1936.

63. Goldman to Stella Ballantine, July 6, 1936, Rudolf Rocker Archive.

64. "Ici Repose / Alexander Berkman / Né le 21 November 1870 / Décédé le 28 Juin 1936 / Son Rève Etait D'un Monde Nouveau, Libre et Beau / Sa vie entière une Lutte sans Trève / Pour le Triomphe de Son Ideal." June 30, 1936 was a Tuesday.

65. Goldman to Stella Ballantine, July 6, 1936, Rudolf Rocker Archive.

66. Goldman to Ballantine, July 25, 1936, Goldman Papers.

67. Goldman to John Cowper Powys, August 3, 1936, Nettlau Archive.

68. Goldman to Max Nettlau, July 12, 1936, Nettlau Archive.

69. *Alexander Berkman: Rebel and Anarchist* (New York: Alexander Berkman Memorial Committee and Jewish Education, July 1936); Goldman to Beatrice Weinberger, July 1936, Harry Weinberger Papers, Yale University; Thomas H. Bell to Frank Scully, July 28 and August 18, 1936, Paul Avrich Collection.

70. Goldman, "Alexander Berkman's Last Days," *Vanguard* (New York), August–September 1936. The original is in the New York Public Library.

71. Goldman to Abraham Zubrin, August 12, 1936, Goldman Archive.

72. Goldman to Gwyneth King Roe, August 12, 1936, State Historical Society of Wisconsin, Madison; copy in Goldman Archive.

73. "Still an Anarchist, But—Red Flame Is Only a Glow When Emma Goldman Returns at 68 [*sic*]," *Burlington Daily Times-News,* February 9, 1934.

30. Waldheim

1. Emma Goldman to Augustin Souchy, August 21, 1936, Goldman Archive, International Institute of Social History, Amsterdam.

2. Goldman to Joe Desser, August 23, 1936, Goldman Archive.

3. Goldman to A. L. Ross, August 29, 1936, Goldman Archive.

4. Goldman to Stella Ballantine, August 29, 1936, Goldman Archive.

5. Goldman to Dear Comrades, September 9, 1936, Nettlau Archive, International Institute of Social History, Amsterdam.

6. Goldman to Mark Mratchny, September 23, 1936, Mratchny Papers, Joseph A. Labadie Collection, Harlan Hatcher Library, University of Michigan.

7. Goldman to M. Eleanor Fitzgerald, September 25, 1936, Rudolf Rocker Archive, International Institute of Social History, Amsterdam.

8. Others whom Goldman encountered included Eusebio Carbo, German anarchist Helmut Rudiger, and Italian anarchist and professor Camillo Berneri, who was killed in 1937. Diego de Santillan was the pseudonym of Sinesio Vaudilio García Fernández.

9. "Emma Goldman Visits Spain to Gather Data," *San Antonio Express,* October 24, 1936.

10. "Leader's Legend Still Marches On," *North Adams Transcript,* March 13, 1937.

11. The Pacific Street Film Collection of New York City has a copy of the film; see also Goldman to Stella Ballantine, December 1936, Goldman Papers, New York Public Library: "You will hear my voice in the Durruti film."

12. "Leader's Legend Still Marches On," *North Adams Transcript,* March 13, 1937.

13. Goldman to Dear Comrades, January 21, 1937, released on January 25, 1937, under the heading "Spain and the World," Nettlau Archives.

14. Ibid.

15. Elmer Peterson, "Emma Goldman Is Here to Work in Spanish Cause," *Helena Daily Independent,* January 17, 1937.

16. Goldman to Comité Nacional CNT-FAI, May 3, 1937, Goldman Archive.

17. "Naïve Anarchists: Emma Goldman Writes of Conditions in Spain," Letters to the Editor, *New York Times,* July 4, 1937.

18. Goldman to Edward Ballantine, January 1, 1939, Goldman Archive.

19. Goldman to Max Nettlau, February 4, 1939, Nettlau Archive.

20. *Windsor Star* and *Detroit News,* May 19, 1939.

21. Paul Avrich interviews with Attilio Bortolotti, Toronto, November 29, 1972; Miami Beach, December 10, 1988, and January 19, 1990.

22. Goldman to Dear Comrades, June 27, 1939.

23. Roger A. Bruns, *The Damndest Radical* (Champaign: University of Illinois Press, 1987), 288.

24. Paul Avrich interviews with Attilio Bortolotti.

25. Cohen was well known for his work on civil liberties and the labor movement.

26. Paul Avrich interviews with Attilio Bortolotti.

27. Goldman to Rose Bernstein, October 28, 1939, Joseph A. Labadie Collection, Harlan Hatcher Library, University of Michigan.

28. Paul Avrich interviews with Attilio Bortolotti.

29. Paul Avrich interview with Ahrne Thorne, Bronx, N.Y., October 2, 1979.

30. Ibid. Dorothy Rogers was Goldman's comrade and assistant.

31. "Emma Goldman Ill: Radical Writer and Lecturer Suffers Stroke in Toronto," *New York Times,* February 21, 1940.

32. Dien Meelis to Leon Malmed, February 29, 1940, Schlesinger Library, Radcliffe College.

33. Paul Avrich interviews with Attilio Bortolotti.

34. Paul Avrich interview with Ahrne Thorne.

35. Dien Meelis to Leon Malmed, February 29, 1940.

36. Paul Avrich interview with Millie Grobstein, Brooklyn, N.Y., April 20, 1975.

37. Paul Avrich interview with Ahrne Thorne.

38. Fitzgerald continued her work in the theater as a manager and publicist, living in New York City, Connecticut, and Wisconsin. She died of cancer in 1955.

39. Paul Avrich interview with Ahrne Thorne.

40. Ibid.

41. "Emma Goldman, Anarchist, Dead," *New York Times,* May 14, 1940.

42. Ben Reitman to Leroy Oberman, May 16, 1940, Ben Lewis Reitman Papers, Richard J. Daley Library, University of Illinois at Chicago; Bruns, *The Damndest Radical,* 289.

43. Paul Avrich interview with Arthur Leonard Ross, New York City, February 3, 1974.

44. "Emma Goldman Funeral," *New York Times,* May 16, 1940.

45. "Burial on U.S. Soil for Emma Goldman," *New York Times,* May 18, 1940.

46. "Modest Stein, 87, Dies," *New York Times,* February 27, 1958.

47. Paul Avrich interview with Ahrne Thorne.

48. Paul Avrich interview with Freda Diamond, New York City, May 13, 1983.

49. Harry Weinberger, *Emma Goldman* (Berkeley Heights, N.J.: Oriole Press, 1940), 2.

50. Goldman to Alexander Berkman, November 19, 1935, Berkman Archive, International Institute of Social History, Amsterdam.

51. Berkman to Goldman, November 24, 1935, Berkman Archive.

Acknowledgments

It has been my good fortune to have known a number of men and women who have discussed my work on this book, have given me the benefit of their knowledge of the lives of Alexander Berkman and Emma Goldman, and have placed at my disposal documents and information that could not be obtained elsewhere: Stephen Cole, Richard Drinnon, Federico Arcos, Mark Benenson, Leo Hershkowitz, Richard Polenberg, and Joshua Freeman. Others who have aided me in important ways are Abe Ascher, Nunzio Pernicone, Malcolm Mason, Candace Falk, Gary Doebler, Julie Herrada, and Yaffe Eliach. I am grateful for their kind assistance.

Paul Avrich

My thanks to the generous Scott Moyers, who trained his keen eye on a sprawling manuscript, and to the great Andrew Wylie. To Joyce Seltzer, astute and dedicated, who appreciated Emma and Sasha both as revolutionaries and as human beings. To the rest of the team at Harvard University Press, especially Brian Distelberg, Margaux Leonard, Ann Hawthorne, and Edward Wade.

To Ina Avrich for her good humor; Bianca and Dan Harris, encouraging and engaged; Howard Wolfson and Terri McCullough, supportive and kind; John Heilemann and Diana Rhoten, a dazzling duo; Debbie Halperin and Gil Fuchsberg, spirited and savvy; Morton Halperin and Diane Orentlicher, gracious and wise.

Heartfelt gratitude to Kyle Froman, Iva Zoric, Yvette Vega, Fred Hochberg, Tom Healy, John F. Harris, Ann O'Hanlon, Adam Nagourney, Ben

Kushner, Andrew Kirtzman, Tim Blanco, and Gary Foster. And special thanks to Carol Lipis and Jane Avrich.

With deep appreciation to the Labadie Collection at the University of Michigan; Columbia University, Special Collections Division; the Joseph Ishill Collection at Harvard University; the Library of Congress; the New York Public Library; the Chicago History Museum; the University of California at Berkeley; the Tamiment Library at New York University; and the International Institute of Social History, Amsterdam, The Netherlands.

To my father, for his magnificent work.

And to Mark Halperin, who patiently listened to chapters, paragraphs, phrases, words, and syllables. He never failed to assure me of the importance of the story, the power of great characters, and the value of the project. His gifts as a writer and journalist, his merits as a wag and a sage, have been a constant font of inspiration and a steady source of strength.

KAREN AVRICH

Index